Trinity College Dublin
1592–1952

An academic history

1 Trinity College from the air, 1946. The photograph is taken looking eastwards. The West Front is prominent, with a bus and a tram passing in front of it in College Green. Behind it is the Front Square, into which project the Chapel (left) and the Examination Hall (right). Beyond the Chapel and further recessed is the Dining Hall, but only the roof can be seen. Recessed behind the Examination Hall is the octagonal reading-room of 1937. The Campanile marks the junction of Front and Library Squares; the latter is flanked on the right by the Library, on the left by the Graduates' Memorial Building, and at the back by the Rubrics. Beyond the Rubrics lies the New Square, its south side formed by the Museum Building (chimney-stacks prominent), and beyond the New Square the football field. To the left of the Library Square is Botany Bay. In the right foreground of the photograph is the cubical block of the Provost's House; between its garden and the Fellows' Garden is the small magnetical observatory. Beyond the Fellows' Garden is the cricket field, and beyond this and the football field, near the eastern boundary, are various scientific and medical laboratories and offices.

Since the date of this photograph the Fellows' Garden has been converted into Fellows' Square by buildings on its east and south side, and the magnetical observatory has been removed.

Trinity College, Dublin

1592–1952

An academic history

R.B. McDOWELL
Senior Fellow of the College and
Erasmus Smith's Professor of Oratory

AND

D.A. WEBB
Fellow Emeritus of the College and
Honorary Professor of Systematic Botany

WITH A FOREWORD BY

F.S.L. LYONS
Provost of Trinity College Dublin

CAMBRIDGE UNIVERSITY PRESS

Cambridge
London   New York   New Rochelle
Melbourne   Sydney

Published by the Press Syndicate of the University of Cambridge
The Pitt Building, Trumpington Street, Cambridge CB2 1RP
32 East 57th Street, New York, NY 10022, USA
296 Beaconsfield Parade, Middle Park, Melbourne 3206, Australia

First published 1982

Printed in Great Britain at the University Press, Cambridge

Library of Congress catalogue card number: 81-12262

British Library Cataloguing in Publication Data
McDowell, R.B.
Trinity College Dublin, 1592–1952.
1. Trinity College (*Dublin*) – History
I. Title   II. Webb, D.A.
378.418′35   LF902
ISBN 0 521 23931 1

Contents

List of plates   *page* xi
List of figures   xiii
Foreword by F. S. L. Lyons, Provost of Trinity College   xv
Preface   xix
Acknowledgments   xxiii

1   Early days: 1592–1640   1

    (i)   The foundation of the College   1
   (ii)   The relation between College and University   4
  (iii)   Courses and teaching, 1594–1634   5
  (iv)   The teaching of Irish   9
   (v)   Scholarly achievement in the early years   10
  (vi)   Laud's reforms   13

2   Sedition, privy conspiracy and rebellion: 1640–1717   17

    (i)   The Civil War and the Commonwealth   17
   (ii)   The College after the Restoration   21
  (iii)   Provosts Ward, Marsh and Huntington   23
  (iv)   Scholarship in the reign of Charles II   24
   (v)   The reign of James II   27
  (vi)   Provosts Ashe and George Browne; the scientific movement   29
  (vii)   The struggle between Whigs and Tories, 1698–1717   32

3   Georgian stasis and Georgian splendour: 1717–1794   37

    (i)   The College under Provost Baldwin   37
   (ii)   Academic developments, 1700–1750   41
  (iii)   Erasmus Smith's Professorships   44
  (iv)   The undergraduate course in 1736   45
   (v)   Provost Andrews, and the shift from solidity to elegance   49
  (vi)   Provost Hely-Hutchinson   53
  (vii)   The chairs of Modern Languages and of Music   56

Contents

(viii) The Regius Professorship of Greek, and further foundations of the Erasmus Smith trustees   58

(ix) Classical and literary publications in the late eighteenth century   61

(x) Mathematics and astronomy in the late eighteenth century   63

(xi) The chair of Feudal and English Law   65

(xii) The foundation of the Royal Irish Academy   66

(xiii) Developments in the undergraduate course, 1736–1792   69

4 Limbo: 1794–1830   74

(i) The turn of the century   74

(ii) Provost Murray; the rising of 1798 and the Union   75

(iii) Provosts and Fellows, 1799–1831; decline of intellectual activity in post-Union Dublin   78

(iv) Great increase in student numbers, 1801–1825   85

(v) Developments in the medical school; James Macartney   87

(vi) Conservative tone of the period   89

5 The College in 1830   93

(i) The physical aspect   93

(ii) The Chancellor, Vice-Chancellor, Visitors and Senate   95

(iii) The Provost and Senior Fellows   97

(iv) The Junior Fellows   103

(v) The Professors and lecturers   110

(vi) The students   113

(vii) The entrance examination and undergraduate course   118

(viii) Scholarships and prizes   120

(ix) The examination system   122

(x) The examination for Fellowship   127

(xi) Lectures and tutorial classes   129

(xii) Private tuition   132

(xiii) Textbooks and cram-books   133

(xiv) The professional schools   134

(xv) The Library   145

(xvi) Conclusion   147

6 Reform under Bartholomew Lloyd: 1831–1837   152

(i) Appointment and character of Lloyd   152

(ii) Circumstances favouring reform   154

(iii) Conservative opposition on the Board   157

(iv) The new mathematics, and new conditions for the mathematical chairs   159

(v) The reorganization of the Divinity School   161

(vi) Archbishop Whateley's projected Divinity College   165

(vii) The chair of Political Economy   168

(viii) The chair of Moral Philosophy   169

Contents

(ix)   Changes in terms and vacations   171
(x)   Institution of moderatorships and honor courses   172
(xi)   The new tutorial system   174
(xii)   The building of the New Square   176

7 Development in early Victorian times: 1837–1851   177

(i)   Appointment of Sadleir as Provost   177
(ii)   Repeal of the celibacy statute   177
(iii)   The non-tutor Fellows   179
(iv)   Foundation of the School of Engineering   180
(v)   The new chair of Natural Philosophy   185
(vi)   Developments in the Medical School   186
(vii)   New chairs associated with the Divinity School   189
(viii)   The awakening of the Law School   193
(ix)   The chair of Music   194
(x)   The Museum, and the growth of natural science   194
(xi)   Changes in the undergraduate course   198
(xii)   General increase in scholarly activity and diversity   198
(xiii)   1848: the spectre of revolution   200

8 The Royal Commission and its aftermath: 1851–1860   202

(i)   The genesis of the Commission   202
(ii)   Its appointment and members   204
(iii)   Its proceedings, and its reception by the College   206
(iv)   General confidence in the Board   209
(v)   Recommendations requiring action by Parliament   212
(vi)   The establishment of non-foundation scholarships   213
(vii)   Other recommendations requiring action by the Board   215
(viii)   Recommendations requiring the issue of Letters Patent   215
(ix)   The problem of lay Fellowships   217
(x)   Recommendations ignored by the Board   219
(xi)   The case of Basilio Angeli   224
(xii)   1858: a year of troubles   225
(xiii)   New moderatorships   229
(xiv)   Changes in the Fellowship examination   231
(xv)   The Indian Civil Service class, and the chairs of Sanskrit and
Arabic   232
(xvi)   The Museum Building and the Campanile   236

9 Shifting landmarks: 1861–1880   238

(i)   The intellectual climate of 1861   238
(ii)   The impact of the intellectual climate on Trinity College   239
(iii)   Ultramontanism and the growth of Catholic claims   243
(iv)   Disestablishment   244
(v)   The Irish University Question   246
(vi)   Possible solutions   248

Contents

(vii)   Fawcett's campaign for the abolition of religious tests   249
(viii) The defeat of Gladstone's University Bill   252
(ix)   Fawcett's Act and its effects   255
(x)   The University Council   258
(xi)   Discontent among the Junior Fellows; the problem of
        'stagnation'   259
(xii)   Provost Humphrey Lloyd; encouragement of research   263
(xiii) The rise of the classical school   265
(xiv)   Philosophy in the late nineteenth century   268
(xv)   Developments in Modern Languages and Literature   270
(xvi)   Developments in Mathematics, Science and Medicine   273
(xvii) Todd and the College Library   276

10   The end of the Victorian age: 1881–1900   279

(i)   Tensions in the political world   279
(ii)   Calm in the academic world   283
(iii)   Provost Jellett   284
(iv)   'Stagnation' again   287
(v)   The College in 1892: the physical aspect   289
(vi)   The Chancellor, Vice-Chancellor and Board   290
(vii)   The Junior Fellows   298
(viii) The non-Fellow Professors   309
(ix)   The assistants   321
(x)   The students   322
(xi)   The academic courses   326
(xii)   Student life in 1892   331
(xiii) The Tercentenary celebrations   335
(xiv)   The Graduates' Memorial Building   339

11   The admission of women   341

(i)   The background   341
(ii)   The campaign   344
(iii)   The aftermath   349

12   The last days of the Ascendancy: 1901–1919   354

(i)   The turn of the century and the death of Provost Salmon   354
(ii)   The struggle for the succession and the victory of Traill   355
(iii)   The Irish University Question once more; Archbishop Walsh   359
(iv)   Trinity College and the Gaelic movement   363
(v)   The Royal Commission of 1901   365
(vi)   The Royal Commission of 1906   368
(vii)   Bryce, Birrell, and the final solution   376
(viii) The dispute with the Church of Ireland over the Divinity
        School   379

Contents

(ix)	Relations with the Presbyterians	383
(x)	The drift towards secularization	384
(xi)	The agitation for constitutional reform, and the Letters Patent of 1911	387
(xii)	Decline in the quality of Fellows, and problems of the Fellowship examination	396
(xiii)	Better facilities for the sciences	405
(xiv)	Progress in History and stagnation in Law	411
(xv)	Academic developments on the periphery	414
(xvi)	War and insurrection; Mahaffy as Provost	418

13 Low profile: 1919–1947 · 423

(i)	Provost Bernard	423
(ii)	The financial crisis of 1919–1923	425
(iii)·	The policy of low profile, and the problems of adjustment for ex-Unionists	429
(iv)	Flags, toasts and anthems	433
(v)	The new system for election to Fellowship	434
(vi)	Provosts Gwynn and Thrift, and other administrative officers	439
(vii)	A contented College	444
(viii)	Changes in the pass course	445
(ix)	Changes in the honor and professional courses	448
(x)	Teaching and scholarship between the wars	450
(xi)	Higher degrees	460
(xii)	War and neutrality	463
(xiii)	Provost Alton	467
(xiv)	Archbishop McQuaid	469
(xv)	The Library crisis	471
(xvi)	Post-war finance and the government grant	473
(xvii)	Changes in student numbers and *provenance*	475

14 Epilogue: 1947–1952 · 477

(i)	Introduction	477
(ii)	Continuing financial problems	477
(iii)	Growing discontent among the academic staff	480
(iv)	The death of Alton and the appointment of McConnell; the 'palace revolution'	490

Appendix 1. Provosts of Trinity College since the foundation	498
Appendix 2. Statistics relating to students	499
Appendix 3. College finance and academic salaries	509
Notes	516
Bibliography	557
Index	567

Plates

1   Trinity College from the air, 1946   *frontispiece*
2   James Ussher, Archbishop of Armagh; Vice-Chancellor,
    1615–46   *page* 11
3   William Laud, Archbishop of Canterbury; Chancellor,
    1633–45   14
4   John Stearne, with a bust of Hippocrates; Professor of
    Physic, 1662–9   20
5   Henry Dodwell, Fellow, 1662–6   26
6   Cenotaph of Richard Baldwin, Provost, 1717–58   35
7   First and last paragraphs of the MS draft of *The principles
    of human knowledge* by George Berkeley, Fellow, 1707–24   39
8   'A bird's-eye perspective plan of Trinity College park
    and gardens' (*c.* 1779)   51
9   John Hely-Hutchinson, Provost, 1774–94   54
10 William Magee, Archbishop of Dublin; Fellow, 1788–
    1812   84
11 (a) Patrick Delany, Fellow, 1709–28   94
    (b) William Clement, Fellow, 1733–82   94
    (c) Sir William Rowan Hamilton, Professor of
        Astronomy, 1827–65   94
    (d) James McCullagh, Fellow, 1832–47   94
12 Two passages from the notebooks of Sir William Rowan
    Hamilton, recording the invention of quaternions   112
13 The Front Square during a quarterly examination
    (*c.* 1819)   122
14 Bartholomew Lloyd, Provost, 1831–7   153
15 Franc Sadleir, Provost, 1837–51   156
16 The College Museum (*c.* 1819)   195
17 Rudolph Thomas Siegfried, lecturer in Sanskrit and
    Comparative Philology, 1858–63   233
18 Mir Alaud Ali, Professor of Arabic (and later also of
    Persian and Hindustani), 1861–98   235

List of plates

19	John Pentland Mahaffy, Provost, 1914–19	266
20	Samuel Haughton, Fellow, 1844–97	297
21	George Francis Fitzgerald, Fellow, 1877–1901	306
22	Sir Robert Ball, Professor of Astronomy, 1874–92	316
23	Officers of the College Theological Society, 1891	319
24	The Elizabethan Society	350
25	Thomas Thompson Gray, Fellow, 1862–1924	407
26	John Joly, Professor of Geology, 1897–1933	409
27	Edward John Gwynn, Provost, 1927–37	440
28	Ernest Henry Alton, Provost, 1942–52	468

Figures

1 Annual matriculations, 1668–1950, plotted as five-year
  running averages   *page* 500
2 Number of qualifications awarded annually in Divinity,
  Medicine and Engineering, plotted as five-year running
  averages   502
3 Annual matriculations of Roman Catholics and
  Presbyterians, and of all non-Anglicans (including non-
  Christians), plotted as five-year running averages   504
4 Five-year averages for total income of the College, income
  from endowments, and annual surplus or deficit   510

Foreword

I deem it a pleasure and an honour to be asked to write a foreword to this history of Trinity College, Dublin, partly because the authors and I have been friends for some thirty years and also because their subject stirs chords of pride and fondness in my heart, as in the heart of every Trinity man who grew up in the old, intimate College of which they write.

Trinity College is approaching its four-hundredth birthday and this book may be regarded as a preliminary salute which differs from most such celebrations by being handsomely ahead of the anniversary date of 1992. It is not, of course, the only history of a College which has inspired much scholarly investigation over the past four centuries, but it is distinguished from all its predecessors by the authors' determination to view their university as what it is and always ought to be – a place of learning devoted to the advancement of knowledge, even if this has sometimes seemed to proceed by erratic, not to say eccentric, fits and starts. Ireland being Ireland, it has not been possible to exclude politics altogether, or to ignore the fact that in the course of its evolution Trinity has been a symbol of various things to various people, but by making this an 'academic history' Dr Webb and Dr McDowell have struck out a new and fruitful line of research.

The panorama they present is indeed impressive. We can follow the College from its earliest beginnings as a highly precarious Elizabethan foundation, through the very nearly fatal shocks of the seventeenth century to the splendours of its Georgian era (so magnificently embodied to this day in its principal buildings), and thence to the more sober, but also more solid triumphs of the nineteenth and early twentieth centuries. Thereafter came a change, as the College sought to adjust itself to the stressful and potentially dangerous circumstances of Irish independence. This period too is dealt with here, but in a suitably low key, for, as the authors make clear, the real adaptation of Trinity to the new Ireland began where their story ends, with the accession of Dr A.J. McConnell to the provostship in 1952; the revolution then set in motion still continues and cannot properly be evaluated for many years to come.

An ancient College is rich in folklore and in individual mannerisms. Both are given their full due here, but so also are the labours of those who worked prosaically to keep Trinity abreast of the always changing world of scholarship. In this they did not always succeed, for financial stringency and provincial isolation have sometimes taken their toll, but this history demonstrates conclusively that at certain crucial periods – for example, the late eighteenth and mid nineteenth centuries – Trinity came to terms with modernity much better than did either Oxford or Cambridge, against which august institutions the College has always rightly measured itself. And although the authors perhaps allow themselves a little mild chauvinism in this regard, they make a valuable point when they indicate that while all three universities underwent commissions of inquiry during the nineteenth century, Trinity's record was such that she did not have to undergo the often traumatic changes of her elder sisters. Ultimately, of course, the weight of numbers and of endowments enabled Oxford and Cambridge to pull ahead, but in the academic boat race of which we have here such a vivid description the Lady Elizabeth made a very respectable showing.*

A word should be added about the authors. Both are distinguished sons of the house and both have displayed throughout their careers that easy versatility which they themselves have identified as the hallmark of the older Trinity tradition. Dr Webb, besides possessing the most incisive mind of his generation in College, has achieved international fame as a botanist and has lifted his subject to new heights during his tenure of the chair of Botany. He has also devoted himself to protecting and enlarging the amenities of the College, especially those of the Common Room, and few aspects of our communal living have not benefited from his deep attachment to the place. Dr McDowell is a renowned and most prolific historian who, though affectionately regarded as embodying many of the attributes of the archetypal bookish don, also proved to be one of the most effective Junior Deans in the modern history of the College, this in itself being a tribute to his remarkable ability to meet the young on their own terms.

It is not to be expected or desired that two such quintessential 'College men' should entirely exclude themselves and their points of view from their book. They are fair-minded and open-minded, but, as the Provost who has seen them in action on the Board (the governing

---

*The Lady Elizabeth, as Trinity men will know but others may not, is the name of the London offshoot of the Boat Club; it is named, of course, after the foundress of the College.

body of Trinity), I would identify their attitude towards the most recent phases of Trinity's evolution as somewhat to the right of centre. Needless to say, this does not affect their history, except perhaps in the closing pages, but it does allow them to suffuse the old Trinity which bred them with the gentle glow of an unmistakable nostalgia. This nostalgia will be balm to the many Trinity men who read this book and even others, who are not of our company, will appreciate the characteristic blend of irony and affection which is the very essence of the book. Dr Webb and Dr McDowell are very far from being simply *laudatores temporis acti*, but that there is much to be praised they, and we, have no doubts. Would that one could be sure that generations still to come will share their *pietas* in equal measure.

March, 1981   F.S.L. LYONS

Preface

There are many pitfalls in the path of the historian of a College, and not the least of these is to make the history a work of *pietas* rather than of serious scholarship. We have done our best to avoid this. We yield to none in our affection for our *alma mater*, but for that very reason we believe that her history deserves a more objective and balanced treatment than it has hitherto received, and we are confident that she will appear handsome, even when delineated 'warts and all'. A college or a university (and T.C.D. is both) exists for a purpose, which may change from century to century but which deserves to be investigated and recorded. Its educational ideals change with the times, or remain obstinately unchanging in spite of them, and its success in achieving these ideals varies from generation to generation. So also do its aspirations and achievements in scholarship. If, as is the case with Dublin, it has for long a monopoly of higher education in its country, it does much to mould public opinion on intellectual matters, and in its turn it is affected in varying degree by changes in the *Zeitgeist*. It may take the lead in a political change; more often it accommodates itself reluctantly to a change which its members find distasteful.

It is these matters which we have tried to chronicle. Our history regards Trinity College primarily as an educational machine and a centre of learning, but also as a sounding-board for the religious, political and social questions agitating the society in which it is placed, from which it draws its students, and to which it sends out its graduates. We do not disdain the study of personalities, as there are few causes which have not been moulded, deflected, frustrated or brought to victory by a striking or subtle personality; and even minor characters can be revealing indicators of the society which generates them or tolerates them. But we do not cherish characters as a novelist might. We regard their reading, their writing, their teaching, their administration and their speeches as more important than their table manners or their matrimonial adventures. It is to indicate this that we have subtitled our history with the adjective 'academic'.

We have passed over the early years of the College's history relatively quickly, partly because they have been treated more fully by our predecessors than have recent centuries, and partly because it seemed unlikely that further research would add significantly to the rather scanty information now available on the educational aims and achievements of the College in its first hundred years. Our terminal date was fixed at 1952, for that year forms a watershed in College history comparable to 1831. In 1952 the impact of the post-war world of social welfare and university expansion, coupled with the death of Alton and his replacement as Provost by McConnell, ushered in a period of rapid and far-reaching change which, as we write, is still in progress, and which cannot be seen in proper perspective until a few more decades have elapsed. But we believe that it is now possible to view the years leading up to 1952 with relative detachment. To write of one's near-contemporaries in a world as small as that of Trinity is, of course, to tread in a minefield; we can only say that we have done our best to follow Othello's excellent advice to his biographers:

> Nothing extenuate,
> Nor set down aught in malice.

We have tried to maintain a similarly detached attitude to political and religious issues throughout the work. To praise or blame men for following the tradition in which they were brought up, or for revolting against it, is to desert history for propaganda and evangelism. A political viewpoint can, of course, be held generously or ungenerously, fanatically or realistically, anachronistically, opportunely or prematurely, and for these variations some praise or blame may be justifiable. That Trinity College was preponderantly Anglican through much of its history and staunchly Unionist from 1801 to 1921 are facts about which there can be no debate, and to suggest (as has lately been fashionable in some circles) that Tone and Hyde were more typical of its graduates than were Elrington and Salmon is plainly ridiculous. But although the College dissociated itself from its dissidents and occasionally expelled them, it persecuted them with much less severity than did many ruling castes elsewhere; Hyde and Salmon had more in common with each other than either had with F.E. Smith or Parnell. Perhaps it would have been better for Ireland and for Trinity if Provost Baldwin had been an advocate of Catholic emancipation and Provost Traill a Home Ruler, but to demand this of them is as foolish as to demand from Cardinal Cullen the ecumenicism of Pope John XXIII, or from De Valera the pragmatism of Cavour. We deal with history, not with the 'ifs' of history. It is only human to view certain attitudes or actions with distaste, but distaste is not in itself an adequate basis for moral condemnation. We ask the reader, therefore, to condemn no man unless he is confident that, in that man's place and with his upbringing, the reader himself would have behaved more wisely or more nobly.

Acknowledgments

We are very grateful to Dr F. S. L. Lyons for kindly writing a foreword to our book, and also to him and to Dr W.B. Stanford for reading through the entire typescript and offering valuable criticisms and suggestions. Dr E.J. McParland of the Department of Fine Arts gave us invaluable help in the preparation and assembling of the illustrations, and to him and to the staff of the College photographic centre we are greatly indebted for having taken so much trouble on our behalf.

It would have been impossible for us to have made such extensive use of the College muniments if they had not been so ably sorted and catalogued by Miss Margaret Griffith shortly before we started work on them. We must also thank Mr William O'Sullivan, Keeper of Manuscripts, and his staff for providing us with such excellent working conditions and facilitating our researches in every way. Mr Giltrap, Secretary to the College, made our work on the later chapters much easier by sending recent muniments still in his charge to the Library on long loan.

We must acknowledge our indebtedness to many of our contemporaries for their patient replies to our frequent questions, and especially to the Most Revd G.O. Simms for reading the text of chapter 13 and for correcting or supplementing our memories of life in the College in the early thirties.

We are grateful to the following institutions for permission to reproduce paintings in their possession: the Fitzwilliam Museum, Cambridge (plate 3), the Bodleian Library, Oxford (plate 5), the National Gallery of Ireland (plate 9), the Royal Irish Academy (plate 14), the Elizabethan Society (plate 24), and the Friendly Brothers of St Patrick (plate 27). Extracts from the Clarendon papers are published by kind permission of Lord Clarendon, and from the Bonar Law papers by permission of the House of Lords Records Office. We are grateful to the Board of Trinity College for permission to reproduce the plates not enumerated above, and for general encouragement and help.

Some parts of chapters 1–5 appeared as articles in *Hermathena*, and we are indebted to the editor for permission to reprint them here.

1

Early Days
1592–1640[1]

(i)

If the foundation of a university be taken as marking the final emergence of any part of Europe from the barren disorder of the Dark Ages into the fullness of medieval civilization, then the lack of such an institution in Ireland as late as 1590 reveals the miserably indecisive result of the long and wasteful struggle which had been waged there since the arrival of the Normans. The absence of a university did not, of course, mean that learning had been totally neglected. The monasteries, the bardic schools, and to some extent the households of the great Gaelic princes and Anglo-Norman nobles provided centres in which the rudiments of knowledge and culture might be acquired, ideas exchanged, and manuscripts collected, copied and edited. But none of these places – Youghal with its college, Maynooth with its library, Clonmacnoise with its painstaking annalists – could be compared for a moment with Oxford, Paris or Bologna. An Irishman who wished to enjoy the intellectual stimulus of a medieval university had to betake himself to England or the Continent. At intervals during the fourteenth and fifteenth centuries attempts were made to found a university in Dublin, but they received little support in Ireland. The English-speaking colony of the Pale was too small and too hard-pressed to find the leisure, the wealth or the sense of security necessary for such a project; and the Irish-speaking majority was naturally indifferent towards a proposal to found a university in the only part of the country in which the alien immigrants had successfully resisted assimilation. The most effective of these attempts produced in or about 1320 a theological college, which can be fairly described as of university status, in close association with St Patrick's Cathedral. It flourished for a few decades, but it eventually petered out from lack of funds.[2] Its only effect was, paradoxically, to delay the foundation of a university for half a century as it produced an *idée fixe* that the expenses must be defrayed from the revenues of the Cathedral, and this was successfully

1

resisted by the powerful ecclesiastics in possession of these revenues.

But by the rise and consolidation of the Tudor monarchy the general picture was transformed. In the course of the sixteenth century a group of resolute soldiers and civil servants, capable exponents of the new administrative techniques, subjected most of Ireland to the authority of the English crown. As a result of their labours Dublin gained in importance and prestige. For two centuries its citizens had gazed apprehensively at the hinterland, where, beyond the borders of a narrow and diminishing Pale, turbulent and often hostile septs despised English custom and flouted English law. But by 1590 the royal writ ran throughout three provinces, and Dublin, the centre of military, judicial and civil administration, was well on the way to becoming a real capital. Its population comprised not only the merchants and craftsmen clustered round the port, but also soldiers, civil servants, lawyers and divines. No other town in Ireland could compare with it in wealth, security or culture, so that if an Irish university were to be founded it would certainly be in Dublin. Accordingly in 1591 the Corporation of Dublin, inspired principally by Henry Ussher, Archdeacon of Dublin, and Luke Challoner, a learned and energetic divine who had formerly been a Fellow of Trinity College, Cambridge, set aside as the site for a college the lands and dilapidated buildings of the Augustinian priory of All Hallows, which had been granted to the city at the dissolution of the monasteries. Soon afterwards they petitioned the Irish Council to assist them in obtaining from the Queen a charter for the new foundation.

In taking these steps the citizens were probably actuated by more than a single motive. They no doubt desired, as they stated in their petition to the Council, to retain in Ireland those potentially valuable citizens, categorized as 'good wittes', who had hitherto been frustrated or forced abroad. But we may guess that they were also to some extent moved by the economic arguments with which Adam Loftus, the worldly-wise Archbishop of Dublin, had commended the scheme to them: colleges might be expected to swell the volume of trade, as they had clearly done at Oxford and Cambridge, and to reverse the decay in prosperity which had followed the dissolution of the monasteries.

For nearly half a century the Irish administration had been giving intermittent attention to the question of higher education. In such an age of fierce ideological conflict learning was intimately related to politics; and it was clear that education might be used in Ireland as a powerful auxiliary to military force, by breaking down the two great barriers to the spread of English influence: Catholicism and the Gaelic cultural tradition. George Browne, the first Reformed Archbishop of Dublin, and Perrot and Sidney, two of the more successful Elizabethan chief governors, had all been anxious to see a university founded in Dublin, but their successive projects had foundered, as has been mentioned above, on the difficulty of sequestering the revenues of St Patrick's Cathedral. The Queen and the English Council, though prodigal with their advice and good will, never offered financial backing for it. It was only in 1591, thanks to the initiative of the Dublin Corporation and to the prospect of obtaining from the now peaceful country the necessary money by a public appeal for subscriptions, that the project seemed at last feasible. The Irish Council gave its approval, and its recommendation, together with the citizens' offer as a solid proof that the foundation was desired and would be supported, was sufficient to persuade the Queen to issue a charter. On 3 March 1592,[3] 'the College of the Holy and Undivided Trinity near Dublin' was incorporated as 'the mother of a university', with the aim of providing 'education, training and instruction of youths and students in the arts and faculties . . . that they may be the better assisted in the study of the liberal arts and the cultivation of virtue and religion'.[4]

Only three Fellows and three Scholars were named in the charter, but their names were given *nomine plurium*, with the idea that the numbers should be increased as soon as the necessary finance was available. A modest expansion took place quite soon, as the confiscations consequent on political upheavals in the first fifteen years of the College's existence placed in the hands of the Crown large tracts of land (though mainly of indifferent quality) which it was prepared to use in the endowment of an institution which could be trusted to consolidate in the religious and cultural spheres the fruits of victory in the field. During the provostship of Temple, and probably before 1620, the number of Fellows had been increased to sixteen and they had been formally divided into seven Senior and nine Junior. The former, together with the Provost, formed the governing body of the College, usually known as the Board. The rate of increase in the number of Scholars is not so easy to estimate; the fragmentary data available from the 'Particular book'[5] suggest that there had been a total of fifty-one Scholars up to 1609, and by 1621–3 an annual admission of about sixteen implies that the number of seventy, which became fixed permanently by the charter of 1637, had been almost, if not completely attained. Soon after this it would appear that the practice of admitting students other than Scholars was initiated, some as sizars, some as pensioners, some as fellow-commoners, and some under the enigmatic title of *scholarium commensales*. The first substantial addition to the original buildings took place under Provost Chappell in 1627–41, but whether, when it was completed, all students could be accommodated *intra muros* we cannot tell.

The relationship between the University of Dublin and Trinity College is at first sight rather puzzling, and has been interpreted in more ways than one. To an Oxford or Cambridge man it seems obvious that there is in Dublin a university essentially similar to his own, but containing, by the accidents of history, only one college. And as the founders and early Fellows were Cambridge men, most of them from Trinity College, it would not have been surprising if they had fashioned college and university in such a way as to correspond in essentials with those with which they were familiar. But it cannot be denied that the University of Dublin, as distinct from Trinity College, has always been a most elusive and shadowy entity, and has never had even a well-grounded formal existence.[6] Sir Joseph Napier[7] tried to demonstrate that the University was, from the date on which the first degrees were conferred, a corporation distinct from (though not independent of) Trinity College. But the strained, and in places almost mystical reasoning of this practical lawyer must be viewed in its historical context: he wrote at a time when Gladstone offered a very real threat of including Trinity College as one college in a new, *omnium-gatherum* university. From a legal point of view the quietus to Napier's interpretation was given by the Master of the Rolls (Andrew Marshall Porter) in 1888, when he ruled that a bequest to 'the Corporation of the University of Dublin' vested in Trinity College.[8]

The only realistic interpretation, therefore, is that, whatever may have been the intentions of the Crown and its advisers with respect to the foundation of other colleges, and whatever the interpretation they gave to the mysterious phrase *mater universitatis* which is used of the College in the foundation charter, in point of fact the College was from its foundation vested with the powers, functions and status of a university, so that the single corporation then established must be regarded as a unitary body with collegiate and university aspects. Confirmation of this view is given by the wording of the Letters Patent of 1613 (which gave to the College representation in Parliament),[9] and by the fact that, about the same time, both the Provost and the Chancellor, though with different motives, wished to secure separate charters for the College and University, but were prevented from doing so by the Fellows.[10]

The anomalous structure of the University of Dublin is, however, more easily understood if it is realised that although it is, in one sense, the last of the medieval universities, and has therefore many formal resemblances to Oxford and Cambridge, it may with equal truth be regarded as the first of the colonial colleges which were, during the next two centuries, to be founded overseas. The thrifty Puritans of Dublin, like the founders of Harvard and Yale, realized that the available resources could support only one college. They saw to it, therefore, that their single foundation was able to discharge the functions of both a college and a university; and their indifference to the precise legal form by which this design might be carried out is reflected in the ambiguous wording of the Elizabethan charter.

(iii)

Of the specific means adopted by the rulers of the College in its early years to give effect to the founders' intentions – the promotion among the youth of Ireland, whether of English or Irish parentage, of civility, learning and Protestant piety – we can form some idea from the statutes of the early seventeenth century.[11] Undergraduates were then, as now, divided into four annual classes, which were lectured separately. The subject-matter of their formal lectures was that part of the curriculum which was later to be classified as Science, that is such branches of learning as would fall today under the heads of mathematics, physics and philosophy. The first year was lectured on rhetoric and the simpler, mainly linguistic aspects of logic; the second year on the controversies concerned with the nature and methods of logical reasoning. The third year was devoted to natural science, still presented in a mainly medieval dress; and the fourth to psychology and ethics. These lectures were of a catechetical nature, part of the time being devoted to exposition and part to questioning the students. Once a week the student was required to furnish an exercise, or to prepare and deliver a declamation on the subjects on which he was lectured. Undergraduates of the two senior years were required to take a regular part in the disputations, which were performed in the traditional manner, with respondent, opponents and moderator. These were for the most part private collegiate exercises; but some of them were public university functions of greater formality. Satisfactory performance in the latter was the principal requirement for a degree. Further instruction of a more personal and private character was given by each tutor to his own pupils in his chambers; here attention was presumably paid to the more literary part of the course. This instruction bore fruit in a weekly Latin essay on the student's work, a weekly Latin composition in prose or verse, and an occasional Latin declamation on a set theme.

The authors of these early statutes clearly wished to give the undergraduate a thorough grounding not only in Latin but also in Greek and Hebrew – the trilingual basis of biblical study and theological scholarship. In the university statutes we accordingly find that a good knowledge of New Testament Greek and some knowledge of Hebrew was required of candidates for the B.A. degree. The teaching of Greek was probably effective at times, at least after 1637, but the reiteration in 1659 and again in 1664 of the necessity of proficiency in Greek suggests that this regulation was difficult to enforce. In the case of Hebrew the difficulties in finding a sufficient number of competent teachers seem to have been too great. In spite of this and later attempts to incorporate it into the regular course,[12] Hebrew has in practice remained, except for very brief periods, an optional subject of study, even for ordinands,[13] though a fairly liberal provision of prizes has ensured that its study has never died out.

It had already become customary by 1600 for the majority of students at Oxford and Cambridge who did not intend to enter academic life or proceed to ordination to leave college after taking their B.A., instead of, as formerly, regarding the master's degree as the normal conclusion of their studies.[14] Nevertheless, the proportion of ordinands was high, and the M.A. degree was not then, as it is now, a formality; accordingly the studies prescribed for resident bachelors form an important supplement to the undergraduate course. At Dublin the bachelor was bound to attend lectures in political science and mathematics, to take part in disputations on mathematical and physical topics, and to deliver prelections on all three subjects. He had also, to qualify himself for his M.A. degree, to give evidence of progress in the study of Greek and Hebrew. Only after he had become a Master was he fit to begin the study of Divinity

In their ideas of the nature of the studies necessary to constitute a university education and of the manner in which they should be taught, the men who framed these early statutes were, of course, largely influenced by their own experience of university life at Cambridge. But they did not copy slavishly from the regulations of the older university or its colleges. A comparison of the statutes of 1629 with those of Cambridge University (1570) or Trinity College, Cambridge (1560)[15] shows that the curriculum was recast in such a way as to take account both of the changes in thought during the past half-century, and of the different needs that had to be met in the new environment. The Irish schools were much inferior to the English, and (partly as a consequence of this) the undergraduates of Dublin were younger than those of Cambridge, and thus doubly worse prepared. The freshman's mind could be treated almost as a *tabula rasa*, and it was reasonable, therefore, to devote the first two years to teaching him how to think and express himself. It was time enough later, when he became a sophister, to provide him with material on which to exercise his now trained faculties. But as it was realized that his university career might well end with his B.A., it was necessary, in order to give his course some symmetry and completeness, to bring down to under-graduate level some studies which were at Oxford and Cambridge reserved to the graduate. In the entire omission of mathematics from the undergraduate course Dublin did not differ from the English universities; for though it had been introduced as a first-year study at Cambridge about 1550, when Platonic philosophy was in the ascendant, it did not long survive the sneers of those scholars who despised it for its practical utility.[16]

In one important respect the early teaching in Dublin looked forward rather than backward – in the emphasis laid on university and tutorial lectures as the main instrument of instruction. The disputations are there and they form an important element in the student's education, but the lectures are at least as important. In Trinity College, Cambridge, however, it is made clear that the disputations are paramount, and that tutorial instruction is provided chiefly to help the student to acquit himself creditably in Hall on the following day.

No textbooks are named in the original statutes, and in many of the subjects the matter of the lectures can only be guessed at. But in the case of logic, the staple diet of the freshman years, we are on firmer ground. The conjunction of rhetoric with logic, and the use of the terms *inventio* and *judicium* make it clear that the logical methods taught were those of Petrus Ramus. The *Dialectica* of Ramus, violently anti-Aristotelian in tone, and much simpler for the student (and correspondingly superficial, according to his opponents) than the school-men's treatises which it replaced, had, especially since the death of the author in the massacre of St Bartholomew, swept through the Protestant universities of Europe. The first five Provosts of Trinity College were Cambridge men, and Ramist logic had been firmly established since about 1580 as the dominant school at Cambridge.[17] Loftus was perhaps too old and too isolated to have been affected by the movement, but his successors, Walter Travers and Henry Alvey, were younger men who had recently been in touch with Cambridge thought, and William Temple, the fourth Provost (1609–27), was a keen Ramist, who had published as early as 1584 an edition of the *Dialectica* with notes. This had soon become a popular textbook, and we may be sure that it was the basis of logical teaching in Dublin in the early seventeenth century. In most of the Protestant universities the reign of Ramus lasted for nearly a century, and was only brought to an end by the gradual acceptance of Baconian and Cartesian modes of thought. But in Dublin, as we shall see, he was prematurely dethroned by an Aristotelian counter-revolution.

Taken as a whole, the curriculum prescribed in the earliest statutes is marked by the conservative tendency which was to prevail in university education for the next two centuries. The systematic teaching of Greek and the time devoted to Latin composition reflect in some small degree a Renaissance interest in the literature of the ancient world; but in its essential structure this curriculum, planned three-quarters of a century after the death of Erasmus, is still infused with the thought of the Middle Ages.

This need not surprise us if we agree with Maurice Craig that the Renaissance made its singularly belated entry to Ireland when the great Duke of Ormonde 'stepped out of his pinnace on to the sands of Dublin Bay' in 1662 to resume his interrupted viceroyalty.[18] Craig is thinking primarily in terms of architecture, for while Longleat was building, and even in the early days of Inigo Jones, an Irish architect would have seldom been able to find a purchaser for anything but a strongly fortified tower house. But the aphorism applies almost as truly to letters. By 1662, of course, the original ideals of the Renaissance were *vieux jeu* elsewhere, and consequently there was never heard in Ireland anything but a very faint echo of that enthusiastic and uncritical admiration of ancient literature which had spread from Italy to northern Europe early in the sixteenth century. Latin was, indeed, cultivated in Trinity College as the international language of scholarship, but it was only rarely that a writer felt obliged to take Cicero rather than St Jerome as the model for his style. Greek was studied deeply only by a few, and primarily as the language of the New Testament, the Septuagint and the Eastern fathers. By 1592 the Reformation had replaced the Renaissance as the main focus of intellectual interest and debate, and it is natural, therefore, that in the half-century following its foundation the scholarship of Trinity College should have been confined almost entirely to theology and biblical studies. Admittedly the intention had been to teach law and medicine as well as divinity, but lack of endowment, together with a lack of sustained effort on the part of successive Provosts, prevented the development of these schools, even on a modest scale, until after the Restoration. Ireland was still a frontier land where Catholicism and Protestantism were struggling for total victory, and the College was seen primarily as a training school from which Protestant divines, well armed for battle, should go into parishes throughout the country.

Within the spectrum of British Protestantism it was at this time Puritanism – strenuous, serious, learned, and firmly determined to mould men's minds and characters – that was the most powerful force. Trinity offered to an English Puritan a place which was near the front line of battle against Rome, but in which he would be free from most of the unwelcome harassment from Lambeth or Whitehall to which he was from time to time subjected at home. It was natural enough, therefore, that when Loftus gave up his nominal tenure of the Provost-ship in 1594 the next four Provosts should be Puritans from England: Travers, indeed, has some claim to be regarded as the intellectual leader of the movement in England, and his *Ecclesiastical discipline* (1574) was an indispensable handbook for his followers (not least because its clear English replaced the heavy Latin of Calvin). In Dublin, however, these men spent most of their time in struggling, with very limited success, with financial, disciplinary and constitutional problems, and such scholarly works as they produced were achieved in less exacting surroundings.

(iv)

One respect in which local conditions suggested an addition to the curriculum current in the English universities was the provision of some instruction in Irish. This was prompted, not by any philological or literary enthusiasm, but in the interests of religion, and perhaps to a small extent also of other aspects of 'civilitie'. The same impulse that led Luther to publish his German Bible led William Daniel, one of the early Fellows, seventy years later, to translate into Irish the New Testament and the Book of Common Prayer.[19] Some years later Provost Bedell prepared an Irish version of the Old Testament, though this was not printed till 1685. During Bedell's brief tenure of the Provostship (1627–9) it was decreed that there should be an Irish lecture in Hall and Irish prayers in the Chapel on holy days. His enthusiasm must have been passed on to at least a few of his colleagues, for a year after his resignation an Irish chapter of the New Testament was ordered to be read by a Scholar during dinner.[20] Apart from the obvious desire to provide clergy who were to serve outside the Dublin area with a medium through which they could preach the reformed faith so as to be understood by all, one may surmise that there may also have been some idea of making Irish-speaking students feel at home in College, and of preventing them from identifying Protestantism too strongly with a foreign culture. But to most Englishmen this identification was almost axiomatic, and with the advent of Provost Chappell in 1634 interest in the teaching of Irish seems to have died out. Nearly fifty years later, during the provostship of Narcissus Marsh, a brief attempt was made to revive instruction in Irish, at any rate for enthusiasts. Paul Higgins, a native speaker, was employed to preach a monthly sermon in Irish and to instruct Scholars 'who had a mind to learn' to read and write the language. But by this time the first rays of the Enlightenment were beginning to illuminate the eastern horizon, and men felt less inclination to waste their energies on a subject so remote from the world of Descartes, Locke, Newton and the Royal Society. Higgins seems to have made one disciple in John Hall, a Kerryman and probably a native speaker, who was a student under Marsh and subsequently a Fellow. For a few years he employed at his own expense a man named Dinny to give lessons in Irish to such members of the College as wanted it, and from 1708 Charles Lynegar taught Irish in a semi-official capacity for a few years, but the subject then lapsed, and was not revived till well over a century later.[21]

(v)

Any attempt to assess the scholarship displayed by the Fellows of the first fifty years during their period of residence in the College is handicapped by the defective nature of the early records, which give very little information of the length of tenure of the Fellowships. It must be recalled that at this period many of the Scholars entered College in their early teens[22] and took their M.A. degree, therefore, a year or two before the canonical age for ordination. Fellowship, for those who were elected, usually followed closely on the Master's degree, and sometimes preceded it, so that its tenure was spent partly in awaiting ordination and partly in looking for a suitable living. Roughly speaking, therefore, it may be said that in terms of age and maturity the undergraduates, graduate students and Fellows of those days corresponded respectively to the schoolboys, undergraduates and graduate students of today. A fair number of Fellows seemed to have stayed for the full term of seven years permitted by the Elizabethan charter, but only a very few managed to stay on longer. It is not surprising therefore, that the literary output of those actually in possession of Fellowships was small.

James Ussher towers head and shoulders above the other early Fellows, both by the width and profundity of his scholarship and by the extent of his influence on College policy. His name, if it is remembered at all by intellectuals today, is usually mentioned with a pitying smile as that of the man who taught that the world was created in 4004 B.C. But the smile is misplaced. If one grants the premise that the Pentateuch is a historical record to be interpreted literally (and it is a premise that nobody at that time would deny; Cromwell and Charles I could agree on that, if on nothing else), then 4004 B.C. is a more rational deduction from the tangled and sometimes inconsistent biographies of the patriarchs than any other date that had hitherto been suggested. Ussher went very deeply into the problems of chronology, but also of geography, linguistics, church history and controversial theology, and

2   James Ussher, Archbishop of Armagh. Vice-Chancellor, 1615–46.

he soon earned for himself the reputation of the most learned man in
the realm. Although he held his Fellowship for only five years, he was
appointed in 1607, while still resident in Dublin, as Professor of
Divinity (usually referred to as Professor of Theological Controversies –
a nice commentary on the intellectual atmosphere of the age),[23] and he
held this post till he became a bishop in 1621. He was also Vice-
Chancellor of the University from 1615, nominally till 1646 and effectively till 1640, when he left Ireland never to return. In this latter
capacity he was largely responsible for the appointment of Bedell and
Chappell as Provosts and Laud as Chancellor, and he helped to mediate
between Laud and the College. Although he was a better scholar than

administrator his honesty, modesty and good temper made him acceptable to both sides in many of the controversies of the day, and he was
thus able to combine a mainly Calvinist theology with a defence of
episcopacy and a tolerance of a certain amount of ritual. There was no
real *via media* in the conflicts of 1640–60, but Ussher found a near
approximation to one, so that, although he never renounced his episcopal rank, Cromwell ordered that he should be buried in Westminster
Abbey and allowed the Anglican liturgy to be used at the graveside.

His brother Ambrose provides a rather pathetic contrast. An equally
devoted scholar, and not far behind in his breadth of learning he seems
never to have looked beyond his study window. He prepared an
original translation of the Old Testament from the Hebrew, and completed it just as the Authorized Version appeared; naturally enough it
did not find a publisher. Besides this a large pile of manuscripts on
theology, politics, Arabic and astronomy, still surviving in the College
Library, bears witness to his industry, but his only work to appear in
print was his *Brief catechism*.

When James Ussher vacated the Professorship of Divinity in 1621
two abortive attempts were made to find a successor in England. In
May the Board appointed John Preston of Queen's College, Cambridge,
to the post, but by this time he had his eye on the Mastership of
Emmanuel (which he secured the following year) and presumably
declined. A second attempt was made in August by the election of
Samuel Ward of Ipswich, a well-known and extreme Puritan preacher,
always in trouble with the authorities but usually protected by his local
popularity. Unfortunately the invitation was issued in the one year in
which this popularity failed to protect him, for he had been jailed for
circulating an anti-Spanish cartoon which had incensed the Spanish
Ambassador. There is no evidence that he came to Dublin, and if he did
it must have been for a very short time. In 1623, therefore, the Board
settled for a local man and one of their own number, Joshua Hoyle.
Hoyle, who may perhaps have spent a short time at Magdalen Hall,
Oxford, before coming to Dublin, had been a Fellow since 1617. His
sermons were said to be well stocked (over-stocked in the opinion of
some) with learning, but his only writing to have survived, *A reioynder
to Master Malone's reply concerning reall presence*,[24] published just
before the outbreak of the rebellion, shows him as a racy and hard-
hitting controversialist. He lost no time in putting Bellarmine in his
place and, in his preface, trounced with gusto the Jesuits, 'those
croaking Egyptian frogs', driving them 'from the scriptures to the
fathers, from the fathers to their uncles the schoolmen and from them
to history'. But in 1641 even Hoyle's vigorous methods were replaced
by more literal apostolic blows and knocks, and he retreated to Oxford,

where, under Parliamentary auspices, he became Professor of Divinity and Master of University College. No successor was appointed until after the Restoration, but this was in part due to the fact that under the Commonwealth Provost Winter made himself responsible for much of the teaching in Divinity.

Before 1637 there was no statutory obligation for Fellows to take holy orders, and in the first thirty years of the College there were eight who remained laymen. James Fullerton and James Hamilton, appointed soon after the foundation, were Scots who kept a school in Dublin, at which James Ussher, among others, was educated. They seem to have been primarily political agents of James VI, sent over to win support in Ireland for his succession when the Queen at length should die. They were astute men of business, and in the intervals of carving out their own careers they gave, from time to time, valuable help to the struggling College. Fullerton was buried in Westminster Abbey, and Hamilton became a wealthy peer in Co. Down. Of the remainder, Henry Bourchier inherited from his cousin the earldom of Bath and became Privy Seal during the Civil War. He was one of those charged with defending Oxford for the King, but according to Clarendon was an unenthusiastic Royalist, and only opposed the Parliamentary forces 'out of the morosity of his nature'. Maurice Eustace became Speaker of the House of Commons and later Lord Chancellor of Ireland, and three others became judges. They can have learnt little law in Trinity, but the fact that so many of these laymen had successful careers suggests that their general education there stood them in good stead. Soon after 1620 it would seem that either moral or financial pressure to take orders must have increased, as no laymen are to be found among the Fellows elected between 1622 and 1651. The statutes of 1637 dispelled any ambiguities; henceforth all Fellows were to take orders except two, who could remain laymen. One of these (the Jurist) was supposed to devote his energies to the study of law, the other (the Medicus) to medicine. A second Jurist's place was established in 1761.

(vi)

In 1637 the Chancellorship of the University fell vacant, and Laud was urged both by Wentworth and by the Vice-Chancellor (Archbishop Ussher) to accept it. He agreed, on condition that he was given a free hand in revising the statutes of the College, which he declared (with some justification) to have hitherto 'been as ill governed as any college in Christendom, or worse'.[25] Laud was an untiring worker in the field of academic administration and reform; no task was too great for his industry, no detail too small for his attention. He had by this time

3 William Laud, Archbishop of Canterbury. Chancellor, 1633–45.
(After Sir Anthony van Dyck, Fitzwilliam Museum, Cambridge.)

almost completed his revision of the Oxford statutes, and was soon to
assert, in the face of great opposition, his right to visit Cambridge. The
problems of Dublin did not detain him for long. In 1634 he paved the
way by installing a Provost of his own way of thinking; in 1636 he
began the revision of the statutes; and by 1637 the Elizabethan charter
had been surrendered[26] and a new charter and a new code of statutes

14

were in force. Attention has been paid by historians mainly to the constitutional changes whereby, in accordance with the monarchical principles of the new Chancellor, the powers of the Crown and of the Provost were considerably increased;[27] but the educational changes are no less striking. Laud was a high-churchman, an authoritarian and an Oxford man. Ramus stood for Puritanism, for intellectual rebellion and for Cambridge influence. In the new version of the chapter *De classium scholasticis exercitiis* we find, therefore, an Aristotelian tone imposed throughout the course. The *Isagoge* of Porphyrius, the traditional introduction to Aristotle's logic, was prescribed for the first year; the other classes read Aristotle himself, with an injunction to the lecturer not to wander far from the text. But the order in which the different sciences were studied was the same as before: the second year was to be lectured on some part of the *Organon*, the third on the *Physics*, and the fourth on the metaphysical works, except during Lent, when these were to be replaced by the *Nicomachean ethics*. The arrangements for the students' exercises and disputations were also left unchanged, except that disputations were enjoined for freshmen as well as sophisters, and that the use of rhetorical flourishes in the putting forward of arguments was deprecated. The subjects assigned to the bachelors were unchanged, but a useful provision in the new statutes ensured that two of the Fellows should be detailed to lecture on Greek.

The sweeping constitutional changes which accompanied this revision of the curriculum were not due merely to the officiousness of the new Chancellor. The forty-five years since the foundation had not been entirely happy ones, and reforms were plainly needed if the College was ever to justify the hopes of its founders. The faculties of law and medicine still existed only on paper, and although in arts and divinity sound teaching had been given and a few works of scholarship had been produced, it was obvious that much of the energies of the Provosts and Fellows had been diverted into other channels. For this the parsimonious attitude of the Government was partly to blame. Persistent and skilful pleading at Court had been necessary to secure the grants of land required as an endowment, and the subsequent negotiations with the tenants of the new estates – many of which had been devastated in the Elizabethan wars – were prolonged and tiresome. But besides all this the time devoted to quarrels among the Fellows had been disproportionate, even for an academic society. Usually the dispute turned on the powers of the Provost or the interpretation of the statutes, which were surprisingly vague and ambiguous even on matters as important as the mode of election of the Provost. But if these legal niceties, coupled with personal animosities, failed to rally their parties the leaders could always fall back on *odium*

15

theologicum, and in Dublin, as elsewhere, charges and counter-charges of Arminianism and Calvinism formed the backbone of early seventeenth-century controversy.

The Provost appointed in 1634 at Laud's instance (and with the consent of Ussher, though he may have regretted it later) was William Chappell, most widely remembered as Milton's tutor at Christ's and the 'old Damoetas' of his *Lycidas*.[28] He had been brought over to Dublin from Cambridge as early as 1612 to act as Dean and Catechist, but he seems to have returned after about a year. Although some of his actions as Provost were almost as high-handed as those by which Strafford and Laud had secured his election, he restored order to the College; and, as he was a good administrator who was *persona grata* to the Government, the College prospered under his rule. We can take with several grains of salt the entry in the Register on his departure, which praises him for having

gratiously reformed the students, happily promoted new Statutes and rich amplifying of the buildings . . . and wonderfully increased the College Plate and stocke, reduced all things into a blessed order, and faithfully governed by the space of sixe yeares as a glorious pattern of sobriety, justice and godlyness.

Beneath the flattery, however, there is a fair foundation of truth.

2

Sedition, privy conspiracy and rebellion
1640–1717

(i)

When Chappell resigned the Provostship in 1640[1] the political balance was shifting fast. Strafford's enemies were gathering round him and Laud's position was becoming insecure. The new Provost (Richard Washington, an Oxford man[2]) sat tight and waited on events; but events, fifteen months after his arrival, took the form of the rebellion of 1641, and he fled to England, never to return, accompanied by many of the Fellows. Although Dublin was held by the Crown, almost all the College lands and the livings to which it had the presentation were in rebel hands. Matriculations dried up to a trickle, and the few entries in the Register of this period mostly relate to the sale of plate. By 1644 the Chancellor was in the Tower awaiting execution, the Vice-Chancellor resident in England, and there was still no Provost. Next year saw the appointment of the Marquess of Ormonde as Chancellor and Anthony Martin (a former Fellow, now Bishop of Meath, but expelled from his diocese by the rebels) as Provost, followed by the appointment as Vice-Chancellor in 1646 of Henry Jones, a former Fellow and now Bishop of Clogher. But the anarchy in the country, in which several armies were marching and counter-marching, frustrated the hopes which the appointment of these men had raised, and the final blow came in 1650, when the plague visited Dublin and claimed Provost Martin as one of its victims.

When the plague had ceased in 1651 and the military victories of Cromwell were sufficiently assured to allow the Parliamentary Commissioners to turn their attention to the College, they had first to ask themselves was there still a college in being to be revived. There was, but only just. Their first step was a wise one: they appointed as Provost Samuel Winter, who was, like Martin and Bedell, a graduate of Emmanuel College, the main nursery of Puritanism in Cambridge. Winter was a devoted, scholarly and relatively tolerant ruler, and under his rule some progress towards revival was made. The finances improved, thanks largely to journeys undertaken by the Provost

17

himself to Donegal and Kerry to make arrangements for the regular collection of rents. A few former Fellows were induced to return; some new Fellows and Professors were appointed; and although the number of students remained pitifully small till about 1657 the educational machine was coaxed into motion again.

In England the Civil War had presented to clergy of the school of Ussher an almost intolerable dilemma, for the creeds and religious practices of the King and of Cromwell were to them equally distasteful. But no middle course was open, and either their principles or circumstances forced them to take sides. We find, therefore, the names of ex-Fellows of Trinity both in the Royalist and the Parliamentary camps. In Ireland, however, the dilemma was not so acute, for although Royalists fought against Parliamentarians there were intervals in which they combined forces to fight together against the Catholics, and later to suppress the Anabaptists. There were among the Fellows and ex-Fellows a few extremists on either side, but most of them were, like Ussher, prepared to tolerate the rule of either King or Protector in the knowledge that at such a safe distance from the seat of power the principles of neither would be applied with remorseless rigour, and that their consciences would have at least a little freedom for manoeuvre. Moreover, Henry Cromwell, who was *de facto* Lord Deputy in Ireland for about six years, although personally very loyal to his father, seems to have held his political and religious beliefs in a very diluted form.

There was not, in consequence, a complete purge of the Fellows either at the establishment of the Commonwealth or at the Restoration. A few of those who served under two masters may have been time-servers, but others were genuinely moderate men, prepared to endure either regime so long as it did not proceed to extremes. We read, therefore, of men like Caesar Williamson, who fought with the King's army at Edgehill despite his holy orders, served as Fellow under Winter for the last seven years of the Commonwealth, was confirmed in his office at the Restoration, and ended his life as Dean of Cashel; or Nathaniel Hoyle, who remained at his post in 1641 and, as Vice-Provost, administered the College in the difficult years of 1641–4, retired to Oxford for a few years but reappeared as a Fellow in 1652, and was confirmed at the Restoration, though he resigned the following year. Henry Jones, again, appointed Vice-Chancellor by Ormonde, although his brother was one of Cromwell's Major-Generals, had been made Bishop of Clogher in 1645; during the Commonwealth he tactfully dropped the style and title of bishop, but in 1661 he shook the dust off his rochet, and although he was not reappointed as Vice-Chancellor he was soon promoted to the see of Meath.

The records of the men who held Fellowship under Winter are sadly defective, but it would seem that although a few were former students of the College the majority were brought over from England, These included Samuel Mather, a former Fellow of Harvard and a prolific writer in the Puritan interest, but his connexion with the College seems to have been little more than nominal. By far the most able was John Stearne, who had been elected a Scholar in 1641, but left for England on the outbreak of the rebellion and completed his education at Cambridge, where he seems to have learnt medicine, and later at Oxford. Although he had moved in Royalist circles in England he was appointed to a Fellowship in Dublin by order of the Parliamentary Commissioners in 1651. He practised as a doctor in the city, but found time also to discharge in College the duties of Registrar, and later of Professor of Hebrew.[3] Shortly before the Restoration he resigned his Fellowship and married, but in 1660 he was reappointed by *mandamus*, with a dispensation from the requirement of celibacy, and in 1662 he became Professor of Physic. This gave him the status necessary to found the College of Physicians, which was originally housed in 'Trinity Hall', a building only a stone's throw from Trinity College; it had been originally built as a Bridewell, and was used intermittently and rather ineffectively as a hall of residence for students of Trinity. The College of Physicians was intended as a medical school subordinate to Trinity College, but after Stearne's death it drifted into a position of virtual independence, largely because the University was unable to supply qualified physicians to manage it.[4] Stearne, however, saw it receive its Royal charter two years before his early death at the age of forty-five; and meanwhile he had written a series of remarkable books on philosophy and theology, in which a gallant attempt was made to combine the tenets of Stoicism with those of Christianity.

Stearne was encouraged in his earlier years in College by Winter, who clearly wished to broaden the range of subjects studied and taught there. Regulations were introduced, with at least some temporary success, for the more effective study of Greek and Hebrew, and four Professorships – of Law, Physic, Oratory and Mathematics – appear to have been established during Winter's provostship. Of the first three we know nothing; the only evidence of their existence is provision for their salaries in a budget of 1658.[5] But with Mathematics we are on firmer ground, and the establishment of this chair provides an early example of the pressure exercised by a government on a university in favour of vocational rather than liberal education. The victory of Cromwell's army had given, as the Parliamentary Commissioners rather coyly expressed it, 'a great occasion for surveying the lands of Ireland', and it was made clear when Miles Sumner, a former Scholar of

4   John Stearne, with a bust of Hippocrates. Professor of Physic, 1662–9.
(Painter unknown, Trinity College.)

the College, who had fought with the Parliamentary army in England,
was appointed to the post that his chief duty would be to train students
in the technique of surveying; even soldiers were allowed to attend his
lectures.

Generally speaking Winter, as behoves a good Puritan, strove to
make the College a society of God-fearing, sober-living and diligent

men and boys, and he succeeded as well as the difficulty of the times would allow. He seems to have imposed a stricter discipline than his predecessors, and this was no easy task, as disorderly behaviour on a scale larger than that which can be considered normal for a university was a problem during most of the seventeenth and the first half of the eighteenth century. One is tempted, perhaps, to overestimate the amount of indiscipline from the detail in which punishments are recorded in pages of the Register, which often contain little else, and in a large number of the entries the offences are no worse than fisticuffs in the College, frequenting ale-houses in the town, or failing to give to the Fellows the statutory marks of respect. But more serious crimes are not infrequent. Part of the trouble was that whereas the towns of Oxford and Cambridge had grown up round the universities, which had permitted the establishment at an early date of proctorial rights of search and arrest in the town, Dublin was too large a city at the time of the foundation of Trinity College for the imposition of such rights to be tolerated or effectively enforced. On the other hand, being a residential college, it had to look after the morals of its students in a way which the Scottish universities could ignore.

A further difficulty arose from the fact that, whereas the pains and penalties prescribed in the early statutes (including whippings and canings) were designed for students almost entirely of what we now regard as secondary-school age, as the century proceeded the age of matriculation became much more variable, so that in the latter part of the Commonwealth, while 20 per cent of the students were under sixteen at entry 30 per cent were over nineteen. It was difficult to devise a disciplinary code for such a mixed body. The Government from time to time showed concern at the lack of discipline, and it was even suggested in 1682 that it might be wise to transfer the College to the newly built Royal Hospital at Kilmainham, which would be further from the temptations of city life.[6] A permanent improvement had to await the development around 1750 of a higher standard of elegance in society in general and a contempt for the grosser forms of rowdyism. But under Winter there was a brief period when the dominant section of society approved of strict discipline in all aspects of life, and this was to some extent reflected in the College.

(ii)

The Restoration brought about some change in the personnel of the College but not a drastic purge. Of those in positions of authority in 1660 only one had a regular title to his post; that was the Vice-Provost, Nathaniel Hoyle, who had been elected a Fellow in 1631 and had taken the oath under the new statutes in 1637. He had discharged the duties of Fellow continuously, except for a period of about five years during the Civil War, which he had spent at Oxford. Although he was a strong Puritan, who got into trouble under Chappell for refusing to wear a surplice, he was confirmed as Senior Fellow in 1660. But the Provost and all the other Fellows had either been appointed by procedures which were irregular in terms of the Laudian statutes, or else had failed to take the prescribed oath. Their places were, therefore, declared vacant, but it was made clear that those who were prepared to conform to the Anglican liturgy and to take the necessary oaths would be reappointed.

Nine of the Fellows accepted these conditions, and the position was regularized by a King's Letter of December 1660, appointing five new Senior Fellows,[7] and empowering them to elect suitable Junior Fellows, though the same letter directed them to give one of these places to a physician with the unlikely name of Lambert Gougleman. He was not a burden to the College for long, as he seems to have resigned in 1661 for a destination which history does not record.

Meanwhile Thomas Seele had been provisionally appointed as Provost, and this was formally confirmed in January 1661. He had been elected a Fellow under Chappell, and was evidently of Royalist sympathies, as he remained at his post till 1647 and spent the Commonwealth period as a preacher in Dublin, celebrating the Anglican liturgy whenever circumstances permitted. From 1666 till his death in 1675 he combined the post of Provost with that of Dean of St Patrick's,[8] but neither College nor Cathedral seems to have suffered from neglect during the period of his dual role.

The Restoration was not only a political event of the first importance; its significance in the religious sphere was almost as great. Both the mitre and the crown were rescued from the dust into which they had been trodden by impious men, and the mutual support which they afforded each other – recognized long ago by James I in his well-known epigram: No Bishop, no King – meant that Anglicanism, in Ireland as well as in England, was now the Established Church in a far more precise and effective sense than it had hitherto been. The new dispensation was well summed up at the spectacular ceremony in St Patrick's Cathedral in 1661, when twelve bishops were consecrated to fill the sees left vacant during the Commonwealth.[9] The anthem, specially written for the occasion by the Dean, had as its refrain:

> Angels look down, and joye to see
> Here, as above, a Monarchie;
> Angels look down, and joye to see
> Here, as above, a Hierarchie.

The days of the ambiguous Puritanism of Temple were over; Trinity College was to be staunchly Anglican for the next two centuries. The degree of toleration extended to dissenters might vary from time to time, but there was to be no place for them in the Corporation.

But although the Restoration brought constitutional stability to the College it was some years before this was followed by material prosperity. Its relative affluence in the last two years of the Commonwealth rested on insecure foundations, for it had been awarded part of the revenues of the Archbishopric of Dublin and of St Patrick's Cathedral, and these, of course, had to be handed back. Although in the early years of Charles II it received some grants, it was one thing to be given a grant by the King, but it was quite another thing to extort the cash from the civil servants or the rents from the tenants of the new lands. For three successive years (1664–6) vacancies in the body of Fellows were left unfilled because of insufficient funds, and in 1666 the election of Scholars also was deferred. At this point the Government stepped in: four Fellows were appointed by King's Letter early in 1667, and a few months later the Archbishop of Dublin, presumably in his capacity of Visitor, ordered the election of thirty-two Scholars. Somehow or other the finances recovered fairly soon and for the remainder of the reign of Charles II the College enjoyed a modest but steadily increasing prosperity. The annual average of matriculations, which in 1665 had stood at about thirty-five, had reached fifty by 1674 and sixty-five by 1683.[10] By this time the College was bursting at the seams, and an extension to the buildings was clearly needed. Bequests and gifts for this purpose began to come in, and a new and larger Chapel was consecrated in 1684. It was to have been followed by a new Hall, which was to serve for examinations and disputations as well as the service of Commons, but this, and much of the additions to the residential accommodation which had been planned at the same time, had to be postponed on account of the rapid reversal of the College's fortunes around 1686, and the building programme was not resumed until near the end of the century.

(iii)

On Seele's death Michael Ward was appointed Provost. Of English birth, but educated in the College, he had a meteoric rise to high office, which is apparently to be attributed to what Ware calls his 'great sagacity in dexterously managing proper conjunctures'. Fellow at nineteen, Professor of Divinity at twenty-seven, he was admitted as Provost at the unprecedentedly early age of thirty-one. But after less than four years he was made a bishop, and died as Bishop of Derry at the age of thirty-eight. When he resigned the Provostship in 1678 there were among the Senior Fellows at least three (William Palliser, Nathaniel Foy and George Browne) who might have been reasonably considered *papabili*, but Ormonde turned to Oxford for a successor, Cambridge presumably being still considered too tainted with Puritanism. He chose Narcissus Marsh, a fastidious and cultured man of wide scholarship, but ill at ease in the Dublin of that day. His laments provide an interesting early example of the perennial complaint of academic men today – that the burdens of administration interfere with their research.[11] After four years he was obviously glad to escape to a bishopric, and he ended his life more happily and more fruitfully as Archbishop successively of Dublin and Armagh. But on his resignation in 1683 Oxford was dragged once more for a possible Provost, and Richard Huntington, a distinguished orientalist who had lived for eleven years in Syria and had collected many manuscripts there, was with great difficulty persuaded to leave his Fellowship at Merton and come to Dublin. He seems to have enjoyed his life in Ireland even less than Marsh, but this was in part because he had to endure the harassment of the College which took place in the reign of James II, and at the end of the long vacation of 1688, when affairs in England were plainly heading towards a crisis, he prudently remained there and did not return to Dublin till the Battle of the Boyne had been fought and won two years later. In 1692 he was glad to resign the Provostship for a modest country parsonage in Essex, and although he allowed himself to be appointed Bishop of Raphoe in 1701, renewed experience of Ireland was too much for him, and he died twelve days after his consecration in Dublin.

Both Marsh and Huntington were good scholars and conscientious men, but their terms as Provost can hardly be regarded as successful on account of their strong dislike of their duties and their surroundings. From 1692 onwards the Crown consistently appointed graduates of the College, who were in most cases Irishmen, and even if these included one or two mediocrities the change in policy was a wise one.

(iv)

The eclipse of the Puritan tradition in Trinity College redirected its theological scholarship, but did not abolish it. Among the Fellows elected during the reign of Charles II, Anthony Dopping, Thomas Pullen and Samuel Foley upheld the Anglican cause both in writing and action. They had all left College before the accession of James II, but all spoke out boldly during his reign, Foley suffering imprisonment and Pullen attainder for their uncompromising words; Dopping, as Bishop of Meath, was treated with more caution by the Government, and he was in a position to give some help to the College in those difficult days. A far more outstanding scholar, however, than any of these was Henry Dodwell, elected Fellow in 1662. He had to resign four years later as he was unwilling to take holy orders, not from any doctrinal objection, but because of a sense of personal unworthiness. He went to Oxford, where for a short time he held the Camden Professorship of History, but in 1690 his tender conscience again interfered with his career, as he refused to take the oath of allegiance to King William and joined the non-jurors. He wrote extensively on ancient history, geography and chronology, as well as on ecclesiastical politics, and it was a misfortune for Dublin that no lay Fellowship was available for him in 1666. The place of *Medicus* was worthily occupied by John Stearne; that of *Jurista*, however, was held by Henry Styles, who, in the eyes of at least some of his contemporaries, was little more than a plausible rogue.

Styles proceeded to deacon's orders, but having obtained the Jurist's place he felt in no hurry to become a priest. This did not, however, prevent him from securing a prebend in the diocese of Dublin. When Michael Boyle succeeded as Archbishop in 1663 he inquired into this irregular situation (undeterred by the fact that he had himself held six benefices while Bishop of Cork). He was met with assurances that Styles's full ordination might be expected any moment, and vague assurances of this kind were renewed from year to year. In 1670 Boyle lost patience and evicted Styles from his prebend, but meanwhile the latter, who had been appointed Professor of Laws in 1662, managed to extract from the Crown a King's Letter directing the College to pay him a salary of £40 a year as Professor. In 1683, when the resignation of Provost Marsh was expected, Styles, who had been Vice-Provost for some years, was talked of as a likely successor, and was recommended for the post to Ormonde by his son, Lord Arran, who was deputizing for him in Dublin. To Arran, Styles had repeated the assurances of twenty years earlier, that of course he would take priest's orders but did not want to do so just now for fear it might be misinterpreted, and Arran was naive enough to believe him. Styles would certainly have secured the Provostship had not Archbishop Boyle, now at Armagh, got to hear of the proposal. In a letter to Ormonde dated 26 January 1683, he gives his opinion of Styles in no uncertain terms. He has 'irregularities (at least) in his religion'; he has not received the sacrament for several years; he is 'no good liver, but vicious in his life and conversation'.

5 Henry Dodwell. Fellow, 1662–6. (Painter unknown, Bodleian Library, Oxford.)

When this was transmitted to Arran he mildly commented that if it was true it was a wonder that Styles had not been put out of the College. It is possible that some of the Primate's charges were exaggerated, for Arran casually remarks in the same letter that 'Mr Troy, a relation of the Primate's, is looked on as a very unfit man.'[12] At all events, Ormonde sent to Oxford for a Provost and Styles died three years later, a disappointed man. Whatever impression he may have made on the teaching or study of law in the University is not discernible after the lapse of three centuries.

A very different type of man was also at this period a Fellow for a few years in deacon's orders only. This was Thomas Sheridan, one of the Fellows appointed by the Crown in 1667. He came of Protestant but largely native stock in Co. Cavan. Two of his brothers became bishops; one joined the non-jurors, the other died before the issue arose. Thomas Sheridan perforce resigned his Fellowship and went to England, where he became friendly with James II before his accession, and remained faithful to him through all subsequent turns of fortune, serving as his Chief Secretary in Ireland, and following him into exile. An honorary Doctor of Oxford and a Fellow of the Royal Society, he sacrificed a promising career in the interests of that devoted loyalty which even the least attractive of the Stuarts were able to inspire, and in Sheridan's case it is all the more remarkable as he retained his Anglican faith throughout.

Not all the Fellows of the period were, however, obsessed with political or religious controversy or with the quest for preferment. The more open and leisured temper of the age shows itself in the emergence on a small scale of what may be termed *belles-lettres* among their literary compositions. John Jones, elected Fellow in 1662, published, while still a Fellow, elegies on the deaths of two noblemen, one in Latin, the other in English.[13] They are full of rather creaking metaphysical conceits, but there is a clear striving after grace and elegance. Some years later Richard Lyngard, Professor of Divinity, wrote a small treatise addressed to a young nobleman leaving the University for the wider world. Its general tone is worldly-wise, and in some respects it anticipates Lord Chesterfield, though without his cynicism. But what is most striking is that although a religious faith is assumed it is not directly alluded to; though written in the age of Bunyan, it points forward to that of Addison.

(v)

The accession of James II presented members of the Established Church with an awkward situation, concerning which their doctrines left them in some doubt. They were certainly still bound to obedience to the King, but the mutually sustaining bond between the crown and the mitre was clearly put in jeopardy if the wearers disagreed on fundamentals. And it was not easy to defend, or even feel happy with a situation in which, under the terms of the Test Act, no dissenter was allowed to serve the King, whereas the King could be the most conspicuous dissenter in the realm. Were his beliefs really less important than those of an alderman or militia captain?

These questions made many of the Anglican clergy uneasy, but their loyalty, even if it had now become intellectual rather than emotional, stood firm at first. In Ireland the hope that, as in two previous crises, the lines of party division might be less acute than in England was tempered by the reflection that if the King proposed to gratify his Catholic subjects at the expense of the Protestants, Ireland would be the most convenient place for him to start. The first attempt to use the College in the furtherance of this policy took place even before Tyrconnell had been appointed Lord Deputy; it took the form of a direction to admit one Arthur Greene to a lecturership in Irish with a supposed stipend of £30 a year, and to pay him several years' arrears of salary. The Board replied that there was no such lecturership and no such endowment, and the matter was allowed to drop. Eighteen months later there was a more serious danger signal: less than a year after the eviction of the Fellows of Magdalen College, Oxford, a *mandamus* arrived ordering the admission of Bernard Doyle to a vacant Fellowship. But the King, characteristically relying on the advice of those more stupid even than himself, had made exactly the same error as that which had foiled his first assault on Magdalen: he had extended his patronage in favour of a man of such notoriously dissolute life that a defence was impossible, and Doyle had been so badly coached in his part that he refused to take the Fellow's oath, which even the *mandamus* required of him. Meanwhile the College had become involved in a tedious and complex dispute with the Government over an attempted sale of plate. In spite of the political uncertainty and the first signs of what was to prove a serious fall in student numbers, the Board wished to proceed with its plan for building more chambers for residents, and decided to raise £2,000 for this purpose by the sale of plate. As it was likely to fetch a much higher price in London than in Dublin it was consigned to England, but the Government, suspecting, not altogether unreasonably, that the College was really concerned with moving its assets out of the kingdom, detained the plate at the Custom House. After much argument and recrimination the plate was sold in Dublin for less than £1,000, and the money was put, not into buildings but into land.

There was no more direct harassment until after the King had lost his English throne. But by the beginning of 1689 the College was in desperate straits for money: no rents were coming in, and plate could not be sold for anything like its real value. The Fellows and Scholars were put on starvation rations and arrangements were made to send the muniments and the Library manuscripts to England. In February the College was searched by the Army and all arms and horses commandeered, and on 1 March most of the Fellows left for England, leaving behind the Vice-Provost and four others, but of this gallant band three were to die within the next fifteen months. Arthur Greene, the rejected lecturer in Irish, turned up again in June, this time demanding a Senior Fellowship. The Fellows again stood firm, and as Fellowship by now implied only meagre rations and a very speculative salary his case was not further pressed. Finally, in September 1689, the Fellows and Scholars were turned out and the College occupied by the Jacobite army as a barracks and prison. Deliverance came in the following July with the Battle of the Boyne and the flight of King James, and a fortnight later the Provost and the remaining Fellows returned from England.

(vi)

They returned to a College thoroughly wrecked by the senseless vandalism which almost inevitably accompanies a military occupation of fine buildings. Fortunately the determination and presence of mind of two priests, Teigue MacCarthy and Michael Moore, saved the Library and its contents from any substantial damage. Moore had been appointed as Head of the College on the advice of the Irish bishops, but some months before the Boyne he fell foul of the Jesuits and was expelled from Ireland by the King. In France his considerable learning was better appreciated, and he ended his life as Rector of the University of Paris.

No Fellows or Scholars could be appointed in 1691, but the College's depleted coffers began to fill up fairly rapidly, and the student numbers increased steadily over the next few years until in 1696 the annual intake was higher than ever before. From 1692 onwards vacant Fellowships were filled by the regular method of election, and the practice, for which all the Stuarts had an unfortunate weakness, of issuing dispensations from their own statutes and appointing individual Fellows by *mandamus* was happily allowed to die out.

When Huntington returned to England in 1692 St George Ashe, one of the Senior Fellows, though only thirty-four years old, was appointed Provost in his place. Ashe was a man of alert mind and wide intellectual interests, and although his writings do not amount to much he had a considerable effect on the intellectual atmosphere of the College by his awareness of the rapid growth of natural science and of the new currents in philosophy. He was a prominent member of the Dublin Philosophical Society, which was in existence (though with some interruptions) from 1683 to 1708; its aims were similar to those of the Royal Society of London, of which several of its members were Fellows.[14] The Society played a leading part in the intellectual life of Dublin during the reigns of William III and Anne, and though its connexion with the College of Physicians was even closer than with the University the fact that at one time or another twelve Fellows of Trinity College were members during their tenure of fellowship meant that it introduced a new note into academic scholarship.

As in London, so in Dublin, there were two strands in the scientific movement. One, originating with Boyle and Newton, was mathematical in its method and strove to establish laws of as wide a generality as possible. This demanded a good mathematical background, which was rather rare in Dublin; but the situation had recently improved, as the Professorship of Mathematics, founded during the Commonwealth, had persisted after the Restoration and was still held by Miles Sumner until his death in 1685. Meanwhile it had secured an endowment by being amalgamated with the Lecturership in Mathematics founded in 1668 by the Earl of Donegall, and after Sumner's death Ashe had held the Donegall lecturership until he became Provost. The second strand, originating with Ray and Hooke, was based on a fascination with the diversity of Nature and strove to chronicle it and chart it. It was natural that in the early days of such inquiries there should have been some confusion between the significant and the trivial, between the folk-tale and the established fact. Ashe was eclectic in his scientific enthusiasms, and we find, therefore, that his contributions to the *Transactions* of the Royal Society range from geometrical demonstrations through astronomical observations to a note on a dew, 'soft, clammy and of a dark yellow', which had fallen in Munster and Leinster.

In educational matters Ashe was a reformer, but not a revolutionary. His interest in natural philosophy and his desire to promote it did not lead him to reject the traditional view of classics, logic and ethics as the basis of university education. But he was anxious that instruction in these subjects should be up to date, and when William Molyneux, one of his friends in the Dublin Philosophical Society, introduced him to Locke's *Essay concerning humane understanding* he was enthusiastic.[15] The development of Berkeley's thought twenty years later might well have proceeded less surely if Locke's ideas had not, thanks to Ashe, become familiar in College.

Promotion to the Bench was at this time rapid for Fellows or ex-Fellows of any ability,[16] and Ashe, after less than three years as

Provost, left the College to become a bishop. He was succeeded by the Vice-Provost, George Browne, who was senior to Ashe but had been passed over in 1692. Browne, in his turn, was Provost for less than four years; he died in 1699, at least in part from injuries sustained in an attempt to quell a riot in the previous year. He is one of those men, baffling to historians, who evidently made a strong impression on their contemporaries, but have left behind virtually nothing by which that impression can be objectively assessed. According to Hely-Hutchinson,[17] although he 'does not appear to have been distinguished as a preacher or to have given any other proofs of his superior abilities', nevertheless he 'had the reputation of being the best president that ever filled this station . . . and his memory is revered today in college'. Hely-Hutchinson was a student only forty-five years after Browne's death, and that is not too long for an institutional memory, but it is possible that he was, at least in part, influenced by Browne's epitaph, which, even by the standards of the day, is remarkably full and laudatory.

There is scarcely any evidence extant from which we can deduce the nature of the teaching given in Trinity College in the late seventeenth century. Every detail of the educational provisions of the Laudian statutes remained technically in force until 1761, when the Crown conceded to the College the right to change them. But many of their clauses must have, in practice, lapsed long before this; indeed it is probable that in the matter of courses and textbooks the strict observance of the statutes did not long survive their author. Winter and his colleagues cared little for Aristotle and less for Laud, and though the Restoration saw nominally a return to the status quo, by this time the world of the scholastics was dead beyond recall and it was impossible to ignore completely Bacon or Descartes. At the same time the emphasis in scholarship was shifting from logic to mathematics and linguistics. All these changes must have been reflected to some extent in the teaching given in Dublin towards the end of the century, and especially under Provost Ashe, who may well have introduced some of the textbooks to be noticed below in connexion with the undergraduate course in 1736. Nevertheless, the Laudian statutes, ignored though they may have been in many points of detail, exercised by their mere persistence a powerful influence on the curriculum, and it will be seen later that even in 1830 the educational framework of the College rested quite clearly on foundations which had been laid by Temple and modified by Laud.

It is apparent from a letter written in 1703 by a somewhat precocious undergraduate critic that even at that date the pure milk of Aristotelian logic had been somewhat heavily diluted.[18] He complains that the philosophical teaching consists of a farrago of conflicting hypotheses from Aristotle, Descartes, Colbert, Epicurus, Gassendi, Malebranche and Locke. Plato, he asserts, was made little of, and Bacon and Boyle ignored. We cannot suppose that all these authors were read by the ordinary undergraduate; some of them were probably merely mentioned in passing, as glosses on Aristotle's text. But the method of teaching was clearly shifting from the scholastic and dogmatic to the historical and eclectic, and some attention was being paid to contemporary writers. The Renaissance may have tarried for two centuries on its way to Ireland: the Enlightenment was not to be so long delayed.

(vii)

In Dublin, however, the period from 1701 to 1714 represents not so much the beginning of the eighteenth century as the winding-up of the seventeenth. King James and King William continued to dominate politics after their deaths, and with the Catholics firmly clamped down under the penal laws theological controversy broke out with renewed vigour in quarrels between Anglicans and Presbyterians.

In retrospect we see this period as dominated in the intellectual sphere by the figure of George Berkeley, who wrote between his election to Fellowship in 1707 and his prolonged leave of absence starting in 1713, most of the works on which his fame rests today. But he remains a strangely isolated figure, who, though revered by his friends, founded no school, was the centre of no circle, and had little immediate effect on philosophical thought in Dublin. His works were not seriously discussed in Trinity College until 1837, and they did not form part of the moderatorship course until 1910. This is partly, perhaps, because his method was Socratic rather than systematic, and partly because his doctrines were for long regarded even by men more subtle-minded than Dr Johnson as fantastical, and by some, after the use Hume made of them, as dangerous.

The Provost under whom Berkeley entered as a student was Peter Browne, who succeeded his namesake in 1699.[19] He was a brilliant preacher, and was already well known as the author of one of the best rebuttals of Toland's *Christianity not mysterious*; in his later years he wrote further metaphysical and theological works, again partly directed against Toland. He was better known, however, for a series of pamphlets which he published after he had left Dublin to become Bishop of Cork. These, though ostensibly religious and philosophical in their argument, were in fact political, for they attacked the practice of drinking to the memory of the dead. And in Ireland after 1702 that could mean only one thing.

32

In England the struggle between Whig and Tory in the reign of Queen Anne showed party politics at its most intense and ruthless, but in Ireland it had an extra dimension. The Whigs saw the Tories as friends of the Jacobites, and in Ireland the aims of the Jacobites threatened not only the civil liberties of Protestants, but the tenure of their lands and their very existence. This led to the development of a narrow Whig orthodoxy which punished very severely the smallest deviation from its tenets or the most casual jokes at the expense of its heroes. Although the College had wholeheartedly welcomed the Williamite settlement (naturally enough, after its experiences in 1689–90), some of its members soon began to chafe against the assumption that even such moderate Tory principles as taking a firm line with Presbyterians or querying the necessity of supporting the Dutch in every crisis indicated a sympathy with Jacobitism; and of course the more often the assumption was made the more it tended to create that sympathy with Jacobitism which it assumed. Peter Browne was a moderate Tory, loyal to Queen Anne, and prepared to accept the Hanoverian succession with at most a grimace of distaste, but he resented the posthumous deification of William III. His sentiments seem to have been well enough known at the time he resigned the Provostship, as during his consecration in the College Chapel another bishop (and a former colleague of Browne's) created a disorderly scene which can only have been inspired by excessive Whiggish zeal; and after his pamphlets had appeared he became an object of execration to all good Whigs. Even after his death the toast to the 'glorious, pious and immortal memory', after reciting the various benefits which the rule of King William had brought to the nation, used to end 'and a fig for the Bishop of Cork'.

Some of the younger members of the University chafed even more impatiently than did the Provost against the repressive rule of the Whigs and, being like many young men not averse from a little opposition for its own sake, used political sentiments to which they may have felt little real attachment as an excuse for behaving outrageously and taunting their elders. This led to an explosion in 1708. At a supper before the conferring of degrees a Scot named Edward Forbes, who was to receive his M.A. on the morrow, declined to drink the toast to the memory of King William, and in justifying himself compared the King unfavourably with a highwayman named Balfe, who had recently been hanged. To orthodox Whigs this was not merely sedition: it was tantamount to blasphemy. Forbes was accordingly expelled from the College by the Board, which also induced the Senate to deprive him of his degrees.[20] Various attempts were made to have this sentence reversed, but all were relentlessly crushed, and were made the occasion for imposing a complete veto on the discussion by the Senate of any motion which had not been previously approved by the Board – a regulation which survives to this day. Over the next few years a number of students were expelled for what in some cases were probably no more than drunken acts of vandalism, such as wrenching the baton from the hand of King William's statue in College Green; others for what was at worst mischievous curiosity, in copying or merely reading a lampoon on George I, entitled 'Nero Secundus'. Open disloyalty to the established government had certainly to be discountenanced and punished, but one feels that it might have been done with a lighter touch. Not for the last time, however, it was possible to justify subservience to the Government by the plea of financial necessity, for the Irish House of Commons in 1709 petitioned the Queen to give £5,000 towards a College Library on the express grounds that the College stood for 'good literature and sound Revolution principles', citing as an example the degradation of Forbes.[21]

Peter Browne must have been glad enough to escape from this atmosphere and he left Dublin for Cork in 1710. He is said to have owed his promotion to the Bench directly to the Queen, who was impressed by his preaching; she also promised that he could nominate his successor as Provost. He rather unwisely chose Benjamin Pratt, one year his junior among the Fellows, and also a Tory; and the Queen was true to her word, despite the most strenuous efforts of the Lord-Lieutenant (Wharton) to block the appointment. Pratt was a man of wit, wealth and learning, who had been domestic chaplain to the second Duke of Ormonde, and who moved freely in London society.[22] He seems, however, to have been somewhat irresponsible and indolent; the social attractions of London tempted him to absent himself from the College for long periods, which enabled his two successive Vice-Provosts, John Hall and Richard Baldwin, to tighten the Whig grip on the College and gradually to make Pratt's position untenable. They had an ally in William King, Archbishop of Dublin, who was itching to use his powers as Visitor to purge the College of Tories, but who could do nothing without the initiative of the Chancellor or Vice-Chancellor, neither of whom shared his crusading zeal. In 1714, however, when the Queen died and George I succeeded without any fuss, Pratt must have seen that unless he was prepared to trim his sails very completely his days as Provost were numbered. He seems, nevertheless, to have decided on a last fling, and returned to College for a large part of 1715. In the Register for April or May of that year are three censures on students, written in a hand different from those that precede them, and very probably that of Pratt himself. One of these is for a purely disciplinary offence, but one is a sentence of expulsion for maintaining

6 Cenotaph of Richard Baldwin, Provost, 1717–58. Executed in Rome, 1771–81. The white marble group rests on a black marble sarcophagus, and is backed by a red porphyry pyramid. (Christopher Hewetson, Examination Hall of Trinity College.)

in public debate that Cromwell was preferable to Charles I, and another of censure for drinking damnation to the Bishop of Cork. Neither sentiment could be publicly defended by a responsible Whig, but neither would have incurred from him more than a mild reprimand for allowing zeal in a righteous cause to outrun discretion. Such defiance from the College could not be permitted, and a few weeks later, on the eve of Trinity Monday, a *mandamus* from the Castle arrived, forbidding the election of Fellow and Scholars, ostensibly on the rather flimsy

35

ground that the recent disorder had been such that the candidates had been unable to concentrate on their work, but actually as a mark of displeasure and an insurance against the election of Tory voters. Pratt managed to hang on for two more years, but in June 1717, he was hustled out to a mere deanery by the threat of a visitation (the Duke of Ormonde having by now been attainted and replaced as Chancellor by the Prince of Wales); and the affair was so skilfully managed that a subscription of £1,000 towards the new library was extorted from the departing Provost. Baldwin succeeded him; what opposition remained was driven underground, and the Whigs ruled unchallenged.

3

Georgian stasis and Georgian splendour

1717–1794

(i)

In the period of fifty-seven years which followed the Restoration the College had seen eight Provosts come and go, of whom only two had died in office. In the succeeding seventy-seven years it was ruled by only three, and none of these resigned for preferment elsewhere. It is inevitable that the history of the College in the eighteenth century should be told largely in terms of these three Provosts, all of them, though in very different ways, men of ability and force of character: Richard Baldwin (1717–58), Francis Andrews (1758–74) and John Hely-Hutchinson (1774–94).

Baldwin was a man of obscure and probably humble origin, who won his way to the top by vigour, determination, single-mindedness and courage. Newly graduated in 1689, he fled to England during the Jacobite occupation of the College. The impression made on the young man by those years was permanent, and when he returned to Ireland to work for Fellowship he was already filled with his lifelong determination to uphold the principles of the Revolution, to crush the Jacobites wherever they might appear, and to use the College, whatever his colleagues might think, as an instrument to assist in this aim. In the closing years of Queen Anne's reign, when others besides the Vicar of Bray thought it expedient to look for Tory favour, Baldwin made no secret of his staunchly Whig opinions, and in 1717 he reaped his reward.

His rule as Provost was arbitrary, and at times harsh, but although he often stretched and sometimes plainly violated the statutes, it was always to forward in the College or in the country his narrow but intense vision of orderly rule in the Protestant interest, and never could his enemies accuse him of feathering his own nest or of promoting favourites for other than strictly political ends. He lived frugally, and the considerable fortune which he accumulated was bequeathed to the College. He was accordingly, though little loved, generally respected, and the respect for his integrity was increased by the heavy *gravitas* of his presence and by his courage, which yielded neither to Lord-Lieutenant, bishops, Fellows, or even the Dublin mob. He was in many respects a forerunner of the more severe type of Victorian head-master, with sound but unimaginative scholarship and an insistence on hard work and the observance of a strict disciplinary code.

The enforcement of this code was, even for a man of Baldwin's determination and severity, no easy matter. Beneath the stodgy surface of early Georgian Dublin lay an underworld of riots and drunken brawls among half-educated would-be gentlemen. The students of Trinity were all too easily drawn into these, and the tradition of indiscipline started by the political tensions in the reign of Queen Anne lasted long after the political motivation had vanished. The Register, therefore, up to about 1740 is rich in records of expulsions, gatings and censures. It was only towards the end of Baldwin's provostship that this bad tradition was broken and student misbehaviour reduced to what may be considered a normal level. This was achieved partly by a general improvement in the standards of behaviour of society in general, and partly by the reaction which followed an incident in 1734, when the rowdies overreached themselves and killed one of the Fellows (not without some provocation).

Baldwin's preoccupation with discipline and political orthodoxy was, even if marked by excessive zeal, to some extent excusable. But it left him little time to promote scholarship, and it is doubtful whether even in easier times he would have achieved much in this sphere. He was determined that students should attend their classes regularly and be submitted to strict examination, but there his interest in scholarship ended, and although he cannot be called a philistine his exaggerated distrust of independence of thought served to stifle such gleams of originality as may have been shown by the Fellows of the time. Several of them, including the two ablest, Richard Helsham and Patrick Delany,[1] were members of Swift's circle, a group of men who had been driven by the narrow and heavy Whig orthodoxy represented by Baldwin into rather futile and cantankerous political opposition, and trivial punning and parlour games. Between these men and Baldwin there was open enmity, and Delany's resignation of his Fellowship was certainly accelerated by the public humiliation to which Baldwin subjected him.

But it must be confessed that few of the Fellows of the time showed evidence of even a blighted promise or of intellectual creativity. Several, no doubt, were kind tutors or good teachers, and well-read men,[2] and one at least, Claudius Gilbert, an indefatigable and dis-criminating book collector. But they lacked either the imagination or the energy, or both, to publish as much as a sermon or an elementary

7 First and last paragraphs of the MS draft of *The principles of human knowledge* by George Berkeley, Fellow, 1707–24. (Library of Trinity College.)

textbook. During a period of thirty-two years, from 1722 to 1753 inclusive (that is to say, for three quarters of Baldwin's term as Provost), we cannot trace a single publication written by anybody who was at the time in possession of a Fellowship.[3] Later on, from about 1780 onwards, the excuse was pleaded that the burden of tutorial duties was so heavy as to leave neither time nor energy for scholarship; and in the late eighteenth and certainly in the early nineteenth century this excuse had, though often overstressed, some validity. But in Baldwin's time, when the average chamber varied from twenty-five to thirty pupils and for some tutors must have been much smaller, it does not seem convincing, especially as Senior Fellowship came at an early age. Moreover, although at other times Fellows who had been silent in

Dublin were prolific in scholarly works after they had moved to Ulster rectories, this was not true of the period under review. None of the twenty-five Fellows elected from 1716 to 1734 appear to have published a line at any time in their lives. Delany and Robert Clayton, elected somewhat earlier, were prolific enough after they had left College, though in Clayton's case it might have been better if he kept silent, as his writings progressed from originality through eccentricity to what was generally adjudged to be heresy, and it was probably only his timely death that spared him from being turned out of his bishopric. It was in this second quarter of the eighteenth century (and not, as Mahaffy with a reckless disregard of the evidence would have us believe, in 1795–1830[4]) that Trinity College earned for itself the nickname of the 'Silent Sister', and although the reproach lived on long after it had ceased to be true, it was at this period deserved.

Although Baldwin survived into the age of Lord Chesterfield, he was, at least in middle life, typical of his times. Most of us, when we try to conjure up an image of the eighteenth century, think in terms of serenity, elegance and grace, and such names as those of Gibbon, Pope, Gainsborough, Watteau, Haydn and the Adam brothers are uppermost in our minds. What we overlook is that of these names all save that of Pope belong to the latter half of the century. The first half, even in England, was characterized more by solidity and weight than by elegance and grace. It was a time of apple dumplings and full-bottomed wigs, of somnolent latitudinarians in lawn sleeves and tedious dramas in blank verse. It had its men of genius and talent, but they were isolated peaks rising from a society not generally distinguished for its liveliness or originality in matters of culture. Bagehot has well said of the age that it possessed a 'sleepy, supine sagacity', and that our pleasure in looking back on it is the pleasure of contemplating 'a large lazy animal lying in the placid shade, without anxiety for the future and chewing the cud of the past'.[5]

In Ireland the dominant tone was as weighty, but it was less sleepy and more watchful, for revolt against Whig orthodoxy threatened greater dangers than in England. And although it is true to say that there grew up in the second quarter of the century in Dublin the spirit, style and sense of values which we now associate with the epithet 'Georgian', this spirit had a long, latent period of gestation, and only in architecture did it manifest itself clearly much before 1750. It was more by good fortune than by the wide diffusion of a cultivated and discriminating taste that Pearce and Cassels were at hand to adorn the city and country with so many noble buildings, for their patrons, unless they went to England, had not much choice of architects at home. And the men who used or lived in these buildings in their early years had, with a few exceptions, merely the conventional good taste that expressed itself in a dislike of ornament or innovation. It is perhaps significant that of the contributions by Cassels to the architecture of the College it was the Dining Hall, a handsome building, but built for a primarily utilitarian purpose, that was commissioned by the Board; the University Press was the gift of a private benefactor.

But although it was started before he became Provost it is the Library which is the real monument of the Baldwin epoch. It shows in its detail all the severity which characterized good taste in the reign of George I and it owes much of its impressiveness to its mere size. An architectural critic, in praising its 'measured reticence' has aptly compared it to a 'powerhouse or warehouse of learning';[6] and it thus provides the most complete contrast that is possible with its rival for the title of the most splendid university library interior in Europe, that of the University of Coimbra, which delights the eye by its highly coloured and light-hearted rococo charm. Although Baldwin can have spent little time in the Library, and is not outstanding for the encouragement he gave to its use by others, he probably deserves much of the credit for planning it on such a magnificent scale and for inducing the Government to provide the funds. In some respects, therefore, it is a fitting memorial to him.

(ii)

The first half of the century was not, in spite of what has been said above, a time of complete academic stagnation, and Dublin never sank into the deep torpor which descended on Oxford and Cambridge. Between 1700 and 1750 a number of new academic posts were established, and although they produced little immediate effect they provided a foundation on which some sound scholarship could be based later on, for the early Georgian period was, as we have suggested, in part a time of silent gestation. In 1700 the academic staff consisted of nineteen persons – the Provost, seventeen Fellows and the Regius Professor of Physic. The Professorships of Divinity and of Civil and Canon Law, as well as the Donegall lecturership in Mathematics, were also in existence at this time, but these three posts were always held by Fellows. By 1750 not only had the number of Fellows been increased to twenty, but the foundation during the previous half-century of ten new Professorships or lecturerships, of which only four were held by Fellows, brought the total number of the academic staff up to twenty-eight. Furthermore, the augmentation in the number of University appointments held by Fellows, though it did not add to the total number of teachers, is an indication of the increasing variety of subjects in which systematic instruction was given.

Of these new posts the earliest, and in some ways the most important, were the lecturerships (raised in 1785 to the dignity of Professorships) in Anatomy, Chemistry and Botany, which were established in 1711 in connexion with the School of Physic. The early history of this school, which was controlled jointly by Trinity College and the College of Physicians in Ireland, is too complex to permit of more than the barest summary here. The only provision made for medicine in the early statutes was a clause, dating probably from the time of Provost Temple, which enjoins that one of the Fellows shall devote himself to medicine, and shall be excused from the obligation of taking holy orders. (Another Fellow was similarly detailed to the study of law.) It must be remembered that in those days a Fellowship was in most cases a short-term appointment held by a fairly young man, and that it corresponded in some respects to what later came to be called a studentship. The provision, therefore, of this post of *Medicus*, though it provided some small stimulus for the study of medicine within the University, did practically nothing to provide for its teaching. Nor was the arrangement from any point of view a great success, for several of the *Medici* of the seventeenth century did not proceed to a medical degree, and on the death of William Clement in 1782 the post was allowed (in defiance of the statutes) to remain vacant for over seven years.

On the other hand the Regius Professorship of Physic, which had existed, though on a somewhat informal basis, since 1662, was usually held by a competent practising physician who had little effective contact with the University. John Stearne, the founder of the Royal College of Physicians, was exceptional in holding both the Professorship and the post of *Medicus*, and in being at once a Fellow, a sound physician, and a man anxious to establish an efficient medical school in the University. But after his death in 1669 the College of Physicians, which had been founded as a daughter college under the name of Trinity Hall, drifted away from Trinity College into a position of virtual independence; and the relations for the next two centuries between the two bodies, which acted sometimes in harmony, but more often in opposition, each jealous of the other but unable to do without its rival, provide a tangled chapter in the history of medical education.[7]

Although the medical school remained small throughout the eighteenth century and gave little indication of the fame that it was later to win for the University, the year 1711 was an important landmark in its history. For the building of an anatomy-house in the College Park and the appointment of the three lecturers mentioned above meant that the College now provided both for its own students in arts, and for others, regular instruction within its walls in what would now be called the pre-clinical departments of medical study. George Cleghorn, author of a minor classic on the epidemic diseases of Minorca, who taught anatomy in the school from 1753 to 1789, was a man of great ability and wide reputation; but with this exception the instruction in anatomy, chemistry and botany was, for the greater part of the eighteenth century, in the hands of somewhat undistinguished men. But if they lacked genius they at least possessed reasonable qualifications for their posts and showed some diligence in carrying out their duties. Clement, who was lecturer in Botany from 1733 to 1763, was also, at one time or another during this period, tutor, Senior Fellow, lecturer in Physics, lecturer in Mathematics, auditor, librarian, Vice-Provost, Regius Professor of Physic and Member of Parliament. Such a life cannot have left much time for extensive researches in botany. But Clement at least resided in Dublin and delivered lectures, and his record compared well with contemporaries elsewhere. Humphrey Sibthorpe, Professor of Botany at Oxford from 1748 to 1784, is believed to have delivered only a single lecture, and John Martyn, his Cambridge colleague, though he lectured for the first year after his appointment, lapsed in 1734 into a silence which lasted till his retirement in 1762.[8]

Clinical teaching at this period lay, in so far as it existed on any organized basis, in the hands of the Regius Professor of Physic and of the various King's Professors. The Regius Professor, as we have seen, was in no real sense an academic teacher and although such men as Thomas Molyneux (1711–33), Richard Helsham (1733–38) and Bryan Robinson (1745–54) were polymaths with wide-ranging intellectual interests, they contributed more to the general culture of Dublin than to that of the University, where their principal duties lay in presiding at the formalities which preceded the conferring of medical degrees.

The King's Professorships were established by the bequest of Sir Patrick Dun, who died in 1713. But litigation and legislation were alike necessary before the estate could be used for the endowment of the chairs, and in any case no funds were available as long as Dun's widow, who had a life interest in the estate, survived him. Accordingly the King's Professorship of the Practice of Medicine, though formally established in 1717, was not endowed until 1749. In this year King's Professorships of Materia Medica and of Chirurgery and Midwifery were also founded, though the latter was allowed to lapse after the death of its first occupant. Finally there was added in 1786 the King's Professorship of the Institutes of Medicine.[9] The right of appointment to these chairs was vested from their foundation, not in the Board of Trinity College, but in the Royal College of Physicians, a reminder of the dual nature of the Medical School. They stood, therefore, somewhat apart from the other Professorships, being more professional and less academic. Indeed, for the greater part of the eighteenth century their connexion with the University was extremely tenuous; for the King's Professors, though they frequently examined at the Royal College of Physicians candidates for medical degrees, rarely, if ever, lectured in Trinity College.

(iii)

The remaining four Professorships or lecturerships established between 1700 and 1750 were always held by Fellows. One of these was a Lecturership in Divinity, established in 1718 by a gift from William King, Archbishop of Dublin, and further endowed by a bequest on his death in 1729. Throughout the eighteenth century the post circulated rapidly among the Senior Fellows, with an average tenure of less than three years. The other three posts were endowed, not by an individual benefactor, but by an educational trust.

The statutes of 1637 had made provision for a lecturer in Hebrew as soon as an endowment could be found to support him, and we have seen that in the absence of such endowment the attempts to maintain teaching in the subject were sporadic and short-lived. The hint was eventually taken by the trustees of the estate of Erasmus Smith, a successful speculator in land who bequeathed large sums in trust to found and endow schools throughout the country, and about 1710 they provided a small sum to endow the lecturership in Hebrew. By 1723 the money was coming in so fast that they were looking round for new and appropriate ways for spending it, and an Act of Parliament was passed empowering them to devote their surplus to the endowment of three new Fellowships in Trinity College, and also to the foundation of two new Professorships, one of Oratory and History, the other of Natural and Experimental Philosophy (*i.e.* mechanics and physics). The idea, evidently, was to broaden somewhat the scope of the academic curriculum, but it wisely restricted itself to subjects cognate to those already taught.

The Act specified that the Professors were to be elected by the Board on the results of a public examination, and that during their tenure they were to deliver four lectures a year, of which two were to be sent to the Governors of Erasmus Smith's schools, who could publish them if they thought fit. The duties were not very arduous, but the salary was only thirty-five pounds a year. As with so many Acts of Parliament which set out to regulate in minute detail the conduct of academic affairs, some of these provisions appear to have been ignored from a very early date. At any rate we can find no evidence of lectures having been published until Helsham's whole course was published after his death in 1739.

The first two Professors, who were presumably elected in strict conformity with the terms of the Act, were both able men: Patrick Delany (Oratory and History) and Richard Helsham (Natural and Experimental Philosophy). Both belonged to the opposition party to Baldwin, and it is unlikely that either would have been appointed if the Board had had a free hand. If Delany did, in fact, lecture on Oratory, we may be sure that the lectures were lively and interesting. Helsham, who was described by Swift as 'an ingenious and good-humoured Physician, a fine gentleman, an excellent scholar'[10] gave a lucid and up-to-date course of lectures, which, soon after their publication in 1739, became a popular textbook. During the rest of the century the chair of Natural and Experimental Philosophy had its ups and downs, but the downs were more prolonged than the ups, Hugh Hamilton (1759–69) and Matthew Young (1786–99) being the only Professors of any real distinction. The peculiar and rather depressing history of the other chair will be examined later.

It is curious that the year 1724, in which the Professorship of Oratory and History was established, saw also the foundation of the Regius Professorships of Modern History at Oxford and Cambridge. But the Dublin chair is the senior by about six months, and the close proximity of the two events would seem to be a pure coincidence, for the circumstances of the two foundations were very different. In Dublin the initiative was taken by an enterprising educational trust; in England the munificence of the Crown was prompted by the Government's desire to find a respectable means of instilling Whig doctrine into the universities and to provide a suitable training, with the right political background, for men who were to travel abroad, either as diplomats, or as tutors to young noblemen making the grand tour. The Professors were accordingly provided with assistants, who were to lecture on modern languages. These Regius Professorships were not a great success in their early years, and in Cambridge no lectures on modern history were delivered before 1773.[11]

(iv)

The earliest date in the eighteenth century for which we possess a complete record of the undergraduate course is 1736.[12] The work of each term is classified, as before, under two heads, Classics and Science. In Classics the four years' reading covers a full and varied course: the *Aeneid* and *Georgics*, Horace, Juvenal, Terence, all Livy, Tacitus, Suetonius, Sallust, Caesar, some Cicero or Pliny, Velleius and Justin; the *Iliad* and *Odyssey*, three plays of Sophocles, Lucian, Demosthenes, Longinus on the Sublime, some Xenophon and Theocritus and one or two other authors. Cicero and the Greek tragedians are poorly represented, and the Greek historians, unless Xenophon's *Cyropaedia* is to be rated as history, are entirely omitted. Greek, however, was one of the subjects required for a master's degree, so that students who remained in residence after they had taken their B.A. may have had an opportunity to fill some of these gaps.

The study of the classics has changed over the last four centuries less than that of any other subject, and the authors read most widely by the earliest scholars of the Renaissance are, on the whole, those that the undergraduate reads today. We must not, therefore, be suspected of anti-classical bias if, both here and later in our narrative, we dwell more briefly on the classics than on the other subjects of the undergraduate curriculum. Changes in the set books of Greek and Latin authors indicate very often nothing more than the personal tastes of the College authorities of the day. Changes in the Science course are at once more intricate and more significant.

In 1736 the undergraduate course in Science was clearly still modelled on the course prescribed by Laud a century before. Logic was studied in the first two years, natural science in the third and ethics in the fourth. But the textbooks had been changed, and Aristotle, though his influence still lingered, was no longer studied directly.

Three separate works on logic are prescribed. The Junior Freshman year was devoted entirely to the *Institutiones logicae* of Burgersdicius; the Senior Freshmen studied Le Clerc's *Logica, sive ars ratiocinandi*[13] and extracts from the *Logica* of Smiglecius. 'The very names of the scholars of those days', says Lytton Strachey,[14] writing of the same period, 'had something about them at once terrifying and preposterous', and one must be on one's guard against the easy assumption that the scholarship of these men was as ridiculous as their names. Burgersdicius and Smiglecius were the two most distinguished of the *Systematici*, the logicians of the early seventeenth century, who, though they usually considered themselves to be Aristotelian and anti-Ramist, had been to some extent influenced by both sides in the Ramist controversy. Burgersdicius (or Burgersdijk) was a professor at Leyden, who published his treatise there in 1626; it was reprinted at Cambridge in 1637 and several times later. Smiglecius (Smiglecki), a Polish Jesuit, published his *Logica* in 1618. The two books are essentially similar in their aims and methods, though that by Smiglecius is the more detailed and discursive; and both contain, as well as what we understand by logic today, a good deal of grammar and metaphysics. Both soon weary the modern reader with their crabbed pedantry, and neither can have been calculated, even two centuries ago, to arouse much enthusiasm in the undergraduate. Goldsmith's bitter reference to 'the dreary subtleties of Smiglecius'[15] might indicate only the memories of an unwilling and idle student, but the diligent Burke is scarcely more affectionate when he refers ironically at the age of fifteen to 'that sprightly Dutchman Burgersdyck'.[16]

But treatises such as these, though perhaps somewhat old-fashioned in 1736, were by no means anachronistic. Even a century later, in the time of Sir William Hamilton, their names were still well known. Burgersdicius was certainly studied at Cambridge in 1717, and probably up to about 1740,[17] and at Oxford Smiglecius survived into the latter half of the eighteenth century,[18] for the universities were slow to recognise the challenge of Descartes and Locke to the primacy of Aristotle in this field. Lockian logic was, however, represented in the course which we are considering by Le Clerc, a French Protestant theologian and polymath who settled in Amsterdam and there made friends with Locke during his period of exile. His *Logic* and his *Physics* (which is described below) are, like most of his works, sound, clear and competent, if not particularly inspired. They had been published in English editions in 1692 and 1700 respectively, and both were well known at Cambridge.[19]

The prescribed books for the natural science of the Junior Sophister year were Wells's *Astronomy*, the *Universal geography* of Varenius, part of the *Physics* of Le Clerc, and Colbert's *General physics*.[20] Edward Wells, an Oxford man, was the author of several textbooks. His *Young gentleman's astronomy, chronology and dialling* was first published in 1712. Varenius (Bernhardt Varen) was a Fleming whose *Geographia universalis*, published originally in Holland in 1650, the year of his death, was at first neglected, but after it had been edited, first by Newton and then by Jurin, became widely known and was studied throughout Western Europe in the early part of the eighteenth century. An English translation appeared in 1733, and was reissued in 1734 and 1736. The book deals, not with the specific geographical features of different regions, but with the general principles of geography and cartography. Le Clerc's *Physics* covers a great variety of topics – astronomy, geology, geography, meteorology, biology and mechanics, as well as physics as the word is understood today. But it is probable that the student's attention was directed mainly to the last book, which covers mechanics and physics.

It should be observed that this course for Junior Sophisters, though it still makes some pretence at covering the whole domain of natural science, was yearly becoming under Newtonian influence more and more mathematical. Nevertheless it was prescribed for youths who had, for the most part, received no mathematical training whatsoever. Geometry was not introduced into the undergraduate course until about 1760, and algebra not until 1808. Nor did the students of this time come up to College with any satisfactory knowledge of mathematics, for the schools, in Ireland as in England, taught little but classics.[21] The first-class man, who had in mind the possibility of a Fellowship, must have learnt a fair amount of mathematics as an undergraduate (though the greater part would be reserved for his postgraduate study), and may have got some help from his tutor. But the average student must be presumed to have simply picked up, along with his astronomy and his optics, the geometrical theorems and trigonometrical formulae which he required, and to have mastered them more by an effort of memory than by any full understanding of the principles involved.

The Science of the final year consisted of ethics and metaphysics; and once more four books are prescribed, one for each term. They are the *Ethics* of Eustachius, selections from the *Metaphysics* of Baronius, Sanderson's *Prelections* and 'the small Puffendorf'. Eustachius (Father Eustache de St Paul) was a French Cistercian who died in 1613. His *Ethica, sive summa moralis disciplinae* first appeared in England in a Cambridge edition of 1655, but may well have been studied there earlier in French editions. It lasted on as a textbook at Cambridge until 1712 at least.[22] That in an institution as staunchly and self-consciously Protestant as Trinity College, Dublin, there should be chosen as a textbook in a potentially controversial subject such as ethics a work by a Catholic monastic writer is a remarkable tribute to the extent to which a unitary European culture had, at the level of serious scholarship, survived the century of the wars of religion.

The remaining authors of the year were, however, good Protestants. Baronius, who must not be confused with either of his contemporary namesakes, the cardinal and ecclesiastical historian, or the French Dominican author of *Ethica Christiana*, was Robert Baron, Professor of Divinity at Marischal College, Aberdeen, who died in 1639, though his *Metaphysica generalis* was not published until 1657. It is written from an avowedly theological standpoint. The author was regarded very highly by his contemporaries, but the latest edition of his book which we have traced is that published in Cambridge in 1685, and its retention on the Dublin course as late as 1736 must be regarded as a local eccentricity. Robert Sanderson, Bishop of Lincoln, delivered his prelections while Regius Professor of Divinity at Oxford in 1646–7. The two series, *De juramenti promissorii obligatione* and *De obligatione conscientiae* form together one of the few extensive Anglican treatises on casuistry. They were widely used in the universities in the early eighteenth century, and of course the topic of the first series was one which was acutely troubling many consciences in 1689 and in 1714.

48

Finally 'the small Puffendorf', which may be confidently identified as the Dublin duodecimo edition of 1716 of Pufendorf's *The whole duty of man*,[23] introduced the student to the ground where ethics and jurisprudence meet.

Surveying this course as a whole one cannot fail to be impressed by two of its features. The first is its cosmopolitanism. Of the ten books named in the Science course seven had been written on the Continent (three in France, two in the Low Countries, and one each in Germany and Poland), while of the three published originally in Britain two came from Oxford and one from Aberdeen. Scholarship in Dublin, it would seem, had not yet found its feet with sufficient sureness to generate textbooks for its own students, although, as we shall see, it was not long after 1736 that this industry was started, and for a century and a half the College produced a spate of works, in many cases partly subsidized by the Board, ranging from cram-books to advanced textbooks, many of which were used by other universities. The second feature, which is in some part responsible for the first, is its uniformly conservative tendency. By 1736 the measured rationalism of the eighteenth century had become well established as the prevailing intellectual mood in England, and Ireland was not far behind; yet most of the books that have been described above are much more characteristic of the previous century, being tortuous in their style, theological in their approach, and controversial in their tone. Only the scientific books were, indeed, in any sense up to date; of the others none were written less than thirty-five, and four were written more than a hundred years earlier. Pufendorf is the only truly secular writer amongst them, and he alone points forward to the future. For in the dry and systematic pages of the German jurist one can discern an early manifestation of that particular type of rationalism which was soon to blossom as the gospel of the Enlightenment.

(v)

When Edmund Burke came to Trinity in 1744 to be examined for entrance he was introduced to Provost Baldwin, whom he described as 'an old, sickly-looking man'.[24] But the appearance was deceptive; Baldwin lived on for a further fourteen years and was well over ninety when he died.[25] He was the first Provost since Temple to live on in the College into old age, and it may be wondered at that such a powerful figure whose politics were acceptable to the Government was not promoted to a bishopric, as had been four of his predecessors since the Restoration. The explanation may have been in part that the Government felt it important to have a strong and politically sound man in charge of the College and saw no satisfactory successor. But it was also because a change in policy had made the Government anxious to fill as many Irish sees as possible with Englishmen. An Irishman, even if he was a staunch Whig, was considered a bad risk politically. The responsibility for this policy is often fastened on Archbishop Boulter,[26] who was Primate from 1724 to 1742, but although he expressed himself repeatedly and freely in his letters in favour of English rather than Irish candidates, he did not always get his way with the Viceroy, and it was only in his last years, and even more markedly under his successors, Hoadly, Stone and Robinson, that the disparity between English and Irish on the Bench became really conspicuous. At all events, Baldwin was passed over and died as Provost.[27]

Like his four immediate predecessors Baldwin had been appointed from the ranks of the Senior Fellows, but if this precedent was to be followed in 1758 it could only be at the cost of defying another precedent, which, unlike the first, rested on a provision in the statutes, namely that the Provost should be in holy orders. For in 1758 only four of the seven Senior Fellows were in orders, and of these Lawson was dying and Disney, Mercier and Wilder seem to have been men of no distinction whatsoever. The three laymen, on the other hand, were all men of ability: William Clement, *Medicus*, Francis Stoughton Sullivan, *Jurista*, and Francis Andrews, who had received a dispensation permitting him to hold his Fellowship as a layman. And as the temper of the age was moving away from a predominantly theological emphasis in education, the appointment of Andrews (who had by far the most political influence among the three laymen) seems to have caused little comment.

Although it was said that Baldwin kept his mental faculties unimpaired to the end, it seems probable that his effective personal rule over the College ended at latest in 1753. In that year Pelissier, who was a faithful mirror of Baldwin's policies,[28] resigned his Fellowship and was replaced as Vice-Provost by the more independent Clement. It is surely significant that it was in this same year that the College received the first of the parliamentary grants, which were to amount to £45,000 in all, towards the rebuilding of the Front Square (or Parliament Square, as it was often called till recently) on a scale to match the Library, but with the more gracious elegance of the new age. It seems very probable that the College had Clement and Andrews to thank for this conception and its execution.

And by 1753 the ice of early Georgian Dublin was breaking up fast. The siege mentality which had dominated Irish Protestantism since 1641 had at last disappeared, for even the most nervous Whig can hardly have taken seriously after about 1750 the threat of a Jacobite

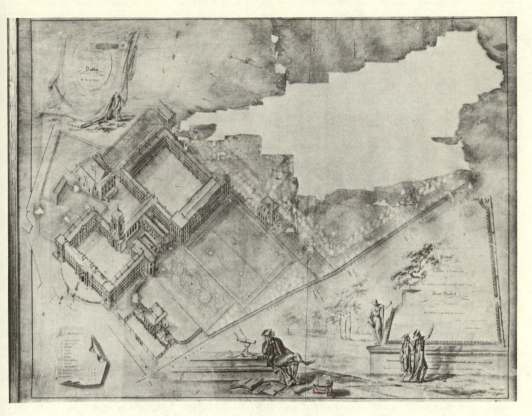

8 'A bird's-eye perspective plan of Trinity College park and gardens',
c. 1779 (Samuel Byron). Comparison with the frontispiece will show that
the Front Square (except its north-eastern portion), Library, Dining Hall,
Rubrics and Provost's House are virtually unchanged. Of the buildings
here shown, the Chapel, projecting into the Front Square, and the Hall
behind it, have been demolished; so also have two small connecting
ranges running north from the Chapel and south from the Hall, and the
range which then formed the western boundary of the Library Square,
while the range on its northern boundary ('Rotten Row') has been
replaced by the Graduates' Memorial Building. The building furthest to
the right is the old Anatomy House, with its physic garden to the south of
it. Both these have gone, but the Printing House, beyond the north-east
corner of the Library Square still stands, though it is invisible in the
frontispiece.

The artist's licence has allowed him to represent the Examination Hall
as complete; it was actually only half-built at the time.

restoration, and the Ascendancy was by now so firmly established that some relaxation of the penal laws could be contemplated. There grew up accordingly a new spirit, confident, expansive and relatively tolerant, with its exuberance tempered in art and literature, if not always in life, by the canons of classical good taste. It is the spirit traditionally associated with Georgian Dublin, of which the buildings form the most conspicuous record. Although, as we have seen, architecture showed a somewhat precocious development of this spirit, the great majority of the buildings which give to Dublin its Georgian character date from the latter half of the century. The culture which thus arose in the world of Protestant Ireland when it had ceased to be obsessed by menaces to its stability found itself by good fortune in harmony with the spirit of the age, for the accepted patterns of eighteenth-century culture were still aristocratic, but no longer martial. The disciplined luxury, rational thinking, elegant living and independence of spirit that characterized later Georgian society in Ireland were the qualities which were at that time prized beyond her shores. It had, of course, its seamy side of drunken arrogance and spendthrift eccentricity, but this was more conspicuous in the country than in the capital, where the tolerance of society for such antics had its limits. In Dublin at least there could be seen again, after the lapse of nine hundred years, a culture which was distinctively Irish and yet wholly European.

Provost Andrews was in every respect the embodiment of his age. His energy was sufficient for him to practise successfully at the Bar throughout his years as a Fellow and to sit in Parliament throughout his years as Provost without incurring – admittedly by the rather easy-going standards of the day – any censure for neglect of his academic duties. And although a persistent Derry accent and a lack of polish in his manners[29] betrayed his provincial origins he was able, thanks to his wit, taste, genuine if somewhat superficial scholarship, geniality and *savoir-faire* to mix confidently and successfully with high society in Dublin, London, Vienna and Rome. To such contacts the University owed the appointment of Lord Mornington as Professor of Music in 1764 and the Duke of Bedford as Chancellor a year later. Andrews was equally at home with politicians, scholars or *littérateurs*, and without offensive ostentation or snobbishness he pulled the College out of its rather fusty obscurity into the world of Society. Only three years after his appointment as Provost a sophisticated visitor accustomed to Court society in London described 'a most magnificent entertainment at the College' in a room 'extreme elegant and well lighted up, with a profusion of wax lights, claret and scarlet gowns'.[30] In Baldwin's day he would have found the entertainment more frugal.

With these ends in view Andrews built for himself and his successors, as soon as the rebuilding of the Front Square had been completed, a magnificent nobleman's mansion, beside the College but detached from it, and here he entertained lavishly. Although at times he overplayed the role of *bon viveur* he ruled the College efficiently and sympathetically on an easy rein, and by his tact, forbearance and common sense he spared himself and his colleagues the constitutional disputes on which his successor, and to some extent his predecessor, had to waste so much of their energies. Although he was more a man of the world than a scholar his eighteen years as Fellow had made him familiar with the nature of scholarship and the crotchets and foibles of scholars, and he used his experience to good effect.

(vi)

Provost Andrews died in 1774, the victim, it is said, of too continuous a regime of giving and receiving hospitality. Less than five weeks later his successor was announced, and to the astonishment of all Dublin this was John Hely-Hutchinson, a married layman, a busy and ambitious lawyer and Member of Parliament, who, since his graduation thirty years earlier, had had no connexion with academic life. His appointment was the by-product of a piece of ministerial jobbery which is difficult to parallel, even in the annals of the eighteenth century. The story has often been told, and can be briefly summarized here. The Viceroy and the Chief Secretary had at this time two men whom they wished to oblige or placate, but only one political post at their disposal. But the office of Prime Serjeant would do nicely for the other, so its occupant, Hely-Hutchinson, was induced to relinquish it in return for the Provostship, together with a sinecure the salary of which was raised from £6 to £1,000.

The appointment of a married man, in defiance of the statutes, was unprecedented, but could be justified on the grounds that most of the men who might normally be considered for the post were also married.[31] The prospect of nursemaids and squalling brats in the squares was made much of by the satirists, but equally unprecedented and much more serious was the appointment of a man with no academic experience. Every previous Provost since Adam Loftus had been a Fellow either of this College or of another at Oxford or Cambridge; and, although the Senior Fellows in 1774 were not a very bright lot, Leland and Clement might have been reasonably considered as qualified for the post, as were one or two of the ex-Fellows such as Hugh Hamilton. A case could be made, perhaps, for appointing, at least occasionally, a man of the world rather than a don, but only on two conditions: that he

9 John Hely-Hutchinson. Provost, 1774–94. (Sir Joshua Reynolds, courtesy of the National Gallery of Ireland.)

should regard the Provostship as a full-time post and subordinate to it all his other interests, and that he should realize that a college and a university have their own tempo and way of life, different from those of the Bar or Parliament. Neither condition was fulfilled by the new Provost. Although he devoted from time to time considerable attention to academic affairs, he used the Provost's House primarily as a comfortable and conveniently placed base from which to continue his political and parliamentary business, and found the Provost's salary a trifling but welcome addition to the income derived from his sinecure, the Secretaryship of State (of which he obtained the reversion in 1777), and his wife's very considerable fortune.

Hely-Hutchinson's talents and defects are so clear that an assessment of his character and his rule as Provost serves chiefly to reveal the writer's sense of values. It is plainly untrue to represent him, as does Patrick Duigenan,[32] as an illiterate tyrant and social climber with no redeeming virtues; it is also false to portray him as a liberal and cultured reformer, frustrated only by the jealousy and malice of stick-in-the-mud Fellows.[33] The truth is less simple. On the one hand he was intelligent and energetic, with liberal and original views on economic and political questions; he had some literary taste and style; he was a shrewd financial administrator; and his domestic life was respectable and happy. These talents were realized to the advantage of the College in his improvement of the income from the estates; his bringing to a successful conclusion the rebuilding of the Front Square; his establishment of the Medical School on a more secure basis by the School of Physic Act of 1785; his introduction of efficient procedures to the meetings of the Board; and his querying of the unchanging subject-matter of academic education.

But against these qualities we must set two defects, which he possessed in such extraordinary measure as to obscure and in part to frustrate his good qualities. The first was his insatiable appetite for office, money and power. This appetite is shown by a few prominent men in every generation, and in few periods has it been more conspicuous than in the late eighteenth century, but in Hely-Hutchinson it was developed to a degree that surprised and shocked even his contemporaries. Their reaction is summed up in Lord North's well-known epigram: he remarked to George III that 'if you were to give this man the whole of Britain and Ireland for his estate he would solicit the Isle of Man for a potato-garden'. His second defect was a monumental lack of any sense of shame or delicacy in the methods he chose to forward his personal interests, and the hectoring and bullying manner he used without scruple towards those whom he thought to be in his power and who showed the least sign of opposition or even independence. His insensitivity was such that he seems to have been genuinely surprised at the depth of the resentment which this behaviour engendered. Making all possible allowance for exaggeration and malice in the writings of his enemies, it is abundantly clear that he repeatedly used the very wide discretionary powers of the Provost, such as assignment of pupils or rooms, granting leave of absence, timing of meetings of the Board, and interposing a veto at elections to Fellowship or Scholarship, to reward his friends and to cow his enemies. The College was a constituency which returned two Members to Parliament, the electors being limited to the Provost, Fellows and such Scholars as were of age; and in the weeks before the elections of 1776 and 1790 no Fellow or Scholar could do business with the Provost without answering a preliminary inquiry as to his voting intentions. On the answer depended the success or failure of the interview, for at each of these elections one of the candidates was a son of the Provost.

For many of his arbitrary actions the Provost could cite precedents from Baldwin's rule, but he overlooked the fact that the more recent and tolerant rule of Andrews and the changing spirit of the times combined to make these precedents unacceptable in his own day. An action which in 1730 would have elicited only a tentative protest aroused in 1780 a storm of indignation. In consequence the College spent a large part of his provostship in a state of open or thinly disguised civil war, comparable to the condition of Trinity College, Cambridge, under Bentley fifty years earlier. Although the Provost won many tactical victories he was defeated on three major issues,[34] and the result of his injudicious use of privilege was to leave the Provostship a less powerful office than it had been when he succeeded to it. Naturally, if regrettably, most of the Fellows tended to oppose his wise as well as his foolish suggestions for change, and although he promoted some useful reforms he would have done much more if he had been able to see the virtues of government by consent. He would also have released for scholarship or more assiduous tuition much of the time and energy dissipated in cabals and indignation meetings. By the time he died it was too late for any extensive programme of agreed reform, for the year of his death saw also the reign and death of Robespierre, which added some new and disagreeable nuances to the concept of reform and ushered in thirty-five years of Tory dominance.

(vii)

Too much, perhaps, has been made by historians and pamphleteers of one aspect of Hely-Hutchinson's provostship – his attempts to promote within the College walls the acquisition of such 'gentlemanly' accomplishments as riding, fencing, dancing and the speaking of foreign languages. In this aim he was not as original a pioneer as might be supposed, for in 1759 a scheme had been launched by Thomas Sheridan and supported by two Fellows of the College, Thomas Leland and Gabriel Stokes, to start a post-graduate college as a sort of finishing-school, in which various gentlemanly accomplishments should be taught, though the emphasis here was on accomplishments that would fit the pupil for the *salon* rather than the hunting field or the ballroom, and especially on oratory and composition.[35] The first volume of lampoons against the Provost owes its title *Pranceriana*[36] to the ridicule heaped on the proposal for a riding-school in College, but there is to a modern mind nothing more ridiculous in this than in providing a squash-court at the present time – provided, of course, in each case that its use is to supplement and not in any measure to replace the normal academic course. Instruction in fencing was open to more cogent objections, for it was not then, as now, a mere display of physical skill, but a preparation for duelling. Hely-Hutchinson had himself fought a duel, and perhaps failed to realize that by 1774 opinion among the more serious-minded members even of high society was hardening against duelling, and among the middle class was almost entirely disapproving. Tutors regarded it as part of their duty to dissuade would-be duellists among their pupils, and they naturally resented the ground being cut away from under their feet by the Provost.

His motive for proposing these activities was not merely to enable the minor gentry who graduated in Dublin (and who at that time constituted a substantial fraction of the student population) to disguise their provincial origins, but also to accomplish something which might be expected to appeal more to a modern appointments board than to an eighteenth-century Provost. This was to fit members of the middle class to take posts as tutors to the 'Nobility and principal Gentry'. He adds that 'it will be well known what beneficial consequences are frequently derived to the Tutors from such connexions'.[37]

The Professorships of French and German and of Italian and Spanish, which were established and paid for by the Crown at Hely-Hutchinson's request, were founded with the same motive, and are introduced in the Provost's justificatory pamphlet in the same paragraph. A modern professor of Spanish would probably resent being put into the same category as a fencing instructor, but in the eighteenth century such a classification seemed entirely natural. Dublin makes much of the fact that it was the first university in these islands to establish professorships in modern languages, but the priority depends on an accident in nomenclature. The assistants appointed in 1724 to the Regius Professors of Modern History at Oxford and Cambridge discharged the same functions, with much the same ends in view; and in the eighteenth century the distinction between professor and lecturer counted for little, especially when foreigners were concerned. The activity of these men was strictly extra-curricular, and they were really only licensed grinders[38] who were given rooms in College and free commons; they had to supplement their slender salary and the small income they derived from undergraduates' fees by taking in other pupils from outside the College. Antonio Vieyra, the first Professor of Italian and Spanish (1776–97), was a linguist of some note; before his appointment he had written a grammar and a dictionary of Portuguese, and he followed this later with philological works on Arabic and Persian. But with this exception the Professors were, until 1866, language teachers of no literary pretensions, and it would be a great mistake to suppose from their title that the youth at Dublin was at this time being instructed as part of their course in the prosody of Racine or the political background of the *Divine Comedy*. It was not till 1871 that any modern European language was taught as part of the requirements for a degree.

Equally peripheral, but with an occupant of a very different type, was the chair of Music, founded in 1764 by Provost Andrews as part of his campaign to bring the College into the world of fashion. The first Professor was the Earl of Mornington, who was later to attain greater fame as the father of the first Duke of Wellington, Socially speaking he was a respectable, if not particularly prominent member of the Irish peerage, but intellectually and culturally he was far above the average for that body. Mrs Delany, who was his godmother, wrote of him at the age of thirteen that 'he is a very good scholar, and whatever he undertakes he masters it most surprisingly. He began with the fiddle last year and now plays everything at sight'.[39] In later life he was a musician whose compositions are well above the usual amateur standard, and he is said to have owed his earldom to the impression his musical talents made on the youthful George III.[40] His role as Professor, however, was purely honorary; he was not expected to teach or examine, nor was he insulted with the customary salary of £100 a year; all that was expected of him was an occasional composition, such as that which he provided for the installation of the Duke of Bedford as Chancellor. Nevertheless, the appointment, if it did nothing else, showed that the University considered music a respectable subject worth honouring. Mornington resigned in 1774, five days before the death of Andrews, probably because it was at about this time that he made England his principal place of residence. One might have expected Hely-Hutchinson to have continued the chair on the grounds that music, as well as fencing, was an elegant social accomplishment; but he had too many other irons in the fire, and no more was heard of music in College for seventy years.

(viii)

Academic innovation under Andrews and Hely-Hutchinson was not, however, entirely concerned with social elegance, and between 1761 and 1792 there were established a number of new Professorships in subjects whose academic respectability could not be questioned. Some of these were merely the conferring of professorial rank on what had hitherto been lecturerships. This was the case with Anatomy, Chemistry and Botany, in which the lecturerships founded in 1711 were converted to Professorships by the School of Physic Act of 1785. The change in status produced no immediate improvement in the quality of the men appointed to fill the posts; in Anatomy, indeed, George Cleghorn, who had been lecturer since 1761 and who enjoyed the Professorship for five years till his death in 1790, was far more distinguished than either of the next two occupants.

The Medical School presented special problems arising from its connexion with the College of Physicians and from the necessity of conforming with the conditions of Sir Patrick Dun's bequest, but in the case of Greek and Hebrew the tale is not very different. In 1761 Letters Patent were issued converting the lecturership in Greek, which had been specified in the Laudian statutes but which survived only on an informal basis, and probably only intermittently, into a Regius Professorship which was to be filled by one of the Senior Fellows. A few months later the Governors of the Erasmus Smith schools, whose income still showed a large surplus, gave a further endowment to the College, founding two new Fellowships and also providing funds for the upgrading of their lecturership in Hebrew to a Professorship, for the foundation of a new chair of Mathematics, and for the division of the Professorship of Oratory and History into two separate Professorships, one of Oratory and the other of Modern History. The chairs of Mathematics, Greek, Hebrew and Modern History all proved their worth in the course of time and were eventually filled by distinguished occupants, but only after the lapse of several decades. Greek, in particular, suffered from the treatment of the Regius Professorship as a routine teaching office to be circulated rapidly among the Senior Fellows. The fact that the only scholarly work produced by the first Regius Professor (Theaker Wilder) was an edition of Newton's *Universal Arithmetic*, while the new chair of Mathematics was given to John Stokes, joint editor of the *Philippics* of Demosthenes, demonstrates indeed the polymath tradition of the College, but also the low esteem in which the chairs were held. It was not until 1792 for Greek and 1795 for Mathematics that a Professor was chosen who had any real aptitude for the subject. Hebrew for some years fared little better; the first three Professors have left for posterity nothing by which their learning can be judged; the fourth, William Hales, wrote copiously on almost every subject except Hebrew; and it was only after the appointment of Gerald Fitzgerald in 1790 that any works on the subject issued from the College.

The chair of Oratory and Modern History also showed a somewhat paradoxical development. From 1722 to 1750 it was held by non-entities, but John Lawson, who was appointed in 1750, gave a course of lectures, published, in part posthumously, as *Lectures concerning oratory* (1758–9), which, although concerned mainly with classical orators, examined the subject very thoroughly and quoted widely from modern authors.[41] But it was the orators of classical Greece which mainly won his admiration, and he exalted these at the expense of their Roman successors in such a way as to provoke some controversy. A few years earlier Thomas Leland, a Fellow of only eight years' standing, had produced in 1754 (with the co-operation of his contemporary, John Stokes) an edition of the *Philippics* of Demosthenes, a work which, apart from its intrinsic merits, deserves some notice as that which broke the long silence of the Fellows to which we have drawn attention above. Although Leland published a rather tedious *apologia* for oratory ten years later, his main interest and his most substantial writings were in the field of history. These included a very successful life of King Philip of Macedon (1758) and a useful if somewhat pedestrian *History of Ireland* (1773); and he was even a pioneer in the field of historical fiction with his *Longsword, Earl of Salisbury; a historical romance* (1762). In the year when this appeared the chair of Oratory and History (to which Leland had been appointed in 1761) was divided, separate Professorships of Oratory and of Modern History being established. But it was Oratory which inappropriately fell to Leland, the chair of Modern History being assigned to William Andrews,[42] who does not seem to have had any particular qualifications for the post. Thereafter the history of both chairs for the next century makes rather depressing reading. Andrews's two successors did something to justify their appointment, for Michael Kearney, interpreting the title of his chair rather liberally, gave a short course on Roman history which won him a great reputation for learning, and his successor, Henry Dabzac (1778–90) lectured on the constitutional history of England. But probably from 1790 and certainly from 1799, following the appointment of Hodgkinson, the chair became a virtual sinecure, and it was not until Barlow was appointed in 1860 that it was occupied by anybody who could reasonably be described as a historian. Hodgkinson's tenure, however, was indirectly of benefit to the subject, for, since he made it clear from the start that he was not going to lecture, George Miller, a pioneer in the constitutional history of the College, was appointed as his assistant, and for twelve years he gave an ambitious course of lectures which drew a larger and larger audience as the years went by. The substance of this course was later published as *Lectures on the philosophy of modern history*, and although the rather pietistic basis of his philosophy is not very convincing the work commands respect as an early and bold attempt at a synoptic review of the whole course of history up to the author's lifetime.

Of the Professors of Oratory subsequent to Leland little need be said. At first they delivered routine lectures to resident Bachelors, but gradually the office seems to have become a sinecure, and can certainly be so described during the latter part of the long tenure (1816–52) by Richard MacDonnell, the future Provost. It was not until John Kells Ingram was appointed in 1862 that it once more showed some life and served as the precursor of the chair of English Literature.

(ix)

The Demosthenes edited by Leland and Stokes and Lawson's *Lectures on oratory* are the first works of what may fairly be called classical scholarship to have been published from Trinity College. Leland followed up this promising start by a very popular translation of Demosthenes, which ran through many editions, as well as the life of Philip of Macedon mentioned earlier. These two pioneers were soon to be joined by Joseph Stock, who published editions of several Greek authors and also of Tacitus, in addition to biblical commentaries.[43] The classical school, however, in spite of this promising start, did not prove a very sturdy growth; the work of Stock was followed only by a few articles on classical themes by Arthur Browne in the early publications of the Royal Irish Academy, the editions of classical authors ground out by the unfortunate and impoverished John Walker after his expulsion from College (see p. 110), and the important corpus of inscriptions, together with a number of editions and translations, published by John Kennedy-Baillie in the two decades following the resignation of his Fellowship in 1831. After this there was nothing till Mahaffy started his work on Greek history in 1869. This failure to develop a continuous tradition of classical scholarship was due partly to the relegation of the chair of Greek to the status of a consolation prize for a Senior Fellow who did not get one of the more lucrative administrative offices, and partly because of the growing ascendancy of mathematics in the examination for Fellowship. Although this did not reach its fullest development until the second quarter of the nineteenth century, it was already making itself felt by about 1780. Nevertheless, in spite of its rather short life, the efflorescence of classical scholarship in the eighteenth century served to make Trinity College much better known to the polite world than it had been for half a century.[44]

Leland held his Fellowship for thirty-five years and died soon after his retirement, but Stock published most of his classical work after he had resigned on a living, and much of it indeed from the episcopal palace of Killala and later of Waterford. Such publications do not in the strictest sense form part of the corpus of Trinity College scholarship, but they enable us to assess the learning and originality of men who must have displayed these qualities to some extent in their earlier life as tutors. This disjunction of academic writing from academic life provides some evidence that the complaint which was now becoming widely voiced[45] and was to continue for three-quarters of a century – that the labour of lecturing, examining and looking after his pupils left a tutor no time or energy for scholarship – was not without substance, even if it was often exaggerated. Of the thirty-five Fellows elected between 1751 and 1780 thirteen published some reasonably substantial scholarly work, but the publications of six of these date mostly (and in several cases entirely) from after their retirement to a living. Apart from the classical studies already mentioned books on subjects as diverse as mathematics, chemistry, politics, agriculture, chronology, physics and theology poured forth in a steady stream from the rectories of the College livings, and demonstrated how strong was the *cacoethes scribendi* among the Fellows once they were freed from the distraction of College duties. Among these 'post-academic' writings those of William Richardson and William Hales are outstanding for their volume. Richardson kept silent for his first twenty years at Clonfeacle, but in the remaining twenty years of his life he published a spate of books and papers on agriculture, botany and geology, in which his enthusiasm did not find itself inhibited by his lack of grasp of some of the basic facts. But Hales was a serious and well-informed scholar. He had written books on physics, astronomy and algebra before he retired in 1787, but thereafter the range of his interests widened rapidly, and in retirement he produced more than a dozen works on a variety of subjects. Some of these were rather austerely conservative tracts on politics or ecclesiastical affairs, in which Catholics, Methodists and the disciples of Paine were castigated with impartial severity; and his somewhat misleadingly named *The Inspector, or select literary intelligence for the vulgar* comes into this category, for it consists of two essays, one refuting 'French philosophism, German illuminism and English utilitarianism' and the other confuting the first attempts at biblical criticism which were then current. But all his other works are as nothing beside his massive *Analysis of chronology* (1809–12), which fills 2,400 quarto pages with closely reasoned argument. Not only does it display throughout an intimate knowledge of Greek, Hebrew, astronomy and history, but the author is not afraid to plunge into the intricacies of Chaldean, Persian and Turkish calendars. His arrival at 5 B.C. for the date of the Nativity (only a year different from that generally accepted today) illustrates the acuity of his reasoning, and he pushes the creation back from Ussher's 4004 to 5411 B.C. But on the whole the reader feels that the author's isolation has prevented his judgment from matching his learning. That a book of this kind could be written at all from the rectory of Killeshandra represents a remarkable *tour de force*, but one suspects that if it had been written in proximity to a common-room containing other scholars the erudition might have been used to better effect.

(x)

We have seen that Greek studies showed a healthy development in spite of the absence of any support from successive Regius Professors. The same would appear superficially to be true of mathematics, but there was an important difference. After the first holder of the Erasmus Smith chair of Mathematics had served for two years he was replaced by Richard Murray in 1764, and Murray was left in undisturbed possession until his appointment as Provost in 1795. Although his mathematical works are few and slight his tenure was not without influence on the subject, as, living as he did in College the life of an unworldly and unambitious bachelor, he was able to devote much of his energies to improving the mathematical knowledge and skill of a whole generation of candidates for Fellowship, and he may be said to be the founder, in this unspectacular sense, of the school of mathematics, theoretical physics and astronomy which was to dominate Dublin scholarship for a full century. Hugh Hamilton was only two years junior to Murray, and perhaps owed little to his teaching; his treatise on conic sections, published in 1758, was the first work of a mathematical nature to be published from the College for nearly twenty years, and although it is not strikingly original its lucidity won it some reputation in its day. This was even truer of his *Four introductory lectures on natural philosophy*, published after he had succeeded to the chair of Physics; it was used as a textbook at Cambridge towards the end of the century, and was retained on the undergraduate course in Dublin till about 1825.

Hales and Young, however, certainly owed something to Murray's teaching. Hales's treatises on sound (1778) and planetary motion (1782) mark some real progress in knowledge, and his *Analysis aequationum* (1786) was much esteemed by Lagrange, who wrote a very complimentary letter to the author. After his retirement, however, his conservative views, to which reference has already been made, got the upper hand, and his *Analysis fluxionum*, an attempt to defend and expand Newton's notation of fluxions, must be regarded as old-fashioned, and indeed reactionary. Matthew Young, however, had begun publication in 1784; he succeeded to the chair of Physics in 1786 and continued until his premature death in 1800 with a wide variety of books and papers on physics, mechanics, geometry and astronomy, in more than one of which he acknowledges his debt to Murray. None of them are of very great weight, but they reveal an acute and inquiring mind, especially if it is realized that they were interspersed with a new translation of the Psalms, two influential tracts on the constitutional law of the College, and essays on topics as diverse as ancient Irish poetry and the origins of the Gothic arch. Young was a polymath of erudition, piety and charm, who had been made a bishop only a few months before his fatal illness began, and his early death was a serious loss to the Church and Irish scholarship.

There remain to be considered two Professorships in subjects forming part of the traditional academic curriculum which were founded in the latter part of the eighteenth century but which unlike those which we have already detailed, were not normally held by Fellows.[46] These were the chairs of Astronomy and of Feudal and English Law.

The traditional connexion of astronomy with natural theology and the moral law, enunciated in the nineteenth psalm and soon to be strikingly reaffirmed by Kant, made the science a fashionable one among the clerical educationalists of the time. Furthermore, its necessary apparatus was more imposing and less messy than that of the other physical sciences, and the great name of Newton had given it a prestige which, especially in Whig circles, counted for much. The Savilian Professorship of Astronomy at Oxford had been founded as long ago as 1619; at Cambridge the Plumerian Professorship was established in 1704 and the Lowndean Professorship had been added in 1749. A chair of Astronomy at Dublin was clearly overdue.[47] But an observatory is an expensive item, and the University had to wait for a suitable benefaction. This was eventually provided by the will of Provost Andrews (d. 1774), who bequeathed a sufficient sum to build an observatory and endow a chair, whose occupant was to be known as the 'Astronomer Royal of Ireland on the foundation of Dr Andrews'. The litigation which at this time seems to have dogged so many charitable bequests delayed the building by a few years; but by 1783 the observatory at Dunsink, which stood on a ridge a few miles north of Dublin, was built and partly equipped, and Henry Ussher had been appointed the first Professor. He had, at Andrews's request, been studying the subject for many years before his appointment, and he published a few observations and notes on astronomical technique. At his death in 1790 the Senior Fellows wished to appoint as his successor John Stack, who had published a small amount of work on optics; but Hely-Hutchinson interposed his veto and, after the usual exchange of recriminations, induced them to elect a young Cambridge graduate, John Brinkley. The Provost's choice was in this case a sound one, as Brinkley was a first-rate astronomer. His textbook, first published in 1813, was still being reprinted three-quarters of a century later, and although his successor, Sir William Rowan Hamilton, brought by his mathematical researches an even wider fame to Dunsink, it was during Brinkley's tenure of the Professorship that Dublin made its most substantial contribution to astronomical knowledge.

(xi)

A Regius Professorship of Feudal and English Law was established in 1761 by the same Letters Patent that set up the Regius Professorship of Greek, but with more practical ends in view. In 1753 Blackstone had begun his lectures on English law at Oxford, and five years later was appointed as the first Vinerian Professor. The chair was such a success that the Crown decided to found a similar one in Dublin,[48] with the idea of providing a legal education which, while retaining an academic flavour, would have more relevance to the daily business of the courts than the lectures (when there were any) of the Professor of Civil and Canon Law. For the latter post had become a virtual sinecure, held usually by a Senior Fellow, who had often little interest in the subject. The new foundation represented, in fact, the beginnings of a professional school as the term is understood today. To ensure a close connexion between the Professorship and the life of the practising barrister it was decreed that only a barrister of two years' standing should be eligible; and in order that he should not be occupied with tutorial business it was decreed that a Fellow elected to the post must *ipso facto* vacate his Fellowship. Francis Sullivan, appointed as the first Professor, was, according to Hely-Hutchinson, 'a man of very superior abilities, of singular simplicity of manners but of invincible indolence'.[49] Nevertheless, he managed during his brief tenure of the chair (for he died at the age of fifty-one) to write, deliver, and leave in a state fit for posthumous publication a course of lectures which appeared in 1772 as *An historical treatise on the feudal law, and the constitution and laws of England*. It did not possess the magisterial authority of Blackstone, but this was in part due to the fact that it was delivered to a less sophisticated audience, who had as yet no experience of one of the Inns of Court. Sullivan was anxious on the one hand to see to it that the budding lawyer received some of his professional education in an academic atmosphere and with collegiate discipline, rather than as a mere apprentice, and on the other hand to emphasize the links between law and history and philosophy, so that it should be regarded as a subject fit to form part of the general education of a gentleman, by which he would be the better fitted to discharge his duties as landlord, Member of Parliament, magistrate or divine. For some reason the lectures attracted little attention in Ireland for the first few years after their publication, and it was only after they had received favourable citation from Bar and Bench in England that they became appreciated in Dublin.

The next Professor, Patrick Palmer,[50] seems to have been simply a run-of-the-mill barrister, but when he died in 1776 he was succeeded by Patrick Duigenan, who certainly cannot be described in those terms. Reference has already been made to him as one of the bitterest of Hely-Hutchinson's enemies, and his appointment to the chair served the interests of both disputants; it removed from the Board the Provost's most formidable opponent, and it left Duigenan less open to reprisals on the part of the Provost. Doubtless his lectures were spiced with entertaining anecdotes from the courts, and his students may have learned useful tips on how to browbeat a witness or bamboozle a jury, but it soon became questionable whether a busy political lawyer necessarily made a better professor of law than an indolent elderly clergyman. Duigenan was an able lawyer, and ended his life as Judge of the Prerogative Court, but he contributed more to the entertainment than to the education of Dublin,

(xii)

In 1785, half-way through Hely-Hutchinson's provostship, the Royal Irish Academy was founded, an event which was at once an indication of the liveliness and variety of scholarship in Dublin at the time and a stimulus to its further development and diversification. The Fellows and Professors of Trinity played a full part in its foundation and in contributing to the early numbers of its *Transactions*, and Robert Burrowes, a very junior Fellow still in his twenties, was invited by Lord Charlemont, the first President of the Academy, to write the preface to the first volume. The Academy was founded to promote scholarly work in science, polite literature and antiquities, a policy to which it still remains faithful, but in its early years the criteria of what constituted scholarship were less severe than they are today, and the early volumes of the *Transactions* combine the functions of the proceedings of a learned society with those of a literary quarterly. This encouraged the scholars of the day to vary their more technical output with writings which one may classify as *belles-lettres*. Even before the Academy was founded there were signs of such a development, for Gerald Fitzgerald had published in 1773 a rather charming poem entitled *The academic sportsman*. It describes a winter day's shooting, the writer setting out early in the frost with his dog, walking to Milltown and there potting a few snipe and woodcock, having a simple meal in a cottage amid a general ambience of Rousseauesque contentment, but nevertheless being glad enough to see the spires of the city again and to dine on Commons and enjoy a bowl of punch with his colleagues, Though full of standard eighteenth-century imagery the poem paints a vivid picture, and above all leaves one with the impression that the author is a most agreeable man. It was republished in 1790 with some other poems, two of them infused with a rather vague romantic patriotism from the Volunteer movement and the constitutional changes of 1782. The fourth poem, 'The Injured Islanders', is of more interest; it treats of the 'fatal impact' of European civilization on the natives of Tahiti (chosen, perhaps, in preference to other Pacific islands because the French, rather than the British, could be made the villains of the piece), and although the language is stilted and the Polynesians are naively portrayed as entirely noble savages, a generous sympathy is evident, as well as a perceptiveness which places Fitzgerald among the first to see and deplore this aspect of the voyages of exploration.

In a very different style, but also far removed from the standard academic publication of the day, are the *Letters concerning the north coast of Antrim*, published by William Hamilton in 1784 while still a Fellow. The author is hard-headed enough to see that here the local savages are not entirely noble, but he presents, fairly enough, a mixture of geology, antiquities, and social and economic facts in a work which is both informative and readable. Unfortunately for himself as well as for Irish scholarship Hamilton's interests shifted to politics after his retirement to a Donegal rectory; his *Letters on the French Revolution* (1793) proclaim him a stern law-and-order man, and he discharged the duties of a magistrate in a very anarchic part of the country with great courage, but with more zeal than discretion, until he was murdered by a band of United Irishmen in 1797.

It was, however, the *Transactions* of the Royal Irish Academy that provided the main outlet for writings of this type, and the early volumes contain, as well as papers on astronomical technique by Henry Ussher, on algebra, optics and hydrodynamics by Young, and on Roman history and Greek tenses by Arthur Browne, a number of literary essays by the Fellows of the day. Both George Miller and Richard Stack joined in the then fashionable pastime of writing essays on the Sublime, few of which demonstrated more than that the word could be variously interpreted; Stack also contributed a long review-article on the character of Falstaff. Burrowes, in addition to the preface, contributed to the first volume a vigorous attack on the style of Samuel Johnson, then but recently dead and still regarded by many as the Grand Cham of English letters. Burrowes starts by declaring that 'of all the faults of stile obscurity must be the most obvious and offensive', but in his condemnation of Johnson's polysyllabic Latinisms he includes not only such words as *obtund* and *empyreumatic*, but also such useful coinages, as *narcotic*, *resuscitation* and *horticulture* which we would find it difficult to do without. Nevertheless, the rashness of this attack by a young man was largely justified by the excellence of Burrowes's own style. In the preface to which reference has been made he explains in what must be one of the most limpid and urbane understatements in the whole of Augustan prose the absence from Ireland until a recent date of the sort of culture which Academy was founded to promote:

The important changes which took place in the government upon the invasion by Henry the Second were not carried out with so little disturbance, as to permit the nation to apply itself immediately to the peaceful employments of literary enquiry: nor could it reasonably be presumed that two classes of inhabitants entirely dissimilar in their inclination and habits, and afterwards more widely separated by a difference in religion, should be readily prevailed on to lay aside their mutual enmity, and unite in the pursuit of speculative science.

Nor were there many men of the day who could unite the mathematical knowledge with the elegance of expression which he displays in his justification of pure science against the demands of those who wish for its immediate application:

There is no apparent connection between duration and the cycloidal arch, the properties of which duly attended to have furnished us with our best regulated methods of measuring time: and he who has made himself master of the nature and affections of the logarithmic curve, is not aware that he has advanced considerably towards ascertaining the proportionable density of the air at its various distances from the surface of the earth.

Burrowes was a man of considerable, but somewhat intermittent and at times eccentric literary talent. He left College in 1796, spent twenty years as headmaster of Portora, one of the leading schools of Ireland, and a further twenty years as Dean of Cork. He published four volumes of sermons, full of lucidly expressed good sense, and is also the reputed author of various ballads, including *The night before Larry was stretched*. While still a Fellow he was rash enough to reply to an absurd pamphlet by Theophilus Swift, denouncing the College for having failed his son in an examination. Swift had been imprisoned for libel, but Burrowes also expressed himself too freely and was committed to Newgate where, according to legend, he and Swift, being the only two gentlemen in residence, had to share the same cell.

It will be clear from the above that the latter part of the eighteenth century saw not only a remarkable development of scholarly activity in the College, but a no less remarkable widening of its range. But the number of students who were directly affected by this diversification was small. Fellowship candidates and a few other graduate students benefited from the increased range of professorial lectures, but although an occasional able undergraduate would have his horizons widened by conversation with or loan of books from a sympathetic tutor, the majority remained circumscribed in their studies by the limits of the undergraduate course. If an undergraduate had the inclination and could find the time to attend lectures in history or botany, so much the better, but he was not to suppose that these elegant fripperies could, any more than could riding or fencing, replace the solid ground work of the classics, mathematics, natural philosophy, logic and ethics which he must study for his B.A. In these subjects he was instructed mainly by his tutor, and although tutorial and professorial lectures did not come into the same sharp conflict as at Oxford and Cambridge it was understood that the tutorial lectures had the stronger claim on the undergraduate's attention. To the developments in the B.A. course since 1736 we must therefore turn our attention.

The changes in the classical course do not call for much comment. The most far-reaching revision was that of 1759, prompted perhaps by the succession of Andrews to the Provostship. Two plays of Euripides and twelve of Plutarch's *Lives* were added to the course, and Xenophon, Demosthenes and Cicero given more generous representation. On the other hand the *Odyssey* was completely dropped, as were also Suetonius and some of the minor Greek authors, while parts of the *Iliad* and *Aeneid* were transferred back to the course which was supposed to have been studied before entrance. By 1793 a rather more careful revision had taken place; several authors who had formerly been read in full were read now only in part, and it had thus been made possible to find room for Herodotus and Thucydides, two dialogues of Plato, some plays of Plautus, and extracts from Quintilian. For the first time the course appears, by modern standards, a reasonably balanced one.

For our knowledge of the Science taught in the latter part of the eighteenth century we are dependent largely on the record of the course for 1793,[51] and on a critical pamphlet published in the preceding year by Robert Burrowes,[52] a Junior Fellow whose writings we have already discussed. The most important development was the introduction of mathematics. Arithmetic, it was somewhat over-optimistically presumed, had been taught at school; algebra was still ignored; but since about 1760 Euclid had been taught in the Freshman years.[53] The Junior Freshmen were examined in the first three books, the Senior Freshmen in books five and six.

The rest of the Science of the Freshman years consisted, as before, of logic; but by 1792 Smiglecius and Burgersdicius had disappeared from the course, as had also Heerebord, whose commentary on Burgersdicius had, about the middle of the century, replaced the original text. They were replaced by an indigenous product, the *Artis logicae compendium* of Richard Murray, published (anonymously) *in usum iuventutis Collegii Dublinensis*. This book which, first in its original Latin edition and later in various successive translations and expansions, remained for over a century part of the undergraduate course, is still purely Aristotelian in its treatment; but it is shorter, simpler and clearer than its predecessors. Though vehemently attacked by nineteenth-century reformers, it is probably a not unfavourable sample of the logical primers of its day.[54]

But besides the improvement in the presentation of traditional logic another and more important change had taken place; three terms of the Senior Freshman year were now devoted to Locke's *Essay concerning humane understanding*, which, as Burrowes points out, vilifies and derides those ideas of syllogism, mode and figure which Murray analyses and classifies with such loving care. The explanation of the inconsistency is clear enough; academic conservatism demanded that the traditional framework should be retained, but could not shut out completely the powerful spirit of an age which regarded Locke as one of its prophets. It is interesting to notice that when in 1908 this illogical union of logicians was broken up it was Locke's *Essay* which disappeared while traditional Aristotelian logic, as mediated by Abbott's *Handbook*, survived.[55]

The Natural Science of the Junior Sophister year had by 1793 become frankly restricted to the more mathematical sciences – astronomy, mechanics and physics. Astronomy covered one term; the textbook prescribed was that of John Keill, a former Savilian Professor at Oxford. It was first published in Latin in 1718, and in English three years later. It was a good book in its day, but Burrowes complains reasonably enough that in 1792 it was seriously out of date. In the same year, however, Brinkley was appointed Professor of Astronomy, and although his textbook was not published until 1808 we may feel sure that the presence of a brilliant young man fresh from Cambridge and Greenwich soon helped to modernize the lectures in this subject and to fill the gaps left by Keill.

Mechanics and hydrostatics were studied in the second and third terms from the published lectures of Richard Helsham (1739) and Hugh Hamilton (1767), both former Fellows. Hamilton has been mentioned above (p. 63); Helsham, who belongs to an earlier generation, was perhaps a man of even greater ability, though he wrote nothing but these lectures, which were published posthumously. He was a doctor who occupied simultaneously the chair of Natural and Experimental Philosophy and the Regius chair of Physic. He had the rare distinction of receiving the honorary freedom of the city of Dublin for helping it with problems of its water supply, and also a present of plate from the College of Physicians for the excellence of his lectures. His textbook was deservedly popular, and was used at Cambridge, as was Hamilton's; part of it remained on the Dublin course as late as 1849. The most up-to-date of the physical textbooks was the *Optics*[56] of John Stack, also a Fellow, who had been Brinkley's rival for the chair of Astronomy. It too persisted until 1849. Burrowes objects to it as too austere and advanced for the average student, but his criticism is here, perhaps, rather captious.

The course of ethics studied in the Senior Sophister year shows an even more pronounced change from that of fifty years earlier, and reflects strongly the spirit of the age. The medieval overtones in Eustachius and Baronius are no longer to be heard; all is clear, rational and enlightened. Only one of the four books is directly concerned with religion: this is John Conybeare's *Defence of revealed religion*, which had appeared in 1732 as one of the numerous replies to Tindal's *Christianity as old as the Creation*, a deistical manifesto which caused a considerable furore on its appearance in 1730. Conybeare's *Defence* is a sound, though scarcely a remarkable book, and its choice as the matter for the last term's reading and the final examination was reasonable enough as a means of crowning the student's recently acquired knowledge with a final layer of orthodoxy, which might well be needed in an ever more free-thinking world. It was preceded by Cicero's *De officiis* (studied for its matter, not its form), Burlamaqui's *Principles of natural law*, and Locke's *Essay on government*. Of Tully's *Offices* (to use the contemporary nomenclature) Burrowes remarks very sententiously that it is presumably prescribed 'as a specimen of the ancient mode of treating the Science of Morality; for I cannot imagine that a Heathen treatise on Morals could have been introduced for the purpose of giving actual instruction in their duty, to those who have been bred up in the light of Christian knowledge and to the purity of the Gospel'. This may possibly be intended as irony, for there is little doubt that in the literary circles of the day Cicero was rated almost as an honorary Christian (eighteenth-century brand). The prestige of his name and the reflection that Conybeare was to follow him in the course were enough

71

to quell any qualms such as Burrowes suggests, and it was only in 1833 that he was displaced by Paley's *Evidences*.

The *Principes du droit naturel* of Burlamaqui, a Geneva professor, had been published in 1747, was translated into English in the following year, and rapidly became popular in the British Isles. Its principles of rational and rather superficial utilitarianism harmonized adequately with the rest of the course. The introduction of Locke's *Essay on government* under the head of ethics represented a daring, and indeed a rash innovation. It is doubtful whether a treatise on political science, which was then regarded as scarcely an academic subject, would have been included, had it not been for the symbolic renown of the author's name. Prestige, indeed, seems to have counted for more than relevance; for Locke's detailed argument in refutation of the theory of the divine right of kings found itself somewhat eclipsed in 1793 by the more forcible arguments favoured in Paris. Moreover it was not the political principle which had the highest priority for a College whose orthodoxy was at that very moment shifting from Whig to Tory, and it was not long, as we shall see, before some awkward phrases in the *Essay* had to be explained away.

Mathematical precision in demonstration, an appreciation of the ordered harmony of the universe, rational empiricism as a habit of thought, liberal oligarchy as the basis of government, the avoidance alike of deism, enthusiasm and superstition – these were the principles which the College attempted, even in the last stormy decade of the century, to impress upon its students; and its obvious failure in the case of such men as Robert Emmett and Tom Moore should not blind us to its general success. The two figures which dominated the curriculum, and through it the whole intellectual world of Georgian Dublin, were those of Newton and Locke.

All universities are (or, should we say, till recently were) conservative, and Dublin was not exceptional in still pinning its faith, as late as 1793, to these two geniuses of the seventeenth century.[57] But it was, perhaps, exceptional in the single-mindedness of its devotion; even to Cambridge, the *alma mater* of Newton and almost the adopted mother of Locke,[58] it yielded nothing in this respect. With eighteenth-century Oxford, where mathematics was largely neglected, and where Locke was read 'with caution and reserve'.[59] there is no comparison. The explanation is, of course, largely political. Newton and Locke were the patron saints of the intellectual world of the Whigs, and, in the words of a pamphlet of 1783, since the accession of the House of Hanover 'the College of Dublin has ever peculiarly merited the name of a Whig university'.[60] In 1794 we find the Reverend William Jones of Nayland complaining to Boswell that the whole Irish edition of his *Essay on the first principles of natural philosophy*[61] (admittedly a heterodox and eccentric work) lay dead on the booksellers' hands, 'there being in the University of Dublin some leading mathematicians who kept guard for the system of attractions more severely than Newton himself did, and would not suffer a heretic to land upon their coast'.[62] Although Locke was not included in the undergraduate course until the middle of the eighteenth century, his *Essay concerning humane understanding* had been favourably received in the College during the author's lifetime, (p. 30). Two notebooks[63] of Michael Wycherley, who graduated in 1782, have survived to show that the preponderance of Newton and Locke did not exist only on paper, but was very real for the student. The books are not lecture notes, but have been carefully written up for revision, and in the larger book we find that 118 pages are devoted to Locke, the remaining 34 being shared between Cicero's *De officiis*, logic and physics, while in the smaller book a further 43 pages are devoted to Locke and the remainder to astronomy.

4

Limbo
1794–1830

(i)

Throughout Western Europe the contrast between the spirit of the eighteenth and that of the nineteenth century is obvious. No society, no matter how remote and sheltered, could preserve unchanged its intellectual climate, its political assumptions or its social structure in the face of the combined forces of the French Revolution, the Romantic movement and the growth of industry and science. But whereas in many countries the boundary between the old world and the new is best drawn at 1789 or at 1806, and in some (as in England) cannot well be attributed to any particular year, in Ireland the historian is more fortunate, and can regard 1800 as truly representing the end of the eighteenth century. It is true that some aspects of the style, the manners and the modes of thought of Georgian Ireland lived on with remarkable tenacity until late in the Victorian epoch, and are perhaps not wholly dead even today. Nevertheless, the passing of the Act of Union is more than a constitutional landmark; it is the watershed about which modern Irish history inevitably divides.

Within the University, however, the secular year has not the same significance. The rebellion of 1798 and the Act of Union were not, of course, without effect; but they were little more than temporary, if unpleasant shocks.[1] The disintegration of the aristocratic society of Dublin, which was one of the most immediate and conspicuous consequences of the Union, soon made itself felt in College by the smaller proportion of students of noble birth (despite the startling increase in the number of Irish peers over the preceding quarter-century); but this change served merely to trim the frills of a society which was, even under Hely-Hutchinson, essentially middle-class.[2] The aristocracy never imposed its standards and conventions on the College to the extent that it did on at least the more fashionable colleges of Oxford and Cambridge. The College of 1810 did not look or feel very different from that of 1795.

For the College historian, therefore, 1794 and 1831 are the dates

74

which symbolize, more aptly than does 1800, the passing of the eighteenth century and the advent of the nineteenth. In the former year Hely-Hutchinson died, and was succeeded in the Provostship by Richard Murray, a respectable and scholarly, but obscure and unworldly Senior Fellow. Dons, in Dublin as elsewhere, were at that time an old-fashioned tribe, and it would be misleading to say that 1794 saw the end in Trinity of either the manners or the outlook of the eighteenth century. But it foreshadowed the end, as far as the College was concerned, of the brilliance of the late-Georgian culture which we have described above. For a generation academic society went, as it were, to ground, and lived in a limbo that was characteristic of neither century. Only in 1831, when Bartholomew Lloyd became Provost and inaugurated a number of important and far-sighted reforms, did there clearly emerge in College the attitude towards education and scholarship which was to characterize the nineteenth century.

(ii)

More than a year before the death of Hely-Hutchinson the Fellows were already putting their heads together to concert a scheme for preventing the Provostship being again used, to the detriment of the College, as a cog in the intricate machine of government patronage. In the summer of 1793 the Provost's retirement was expected, and it was rumoured that the Government intended to give the post to Arthur Wolfe (later Lord Kilwarden), who was then Attorney-General. The Fellows resolved that this must not come to pass. There is no doubt that self-interest played some part in bringing them to to this resolve, but the strength and virtual unanimity of their decision that an outsider should not again be appointed Provost provides more damning evidence of the faults of Hely-Hutchinson's rule than do whole volumes of pamphlets and lampoons.

The strategy of their campaign was involved and delicate, for it was essential that Fitzgibbon,[3] their natural channel of approach to the Crown's advisers, should be short-circuited. Accordingly, a deputation of four Fellows was appointed to go over to London and endeavour to establish their point there. They wrote to the Marquis of Abercorn; they interviewed Pitt and Dundas; they left cards on the Duke of Gloucester, Chancellor of the University; they explained matters to Burke, who, though sympathetic throughout, was very discouraging at first; they waited on the King at a *levée*; and they came back without any clear indication of success. As things turned out the Provost did not resign, and there was a year's uneasy waiting until, in September 1794, news of his death at Buxton reached Dublin. The Fellows thought it unwise to repeat their lobbying on any extensive scale, but they craftily sent one of the laymen amongst them to the Duke of Portland to urge on him the desirability of a clerical Provost. The Government cheerfully assented to this argument, and proceeded on the strength of it to sound William Bennett, the newly appointed Bishop of Cloyne, on the subject. College was aghast at the news, for whatever dispensations from the statutes had been feared the idea that a Provost could also hold a bishopric was unheard of; and in any case the prospect of being ruled not merely by an outsider but by an English careerist was too much to stomach. When it became known that the Bishop's housekeeper had inspected the Provost's House the Fellows held a last, desperate meeting, at which they resolved on an ultimatum. They sent two of their number to inform the Bishop that if he were to be appointed it would be war to the knife, and that he would not know a minute's peace. The Bishop was shaken, and, following a change in the Lord-Lieutenancy, in January 1795 the Government, largely through the good offices of Burke, appointed the Fellows' candidate – Richard Murray, the Vice-Provost.[4]

Murray was an elderly clergyman who had spent all his life in the College, kindly and upright, if somewhat peppery, erudite in a provincial way, modest and diffident to a fault – in all respects, in fact, the antithesis of his predecessor. He was, as we have seen, an effective teacher of mathematics to advanced students, and is also remembered as the author of the elementary treatise on logic which we have noted in the undergraduate course for 1793. He was neither a great Provost nor a great man, but he gave the College what it most needed – peace; and he helped to steer it successfully through the somewhat explosive situation created by the visitation of 1798.

There is a tendency today to view the growth of the United Irishmen and the rebellion of 1798 as just one episode, one of the most colourful perhaps, in the long struggle between Irish nationalism and English imperialism. But it must not be forgotten that these events were inspired not only by the ancient enmity, but also by the ferment produced by the arrival in Ireland of the ideas of the French Revolution. Romanticism, radicalism and a new-born and militant rationalism combined to form a powerful mixture which welled up like lava through the cracks in the Augustan world which had seemed so stable. Intellectuals all over Europe were struggling to interpret, forward and direct a movement which was rapidly reshaping both the structure of society and the philosophy of the individual. It was not long before some of the tremors caused by this upheaval reached the squares of Trinity College. Politically exuberant undergraduates addressed a memorial to Grattan in favour of Catholic emancipation and appeared amidst applause at a Catholic gathering;[5] some of the younger graduates became more seriously inspired by the new ideas; a few even of the Fellows were impressed by *The rights of man*.[6] But the political deadlock and growing tension of the seventeen-nineties brought it about that liberalism soon came very near to treason. A brawl in the College with political undertones and involving two Scholars who were openly sympathetic to the United Irishmen sparked off the final crisis. The Scholars were expelled, though Arthur Browne, one of the Senior Fellows, openly stated that he thought this sentence too severe. The controversy came to the ears of Lord Clare, who determined that the College must be purged of sedition, and ordered a general visitation at which he presided.

Although Clare was the driving force, the general purpose of the visitation, though not the severity of its sentences, was approved by the College as a whole. It resulted in the expulsion of a score of undergraduates and a censure on two of the Fellows. Whitley Stokes, an amiable, courageous and upright man, but with his full share of the political ingenuousness characteristic of the academic liberal, had moved freely in radical circles in the early years of the decade, but as the rebellion drew near and radicalism became more extreme he shifted to the right.[7] At the visitation, however, when he was the most senior of the Junior Fellows, his past associations and his outspoken independence earned him a censure and a period of degradation.[8] His senior colleague, Arthur Browne, was also severely rebuked for his public criticism of the Board's sentence.

Accounts of these proceedings, with their merciless and inquisitorial atmosphere, make distasteful reading today, but it must be allowed that the fears of the College authorities, though perhaps exaggerated, had a basis in fact. The country was on the brink of what turned out to be a serious armed rising supported by a foreign invasion, and the ideas of the revolutionary leaders must have appeared, even to the moderate conservatives who made up the majority of the Fellows, about as objectionable as they could be. Their loyalty was scandalized by open admiration of the ideology of a government with whom their Sovereign was at war; their clerical ears were offended by outspoken defence of infidelity; their Protestantism felt itself menaced by ever-widening Catholic claims; and their pockets were threatened by the prospects of an agrarian revolution. What made the situation particularly embarrassing was that many of these new doctrines were represented plausibly enough as a logical development of the Whig faith on which the College had lived for eighty years. It seemed that those very principles on which the College had relied to keep out the Jacobites might now betray it by letting in the Jacobins. For what was *The rights of man* but an extension of what Locke had had written in his *Essay on government*? So thought William Magee, the future Archbishop of Dublin, who was no revolutionary. 'In Paine', he wrote, 'whatever is good is not new, whatever is new is bad ... he may be called Locke run mad.'[9] Thomas Elrington, the most vigorous of the younger Tory Fellows, took up the challenge and brought out in 1798 an edition of the *Essay* in which the dangerous passages were carefully explained away.[10] He writes in the preface:

We are told by citizen Thomas Paine that *whatever the people have a mind to do they have a right to do*; and in support of this system the authority of Locke has been very confidently cited. It must be acknowledged that the venerable Advocate of political freedom has sometimes unguardedly expressed himself in such a manner as to render it difficult to free him from the charge of favouring this mischievous theory ... But an accurate examination will prove that the word *people* was used by him in a sense far more limited than by the followers of Paine; that the term was used to signify only those who were possessed of such property as was sufficient to secure their fidelity to the interests of the state.

Others took comfort from the fact that Burke was still a Whig, albeit now an 'Old Whig'; and in 1790 the College, which had viewed with indifference throughout the American War and the earlier part of the trial of Warren Hastings the career of her eminent son, hastened, within a month of its publication, to offer to the author of *Reflections on the Revolution in France* an honorary degree. It was almost too easy for the radical press in Dublin to find the appropriate comment. When in 1799 the portrait of Grattan, who had been politically ruined by the rising of the previous year, was taken down from the wall of the Examination Hall and replaced by a portrait of the Earl of Clare the break with the days of Andrews and Hely-Hutchinson was complete.

(iii)

In the same year of tense, uneasy waiting between the rebellion and the Union, Provost Murray died. His four successors in office – John Kearney (1799–1806), George Hall (1806–11), Thomas Elrington (1811–20) and Samuel Kyle (1820–31) – had much in common in their careers. All had been Senior Fellows before their appointment as Provost,[11] and all, after a relatively brief sojourn in the Provost's House, left it for the episcopal Bench.[12] Of Kearney it has been rather quaintly said by an earlier historian of the College that he 'was always remarkable for his close attention to whatever might be considered likely to forward his improvement'.[13] But he was not a mere place-hunter, and the accounts of his contemporaries portray a man of wit and literary taste, well known in both Dublin and London society, and gratefully remembered by Moore as one of the few members of the

College to encourage his early literary efforts.[14] Hall, an Englishman who had migrated to Ireland on leaving school, presents, after a century and a half, a dimmer figure; but one forms the impression of a quiet, grave, perhaps rather severe administrator, trusted by his colleagues. Elrington is the most outstanding but scarcely the most attractive of the four. The *Dictionary of National Biography* refers to him as 'an active and useful prelate of the Irish Church', which is true enough, but there is a grain of truth also in Cloncurry's memory of 'a learned man, but stupid and blockish, and thoroughly imbued with the narrowest bigotries of his class and position'.[15] In addition to the edition of Locke referred to above he published a very popular edition of Euclid in 1793 and later, while Provost, a couple of classical texts; and throughout his later life there came from his pen a veritable snowstorm of pamphlets, sermons and charges, dealing with tithes, Roman claims, and any issue in which he scented danger for the Establishment or the Union. As Provost he appears for the most part as a rigid reactionary who represented only too faithfully the nervous repressiveness of the post-Waterloo years; and it is clear that his ever-present fear of 'the Revolution' led him to distrust intellectual independence in young men and to see in the most innocent assembly of students the seeds of a Jacobin club. It was during his provostship, in 1815, that the Historical Society was expelled from College and forced to continue its existence outside the walls. Nor was it only liberals who chafed under his rule. Thomes Prior, a very solidly conservative Senior Fellow, who had quarrelled with the Provost over a supposed slight, refers to him in his diary around 1818 as a 'tyrannical knave' and a 'beastly tyrant', and refers to his 'savage and corrupt nature'.[16] In view of the acerbity of Prior's comments on his other colleagues these phrases need not be taken too literally, but it is clear that Elrington was neither conciliatory nor obviously kindly. It must, on the other hand, be admitted that when he died a meeting convoked to found a prize in his memory was very largely attended and produced a substantial sum of money; also that just before Elrington's death Prior forgave and forgot, and summed him up as 'a thoroughly honest man, sturdily attached to the British Constitution in Church and State'.[17] But liberal triumphs have a wonderful power of healing rifts among conservatives.

Kyle was also a Tory, but he did not parade his sentiments so conspicuously; he could be represented by his enemies as a schemer, but not as a tyrant. He owed his appointment as Provost over the head of his senior and more distinguished colleague, Bartholomew Lloyd, to his greater 'soundness' on Catholic emancipation at a time when a firm stand against the proposal was necessary to preserve the rather precarious equilibrium of Lord Liverpool's cabinet.[18]

The period of thirty-two years that is covered by the rule of these four Provosts forms a well-defined if somewhat obscure chapter in the history of the College. It represents, as has been suggested above, a sort of twilight between the glittering magnificence of the eighteenth and the solid splendour of the nineteenth century. It is a prosaic, unimaginative, and in some respects inglorious chapter, but it does not merit all the abuse that it has received. When Mahaffy describes the history of this period as 'the least creditable in all the three centuries', the general atmosphere of the College as 'unwholesome', 'stagnant' and 'disgraceful', and its rulers as 'criminally supine',[19] he is not only showing a standard reaction against the manners and fashions of two generations past, but he is also, as all too often in his writings, fighting in history the battles of his own day.[20] Even if it be granted that the great increase in student numbers between 1800 and 1830 was due mainly to external factors, a period in which the student population is more than trebled can hardly be regarded as the most disastrous in the history of the College. Nor was its intellectual achievement at this time by any means contemptible. The work of Magee, Richard Graves and C.R. Elrington in theology, of Young, Brinkley, Bartholomew Lloyd and Harte in the mathematical sciences, of Walker and Kennedy in classics, Browne in law, and Whitley Stokes and Macartney in medicine was mostly done between 1795 and 1830. Together it forms a corpus of scholarship which is at the lowest respectable, and is in part distinguished.

It is pertinent also to point out that in the early part of this period the Board contained more distinguished men than at any other time in the history of the College. From 1795 to 1811 its eight members included usually six and never less than five men whose achievement was sufficient to win them an entry in the *Dictionary of National Biography*. Thus, though Trinity College, Dublin, cannot rival the astonishing claim of its Cambridge namesake that 'this most illustrious foundation has alone produced more distinguished and eminent characters than the whole University of Oxford, nay, it may be added, than all Christendom',[21] it can safely claim that in the early years of the nineteenth century its governing body included more distinguished men than that of any college at Oxford or Cambridge – not, it must be allowed, at this particular period a very exacting challenge. Five of these men (John Kearney, Young, Hall, Thomas Elrington and Magee) were future bishops, while Barrett, Whitley Stokes, Graves and Browne won at least a local renown by their writings. Nor did any of the men appointed to bishoprics owe their promotion to influence; they were sons of clergymen, merchants or of very minor country gentry, and they competed successfully on their merits against the cousins of peers and the chaplains of viceroys.

A sketch of Young's work has already been given and the three future bishops who were also Provosts have been noticed above; something will be said of Stokes and Graves in the next chapter. It is here convenient to give some account of the work of Browne, Barrett and Magee.

Arthur Browne, who held a Fellowship from 1777 to 1805 and the Regius Professorship of Laws for the last twenty years of that period, was a man of remarkable talent and energy. Born and brought up in New England, whither his grandfather had been persuaded to emigrate by Berkeley, he graduated in Dublin at the age of nineteen, won his Fellowship a year later, and before he was thirty had established himself as a successful barrister, M.P. for the University and Regius Professor. He set a new precedent by taking seriously the duties of the chair, and in 1798–9 published treatises on the civil and ecclesiastical law which were well received in Dublin and were reprinted and revised after his death both in England and the United States. In Parliament he was respected for his independence, and he courted ministerial displeasure on more than one occasion by standing up for civil liberties. But his loyalty was never in doubt, and, when a yeomanry corps was set up in College, Browne was unanimously chosen as its captain. On the question of the Union he hesitated for some time, but at the final vote, although he realized that most of his constituents took a contrary view, he came down in favour of it, from a conviction that it gave the best promise of peaceful progress for Ireland. Unlike many members who received a peerage for this service he was rewarded only by the loss of his seat, as the representation of the University was reduced from two to one and Knox, his fellow-Member, retained his seat under the terms of the Act of Union. Apart from his legal and parliamentary work Browne was a man of very wide culture; philosophy was his hobby, and his writings, as well as the auction catalogue of his library, show that he read widely and fluently in Greek, Latin, French, Italian and Spanish, and had more than a nodding acquaintance with German, Hebrew and Persian. He published in 1798 two volumes of essays which were, he tells us, 'put together as evening amusements in melancholy inns' in the course of 'a long and solitary journey into a remote and unfrequented corner of Ireland'. If at times the sentiments are somewhat naive, the tone is always urbane and the style fresh and unpretentious; the essays leave with the reader the impression – confirmed by the opinions of his contemporaries – of an agreeable companion and good conversationalist, and of a man who combined, as happens all too rarely, charm with integrity. Unfortunately, like Young, Browne died before he was fifty,[22] at the height of his powers and reputation.

John (but universally remembered as 'Jacky') Barrett was elected

Fellow a year later than Browne, but granted that they were both scholars he presents as vivid a contrast as can well be imagined. He is famed, not as a scholar, but as an eccentric, and innumerable stories are told of his miserliness, his provincial expletives, his slovenly dress, his absorption in books and his ignorance of the world outside the College walls.[23] All these characteristics have been doubtless somewhat exaggerated in legend, but there is ample testimony to the fact that during his lifetime he was regarded as an eccentric of the first order, and it seems true that with extremely rare exceptions his daily peregrinations took place within the quadrilateral defined by the Library, the Chapel, the Dining Hall and his rooms. Although some of the stories told of him may well be true, he soon attained the status (as did later Provost Mahaffy) of a character to whom stories are attributed when the narrator has forgotten to whom they originally referred. His renown as a 'character' has, however, somewhat unfortunately eclipsed his other claims on our remembrance. He was for many years Librarian, and although he had no talent for administration he rescued from oblivion many valuable books and manuscripts, and was the first person to attempt seriously to put in order the muniments relating to the history of the College. His most spectacular discovery in the Library was a very early version of St Matthew's Gospel (now known to scholars as Codex Z) in which the writing had been partially erased and written over with extracts from the Greek fathers several centuries later. Barrett, although he made some mistakes, was fairly successful in deciphering the original text; enough, certainly, to demonstrate its importance. He also published an account of the early life of Swift, and a treatise on the zodiac, which has been unjustly ridiculed as implying his belief in astrology and magic. It is, in fact, a somewhat eccentric but objective inquiry into the origin of the myths and beliefs associated with the zodiac, and can be regarded as a pioneer work in the field of comparative religion.

Barrett's work suffered to some extent from his self-imposed isolation, almost as severe as that which geographical isolation imposed on scholarly ex-Fellows such as Hales, but his scholarship, if at times unbalanced, was profound. It fell to his lot, less than three months before his death, to receive George IV in the Library on the occasion of his visit to Dublin in 1821, and to show him its treasures. They must have formed a remarkable pair. Barrett welcomed the King with a Latin oration, but what small talk, if any, then took place between the First Gentleman of Europe and the most dilapidated scholar of Europe history does not relate.

William Magee, although only ten years junior to Barrett and Browne, belongs much more clearly to the nineteenth century: in place of tolerant urbanity or scholarly absorption we find a hard-headed, if at times apprehensive defence of the Establishment. He was a popular and extremely conscientious tutor, but he was something of a perfectionist, who believed that a rule should admit of no exception, and he carried out his College duties (and later his duties as bishop) in the manner of a brisk and genial schoolmaster who is, however, determined to stand no nonsense. He published in 1801, at the age of thirty-seven, a substantial treatise on the Atonement, which, though it strikes the modern reader as exhaustive rather than very original or illuminating, was well received and ran through seven editions. He resigned on a living in 1812, and was seriously considered for an English bishopric soon afterwards. But nothing came of this, and after spells as Dean of Cork and Bishop of Raphoe he ended his life as Archbishop of Dublin, from 1822 to 1831. Here he found plenty of scope for his administrative energy, for the diocese, having been for many years under an archbishop who was insane, was in a bad way. A good part of his energies was, however, dissipated in what now appears a somewhat obsessive anti-Romanism and he found himself fighting on two fronts as a result of an incautious remark in his first charge to the clergy of his archdiocese, when he referred to his flock as 'hemmed in by two descriptions of professing Christians, the one possessing a Church without what we can call a religion, and the other possessing a religion without what we can call a Church'. In his serious and intense but by no means emotional Protestantism he was typical of his age, and his conviction, sincerity and eloquence must have played no small part in establishing this attitude as the dominant one in Trinity College in the early nineteenth century.

After the resignation of Magee in 1812 the quality of the Fellows co-opted to the Board fell off rapidly, and within a few years mediocrity was firmly established in the saddle. Moreover, it cannot be denied that even while there were still some men of great ability on the Board there crept into the College soon after the Union a certain provincial drabness in matters of taste and style. There were intermittent attempts at display but the effects were heavy, and in part vulgar, rather than elegant or inspired.[24] No buildings of which we now feel proud were erected in the College between 1795 and 1831. Even the work of maintenance was not well seen to, for when the old Chapel was demolished in 1798 the recumbent alabaster effigy of Luke Challoner was turned out of doors to dissolve in the city rain, and the great bell was housed for half a century in a ramshackle and undignified penthouse. The most substantial legacy of the period is the square which from its earliest days has been nicknamed Botany Bay,[25] and though the buildings have at times suffered unfairly from the squalor of the space

10 William Magee, Archbishop of Dublin. Fellow, 1788–1812. (H. Wyatt, Trinity College.)

which they enclosed, their flat, characterless face of dark, rough-hewn limestone speaks all too clearly of the new spirit that was abroad. Instead of the confident expansiveness of Georgian days there is a practical, cautious and unimaginative adjustment of ends to means.

But this new spirit was not peculiar to the College; it pervaded the whole life of Dublin. The constitutional and social cataclysm of the

Union conspired with the growing disparity between England and Ireland in wealth and population to change Dublin from a capital to a provincial city. It is easy to exaggerate the force of the blow which the Union dealt to society and culture in Dublin. The city was prosperous; the Bar was crowded with wits; Francis Johnston was designing fine buildings; there was still a vice-regal court. But the peers who deserted Dublin for London were numerous enough to leave a conspicuous gap; the absence of a parliament deprived society of its 'season'; the vice-regal balls were not quite what they were; and, deprived of many of its patrons, the world of culture soon languished. The decline spread quickly from Dublin throughout the country, and soon after 1800 the Irish landlord was transformed with remarkable suddenness from a cultured, if somewhat provincial gentleman to a philistine whose only interests were soldiering and sport.[26] This was perhaps due in part to the very success of the Augustan civilization in Ireland, which rendered the Romantic movement unacceptable, isolated the country from contemporary culture in England, and drove it back on admiration of its own past. At all events no Irish Romantics except Moore arose to replace Burke, Goldsmith and Sheridan; there is indeed a very remarkable lack of great Irishmen in any walk of life born in the last decades of the eighteenth century.[27] All these factors combined to produce in the atmosphere of Dublin a change which is at once obvious if the society of Barrington's *Reminiscences* be compared with that of Lever's early novels. Barrington, admittedly, was writing for a Regency public which liked its memoirs well spiced and garnished, but all the same the contrast is significant. The society described by Barrington is exuberant, self-assured, and never lacking in poise. Lever's, though full of high spirits, is shaded by philistinism and shabby-gentility. And on a more serious level a similar change can be seen. The outlook of the eighteenth century was essentially aristocratic – at its best spacious, self-confident and generous, at its worst short-sighted, arrogant and spendthrift. The Irish Protestant of the early nineteenth century soon developed the virtues and vices of the middle class, and with them an outlook on politics and religion that was at once deeper and narrower than that of his father.

(iv)

It was during this superficially rather colourless period, however, that the College underwent a startling change which has been ignored by all her historians. This was a very rapid and sustained increase in the number of students, which meant that from about 1813 onwards the College was operating on a scale hitherto undreamed of; and, although the highest numbers were not sustained, the fluctuations during the remainder of the nineteenth century and the early part of the twentieth took place over a range which exceeded the maximum of the eighteenth century. From 1700 to 1765 the annual intake of students had fluctuated between 70 and 110, but about 1765 the number began to increase and by 1790 had almost reached 200.[28] A sharp decline then followed for reasons that are not entirely clear, for although the uncertainties of 1798–1800 intensified it, it had started while the political horizon still seemed clear. Recovery, however, began soon after the Union, and by 1811 the annual intake was back to the level of 1790. Thereafter the expansion continued with ever-increasing speed; by 1817 the annual intake had reached 300 and by 1820 more than 400, finally attaining in 1824 a figure of 466, which was not to be equalled until after the Second World War. Subsequent rises and falls are not without their interest; they will be mentioned later and are given in detail in appendix 2, but this more than fourfold increase in size within a period of twenty-five years is by far the most spectacular change in College numbers during its entire history. Its causes are very obscure. Admittedly the population was increasing very rapidly over the same period, but although it continued to increase at much the same rate between 1825 and 1845 the College numbers show a decline over these decades. Moreover, the rising curve shows neither hesitation nor acceleration at the coming of peace in 1815, the event from which so many economic changes can be dated. Nor can the rise be due to any specifically Irish cause, as the curve for the University of Cambridge follows closely on that of Dublin.[29] The annual intake at Cambridge had been over twice that of Dublin in 1700, but it dropped fairly steadily thereafter, and by 1772 was overtaken by the rising curve of Dublin. From 1770 the two universities differed little in size, and, as in Dublin so in Cambridge, there was a fall during the seventeen-nineties, followed by a rapid and steady increase after 1800. The two rising curves coincide with almost uncanny accuracy, that for Dublin lagging some four years behind on account of its lower minimum in 1800, but eventually catching up in 1817. For eight years thereafter the differences are negligible, but whereas 1825 is for Dublin a peak it is for Cambridge only the beginnings of a plateau, which persists until a further rise began about 1860 (for detailed figures see pp. 499–501). It is plain that some social force, as yet unidentified, produced in both universities the same rapid expansion in the first quarter of the nineteenth century.

It is not only the historians who have ignored this phenomenon;[30] the College records give no obvious indication of the strains to which this expansion must have subjected the academic machine – strains surely as great as those on which so much breath and ink was devoted from 1950 onwards. Even if allowance is made for the creation of three new Fellowships in 1808–11, and for the fact that it was probably in this period that the proportion of non-resident students rose considerably, the work of the tutors in examining, and to some extent in lecturing this unprecedented throng must have increased enormously; as also, of course, did their emoluments. Both alike, however, seem to have been received with the same silent sang-froid.

(v)

The first thirty years of the century saw relatively few changes in the constitution, the teaching methods or the curriculum of the University. In one school, however, there were some important developments, and that was the school in which they were most needed, the School of Physic. The year 1795 found the University sadly bogged down in a dispute with the College of Physicians, and the School of Physic, which was jointly administered by the two disputants, naturally suffered. The legislation of 1785, which attempted to make provision for the joint administration of Sir Patrick Dun's estate, and in particular to implement his desire for the establishment of clinical lectures, was a failure, because the only hospital in Dublin suitable for the purpose refused co-operation. When the College of Physicians tried to solve the difficulty by transferring a few patients to a house in Clarendon Street and calling it a hospital the University Professors refused to recognize it.

Meanwhile the process of obtaining a medical degree had been reduced to a ritual of almost byzantine complexity. The regulations approved by the Board in 1793 prescribed that the student should first produce to the Registrar testimonials of attendance over a period of three years at medical classes in a university (not necessarily Dublin), and also of attendance at clinical lectures in Dublin and at one course given by each of the six Professors of the Dublin School of Physic; he was then given by the Board a *liceat ad examinandum*, which he presented to the Registrar of the College of Physicians, who arranged for him to be examined (*viva voce* and in Latin) by Fellows of that College, accompanied by the Regius Professor. If they were satisfied he next presented a thesis in Latin (on a subject previously approved by one of the University Professors) to the appropriate King's Professor, and if the latter approved the thesis the candidate received from the College of Physicians a certificate that he was *idoneus . . . qui admittatur ad praestanda exercitia*. He next had to pay to the Senior Proctor a fee of £21 8s. 6d. and present the certificate to be countersigned by the Registrar of Trinity College. It was then presented to the Regius Professor, who fixed a time for the performance of the 'acts' in public in the College hall. They consisted of disputations 'according to the usage of the University' and the reading (for the degree of M.B.) of two pre-lections. For the degree of M.D. there had to be four prelections, and printed copies of one of these had to be sent to the holders of eighteen designated offices.

The grotesque complexity of these arrangements arose mainly from the jealousy of the two Colleges and their refusal to trust each other. Trinity College wished to keep up the ancient formalities, while realiz-ing that it had not the expertise to examine thoroughly in medicine, while the College of Physicians was determined to maintain its right of independent judgment and not to become a mere cog in the machine of university procedure. Clearly a complete ignoramus or imposter would have been stopped at some point in this ritual, but at what stage, if any, an assurance was obtained that the candidate was really fit to practise medicine is far from clear. And what made the procedure all the more absurd was that the number of candidates for medical degrees averaged at this time less than two a year. The would-be doctors of Ireland, as of England, went to Edinburgh, whose medical school was then at the height of its fame; there they got good teaching and a medical degree without any requirements to take examinations in arts subjects. In 1795, in fact, all the King's Professors and one of the University Professors were medical graduates of Edinburgh, though some of them had first taken their B.A. degree in Dublin.

The first step towards an improvement of this position was the passing of a new School of Physic Act in 1800, by an Irish parliament already under sentence of death. It was the result of a somewhat adverse report on the College of Physicians by a committee of the House of Lords, which in its turn owed its appointment to the persistent lobbying of Robert Perceval, the University Professor of Chemistry. The most important provision of the Act was that all surplus funds from Dun's estate, after the King's Professors had been paid £100 a year each, were to go to the building of a hospital suitable for clinical teaching. The duties and mode of election of both King's and University Professors were also laid down in some detail. The provisions of an Act of 1747 which excluded Catholics from the King's Professorships were repealed, and the posts were declared open to all Christians; the University Professorships, on the other hand, were restricted to 'Protestants of all nations'.

Although it was to be bitterly attacked some fifty or sixty years after its enactment (by which time some of its provisions were, indeed, obsolete and irksome), the Act of 1800 at least restored peace to the

School of Physic. While Dun's Hospital was being built arrangements were made for clinical lectures in the Meath and Steevens's Hospitals, and around 1815 they were transferred to the new building. When the coffers of Dun's estate, which had been depleted by the building, filled up again, the long postponed King's Professorship of Midwifery was established in 1827.

Perceval was at the turn of the century a vigorous and effective teacher of chemistry, as well as a successful academic politician; his colleague in botany (Robert Scott), though diligent at his subject, played little part in the general development of the school, and William Hartigan, the Professor of Anatomy, was a very minor figure. The situation was transformed, however, when on Hartigan's death in 1812, James Macartney was appointed as his successor. Macartney was a radical Presbyterian from the north, who had studied mainly in London, and who for the past ten years had rather improbably combined the post of surgeon to the Radnor Militia with that of lecturer in comparative anatomy at St Bartholomew's Hospital. As soon as he started lecturing in Dublin the number of students increased rapidly, and by 1820 he was having to duplicate his lectures from lack of seating accommodation. He urged on the Board the necessity of greatly enlarged premises for the Medical School in general, and soon carried his point in principle. There was some delay from arguments over the best site, but the building of a new medical school at the east end of the College Park was begun in 1823 and completed two years later. The building was rather grim and prison-like, but at least it was spacious and served its purpose; some parts of it survive to this day, where the departments of anatomy and chemistry meet.

It would be wrong to attribute entirely to Macartney's reputation the great increase in the number of medical students during his professorship,[31] as the numbers in arts were rising rapidly at the same time, but there is no doubt that he attracted many Irish students who would otherwise have gone to Edinburgh, and even a few from England and Scotland.[32] William Stokes was later to refer rather ungenerously to the Medical School of 1820 as 'a grammar school of anatomy and book medicine and little more,'[33] but it was Macartney's grammar of anatomy which drew in the students who were to profit later from the clinical teaching of Graves and Stokes himself.

(vi)

In other departments of College life this period is somewhat uneventful and unenterprising, but it was not one of complete stagnation. A number of small changes made in the academic machinery indicate that the Board showed at least a sporadic desire to improve the efficiency of the College and to eliminate obvious anachronisms. The introduction of algebra into the B.A. course, long overdue, dates from 1808. In the same year three new Fellowships were established, which helped to provide more tutors for the ever-increasing influx of undergraduates. In 1814 the Board decided that a blind and absentee septuagenarian could not adequately perform the duties of Regius Professor of Divinity, and obtained Letters Patent which pensioned him off and re-established the office on a new basis, with guarantees that the duties would be properly performed.[34] Five years later it obtained from the Crown power to remit the statutory fines imposed on resident Doctors and Masters for failing to perform the commonplaces and disputations prescribed by Laud.

More important ultimately than any of these was an apparently small change in the arrangements for awarding the medals at the B.A. degree examination. From about 1730 onwards premiums had been awarded at each terminal examination to the best answerer in each of the divisions into which each annual class was arbitrarily divided for examination purposes. The competition for these premiums was keen, and it provided the basis for an informal distinction between pass-men and honors-men, for those who competed seriously for the premium had to be prepared for more numerous and more searching questions than were put to those who were merely seeking a pass. In 1793 it had been decided that, in addition to the term premiums, a gold medal should be given at graduation to every student who had an unbroken record of excellent answering in every one of his sixteen term examinations.[35] By this means a reward was provided for the really first-class man who happened to have in his division an even more brilliant rival.

But in 1815 it was announced that the medals would in future be awarded on a new basis. At the B.A. examination undergraduates who had won a premium at any of their earlier examinations were segregated into a separate division, which was examined more rigorously and on a more advanced and extensive course. The names of these honors-men, as we should now call them, were put at the head of the list of the year's graduates, distinguished as *primarii in sua classe*, and they were arranged in an order determined by their answering. Two gold medals were awarded, one to the best answerer in Classics, and one to the best in Science (*i.e.* mathematics and philosophy). The scheme had some obvious defects, but it contained the germ of the modern idea of an honors degree. For the first time honors-men are classed in an order determined by their answering, and for the first time a limited amount of specialization is encouraged and provided for.

These various changes show that some life was stirring in the College in the early nineteenth century, but they can hardly be said to add up to a very impressive programme of reform. They were probably less extensive than the changes brought about at Oxford between 1800 and 1810, or at Cambridge between 1820 and 1830. But before we pass adverse judgment on the rulers of Trinity during this epoch we should remember two things: that the times were everywhere unfavourable for reform, and that the need for reform was not nearly so pressing in Dublin as at Oxford or Cambridge.

Both before and after Waterloo circumstances in Great Britain and Ireland favoured a conservative rather than a radical outlook, and by 1810 or thereabouts political orthodoxy in the University and in most of the Protestant world outside its walls was as staunchly Tory as it had been staunchly Whig a generation earlier. The excesses of the Jacobins had produced a widespread revulsion, and at times panic. The Napoleonic war, though far from totalitarian by modern standards, was a serious business; and the necessity of winning it at all costs gave the Tories an excellent excuse for postponing inevitable reforms. Finally, when the war was won, the physical resources, as well as the moral prestige as victors, of the powers of the Holy Alliance established conservatism in the saddle as the only respectable creed; the Corsican ogre was officially branded as a man of the left. In Ireland some local factors tended in the same direction. The existence of the Protestant Ascendancy, still protected by discriminatory laws, made the division between privileged and unprivileged classes sharper than in England, and by emphasizing the precarious position of the former tempted them constantly towards a policy of repression. The rising of 1798, partly under Jacobin auspices, and the recurrence of rebellion in 1803 made it easy to represent liberalism as the first step towards treason. And finally the tension was increased by the steady growth of agrarian unrest. The foundations of this had been laid by the Cromwellian and Williamite settlements; but it was reinforced in the early nineteenth century by rapidly increasing population pressure, by the dislocation of prices and rents caused by the boom and slump of the war, and by agitation over the chronic and natural grievance of the Catholic tenants – payment of tithe.

It is true that another side of the picture existed, for many of the liberal and reforming movements that characterized the Victorian age had their origins in Regency times. But before 1830 the conservative note was the dominant one, in the political and intellectual worlds alike. In Dublin, moreover, a conservative policy in academic matters invited less criticism than did a similar policy in Oxford or Cambridge. The worst that can be said of the rulers of Trinity at this time is that they jogged along unimaginatively and rather more slowly than did the world outside their walls. Even conservatives are tempted to occasional reforms if the institutions thereby affected are not too venerable; and Trinity was, in this conservative age, spared by her relative modernity from the devoted fanaticism which paralysed reform in the English universities by seeing in any proposal to revise a statute that had been obsolete for centuries an attack on the very heart of the collegiate system. Sentimental devotion to founders' intentions, vested interests surviving from a vanished social order, independent colleges suspicious of any attempt at co-ordination, veneration for ancient statutes and practices simply because they were ancient – none of these affected seriously a unitary institution which, though founded in Elizabethan days, had been so extensively developed, rebuilt and reshaped during the eighteenth century as to be dominated by the spirit of the latter. But by 1830 the atmosphere of the College, though in no way medieval, was scarcely up to date; it was no closer in spirit to the new Colleges just founded in London than it was to Oxford and Cambridge. The world of Andrews and Hely-Hutchinson, perpetuated in the buildings, the furnishings, and in much of the teaching and organization of the College, did not possess for the men of this generation the glamour with which we invest it. For the reformer the problem was not to awake from a centuries-old slumber, but to cast off the by now rather stuffy influence of the day before yesterday. It is worth while pausing, before we examine the changes which the Victorian era was to bring to Trinity, to review in some detail this humdrum, busy phase of its history, when it filled the role of the slightly rusty but generally serviceable Redbrick University of the day.

5

The College in 1830

(i)

If at this point we interrupt the progress of our narrative with a static chapter, it is in conscious and unashamed imitation of an earlier and greater historian who used the device with such success. By this means we can knit together at a single point the threads of what must perforce be separate narratives of the various parts of the University, and thereby enable the reader more easily to apprehend the nature of the whole. For this purpose the year 1830 is the most convenient. It represents the boundary between the relatively stable period which we have just described and the succeeding period of rapid development and reform which followed the simultaneous political triumph of the Whigs and the appointment of Bartholomew Lloyd as Provost. But although we shall attempt in this chapter to portray as accurately as we can the institutions, personalities and atmosphere of the year 1830, it will be necessary at times, to set the picture in a true perspective and to avoid needless repetition, to glance backwards or forwards for a decade or more.

To consider first the physical aspect of the College, it lay no longer 'near Dublin' but well embedded in it. On the north and north-east reclamation of estuarine sloblands had created an extensive quarter of docks and warehouses. On the west a broad commercial thoroughfare led to the old city. On the south the College was separated from Nassau Street by a crooked and in places dilapidated brick wall; Nassau Street itself was still narrow and ill-paved, but beyond it were fashionable streets passing over from private residences to shops. To the south-east and east the squares and sober streets occupied largely by the professional classes stretched as far as the Grand Canal and were continued by the prosperous suburbs on its further bank.

The principal, western part of the College had already taken on much of its present form, and the refacing of the Library with granite (to replace the original sandstone, which had weathered badly) was nearing completion. Front Square and Library Square were much as we

93

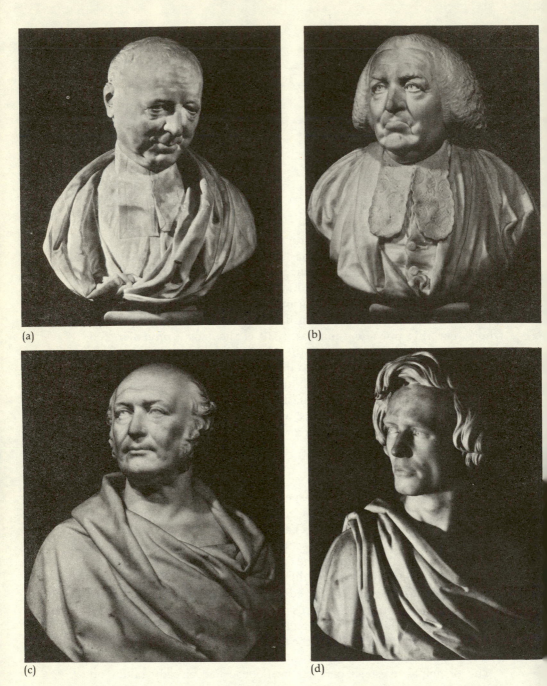

(a)

(b)

(c)

(d)

11   (a) Patrick Delany, Fellow, 1709–28. (John van Nost.)
       (b) William Clement, Fellow, 1733–82. (Edward Smyth.)
       (c) Sir William Rowan Hamilton, Professor of Astronomy, 1827–65.
           (J.H. Foley.)
       (d) James McCullagh, Fellow, 1832–47. (Christopher Moore.)

know them today, except that they were imperfectly separated by a red-brick range which ran north and south though with a gap in the middle (where the Campanile now stands), marking the site of the Old Hall and Chapel demolished over thirty years earlier. There was a similar red-brick range on the site now occupied by the Graduates' Memorial Building. To the south of these squares the back windows of the Provost's House looked out over a spacious, if somewhat dreary Fellows' garden as far as the wall of the College Park, where the old anatomy house had recently been pulled down. Eastwards from Library Square the nearer part of the College Park was laid out with trees and walks, but soon merged into a neglected and ill-drained 'wilderness' where an occasional snipe or curlew might still be seen. At the south-east corner of the Park, and opening on Park Street (the present Lincoln Place) but walled off from the rest of the College[1], stood the new medical school.

(ii)

To turn now to the administrative structure which these buildings housed, the machinery of the University, as distinct from the College, need not detain us long. Its functions were few and mainly formal, and it lay completely under the control of the Board of Trinity College. At the head of the University was the Chancellor, Ernest Augustus, Duke of Cumberland, the last of a series of Hanoverian princes who had, with a single brief interlude, held the post for well over a century. The election in 1715 of the Prince of Wales (later George II) to the Chancellorship was simply an attempt to advertise the resolute Whiggery of the University, and to dissociate it from the Jacobite vagaries of the previous Chancellor, the second Duke of Ormonde. But the election set a precedent from which it was difficult to depart without an appearance of disloyalty. When in 1786 the Chancellor (the Duke of Gloucester) was believed to be dying, John Kearney, then a Senior Fellow, besought the Earl of Charlemont to allow himself to be nominated, on the grounds that a Royal Duke 'might neglect such petty objects as we are',[2] but the majority of the Board was prepared to endure the neglect, and doubtless preferred a royal absentee to an Irishman who might prove a busybody – a certain King Log to a possible King Stork. When the Duke did in fact die in 1805 the Board, actuated either by courageous but by now inopportune Whiggery, or else by singular obtuseness, proposed to elect the Prince of Wales, whose unpopularity with his father and with the Government was then at its height. They were rebuked by the Lord-Lieutenant, and informed that if a Royal Duke were to be elected the choice must lie

95

with the King. The Board swallowed the snub, and consented to the choice of the Duke of Cumberland.[3] By 1830 he had become a symbolical ogre of reaction, debarred from the succession only by the slender barrier of the life of the young Princess Victoria. He was perhaps the most unpopular man in England, though in Irish Protestant circles his extreme Orange views were regarded with more tolerance. In the affairs of the University, however, he was little more than a figurehead, who was only very occasionally consulted on formal matters or lobbied either to procure Court favours (if he happened to be on speaking terms with the King) or to assist in blocking a liberal measure. Even his removal to Hanover for the last fourteen years of his life can have made very little difference.

The Vice-Chancellor was appointed by the Chancellor, and automatically vacated office when a new Chancellor took office. The Chancellor normally consulted the wishes of the College in filling a vacancy in the office, but at least on one occasion he failed to do so.[4] In 1830 the Vice-Chancellor was Lord John George Beresford, Archbishop of Armagh; his appointment in the previous year marked a temporary reversion to the practice which had been invariable from 1615 to 1791 of choosing an ecclesiastic for this post. (From 1791 to 1829 it had been filled by a judge, either the Lord Chancellor of Ireland or the Lord Chief Justice.) Beresford, though at times a bit starchy and pompous, proved himself as Vice-Chancellor and later as Chancellor a good friend to the College and often a wise counsellor.

The Visitors of the University and College were the Vice-Chancellor[5] and the Archbishop of Dublin, *ex officio*. The curious arrangement of having two Visitors, without any clear statutory direction as to what should happen if they disagreed, seems unparalleled elsewhere. Besides discharging the functions of a final court of appeal they were required by the Caroline statutes to conduct visitations of general inquiry every three years. In 1811 annual instead of triennial visitations were decreed, and this arrangement lasted till 1833, when the Visitors were released from any obligation to visit unless they wished to do so, or unless an appeal or *dubium* was referred to them for decision. By 1830 the annual visitations had become a tedious and usually meaningless ritual.[6] Only a handful of appeals had come before them at these regular visitations, and the regularity with which the Visitors found in favour of the Board did not encourage their increase. Some of the complaints were trivial or ill-founded, but others of more substance (such as a protest by the Junior Fellows and Scholars against the Board's practice of sending loyal addresses and other communications of political significance in the name of the Provost, Fellows and Scholars without consulting the major part of this body) met with the same fate. The consent of the Visitors was also required for certain regulations of the Board (mainly those relating to salaries) which were classified as decrees. Occasionally the Visitors made the Board modify their original proposals, but usually the consent was given as a matter of course. The requirement, however, provided at least a partial guarantee against the members of the Board acting too flagrantly in their own interests.

The Senate of the University was an ineffectual body whose meetings were confined to the formal proceedings at which degrees were granted and conferred. Until its incorporation in 1857 its status and composition were ill-defined, and its activities were governed by a curious code of *Consuetudines, sive Regulae* of unknown origin, which were in some points at variance with the College statutes. For a brief period in the early eighteenth century an attempt had been made to use the meetings of the Senate as a forum for political demonstrations, but the scandal thereby produced resulted in a rigid interpretation of the rule which forbade any grace to be moved unless it had the previous consent of the Board. The Senate, therefore, had limited powers of veto, but none of initiative, and it was thereby prevented from developing (except on a very few occasions later in the century, with the consent of the Board) into a body whose meetings might serve for the discussion of policy by the University at large.

(iii)

The entire government of the College and University lay, in practice, in the hands of the Board, that is, the Provost and the seven most senior of the Fellows. To them were entrusted powers that were analogous in Cambridge terms to those of the Seniority of Trinity and the Caput of the Senate combined. Similarly the position of the Provost was (and still is) comparable to that of a Master of Trinity who is permanently Vice-Chancellor. A number of important powers of veto had been reserved to the Provost in the statutes, but the constitutional struggles of the eighteenth century, coupled with the injudicious use of the veto made at times by Baldwin and Hely-Hutchinson, and even on a few occasions by Andrews, had resulted in rulings which deprived the Provost of any substantial sphere of independent action, and the commanding position which he usually occupied in the College and University was due more to the respect conceded to his office than to any precise legal rights.

The Board in 1830 consisted of Samuel Kyle, Provost; Francis Hodgkinson, Vice-Provost, Regius Professor of Civil Law and Erasmus Smith's Professor of Modern History; Robert Phipps, Registrar;

Thomas Prior, Regius Professor of Greek and Archbishop King's Lecturer in Divinity; Bartholomew Lloyd, Senior Lecturer[7] and Erasmus Smith's Professor of Natural and Experimental Philosophy; Henry Wray, Senior Proctor; Franc Sadleir, Bursar, Librarian, Erasmus Smith's Professor of Mathematics and Donnellan Lecturer; and Charles William Wall, Senior Dean and Professor of Hebrew. Hodgkinson and Phipps were laymen; the others were in orders. Hodgkinson, the eldest, was seventy-three; Wall, the youngest, was fifty.

They were, on the whole, an undistinguished lot – a sad falling-off from the Boards of a generation ago. Lloyd was, indeed, a man of remarkable ability and vision, and Sadleir, if a place-hunter, was a shrewd and industrious one, with some talent for administration. Both these future Provosts will be dealt with more fully in the next chapter. But the impress which the others have left on the pages of history is a faint one. Kyle was a competent, but not an outstanding man, who had been appointed, as we have seen, mainly on political grounds, but in spite of his extreme views he managed, thanks to a bland manner and the ability to keep his mouth shut, to avoid any violent controversy.[8] Hodgkinson, who had sat on the Board since before the Union, was no trouble to anybody so long as he accumulated enough sinecures, dispensations and leaves of absence. Prior was a convinced and earnest conservative whose very jaundiced view of nearly all his colleagues has been enshrined for posterity in his diaries. He fancied himself as a likely Provost both in 1820 and in 1831, and ascribed his failure to almost every cause except that which is clear to us now – that he had no ascertainable qualifications for the post. Phipps was a cantankerous and elderly bachelor whose main recreation was entering his dissent in the minutes. Wall, a generous benefactor of the College, was a genuine scholar, whose five volumes on Hebrew orthography brought him some reputation in his day. Wray, whose memory has been kept alive by a substantial prize for students of philosophy founded by the piety of his widow, made an unfortunate impression on at least one of his contemporaries. J.W. Croker, the not over-squeamish candidate for the University seat in the election of 1818, alleged that Wray was withholding the promise of his vote until he had secured a job for his brother-in-law, and declared that 'in all my election practice I have never seen or heard such filthy venality as in this Doctor of Divinity'.[9] Croker's righteous indignation is indeed suspect, but it is remarkable that in the three elections of 1827–31 Wray voted each time for a different candidate.

In the hands of these eight men were centralized all the judicial, executive and legislative powers that lay within the competence of the College. They appointed to all academic posts except the Provostship (which was reserved to the Crown), but including the Chancellorship. When statutory change was desired it was the Board which petitioned the Lord-Lieutenant for a King's Letter. As a judicial body they were subordinate only to the Visitors as a court of appeal. They had complete control of all the finances, subject only to a few minor restraints from certain acts of parliament. And not only did they discharge, as a body, executive functions, but they appointed from their own ranks all the major executive officers – Vice-Provost, Librarian, Registrar, Senior Lecturer and Bursar. In addition to these major offices the Senior Fellows also shared out between them the lesser offices of Senior Dean, Senior Proctor, Catechist and Auditor.[10]

The librarianship was usually given to the Senior Fellow who had the most taste or aptitude for the post, and the Librarians of the nineteenth century – Barrett, Sadleir, Wall, Todd, Ingram, Abbot – were, with the exception of Sadleir, men who had a feeling for and love of books.[11] But the other offices were distributed not on any principle of suitability, but on the ancient principle of Buggins's turn. This was exposed to public scrutiny in 1870, when a rebuke from the Board to the Junior Fellows on the inefficiency of one of their officers stung the Juniors into inquiring how the posts reserved for the Seniors were filled. Could they be assured, they asked the Visitors, that in every case the electors voted, as the statutes required, for the most suitable candidate?[12] The answer was that the elections were regulated not by the statutes but by 'immemorial custom', by which the offices of Senior Lecturer and Bursar (which brought in the most money, as the holder received, as well as a salary, poundages on fees and rent respectively) rotated among the Senior Fellows on a two-year tenure, while the five remaining Senior Fellows were given in order of seniority their pick among the remaining offices. As the vice-provostship was the most lucrative of these it was, almost without exception, held by the most senior of the Fellows, and at first sight it seems puzzling that Hodgkinson, of all men, who had been Vice-Provost since 1821, should have stepped down for a year in 1832 and taken the senior proctorship instead. A little reflection supplies the explanation. In 1832, as a consequence of the Reform Act, a large number of graduates were taking their M.A. degrees so as to qualify as university electors. And for every M.A. the Senior Proctor got £2 10s.

It would seem that occasionally these conventions were broken so as to debar from an office a Fellow who, from failing health or other reasons, was totally unsuited to it, and obscure deals and exchanges took place from time to time which resulted in relatively long tenures by the same man, as when MacDonnell held the bursarship for eight years from 1836. But as a rule the rotation was rapid; the senior lecturership was never held for more than two consecutive years by the same man between 1845 and 1860. This meant that although the routine duties of the various offices were for the most part carried out fairly conscientiously, there was no chance for anyone to develop a coherent administrative policy or to increase his efficiency by experience.

In addition to these administrative offices, a fair number of Professorships and lecturerships were held by the Senior Fellows at this time. The chair of Modern History was by now a complete sine-cure, and the Regius Professorship of Civil Law involved only some trivial examining duties; both these posts had for many years been appropriated by Hodgkinson. Erasmus Smith's Professor of Mathe-matics was usually elected from among the Senior Fellows, though Bartholomew Lloyd had been elected to the post while still a Junior Fellow. The holder, even if past his prime, had in most cases been a good mathematician in his day, but there was some doubt as to whether this was true of Sadleir, who occupied the chair in 1830. The Professor of Natural and Experimental Philosophy (*i.e.* physics) on the same foundation was bound by Act of Parliament to be chosen on the results of an examination, and its record, therefore, was fairly good. In 1830 it was held by Bartholomew Lloyd, about whose competence there could be no doubt, and he was exceptional in having been elected to it as a Senior Fellow, having vacated the chair of Mathematics for this pur-pose in 1822. The chair of Hebrew was held by Wall, who was a sound scholar in the subject; apart from the inevitable tenure for three years by Sadleir the post had hitherto been filled reasonably enough. Finally, the Regius Professor of Greek and Archbishop King's Lecturer in Divinity were always chosen from among the Senior Fellows, the former by statute, the latter by custom, but they were not regarded as anything more than routine teaching posts to be held for two years or so, and they rotated among the Senior Fellows fairly rapidly. As with administrative offices, although the routine duties of the post were carried out with efficiency, if not always with zeal, the frequent exchanges discouraged any growth of expertise.

Although the Board at this time, as far as can be deduced from the rather curt records of the Register, occasionally discussed at length important educational or administrative issues, much of its time was taken up by matters which we should nowadays regard as more suitably deputed to officers or committees. Among these the manage-ment of the College estates loomed largest, and it formed, indeed, the most frequent item in the Board's business.[13] As the leases were restricted by law to a period not exceeding twenty-one years, renewals appeared on the agenda almost every month, and although many of these doubtless went through automatically on the Bursar's recommendation their terms were now and then debated and voted on. Long paragraphs appear from time to time detailing the number of trees planted on a College holding, with its financial implications. Nor did the Board escape the philanthropic burdens which custom placed on landlords; it was in constant receipt of requests for contributions towards the cost of a church, a school or a pier for a parish in which it held some land, and these requests usually received a favourable reception, though the sums voted were small. Awards of prizes and testimonials, the granting or withholding of academic credits, and the approval of degrees account, reasonably enough, for a good deal of the remaining business, and when all else failed the Board could always fall back on the apparently fascinating recreation of appointing and dismissing porters. As for academic offices, so also for the right to nominate to a vacant place among the porters there was a system of rotation among the Senior Fellows. That the system was not very happy in its operation was shown by the frequency of dismissals, the charges ranging from simple drunkenness, through assault and battery, to seduction of a fellow porter's wife. In this last instance the Board showed a fine impartiality: both porters were dismissed, one for adultery and the other for keeping a disorderly house.

Thanks partly to the concentration in their hands of so many offices, the Provost and Senior Fellows formed in the early nineteenth century an élite of wealth as well as of power. The income of the Provost would seem at this time to have been rather more than £3,000 a year (in addition to a free house); those of the Senior Fellows probably averaged about £1,800 a year.[14] A considerable fraction of this wealth was derived from a curious source which, though not without its parallels in other institutions, reflected little credit on successive generations of Senior Fellows. When each short-term lease fell in, if, as was usual at this time, the value of the land had increased, the College could either raise the rent, or renew at a rent below the market value on payment of a fine by the tenant. The rents went to the common fund of the College, but the renewal fines were divided between the Provost and Senior Fellows, and to the Provost and Senior Fellows was entrusted the decision as to which course should be adopted. It is not surprising that in 1850, when this short-sighted system of legalized embezzlement was abolished, the College estates were found to be let at rents which represented only about a third of their real value.

All these factors served to separate the Board very sharply from the rest of the College, in the same way as at this period the Heads of Houses formed a distinct caste at Oxford and Cambridge. The constant, if often ill-informed criticism to which the Board was naturally exposed[15] tended to reinforce the class-consciousness of its members, to produce in it a strong *esprit de corps* which was, on account of the slow rate of change of its membership at this time,[16] the easier to maintain, and to lead its members to hide their individual differences behind the facade of collective decisions.

The income of the College, and *a fortiori* of the Senior Fellows, had risen very sharply in the first quarter of the nineteenth century. This had helped to produce a rather unexpected change in the composition of the Board. The College had in its gift a number of livings,[17] and it was the custom to offer each one, as it became vacant, to the Fellows in order of seniority (laymen, of course, excepted). These livings varied greatly in value, but the best of them were very well endowed; at least six were worth upwards of £1,500 a year, and a further seven or eight over £1,000.[18] During the eighteenth century the great majority of the Fellows retired after a tenure of Fellowship averaging fifteen to twenty years to one of these country rectories, where they were free to marry, and in many cases enjoyed a better income for less laborious work. This produced a rapid renewal in the personnel of the Board; of the Fellows co-opted to Senior Fellowship in the course of the eighteenth century two thirds resigned, after sitting on the Board for an average period of ten years, for a College living. But the improved financial status of Senior Fellowship began to reduce the rate of turnover soon after 1800; the number of livings which a Senior Fellow was prepared to accept grew smaller and smaller, so that unusual longevity in the occupants of a few of these better livings would stabilize the composition of the Board for long periods. By 1830 the system had come to a standstill, for James Wilson, who accepted Clonfeacle in 1824,[19] was the last Senior Fellow in the history of the College to resign on a living.[20]

The average age of the Senior Fellows shows, in consequence, a very steep rise over this period. William Magee, in 1800, was the last man to be co-opted Senior Fellow while still in his thirties; by 1830 the prospects of reaching the Board before the age of fifty had become remote.[21] About 1710 the average age of members of the Board had scarcely been over forty. Between 1775 and 1810 it lay close to fifty. By 1830 it had risen to exactly sixty. It was perhaps surprising that it was not higher, as there was no precedent for retirement on the grounds of age or infirmity, and no provisions for a pension. A Senior Fellow unable to attend Board meetings ceased as a rule to hold any offices, but he still drew the basic Senior Fellow's salary.[22] Toleken, who, according to his obituaries, suffered from poor health throughout his life, was the first Senior Fellow to resign on grounds of infirmity. He did so in 1880, at the age of seventy-seven and survived until he was eighty-four.[23]

By modern standards the somewhat elderly men who sat on the Board in 1830 were over-generously rewarded for their not very exacting duties, and their monopoly of so many offices blocked various reforms and developments which their juniors might have promoted. But before we condemn them or the system too harshly three extenuating circumstances should be borne in mind. Firstly, there had been very few new appropriations of power; the system had developed by imperceptible changes from one which had worked very well in the seventeenth century, when the Junior Fellows were immature birds of passage and the government of the College was quite rightly entrusted to those who had at least seven years' experience of it. Each succeeding generation saw this state of affairs slightly transformed, but at no time was the change sudden enough to call clearly for action. Secondly, although the Senior Fellows had it in their power to release to their juniors a few minor plums of office, the more lucrative posts were confined to the Senior Fellows by statute. Doubtless the Board could have (and should have) petitioned the Crown for a change in these provisions, but one cannot criticize anyone very severely for not taking the initiative in promoting legislation designed to reduce his own emoluments. Finally, although a few Senior Fellows, like Hodgkinson, appear to have been lazy, and a few, like Sadleir, were grasping, the great majority carried out the duties of their various offices in a regular if unimaginative way, and in most cases they attended Board meetings regularly through the year, with only rare absences.[24] Above all, they resided in Dublin, and in many cases in the College, and in this respect they shone as models of industry in comparison with the Seniority of Trinity College, Cambridge, at the same period. There the idea of requiring an undertaking to reside in Cambridge before a man was co-opted to the governing body was dismissed, even by the University Registrary, as 'an absurd and romantic notion', and as late as 1860 a meeting of the Seniority attended by all its members was regarded as a remarkable and almost unprecedented event.[25]

(iv)

The Junior Fellows numbered at this time eighteen. They were responsible for the greater part of the teaching and examining, and for the general supervision of the students. They were, with one or two exceptions, tutors; and were required in this capacity by the statutes not only to act as moral guardians of their pupils and to represent them in all transactions with the higher authorities of the College, but also to give them the tuition necessary to see them through their College course: *tutores quae discenda sunt, pupillos suos per singulos dies sedulo doceant, quaeque etiam agenda sunt, moneant.*[26] The con-scientiousness with which these duties were performed and the manner adopted towards their pupils varied widely, of course, from one tutor to another. A good deal of irregularity seems, in many cases, to have been permitted to both pupil and tutor in their attendance at tutorial classes. Magee (later Archbishop of Dublin) won many pupils, if we are to believe his biographer, by the charm of his manner; 'the apparently unwearied courteous attention which he paid to those that were speaking to him was often a subject of surprise and just admiration'.[27] J.T. O'Brien, who also became a bishop, had a different technique: 'His usual salutation to his pupils at his door (for he seldom asked them in), "Well, Sir!", is said not to have been discontinued in the Palace study at Kilkenny to men who had come many miles to speak to him on diocesan business.'[28] Richard Graves not only remitted the fees of a large number of his poorer pupils, but found himself in many cases out of pocket on their behalf;[29] and there were doubtless others who showed a similar generosity.

Over and above their tutorial duties the Junior Fellows had to provide from among their ranks a Junior Dean, a Junior Bursar and Registrar of Chambers, and a few other minor administrative offices, and to fill one or two Professorships and over twenty lecturing posts – Greek lecturers, morning lecturers in Science, assistants to the Catechist (who gave religious instruction), assistant lecturers in Hebrew, Divinity and Mathematics, and University preachers. They had four times a year to examine between them the whole body of undergraduates in the quarterly examinations, which were strenuous *viva voce* affairs lasting for eight days; and they had to assist the Provost and Senior Fellows in examining prize candidates and divinity students. Academic men are apt to complain, perhaps more frequently than most, of overwork, but when the Fellows of Trinity were taunted, as they constantly were, with the paucity of their literary productions they could at this period reply with some justice that 'the College of Dublin exacts the most overwhelming labour from its Fellows ... by the mental treadmill of the classes and daily lectures'.[30] In 1808–11 the number of tutors had been increased by three, but the enormous growth in the number of students since 1800 meant that in 1830 the tutors, with an average of over 100 pupils each, were busier than they had ever been before. Rowan Hamilton, who accepted the chair of Astronomy in 1827 on condition that he did not compete for Fellowship, justified his choice later by saying 'as a Fellow, on the present system, I would either have had no time for pursuing Science, or must have made that time by exertions at extra hours, and to the injury of health'.[31] Thomas Romney Robinson was even more plaintive. He writes in 1820:

Under the system pursued at present in Trinity College, its Fellows can scarcely be expected to devote themselves to any work of research or even of compilation; constantly employed in the duties of tuition, which harass the mind more than the most abstract studies, they can have but little inclination, at the close of the day, to commence a new career of labour. How different is this from the state of the English Universities ...[32]

The Fellows were recruited on the results of an examination which, except perhaps that for admission to the Chinese civil service, had a good claim to its reputation as the most gruelling public examination in the world. It was also one of the fairest, for although it may be argued that an examination of this type was not an ideal way of selecting the best scholars or teachers, it was never once suggested throughout the entire nineteenth century that a candidate's success had been furthered by favour or influence. Any B.A. was eligible to compete. Sometimes a brilliant man would be successful after one or two years' reading; more often four or five were needed.[33] Magee used to read from early morning till ten at night, then go out to a ball for a few hours' relaxation and exercise, and return to resume his reading.[34] Phelan, who on account of poverty had to spend much of his time in giving private tuition, used to work from 4 a.m. to 10 p.m., his only relaxation being in varying his labours. After four years of this without success he retired to the country, but when a vacancy occurred three years later he was persuaded by his friends to make one more attempt, and was successful after six weeks' work.[35]

The examination was held in Whitsun week, and a speculative element was supplied by the fact that Fellowships were offered only as places came vacant. There was, therefore, uncertainty up to the last moment as to how many Fellowships would be available each year, and the unexpected death or resignation of a Fellow in April or May in a year in which no place had hitherto fallen vacant would precipitate a sudden flurry among examiners and candidates alike. Sometimes three years would pass without a vacancy; sometimes there would be three places to be filled at once. For a man who had just failed and was willing to try again the prospect of having to await the unpredictable incidence of death among ex-Fellows in remote Ulster rectories,[36] while new competitors were coming forward from among his juniors, produced a tension which, coupled with the necessary hard work, was too much for some constitutions. Men as able as John Jebb, later Bishop of Limerick, and Thomas Lefroy, later Chief Justice, broke down under the strain and retired from the fray.

The excitement mounted through the four days in Whitsun week in which the examination was conducted, usually before a large and interested audience (who laid heavy bets on the result), and reached its climax in the solemn announcement by the Provost on Trinity

Monday. In one case at least the news of the result had effects which verged on the miraculous: Miss Plunket, an elderly friend of Magee's who had long been bedridden with rheumatism, when she heard the messenger give at her door the knock that indicated Magee's election leapt from her bed and met the astonished messenger on the landing.[37]

The Fellows were by this time required by the statutes to remain celibate and, except for the *Medicus* and the two *Juristae*, who could remain laymen, to be ordained within three years of their M.A. degree.[38] A few of the Fellows obtained – by the use of what influence we cannot now tell – dispensations from the requirement to take orders, and such dispensations became rather more frequent as the century proceeded, until the requirement was swept away by Fawcett's Act in 1873. But up to the year 1866 the number of Fellows who were in orders (or who were to take orders a year or two later) never fell below three quarters of the total.

With regard to the rule of celibacy, the position in the early nineteenth century was curious, and indeed rather ludicrous. The meaning of the statute was plain enough, but as its wording was somewhat ambiguous[39] there had grown up among the Fellows from about 1750 onwards a practice of contracting semi-clandestine marriages. The Provost, and doubtless the Visitors, were well aware of the existence of the Fellows' wives, but the appearances were preserved. The wives were not acknowledged as such inside the College, and in academic society they preserved their maiden name with the prefix of Mrs. The sons of Fellows, when they entered College and were asked their father's profession, usually returned the non-committal *Clericus*, unless the father had by this time retired to a living, in which case *olim hujus Collegii Socius* could safely be added. Although the fear of expulsion was not a very real one, the position of these married Fellows was always a trifle precarious. When, as has been related in the last chapter, some of them waited on the Bishop of Cloyne in 1794 to point out that it was contrary to the statutes to hold the provostship simultaneously with a bishopric, a brief reference by the Bishop to their wives was enough to close that line of argument. A few of the more cautious went to the trouble of obtaining a dispensation before marrying,[40] but the majority, feeling rightly that there was safety in numbers, cheerfully took upon themselves the responsibility of interpreting the statute liberally. The able and ambitious Magee fell in love after he had been a Fellow for a few years; at first 'with all the impatience of a lover he commanded his ardour and resolved to wait for an adequate living', for he did not consider that his income as a Fellow would allow him to support a wife; but before long 'strong inclinations gradually modified and at last set aside the scruples and delays of cold and calculating prudence',[41] and he married. Throughout this trying engagement the celibacy statute does not seem to have entered into his calculations.

By 1811 no fewer than sixteen out of the twenty-five Fellows were married. Provost Hall decided that the flouting of the plain meaning of the statutes in a matter liable to cause irreverent amusement should no longer be tolerated, and obtained, only a few days before his resignation, Letters Patent which imposed the obligation of celibacy in terms which admitted of no evasion. He took this unpopular step on his own initiative, without consulting the Board or the Visitors. Under the new statute the married Fellows were given a full indemnity; and in 1812 supplementary Letters Patent recognised the vested right to matrimony of all the existing unmarried Fellows (who, it was argued, had competed for Fellowship on the understanding that it was compatible with matrimony), provided that they openly announced their marriages. But among the Fellows elected after 1812 this rigid reimposition of an antiquated rule soon led to complaints, and already in 1818 it had become an issue at a parliamentary election.[42] The celibacy statute was finally repealed in 1840, not without a protest from the Scholars, who feared that the main incentive for the resignation of Fellows would vanish with it, and that the frequency of vacancies would be greatly reduced. Their fears were reasonable, for there is no doubt that the rigid enforcement of celibacy for twenty-eight years, combined with the tendency, already referred to, for Senior Fellows to be less eager to resign on livings, was responsible for a marked increase in the years around 1830 in the number of resignations of Junior Fellows. Of the eighteen Fellows elected between 1812 and 1830 four died relatively young, twelve resigned after an average tenure of ten years, and only two stayed on to become Senior Fellows.

To the lay Fellows the College had no patronage to offer, and a larger proportion of them remained permanently in academic life. But in the early nineteenth century two lay Fellows, both lawyers, resigned their Fellowships as young men to occupy in succession the chair of Feudal and English Law, which served as a stepping-stone to a successful professional career outside the University. P.C. Crampton became a judge of the Queen's Bench after a short term as Solicitor-General; Mountiford Longfield specialized in the law of real property, and when the Landed Estates Court was set up he became one of its judges. It is interesting to note that both these men turned in their old age to topics with which their early academic life must have familiarized them. Crampton published shortly before his death two theological essays, and Longfield an elementary treatise on mathematical series.

But for most of the Fellows it was the episcopal rather than the judicial Bench that represented the summit of their reasonable ambitions. In the closing years of the seventeenth century Trinity College had supplied most of the bishops for Irish sees, and there were for several years at this time nine ex-Fellows simultaneously on the Bench. In the early eighteenth century this river of patronage began to diminish, and when the Whig governments settled firmly on a policy of appointing Englishmen to Irish sees it dried up altogether. After the appointment of Stopford to Cloyne in 1735 a period of nearly half a century elapsed in which no Fellow or ex-Fellow was made a bishop. In the disturbed years at the close of the century, when Irish sees had become less attractive in English eyes, one Fellow and two ex-Fellows were appointed in rapid succession: Hugh Hamilton, the author of a textbook on physics referred to earlier, and of a very elegant treatise on conic sections, in 1796; Stock (p. 61) in 1798; and Young (p. 63) in 1799. After the Union another period of comparative neglect set in, for although Provosts were regularly promoted to bishoprics the only other ex-Fellow to reach the Bench between 1799 and 1836 was Magee, who was appointed to Raphoe in 1819 and translated to Dublin three years later.

George IV, a keen, if at times erratic student of the problems of ecclesiastical patronage, had indeed pointed out that 'however respectable the university of Dublin might be it could scarcely be considered sufficiently adequate to supply all the demands of the Irish Church'.[43] But he was sufficiently impressed by the lavish entertainment he had been given by the College on the occasion of his visit to Ireland in 1821 to resolve to bestow on one of its members the next vacant bishopric. Nothing happened for five years, and when eventually the promise was made good local politics gave it an unexpected twist. The new bishop of Cloyne was not to be a Fellow or ex-Fellow, but John Brinkley, Professor of Astronomy. The explanation lay apparently in the ambitions of Goulbourn, the Chief Secretary, to represent the University of Cambridge in Parliament; for by nominating a Cambridge graduate with a post at Dublin he was able to further his own purpose while nominally gratifying the King's whim.[44]

In the mid-nineteenth century the tide of patronage was once more to flow in favour of the Fellows before its final disappearance at Disestablishment, and there were in 1830 four future bishops among the Junior Fellows: Sandes, O'Brien, J.H. Singer and Griffin.[45]

Most of the Fellows who retired to livings spent the rest of their lives there as country rectors, distinguished from their neighbours only by the memory of a great prize that they had once won, and by the erudition or obscurity of their sermons. But in those days even a diligent and conscientious rector usually had a fair amount of leisure, and some of the ex-Fellows carried on in their parishes scholarly work which had been begun in College but which all too often had been crowded out by the pressure of tutorial duties. Of these the most remarkable in the period under review are Edward Hincks and Thomas Romney Robinson. Neither published anything of consequence while a Fellow, but in later life Hincks, from his rectory in Killyleagh, whither the inscribed stones were brought to him by barge, did brilliant and pioneer work in the deciphering of hieroglyphic and cuneiform inscriptions; while Robinson, from Armagh, published the astronomical results which were to win for him the Royal Medal of the Royal Society.

But there was one of the ex-Fellows of this period to whose fiery spirit tutorial duties, quiet scholarship and the life of a country parish were alike unsatisfying. Arthur Hugh Kenney, after ten years as a tutor, retired to the country and soon became Dean of Achonry. In 1820 he pressed on the Government his claims to be made Provost with a vigour that was unhampered by any false modesty,[46] and when they were ignored he shook the dust of Ireland from his feet and became rector of a busy London parish. Meanwhile he had taken up pamphleteering in the Protestant and High Tory interest: *An enquiry into some doctrines maintained by the Church of Rome* was followed by *Principles and practice of pretended reformers in Church and State* (an uninhibited defence of the Peterloo massacre) and *The dangerous nature of popish power*; also, more quaintly, *Letters on prejudice* and *A defence of religious liberty*, whose titles require, however, to be interpreted in the light of the author's concepts of prejudice and liberty. In later life he turned to less controversial matters (including the memoir of Magee, to which reference has several times been made above). Perhaps the change was brought about by misfortune, for 'adverse circumstances and pecuniary difficulties arising, his living was sequestered',[47] and the would-be Provost died dodging his creditors at Boulogne.

It must not be inferred, of course, that the typical Fellow of the time had either the genius of Hincks or Kenney's passion for the limelight. Most of them were much dimmer luminaries. Of the eighteen men who were Junior Fellows in 1830, five made reasonably substantial contributions to the scholarship of their day,[48] four others published at least a few pamphlets or sermons, but nine evaded the critical judgment of posterity by refraining from the printed word.[49] It is not, by modern standards, an impressive record, but it is doubtful whether any Oxford or Cambridge college would at this time have made a much better showing. Trinity College, Dublin, still bore in the early nineteenth century the reproachful sobriquet of 'the silent sister', which implied that her scholarly output was not proportionate to her size and resources. That there was some substance in the charge cannot be denied, but it was often greatly exaggerated. Critics seemed to forget that although in the number of its students Dublin was, between 1775 and 1835, comparable to the English universities, its financial resources, and consequently the number of its Fellows and Professors, were greatly inferior. This meant that not only had it fewer potential authors, but also that they had much heavier teaching duties. The fair comparison would have been with about three colleges from Oxford or Cambridge, and not with the entire universities. It should also be remembered that at this period the reputation in the world at large of a learned society depended far more on its achievements in classical scholarship than in any other field. In mathematics, physics, astronomy and biblical scholarship Dublin had nothing to be ashamed of, but thanks to the mathematical bias of the Fellowship examination few of the more scholarly Fellows of Trinity between 1760 and 1860 paid any attention to the classics.[50]

There were, in fact, between the resignation of Stock in 1779 and the election of Ferrar eighty years later only two Fellows who published anything of consequence in this field. John Walker, who wrote on Horatian metres as well as editing Livy, Lucian, Pindar and the Odyssey, might have earned wider fame as a scholar had not poverty driven him to hack-work; for he was expelled from his Fellowship in 1804 for declaring to the Provost that he could not conscientiously remain a member of the Established Church, and subsequently founded the very strict Calvinistic sect known as the Separatists or Walkerites.[51] James Kennedy (later Kennedy-Baillie), who held a Fellowship from 1817 to 1831, fell a victim not to poverty but to wealth. The author of three weighty tomes on Greek inscriptions (many of them copied during an extensive tour of Greece and Turkey), of prelections on Greek literature, and of editions of Demosthenes, the *Iliad* and the *Agamemnon*, was also a vain and pompous snob. His researches into his own genealogy led him to claim relationship with the Marquis of Ailsa, to whom he offered to leave his considerable property if he would acknowledge the relationship. But the Marquis was not to be bribed, and the disgruntled scholar was forced to end his days in the middle-class environment of a Tyrone rectory.[52]

(v)

In addition to the twenty-five Fellows, the teaching staff of the University included in 1830 thirteen Professors who did not hold a Fellowship. Three of these were ex-Fellows of whom two (C.R. Elrington, Regius Professor of Divinity, and P.C. Crampton, Regius Professor of Feudal and English Law) had resigned their Fellowships as a statutory condition of succeeding to their chairs; the third (Whitley Stokes, Regius Professor of Physic) resigned mainly on account of religious scruples. The Professors who had never held Fellowships were the three University Professors and four King's Professors in the School of Physic, the two Professors of modern languages, and William Rowan Hamilton, the Professor of Astronomy and Astronomer Royal of Ireland.

All these men except Elrington were isolated from their colleagues and the general life of the College by academic or social barriers or by geographical distance. The attitude was then dominant, and destined to survive, albeit with progressive dilution, for another century, which regarded professors of all subjects other than those taught in the seventeenth century as technical experts hired to discharge specialized teaching duties, but not qualified to participate in the general direction of academic affairs. The Professors were, accordingly, firmly subordinated to the Fellows, constitutionally, financially, and to some extent socially.[53] In the case of the medical Professors this attitude of exclusion was reinforced by their isolation in space, for they worked mainly in hospitals or at the far end of the College Park. Crampton was occupied in the courts for much of the day, and in any case his interests at this time were largely political, and of a shade of politics not likely to make him welcome at the dining-tables of many of the Fellows. Further consideration of these Professors in the faculties of Divinity, Law and Medicine is best deferred till we come to review the professional schools.

In 1830 the successors of Hely-Hutchinson's language Professors were Charles Williomier, Professor of French and German, and Evasio Radice, Professor of Italian and Spanish. They were, as we have seen, merely licensed private tutors without serious literary pretensions, and their contacts with the Fellows must have been few and superficial.

In the case of Hamilton the isolation was only geographical, for he was on terms of close friendship with several of the Fellows, and his subject was one which formed part of the undergraduate course. But the fact that he lived and worked in the observatory at Dunsink, five miles from the College, meant that, apart from brief appearances to give his lectures, he was seldom within its walls. For him this isolation was for the most part welcome, as he preferred country air and freedom from distraction, but it meant that his influence on the mathematical world of Dublin was exerted more through the Royal Irish Academy than in Trinity College.

The story of the early life of Hamilton has often been told, but as he was, without question, one of the leading intellects of the nineteenth century, it requires some notice here. He first showed his extraor-

120   *Quaternions.*   (See paper next but one)

[handwritten notebook passage, partly legible] ... this morning, was led to what seems to me a theory of quaternions which may have interesting developments. Couples being supposed known & known to be representable by points in a plane, so that ... it is natural to conceive that there may be another sort of ... perpendicular to the plane itself; ... let this be j; so that $j^2 = -1$, as well as $i^2 = -1$. A point may ...

[handwritten notebook passage] The multiplication-assumptions, or definitions, were therefore collected to be:

$$i^2 = j^2 = k^2 = -1; \quad ij = k, \; jk = i, \; ki = j;$$
$$ji = -k, \; kj = -i, \; ik = -j.$$

And thus we are led, or tempted, to assume as the formula for the multiplying of 2 quaternions, the following:

$$(a + ib + jc + kd)(\alpha + i\beta + j\gamma + k\delta) =$$
$$a\alpha - b\beta - c\gamma - d\delta + i(a\beta + b\alpha + c\delta - d\gamma)$$
$$+ j(a\gamma - b\delta + c\alpha + d\beta) + k(a\delta + b\gamma - c\beta + d\alpha).$$

12   Two passages from the note books of Sir William Rowan Hamilton, recording the invention of quaternions. (Library of Trinity College.)

dinary talents as an infant prodigy in the linguistic sphere, the number of languages of which he had a fair mastery keeping pace with his years until he was about twelve. His mind then turned to mathematics (in which he was almost entirely self-taught) and astronomy; at sixteen we find him detecting an error in Laplace, and at nineteen, in his second year in College, sending to the Academy an original paper in optics. Although some revision and expansion were recommended, it was regarded by two of the mathematical Fellows as 'novel and highly interesting'. From then onwards he was watched as a coming man, certain to win Fellowship in a few years, and expected by many to perform the unprecedented feat of winning at his degree examination both the gold medals, one for Classics and one for Science. But when, at the beginning of his final year, Brinkley, the Professor of Astronomy, accepted the bishopric of Cloyne, several members of the Board determined that Hamilton should succeed him. Seldom can electors have had such an *embarras de richesse*, for among those interested in the post

112

was George Airy, already Lucasian Professor at Cambridge and soon to become Astronomer Royal in Britain; and although he lost interest when he found that the salary was smaller than he had expected, there is little doubt that the Board could have secured him for an extra £200 a year. Hamilton, therefore, still two months short of his twenty-second birthday, was unanimously elected, on condition that he did not stand for Fellowship and took his degree immediately, at an examination at which no medals were awarded. It was a difficult decision for such a young man, but he scarcely hesitated, and never regretted his choice.

By 1830 he was, at the age of twenty-five, a mathematician, not of promise but of substantial achievement. Although he is famous primarily for his invention of quaternions, which absorbed most of his creative energies from 1843 onwards, there are many mathematicians who consider that although these represent an imaginative achievement difficult to parallel, his earlier work on optics (which was nearing completion in 1830) and in dynamics (which occupied him from 1834 to 1839) has been of greater service in the general development of mathematics. There is no doubt that for these abstruse researches he found in Dunsink an almost ideal environment,[54] and that his appointment to the post brought fame alike to Hamilton and to the College. The only loser was astronomy, for, although in his earlier years as Professor Hamilton was interested in the observational side of the science as well as the analytical, he was handicapped by a lack of training in the use and design of instruments, and during his tenure of the chair the reputation of Dunsink as an observatory gradually declined.

(vi)

It is time now to turn from the teachers to the taught, and to attempt a brief survey of the student population of the College in 1830. Their number in this year stood very close to its maximum for the nineteenth century. From 1800 to 1826 the number of annual entrances rose rapidly and fairly steadily from 103 to 496, and for the next two decades it fluctuated irregularly around 350–400, until a rather sharp decline set in about 1844. In 1830 the number of undergraduates and resident bachelors on the College books must have numbered about 1,750.[55] The average age of the students had for long been rising steadily, but very slowly. During the decade 1820–29 11 per cent had entered at under sixteen, 26 per cent at sixteen, 29 per cent at seventeen, 14 per cent at eighteen and 20 per cent at nineteen or over. The median age was about 17.4, only a few months less than the corresponding figure for a century later, but the spread was greater, and consequently about a fifth of the undergraduate population at any given moment had not yet passed from what we regard today as school age.

Students were divided for academic purposes into the four annual undergraduate classes of Junior and Senior Freshmen and Junior and Senior Sophisters, and after graduation into Junior, Middle and Senior Bachelors. Of the bachelors a large proportion were Junior Bachelors preparing for ordination. The Scholars, who were elected not at entrance, but usually in their third year, took precedence over the other students as members of the foundation.

The students were also graded socially into noblemen, fellow-commoners, pensioners (ordinary students) and sizars. A peer, peer's son or baronet could, if he or his father so chose, matriculate as *nobilis ipse*, *filius nobilis* or *eques*, and if he did so was entitled, on payment of four times the pensioner's fee,[56] to wear a cap with a gold tassel and a gown scarcely less gorgeous than the Chancellor's, to dine at the Fellows' table, and to take his degree in two years instead of four. The rank of fellow-commoner was open to anyone who cared to pay for it. He too, in exchange for double the pensioner's fee, dined at the Fellows' table, wore a gown devoid of gold, but well frogged and braided, and was allowed to take his degree six months earlier than the pensioners. The fellow-commoners included, no doubt, some sons of parvenus and social climbers, as well as the sons of some impoverished noblemen, but broadly speaking the categories of nobleman, fellow-commoner and pensioner coincided fairly well with the aristocracy, gentry and middle class among the students. At this time about 30 per cent of the students described their fathers as 'gentlemen'; 40 per cent were the sons of clergy, professional men or army officers, 18 per cent of tradesmen, 8 per cent of farmers, and 4 per cent of minor civil servants or clerks. The number of fellow-commoners, though diminishing, was still fairly high (about 18 per cent of the total). In 1825 inquiries made by Daniel O'Connell led him to conclude that 'it was unpleasant to a young gentleman to be a pensioner'[57] and the King of the Beggars entered his sons as fellow-commoners.

The sizars were students of limited means who were awarded a sizarship at entrance on the results of a special examination (at this time in classics alone). Their status had originally been much inferior to that of other students; they had been lodged in garrets and had been obliged to wait on the Fellows at commons, and to dine on their leavings. By the early nineteenth century most of these humiliating conditions had fallen into disuse, and in 1819 even a painfully class-conscious sizar, smarting under a grievance, could declare that 'the only thing that could be considered in the slightest degree painful to the most delicate feelings is that their hour of dining is later than that of the other students, and that the joints served up to them are those removed from the Fellows' table. The vegetables are, however, dressed for themselves, and a clean cloth is laid for them on a separate table, and they have the attendance of the porters.'[58]

At this time 92 per cent of the students had been born in Ireland. Of these rather more than a quarter came from Dublin city, a quarter from Munster, a fifth from Leinster outside Dublin, and smaller contingents from Ulster and Connaught. The proportion of Munstermen, though high, was sinking, for at the beginning of the century this province had provided 35 per cent of all the students.[59]

In 1830, as at the present day, the majority of the students lived outside the walls, either at home, with relations, or in lodgings. In 1775 the College buildings had been able to house 225 students out of a total of 598 on the books.[60] The buildings of Botany Bay added about 140 to the number of students which the College could accommodate, but meanwhile the total number had been nearly trebled, so that in 1830 it was only about one student in five who lived in College at any one time, though doubtless the proportion who held rooms at one time or another in their student career was nearer one in three. But not all of those who lived outside the College were in the city, or even in its neighbourhood. The University of Dublin was at this time unique among British universities (and so remained till London followed its example in 1858) in permitting a student to qualify for a degree merely by passing periodical examinations, without requiring him to attend lectures or to reside in the city, and without inquiry as to what tuition he received. Exactly when or how this system originated is hard to tell; it was certainly, as nineteenth-century critics were not slow to point out,[61] at variance alike with the letter and with the spirit of the original statutes. But it appears that probably in the latter part of the eighteenth century the term examinations, to which great importance had always been attached, were allowed to usurp from attendance at lectures and tutorial classes the right to qualify a student for his degree. The average age at which boys came up to Trinity was at that time fifteen to sixteen, and a considerable number were only thirteen or fourteen. The College had, therefore, much of the atmosphere of a boarding school, with the tutors discharging the quasi-parental functions of housemasters. When, probably at some date near 1760, the number of boys who sought a university degree began to exceed those who could be accommodated *intra muros* a difficult problem arose. Some could be sent to live with relations or trusted friends in Dublin, and a few were taken by their tutors to live with them, but there remained a fraction who, if they were to reside in Dublin at all during term, would have to live unsupervised in lodgings, in a capital city which was too large for the

University to attempt, as it did with some success at Oxford and Cambridge, to exercise disciplinary jurisdiction outside the College walls. Parents were naturally unwilling to expose their sons in their early teens to hazards of this kind, and must, for this reason if for no other, have welcomed an arrangement whereby the boy could be taught at home by his father, a tutor, or the local rector, and spend in Dublin only two or three nights each quarter when the date of his examination came round. Nor would the financial advantages of such an arrangement be overlooked in a country whose middle class was as poor as that of Ireland.

As the nineteenth century progressed the average age of the under-graduate slowly but steadily rose, and over the same period the growth of evangelical piety and middle-class responsibility made Dublin a much less dangerous place for an unsupervised youngster than it had been in its Georgian heyday. By 1830, therefore, it would seem that a considerable proportion of the students were living in lodgings, and the number not resident in Dublin was not very large. But it was almost immediately to be reinforced from a new source. From 1770 to 1820 the proportion of undergraduates who matriculated at the age of twenty-one or over had been fairly constant at 5 per cent. But after 1820 it began to rise: by 1830 it was about 8 per cent and by 1850 17 per cent — more than a sixth of the total. These undergraduates of mature age were mostly men who were already earning their living; most of them were domiciled in Great Britain (especially the north-western counties of England), and they gladly seized on an opportunity, to which at this time there was no alternative, of reading for a degree in their spare time without having to abandon their employment. These formed the nucleus of the non-residents, but the number was swollen by 'the very needy provincial Protestants, who cannot afford to leave the paternal farm or counter and take up their abode in Dublin as students, and the sons of rich people who wish their sons to live at home, and who can afford to have tutors at home to teach them, but who desire to give them an objective point, and find it in a non-residential degree at Trinity College'.[62]

In the fifties and sixties nearly a fifth of those who graduated had never attended classes in the College. But the proportion of non-residents was much higher than this figure would suggest, for among them a much larger percentage than among the residents failed to complete their course. In 1852 only 636 out of 1,217 undergraduates were returned as resident in the city or suburbs.[63] Even in 1872 it was estimated that well over a quarter of the undergraduates attended no lectures at all.[64] But from about that date onwards the growth of the other Irish universities, the development of London into a vast examining university, and the foundation of provincial universities in England all helped to reduce the number of non-residents at Dublin, and although a handful persisted up to the middle of this century, the external student was already by 1900 ceasing to form an important or conspicuous element in the University.[65]

The non-residents obtained a degree, but little else. Their academic career was usually undistinguished, and the proportion of prize-men or honors-men among them was minute. They were referred to contemptuously as 'back-stairs men' and their achievement as a 'steamboat degree', since most of them lived in England. Nor did their existence do much to enhance the reputation of the University, whose official spokesmen usually did their best to play down their numbers and their significance. It is doubtful whether the financial gain accruing from students of this type, who paid the full fees but required little attention, outweighed the inevitable depreciation of the public estimate of a Dublin degree. The Dublin non-residents were no worse an excrescence on the university system than were the young noblemen who went to Oxford or Cambridge for everything *except* a degree; but inevitably a university which was ostensibly resident in the same sense as were Oxford and Cambridge, but which granted degrees without requiring residence or supervision of any kind, exposed itself to severe criticism. Bishop Butler of Lichfield was not a sweet-tempered man, and he had no love for the Irish, but he was not entirely unjustified when he wrote to a Dublin graduate seeking ordination that 'it is very hard upon young men who are waiting for orders and who have been at the expense of a regular college education and have kept three and a half years' residence there, that they should be superseded by candidates that have never resided at College, and thus have had no regular academic education, but have merely gone up for a few days to sit and pass at a general examination'.[66]

Nevertheless, for some time Trinity College performed efficiently enough for a number of men for whom there was no alternative the limited and arid functions of an examining university. It is also true that before about 1860 one must set in balance against the non-residents the fact that the resident students at Dublin were much more closely supervised in their studies than were their contemporaries at Oxford and Cambridge. The 'regular academic education' which the Bishop attributed to English graduates was, indeed, achieved in the immediate neighbourhood of Oxford and Cambridge, but in many cases more on the river, with the local hunts, and in the supper-rooms of the town than in the lecture-room or tutor's study.

(vii)

'The mode of entrance to this University', we used to be informed by the College Calendar as recently as 1952, 'is by passing an examination'; and so it was in 1830, when central clearing-houses and leaving certificates had not yet dawned on the imagination of even the most progressive reformer. In this respect the virtual coincidence of College and University in Dublin spared it the dispute which agitated Cambridge for many years: whether there should be a general university examination, as distinct from those held by the colleges.[67] But it must not be inferred that Dublin thereby maintained the exalted entrance standard for which the Cambridge reformers were striving. Its examination, though imposing enough on paper, was conducted more in the spirit of the college examinations at Oxford and Cambridge, and rarely were more than two or three per cent of the candidates refused admission. The policy of the College was then, as indeed it remained in some degree till very recently, to select and reject not at matriculation but at later examinations, when the educational machine should have had an opportunity of raising all but the unteachable to a reasonable standard, if not of culture and scholarship, then at least of literacy and information.

The entrance examination of 1830 was still confined to classical texts. Whether this postponement of all other subjects of study represented a deliberate educational policy, or whether it was merely a recognition of the fact that the schools still[68] taught little else than classics, it is hard to say, for it seems to have been always taken for granted. But within this restricted field the course was fairly extensive: it comprised the Gospels and the Acts in Greek, eight books of the *Iliad* and some Xenophon and Lucian, six books of the *Aeneid* and three eclogues, Horace's lyric poetry, and selections from Juvenal, Terence, Sallust and Livy. We may conclude that the average freshman at matriculation was fairly well grounded in Greek and Latin grammar and had at least a nodding acquaintance with a representative selection of ancient literature.

Sizars were elected on the results of a more searching examination on a similar course, to which were added, however, the remaining books of the *Iliad* and *Aeneid*. There were also awarded at entrance prizes for 'such young gentlemen who understand Hebrew',[69] and who acquitted themselves satisfactorily at an examination in elementary grammar and the first six psalms.

Once he had entered the student embarked on the standard four-year undergraduate course, which did not yet permit of any choice of subjects. There were, indeed, some optional additions which served as

118

outlets and rewards for talent and industry; details of these are given in the next section. But for the dullard and the genius, the born mathematician and the man of literary tastes, the same basic ration was prescribed; and the prizes at the quarterly examinations were to be won mainly by the painstaking and intensive study of that same course which was read superficially for a pass, and only to a small extent by wider reading.

Since 1793, the year in which we last reviewed it, the undergraduate course had been revised only in detail, and the structure originally prescribed in 1629 can still be discerned two centuries later.[70] In Classics the most notable change is the very generous treatment now given to Greek tragedy. In 1830 six plays of Sophocles and six of Euripides were read in the course of the Senior Freshman and Sophister years, but Plato and Thucydides had been jettisoned to make room for them. The excision from the course by Provost Elrington of Terence's *Eunuch* as unsuitable for tender minds is, perhaps, symbolical of the difference in taste between the eighteenth and the nineteenth century.

The Science of the Freshman years was still based on Murray's *Logic* and Locke's *Essay concerning humane understanding*, together with Euclid and, since about 1808, some algebra. In the physical science of the Junior Sophister year the scope of the course remained unchanged, as indeed did two of the prescribed books – Stack's *Optics* and Helsham's chapters on hydrostatics and pneumatics, despite the fact that the latter were by now almost a century old. But instead of the remainder of Helsham and Hugh Hamilton's lectures on mechanics, Bartholomew Lloyd's *Elementary treatise of mechanical philosophy* was prescribed;[71] and Brinkley's *Treatise on astronomy* (first published in 1808 and many times reprinted and re-edited) had replaced the out-of-date Keill.

In the ethics of the final year, two of the books from 1793 – Cicero's *De officiis* and Burlamaqui's *Natural law* – had survived. But Conybeare had been replaced by a rather similar work, referred to in the jargon of the day as 'Leland and Porteus'. This was an edition, published in Dublin in 1818, of two separate works bound together: an abridgement of John Leland's *The advantage and necessity of the Christian revelation, shown from the state of religion in the antient heathen world*, originally published in 1764; and the *Evidences for the truth and divine origins of the Christian religion* of Beilby Porteus, Bishop of London, published in 1800 and many times reprinted. The latter was justly popular, for it is, if not very profound, an admirably clear and well-marshalled piece of apologetics. The former, written by a Dublin nonconformist minister, was a curious survival from the deistical controversies of the previous century. Locke's *Essay on government* had been dropped, either as needless, or else as dangerous, despite Elrington's Tory glosses on the text, and in its place had appeared the subtle (some would say over-subtle) *Analogy* of Bishop Joshua Butler, which persisted on the undergraduate course until 1908, and was prescribed for Divinity students as recently as 1963.

Such was the course which all undergraduates, wherever their aspirations might lie, were bound to study, and at least in some small degree to master. If it appears to us today as dry, narrow and unenterprising, one must admit that it was at least well-balanced. Dublin compares favourably in this respect with the English universities, where at this time classics at Oxford and mathematics at Cambridge still retained a complete ascendancy over all other subjects. A Dublin graduate of the time might not be very deeply or very widely read, but there were three fields – mathematics and physics, classics, and philosophy – in which he could hardly be a complete ignoramus. Furthermore his course, by concentrating on the more rigorous type of learning (the only exception being the ethics of the final year), provided a genuine opportunity for mental training and discipline, and avoided the diffuse and over-eclectic comprehensiveness of the Scottish universities, which, according to Dr Johnson (hardly an unbiased critic perhaps), gave everyone a mouthful and no one a bellyful of learning.[72]

(viii)

This compulsory course, being tempered to the capacity of the weaker pass-man, left the able undergraduate with a fair surplus of time and energy to devote to other academic pursuits. Such additional reading was encouraged by the College in three ways. The first, and least important, was the existence of professorial lectures in modern languages and natural history, in connexion with which small prizes were awarded. (The professorial lectures in other subjects were designed for graduates or professional students, or were given in connexion with the medal course, which is described below.) The second was by the award of foundation Scholarships, and the third by the award of gold medals at the degree examination.

Scholarships were competed for, not at entrance but about half-way through the student's undergraduate career. Trinity is exceptional in adhering to this system today though it also offers exhibitions at entrance; but in 1830 the open entrance scholarship was unkown.[73] The obvious disadvantage of postponing the award in a college from which the majority of students go down immediately after graduation was not a serious one in 1830, when a considerable fraction stayed on for a year or two as bachelors, reading for ordination or preparing for the Bar; and the advantages of postponement in a country in which the schools were hardly adequate to select and train the boys of greatest ability were clear enough. In the period around 1830 the examination, which was held just before Whitsun so as to permit the election of the new Scholars on Trinity Monday, was taken, in all but a few exceptional cases, in the Junior Sophister year. It was a competitive examination for a fixed number of vacancies, the total number of Scholars being fixed by the charter at seventy, so that about fifteen were elected each year. The subject-matter was confined by statute to the classics, and it was not until 1856 that any change was made in this provision. The course comprised all the classical authors prescribed for entrance and for the undergraduate course up to the middle of the Junior Sophister year. There was, therefore, nothing new for most of the candidates to read; but they had to submit to a very searching examination on the fairly lengthy list of classical texts which they were supposed by this time to have mastered. Success at the Scholarship examination was rewarded by free Commons, rooms at reduced rent, reduced fees, a salary of £18 9s. 3d. per annum, and the right to wear a velvet cap and graduate's gown. The scholarship continued until its holder became of M.A. standing.

The special courses for the gold medals at degree were, as has been described in the previous chapter, instituted in 1815. Competition for the medals was restricted to those students who had already proved their merit by winning a premium at a term examination; they were distinguished in the degree lists as *primarii in sua classe* and were examined at the degree examination, not only more searchingly, but on a much wider course. In both Classics and Science a respectable standard was expected, but the award of two medals, one for each subject, encouraged some degree of specialization. In Classics only a few texts additional to those of the ordinary course were prescribed (some Aristotle, a play of Aeschylus, Cicero's *De oratore*, and the *Ars poetica* of Horace), but candidates for the medal were advised to be 'prepared in an extensive course of History, and should be well acquainted with the Prosody and other niceties of the Greek language, besides the nature and history of Greek drama ... It is also requisite to possess an acquaintance with the Classical English poets, and to be practised in Latin composition at least.'[74] For the Science medal nothing beyond the pass course seems to have been required in logic or ethics, but in mathematics and physics the demands were formidable enough – conic sections, analytical geometry, differential and

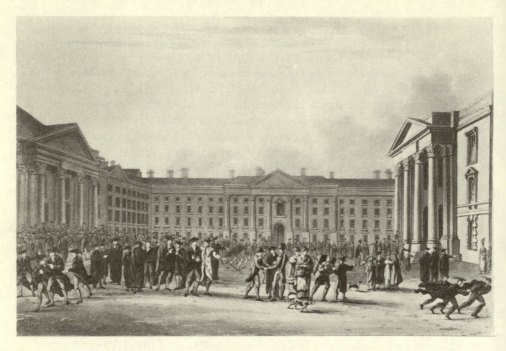

13 The Front Square during a quarterly examination, c. 1819. (W.B.S. Taylor, published in *A history of the University of Dublin*.)

integral calculus, and fairly advanced work in algebra, trigonometry, astronomy and optics.

(ix)

For a good performance in the medal examination one or two years' fairly continuous work was necessary, which was then tested in a single examination. But the progress of the undergraduate in his ordinary course was subjected to regular and frequent scrutiny by means of quarterly examinations.[75] Examinations have always played a more prominent part in university life at Dublin than at Oxford and Cambridge, and the difference can be traced back as far as the early seventeenth century. The Tudor statutes of Oxford and Cambridge both contain strongly worded provisions insisting on regular attendance at lectures, but they make little or no reference to examinations,[76] other than the 'exercises' for the various degrees, which were cast in the medieval mould of the disputation or oration. Laud, when he revised the Oxford statutes in 1636, insisted on examinations being held for the various degrees, but these rapidly fell into disuse or absurdity. In Dublin, however, his statutes of 1637, which make express provision for the testing of the knowledge of the Scholars (who comprised at this time most of the students) by terminal public examinations in the College hall,[77] were observed both in letter and spirit. Dublin, in fact, possesses the questionable distinction of being the cradle of the public examination system.[78]

This was, of course, the chief factor which permitted the development of Dublin into an optionally resident university; the frequent examinations provided some guarantee that the student, even if working unsupervised, was making regular progress on an ordered course, and thus enabled at least a prima-facie case for the non-resident student to be made out. In the location of the university in a considerable city Dublin resembled Edinburgh and Glasgow rather than Oxford or Cambridge, and the report of the Royal Commission on the Scottish Universities in 1831 voiced the general public opinion of the time when it remarked that students

resort to the College during the hours of teaching in the Classes which they attend, and when that attendance is over are lost in the crowds of these populous cities. This consideration must forcibly point out the importance of the degree of attention which may be paid, during the hours of teaching, to the diligence and progress of the Students; the necessity of constant and unremitting examinations by the Professors; and the great evil of the instruction being limited to reading a Lecture to a numerous Class, with whose progress and diligence the Professor is imperfectly acquainted.[79]

In 1830 the quarterly examinations were about at the zenith of their importance and size. In earlier years they had been more haphazard and ill-organized, and had involved a smaller number of students; and as the nineteenth century progressed they were gradually eclipsed in esteem, and eventually in size, by the honor examinations. But at the time of which we write the week that preceded each term was full of indescribable ferment and bustle, with two or three hundred students from the country or from England who were never seen in College at other times helping to crowd the squares, with Masters of Arts (who assisted the Fellows as examiners when needed) emerging from their burrows in obscure corners of Botany Bay, and with undergraduates running to and fro between the examination hall and their books or their grinder for a last-minute tip, or shuffling together their hastily composed or dearly bought themes, while the great bell of the College from its ramshackle penthouse in Botany Bay tolled out its solemn, almost funereal note.[80] This spirit is well conveyed in plate 13. The buildings merely form a background for the almost Breughel-like crowd of busy figures flitting back and forth; and the whole presents a striking contrast to the peaceful, static and sometimes even sombre atmosphere of other prints of the College.

The examination of each class lasted two days, and the hours (8 to 10 and 2 to 4 each day) were still those laid down by Laud, though they were no longer statutorily binding. For the purpose of the examination each class was split into a number of divisions, and to each division, containing thirty to forty students, were assigned two examiners, one for Classics and one for Science. Both questions and answers were almost entirely *viva voce*, the only written work being the classical compositions for the medal examination and, in the ordinary examinations, the 'theme' (*i.e.* Latin essay) which was set by the classical examiner on the first day and had to be handed in by the following afternoon. Dublin was in this respect somewhat behind the times, though not as much as one might suppose. For although in the Senate-House examination at Cambridge the answers had been written since about 1790, and at Oxford the increase in the number of candidates and the various reforms in the years between 1800 and 1830 had meant that in the Final Schools written work had gradually supplanted oral answers, it must be remembered that these were both final degree examinations, and more serious, therefore, than one of the quarterly examinations at Dublin. Responsions at Oxford and the Previous Examination and the annual college examinations at Cambridge[81] were largely, if not entirely *viva voce*. It was, therefore, only in the retention of *viva voce* methods for the Fellowship and medal examinations that Dublin could be said to be clearly old-fashioned.

As for the printed examination paper, that was a very recent invention which had first been seen at Cambridge only three years earlier. Previous to 1827 (and still in 1830 at Oxford) the questions had been dictated to the candidates, and each examiner proposed his own questions. The simple device which we take so much for granted today was hailed at the time with the enthusiasm which the next generation gave to the steamship or the electric telegraph. 'I do not believe', wrote one enthusiast in 1837, 'that the wit of man could by any possibility invent a plan more admirably adapted than the one we have been discussing to call forth and develop the talents of young men. Its effects have certainly been most wonderful, and it is to its successful application that Cambridge owes its glory and renown as the cradle of genius and the temple of literature and science.'[82] His raptures might have been more restrained had he known that only thirty years later even friendly critics would have deplored the narrowing effect on the reading of the undergraduate of the emphasis placed at Cambridge on examinations and placing.[83] In Dublin the questions proposed *viva voce* in the medal divinity and Fellowship examinations were usually printed *after* the examination, being furnished to the printer either by the examiner from his own notes, or (in the case of Fellowship) by reporters who attended the examination for this purpose.

A clear insight into the actual conduct of the quarterly examinations at this time can be obtained from a pamphlet written in 1828 by Richard MacDonnell,[84] later Provost, but at that time a Junior Fellow. It is one of the very few pamphlets of the early nineteenth century to make proposals for academic reform in Trinity College. MacDonnell, who was a practical, businesslike man and perhaps, thanks to a few years' practice at the Bar, more in touch with the outside world than were most of his colleagues, found four principal defects in the current method of examining, and there is little doubt that all his criticisms were reasonable. In the first place, the system of divisions, each with its different examiners, introduced a needless element of chance. 'In one division an honor is often lost on *valde in omnibus*, whilst in another it is got on *benes* . . . It is frequently said (and a Fellow who is a tutor often hears it), "I am quite safe; Mr A. is my examiner" while another says "I will stay out the remainder of the examination, there is no use going in, Mr. B. is my examiner." ' Furthermore, certain examiners who fancied they knew from previous experience who was the best man in the division would not subject other aspirants to honors to questions sufficiently searching to reveal their talents. Secondly, the system was extremely wasteful in time: 'The time in which any individual not a candidate for honors is occupied by either of the two examiners, cannot out of eight hours exceed ten minutes . . . The effect is that many of the students pass the time in conversation, drawing with their pencils, or cutting the tables.' Thirdly, the arrangements with regard to the theme were obviously open to corruption; it was impossible to ensure that a composition was really the work of the student whose name it bore, and it was well known that there was a regular traffic in them. Finally, the course was more ambitious than the capacity of the weaker student warranted:

At the beginning of the Senior Sophister year we require from the [indifferent] student in addition to his science two plays of Sophocles and five books of Livy. The consequence is that he despairs of accomplishing the entire. The Livy is too long to be attempted, and he prepares in a slovenly way a few passages of the Sophocles in the hope that the examiner may fall on one of them. Had half a play in the Greek and one book of Livy been assigned to him, the Examiner might reasonably have been strict, the business would have been prepared, and the student's scholarship improved.

Viva voce methods always tend to encourage an inquiry into accurate knowledge of detail rather than broad grasp of principle, and to favour the alert and analytical at the expense of the diffuse and imaginative mind. Examinations in Trinity in the early nineteenth century bore full witness to the truth of this generalization, and the tradition thus established showed great tenacity even after the introduction of written answers and printed papers. Furthermore, though the medal and Fellowship examinations contained many questions which can be fairly described as problems, there was a tendency to examine the honors-man in part and the pass-man almost entirely on books rather than on the subjects covered by the books. Question after question recurs in the form: 'State Facciolati's distinction between enthymeme and syllogism, and show that it does not agree with Aristotle's', or 'Remarkable contradiction in Mosheim about the time of the existence of the Waldenses?', or *'In quemnam errorem incidit Dominus Lardner quoad hasce tres radices?'* The chief upholder of these examining methods in later years was Joseph Carson (Fellow, 1837–98), who was in this, as in some other respects, a survival of the pre-Victorian world into late Victorian times. Two stories, both well-authenticated,[85] are told of his remorseless insistence as an examiner on accurate and detailed knowledge of the prescribed books. In the *viva voce* for classical moderatorship in 1891 he asked: 'What does Grote say of the effect of the battle of Mantineia?' In vain did the well-informed candidates suggest that its effect was to restore the reputation of Sparta throughout Greece, or to precipitate a *coup d'état* in Argos; that was not what Grote had said. 'Its effect throughout Greece was prodigious', says Grote,[86] and no other word than 'prodigious' secured a mark. On another occasion a divinity student, being examined on the Old Testament, was asked how many knives did the Jews bring up out of captivity.[87] He did not know. 'You don't know?' said Carson. 'You're going out to teach your flock, and you don't know how many knives the Jews brought up out of captivity!'

The results of the quarterly examinations took the form of 'judgments', pronounced separately by each of the two examiners. These ranged from *optime* (very sparingly awarded) through *valde bene*, *bene*, *satis bene*, *mediocriter*, *vix mediocriter* and *male* to *pessime*. A candidate who obtained a judgment below *mediocriter* was 'cautioned', and lost his examination; if he got two such judgments he was put down to the bottom of his yearly class, and if cautioned again at the next examination was degraded into the class below, that is he lost his year. Although the standard of examining could hardly be called severe, the number of candidates cautioned at each examination (which at this time averaged eight to ten per cent) rendered the ordeal a very real one to the idler or dunce.

At the other end of the scale the competition for premiums was intense. A premium, which took the form of books to the value of two pounds,[88] was awarded to the best student of each division at every examination, but no matter how brilliant his answering in one subject he could not be awarded a premium unless he attained at least to *satis bene* in the others. No student could win more than one premium in the course of an academic year; if he had already won one and was entitled by his answering to another he was given a certificate instead; and for the Michaelmas certificate (the last of the academic year) the competition was especially keen.[89] Richard Graves, when he had won a premium or certificate used to write 'Victory' round the seal of the letter in which he announced the news to his parents;[90] and an undergraduate writing home in 1810 described how he saw 'a fine lad there, the son of Saurin (Attorney-General) actually crying at losing the premium in my division.'[91]

Attendance at the quarterly examinations was normally compulsory, but the only sanction imposed on those who had kept the preceding term by lectures was a fine of five shillings, and in fact only seventy to seventy-five per cent of the class attended any one examination. It was necessary, however, in order to proceed to a B.A. to save (*i.e.* pass) at least eleven quarterly examinations (of which five had to be in the freshman years), so that it was unwise to be absent from many. The Michaelmas examination of the Senior Sophister year, although candidates attending it were said to be 'answering for their degree', did not differ in scope or severity from any that had gone before it. There was, in fact, no degree examination as we understand the term today: qualifying for one's degree was a gradual, cumulative process. This meant that the regulation whereby a fellow-commoner could take his degree after three and a half years, and a nobleman after two, was not quite as outrageous as it seems. These privileged persons were allowed to abbreviate their course by jumping a smaller number of hurdles, but the average height of the hurdles was the same as for the pensioner. The fellow-commoner did, however, derive another advantage if he was a candidate for honors, for in April, the month in which he answered for his degree, a separate gold medal examination was held, at which the competition was considerably less severe than at Michaelmas.

(x)

For the medal examination the course was, as we have seen, of real honors standard, and gave plenty of scope for the brilliant student to display his ability. But the climax of the system was the examination for Fellowship, in preparation for which the ablest men of the day spent an average of three or four years in fairly intensive reading.[92] The technique of the examination was still somewhat primitive, being conducted entirely *viva voce* and in Latin (which in the mathematical parts was scarcely of Ciceronian quality), the examiners being the Provost and the seven senior Fellows. Archbishop Whately, who was the very archetype of Bernard Shaw's Broadbent – the generous and kindly but insensitive Englishman, who makes himself unpopular in Ireland by his complacency, tactlessness and genuine amazement that the Irish do not at once imitate whatever is the latest reform to have been adopted in England – has left us a characteristic comment on the examination. 'I had the *amusement*', he writes in 1832, 'of hearing an examination (one day of it) for the Trinity College Fellowships. It is very strange to us Oxford men, and, *we* should think, very absurd – being in Latin, all oral, and all the candidates together, jostling each other. It was a matter of curiosity to hear for the first time an examination in my . . . *Logic*.'[93] But absurd though it may have been by Oriel standards, it managed, on the whole, to secure the election of the ablest men, and Whately could have found closer at hand in Oxford systems open to far more damaging criticism, for in many of the colleges election to Fellowships in 1830 was still by favour and influence 'with no damned nonsense about merit'.[94]

The subjects for the Fellowship examination were prescribed by the Laudian statutes, and these provisions were still observed in 1830, at least in form. The examination was to last for four days, with two sessions of two hours each every day. The first day was to be devoted to logic and mathematics, the second to natural philosophy and ethics, the third to *litterae humaniores*, [95] and the fourth to classical composition. But at some time about the middle of the eighteenth century mathematics and theoretical physics had begun to be regarded as more important than the other subjects, and this tendency continued until in 1830 they had obtained a complete ascendancy.[96] Ethics and logic came next in importance, and it was seldom that the examination on the third and fourth days counted for much towards the result, unless to decide between two candidates whose answering had hitherto been very nearly equal; it was, in fact, only the questions proposed on the first two days that were printed after the examination as a guide for future candidates.

This privileged position accorded to mathematical studies at the Fellowship examination naturally affected the balance of studies in the University as a whole. Not only did it mean that men of mathematical rather than literary ability preponderated among the academic staff, but also it led to the diversion of ambitious students of all-round ability from literary into mathematical reading. During the eighteen years in which the medal system, as we have described it, was in operation (1815–32), nine of the Science medallists were later elected to Fellowship but only one medallist in Classics (John Darley, Fellow 1823–32). Nevertheless, two factors operated to keep classical studies alive in the University, and to prevent the predominance of mathematics from reaching the extreme form which it still held at Cambridge. One was the existence of the classical medal at the degree examination; the other the fact that Scholarship was awarded purely on Classics. Of the twenty-five men who held Fellowship in 1830, all but six had been Scholars and must, therefore, have laid down a sound foundation of classical reading before they turned to the mathematical studies necessary for Fellowship. This curious disharmony between the requirements of the Scholarship and the Fellowship examinations lasted until 1855, and did much to establish the polymath tradition on which the fame of Trinity College in the latter part of the nineteenth century so largely rested.[97]

(xi)

For a minority of students, as we have seen, this world of examinations represented the whole of the academic machine. But on the majority — those who lived in College or in the city during term-time — there was imposed the duty of more or less regular attendance on the religious and secular instruction provided for them. Details of the regulations governing this attendance may be found in the *Discipline of Dublin University* (see p. 528) which, being a practical and unofficial guide, may be trusted to give a fair picture of the *de facto* requirements.

Attendance at Chapel, which was held at the forbidding hour of 6 a.m. (and again at 4 p.m., when the day's work was done), was compulsory for those who lived in College, and even those who lived in the city had to attend four times a week. Doubtless the surplices, which at Oxford covered hunting pink, here often served to hide nightshirts; but the sluggard, although he might sleep in Chapel, could not afford to oversleep too often in his bed without incurring serious censures. The religious instruction of the freshmen was further safeguarded by compulsory catechetical lectures on the Bible and the creeds; these were delivered once a week.

Secular instruction took two forms: college lectures and tutorial classes. The former dealt with the Greek authors and the more difficult or specialized parts of the Science course, while the tutor taught his own pupils the Latin authors and the easier parts of the Science course. Neither took the form of a lecture as the term is understood today. There was, no doubt, some exposition, but the teacher proceeded mainly by questioning his class or by putting them on in turn to translate a passage which they were supposed to have prepared. At the science lecture, which was held daily at 7 a.m., and the Greek lecture, which was held on three days a week at 8 a.m. or 9 a.m. the classes were large, and they seem to have been crowded, noisy and unprofitable affairs: 'Every Monday, Wednesday and Friday', writes an under-graduate in 1809, 'at nine o'clock I attend a Greek lecture (in Homer), from which indeed I derive *no advantage whatever*, for among such a number some may be there for months and never have a question put to them, which has been my case.' At the tutor's classes the numbers were much smaller, and the atmosphere was more informal and homely. 'Every day,' continued the same undergraduate, 'I attend a logic lecture in my tutor's rooms at half past twelve and this is of great use to me. I am going on pretty well with that, and I assure you Mr. Kyle no later than yesterday told me that he was glad to find I could chop logic so well.'[98]

Novels of university life are almost as unreliable for the historian as are school stories, and doubtless the teaching method varied from one tutor to another, but it is perhaps legitimate to regard the account of a tutorial class in *Charles O'Malley*, extravaganza though it undoubtedly is, as derived ultimately from the actual procedure of the period.[99] Even if the fullest allowance is made for academic eccentricity and for the difficulty of heating Georgian buildings, it is doubtful that a tutor would have attempted to conduct a class from beneath the bed-clothes, but the rest of the scene may well be drawn from life. We may picture the tutor, seated in his favourite armchair, and clothed perhaps in a medley of miscellaneous garments, receiving not so much an organized class as ten or twelve private pupils, and firing at them in turn questions on small points of detail. The ease with which Webber substitutes himself for the tutor who has gone away to the country in the middle of term is not to be regarded as pure novelist's licence, as such casual absence seems to have been fairly common. 'No cogni-zance', it was said, 'was taken of irregularity either on the part of the lecturer or the lectured, and consequently there was a great deal of it on both sides. A Fellow was often absent from his class, the class oftener absented themselves from the Fellow.'[100]

By these means the College provided the undergraduate with a reasonably thorough but inevitably pedestrian grounding in the con-tent of his compulsory course. It was calculated to satisfy the needs of the plodder rather than of the scholar. For the boy with sufficient ambition or intellectual curiosity to make him wish to get his teeth into something more substantial there was as yet no organized honors course, and he had to rely largely on private reading to educate himself above the minimum level. There were, however, a few professorial lectures which dealt either more profoundly with the subjects of the undergraduate course, or with subjects which did not fall within its scope. The lectures in divinity, law and Hebrew were designed for

Bachelors, as were also the lectures delivered by the Professor of Mathematics, these latter being especially for the benefit of Fellowship candidates. Lectures in relatively advanced mathematics were, however, given also by the assistants to the Professor, and they were suited to the capacity of the premium-men among the undergraduates. Professorial lectures in Greek were given once a week, and were open to all students. The Professor of Natural Philosophy gave discourses three times a week, but these seem to have been mainly demonstrations of physical and mechanical experiments to illustrate the Junior Sophister course. The Professor of Astronomy also lectured to Junior Sophisters. In Brinkley's day the lectures, though full and fairly exhaustive, seem to have been closely related to the content of the undergraduate course. But with the appointment of Hamilton there came a great change in their atmosphere and content: they were professorial lectures in the fullest sense, and paid no heed to the limitations of the audience. In his introductory lecture he used to sketch 'comprehensive views of the relations of Astronomy to ... all the regions of thought which it touched ... He was wont to indulge himself in refined and eloquent disquisition, in poetic language, quotation and allusion.'[101] But the subsequent lectures were 'rigorously mathematical and demonstrative ... it may be frankly acknowledged that only the learners who had more than ordinary largeness of mind could take in the full profit of his teaching.'[102]

The lectures of the Professors of Botany, Chemistry and Anatomy were open to the public, and they were occasionally attended by students who were not reading medicine. Whitley Stokes was still lecturing on natural history. The Professors of modern languages received pupils in what were probably conversation and composition classes rather than lectures. Modern History also boasted a Professorship, but no lectures were delivered, for the discontinuance of Miller's course in 1811 (p. 60) was not enough to stir the Professor, Francis Hodgkinson, into action. He may perhaps have pleaded the preoccupations of his other chair (Civil and Canon Law), but it seems fairly clear that he did not lecture in that subject either.

In spite of their variety and, at least in some cases, their reasonably good quality, the professorial lectures did not attract large audiences. This was largely because little incentive was provided, for in all but a very few students intellectual curiosity needs to be stimulated and reinforced by fame, financial reward, or exemption from other duties. The prizes in the subjects of the professorial lectures were not very numerous or of great value, and the tutors, almost to a man, would have thought it more profitable for their students to master every detail of the limited undergraduate course, so as to win judgments of *valde bene* or *optime* in their examinations, than to go straying off into topics outside the curriculum.

(xii)

Until quite recent times there existed in every university, no matter how excellent the quality of its official lectures, a residual demand which could be satisfied only by private tuition. The rather sudden elimination of private tuition has not yet attracted the attention of educational historians. Doubtless the development of official tutorial instruction to small classes provides part of the explanation, as does also the diminishing esteem in which examination results are held. And although the average student of today is no poorer than that of a hundred years ago, he thinks he is, and, looking on free academic education as a right, he is reluctant to divert any of his personal funds into remedying its deficiencies. But in 1830 things were very different. It was not only the idler and the dullard who were dependent on the grinder's help, for the aspirant for the highest prizes and honors was also in the habit of supplementing his reading and his lectures with private tuition to a surprising extent. Graduates reading for Fellowship were usually compelled, unless they had private means, to devote some of their time to giving grinds, and there were always plenty of medal candidates willing to employ them. There were usually in addition a number of Masters of Arts who lived in College and devoted their whole time to grinding, their customers ranging from the dullest pass-men to the Fellowship candidates themselves.[103]

This state of affairs was by no means peculiar to Dublin. Private tuition at Cambridge had become by 1830 the principal medium of instruction for the better tripos candidates although in 1781 the Senate had taken the extraordinary step of requiring from honors candidates at the degree examination a declaration that they had not had private tuition within the past two years. The regulation was, of course, quite impossible to enforce, and it was eventually dropped in 1824. But it was not until the number and efficiency of the tutors was increased in the middle of the century that the coach ceased to be the dominant figure in academic teaching at Cambridge and sank back to a subsidiary position.[104]

In Dublin, however, the College tutors, though they doubtless despised the cramming methods of the grinders, looked on them in general as allies rather than rivals. It was generally realized that the College teaching had to be directed at the student of average, or slightly below average capacity, and that there remained gaps at both ends of the scale of ability which were more naturally filled by private tuition than by solitary reading.

(xiii)

The powerful influence of the quarterly examination system on the methods of learning employed at this time in Trinity College may be seen not only in the catechetical nature of the tutorial lectures and in the importance attached to the grinder, but also in the textbooks which were most widely used. In the early nineteenth century the number of classical texts and mathematical, physical or philosophical primers prepared specifically *in usum iuventutis Academiae Dublinensis* was surprisingly large.[105] They varied greatly, of course, in quality. At one end of the scale were scholarly, well-printed texts with commentaries sufficient to make the text comprehensible to the hard-working pass-man. Books of this kind, as for example some of John Walker's classical texts, were in some cases actually commissioned by the Board; and it was customary between 1825 and 1850 for the Board to pay half the cost of production of a textbook written by a Fellow or a Professor for the undergraduate course, without claiming any repayment from royalties. But from the level of thoroughly respectable textbooks one descends by a series of almost imperceptible steps to the veriest cram-books, whose avowed and only purpose is to enable the student, who would otherwise be cautioned, to mouth his way, parrot-wise, through his quarterly examinations. Many of the mathematical and logical works contain 'spot questions' (the compiler being in one case considerate enough to distinguish with an asterisk the questions which 'even the most indolent student would be able to answer'),[106] and some of them proceed entirely by the catechetical method, which, 'though objectionable in many respects is that best suited to the multitude of readers'.[107] In many cases the author admitted in his preface with disarming candour the lowly nature of his labour. 'My exclusive object is to be practically useful', wrote Daniel Spillan in the preface of his translation of Demosthenes (Dublin, 1823). 'I have therefore rendered the author word for word, with the accuracy of a lexicographer, and I have paid no further regard to the diction in which I clothed his ideas than to take care that it should be perfectly intelligible to the meanest capacity.'

The motives which induced men who were often first-class scholars to stoop to this work are to be found, of course, in the steady and considerable sale which a cram-book could be relied on to command, if they paid proper regard to the capacity of the reader and the habits of the examiners. This motive was often admitted in the prefaces with complete frankness. Walker, in particular, parades a plaintive fastidiousness. 'In any literary work in which I am now engaged', he writes, four years after his expulsion from Fellowship, 'I must submit to be controlled by circumstances and not attempt to follow the leaning of my own judgment and taste. Were it otherwise the critic may be assured that this publication would never have seen the light.'[108] An anonymous rival of Walker's, who published in 1826 *The compendium of logic used in the University of Dublin . . . adapted exclusively for the use of students*, is even more outspoken. 'In publishing a commentary on Murray's *Logic*', he writes, 'it is scarcely necessary to disavow any claim to literary or scientific merit. The emoluments of the sale are the only inducements for stooping to the task.' It is all the more pathetic, therefore, to realize how often financial embarrassment continued to dog the footsteps of those scholars who stooped to this means of making a living. Isaac Butt's edition of the *Fasti* (1833) represented but one incident in a lifelong and largely unsuccessful struggle against debt, and Daniel Spillan, who graduated with honors in 1822 and published numerous translations of classical texts as well as medical cram-books, died as a pauper in the St Pancras workhouse. There was, however, one colourful figure of this period who managed to make of his grinding and textbook-writing days in Dublin the useful apprenticeship to a lucrative career. Dionysus Lardner, who graduated in 1816, was one of the first to realize the profitable market that existed in the growing appetite of the middle classes for suitably digested scientific knowledge, and he had, as well as a basis of sound scholarship, a genius for popularization and for enlisting the co-operation of eminent men. His appointment to the chair of Natural Philosophy at University College, London, gave him an assured vantage-point from which to pour out a flood of popular lectures, textbooks and cyclopedias, and his profits from these ventures were more than sufficient to pay a bill of £8,000 for eloping with the wife of a cavalry officer.[109]

(xiv)

The professional schools did not form in 1830 a conspicuous or very important element in the total educational activity of Trinity College; nor were the studies in Divinity, Law and Medicine clearly organized into professional schools in the sense in which the term was to be understood later. But at least in Divinity and Medicine some professional instruction suitable for future clergymen and doctors was provided, and the state of affairs at Dublin, though unsatisfactory, was rather better than at Oxford and Cambridge, where it was virtually impossible in the early nineteenth century to receive any professional training whatsoever.

By the terms of its original charter Trinity College had been intended to conform to the pattern of the medieval universities in so far as it was to give instruction *in omnibus artibus et facultatibus*. To the medieval world instruction in the faculties – the distinct branches of specialized learning useful to society and therefore worthy of serious attention – was the primary aim of the university, and the course in arts was simply a preliminary training in which the requisite mental discipline, habits of thought and intellectual tools were acquired. But the fact that each of these faculties was associated with the practice of a profession, and that the knowledge of each could, therefore, be regarded as the technique of a learned trade, gave rise to a state of affairs which the universities were slow to recognize. From an early date the lawyers and doctors grouped themselves into vocational organizations, and the clergy found in the structure of the Established Church a ready-made organization which could discharge the same functions. These organizations naturally took it upon themselves to regulate the admission of recruits to the ranks of the profession, and to determine the nature of the tests which should qualify for admission. The function of the universities thus became, not by any decision on their part but by force of circumstances, largely confined to the teaching of the liberal arts. In these subjects it was recognized that a university degree was the best qualification that could be obtained, but degrees in divinity, law and medicine came to mean less and less, since they did not *per se* entitle a man to practise as a clergyman, an advocate or a doctor. Ordination by a bishop; calling to the Bar by the Benchers; the grant of a licence by the College of Physicians or the Society of Apothecaries – these were the doors to the learned professions, and over them the universities had no control. Unwilling to recognize this fact, or to make over to others any part of the educational province of which they had a real monopoly in the Middle Ages, the universities preserved through the seventeenth and eighteenth centuries a paper facade of professional instruction which had little reality behind it. This state of affairs led in its turn to the contempt for any learning of direct use in a profession (other than that of schoolmaster) which characterized the more scholarly of the older English universities throughout a large part of the nineteenth century. 'Here's to the higher mathematics, and may they never be of use to anybody' was the traditional Cambridge toast, and it is unfortunate that this attitude, which in its heyday was able to frustrate any reasonable teaching in law and medicine, should eventually have gone down to defeat by the institution of degrees in physical education and hotel management. But a *via media* prevailed from the mid-nineteenth to the mid-twentieth century, and it was achieved by the negotiation of concordats between the universities and the professional bodies. These concordats (which were arrived at earlier in Dublin than at Oxford or Cambridge) naturally differed rather widely in accordance with the needs of each profession.

It must also be remembered in connexion with the professional schools that there had been a gradual abbreviation of the university course between the sixteenth and the nineteenth century. This was to some extent correlated with the increased age at which undergraduates matriculated: the schools gradually took over what had been the earlier part of the university education, but the universities did not respond by any change in the structure of their curriculum. In the early sixteenth century the B.A. was only a milestone, and a university career that did not culminate in a master's degree was regarded as incomplete. In the period between his B.A. and his M.A. the student was expected to attend lectures in those subjects which, though not always strictly professional, were of some relevance to a future career in the professions. But the decline in the activity of the universities, the indifference of the Church to adequate instruction of ordinands, and the development by the professional bodies of professional teaching and examination outside the universities all conspired to render the post-graduate courses academic in the worst sense of the word. The number of graduate students progressively declined, and the universities became reconciled to the atrophy of what had originally been almost half of their curriculum. By the middle of the eighteenth century the only function which the post-graduate courses served, in Dublin at any rate, was to provide a means whereby Scholars or other B.A.s who wished to keep their names on the books could claim that they were in some sense receiving instruction. But by the end of the eighteenth century reform had begun, and by 1830 both the Divinity School and the School of Physic were to some extent cognizant of the needs of the professions which they existed to serve.

The position of the Divinity School was, indeed, relatively satisfactory. Although it was to undergo a rather extensive reform in 1833 it could boast already in 1830 that it had a steady flow of students, an adequate teaching staff, regular and relevant (though doubtless inadequate) instruction, and a working arrangement with the bishops.

The Regius Professor of Divinity in 1830 was Charles Richard Elrington (son of ex-Provost Elrington, who was by then Bishop of Ferns). He had succeeded, a year earlier,[110] to Richard Graves, Dean of Ardagh, an essentially eighteenth-century divine, whose disquisitions on the Pentateuch displayed more of solidity than of profundity or brilliance. Elrington was a favourable and fairly distinguished representative of the Church of Ireland of his day. He was high church by Irish standards, but in a conservative and not an innovative spirit. Although he claimed to have anticipated some of the doctrine of the Tractarians he was no medievalist; he did not seek to improve the Prayer Book of 1662 but merely to conserve it and to see that its rubrics were observed.[111] He was staunchly, if undemonstratively anti-Roman, but perhaps more worried by the excesses of the evangelical movement. He was passionately interested in the education question, and his outspoken opposition to the Government's National Education scheme lost him a bishopric in 1842.[112] But most of his energies in the latter part of his life were devoted to his *magnum opus*, a seventeen-volume edition of the works of his great predecessor, James Ussher.

Both Graves and Elrington had been Fellows at the time of their appointment as Regius Professor, but had been required by statute to resign their Fellowships on appointment. This meant that they were able to accept livings, and both of them did so, for the salary of £1,300 a year attached to the chair, liberal though it was, would not at this time have been sufficient to induce a man to forgo the prospects of a Senior Fellow's emoluments unless it were possible to supplement it. But this pluralism, whatever its effects may have been in the parishes of Raheny or Armagh, does not seem to have seriously injured the interests of the College. Both Professors discharged regularly the statutory duties of their office, which included the delivery of two lectures a week to resident Bachelors, as well as a public prelection each term, and both published, during their tenure of the chair some theological work which, if forgotten today, must have added something to the reputation of the College at the time.

Attendance at the lectures of the Regius Professor was compulsory only for Senior Bachelors (*i.e.* men in their third post-graduate year) who were not studying medicine or law. Ordinands who intended to spend only one post-graduate year in College (and they formed the majority) were recommended to attend these lectures, but not compelled to do so. For Junior and Middle Bachelors there were, however, two divinity lectures a week, delivered by Archbishop King's lecturer and his two assistants. This lecturership was held up to 1833 by one of the Senior Fellows; his assistants were chosen from among the Junior Fellows. The only other lectures which can be considered as forming part of the Divinity course were those in Hebrew. They were prescribed for all resident Bachelors (other than those studying medicine or law), and consisted of six a week for the three classes, delivered by the Professor and his assistants, all of them Fellows.

The number of students passing through the Divinity school at this time was large. Around 1830 the number of graduates preparing for orders at any one time averaged about 115.[113] At the same period the average number of B.A. degrees conferred each year was about 260, so that it would appear (making allowance for the fact that some divinity students spent two or three years in College after graduation) that at least a third of the graduates proceeded to orders. This was sufficient to meet the needs of the Irish church (in the ranks of whose clergy graduates of any other university formed a very small minority – bishops always excepted) and to leave a surplus for export.[114]

The course on which the divinity lectures were based had been drawn up by the Irish bishops in 1790; it took the form of a list of books in which they proposed in future to examine all candidates for ordination. The list had been communicated to the Board, which replied that it would 'cheerfully co-operate as far as depends on them with their Lordships' pious intention', and passed on the list to the Regius Professor of Divinity. The list was not very formidable; it comprised only the Bible (with recommended commentaries), Grotius's *De veritate religionis Christianae* and Secker's *Lectures on the Church Catechism*. Ability to write a Latin prose composition and to construe the Greek Testament was also required.

A further resolution taken by the bishops in 1790, not at first unanimously, but acceded to by all those who were subsequently added to the Bench, bound them not to ordain any graduate of Trinity College who did not produce a testimonium of attendance at a year's divinity lectures.[115] Efforts were made by Graves, while Regius Professor, to induce the bishops to go one step further and to bind themselves to ordain only those who had passed a Divinity School examination on the year's work, but the bishops at this time preferred to keep the examination of candidates in their own hands. A few years later, however, the issue of a testimonium was made conditional on passing an examination as well as attending lectures, and by this means, although the bishops retained the right to examine candidates themselves, the training and testing alike of the intellectual fitness of ordinands passed more or less completely under the control of the College.

If the Divinity School of 1830 was by modern standards somewhat sketchy, the Law School was virtually non-existent. Many of the Dublin barristers of the day were graduates of the University, but they were not heavily indebted to it for their legal education. There were, it is true, two Professorships of Law, and two degrees were granted in the faculty. But the tests for the degrees were simply formal exercises; for their performance the only requirements were some slight knowledge of Latin and a minimum of inventiveness and presence of mind.

Supervising these exercises and presenting for their degrees the uniformly successful candidates were the only duties of the Professor of Civil Law in 1830, for the post had become a virtual sinecure by means of which a further £100 could be added to the salary of one of the Senior Fellows. The Professorship of Feudal and English Law, which had been founded only seventy years earlier, did involve a certain amount of lecturing on common law – sufficient at any rate for Philip Crampton, the Professor of the day, to find it necessary to appoint a deputy when in 1829 he entered on the final burst of political activity in the Liberal interest which won him the post of Solicitor-General in 1832. His lectures before that were doubtless competent enough, and, coming as they did from a practising barrister, were of relevance to the law as it was actually interpreted in the courts. Attendance at them, however, did nothing to shorten or lighten the professional training required of a prospective barrister or solicitor, and his audience consisted mainly of such resident graduate Scholars or Fellowship candidates who preferred (seeing that they were bound to attend some lectures in any case) to receive instruction in law rather than in Hebrew.

There was one small advantage which a student of Trinity enjoyed over a non-university man in reading for the Bar, but it had no connexion with the faculty of law. By an anachronistic survival of Tudor educational policy, which had always been obsessed by the danger of the settlers becoming *Hibernicis ipsis hiberniores*, candidates for the Irish Bar had to reside for eight terms (two years) at one of the English Inns of Court. The requirements of residence had been gradually whittled down, till at this period they were reduced to dining a few nights in Hall, but the irksome necessity of paying eight visits to London remained. For university graduates, however, the number of terms was reduced from eight to six. This meagre concession represented the sum total of the co-operation of the legal profession with the universities, and it was urged with some reason twenty years later that so long as this vexatious regulation remained in force any attempt to create a real school of law in the University of Dublin was bound to fail.

The schools of Divinity and Law, therefore, represented the two extremes in the possible development of an academic faculty into a true professional school. Study in the Divinity School was a necessary condition for proceeding to orders, and a few years after 1830 it became a sufficient condition, the examination required for the testimonium being accepted by the bishops. Study in the Law School (in so far as it was possible at all) may have broadened the mind, but it did nothing to facilitate the student's entry into the legal profession. The Medical

School in 1830 occupied a position intermediate between these two extremes, and no simple formula can express correctly the complex nature of its relation to the medical profession.

The Medical School itself, as we have seen earlier, was strictly speaking the 'School of Physic in Ireland', which lay under the joint control of Trinity College and the Royal College of Physicians. The bequest of Sir Patrick Dun's estate to the joint school had perpetuated its dual nature by giving to each partner an interest in the considerable endowments; and the constitution of the school, its personnel and the nature of its teaching had been somewhat minutely regulated by School of Physic Acts of 1785 and 1800.

Moreover, the structure of the medical profession at this time was complex and ill-defined. The distinctions and relations between physicians, apothecaries, surgeons, midwives, barbers and druggists were still in a state of flux, and rested on a basis that was partly technical and partly social. In Dublin alone there were, in addition to the University, no fewer than three professional groups which examined and granted qualifications. Two of these, the Royal College of Surgeons and the Company of the Apothecaries' Hall, provided teaching as well. The third, the Royal College of Physicians (which had much the highest social prestige of the three), did not teach directly, but had in its right of nominating to the King's Professorships in the School of Physic a major voice in the control of its clinical teaching. Nor does this exhaust the list of medical educational establishments in Dublin, for there were at least six private medical schools in operation in 1830. These were set up by small groups of enterprising physicians and surgeons. They could grant no qualifications, but their students could present themselves for examination to one of the licensing bodies, and in some cases the teaching they offered was at least the equal of that given by the official bodies. They were, however, in many cases short-lived, depending as they did on the professional reputation of one or two men, and their transitory nature may be gauged from the fact that when the Park Street medical school was built in 1824 it was decided to build it in the style of a Methodist meeting-house, so that the building might be the more easily sold if the school was a failure.[116] In fact, however, the school flourished for many years; standing as it did at the back gate of Trinity College it served as a training ground for several men who later held appointments in the School of Physic, and it was nicknamed the 'chapel-at-ease' of Trinity College.

With this professional background it is no wonder that the School of Physic itself was somewhat loosely organized. To us it seems inevitable that chemistry, physics and botany should appear at the beginning of a medical course, that anatomy should come next, and therapeutics and clinical training last. But since medicine, surgery, midwifery and pharmacy were regarded as essentially independent sciences it is not surprising that the student should have been allowed, as he was in 1830, to take the different parts of the medical course in whatever order he pleased. The Medical School was, moreover, in some respects the stepchild among the faculties. The Board of 1830, like most academic bodies, had not yet reconciled itself to the swift growth of experimental method and detailed clinical study which had transformed the study of medicine over the past half-century. So long as medicine was primarily a subject to be studied from books, some of them at least written in Latin, the Board would encourage its study. But a school in which anatomical demonstrations and dissections by the students were given more and more prominence, in which demands by the profession for an increase in the number of years required for a diploma and in the rigour of the final examinations became more and more insistent, and whose demands for space and buildings were renewed as soon as they had been satisifed, soon became a source of tedium and irritation. The difficult behaviour of Macartney, the Professor of Anatomy, did not help. Nor must it be forgotten that the Anatomy Act of 1832 had not yet been passed. The methods of obtaining bodies for dissection were sordid and undignified, and usually involved bribery of sextons and midnight admissions. And although no darker suspicions were justi-fied in Dublin, a world in which the scandal of Burke and Hare at Edinburgh was only two years old was not one in which anatomy was likely to be regarded as the most essential or the most edifying of the sciences by a sequestered coterie of middle-aged, literary-minded clergymen.

Nevertheless, conditions in Dublin in the early nineteenth century were such that the Board was forced to extend to the Medical School more attention and support than they might otherwise have been disposed to give. Dublin was well provided with hospitals, thanks largely to eighteenth-century benevolence, and its professional class had attained since the Union to a dominant social position which could be matched only in Edinburgh. The medical world of Dublin was extensive, active, and relatively powerful. Pressure exerted by the profession as a whole on the Professors in the School of Physic could in some degree be transmitted to the Board; and although procrastination and obscurantism, as well as legal tangles, prevented the school from enjoying the high reputation in Dublin that it could easily have won for itself, this pressure of public opinion, reinforced by a consciousness of the danger that Edinburgh might draw off from Ireland an even larger proportion of students than it already did, prevented the school from sinking into too serious a state of torpor or neglect.

The dominant figure in the Medical School in 1830 was James Macartney, who held the chair of Anatomy from 1813 to 1837, and whose early career we have already sketched. Macartney, unfortunately, besides being a great teacher and a distinguished anatomist, was a doctrinaire and hot-tempered radical, and much of his energies were squandered on quarrels with his medical colleagues and with the Board. By 1830, he had conducted some preliminary skirmishes with the Board, he was at loggerheads with the College of Physicians over examinations, he had been accused of teaching atheism to his students (though he was completely acquitted on this charge), and he had broken his umbrella on the architect of the new medical school. In 1823 there began the final, bitter controversy with the Board over the hour of his lectures, some of which he insisted on giving at three o'clock, the hour assigned to the King's Professor of the Practice of Medicine. The quarrel culminated in 1835 in the locking of the door of the anatomy school from three to four o'clock by order of the Board. Macartney retorted by cutting down the number of his lectures to well below the statutory minimum, and the Board had no option but to force his resignation in 1837.[117] It was the familiar story of the reformer of talent and insight who helps, by his truculence, haste, vanity and refusal to compromise, to strengthen the obscurantism against which he is fighting.

Macartney taught surgery as well as anatomy, and he was responsible for any teaching of physiology that was given. He was, of course, a surgeon by training, and this helped to widen the gap between him and his colleagues, who were all Fellows of the College of Physicians. In 1830 they comprised the Regius Professor of Physic, the Professors of Botany and Chemistry, and the four King's Professors appointed by the College of Physicians. These latter delivered their lectures in Sir Patrick Dun's Hospital, and their connexion with Trinity College was therefore rather tenuous.

The year 1830 saw the death of Edward Hill, who had been Regius Professor for almost half a century. He was by then a somewhat fantastic survival of a bygone age, who seemed to have drifted almost by accident into the world of medicine. His polished calligraphy, his unpublished critical edition of *Paradise Lost*, and his passionate repudiation of any language but Latin as a suitable medium for medical examinations[118] all suggest that his primary interests were literary. The science for which he showed most enthusiasm was botany, and it was as a result of his tireless efforts in the latter part of the eighteenth century that the College botanic garden had been started. When in 1800 he was forced by the new Act to resign either the chair of Botany or the Regius Professorship of Physic he opted to retain the latter; and although Hill was certainly an ornament and a cultural asset to the College, it was perhaps no great loss to the Medical School that the duties of the Regius Professor were little more than nominal.

He was succeeded by Whitley Stokes, to whom we have already referred in connexion with the visitation of 1798. Stokes was a member of one of the most distinguished and long-lasting of the scholarly dynasties of Dublin,[119] and was a man of wide intellectual interests. His primary commitment was to medicine, but botany, zoology, chemistry, politics and economics were all grist to his mill; he was also a deeply religious man. But as in his political, so also in his religious and educational beliefs, he was obstinately unorthodox. He would not send his sons to school or college, but educated them himself with the help of private tutors; and in religion he sympathized with the Calvinistic views of John Walker, though he did not hold them so rigorously. But by 1815, after sitting on the Board for ten years, he began to feel that although he was a layman his religious views were incompatible with his position. The Board, by now ashamed of their harsh treatment of Walker, looked round for an arrangement which would satisfy everybody, and after some financial haggling Stokes resigned his Fellowship on being appointed at a relatively generous salary as lecturer in natural history, a subject on which he had been lecturing for some years on a voluntary basis. As a physician he was inspired more by a humane desire to relieve immediate suffering than by an impulse to benefit future sufferers by advancing the science of medicine; many tales are told of his kindness to the sick poor of Dublin. When he succeeded to the Regius Professorship he was aged sixty-seven, and in this capacity made little mark on the school, but in his earlier years, as King's Professor of the Practice of Medicine, he initiated in Mercer's Hospital the first experiments in clinical teaching, which were to be further developed by his son and R.J. Graves.

The remaining Professors in the school call for little comment. Barker, the Professor of Chemistry, was deservedly esteemed as a physician, especially for his work on fevers, but seems to have had little interest in chemistry, and William Allman, Professor of Botany, was known chiefly for his work in mathematics. Of the King's Professors, Crampton (Materia Medica) and Leahy (Practice of Medicine) have left little mark on medical history,[120] but Montgomery, first holder of the new chair of Midwifery, was an able and successful obstetrician. The fourth chair, that of the Institutes of Medicine (*i.e.* pathology), was held by Robert James Graves, who was among the most outstanding and original figures in European medicine of his day. His name is commemorated by the designation of exophthalmic goitre as Graves's disease, but his most important legacy is the system of clinical instruction which he started in the Meath Hospital, in which a senior student was put in charge of a small number of patients and made to study and report on their progress in detail. His Professorship was among the least important of his activities, and the debt of Trinity College to Graves, perhaps the greatest of those who made the reputation of Dublin as a centre of medical teaching, is largely indirect.

One more employee of Trinity College in 1830 deserves mention here, for he was remotely connected with the Medical School. This was the gardener, James Townsend Mackay. Like almost all good gardeners of the nineteenth century he was a Scot, and although his primary responsibility was to the Botanic Garden, now well established at Ballsbridge, he had also to supervise the maintenance of the College grounds. But he shared the weakness of many other Scottish gardeners in bitterly resenting giving to his masters any of the plants he had grown, ostensibly for their benefit, and the Professor of Botany complained to the Board of his insolence more than once.[121] He also, despite some discouragement from the Board, advertised in rivalry to the official classes of the Professor classes given by himself in the Botanic Garden for a fee. He was, however, tolerated in these misdemeanours because he was not only a good gardener but also, although self-taught, no mean botanist. His pioneer exploration of Connemara and other parts of the west was reported in papers to the Royal Dublin Society and the Royal Irish Academy, and later enshrined in his *Flora Hibernica* of 1836, the first comprehensive account of the flora of Ireland. Moreover, he was commemorated by authorities no less distinguished than the Professor at Cambridge and the Director of Kew in the names *Erica mackaiana* and *Mackaya bella*.

The students in the School of Physic fell into two classes: those who were full members of Trinity College and were reading for a B.A., and those who had matriculated only as medical students and did not intend to proceed to a degree. The latter, who formed the great majority,[122] obtained from the College at the end of their three-year course a diploma,[123] which declared the possessor as *habilis atque idoneus qui Medicinam exerceat*, and which entitled him to present himself to the Royal College of Physicians for examination for a licence. The degree of Bachelor of Medicine had, however, sufficient social cachet attached to it to tempt a minority of the students to present themselves for it. The professional examination was identical with that for the diploma, but the holder of the degree could practise without having to obtain a licence from the College of Physicians. The price the medical graduate paid for this was that, before he could become a Bachelor of Medicine, he had to graduate as Bachelor of Arts, and to take, therefore, the whole series of quarterly examinations which we have described above.

But for the Irish student who wished to write M.D. after his name without first wrestling with logic and astronomy a way of escape lay open. The University of Edinburgh conferred its degrees without requiring any examination in arts, and it was prepared to recognize the courses given in the Dublin School of Physic. It is not surprising, therefore, to find that many Irishmen who had begun their medical studies in Dublin concluded them in Edinburgh, and emerged as Doctors of Medicine of the latter university.[124]

It is interesting to see in this difference of attitude towards the education of doctors a foretaste of the general problem of reconciling the claims of professional and liberal education – a problem which continues to harass our universities today. Dublin could reasonably boast that its medical degrees indicated good general education as well as technical competence, and argue that to lower the standard required in the former would be to degrade the profession and the University alike. But Edinburgh could reasonably retort that as long as other and easier methods of obtaining a professional qualification were open they would be patronized by the majority; that the issue of a diploma by Dublin was a recognition of that fact; and that against the educational guarantee implied by a Dublin degree must be offset the very small number of people who took it. The majority of the faculty at Edinburgh considered, therefore, that it was best to let general education look after itself. But occasionally an unfortunate circumstance made them waver from this attitude, and the Professor of Military Surgery, giving evidence before a Royal Commission, pleaded for some insistence on general education by citing an embarrassing case which must have given some satisfaction in Dublin:

It is not only of the Latin, but of the English language that some of our graduates are ignorant. A short while ago, when Dr Hennen was at the head of the Medical Department of the Army in North Britain, he showed me several communications from the surgeon of a regiment, then stationed in the west of Scotland, which were so defective in point of grammar and spelling that Dr Hennen, with a forbearance, a liberality, and a kindness, which he was but little called upon to exercise, withheld these communications from the Head of the Army Medical Board, and forwarded the substance of them in his own language; the gentleman from whom they came was, I blush to say, a graduate of the University of Edinburgh.[125]

(xv)

It would be wrong to conclude our account of the College in 1830 without some mention of the Library. The considerable output of learned works by ex-Fellows living in country rectories suggests that during the late eighteenth and early nineteenth centuries it was possible for a scholar of reasonable financial prudence to depend mainly on his own library for his sources of information. But to those still at work in the College the College Library formed, of course, a very valuable supplement.

For half a century after its completion the great Long Room must have displayed long stretches of empty shelving. There were constant purchases, but not on a very large scale, and most of the growth during the eighteenth century was the result of gifts or bequests, in many cases from former Fellows or their heirs, and some of them very substantial. In 1802 the Library received its largest single acquisition, and this came, indeed, by purchase, but the greater part of the purchase money was provided by an outside source. This was the library of Greffier Fagel, Grand Pensionary of the Netherlands, who had fled to England when his country was invaded by the French revolutionary armies, and who had to sell his library to maintain himself in exile; thanks to the imaginative generosity of the Erasmus Smith trustees the collection of over 20,000 volumes was acquired by the College.

In 1801, following on the Act of Union, a new Copyright Act secured for the Library a free copy of every work published in the United Kingdom, provided that it was registered at the Stationers' Hall. This did not, however, provide as large a volume of accessions as might have been expected, partly because the books which were *not* registered at the Stationers' Hall included many of those which would have been of most value to the Library, and partly because, despite the efforts of the College's agent in London, many publishers were reluctant to fulfil their obligations, and had to be threatened with legal action at least once. This state of affairs was not to be improved until 1835.

In 1830 the Library contained rather more than 75,000 volumes, and was growing at the rate of about 1,000 a year. To the bibliophile it offered a fair collection of incunabula and other rare early printings; to the scholar a reasonably complete coverage of worthwhile works on those subjects which were recognized as academic. The frequenter of literary by-ways might well find there the book he needed, but there was almost an equal chance that he would not. Only a very few novels, for example, were admitted, and only those of which the author had been dead long enough for his works to rank as classics. Another category which was very thinly represented was that of elementary textbooks, but in this respect the libraries of Oxford, Cambridge and the British Museum were little better. Such books were regarded as of no permanent interest, and at this time none of the great libraries catered for undergraduates. In Dublin admission was confined by statute to resident graduates, and although the Board was prepared to stretch a point by giving temporary admission to respectable scholars from elsewhere vouched for by one of the Fellows, the admission of undergraduates was not to be even discussed for another fifteen years, and not to be granted till 1855 (and then only to the senior classes). The simple needs of undergraduates were, in the opinion of the Board, adequately met by the existence of a lending library, which had been founded nearly a century earlier. Its usefulness varied from time to time as periods of neglect were followed by reorganizations, but it usually provided the student with most of the books he required for the undergraduate course, the professional schools, and at least part of the medal course. But if a budding Hamilton or McCullagh wished to extend his reading beyond narrow limits during his undergraduate days he had to rely on loans from his tutor or a search of the second-hand bookshops.

(xvi)

We have set out above in some detail the structure of the College in 1830, its educational principles and methods, its personalities and the texture of its daily life. Before we resume our narrative we must ask the reader to stand back a few paces from the portrait which we have been building up, so that the most striking features of the subject and its relation to the background may be seen more clearly.

Trinity College, Dublin, possessed few of the picturesque anachronisms and anomalies that distinguished Oxford and Cambridge in the early nineteenth century. Tests, teaching, administration, appointments and finance were conducted on lines which were, though open to criticism in many details, at any rate for the most part rational. There were few departments in which the College was conspicuous for its up-to-date methods, but there were no relics of medievalism, and not very many of the world of the seventeenth century. The members of the Board were, it must be admitted, handsomely remunerated for their not very arduous duties, and more than one office had been allowed to decline into a sinecure. But there was no scandal which cried to Heaven for redress, and no extensive body of impotent discontent. Judged by the standards of equity and integrity which were current in the still unreformed parliament, in the civil service, and in other departments of public life, the Board may be held to have used its wide powers with responsibility and restraint. In the Board Room, the Library, the Bursar's office and the administration generally, the atmosphere was one of caution, verging at times on fustiness or stagnation, of absorption with detail, of petty economies and their resulting inefficiencies, but nevertheless of conscientious execution of day-to-day duties – the atmosphere, in fact, of an old-fashioned firm of solicitors. But with respect to academic studies and the relation between tutor and pupil,

Trinity had more the air of a mid-Victorian public school: boys mostly still in their teens working along fixed courses, with frequent examinations and steady drill-like tuition; dons, nearly all clerical, devoting their energies almost entirely to teaching; daily chapels; crude but plentiful food served in rather Spartan surroundings; a prevailing tone of moral earnestness and low-church piety – there is little in the picture of which Dr Arnold would not have approved.

But in one respect the College differed strikingly, not so much, perhaps, from Arnold's Rugby as from the public schools of later Victorian times: there were no organized games, no attempt to fill every hour of the student's day, and no supervision of his leisure, save for a few disciplinary prohibitions. Even if he was conscientious in his attendance at chapel, lectures, tutorial classes and commons, a number of hours were at his disposal, which only the most diligent spent entirely in study. How the student of 1830 spent his leisure hours is a question to which the answer must be based largely on guesswork, but one thing is certain – it was not in ball games or any competitive sport. To most people today a university without cricket, football, rowing and athletics is difficult to conceive; but to the man of 1830 the vision of a university in which these pursuits were encouraged, subsidized and even revered would have made him rub his eyes in disbelief. The first hint of any interest in such activities is to be found in an application by some students in 1833 for a gymnasium to be built; the request was granted in principle, but the gymnasium did not materialize, and when the request was renewed in 1839 it was peremptorily refused, as was also a request for handball courts ten years later. In 1830 the word 'sport' meant horses and dogs, rods and guns; cricket was the only ball game played by any substantial number of respectable adults, and, partly for climatic reasons, it never obtained a very firm hold in Ireland. It was not until 1842 that a part of the College Park was organized as a cricket field. Football was still a rowdy and undignified scrimmage with no rules; the public schools in England were beginning to hammer it into shape, but had not yet got far. Sculling was still a recreation, though it was soon to develop into a competitive sport. Golf was confined to Scotland; tennis was the preserve of antiquarian eccentrics and bowling of idle aristocrats; lawn tennis had not been invented, and even croquet had not yet arrived on rectory lawns.

How, then, did the student of 1830 amuse himself? Largely, it would seem, indoors; for there were few at this time to stress the health-giving virtues of fresh air and exercise. Wine and card parties, visits to the theatre or music hall, amateur concerts – these are what appear in novels and reminiscences. On a fine day one could take out a boat on the river or in the bay, or try one's luck with a rod on the Dodder, where there were still trout. There may have been improvised cricket or bowling in odd corners of the College Park – the sort of game where numbers are unprescribed, rules elastic and victory unimportant. The richer or more fashionable could now and then try out a horse in the Phoenix Park or take their terriers ratting; the poorer and more serious-minded went for long walks in the country, which began only two miles from the College gates. And on these walks, as well as in fireside discussions, were formed many of those slightly sentimental but entirely asexual friendships which were such an important element in the lives of intellectuals in the Victorian and Edwardian age.

The texture of daily life in Trinity, whether at work or play, fitted in well with the standards and ideals of that section of contemporary Irish society which it was meant to serve. The social tone of Dublin was then (as it has indeed remained since) delicately and in some ways confusingly poised between the metropolitan and the provincial. The Union, which had been adopted rather as the best solution of a difficult and dangerous problem than as a thing desirable in itself, had left a permanent air of frustration and disappointment, even among its supporters. The Georgian glories of the age of Grattan and Charlemont could neither be forgotten nor recreated; and the big houses, which a generation ago had sent their sons to seek their fortune in that political world which had one foot in Dublin and one in London, now sent them to govern West Indian islands or to fight against the Sikhs. Those who stayed at home did so for practical reasons, and did not expect to find romance or adventure in life at the Irish Bar, or in the management of their estate. Trinity, therefore, was able to satisfy the rising middle class without proving too humdrum for the lesser gentry. It was learned but not alarmingly highbrow; its student life was free and easy but certainly not fast; it was traditional without being too inefficient; and above all it was cheap. If it lacked, both in its literary productions and in the manners of its Fellows, some of the graces and metropolitan poise which Hely-Hutchinson had tried to encourage – well, there was little scope for them in the Dublin of 1830, where society tended either towards the stodgy or the raffish. And yet the College was a very long way from the utilitarian technical institutes for which the English radicals were clamouring in London.

It would be a great mistake, however, to suppose that it was only by these secular criteria that Trinity was assessed. Religious interests and ecclesiastical problems assumed a greater importance in the minds of Irishmen during the early nineteenth century than at any period since the civil wars. Trinity College was a society whose senior members were mostly clergymen, and in which a large proportion of the students were future clergymen. It was a pillar of the Establishment, but it was also the nursery of an earnest, if at times, narrow, personal religion of an evangelical cast. In both these respects too it mirrored faithfully the society it served. The privileged position of the Established Church was, of course, resented and criticized by members of other communions, but Catholics and Presbyterians alike were at least glad to know that the College was governed by sober, God-fearing men. Any proposals for secularization, or for the abandonment of the idea of a specifically Christian college and university, would have provoked a storm of shocked amazement outside as well as inside its walls, and would have won little sympathy even among the severest critics of the Establishment. And it must be remembered that the Establishment enshrined a rather complex ideal. It was, indeed, a machine for maintaining by respectable methods the ascendancy of a particular class, and for keeping Papists and Dissenters in their place. But it was much more than this: it was a mutually sustaining alliance between Church and State, and a means of bringing into the political world the virtues of the Anglican *via media*. But by 1830 its foundations were demonstrably insecure. A community which included almost all the landlords, officials and leaders of town and country society, but little more than ten per cent of the population, was inevitably, in an age of rising democracy, both proud and nervous. Something of this can be seen in the portrait of Archbishop Magee in the College Common Room (plate 10). Buoyed up by his lawn sleeves and with the badge of St Patrick glittering on his breast, he looks, none the less, a trifle wary and insecure – an intelligent and sensitive man who might have been a benevolent liberal, scared by the scent of danger into *hauteur* and rigidity.[126]

This, the less attractive side of Irish churchmanship in 1830, appears especially in the relations of the College to the outside world. But within her walls it was the ferment, the earnestness, and the bigoted but sincere sectarianism of the evangelical movement that held sway. Not that the extremists or eccentrics of the movement were in the ascendant; their enthusiastic antics were reprobated by the sober and mainly centre-party divines of the Divinity School.[127] And no doubt there were many undergraduates who lived the carefree and untheological life depicted in *Charles O'Malley*. But a perusal of Victorian biographies and memoirs leaves no doubt that many students of this time experienced while in College the personal conversion which is the corner-stone of the devoted evangelical life; and many others, influenced by their home, their tutors or their College friends, regarded it as natural to devote a large part of their leisure to Sunday schools and Bible classes. Side by side with deep and wide-ranging scholarship there existed an extraordinarily intense conviction that the narrowly defined path of the evangelical to salvation was the only one; and the Protestant ranters on public platforms drew part of their inspiration from gentle, scholarly clerics who thought it wrong to mince their words when speaking of the whore of Babylon. A war on two fronts was always being fought – against high-and-dry churchmanship within the Protestant fold, and against the Roman menace, shortly to be reinforced by traitors from Oxford. This was the period in which the last great effort to convert the mass of the Irish people to Protestantism was being prepared, and it was an effort which appeared at the time to many level-headed judges to have a good chance of success. The consciousness of this great goal casts here and there a mantle of nobility on what would otherwise be crude and shrill polemic; and though it did nothing to moderate the vigour of the attack, it at least kept the anti-Roman propaganda of the Church of Ireland free from the sour, nagging tone that it later acquired when it was clear that the main battle was lost. A few divines of this period may have become so absorbed in the horrors of the Inquisition or the moral obliquity of the Jesuits that they could think of little else. But for the majority of churchmen sectarian controversy was but the surface froth that over-lay a life of simple piety and serious moral endeavour.[128] Vision, imagination, and at times generosity may have been lacking; but the unquestioning faith and the steadfastness in a few simple moral prin-ciples that characterized the Church as a whole was, with scarcely a noticeable dilution by academic scepticism, one of the most striking features of the Trinity College of 1830.

6

Reform under Bartholomew Lloyd
1831–1837

(i)

In 1831 Provost Kyle was appointed Bishop of Cork, and Bartholomew Lloyd was immediately named as his successor. The elevation to the Bench by a new and crusading Whig government of as convinced a Tory as Kyle is somewhat surprising, but it would seem that the Government was prepared to pay the price of a Tory bishop who was, at any rate, discreet and co-operative for the sake of installing in the Provost's House a man who, though not a committed Whig, could be relied on to carry out a policy of reform consonant with that which the Government was proposing in other fields. Lloyd was at this time fifty-nine years old and, politics apart, by far the most suitable and distinguished among the Fellows.

His appointment marks the beginning of a series of important reforms which affected nearly all aspects of the College's educational activities. Within the six and a half years of his provostship the terms and vacations were redistributed on a more rational basis; the tutorial system was reorganized so as to render classes more uniform in size and to reduce the number of subjects which each tutor had to teach; the Divinity course was revised and extended; two new chairs were founded, and two more were converted from part-time to full-time posts; and moderatorships (*i.e.* honor degree examinations in something like the modern sense) were instituted. The succeeding decade (1838–47) saw six more chairs founded or revived and one more converted to a full-time post, and also the foundation of the School of Engineering. A period of relative stagnation gave place to one of rapid reform and development, and conservatives and reformers alike agreed that the change was largely due to Lloyd's initiative.

He is in many ways a pattern to the academic reformer whose real aim is to see that the necessary changes are actually carried through, even at the cost of some delay, and not merely to express his personality or expound his principles. He had to face considerable opposition in College but by a combination of tact, diplomacy and patience he won

152

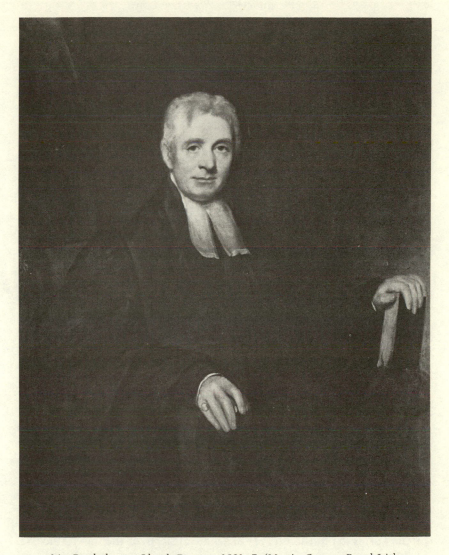

14   Bartholomew Lloyd. Provost, 1831–7. (Martin Cregan, Royal Irish Academy.)

over some of his opponents and outmanoeuvred the rest. He maintained throughout his years of service as Fellow the reputation of a moderate, and bided his time with patience until the prestige he enjoyed as Provost enabled him to get his way with much less controversy than might have been expected. In his portraits there shines out clearly from his face the combination of benign serenity and firm purpose which enabled him to achieve his ends.

(ii)

The atmosphere, apart from a few pockets of entrenched conservatism which we shall examine later, was, of course, more favourable to reform than it had been at any time since 1798. Only two years earlier a Tory government had been forced by pressure of public opinion to grant Catholic emancipation, and in the same month as Lloyd became Provost the Reform Bill was introduced in the House of Commons by Lord John Russell. Privilege and tradition were everywhere at a discount, and there was a general tendency to apply Benthamite criteria of efficiency even to the most venerable institutions, and to require them to show that they were using their resources rationally and equitably. In England the ancient universities presented obvious targets for attack, for although reform had been stirring there intermittently since 1800 it had not made very conspicuous progress. Oxford and Cambridge alike had an oligarchical constitution, a peculiar (and, in the eyes of outsiders, unbalanced) curriculum; both subjected dissenters to severe disabilities; and at both there had arisen from an exaggerated regard for founders' intentions an allocation of scholarships and fellowships which took no account of the redistribution of population since Tudor, or even Lancastrian times. For twenty years they had been under fire from the Whig critics of the *Edinburgh Review*, and these had been recently reinforced by the more ruthless, if less cultured critics of the *Westminster*, who were as blind to the advantages of ancient tradition as they were quick to put a finger on its defects. Higher education, they complained, had scarcely altered since the time of Alfred the Great, and all that could be learnt at Oxford or Cambridge was 'Ovid and Catullus, Homer and drinking, driving curricles or stage-coaches, and rowing boats'. How, they demanded, did this 'conduce towards cotton-spinning; or abolishing the poor-laws; or removing stupid commercial restrictions; or restraining the Holy Alliance?'[1]

In the English universities criticism of this kind served only to spur on the Tories to put themselves in a state of siege for the inevitable trial of strength, which was eventually to culminate in the Royal and Statutory Commissions of the fifties. Dublin, being at once poorer and more business-like, was subjected to much less criticism, but it did not get off scot-free. Many of the conservatives in Trinity were too much worried over the major issues of the Establishment, tithes, the agrarian question and the stability of the Union to feel inclined to take a firm stand on minor matters of internal administration; on such issues, therefore, there was a tendency to be prepared to meet critics half-way. Wall, writing to the Primate in 1832, gives clear evidence of this attitude of distressed appeasement. 'At such a time as this', he writes, 'when so little respect is paid to charters, when there are so many in the House of Commons willing to attack our College, and we can so little rely on being effectively protected by a government that truckles to Mob orators and is sustained by Mob favour. . .'[2]

This is the authentic Tory voice, and Wall, as we shall see, was not alone among the Senior Fellows in his angry feeling of impending doom. Nor were the College electors prepared to trim their sails in 1831–2 to the extent of electing to Parliament P.C. Crampton, the Whig Solicitor-General and former Fellow; they remained faithful to the sitting Member, Thomas Lefroy, who was an extreme Tory.[3] But it must be remembered that the peculiar circumstances of Ireland forced into Toryism many who would in England have been Whigs or even Liberals. With the agrarian, the religious and the constitutional problems which were to form the substance of Irish politics for the next century already standing out in their stark crudity, there was little room for a centre party; and it was difficult for a Protestant clergyman in a College which was a large-scale landlord, no matter what his abstract principles might be, to show himself in a political context as anything but a Tory. Charles Boyton, a Junior Fellow of the day, is a significant figure from this point of view. A frequent and vigorous speaker on Orange platforms, he was really a believer in vigorous action rather than in conservatism, and a very small difference in his political milieu could have made him a radical. This was, perhaps, sensed by Thomas Davis when he paid him a generous tribute.[4]

There were, however, one or two among the Fellows who were prepared to tread a political tightrope by declaring oneself a Protestant Irish Whig. Sandes, who was a member of the Board for most of Lloyd's provostship, reaped his eventual reward from a Whig government and was made a bishop in 1836. But a more influential Whig, also on the Board at this time, was Franc Sadleir, who was to succeed Lloyd as Provost in 1837. The tightly pursed lips and the shrewd, calculating eye to be seen in the excellent portrait of Sadleir in the Provost's House (plate 15) betray indeed the Whig outlook as the poet sees it:

> A levelling, rancorous, rational sort of mind
> That never looked out of the eye of a saint
> Or out of drunkard's eye.[5]

But even his enemies were forced to admit his ability, and the course which he set himself demanded cool courage as well as ability to see it through. He seems to have held his political opinions with sincerity, but with sufficient flexibility to ensure that they did not lead him along the road to martyrdom. The author of a pamphlet on tithe suggesting a

15   Franc Sadleir. Provost, 1837–51. (J.H. Nelson, Trinity College.)

drastic reduction in the Church's revenues, who managed nevertheless
to draw simultaneously the salaries of Senior Fellow, Bursar, Librarian
and Professor of Mathematics, presented an obvious target for Tory
journalists. It would appear that he never displayed much aptitude for
the chair of Mathematics, which he had held since 1821, and although
he added to it in 1833 the Regius Professorship of Greek it was only in
1835 that he was finally bought off with £1,000.[6] 'To Dr Sadleir',

156

commented the *Dublin University Magazine* magnanimously, 'we should be sorry to attach any blame. A sinecurist and pluralist in everything, he acted in the spirit of both characters.' But his critics overreached themselves. It was partly because of his undoubted abilities, but partly because the Viceroy had been shocked at the way the 'poor old man' had been attacked by his political enemies, that Sadleir was given the provostship two years later. Even the *Dublin University Magazine* had to admit that if the Government were going to choose from among their friends Sadleir was undoubtedly the best among them.[7]

One more figure of a reforming turn of mind demands mention here although he did not join the Board till a year before Lloyd's death; but he fairly often attended, before that, as deputy for an absent Senior Fellow. Richard MacDonnell, who was to succeed Sadleir as Provost in 1852, kept clear of active party politics, but he had, at least in his earlier years, a fundamentally Whig outlook, and in College affairs he appears as a busy, practical, rational reformer. We have quoted in the preceding chapter from his common-sense pamphlet on examinations. He originally intended to read for the Bar, and obtained a dispensation from the obligation to take orders, but changed his mind after a few years and was ordained. By the time he became Provost his liberalism was wearing a little thin, but there can be little doubt that twenty years earlier he gave valuable support to Lloyd in helping to implement and popularize his reforms.

(iii)

Between them then, the Whigs, the centre-party men on whom the stresses of Irish politics had pinned a somewhat misleading Tory label, and the Tories whose zeal was tempered by discretion if not by fear, made up the bulk of College opinion, and all were prepared to give at least a hearing to the changes which Lloyd was to propose. But this did not apply to the Board. Four of its eight members, Hodgkinson, Prior, Phipps and Wall, yielded nothing to the young Gladstone in their reputation as stern and unbending Tories, and a fifth (Wray) was at best a centre-party man. On several occasions, therefore, motions proposed by Lloyd were lost on an equality of votes (for the Provost had no casting vote except in elections), and even if MacDonnell was called up to take the place of an absent conservative, the issue might turn on the unpredictable vote of Wray.

Thomas Prior's conservatism was thorough-going, and not confined to academic matters. He had just graduated at the time of the French Revolution, and had had his fill of liberalism then; now, with the July

Monarchy, he saw the same distasteful cycle beginning again, but with threats such as Catholic emancipation and the Reform Bill much nearer home. He was, accordingly, a keen member of the committee of the Brunswick Club, and in order to attend its meetings he was prepared to miss an occasional Board, despite the risk of one of the Provost's nefarious schemes being pushed through in his absence. He truly believed that changes in the academic or administrative affairs of the College were only Catholic emancipation and the Irish Church Temporalities Act writ small, and so he had been driven to conclude that the Provost and his allies on the Board 'are manifestly in collusion with the British revolutionary government to subvert the Protestant establishment of Ireland and to romanize Trinity College in Dublin'. And when, despite his protests, the hour of evensong was changed from 4 p.m. to 9 p.m. he wrote: 'This is a change intended for the subversion of all religion here, devised and directed by an infidel government . . . This I believe to be a lamentable day for our university, *whose sun I believe now sets*; I seriously apprehend a deep scheme for converting it to purposes of Popery, radicalism and infidelity.'[8] Although he fought on, he realized that the times were against him, and one of the few cheerful entries in the latter part of the diary is that for 13 July 1836: 'This day Haliday Bruce made me a present of a nice blunderbus.' When the *jacquerie* arrived he would at least sell his life dearly.

Unfortunately for Prior, however, the conservatism of his three allies on the Board was neither so consistent nor so deeply felt. Hodgkinson had the right principles, but he was easygoing, and so long as he got his sinecures, dispensations and leaves of absence he was not going to put himself about. Besides, he was easily gulled. 'Had a conversation with Hodgkinson', writes Prior, 'on the Provost's revolutionary scheme, which this good old man seemed favourable to because not understanding it, but he departed saying he agreed with me and would not agree to any change not evidently tending to some great good and very gradual in operation, at this time of reform and revolution.'[9] But there was not always an opportunity for such brainwashing. Wall was a flighty young man, only recently turned fifty, who could easily be bought or bamboozled by the Provost. And Phipps, though intensely conservative as regards the minutiae of College life, seems to have had little interest in what went on outside its walls. He made passionate protests against changes as various as the building of the New Square, the foundation of the chair of Irish and the admission of guests to Commons, but he could not be relied on to detect the Whiggery in proposals remote from his own immediate interests, and indeed Prior records with sorrow one occasion when he joined the 'revolutionaries' in a vote relating to a protest against a proposed Tithe Act.[10] Besides, he had no sense of tactics. Prior, at least on some occasions, gave in gracefully when he saw his cause was clearly lost, hoping to gain some goodwill for the next campaign. Phipps, however, positively enjoyed being in a minority of one, and the pages of the Register which record his opinions serve as a permanent warning of the folly of insisting that the reasons for one's dissent should be recorded in the minutes. The Board as a whole might, with a pardonable failure to foresee the future of transport, instruct their parliamentary representative to oppose a bill 'for erecting a railway for steam carriages to the north of the College, and partly on College land', but it was left to Phipps to protest angrily against the decision to cede a small strip on the southern perimeter of College for the widening of Nassau Street, in return for the building by the Corporation of the existing retaining wall and railing. 'The street', so runs his minute, 'has answered as it is for more than fifty years, and I think it improbable – very improbable – that great width will be necessary for the future, by increase in the wealth or population of Dublin.'[11] Had he foreseen the stream of double-decker buses that crowd the street today he might have used a different line of argument, but it would not have made him consent to the change. Like all extreme conservatives he sometimes made shrewd points which ran the risk of being overlooked among the mass of his foolish protests, and he campaigned against jobbery with the single-mindedness of a quarrelsome man for whom nobody is likely to make a job.

In spite of their failure to co-operate closely this quartet made a formidable opposition, but by a combination of patience, diplomacy, conciliation, persistence and opportunism Lloyd managed to outwit them or wear them down, and no major reform which he proposed was blocked by opposition on the Board for more than a few months.

(iv)

Bartholomew Lloyd was appointed Professor of Mathematics in 1813, but in 1822 transferred to the chair of Physics (then largely theoretical and mathematical), which he held until he was appointed Provost. Although he published no original work he had a profound and beneficial influence on mathematical studies in the College, and may, indeed, be regarded as the founder of the distinguished Dublin mathematical school of the nineteenth century.[12] He achieved this result partly by his skill as a teacher and by the pains he took in encouraging his promising pupils,[13] but chiefly by his early appreciation of the great revolution that had been wrought in mathematics by the development of analytical methods in Paris about the turn of the century. Immediately after Lloyd's appointment as Professor in 1813 the works of Lacroix, Poisson and Laplace appeared on the medal and Fellowship courses; fresh textbooks were written, using the new methods and the new notation; and within a very few years Dublin had drawn level with Cambridge and far outstripped Oxford in the profound and up-to-date quality of its mathematical teaching and research.[14] The chief architect of this revolution was undoubtedly Lloyd; he had valuable allies, however, in Brinkley, the Professor of Astronomy, whose writings of the period display a familiarity with continental mathematics, and H.H. Harte, who, both as Fellow (1819–32) and after his retirement to a living, published annotated editions of the major works of Laplace and Poisson.[15] Had Rowan Hamilton or McCullagh been born twenty years earlier their mathematical genius might well have had to waste some years in struggling with an out-of-date system, and both were fully conscious of the debt they owed to Lloyd.

Mathematics, more perhaps than any other subject, requires for the successful prosecution of original work some protection of the scholar from constant interruption by the claims of routine business. Lloyd himself never enjoyed such protection, and perhaps he never sought it; but it was doubtless a realization of this fact, and a desire not to see the original work of his pupils brought to a standstill that prompted him to propose, very soon after his appointment as Provost, the first of his important reforms in the teaching system.

The salaries attached to professorships (with a few exceptions, such as the Regius chair of Divinity) were at this time small, usually £200 a year or less. For non-Fellows these meagre stipends had usually to be supplemented by work done outside the University, though in the medical school a fair income was available from authorized capitation fees levied on the class; Fellow-Professors, on the other hand, derived the major part of their income from tutorial fees. But a tutor was, as we have seen, a very busy man; so that to appoint a Junior Fellow to a chair was largely to sterilize it. Lloyd conceived the idea, obvious enough today but at that time novel, of transforming some, at least, of the arts professorships into something like what we understand by the word today – a well-paid post with moderate lecturing and examining duties, whose occupant is expected to devote a fair amount of his time to advanced teaching and research.

Since Lloyd's elevation to the provostship left vacant the chair of Natural and Experimental Philosophy (*i.e.* physics) it was natural that he should start with it. He proposed that in future the Professor should be released from tutorial duties, and should be paid as Professor a salary of £700 a year. The proposal might well have been adopted without serious controversy, had it not been for one unfortunate circumstance. The Provost's candidate for this new and attractive post was his own son, Humphrey, who had been elected a Junior Fellow in 1824. He was undoubtedly a first-class physicist and well qualified for the chair, but it was inevitable that the coupling of his appointment with the new conditions of tenure should expose the Provost to what Wellington once called 'the senseless outcry against public men for not having overlooked the ties of blood and nature in disposing of the patronage of office'. The painful, and indeed crude course of the controversy may be seen from the appearance at one stage in the draft regulations of a provision that the son of a former professor should be ineligible. But the lack of any rival candidate obviously superior to the younger Lloyd hampered the opposition,[16] and the Provost's quiet tenacity eventually won the day. A last rumble of the dispute was heard, even after the Provost's death, when Wall pointed out in 1840 as an argument against relaxing the celibacy rule that with celibate Fellows such cases of nepotism were unlikely to arise. Fortunately the new Professor rapidly justified both his appointment and the new conditions of tenure,[17] and when four years later Sadleir eventually relinquished the chair of Mathematics it was agreed without dispute that the brilliant young James McCullagh should succeed him under the same conditions of tenure.

(v)

A reorganization of the teaching of Divinity, somewhat similar to what had been achieved in mathematics, was carried out in 1833, again on the Provost's initiative. Hitherto the post of Archbishop King's Lecturer in Divinity had been a post of light routine duties which had been held on a yearly tenure, usually by a Senior Fellow. In 1833 it was decreed that it should in future be held by a Junior Fellow who, like the mathematical professors, should be debarred from holding a tutor-ship and paid a salary of £700 a year in compensation. By this means it was possible to transform the post-graduate instruction in divinity from a one-year to a two-year course. It was permissible to take the first, or junior divinity year while still a Senior Sophister, and for the pass-man this overlap of courses presented no great difficulty. It was, however, only to students who were aged upwards of seventeen and a half at entrance that the arrangement was likely to appeal, since otherwise an abbreviation of the total course to five years would only result in fitting the candidate for ordination before he had attained the canonical age of twenty-three.

Archbishop King's Lecturer, as well as being debarred from holding a tutorship was, naturally enough, forbidden to hold a cure of souls.[18] But in this matter the Provost's logic and good intentions found themselves defeated by the prevailing appetite for ecclesiastical pluralism. The first Lecturer under the new arrangement was J.T. O'Brien, a forceful character to whom we have alluded earlier (p. 104), and after only three years in office he managed to extort from the Board (Phipps, to his credit, dissenting) a dispensation permitting him to retain the Lecturership after he had resigned his Fellowship in order to accept the living of Clondehorkey. The dispensation was later extended to cover the Deanery of Cork, O'Brien having given the Board emphatic assurances that his duties as Dean would be even lighter than those of rector of Clondehorkey. When he became a bishop in 1842 he finally severed his academic ties, but the bad precedent was too easily followed, and his successors in the Lecturership, Thomas McNeece (1842–62) and William Lee (1862–83), accepted livings almost immediately after their appointment, the later holding also the archdeaconry of Dublin. It was only with the appointment of John Gwynn in 1883 that the post became in any strict sense a full-time one; but even as late as 1902–11 there was a period in which J.H. Bernard not only combined its duties with those of Dean of St Patrick's, but succeeded, in the middle of this period, in having the status of the office raised from Lecturer to Professor.

The compliance of the Board in accepting pluralism of this type, despite an adverse recommendation by the Royal Commission of 1851, seems rather surprising; but at least in some cases it would seem that it was the parish rather than the College which suffered. This can be deduced from the rather airy reference, in the otherwise fulsomely eulogistic obituary notice of McNeece, to the parish of Arboe, where 'when disengaged from his labours he spent a considerable portion of his time'.[19] It must also be remembered that the Regius Professor held a cure of souls throughout the first half of the nineteenth century; and it was doubtless argued that if he, with his salary of £1,300 a year, had to console himself with a living as well, how much more so did Archbishop King's Lecturer with his beggarly £700.

The Regius Professor lectured the senior year as a whole, as did Archbishop King's Lecturer the junior year, but these lectures were supplemented by less formal instruction given by their assistants, who were drawn from the ranks of the Junior Fellows, and for these more or less tutorial classes each annual class was divided into two or three divisions. Soon after the new course had been instituted regular examinations were appointed, not only for the testimonium and for rising from the junior to the senior year, but also on a smaller scale at the beginning of each term.

A number of changes were made in the teaching in the first few years, but by 1838 the course had settled down to a pattern which it retained for some decades. The junior year was lectured on the general principles of natural and revealed religion and on the Socinian controversy, while the assistants expounded the Greek text of St Luke and Romans, as well as Pearson on the creed. In the senior year the Regius Professor devoted one term to the criticism and interpretation of the Bible, one to the liturgy and the Thirty-nine Articles, and the last to the Roman controversy. His assistants lectured on the Epistle to the Hebrews, and on Burnet on the Articles. Ecclesiastical history was at first included in the lecture course, but was crowded out after a few years. Students were still examined in the subject, however, those parts of Mosheim being prescribed which covered the patristic period, the Reformation and the seventeenth century (at least as it affected England). Over the history of the medieval church a decent veil appears to have been drawn.

From the list of books prescribed for the examinations, as well as from the writings of the Professors and lecturers, we can infer the prevailing tone of the Divinity course: a conservative, robust, but reasonably balanced Protestantism. There was, needless to say, no flavour of Tractarianism, but neither was there a marked reaction against it; the doings of the ritualists in England provoked disgust but little alarm. And though an evangelical attitude can be detected here and there it was one which had little sympathy with the extremists of revival movements. Most striking, perhaps, is the conservative bias: the course leant heavily on the Caroline divines and the writers of the early eighteenth century, Magee's *Atonement* being the only modern work prescribed. Pearson on the creed, Burnet on the Articles, Wheatly on the Prayer Book, Potter on church government, Newton on prophecy, Paley's *Evidences*, Butler's *Analogy* – this was the solid ballast provided against the blasts of vain doctrine which were whirling on all sides. Even on the Roman controversy a refreshingly sober note was struck by Leslie's *Case stated*[20] – a leisurely and urbane conversation between a Catholic *Lord* and an Anglican *Gent.*, in which the former is gradually reduced to silence by the ever-increasing eloquence of the latter, but is not humiliated or held up to ridicule. In 1844 this was replaced by Jeremy Taylor's *Dissuasive from popery*, but even its more trenchant style of argument must have been considered very thin stuff by the debaters at public meetings or the writers in the rich underworld of ecclesiastical journalism.

For this prevailing atmosphere of sobriety in an age when restraint was not always regarded as a virtue in theological matters C.R. Elrington, who held the Regius Professorship up to 1850, deserved much of the credit. Conservative enough to oppose the Whigs' National Education Board at its first inception, he was also realistic enough to see, some fifteen years later, that the Church Education Society was failing in its attempt to provide alternative schools. His consequent change of policy made him unpopular with his fellow clergy, among whom the issue provoked an intensity of feeling which is not easy to understand today.[21] Nevertheless, he was widely respected for his independent, if cautious views, and there is no doubt that he did the Divinity School a service in preventing it from being pushed by the weight of extreme party views into the provincial eccentricity which many regarded as the only guarantee of a lively apostolic faith.

With such a man at the head, a more robust theological tone could be permitted to the lieutenants; and the first two men to hold Archbishop King's Lecturership under the new conditions may fairly be described as belonging to the school of Kingsley. O'Brien, indeed, engaged in controversy with Newman over Tract 90, though this was only one incident in a long career of polemical writing. His great vigour and undoubted learning did not altogether compensate for the irresponsible and at times eccentric tone of his writings.[22] His celebrated sermons on *Justification by faith* were described by unfriendly critics as pure Lutheranism, and it was hinted that even graver heresies lurked in some of the charges which issued like thunderbolts from the Palace at Kilkenny, where he survived till after Disestablishment. McNeece, who succeeded him in the Lecturership in 1842, was more restrained in his utterances; but the general cast of his mind can be deduced from the epithet 'manly' which recurs in his obituary notices. We are given to understand that, kindly man though he was, he gave short shrift to those who obfuscated the plain truth of the Gospels with the verbal subleties of Tractarian metaphysics.

As the nineteenth century progressed, further additions were made to the staff of the Divinity School by the foundation of the chairs of Irish (1840), Ecclesiastical History (1850) and Pastoral Theology (1888); to these may be added the chair of Biblical Greek (1843), although it was not formally incorporated into the Divinity School until 1909. It is curious to note that in none of these chairs, except that of Biblical Greek, was any initiative taken by the Board, in spite of their real interest in the welfare of the school; the others were all founded by public subscription or private benefaction. This inaction, whatever may have been its basis, serves to emphasize the value and importance of Lloyd's enterprise in initiating a reform in this field; and it is quite likely that if the teaching of Divinity had not been reorganized during his provostship the school would have ceased to exist by the middle of the century.

(vi)

For it was just at this time that the question of the most suitable machinery for the training of ordinands was beginning to receive serious attention in England; and in the thirties it was being widely debated whether this training would best be performed by the universities or by the theological colleges which were beginning to multiply, especially in the cathedral cities.[23] Among the new universities Durham had from its foundation as one of its principal aims a complete and systematic training of ordinands within the university, and King's College, London, was soon to establish a theological faculty. But Oxford and Cambridge were caught by this question in an unfortunate phase of their development, and they allowed themselves to drift into an attitude which was not unfairly compared with that of the dog in the manger. They deplored the foundation of theological colleges elsewhere, but they could not be stirred up into providing within the universities a post-graduate training in theology which would satisfy the public opinion of the day. Cambridge eventually produced its Voluntary Theological Examination, but by that time it was too late; for the party spirit stirred up in the Church of England by the evangelical revival and the Oxford movement seized on the theological colleges as a God-sent opportunity of steering the rising generation of clergy towards one wing or the other. In Ireland there was no pressure from the Tractarian side, but there were many strong Protestants who doubtless thought the theological atmosphere of Trinity much too cautious and high-and-dry; and if it had been possible to claim that there was a vacuum waiting to be filled in the arrangements for the training of the clergy, some of the zeal which found its outlet in the Achill and Connemara missions might well have been diverted into the foundation of a theological college. The matter did, indeed, tremble on a razor's edge for a few years; the threat to the Divinity School came, however, not from the extreme Evangelicals, but from a man whose detachment from and contempt for all parties in the Church was sufficient to make him a centre of controversy as violent as any which raged round Newman or Maurice.

Only six weeks after Lloyd had been admitted as Provost, Richard Whately arrived in Dublin as Archbishop. We have elsewhere (pp. 127–8) made reference to his early contacts with the College; his first impressions of the Irish Church were not much happier, nor were they more tactfully expressed. By his failure to comprehend his milieu, his lack of the patience necessary to await the moment when criticism might be heeded, and his complete confidence in the strength of his own arguments, he soon won a reputation, which was not wholly deserved, for stubborn arrogance and meddling eccentricity. With the added handicap of being a keen liberal (who declared himself above party politics) it is not surprising that his real benevolence, enthusiasm and intellectual fertility found themselves largely sterilized by the opposition which his beliefs and manner had conjured up. In particular it led to a hopeless lack of agreement, or even co-operation, between him and his Primate, Lord John George Beresford, who had two years earlier been appointed Vice-Chancellor of the University. Beresford was a solid aristocrat who had been a bishop for as long as anyone could remember,[24] and who looked down on Whately as the eighteenth upon the nineteenth century, as Christ Church upon Oriel, as a slow-moving Tory on a radical logic-chopper, and above all as an Anglo-Irish nobleman, and a Beresford to boot, on a mere English adventurer, the son of a prebendary of Bristol. On this antagonism one of Whately's favourite schemes was destined to founder.

As soon as the new Archbishop began examining candidates for ordination in his diocese (characteristically refusing to accept the list of books agreed to by most of the Irish bishops as a basis for the examination, and indeed refusing to prescribe any books whatsoever), he perceived, rightly enough, that there was room for improvement in their training. He accordingly formed a scheme for setting up a theological college (which he generously offered to endow from the revenues of his see) in the old Archbishop's palace of St Sepulchre's in Kevin Street. Unfortunately he launched this project in the form of a couple of jaunty letters to the Lord-Lieutenant and Chief Secretary at the precise moment when the new two-year Divinity course in Trinity College was coming into operation; and although there still remained arguments which could be fairly urged in favour of a separate college, his assumption that the time between graduation and ordination was completely wasted, an exaggeration even before 1833, was now quite unwarranted. The proposed seminary was to be loosely associated with Trinity College, and by what appears to have been a genuine misunderstanding the Provost and the Regius Professor of Divinity gave the scheme their support in its early stages; but the Provost, partly under pressure from conservatives on the Board (who were, of course, opposed to the idea from the start), and partly by discovering how little say the Archbishop was going to allow him, or any member of the College, in the planning or management of his seminary, disengaged as gracefully as he could, despite Whately's pained reproaches. In May 1834 he resigned from the position he had accepted as trustee, and joined the great majority of the Fellows[25] in signing a protest to Whately, asking him to desist from interfering with one of the principal objects for which Trinity College was founded. Despite the Archbishop's hint that to insult somebody who stood as high as he did in the esteem of the Government was to court disaster, the opposition from the College and the Primate may have led the Government to hesitate before taking action. At all events nothing happened during the next six months, and the Whigs were then dismissed from office by the King.

When they returned to power a few months later they sent over as Lord-Lieutenant and Chief Secretary, not Wellesley and Littleton, with whom Whately had established such good relations, but two new men; and Whately appears to have lost heart. But in 1839, thinking perhaps that his chances were improved with Sadleir (who had supported him in 1834) in the Provost's House, he revived the project in a form which made the seminary completely independent of Trinity College. Beresford, scenting trouble, wrote to the Chief Secretary for information, but was put off with temporizing replies, and when, on 25 May, he wrote again and more insistently, demanding information so that he could consult his fellow-bishops, he was blandly informed that the sign-manual for the charter of the new college had been affixed a fortnight earlier, when the Government was in the thick of the Bedchamber crisis and very uncertain as to its future. At this point Whately, assured of victory, incautiously went abroad, and Beresford, justly incensed at the uncivil and disingenuous treatment he had received in a matter which, as Melbourne himself had assured him, 'was very important for the whole Church' demanded a reconsideration of the matter *de novo*. He had the support of an undivided Board, for Sadleir, having reaped the reward of his political constancy, seems now to have thought good relations with his colleagues more important than consistent support for the Whigs, and had turned against the scheme. The Primate was also fortified by a statement from another satisfied Whig, Sandes (now Bishop of Cashel) that 'the city of Dublin is beyond all places in the world that which least requires a Divinity Hall, because there is in the city of Dublin the very best Divinity School in the world'. *Pietas* may have led to some exaggeration here, but whereas in 1834 the new Divinity course existed only on paper, by 1839 it had proved its worth, even though it contained too much dogmatic theology for Whately's somewhat latitudinarian tastes. Luckily for Beresford, Lord Ebrington, who had recently been appointed Lord-Lieutenant, sweetened perhaps by the haste with which the College had invited him to dinner and conferred on him an honorary degree, was prepared to examine the situation on its merits, and, presumably on his advice, the Government countermanded the charter. Whately, fortunately, was not the man to nurse a grievance for long, and it is to his credit that he soon re-established friendly relations with the College.[26]

(vii)

He was probably not the first, and certainly not the last would-be educational benefactor to discover to his dismay that, whereas universities are always eager to secure further endowments, they often complain that the particular purpose for which these endowments are designed is ill-advised or unwanted. He may have felt particularly sore over the frustration of this public-spirited, progressive and generous offer (as he saw it) since he had made an earlier venture of the same kind, in which, although his offer was first received with a caution that verged on suspicion, it was accepted, and worked out satisfactorily in the view of the university and the donor alike. This was the creation and endowment of a chair of Political Economy.

This science (which Whately characteristically wanted to re-christen 'Catallactics') was developing rapidly, and was fashionable in liberal circles. Whately himself was keenly interested in it, and had been appointed, only a year before his elevation to the archbishopric, to the newly created Drummond Lecturership in Political Economy at Oxford. He therefore saw immediately as a defect in Trinity College the absence of any teaching in the subject. In the spring of 1832 he suggested that a chair should be established on a part-time basis, with a maximum tenure of five years, and he offered to provide a stipend of £100 per annum – a payment which he continued up to his death. The duties of the Professor would be to deliver an annual course of lectures, of which at least one was to be published.

A few years later Whately related with complacent amusement the manner in which his offer had been received. There has been some fears that no suitable candidate for the chair would be forthcoming, and the Provost had volunteered the information that 'it had been suggested to him that in the absence of any person having a full knowledge of the science a person should be selected . . . who should be of sound and safe conservative views'. The Archbishop professed himself 'appalled at the introduction of party politics into a subject of abstract science'.[27] There was, however, no shortage of candidates professional enough to satisfy the donor and at the same time not so radical as to alarm the Board; the first two, indeed, were Tories. The first Professor, appointed later in 1832, was Mountiford Longfield, a Junior Fellow of seven years' standing, who resigned his Fellowship two years later on appointment to the Regius Professorship of Feudal and English Law, a post which he retained even when he became a judge in 1858.[28] He set the tone for his successors in the Whately Professorship, for they were all, for many years, members of the Irish Bar, and most of them were men of some distinction. Longfield was succeeded in 1836 by Isaac Butt, who is remembered today chiefly as the leader of the Home Rule party in the seventies, but who was also, besides being a busy lawyer, a prolific writer on history, politics, economics, law and education, and the editor of a classical text. His successor, J.A. Lawson, made his career at the Bar, and later as a judge, but the next two Professors, W.N. Hancock and R.H. Walsh made their reputations primarily in the field of economics, as did Walsh's successor, J.E. Cairnes, who at the time of his early death in 1875 was perhaps the most outstanding economist in the British Isles, despite the fact that his working life in the subject was less than twenty years. His Dublin lectures formed the basis of a valuable study of the fundamentals of economic thinking, and he won a wider audience with *The slave power* (1862), a trenchant and influential attack on the Confederate States.

The legal background shared by all these Professors accounts, perhaps, for their preference for inductive over deductive reasoning, which has been seen as a characteristic of the Dublin school.[29] They were happiest in deriving economic principles from current practical problems, of which Ireland furnished many in a particularly stark form. The earlier Professors were conscious of a prejudice against their science as being at best hard-hearted (in view of the prevalence of *laissez-faire* doctrines), and at the worst subversive and positively immoral, and they laboured with some success to establish its respectability alike in intellectual and in ethical terms. Many of their published lectures combine the acute and fresh reasoning which might be expected from intelligent amateurs exploring a novel field of inquiry with the skilful exposition derived from their experience as advocates. They certainly awakened a lively interest in economics in Dublin, which bore fruit in 1847 in the foundation of the Dublin Statistical (later Statistical and Social Enquiry) Society, of which Whately was the first president. For over a century its publications have provided a valuable commentary on Irish economic development.

(viii)

The remaining Professorship to be founded during Lloyd's brief tenure of the provostship – that of Moral Philosophy – was due, not to the activity of outsiders, but to the initiative of the Provost himself. It is a curious anomaly in the structure of the University up to the middle of the eighteenth century that professorships in the principal subjects taught to undergraduates were non-existent. It was assumed, rightly on the whole, that most of the Fellows were capable of teaching them up to the required standard, but the idea was slow to take hold that it might be advantageous to encourage more profound scholarship in these subjects. We find, accordingly, that in 1760 there were Professors of Divinity, Law, Medicine, Hebrew, Physics and History, but none of Mathematics, Greek, Latin, Astronomy or Philosophy, the subjects which composed virtually the whole of the undergraduate course. Mathematics and Astronomy were provided for later in the century by private benefactions, and Greek by Letters Patent, presumably at the request of the College, in 1761. But Latin and Philosophy had to wait till the next century. Since 'Ethics and Logics' formed one of the new honor degrees instituted in 1833, the need for somebody to guide advanced study in these subjects was plain, and accordingly a Professorship of Moral Philosophy was established by the Board in 1837.

In the absence of external endowments, however, the chair had to be a part-time one, with a salary of only £100 a year. None of the existing Fellows had much claim to be taken seriously as a philosopher, so William Archer Butler, who had, only three years earlier, graduated with first place in the first examination for Moderatorship in Ethics and Logics, was appointed. He was simultaneously presented by the College to the most remote (and least well endowed) of its livings in Co. Donegal. Butler was an able man, a profound, if not strikingly original thinker, and was endowed with a most attractive personality. His lectures (published posthumously) show that in addition to an intimate knowledge of Platonic philosophy he had an understanding of Berkeley far removed from the naive and superficial views generally current at that time, a considerable understanding of Kant (though no English translation had yet appeared when he first delivered his course), and at least a nodding acquaintance with Hegel. His early death in 1848 from typhoid fever – a fate which overtook many of the best of the clergy who were active in relief work after the famine – represented a serious loss to the Irish Church and to the intellectual life of the country. But his immediate influence in the College was less than it might have been, for, although he was required to lecture for two terms each year, he was not asked to examine. An old and bad tradition kept the more important examinations in the hands of the Provost and Senior Fellows, and the candidates for Moderatorship or Fellowship in Philosophy were therefore examined for the most part by men not competent to hold the Professorship of the subject. Students will always attend more diligently the classes conducted by their examiners than those given by an outsider, however brilliant, and Butler's audience was largely composed, therefore, of resident Bachelors, who used his lectures as one of the options by which they could keep their terms. As these were mostly divinity students the chair became gradually, if unofficially, regarded as an appendage to the Divinity School, and Butler's successors from 1847 to 1857 were parochial clergymen who were theologians rather than philosophers. From 1857 to 1872 the chair was held by Fellows of some philosophical ability, but their lack of commitment to the subject was shown by the fact that Webb deserted the chair for the Regius Professorship of Laws, and Abbott for the chairs of Biblical Greek and Hebrew. It was not till Thomas Maguire (the first Roman Catholic Fellow) was appointed in 1882 that the Professor of Moral Philosophy began to fill the role that we would expect from the title today.

A lecturership in Biblical Greek (raised in 1843 to the dignity of a Professorship) was founded a few months after Lloyd's death in very similar circumstances and with very similar conditions; it was not formally attached to the Divinity School and divinity students were not compelled to attend the lectures. Provision was made, however, that the lecturer should assist at their examinations, and this meant that the post played from the start a useful if limited role in the Divinity School.

(ix)

A practical and much-needed change initiated by Lloyd soon after his appointment was the reorganization of the academic year. Under Provost Bedell's statutes the College had four terms of almost equal length (eight to nine weeks) and four vacations, each of thirty to thirty-seven days. This was not ecclesiastical enough for Laud, who in any case, like many other Oxford men before and since, found it very difficult to see why any academic arrangements should diverge from the Oxford pattern. The timetable which he imposed on Trinity in 1637, essentially similar to that current at Oxford, was particularly inconvenient, for two of the four terms were defined at one end by a calendar date and at the other by a movable feast of the Church. Hilary Term, in consequence, could vary according to the date of Easter from sixty-nine to an intolerable ninety-seven days, and Trinity Term from fifty to a ridiculous twenty-two. Even the two terms of fixed length were ill-matched, as the Easter Term had forty-one days against seventy-seven for Michaelmas.

These terms were defined by statute, but Lloyd managed to secure the inclusion, in a King's Letter which freed the College from some other clearly anachronistic statutes, of a provision for reorganizing the terms and vacations on something like the Cambridge pattern. From 1834 there were to be three terms in the year, varying in length only from seventy-two to seventy-seven days, with three weeks' vacation at both Christmas and Easter and over three months in the summer.

(x)

This change naturally meant that the work assigned to the various classes for each term had to be redistributed, and Lloyd made use of the opportunity to introduce the most far-reaching of his reforms. In June 1833, three months after the King's Letter had been issued, he secured the consent of the Board to a set of regulations which amounted to a thorough replanning of the undergraduate course. Prior, by what one would hope was a coincidence, had obtained a few weeks' leave of absence for family reasons, and Phipps, for reasons now hidden from us, did not attend the meeting of the Board at which the final decision was taken.

The changes in the actual subjects to be studied were small; those in the books prescribed were more significant. But the real novelty was a clear distinction throughout the course between the studies of honors-men and pass-men, a distinction which, with many changes in detail but none in general principle, was to persist for almost a century and a half until, paradoxically, in our own day it was decided that all academic geese are swans and that the dullest must read for honors on a course devised for the brightest.

Allowance was made for a transitional year in 1833–4; the new course came into full effect in Michaelmas 1834. For pass-men the chief changes were as follows. The position of logic and mathematics in the Freshman years was reversed, so that now Junior Freshmen studied mathematics and Senior Freshmen logic. For the first time elementary trigonometry was incorporated into the mathematical course. Locke's *Essay* and Murray's *Logic* were retained as the set books for the Senior Freshman year. In the Science of the Junior Sophister year the Provost's *Mechanical philosophy* was reserved for the honors-men; for the pass-men there was prescribed the recent and less ambitious text-book on mechanics by James Wood, Dean of Ely, and their course in astronomy and optics was reduced in content. Finally, in the ethics of the last year Paley's *Evidences* was substituted for 'Leland and Porteus' as the work of Christian apologetics. In Latin the only new author to appear was Ovid; Sallust and Persius were eliminated to make room for three books of the *Fasti*. In Greek the changes were more extensive. Herodotus, Thucydides and Plato, who had been dropped earlier in the century, were restored to the course, as were four books of the *Odyssey*;

172

to make room for these Lucian and Longinus were omitted, and the number of tragedies was reduced.

Simultaneously with these changes in the course, improvements were made in the manner in which the term examinations were conducted, most of them based on recommendations in MacDonnell's pamphlet (p. 125). The arbitrary element was eliminated by assigning to each class a single examiner in each subject, and the composition had henceforth to be done in the examination hall. Apart from abolishing the pecuniary traffic in themes, this provided the candidates with an occupation while they were awaiting their turn for *viva voce* examination.

The changes in the course implied for pass-men a substantial diminution in the total of prescribed books, even if the pruning of the classical authors did not go as far as MacDonnell had suggested. For honors-men, on the other hand, a fuller and more advanced course was devised for every term of the four years. The intention was clear: pass-men were to read a more limited and easier course than hitherto, but would be expected to have mastered it thoroughly, while honors-men would read a more varied and extensive course than before, of which, presumably, a less detailed knowledge would be required. They were, however, protected from the temptation to dilettantism or excessive specialization by the requirement that before taking the honor examination they must acquit themselves with distinction in an examination on the pass course, to which the first two days of each terminal examination were devoted. At the end of these two days the examiners of each division were to recommend for examination on the honor course, either in Science or in Classics or in both, those candidates whom they judged to be qualified.

The honor examinations, besides covering much of those parts of the old pass course from which the pass-men were now exempted, demanded also some knowledge in fields which were entirely new. In mathematics there was a little analytical geometry and spherical trigonometry. In logic they were examined on Whately's textbook, and also on *Sketch of the philosophy of the mind* by Thomas Brown, who has been described as the last of the Edinburgh metaphysicians. In physics and astronomy there were no great novelties, but the course was rather more searching and extensive, while in ethics Paley's *Moral philosophy* was added to his *Evidences*, as was also Gisborne's *Principles of moral philosophy*. These last two works were fifty years old, and indicated, perhaps, that in ethics Lloyd was less in touch with contemporary thought than he was with other subjects. As a whole, however, the course can be regarded as reasonably up to date.

The honor course culminated in the degree examination, in which successful candidates were designated Moderators. (The name, which is peculiar to Dublin in this sense, and is still in use to denote a successful candidate at an honor examination for B.A., has its origin in the fact that for many years before 1833 the best performers at the degree examination had been asked to act as chairmen or moderators at the disputations of the less brilliant students.) As with the term examinations, however, it was only after having acquitted himself with distinction at the ordinary degree examination that a student was allowed to compete for a moderatorship.[30] The courses for the latter did not differ very greatly from those for the medals, described earlier (p. 121), but there were some important changes in the new system. Previously, although a medal was awarded to the best man in Science and another to the best in Classics, everybody had to sit the examination in both subjects, and it was necessary to be a good all-rounder to secure a place in the list of *primarii in sua classe* which followed the names of the medallists. Now specialization was encouraged by the award of separate Moderatorships in Classics, in Mathematics (including theoretical physics) and in 'Ethics and Logics', the candidates being examined only in the subject of their choice. The Moderators were divided into two grades, Senior and Junior; all the Seniors were given gold medals, while the Juniors were given silver. The award of each grade was, of course, intended to be made on grounds of absolute merit, but a safeguard against depreciation of the academic currency was inserted in the shape of a regulation which fixed $2\frac{1}{2}$ per cent of the total number of the class as the maximum for Senior Moderators, and 5 per cent for Junior. In the first ten years of the system there were thirty-seven Senior Moderators in Mathematics, twenty in Classics and thirty-eight in Ethics and Logics, while the corresponding figures for Junior Moderatorships were fifteen, fifteen and fifty-nine. The large figures for philosophy, especially among the weaker candidates, suggest that it must have been to some extent a 'soft option', and indeed the prescribed books were neither very testing nor very up to date.

(xi)

The initiation of moderatorships laid the foundations of proper honor teaching, and in the following year an innovation, due largely to the Provost, although it was essentially administrative in its nature, made a great improvement in the standard of teaching for pass-men. This was the new tutorial system. We have seen in the last chapter that an undergraduate received a large part of his instruction from his tutor, who in return received a substantial fee for every pupil in his chamber.

This produced great disparities, both of work and of income. Although the Provost could assign pupils to tutors as he chose, this power had been so abused by Hely-Hutchinson that it was rarely used in the nineteenth century, except in so far as the Provost, with the consent of the Board, fixed an upper limit to the number of pupils which any one tutor might take. The choice of tutor lay, therefore, either with the parents or the schoolmaster of the pupil. And as Provost MacDonnell was later to point out,[31] a tutor's success in attracting pupils would depend not so much on his merits as on 'his habits of life in leading him more into society, the extent of his acquaintance with schoolmasters throughout the country, and, in times of political excitement, his conspicuousness and forwardness in taking a part in political movements'. A life of this kind would leave little time for scholarship, and would not even encourage regular tuition, so that the tutors with the largest classes tended to be those least fitted to teach them. Moreover, even a recluse was not likely to be a really efficient teacher on all parts of the four-year course.

Under the skilful and patient guidance of Lloyd the tutors agreed in 1834 to a new system which rationalized their teaching by introducing a division of labour, and which made their tutorial income depend scarcely at all on their popularity, but almost entirely on their seniority.[32] Each tutor was to lecture on a limited range of subjects for which he had some taste or aptitude, and he was to lecture to the pupils of other tutors besides his own. All tutorial fees were thrown into a common fund, and the tutors were graded by seniority. The five most senior constituted the Senior Grade, the five most junior the Junior Grade, while the remainder, numbering seven in 1834, but soon to be increased to eleven, constituted the Middle Grade. A tutorial dividend from the fees was paid in the ratio of 4 : 3 : 2 to the members of the three grades. The advisory and disciplinary responsibilities of a tutor towards his pupils were not affected.

The new system proved an immediate success. Although there was some grumbling from the older Fellows and graduates (and from the younger, but equally crusty, Tories of the *Dublin University Magazine*) about the loss of the quasi-paternal relationship which was established under the old system, the new arrangement was warmly defended before the Royal Commission in 1852 by nearly all the tutors, including some who would have been likely to have made a good deal more money under the old system. Although a certain element of financial incentive towards acquiring pupils was introduced later, the system established in 1834 lasted for over a century with only minor modifications.

(xii)

The years of Lloyd's provostship saw also a change in the College buildings. More lecture-rooms and more living-space were needed, and as the windfall in M.A. degree fees produced by the otherwise distasteful Reform Act had wisely been added to a small pre-existing buildings fund, the Provost felt himself in a position to ask the Board's consent in November 1833, to advertise for plans and estimates for 'the new buildings contemplated'. This is their first mention in the Register, but it seems to have been agreed some short time before that a new range should be built to the east of the University Press, and that the western range of the Library Square, which was probably in bad condition, and which must have looked rather odd ever since the old Hall had been excised from the middle of it in 1798, should be pulled down. Phipps, of course, dissented from the whole idea, but otherwise the Provost met with no opposition, though it was not until January 1835 that plans were received from Darley, accompanied by an estimate of £7,000. By the end of March the estimate had almost doubled, but in May the Board accepted the plans, with a limit of £14,000 on the cost. Frederick Darley, whose claims to design the range have been summarized as 'genealogically rather than architecturally convincing',[33] put up a granite building which is decent, substantial and dull, and may be taken as representing the running-out of the Palladian tradition in Dublin; the tradition was strong enough to prevent gross eccentricities or errors of taste, but inspiration had dried up to a trickle. By March 1837, before the range had been completed, another was under consideration, and by June the builders had been chosen for what is now the east side of the New Square, to a design similar to the north side but slightly more grandiose. Lloyd died before the second range was started, but one of his successor's first acts was to order building to be started forthwith (January 1838), and just two years later we read of the enclosing and landscaping of the square being completed.

7

Development in early Victorian times
1837–1851

(i)

Bartholomew Lloyd died suddenly in November 1837, and Franc Sadleir was an obvious choice for a Whig government to appoint as his successor. (Had a Tory government been in power Wall might well have been appointed; he was a better scholar than Sadleir, but probably less effective as administrator.) During Sadleir's provostship the pace of reform and development slackened, but it did not by any means come to a halt. The new Provost was, as we have seen earlier, an archetypal Whig, with no desire to make big changes but always alert to the need for small adjustments, and always ready to move (within reason) with the times. His grasp of the principles of orderly administration can be seen in a change of style in the Register soon after his appointment. For the first time we read of the minutes being confirmed and signed; a vacation committee was instituted on more than one occasion, with limited powers to act in the name of the Board; and many details are minuted on which the Register had previously been silent. Under Sadleir's rule, and in most cases with his active encouragement, the celibacy statute was repealed, the Engineering School was founded, the Medical School made notable progress, the number and diversity of interests of the academic staff were considerably increased and the first tentative steps were taken in allowing an element of choice in the pass course for undergraduates. To these, as well as to some changes which occurred during his provostship as the result of outside pressures or the mere passage of time, we must now turn our attention.

(ii)

It was only a few years after its strict enforcement in 1811 that an agitation for a repeal of the celibacy statute had begun. But it was a matter on which the College was divided. The older Fellows, who were either confirmed bachelors or else were married and protected by the indemnity of 1812, saw plainly the advantages of a regulation which

177

prescribed that at least a majority of their colleagues should be wedded only to their muse. They were supported not only by a considerable weight of conservative opinion outside the College, but also by the Scholars, who feared that permission for Fellows to marry would mean fewer resignations, and therefore fewer elections.[1] The attitude of the Scholars is easy to understand, but it was short-sighted, and once they were elected to Fellowship they presumably changed their views. It is not so easy to see why so many others were equally obsessed at this time with the supposed necessity of keeping up a rapid circulation in the Fellowship body by encouraging frequent resignations to country livings; for it was in this, rather than in any ideal of monastic seclusion from the distractions of the world, that the main support of the celibacy statute lay. The fact that as late as 1828 the College spent £14,000 on the purchase of the advowson of Clogherny shows how strong was this obsession, and even the Commissioners of 1851, who censured the Board for this purchase, refer elsewhere to 'the necessity of a rapid circulation in the body in order to have a vacancy every year'.[2] This attitude took as its starting-point the idea of Fellowship not as a career but as a prize, which might launch the winner on one of several careers, of which the academic represented only one possibility and the clerical was the most probable. But we have already seen that a fall in the value of livings and a rise in the emoluments of Fellowship had militated against this 'rapid circulation', and the tithe war and the Irish Ecclesiastical Temporalities Act of 1834[3] had recently tipped the scale further against the livings. The pages of the Register from 1840 onwards show a mounting disquiet as living after living is refused by all the Fellows; everybody felt that something must be done to bring back the happy days of 1820, with their 'rapid circulation', but nobody knew what to do. The Board, and still more the main mass of conservative graduates, was reluctant to admit, even privately, that agrarian and political conditions were such that attempts to patch up the patronage system of the College were a waste of time, for the system was dying. It was, indeed, virtually dead when Disestablishment finally gave it the *coup de grâce* in 1870.

It was natural that a governing body faced with this problem should hesitate before abolishing the strongest stimulus (now that financial gain was small or non-existent) for a Fellow to resign on a living – the fact that only in this way could he get married. But as the years went by the number of compulsory and unwilling celibates increased,[4] and eventually the pressure which they exerted won the day, reinforced by the growth of liberal opinion outside the walls, and even, perhaps, by a feeling that the faithful of such parishes as Clondehorkey and Aghalurcher deserved better than to be ministered to exclusively by incumbents selected originally for their brilliance in mathematics. Sadleir was an open advocate of repeal; a petition for repeal signed by 800 graduates was sent to the Queen in 1839; and in 1840 the necessary Letters Patent were issued, despite the protests of the Primate and a few other angry conservatives.[5]

The Board, in petitioning for repeal, had suggested that celibacy might still be imposed on the nine most junior of the Fellows, hoping that the impatience of at least a few of these would lead to some resignations. But the Crown, ignoring the views of the Board and the Vice-Chancellor alike, adopted a different solution: it noted the increased revenues of the College, and created ten new Fellowships, to be filled up at the rate of one a year over the next decade. This removed any grievance from the existing body of Scholars; and to prevent the Junior Fellows from complaining that this dilution of their ranks would lead to a serious loss of tutorial fees, it was enacted that only four of the new Fellowships should carry the right to a tutorship.

(iii)

The Board debated these proposals on 10 March 1840, and although only four of the eight members approved them, the other four were divided on the nature of their opposition, so that in the end they were grudgingly accepted. It soon became clear that the Government had made (not for the last time) the mistake of regulating too minutely the affairs of an institution with which it was not thoroughly familiar, instead of contenting itself with imposing a broad principle and letting the College work out the details. For the six non-tutor Fellowships were not a success; there was general agreement on this point by 1850. The income of a Junior Fellow (except for two or three who held other well-paid posts) depended almost entirely on his tutorship, so that the non-tutor Fellows had to live on a pittance for some time after their election. In 1850 the income of the tutors ranged from £410 to £1,000 per annum, averaging about £650;[6] but the best paid of the non-tutor Fellows received only £184 from the College, and one of them received only £80. Admittedly their duties were light, and they had plenty of time for private tuition and any other occupation they could find; but it is small wonder that they formed what Provost MacDonnell described to the Commission as 'a nursery of discontent'. At the time of the Commission they were in rather bad odour, having recently addressed to the Board a memorial about their incomes; they had received the chilling reply that they knew perfectly well what the situation was when they started to read for Fellowship, and the fact that they refused College livings worth as much as £500 a year showed that 'the discontent with their transitory position is more than balanced by their prospective advantages'.[7] The non-tutor Fellows replied that although this was true their plea was based on the fact that they had not enough to live on here and now, and that even when they received a tutorship, after a waiting period which could not be exactly predicted but was seldom less than three years, their income rose only slowly to the average of the Junior Grade, so that they would find it difficult to pay off quickly the debts which they were now forced to incur. They did not ask for an income equal or nearly equal to that of the Junior Grade of tutors, but merely for a few crumbs to be tossed to them now. Even this did not move the heart of the Board, but the Commissioners were more sympathetic, declaring that the Board's reply was not likely to satisfy men 'whose only complaint is that their emoluments are unreasonably low, for no other purpose that they can conceive, except to increase the emoluments of other Fellows who have been subject only to the same tests and examinations as themselves'.[8] By 1853 there was general agreement that the experiment had been a failure, but the difficulty of phasing out the non-tutor Fellows without damaging the interests either of the Scholars or of the tutors seemed at first insuperable. In 1856 the Board was still refusing their request for an extra £50 a year, but two years later it obtained powers to reduce their number. By 1870 the number had been reduced to two, at which point it was stabilized, but as the waiting period was now short, and the fees for examining and other services had been increased, the non-tutor Fellows no longer presented a serious problem.

(iv)

If the repeal of the celibacy statute was the most important legislative change to take place under Sadleir's rule, the most important academic development was the founding of the School of Engineering in 1841. The claim has sometimes been made that Dublin was second only to Glasgow in giving university recognition to this subject, but this is not quite true. The first Professor of Engineering at University College, London, was appointed a few months before his colleague in Dublin, and instruction in engineering science, albeit without a professor of the subject, had been given in Durham since 1831 and in King's College, London, since 1838. Nevertheless, the industrial revolution was not as conspicuous a presence in Dublin as it was in Glasgow, Durham and London, and the College showed considerable enterprise in entering on this field as early as it did. It needed the lapse of another half-century before Cambridge instituted its Tripos in Mechanical Sciences.

Although there was a fair amount of old-established light industry in

Dublin which was at this time modernizing its plant, the immediate stimulus was the coming of the railways. By 1841 the great railway boom was in sight; 'railways', it has been said, 'were the cry of the hour, and engineers the want of the day'.[9] Ireland had by this time twelve miles of railway in operation, with the city terminus at the back gate of the College (and indeed repelled only with difficulty from appropriating some of the College land); and half a dozen companies were issuing glowing prospectuses for a greatly increased mileage. It was clear that many supervisors and designers would soon be needed for the large programme of surveying, levelling, earth-moving, tunnelling and bridge-building envisaged. Another factor which may have helped to win acceptance for the University's entry into this unfamiliar field was the suggestion made by a parliamentary committee in 1838 that a polytechnic institute should be founded in Dublin; for academics, reluctant though they often are to admit new subjects to their curriculum, are usually even more reluctant to see other institutions founded to teach them.

Engineering resembles medicine in being a combination of theoretical knowledge and practical skill, and the incorporation of such subjects into a university curriculum always imposes difficult strains on the academic mind. To bridge the gap between the Professor of Physic lecturing and examining, at least in part in Latin, and the practitioner diagnosing and treating disease in a hospital or a tenement was no easy task. So also in engineering; its practitioners had hitherto for the most part worked their way up from the bottom by being apprenticed to builders or mechanical craftsmen, and were not on effective speaking terms with the professors who proved with mathematical rigour theorems in statics or hydrodynamics. To this impasse there was one exception; the Academy at Woolwich had been founded just a century earlier to provide both the theoretical and the practical training necessary for artillery officers and army engineers. But its contacts with the academic world were few.

Undeterred by these difficulties, however, three Junior Fellows sent to the Board in April 1841 a memorandum requesting the foundation of a Professorship of Civil Engineering and suggesting the curriculum for his school. The signatories were Humphrey Lloyd, James McCullagh and Thomas Luby. The first was a physicist of established reputation, who had done good work in optics and was at this time the active director of the magnetic observatory recently erected for him in the Fellows' garden.[10] McCullagh was a brilliant young mathematician and a romantic and idealistic nationalist, anxious for the College to play a full part in the life of the country. Luby was a more pedestrian mathematician, but with a shrewd head for business, and evidently some understanding of public affairs, as he was chosen by the Board nine years later as their emissary to superintend in London the passage through Parliament of an intricate and controversial bill dealing with the College's rights as a landlord.

After less than three months' deliberation the Board agreed to the proposals. Two new Professorships were to be created, one of Civil Engineering[11] and one of 'Chemistry and Geology applied to the arts of construction'. The teaching in mathematics and mechanics was to be given by the existing Fellows.

The motives that lay behind the foundation of the school are clearly set out in the Calendars of its early days. It was set up, we are told, 'with a view of combining, as far as is practicable, the theoretical and practical instruction necessary for the Profession of Civil Engineering, and of imparting to the members of that Profession the other advantages of academical education. With these objects in view it has been deemed advisable that a Student preparing for the Profession of Civil Engineering should be a member of the College and subject to its general discipline.' The students of the new school, however, were to be in the College, but in a sense not of it. In 1841 the idea of conferring a degree in anything but arts or one of the old-established faculties was unheard of, and in any case the course as originally planned was of only two years' duration. Students of engineering were, therefore, to work for a diploma, and their position was to be something like that of the medical students who were working for a diploma but not a degree. Engineering students had to matriculate, and to pass the first year of the undergraduate course in arts (half of which consisted of mathematics anyway); but after that they need study only their professional course. In fact, however, it soon became customary for the majority of students to read the full arts course, and to emerge with a B.A. as well as a diploma in engineering.

After two years' experience it was agreed that two years was insufficient to provide the professional training required, and the course was lengthened to three. The first year's studies comprised mathematics, theoretical mechanics and chemistry; the second, practical mechanics, principles of physics and preliminary work in drawing, surveying and levelling. This last was continued in the final year along with geology, practical engineering, and 'field-work in general', which included visits to works of engineering interest. The lectures in the school were open to all students on the College books.

James Apjohn was appointed as the Professor of Applied Chemistry and Geology immediately after the structure of the school had been decided, and a year later J.B. McNeill was appointed Professor of Civil Engineering. Apjohn, who was a former Scholar of the College and a graduate in medicine, had taught chemistry for some years, first in Cork, and then at the Royal College of Surgeons and the Park Street medical school. He was a very competent chemist, and well able to tackle also the mineralogy which he had to teach, but he had no training in other aspects of geology, and it soon became apparent that it was a mistake to imagine that one man could act as professor of both subjects. In 1844, therefore, the Board founded an independent chair of Geology and Mineralogy, and confirmed Apjohn as Professor of Applied Chemistry alone, with an eye on the fact that Barker, the University Professor of Chemistry, was now an elderly man and would not be reappointed at the end of his current term of office. He was, in fact, pensioned off in 1850, and Apjohn, without any competition, succeeded to his chair, as the first Professor of Chemistry who was primarily a chemist and only secondarily a physician.

The new Professor of Geology and Mineralogy was John Phillips, a nephew of William Smith, 'the father of English geology'. He had assisted his uncle for some years in local surveys, had held the chair of Geology at King's College, London, and had recently been appointed to the staff of the Geological Survey. He hoped to be able to continue his survey work in England during his vacations from Dublin, but this proved impossible, so he asked to be transferred to the Irish Survey. But this also was declared by the Director to be impossible, and, as the Dublin chair carried only a small salary,[12] he resigned in frustration after only fifteen months' tenure, to return to survey work in England and later to take up the chair at Oxford. The straitened resources of the College and the inflexibility of government officials combined to rob Dublin of a man who was not only an extremely able geologist, but also a good administrator and a popular colleague. He was succeeded[13] by Thomas Oldham, a Dublin graduate who had been acting as assistant to the Professor of Engineering, having studied the subject in Edinburgh. By a strange irony he was permitted what had been denied to Phillips, and worked for the Survey as well as for the University. He served both masters well, before leaving in 1850 to achieve wider fame by his work for the Geological Survey of India. His name is commemorated in *Oldhamia antiqua*, an enigmatic fossil (or some would say trace-fossil or pseudo-fossil) in the Cambrian rocks of Bray Head.

McNeill (shortly to become Sir John McNeill), the first Professor of Engineering, was also a man of some distinction. He was an Irishman, but had learnt his trade under Telford in England, and worked as a consulting engineer in London and Glasgow. He got the school off to a good start, but seems to have deputed most of the teaching to his assistants, and spent much of his time as consultant for the Irish railways. He retired from the chair after ten years, and was succeeded by Samuel Downing, a more workaday figure and author of some useful textbooks, who held office for thirty years. McNeill was, however, retained till his death in an honorary, and perhaps occasionally consultative, capacity as 'Professor Extraordinary of Civil Engineering'.

During its first year the new school had to make do with makeshift accommodation, but in 1843, as a consequence of the death of Prior and a reshuffle of rooms among the Senior Fellows, most of the East Chapel building became vacant, and its rooms were allotted to the Schools of Engineering and Natural Philosophy. The latter had been housed for the past twenty years or so in the handsome room over the vestibule of the Dining Hall, which at an earlier date had been the debating hall of the Historical Society; it was now converted to a Fellows' Common Room, a purpose which it still serves.[14] But the engineers soon demanded further space for a drawing school, and in the summer of 1847 a temporary building was run up quickly, at a cost of £357, between the Examination Hall and the Library. It was an early example of a phenomenon which was to become almost universal in the universities of the mid-twentieth century – an inelegant temporary building required for scientific or technological expansion cowering under the disapproving gaze of lofty and classical porticoes or colonnades. But unlike some of its successors it was truly temporary, and was taken down when the Engineering School was moved in 1855 to its permanent quarters in the new Museum Building.

The School was a success from the start. It was inaugurated by an eloquent prelection given by Humphrey Lloyd, consisting of a high-flown paean of praise for applied science as one of the foundation-stones of civilization, and illustrated by a dazzling array of statistics showing that the Great Pyramid and other mighty works of antiquity could have been built almost in the twinkling of an eye with the help of steam power.[15] The school won complimentary tributes from official and professional bodies, and in 1860 it was felt that it had attained to sufficient respectability for the successful student to be rewarded with a licence, publicly awarded at Commencements, instead of a diploma. At the same time the degree of Master in Engineering was instituted for licentiates who were also Bachelors of Arts and who had spent three years in engineering practice. The final step was taken in 1872, when the degree of Bachelor of Engineering replaced the licence for those who had also taken a B.A.[16]

By 1861 some 130 diplomas had been issued. Of the two pupils who completed the course in its first year of operation one, James Barton, designed and erected twelve years later the Boyne viaduct, perhaps the most ambitious bridge in Ireland. More than half the diploma-holders in 1861 were working abroad, twenty of them in India. They were the advance-guard, soon to be joined by graduates from other faculties, of the army of T.C.D. men who were to provide the British Empire for nearly a century, in numbers far exceeding their proportion of the total roll of graduates of the British Isles, with administrators, jurists, doctors, missionaries and engineers. They soon established a lasting tradition that the Dublin graduate, although he might lack some social polish and sophisticated learning, was likely to be resourceful, adaptable, enterprising, and well grounded in the basic knowledge of his subject.

(v)

The death of Prior, apart from liberating accommodation for engineering and physics, had other repercussions in the same field. Humphrey Lloyd was co-opted as Senior Fellow in his place, and thereby automatically vacated Erasmus Smith's Professorship of Natural and Experimental Philosophy. McCullagh was moved across from mathematics to physics, and Charles Graves was elected Erasmus Smith's Professor of Mathematics in his place.[17] McCullagh thus became responsible (with assistance from other Junior Fellows) for the teaching of mechanics and physics in the Engineering School.

Just four years later, on 24 October 1847, the College was shocked to hear of his suicide at the age of forty. There appear to have been two concurrent causes, of which one was political disillusion. The country was laid low by famine; Thomas Davis was dead, and with him the prospects of any realization of the idealistic nationalism which McCullagh had embraced; and McCullagh himself had been decisively rejected by the University electors when he contested one of the seats as a Liberal. At the same time he was growing more and more dissatisfied with the reception given to his mathematical work, despite the award of the Copley medal of the Royal Society in 1842. His mind was fertile in original ideas, but he lacked either the patience or the desire to work out their implications in detail; and when Hamilton or others did this he accused them of stealing his ideas and drifted into a condition near to paranoia. The Board sensed his troubles as early as 1844, and offered him a rise in salary of £100 a year 'for the credit he has done the College by his discoveries in Science', but McCullagh declined it, actuated by a pride which may well have been reinforced by class-consciousness, for he was of humble farming stock, whereas most of his contemporary colleagues (and virtually all in the field of mathematics and physics) were the sons of professional men or minor country gentry.

The year 1847 was also that in which the effects of the famine made themselves felt in all sections of the Irish economy, and shortly before McCullagh's death the Board, with their own finances somewhat straitened, received the unwelcome news that the Erasmus Smith trustees felt themselves compelled to cut down severely their grants for the endowed Professorships. The Board decided, therefore, that the special conditions which had been attached to the Professorship of Natural and Experimental Philosophy would be better transferred to a post over which they had full control, whereas the Erasmus Smith lecturership[18] (for which the methods of appointment and conditions of tenure were regulated by Act of parliament) should, with its reduced endowment, become a relatively minor post, centred mainly on the engineering school and held by one of the tutors. They therefore appointed J.H. Jellett, a Junior Fellow of seven years' standing, to the new post of University Professor of Natural Philosophy, while R.J. Dixon, a somewhat senior but less able man, was appointed to the Erasmus Smith post. Dixon resigned on a living a few years later, and the post was then upgraded again to a full-time Professorship, but this did not lead to mere duplication, as a differentiation was gradually established whereby the University Professor concentrated more on the theoretical part of the field and the Erasmus Smith's Professor on the experimental and practical part, so that eventually the former became, in effect, a professor of Applied Mathematics and the latter a professor of Physics.

(vi)

In the Medical School the most important changes during Sadleir's provostship were the succession of William Stokes to the Regius Professorship in Physic, and the development of surgery as a distinct subject and not a mere apanage of anatomy. Macartney, as we have seen, resigned a few months before the death of Bartholomew Lloyd – a loss to the school, but in some respects a relief. His successor, Robert Harrison, though not of the same calibre as a teacher, made an efficient Professor, and his manual of dissection was widely used in America as well as in Ireland. Although he was by training a surgeon, and no doubt felt himself competent to teach the subject, he suggested to the Board as early as 1842 that a separate course in surgery should be started. The board included this proposal among the heads of a Medical Act, which at that time seemed possible, but the Act did not materialize and nothing came of Harrison's proposal till seven years later, when a revised and greatly improved curriculum for medical students was introduced. The delay was due partly to a tedious wrangle with the Royal College of Physicians, who wished to introduce Medical Jurisprudence as a compulsory element in the course; the Board was unwilling to do this because it held that the curriculum was already full enough. Eventually a curious compromise was reached whereby Medical Jurisprudence was accepted as an optional alternative to Practical Chemistry. On this understanding the four-year curriculum introduced in 1849 consisted of eight full courses, each of six months' duration – Chemistry, Anatomy, Practical Anatomy, Materia Medica, Institutes of Medicine, Practice of Medicine, Surgery, Midwifery; and also two half courses – Botany, and either Medical Jurisprudence or Practical Chemistry. In addition, eighteen months' attendance at hospital was required; this included clinical lectures, but all professorial lectures were henceforth to be delivered in Trinity College and not in Dun's Hospital. Granted that such subjects as bacteriology did not then exist, the course has a fairly modern look, the only archaic features being that the courses could be taken in any order, and (largely in consequence of this) the absence of any examinations apart from the final one.

The plea made by the Board that the curriculum was already heavy enough was, of course, partly based on the fact that the student who wished to obtain a medical degree, and not a mere diploma, had to study the full course in arts. In 1839 the medical Professors petitioned the Board for a lightening of this load, a petition which was at first refused. Later in the year, however, the Board made an astonishing *volte-face* and introduced new regulations which permitted the conferring of the M.B. degree on students who had followed only the first two years of the arts course. This broke through a tradition which had existed since the foundation and which was to continue, apart from this single lapse, until 1926, that no other degree (except in Music) could be conferred unless the recipient was already a Bachelor of Arts. The experiment, however, was not a success. Those who graduated in medicine by the easier course were distinguished (somewhat illogically) as holding a degree by diploma, and they were unable to proceed to the degree of M.D. It became apparent that a breach in academic tradition had been made to satisfy a mere handful of students, and in 1846 the Board quietly reverted to the status quo.

A Professorship of Surgery was set up in 1849 to provide teaching for the new course, and R.W. Smith was appointed as Professor. This started off a dispute with the Royal College of Surgeons, which was at first confined to argument over the conditions under which reciprocal recognition of courses might be granted, an argument which reached deadlock early in 1851. But it soon changed to a more serious issue which was disputed with considerable acrimony. Smith's duties were to teach a little surgery to would-be physicians, so as to fit them to be dispensary doctors or general practitioners. But in February 1851 a group of medical students sent a memorial to the Board requesting the foundation of a School of Surgery, that is to say a course to qualify men as surgeons, for although the day was not far off when medicine and surgery would be generally regarded as branches of the same science, it had not yet arrived. The Board, having satisfied itself that a diploma in surgery based on such a course would be recognized by the Army, the Navy and the East India Company, gave its approval and published the details of a four-year curriculum (which naturally shared many courses with the medical curriculum, but gave more time to surgery and anatomy). In 1852 it set up a second chair, whose occupant was to be styled the University Professor of Surgery,[19] and whose chief duty would be to examine for the diploma. J.W. Cusack was appointed to the post, the first Roman Catholic to hold a Professorship which was entirely under the control of the College.[20] Meanwhile, however, there had been a furious protest from the College of Surgeons, which maintained that it had a monopoly of surgical education and licensing, and that the issue of a diploma in surgery by Trinity College would be not merely unfair but positively illegal. In this protest it was supported by its sister college in London. But the Board, fortified by assurances given by the Attorney-General and no fewer than four other barristers, called the Surgeons' bluff by offering to have the case tried before any legal tribunal in the kingdom, and the Council of the College of Surgeons (embarrassed by the fact that Harrison, Smith and Cusack, the architects of the proposed diploma, were all numbered among its Fellows, Cusack having been President only four years earlier) subsided into angry huffing and puffing and accusations of bad manners.[21] No difficulties arose over the recognition of the diploma, and the progress of the school was marked by the institution of the degrees of M.Ch. and B.Ch. in 1858 and 1872 respectively.

Meanwhile, the main development in medicine had been the succession of William Stokes to the Regius Professorship left vacant by his father's death in 1845. Whitley had been failing for some years, and since 1840 William had been acting first as his assistant and later as his deputy. Graves also competed for the chair, presenting the Board with a difficult choice between two candidates who could both fairly be described as of European reputation. Stokes was elected by four votes to three, and it was a fortunate choice, as it was only a few years after the election that Graves began to suffer from the illness which was to lead to his death in 1853. Stokes's professional reputation was at that time based mainly on the first of his two great works on diseases of the chest,[22] and on his appreciation of the valuable information to be obtained by intelligent use of the stethoscope; his name is perpetuated in the phenomenon known as Cheyne-Stokes breathing. He took his duties as Professor seriously from the start. He introduced to Dun's Hospital the methods of clinical teaching which he had helped Graves to establish in the Meath; he instituted the practice of an inaugural prelection to medical students at the beginning of the academic year, in which the broader aspects of medical education were reviewed; he acted as ambassador for the University in London during the drafting of the Act of 1858, which initiated medical registration and set up the General Medical Council; and he was a pioneer in recognizing the importance of preventive medicine, an interest which bore fruit in the institution in Trinity College in 1870 of the diploma in state medicine (later diploma in public health). His abilities were recognized by the award of honorary degrees from Oxford, Cambridge and Edinburgh, and it is probably true to say that he had a larger share than any other one man in establishing for the medical school the high reputation which it held for half a century after his death.

(vii)

Throughout the period covered by this chapter the central core of instruction in the Divinity School, represented by the lectures of the Regius Professor, Archbishop King's Lecturer and their assistants, showed little change; it still rested on the secure foundations laid in 1833. But this core was supplemented by the foundation of three new Professorships in or closely connected with the school. We have already noticed the chair of Biblical Greek, founded as a lecturership in 1838 and raised to a Professorship in 1843. The two other chairs were those of Irish and Ecclesiastical History.

There had been some teaching of Irish in the first few decades of the College's existence (when it was, of course, a subject of considerable practical importance), but it was terminated by Provost Chappell in 1635, and its revival under Narcissus March in 1690 did not last long. Towards the end of the eighteenth century, however, the romantic spirit which was abroad had brought about a widespread interest in Gaelic literature among the Irish gentry, and the age of Ossian had produced some stimulating and original (if at times fantastic) work on Irish antiquities by amateurs. Henry Flood was sufficiently interested in this element in Ireland's cultural tradition to bequeath a large sum to Trinity College for the endowment of a chair of Irish and the purchase of Irish manuscripts. Had he succeeded in his intention Trinity College would have been the centre of the great scholarly movement of the early nineteenth century which, prosecuted largely by professional men and gentlemen of independent means and with the Royal Irish Academy as its focus, established Irish archaeology and Celtic philology on a scientific basis. But Flood's widow, who had a life interest in the bequest, survived her husband by many years, and when eventually she died the reversion to Trinity College was declared invalid on technical legal grounds.[23]

When the question of Irish studies was again canvassed in College in 1835 it was against a very different background. The zeal shown in the seventeenth century by a few Anglican prelates such as Bedell for providing the Irish with Bibles and Prayer Books in their own language and with an Irish-speaking ministry had gradually evaporated during the eighteenth century. Irish had by then become the language not of a nation, but of a dispossessed fraction of it; it impinged less and less on the consciousness of the average Anglo-Irishman, and not at all on that of the bishops imported from England. On any rational calculus it was likely to vanish within a century or so, and meanwhile the saving of souls was less attractive than writing replies to deists or Socinians. But soon after 1830 the tide turned again, and the Irish Evangelicals woke up to the fact that they had on their doorstep a mission-field second only to India in its potential yield; and in Ireland, as in India, it would best be tilled by preaching in the vernacular. The concern of these men with the spiritual welfare of the Irish poor was very real, even if to us today their methods seem crude and their self-assurance staggering. One of the most energetic of them was le Poer Trench, the last Anglican Archbishop of Tuam. He tried to admit only Irish-speaking clergy to his diocese, and when he failed to win the support of his fellow-bishops in an attempt to found a college to train them he turned to the Irish Society (which had been founded in 1818 to spread a knowledge of the Scriptures among the Irish-speaking peasantry) and persuaded them to set about raising enough money to found a chair of Irish in the Divinity School of Trinity College. The first application came to the Board in 1835. It was rather cautiously received, and was frankly opposed by Phipps, whose distaste for the language on political grounds overrode whatever concern he may have felt about the need to rescue the Connaught peasantry from the bonds of popish superstition. The majority, however, consented to the proposal on condition that the Professor's salary should be endowed by public subscription, the College undertaking to give him free rooms and Commons. The subscriptions were slow in coming in, and eventually the Board agreed to provide thirty pounds a year towards the salary if the subscribers could find seventy pounds, but insisted that this sum must be guaranteed before the chair could be established. At last in 1840 this was accomplished, and the Reverend Thomas Coneys was appointed as the first Professor.

Coneys, who held the chair until 1851, and Daniel Foley, who succeeded him until 1861, were both hard-hitting controversialists of an extreme Protestant type, with some experience of quasi-missionary parishes in the west. Up to 1919 all the Professors were clergymen, and their interest in the Irish language, though real enough, was as a means to an end. Foley, and also his successor Thaddeus O'Mahony, were native speakers and converts from Roman Catholicism. Coneys and Foley both compiled dictionaries which were of some use in their day, but only O'Mahony, who helped to edit the *Ancient laws of Ireland*, made any substantial contribution to Irish scholarship. His successors, James Goodman and J.E.H. Murphy, who held office from 1879 to 1919, seem to have achieved little. By this time, of course, the original motive for the foundation of the chair had lost its cogency, and when the Board rescued the appointment from its clerical doldrums and established it in 1919 as a literary Professorship with a better salary they were bringing about a reform which was at least fifty years overdue.

The third foundation was more obviously useful for the majority of ordinands. Although candidates for the divinity testimonium were set some questions on the history of the Church, there was no systematic teaching on the subject, and they had to learn what they could from the dry pages of Mosheim. In February 1850 the Vice-Chancellor (Primate Beresford) wrote to the Board offering to provide £1,000 towards the endowment of a chair of Ecclesiastical History, on the grounds that it would 'be of the greatest use in preserving the great body of the Clergy from being perplexed and carried away by the errors of the times if they were well acquainted with the history of the introduction of those errors'. The members of the Board were somewhat embarrassed by the offer, as they were at that moment trying to head off the Vice-Chancellor from a proposal which he was urging with some enthusiasm: the institution of a fund to facilitate the retirement of elderly Senior Fellows. Nevertheless, they accepted the offer in principle and asked for time to consider details. Six weeks later they wrote to say that they would be glad to institute a lecturership in the subject (not a Professorship), and that they would make up the salary, with whatever came in from Beresford's endowment, to £100 a year; they regretted that they could not afford more. They offered to Beresford, as a *douceur*, the nomination of the first lecturer. A cheque for £1,000 came by return of post,[24] and with it the nomination of Samuel Butcher, a Junior Fellow of thirteen years' standing, and theologically a sound, centre-party man. On the status of the post the Board backed down, for when the regulations were finally drawn up in November the title was silently altered to Professor. Butcher held the chair for only two years, and then succeeded to the Regius Professorship of Divinity. His successors in the chair were all accomplished scholars, and in several cases men of real distinction, right up to the suppression of the chair in 1964. It must be confessed, however, that to the student two of them, Richard Gibbings (1863–78) and H.J. Lawlor (1898–1933) appeared merely as dry and uninspiring pedants.

Meanwhile the general tone of the school had been changing. The tide of evangelicism was flowing strongly, and C.R. Elrington, the Regius Professor, was finding himself more and more isolated; his style of churchmanship was now derided as high-and-dry. The chief thorn in his flesh was Singer, his exact contemporary as a Fellow, who, after his co-option to the Board in 1840, began to use his prestige as a Senior Fellow to promote rather extreme evangelical opinions in the College. This he did mainly through the Theological Society, which, although it dates its foundation from 1830, did not receive any kind of official recognition until 1852 and has no continuous records before that date. In the forties it consisted of a group of high-minded, earnest evangelicals led by Singer, who held prayer-meetings, talks and services, invited in to their meetings prominent controversialists from outside, and were always on the look-out for brands to be snatched from the burning. Singer seems to have received some support from Smith, the Professor of Biblical Greek, for in November 1849 we find Elrington angrily protesting against his students being circulated during the lectures in biblical Greek with notices of a meeting of the Theological Society to be held in Singer's rooms. At the same time he blocked Singer's application for the chair of Hebrew by pointing out that he was already Erasmus Smith's Professor of Modern History, and that the regulations forbade anyone to hold two chairs on this foundation. Elrington carried both his points on the Board; the circulation of leaflets advertising meetings of societies not recognized by the Board was forbidden, and Todd, who was a high-churchman of Elrington's school, was appointed Professor of Hebrew. But it was a Pyrrhic victory, for Elrington died two months later and Singer was unanimously elected to succeed him. The Theological Society was thereupon given some sort of recognition, on condition that the chair was taken by somebody on the College books, but even as late as 1859 it was refused permission to advertise publicly its inaugural meeting. Singer, however, held the Regius Professorship for only two years, as he was appointed Bishop of Meath in 1852. His successor, Samuel Butcher, although he had some evangelical leanings, was a man of wide sympathies, and under his rule the school soon settled down to a new version of the *via media*. In 1861 the Theological Society was brought effectively under the control of the Divinity Professors and was given full recognition.

(viii)

In 1850 the Board decided that the Regius Professorship of Civil Law, which had been held since the death of Arthur Browne in 1805 as a near-sinecure by a Senior Fellow, and usually by one of the dimmer ones, should be transformed into an effective teaching post, and they laid down as qualifications for the post the possession of the degree of LL.D. and six years' experience as a practising barrister. Two separate factors led to this reform. One was the need to meet, at least in part, the unfriendly comment which in that year was widespread in press and Parliament, and to which even Primate Beresford seemed to lend a sympathetic ear, on the excessive salaries of the Senior Fellows. The other was the receipt of a memorial from the Benchers of the King's Inns which suggested that the University should co-operate with them in setting up an effective school of law. Agreement was soon reached between the two bodies, whereby the Regius Professor of Civil Law was to lecture on Civil Law and General Jurisprudence, the Regius Professor of Feudal and English Law on Equity and Real Property, while the Benchers were to establish two Professorships at the King's Inns, one to be responsible for Constitutional and Criminal Law, the other for the law of Personal Property, Pleading, Practice and Evidence. All courses were to be open to students of Trinity and of the King's Inns alike. This arrangement ensured that instruction in all the main branches of law was available, but a curious provision decreed that, whereas a non-graduate had to produce evidence of attendance at all four courses before being called to the Bar, a graduate need have attended only two – a privilege based more on the necessity for preserving differentials than on any real educational principle.

The new Professor of Civil Law was John Anster, selected from among six applicants for the post. He was a poet and man of letters as well as a barrister, and is best remembered today as a pioneer in the translation of Goethe's *Faust*.[25] Nevertheless, he seems to have discharged his duties efficiently, and his colleague, Mountiford Longfield, was as good an authority on the law of real property as could be found in Ireland.[26]

The new arrangements provided a good start for a Law School, but only a start. Students who were reading for the Bar were still hampered by the necessity of paying six visits to London to eat their dinners at the English Inns, for this naturally diverted them from their studies, disrupted the lecture programme and added to the expense of the course. Moreover, although all four Professors held examinations on their courses, success at these was required neither for admission to the Bar nor for the degrees of LL.B. and LL.D., which were still awarded on 'exercises' which had degenerated to very perfunctory formalities.

(ix)

One more Professorship was revived and put on a permanent basis while Sadleir was Provost. This was the chair of Music. The only previous Professor had been the Earl of Mornington, whose tenure from 1764 to 1774 was, as we have seen, in fact, if not in name, honorary. The revival of the chair in 1847 was indicative of an awakening of Dublin from the musical torpor which had beset it since the Union. The Dublin University Choral Society had been founded a few years earlier, thanks to the initiative of some of the Fellows and the encouragement of Provost Sadleir, and its concerts rapidly became popular both inside and outside the College. The Professor appointed in 1847 was John Smith, an Englishman who came to Dublin as a young man and soon established himself as monarch of the small musical world of Dublin, based on his position as organist to Christ Church Cathedral and to the Chapel Royal. He was clearly a competent musician, but he seems to have made up in self-confidence what he lacked in sensitivity and imagination, as is suggested by his only publication, a short handbook which purported to cover all aspects of theory and composition.[27] He received no salary as Professor, and his appointment merely carried with it the grant of rooms in College, a licence to teach private pupils there, and the duty of examining candidates for the musical degrees, for which he received a very small fee. He was not required to lecture, and did not do so, and the extent of his examining duties may be gauged by the fact that during the seventeen years of his Professorship only six persons proceeded to degrees (other than honorary) in music. It was not until Smith was succeeded by Stewart in 1862 that the College became a real centre of musical life; but the appointment of Smith at least provided the formal basis from which this development could later proceed.

(x)

Within the period of five years from 1840 to 1845 a number of apparently minor posts were filled in such a way as to win rapidly for the University an important place in the world of descriptive biology and scientific natural history. Most of these posts related in one way or another to the Museum.

16   The College Museum, *c.* 1819. (W.B.S. Taylor, published in *A history of the University of Dublin*.)

The College had acquired in its earlier years a few objects of value and scholarly interest, but they seem all to have been kept in the Library. The Museum dates from the acquisition in 1777 of a large number of Polynesian artefacts collected by Dr Patten in the course of Cook's last two voyages and presented by him to the College. It was decided that these should be housed in the large room over the Front Gate, hitherto used for disputations, and to this day known as the Regent House.[28] Further acquisitions of a very miscellaneous nature – the stock-in-trade of the eighteenth-century virtuoso – continued to flow in, but with the advent of the nineteenth century the proportion of natural objects increased and that of works of art and craft decreased, so that the Museum took on a mainly zoological and minera-logical character. Although there was no formal post of curator, Whitley Stokes, when he was made lecturer in Natural History in 1816, was, reasonably enough, put in charge of the Museum; but he had too many interests to find time to advance very far the work of cataloguing and arrangement, and by 1840 he was an elderly invalid.

The initiation of a more active policy with regard to the Museum was promoted by the return to Ireland of Thomas Coulter, a botanist of some distinction.[29] Born in Ireland, he graduated in Medicine in 1820, and then, after two years in Paris, moved to Geneva to work under De Candolle, the leading botanist of Europe. It was from Geneva that he published his monograph of the Dipsacaceae. Later he undertook a thorough and somewhat adventurous botanical exploration of Mexico and California, interrupted for three years during which he acted as manager of a mine. In 1840 he returned to Ireland, intending to work on his collections. Unfortunately part of these, together with most of his notes, were lost in transit, but the residue, together with the French plants, dating from his days in Paris and Geneva,[30] forms the nucleus of the College herbarium.

In June 1840 Coulter was appointed Curator of the botanical part of the Museum at a salary of £100, together with rooms and Commons, and a promise of an increase to £300 when Whitley Stokes should retire or die. In return for this he made over his collections to the College, and undertook to accept the chair of Botany if it should be offered to him. He was allowed £50 a year for purchases. He soon extended his curatorial activities to the shells, and perhaps to other parts of the zoological collections, but he died only three and a half years after his appointment. The Board, as a temporary measure pending the appointment of a new Professor of Botany in the spring of 1844, put the Museum under the charge of the Bursar, except for the minerals, which were entrusted to Apjohn.

In March 1844 two candidates presented themselves for the chair of Botany: G.J. Allman, who was no relation to his predecessor (p. 143) and W.H. Harvey. Allman was a recent medical graduate; he was an accomplished naturalist, but his principal interest lay in the field of marine zoology.[31] Harvey, on the other hand, was by far the best botanist in Ireland and already, at the age of thirty-three, an acknowledged authority on South African plants and on the seaweeds of the British Isles. He had, however, no medical education, and although an honorary M.D. for him was hastily rushed through, the Board evidently considered him unsuitable for a chair in the School of Physic. He was, in fact rejected for the chair of Botany because he was merely a botanist. Allman, however, though prepared to take the classes in botany did not want to divert to the curation of the herbarium any of the time which he might be able to devote to his zoological researches. He therefore gave up £100 of his salary; the Board added £50; and Harvey, who was a frugal bachelor of Quaker upbringing, was content to be appointed as Curator of the Herbarium on this small salary. It was a good bargain for the College, for Harvey, by a combination of flair, personal connexions in the botanical world, and extremely hard work, rapidly built up the herbarium by collection, purchase, exchange, and the gift of duplicates from Kew, with whose Director he was on terms of close personal friendship. Meanwhile his books, full of descriptions of new species and illustrated by lithographs drawn and etched by himself, poured out in a steady stream, and by the time he succeeded to the Professorship of Botany in 1855 his name was well known both in America and Europe.[32]

Botany thus provided for, the Board proceeded in the following month (April 1844) to appoint Robert Ball as Director of the Museum. Ball was a clerk in Dublin Castle, but, although almost entirely self-taught, was also a very keen and well-informed naturalist, and had won for himself a commanding position in the Dublin world of amateur science. His career in the civil service says little for either the intelligence or the sense of justice of the Castle bureaucracy, for this obviously able man (who was later to prove a very efficient Secretary to the Queen's University) was for many years refused promotion on the grounds that he was performing his present duties better than any successor would be likely to do, and was then dismissed in the course of an economy campaign on the grounds that he spent all his spare time on science, which was unbecoming in a public servant. The Castle's loss, however, was the College's gain, for he made excellent use of his years of leisure in ordering the zoological, and to some extent the ethnological collections and making of them at once a scientific reference collection and a popular educational exhibit.[33] The care of the minerals and the fossils he was able to depute to others.

He had his hands full, for apart from purchases made from a surprisingly liberal allowance given him by the Board gifts kept pouring in. The variety of these can be appreciated from the entertaining report which he gave to the Royal Commission of 1851.[34] Confining ourselves to gifts from his colleagues we note that Carson presented an albatross, Hart 'two brazen bombshells used by the Sikhs in the late war', Luby the skull of a man executed for murder, McCullagh 'a nutmeg preserved in Goadby's solution', Stubbs 'a mineral resembling plumbago from Whiddy Island'; while Todd's numerous gifts ranged from two mummy crocodiles to three ancient Scandinavian almanacs. From outside the walls the benefactions were even more bizarre: a pug-dog's skull, some bricks and mortar from the Great Wall of China, and a waterproof dress and cap made from the intestines of the sea-lion by the Indians of Nootka Sound. To preserve the rubbish without letting it swamp the basic collections required tact, discrimination and hard work. It also soon needed more space, but this was provided by the Board by the grant of some rooms adjoining the Regent House.

Meanwhile, as we have seen, Apjohn and Oldham had been recruited to the staff of the Engineering School, and though their teaching had to be down to earth they had time to reduce to order the geological and mineralogical collections, which were later to be moved to the new Museum Building when it was completed in 1855. Apjohn, in particular, made a very complete and useful catalogue of the minerals.

Thus, in the course of a decade, the various departments of the Museum were organized in such a way as to become a credit to the College and a help to education and research in the natural sciences. Though there was an element of luck in the right men being available when there was a niche for them, the Board deserves credit for providing these niches, and for furnishing their occupants with reasonable working conditions and relatively generous grants for purchase. Although the biological sciences were not yet regarded as part of a normal university curriculum, except as handmaids to the professions, their incorporation into the curriculum twenty years later was greatly facilitated by the existence of well-stocked and well-ordered museums.

(xi)

In contrast to the numerous developments in the professional schools and the peripheral fields of scholarship which we have just described, changes in the undergraduate pass and honor courses were relatively few during Sadleir's provostship. There were, however, two significant developments. One was the institution in 1849 of a fourth Moderatorship – in Experimental Physics (which was interpreted so as to include a little chemistry and mineralogy). Concurrently with this there appeared for the first time a small element of choice in the Senior Sophister course for both pass and honor students. Astronomy and Ethics remained compulsory, but from the trio of Classics, Mathematical Physics and Experimental Physics the student was allowed to choose two. Thus the idea of choice in the pass course – an idea to be enormously extended later – made its first appearance. So also did another principle destined to be progressively and widely extended – that of professional privileges. Some small abbreviations of the pass course in the sophister years were permitted to students who were concurrently studying divinity or law, and rather larger concessions to those who were studying medicine.

(xii)

The various scholastic developments which have been chronicled above meant that the academic staff in 1851 was not only much larger than in 1837 (fifty-seven against thirty-six), but also much more varied in its interests. Classics was still neglected, but nearly every other branch of scholarship made a fair showing. It is true that the Professor of Civil Law was writing poems and translating *Faust*, that the Professor of Hebrew spent most of his time studying Irish manuscripts, that the Professor of Astronomy worked on pure mathematics, and that the Professor of Botany is remembered for his treatises on marine animals, but the Dublin tradition of scholarship has always been impatient of pigeon-holes. That Basilio Angeli, the Professor of Italian and Spanish, was found a few years later to be doubtfully literate in his own tongue is a more serious criticism, but apart from this one blot the chairs seem to have been well filled, and the names of Humphrey Lloyd, William Stokes, Rowan Hamilton and W.H. Harvey were well known outside Ireland. As a result of this scholarly activity the general atmosphere of the College had changed considerably since 1830. In that year it could have been compared not altogether unfairly to an intellectual sausage-machine, primarily concerned with ensuring a uniform and tolerable standard in its graduates. In 1851 the machine was still intact, but behind it could be discerned the first lineaments of a modern university.

Furthermore, the standard of teaching must have been improved by the fact that this augmented academic staff was in charge of a considerably diminished student body. In 1830 the student numbers had shrunk slightly from their great peak of 1827, but the decade from 1835 had seen them rise again, and on the eve of the famine there must have been some 1,600 students on the books. But the College suffered, along with the rest of the country, from the disastrous years 1846–8, and in 1852 the number of students was less than 1,400 and was still falling. Rather more than a third were ordinands; perhaps a tenth were reading for a moderatorship; rather less than a tenth were students of medicine or engineering; while the remainder, amounting to some 45 per cent of the whole, contented themselves with the pass course in arts. The last two decades had also seen a considerable rise in the average age at entrance: in 1851 only 11 per cent (as against 37 per cent in 1830) entered before their seventeenth birthday, and as many as 34 per cent were aged nineteen or more at entrance. Of these mature students a large number, perhaps half, were likely to have been 'steamboat' men, who kept their terms by examination only. But although the principles of teaching had undergone no fundamental change, the combined effect of the smaller classes and more mature students was to bring about a gradual replacement of the methods of the schoolroom by those of the lecture-room and tutorial as we understand them today.

The atmosphere of calm and somewhat sedate progress which marked the period of Sadleir's provostship was occasionally ruffled by attacks on the College in the press or in Parliament, but in 1848 it had to weather a more severe disturbance. It is easy to see now with hindsight that, whatever might happen in Paris, Rome or Vienna, the prospects of revolution in Ireland were not very bright. Half the population was on the verge of starvation or impatiently awaiting a passage to America, and the leaders of the Young Ireland group were for the most part unpractical idealists, whose minor skirmishes in 1848 would be long since forgotten, even by the most ardent nationalist, had it not been for the literary talent of Davis and Mitchel. We realize now that more lives were to be at stake from cholera in 1849 than from gunshot in 1848. But the men of the time did not view the situation thus. Several members of the Board were old enough to remember the events of 1798 (the Provost was a Fellowship candidate at the time, and Wall had just been elected a Scholar) when the Bishop of Killala (an ex-Fellow of Trinity) had been held captive in his palace by French troops, and Protestant lives were in danger throughout the county of Wexford. And since the majority of the Board had been adults at the time of Waterloo they tended to regard the French as the natural enemies of the Crown. They saw, therefore, not only rebellion but treason in the appeal for help sent in February by the Young Ireland leaders to the newly established republican government in Paris (which was, of course, far too deeply bogged down in its own difficulties even to contemplate foreign adventures), and composed a strongly worded memorial to the Lord-Lieutenant deprecating such attitudes. There was a clamour from many of the graduates to be associated with the memorial, and it soon received 1,400 signatures. It was proposed that the signatories should bear the document in procession to the Castle, but this was wisely vetoed by the police, and it was handed in quietly on 14 March. The Lord-Lieutenant sent a reply, best summarized in modern idiom, to the effect that he couldn't agree more, but he did not propose any particular course of action. There was then a short lull, but for the first three weeks of April the Board was in almost constant emergency session. It offered rooms for two companies of soldiers to be quartered in the College; it gave orders for the Front Gate to be provided with a new, stout door; it sent 'a skilful and confidential person' to Birmingham to buy two hundred small arms, and instructed the Junior Dean to prepare a list of reliable resident students to whom they could be issued; and it ordered the Bursar to lay in 5 cwt of biscuit, 6 cwt of rice,

5 cwt of salt beef and two dozen hams (MacDonnell dissenting because he though the quantities too small).

But the alarm subsided as quickly as it arose. When the Army asked on 20 April for accommodation for a third company of troops they were told that it could be given if absolutely necessary, but that it would be very inconvenient, and that they could not have the Examination Hall as it was required for examinations. Presumably salt beef and rice appeared frequently on the Commons menu through the summer, and in September the Army reluctantly relinquished their free billets at the request of the Board. In 1850 a contract was accepted to keep the small arms in good order for ten pounds a year, but in 1866 they were offered to the Government.

The effect of these stirring weeks can be detected in the next few years in an undoubted swing to the right in the political attitude of the Board. Pio Nono was not the only man to be cured of his liberalism by the events of 1848, and an echo of the strains of the previous year can be heard in the reply which the Board sent in November 1849 to an innocent suggestion from Primate Beresford that a superannuation fund for Senior Fellows might be instituted. The Board felt 'that such a topic would readily be seized on as a part of a great social change or revolution, and that its discussion would soon become involved in extreme difficulties'. The shock which Metternich received in 1846 at the news of the election of a liberal Pope was as nothing to the discovery by the Board of these dangerous ideas in the mind of their hitherto reliable Vice-Chancellor.

8

The Royal Commission and its aftermath

1851–1860

(i)

The appointment in 1850–1 of Royal Commissions to report on the older universities of England and Ireland[1] was the result of some twenty-five years' pressure from an *ad hoc* coalition of radicals, Catholics, nonconformists and utilitarians. The universities were charged by their critics on the one hand with unfair sectarian exclusiveness, and on the other hand with inefficiency, medievalism and sloth. Dublin was far less vulnerable to the second charge than were Oxford and Cambridge but was more exposed to the first, not because of its greater exclusiveness, but because of its virtual monopoly of higher education.

For Dublin at this time treated dissenters far better than did Oxford or Cambridge. All degrees and a few academic posts were open to Catholics, and almost everything except Fellowship was open to Protestant dissenters whose dissent was not too shrill. All this, however, weighed little against the fact that in Ireland dissent was the religion of the great majority. The Anglican exclusiveness of Oxford and Cambridge could, with some slight plausibility, be defended on the grounds that the Church of England was the religion of the great majority of the people and that in London there was a new and rapidly developing university in which dissenters could seek their careers and, by their endowments, build it up to rival its elder sisters. But, in Ireland, Trinity was not merely the university of a minority: it was one to which there was, up to 1850, no alternative, and which provided (leaving aside sectarian issues) the type of education which the majority wanted.

These facts did not worry the true Tory, but to a pragmatic conservative like Peel they presented a challenge, and in 1845 he made a bold attempt to meet it. Three new colleges, non-residential, completely undenominational, and with a modest, but for the time being adequate subsidy from the Government, were established in Belfast, Cork and Galway, and in 1850 the new colleges were joined together as constituents of a federal Queen's University. Something similar to

London University, but tailored to local needs, was thus provided for Ireland, and at the same time the specifically ecclesiastical needs of Catholics were to be satisfied by a handsome increase in the grant to Maynooth. Peel, who had served as Chief Secretary, was no stranger to the strength and complexity of Irish sectarian animosities, but like many rational, centre-party Englishmen he found it difficult to allow for the small place that reason tends to play in determining the attitude of Irishmen. Nowhere did the Queen's Colleges receive a warm welcome. The Board of Trinity was polite to them, but scarcely cordial, and it worked itself into an unnecessary fuss over two minor issues. It first protested to the Primate against the institution of religious instruction (extra-curricular, of course) for Church of Ireland students in the colleges, scenting in this the germ of three rival divinity schools; six months later it tried hard to excise from the charter of the new university a clause which specified that its offices should be in Dublin, on the grounds that its degrees would be confused with those of Trinity. On the first issue the Primate told the Board fairly bluntly not to be silly, and on the second it received from Dublin Castle a message which, though couched in more ceremonial terms, amounted to much the same thing.[2]

But the attitude of the Catholic majority to these new foundations was more important. It was not long before they were denounced as 'godless colleges', and though the term originated with an English High Tory it was soon taken up by Irish Catholics. Not only would their sons receive there no specifically Catholic instruction, but they were liable to be lectured on history or philosophy by a Presbyterian. The colleges were condemned by Rome before they had fairly got on their feet, and the condemnation was reiterated by the Irish bishops in 1850 in the form of a warning to the faithful of their perils, and a strong dissuasive from attending them. Their establishment, therefore, did little to relieve the pressure on Trinity.

The critics exerting this pressure, though mainly concerned with the exclusion of Catholics from Scholarships and Fellowships in Trinity College, did not disdain to pick on small administrative flaws when they could find them, or could plausibly invent them. The reforms chronicled in the last two chapters were enough to convince any detached observer that as far as charters, statutes, educational practice and the use of income were concerned, Trinity College, though open to criticism on points of detail, needed no radical reconstruction. In Oxford and Cambridge the picture was very different. A fair amount of reform had, it is true, taken place during the past fifty years, but the combination of vested interests in high places, a hard core of dogged conservatives, and absurdly restrictive statutes which even moderate

203

reformers were curiously reluctant to change, had seen to it that the course of reform had been limited and slow. All the same, debates in the House of Commons on these aspects of Oxford and Cambridge seldom failed to assume an Irish dimension. Some of the criticism was designed more to exhibit the wit of the speaker than to expose any real defect. The fact that Liberal opinion had been solidly behind the repeal of the celibacy statute did not prevent Bernal Osborne (a Liberal M.P.) from deriding in 1845 'the gigantic scheme of collegiate connubiality presented by T.C.D.', with few Fellows in Hall and fewer in Chapel, and a Fellow regarded as a 'good catch' by Dublin matchmakers. Since any scheme for Irish university reform needed money Trinity was often scrutinized to see whether some of its revenues could be diverted to other uses, and in such an inquiry the large incomes of the Senior Fellows were an obvious target. The Board could fairly point out that all salaries except the smallest implied definite duties (which was by no means the case at the English universities), and that averaged over his whole working life a Fellow earned no more than a moderately successful professional man. But in spite of this the sight of an elderly clergyman drawing a large income and not even using it to cut a dash, but enjoying bourgeois comfort in Leeson Street and salting down the surplus for his heirs, was calculated to sharpen the pen of any radical pamphleteer.

When Lord John Russell announced in April 1850, that Royal Commissions were to be appointed to inquire into the finances and educational work of Oxford and Cambridge he made no mention of Dublin, conscious, no doubt, of the way in which his predecessor in office had burnt his fingers on Irish University problems. But he was soon nagged into changing his mind, and a similar commission on the University of Dublin was announced late in 1850 and appointed in the following year.

(ii)

The Board reacted to the news with uneasiness but no real alarm. The Registrar immediately wrote to the Lord-Lieutenant, declaring that the members of the Board 'do not shrink from the fullest enquiry, but can see no good results likely to arise from a Commission the members of which are disqualified either by want of knowledge or their pre-conceived notions from forming a fair judgment', and suggesting thirteen names from among whom it was hoped that the Commissioners might be selected. These included three bishops, five judges, a doctor, and as many as three astronomers. The Lord-Lieutenant sent a polite reply indicating that the Government was thinking along the same lines, and in fact, when the names of the Commissioners came to be announced, it transpired that five of the six were drawn from the list submitted by the Board.

The Commissioners were Richard Whately, Archbishop of Dublin, Maziere Brady, Lord Chancellor of Ireland,[3] William Parsons, third Earl of Rosse, James Wilson, Bishop of Cork, Mountiford Longfield, Professor of Feudal and English Law in the University, and Edward Cooper, of Markree Castle, Co. Sligo. Three of them (Brady, Wilson and Longfield) were Dublin graduates, the other three graduates of Oxford, though Rosse had spent two years as an undergraduate in Dublin before migrating to Oxford. Politically they were confined to a fairly narrow band of the spectrum, from easy-going Tory to middle-of-the-road Whig.

Whately needs no introduction to the reader. Although an Oxford graduate, he knew the College well as its Visitor. He had mellowed somewhat from the clever but brash stranger, alarmingly young for an Archbishop, who had burst upon the Dublin scene twenty years earlier, but still had a restless and inquiring mind. He had seen with some satisfaction the dilution of the High Tory attitude which was conspicuous in the College when he arrived, and he can be summed up as a perceptive but not unfriendly critic. Brady was a reliable Whig lawyer who had recently reaped his reward by being appointed Lord Chancellor. He had a keen amateur interest in science, especially geology, and was a prominent figure in the educational world, being one of the Commissioners for National Education and the first Vice-Chancellor of the new Queen's University. Wilson was older than the others. He had graduated in 1802, but had remained for several years in College as a resident Master, presumably earning his living by tuition. After ordination he had spent twenty years in administrative posts, as Secretary first of the Association for the Promotion of Christian Knowledge and later of the Irish Ecclesiastical Commission. He was the only Commissioner whose name had not appeared on the Board's list of suggestions, and he was, perhaps, to some extent *persona non grata*, as he had been closely associated with Whately in his scheme for a Divinity College (p. 165) and had been named in the abortive charter of 1839 as one of its governors.[4] Rosse came of a family of landowners in the midlands who, after a shaky start a hundred years earlier, had established for themselves a reputation for philanthropy and benevolent management of their estates, coupled with a cautiously liberal attitude in politics. He himself was a man of very wide cultural interests, but his fame rests largely on the fact that a few years previously he had built in the grounds of Birr Castle, helped only by the estate workmen, what was to remain for half a century the largest

205

telescope in the world. The astronomical discoveries which he made with it, especially on the spiral nebulae, were of great importance, but the skill and ingenuity which he showed as an engineer in casting and grinding the mirror and devising the supports for it and the tube were at least as remarkable. Longfield was a former Fellow and the first holder of Whately's chair of Political Economy, who had recently been made a Commissioner of encumbered estates. For a number of years he had acted as adviser to the Board on legal and parliamentary matters. Cooper was a country gentleman of a well-known Sligo family, who had travelled in the Near East as a young man and written a book about it, served eleven years as M.P., and was now an amateur astronomer second only to Lord Rosse, with a more modest but useful observatory at his home, Markree Castle.[5]

They formed an able team, whose findings were likely to command respect. They appointed as their secretary W.N. Hancock, an energetic young lawyer from Co. Antrim, who had just finished his five-year term as Whately Professor of Political Economy, and was later to prove a voluminous writer on economics, finance, education and law. He certainly played as large a part as most of the Commissioners in framing the questionnaires, and probably also in drafting the report.

(iii)

The Commission started work in September 1851, but within three months of its first meeting both the Chancellor and the Provost died. The consequent changes, however, made little difference to the nature of the body on which it was to report. The absentee King of Hanover was replaced as Chancellor by Primate Beresford, who had, as Vice-Chancellor, been doing his work for him for the past twenty years, and Francis Blackburne, the Lord Chief Justice, was appointed as Vice-Chancellor. Beresford's election was not, however, unanimous; three members of the Board voted for Lord Derby and one for Lord Rosse.

Franc Sadleir's successor as Provost was Richard MacDonnell, a man of similar outlook and only twelve years younger, and the change led to no obvious alteration in policy. But MacDonnell was appointed only as a *pis aller*. The other names mentioned were those of Todd, Humphrey Lloyd and Longfield. An interestingly frank review of the candidates is given by William Fitzgerald, at that time Professor of Moral Philosophy and later Bishop of Killaloe, in a letter to Archbishop Whately which has somehow found its way into the Bernard papers.[6] Though written on 23 December 1851, it is not entirely full of the Christmas spirit:

Lloyd is not very much of a theologian nor does he often preach, but when he does he preaches well ... He is known through Europe as an experimentalist, and he has a

206

character for rigid integrity combined with gentle manners . . . MacDonnell would not on the whole be a *very* bad appointment. He was a barrister, but his then arrogant manner drove the attornies away. He began in College as a reformer, but has not spirit and activity (he is clever but *very* lazy) or perhaps honesty to carry it on. Still, he has a strong dash of liberality about him and would do a liberal thing to make a show . . . a good bursar and the only one I know who visited the College estates. He is vain and conceited, and his deportment at Divine Service is so grossly inattentive as to give some scandal, but this is a common fault with the senior men in College . . . His worst tendency is to jobs, and especially family jobs . . . Anyone, I do believe, would be better than Todd . . . I have a great regard for him but I am convinced he would throw the whole weight of his position into the Tractarian scale . . . Longfield would no doubt be a good appointment though he is apt to be a little wrong-headed. His appointment, being a layman, would create some panic as if great changes were contemplated.

Evidence that the appointment was made primarily on political grounds is to be found in letters from the Lord-Lieutenant (Lord Clarendon) to Lord John Russell.[7] On 16 December he wrote: 'The seven Senior Fellows . . . are not very eminent men. There are one or two who are liberals or call themselves so. I would think the appointment should not be political and the object should be to do what is best for the College.' On 21 December he wrote again: 'Dr MacDonnell will be the best selection out of indifferent material for Provost. He is of rather liberal politics and was always friendly to Catholic emancipation and the National system of education. The Archbishop is rather inclined to support Dr Longfield, who is certainly the ablest man, but I know if we were to appoint a layman it would raise the greatest uproar, and we could be accused of working to insult and degrade the Church, even though Longfield is a Tory. We might do the College a little good, and ourselves an infinity of harm.' One suspects that between the two letters Clarendon had received a hint from London to drop his silly idealism and have regard to political realities. In fact MacDonnell made a fair Provost, though with some tendency to push unsuitable people into jobs.

The Commission worked steadily for eighteen months and sent in its report early in 1853. Its most active members were the Lord Chancellor, the Archbishop and Professor Longfield, as they alone lived in Dublin. Lord Rosse (who was doubtless preoccupied by his duties as President of the Royal Society) attended only three meetings, but he was mainly responsible for the very detailed and searching questionnaire addressed to the Professor of Astronomy. The answers make rather sorry reading, for Hamilton, with the full consent of the Board, had for years devoted nearly all his time to pure mathematics, and had deputed most of the routine work of the observatory to an elderly and apparently not very efficient assistant.

Here and there at other places in the evidence one can detect a

similar note of embarrassment, as when attempts were made to demonstrate the usefulness of the medieval 'exercises' for degrees, which
were still carried out in a perfunctory manner, or when it had to be
explained that the Bursar's emoluments, amounting to £3,400 in the
past year, were higher than the average. Elsewhere there is, as one
might expect, some window-dressing on the part of the less distinguished Professors. It is doubtful, for example, whether Professor
G.S. Smith's classes in biblical Greek read quite as widely as he gave the
Commissioners to understand in 'Poli Synopsis, Wintle on Daniel,
Hengstenberg's Christology, Masius on Joshua, Bengelii Gnomon,
Oldhausen's Commentaries' and the other weighty works which fill
eight lines of his evidence, or that his lectures on 'the critical labours of
Scholz, Lachmann, Tischendorf, &c.' were quite as profound as he suggests. But on the whole the Commissioners' questions were answered
candidly, clearly and honestly, and the report, with its evidence, forms
a rich source of information, from which we have freely drawn, about
the daily life of the College in mid-century.

The reception accorded to the Commission by members of the College in positions of influence or authority was in general friendly; for
they realized, perhaps with some complacency but also with justice,
that no very widespread dissatisfaction existed with regard to their
teaching or administration, and that nobody who commanded the ear
of the Government was likely to call for very radical changes.[8] In
contrast, therefore, to the cry of 'To your tents, O Israel!' which rang
round Oxford, and to the bitter conflict between reformers and conservatives which rent Cambridge, Dublin displayed a united front and
a reaction which was, if at times a bit starchy, on the whole courteous.
Naturally there can be detected in some of the replies an undercurrent
of resentment at the meddling of busybodies in the machinery of an
institution which worked perfectly well, and a feeling that the University, which could fairly be said to have reformed itself during the
past twenty years, could be trusted to continue in this path by its own
efforts without the help of external commissioners. These feelings were
pithily summed up by George Salmon (later Provost, but then quite a
junior Fellow) in his reply to a circular from the Commissioners which
asked for suggestions:

When called upon by the Commissioners [he wrote] to furnish them with *information*, I
have, in common with other members of the University, cheerfully taken considerable
trouble to procure them what they desired; but when asked to offer *suggestions* I am
bound to remember that the University already possesses a Governing Body to which
the Crown has, by Charter, intrusted the direction of the studies of this institution. I
believe, moreover, that this body . . . is the most competent to pronounce ultimately on
the merits of any suggestions for its improvement. I trust that the result of the

Commission will be to bring before the Board many valuable ideas, to which it will be their duty to give attentive consideration; but as for any suggestion which I may have myself to make, I think it more respectful to the Heads of the University to offer them to them directly, rather than through the intervention of an external body.'[9]

The correct, if somewhat priggish tone of Salmon's reply must have caused some heart-searching among those of his colleagues who had seen in the Commissioners' query a spacious exercise ground for their several educational hobby-horses. Richard Townsend, for example, prefaced 9,000 words of suggestions with an apology that illness and other business had precluded the possibility of his entering into particular details, and necessarily confined him to 'remarks of a very general nature'.[10]

(iv)

Salmon was not alone, however, in the confidence which he reposed in the Board. A very striking feature of the evidence, even when all reasonable allowance has been made for the desire of younger men to win the good opinion of their all-powerful elders, is the picture painted by nearly all the Junior Fellows and the majority of the Professors of the Board as an efficient, sympathetic and progressive governing body. Even the rather sharp complaints which arose from the under-privileged – the non-tutor Fellows and some of the worse paid Professors – were focused on their own specific grievances and were not enlarged into a general denunciation. 'There is scarcely a day', writes Townsend, 'they [the Board] meet for business, on which minor alterations and improvements are not discussed and effected; useless and unnecessary regulations rescinded; existing impediments gradually removed; abuses by degrees corrected; and all the minor details of the different Courses of Study continually arranged and adjusted.' 'During the entire period of my connexion with the University,' declared J.K. Ingram, 'the Board have steadily and vigorously carried out sound and well-considered improvements in almost every department of our system.' G.J. Allman, the Professor of Botany, was confident that 'the active interest manifested by the present Board in all that tends to promote progressive improvement is a sufficient guarantee that the time and mode of bringing these suggestions into operation may be safely left in their hands', and Haughton, a Fellow of only eight years' standing, and of vigorous and independent views, believed that 'the power of altering and improving the Course of Studies has been wisely and judiciously exercised by the Board of Trinity College; and that it is, on the whole, best left in their hands'.[11]

There were a few dissentient voices, but the feeling of general satisfaction in 1852 is undeniable. It was, however, to be of short duration; less than six years later the Board was to be vigorously assailed from all sides, and not least by the Junior Fellows. The temporary harmony of the early fifties arose largely from the fact that the average age of the Board was at this time exceptionally low. In 1852 the oldest member was Wall (sole survivor of the Board of 1830), but although he had headed the list of Senior Fellows for nearly five years he was only seventy-two. The new Provost was sixty-five and after him came a remarkable gap, for Humphrey Lloyd, who stood next[12] on the list of Fellows, was only fifty-two, while the remaining members of the Board (Moore, Luby, Todd, W.D. Sadleir and Hart) were all in their forties. This is an age-distribution in a governing body which would cause no comment today, and appeared to cause no comment at the time, but it would have appeared preposterous to our grandfathers. It was, in fact, a very temporary phenomenon; fifteen years later six of these eight men, fifteen years older, were sitting round the same table, and both the new recruits were over fifty.

Two distinct circumstances combined to produce the juvenile Board of 1852. The first was the strict observance from 1812 to 1840 of the celibacy rule, as has been mentioned earlier. This led to a sharp rise in the number of resignations among Junior Fellows, and temporarily reversed the trend which had been reducing the frequency of retirement to a country living. In the decade 1829–38 no fewer than fourteen men resigned their Fellowships, and this removed from the College most of the potential sexagenarian Fellows of 1852. Their places on the Board were filled by men elected to Fellowship between 1829 and 1835, who, by the time they had reached an age to contemplate marriage, had seen the probable end of celibacy in sight. The second circumstance was a fortuitous statistical chance; the incidence of death among Fellows was higher in the second quarter of the nineteenth century than in either the first or the third. Even if there had been no resignations at all the Board in 1852 could have mustered only two septuagenarians.

In consequence we find that at this date, whatever grievances individual Junior Fellows may have felt, there was no general sense of a war between the generations – a feeling which was to dominate College life fifty years later. It was not surprising, therefore, that those who were satisfied with the Board in practice should have been slow to question the theory of its constitution, and neither in the report nor in the evidence was there (with one exception to be mentioned shortly) any speculation on the question whether the College would continue to be properly and efficiently governed by a Board recruited purely on a basis of seniority. Five Fellows, admittedly very junior ones, had resigned on livings within the five years preceding the Commission's report, and the Commissioners may perhaps be excused for failing to foresee the rapid change which was coming over the Fellowship body. The increase in the number of Fellows, the relative decline in the income of the livings, the abolition of the celibacy rule and the increasing expectation of life all combined to produce the same result. Whereas J.L. Moore, elected Fellow in 1829, had to wait only fifteen years before reaching the Board, Charles Graves, elected in 1836, had to wait twenty-five years, and for William Roberts, elected in 1841, it was thirty-five years. Eventually the fantastic situation was reached by which Benjamin Williamson, elected Fellow in 1852, was still, forty-four years later and now aged sixty-nine, a Junior Fellow with no voice in the government of the College. He was governed by his seniors, and he must bide his time.[13] By a curious irony it was in the very year in which Williamson was elected Fellow that MacDonnell wrote to the Commissioners opposing an increase in the number of Fellows on the grounds that it would defer till too late the co-option to Senior Fellowship, which he described as 'the principal prize'. 'If it were a settled thing that a man was to remain in the fag, and with only the income of a Tutorial Fellowship, for the entire of his life, it would cease to be sought for, as it is at present, by some of the very best men of each class.'[14]

One man alone had the prescience to point out to the Commissioners the probability of the forthcoming change. This was Charles Graves, then a Junior Fellow:

Should the present system continue, and my own life be prolonged till I reach the age of eighty, I shall, perhaps, find myself one of seven Senior Fellows whose united ages amount to 500 years. I fear we should make but a sorry Board, unable to keep pace with the rapid progress of men and things at the close of this century. Age and experience are indeed qualifications which add authority to official rank; but the former may be possessed in a degree which is not compatible with due energy and promptitude of action; and experience itself, so far as it related to things gone by, may be little better than actual ignorance.[15]

Graves's estimate was on the low side, for when he reached the age of eighty (he was by then no longer a Fellow) the united ages of the seven Senior Fellows amounted to 510, and the youngest member of the Board was within a few months of his seventieth birthday. But the Commissioners, impressed with the efficiency of the Board as it stood, seem to have considered this development too remote to call for action, and their report, unlike its two successors, recommended no change in the constitution of the governing body.

(v)

The general tone of the report was very complimentary to the University. The Commissioners found that 'numerous improvements of an important character have been from time to time introduced by the authorities of the College, and that the general state of the University is satisfactory. There is great activity and efficiency in the various departments, and the spirit of improvement has been especially shown in the changes which have been introduced in the course of education, to adapt it to the requirements of the age.' Compliments only slightly less gracious were paid to Oxford and Cambridge in the reports of their Commissioners, but they were followed by some trenchant criticism and by recommendations for far-reaching reforms. In Dublin, however, although there were numerous recommendations they were all on points of detail, and in so far as they implied criticism this was directed as much at past governments as at the College.

These recommendations were set out in thirty-four numbered paragraphs at the end of the report (all but one being unanimous), but some other suggestions were made as *obiter dicta* in the text. It will be convenient to consider them under three heads: those which required an Act of Parliament; those which could be implemented by the College itself; and those which required a Queen's Letter to sanction a change in the statutes.

Since the College was, within a few years of the appearance of the report, to be criticized for its tardiness in initiating the introduction of some of the recommended reforms, it should be recognized that the Government's record in implementing those recommendations which required an Act of Parliament was no better. Nearly all the recommendations under this head were acceptable to the Board, and a private member's bill to implement them was introduced in the House of Commons in May 1856. But the Government declined to facilitate it, and it never got past a first reading. Parliament, however, though it moved slowly, eventually gave most of the concessions which had been recommended. The vexatious clauses of the School of Physic Act were repealed in 1867, by an Act which did away with religious restrictions on the University chairs in the school, rationalized the method of election of the King's Professors and repealed the sadly out-of-date regulations relating to clinical lectures. In the following year the necessity to take the oaths of allegiance and abjuration at graduation was abolished, but it was not until 1885 that legislation was passed relieving Irish law students from the necessity of eating dinners in London. Finally, certain taxes and stamp duties which the Commissioners regarded as an inappropriate burden on scholarship were abolished in the early sixties, but with Gladstone as Chancellor it was too much to hope that the Exchequer would not extract a quid pro quo. This took the form of the withdrawal of an annual Treasury grant of £360, which dated back to the time of Queen Elizabeth, and of the salaries of the Professors of modern languages, which had hitherto been paid by the Crown.

(vi)

The recommended changes which could be implemented by resolution of the Board (in some cases requiring also the consent of the Visitors) were of a very miscellaneous character. One of them, however, stood apart from the rest as of interest to the general public: this was the suggested creation of awards open to dissenters which should be comparable in value and prestige to foundation Scholarships. The operation of religious tests in determining elegibility for Scholarship was in some respects rather anomalous. The test was not, as it had been for degrees before 1794, enforced by an oath repugnant to even an elastic Catholic conscience, but depended simply on the knowledge (based sometimes on hearsay) on the part of the electors of the candidate's religious beliefs and practices. A student who did not attend the College Chapel was, by general consent rather than by any specific statute, considered ineligible, although a very few Catholics who were prepared to put in an occasional appearance at an Anglican service seem in fact to have been elected to Scholarship in the period 1795–1810.[16] A slightly larger number of Protestant dissenters were elected in the same period, thanks either to the Board's turning of a blind eye or to their willingness to receive the sacrament in Chapel at least once; but after about 1810 the attitudes both of the Board and of the dissenting churches became more rigid. One or two of the dissenters murmured, and queried the basis for their exclusion,[17] but it was not until 1843 that the question was pressed to a legal decision. In that year Denis Caulfield Heron was examined for Scholarship, won high marks, but was passed over as one who openly professed Catholicism. He appealed to the Visitors, who at first refused to entertain his appeal, but were later compelled to do so by a *mandamus* from the High Court. That they dismissed it surprised nobody, but whether they did so on sound legal grounds is not entirely clear. Their judgment was, of necessity, based on 'the whole body of College charters and statutes', for they had to concede that although the Caroline statutes very specifically debarred from Fellowship anybody *qui Pontificia religioni, quatenus a Catholica et orthodoxa dissentit, et Romani Pontificis jurisdictioni per solemne et publicum juramentum non renuntiaverit*, there was no corresponding clause in the chapter on the Scholars; nor was there any specifically Anglican clause in the Scholar's oath. It could be fairly commented that the Visitors (who were the two Archbishops of the Church of Ireland), no matter how conscientiously they set about their task, would not easily be able to judge the case dispassionately. Justice may have been done, but not very visibly. Nevertheless, the verdict was generally accepted as an interpretation of the existing law, and the efforts of the dissatisfied dissenters were switched in the direction of legislative reform.

It was natural, therefore, that the Commissioners should discuss the desirability of opening the foundation Scholarships to students of all the churches. They were divided on the point, and therefore made no recommendation, but they unanimously suggested that 'a reasonable number of Exhibitions', open to students of all denominations, should be 'given in the same manner as College Scholarships but without-making the holders members of the Corporation'.[18]

In this they were echoing the near-unanimous attitude of those members or former members of the College who had expressed an opinion on the matter. Provost MacDonnell, indeed, was prepared to throw open the foundation Scholarships, but the Chancellor, the Vice-Chancellor, the majority of the Board, the Bishops of Meath and Ossory and several of the Junior Fellows all reacted to the idea with disapproval – always on the grounds that the Scholars were 'part of the foundation'. In vain did the Provost demonstrate that this was a phrase of little meaning; to some of the Fellows it had, if no practical meaning, a symbolic significance, while others were convinced that to do away with the religious tests for Scholarships was an open invitation to abolish them for Fellowship also. Within twenty years all these distinctions were to become meaningless, but in 1852 they seemed very real, even to intelligent and quite moderate conservatives, and the Commissioners, wisely enough, backed the idea of founding what were later to be called non-foundation scholarships – a programme which was supported by most members of the College, though not in every case with enthusiasm.

The first four non-foundation scholars were elected in 1855, the list being headed by Thomas Maguire, who was later to become the first Catholic Fellow. In this and the ensuing seventeen years, until the distinction between foundation and non-foundation Scholars disappeared in consequence of Fawcett's Act in 1873,[19] a total of 38 non-foundation Scholars were elected, as against 249 Foundation Scholars – a proportion only slightly lower than that which dissenters bore to members of the Established (or recently disestablished) Church in the whole student body.

(vii)

The remaining recommendations which could be implemented by internal legislation were too miscellaneous to permit of easy classification, and too numerous to be dealt with seriatim; we confine ourselves, therefore, to a mention of a few of the more important. A number of suggested changes in courses and examinations were carried out over the next fifteen years, the only one to be rejected was that which suggested the incorporation of a modern language and 'some elementary economics and civics' as compulsory elements in the pass course. This smacked too much of utilitarianism for the Board of 1853; and although modern languages were eventually included in 1876 and economics in 1908 they were optional, not compulsory. An elaborate proposal for the rationalization of most of the degrees was quietly ignored; it was too much to expect a University 260 years old to treat its traditional accolades in such a Whiggish manner, especially as Oxford and Cambridge, with an equally irrational system, showed no signs of changing. Some administrative and financial changes were made rather slowly and grudgingly, the delays being due, at least in part, to tortuous arguments over the supposed vested interests of relatively junior Fellows in the emoluments of offices to which they might one day hope to succeed. Finally, in regard to a recommendation that the statutes should be codified and consolidated the Board was distinctly evasive. Promises alternated with postponements, and eventually the project was forgotten. The task was more difficult and complex than the critics represented it to be, but it was not impossible; and the unsatisfactory state of affairs lasted till 1926 whereby the fundamental law of the College and University could only be deduced by reading backwards through a long collection of documents, noting which clauses of an earlier statute had been repealed by a later one.[20]

(viii)

The matters set out in the last two sections occupied the attention of the Board intermittently for the next twenty years or so, but in the four years immediately succeeding the appearance of the Commissioners' report much of its energies were devoted to preparing drafts of Queen's Letters and to arguing with the Chancellor or the Government, as well as amongst themselves, over their contents. These drafts were designed not only to give effect to some of the statutory changes recommended

215

by the Commissioners, but also to clear away some statutory provisions dating from the seventeenth century which were absurdly restrictive or completely inapplicable to the Victorian world. The Government at first gave the College no guidance as to which of the recommendations it was expected to enshrine in the draft, and the Board, with what turned out to be a somewhat illusory sense of freedom, began to pick and choose between them.

Reasonably enough it decided to deal first with the less controversial matters, but it was not as easy to identify them as at first it seemed. On some issues the Provost differed from the rest of the Board; on others the Junior Fellows (who were reluctantly allowed to discuss the draft more or less at the last moment) dissented. The Chancellor, who was in constant touch by letter with the Provost and with several of the Fellows, was on many issues inclined to support the Provost against the Board, or the Commissioners against both. He served as the channel of communication between the College and the Government, and on the whole he shows up well in the role of honest broker, and in some respects of constitutional monarch. When he thought the Board's decisions unwise he said so, but if the Board persisted he yielded gracefully.[21]

By March 1854, less than nine months after the publication of the report, a draft had been agreed and transmitted to the Chancellor, who forwarded it to the Government, indicating that it had his approval. The Government naturally referred it to its law officers. Unfortunately for the College Maziere Brady, one of the Commissioners, was still Lord Chancellor of Ireland, and in September he wrote to Beresford criticizing the draft severely, partly on account of the large number of recommendations which had been ignored, and partly because (following precedent) it took the form of amendments to the existing statutes and earlier Letters Patent instead of a new code of statutes. The Board replied, justifying itself at great length, but failed to convince the Government, and on 28 September Palmerston informed Beresford that the Government could not proceed in the matter until Brady's objections had been met. Compromises were laboriously hammered out and a clause inserted in the draft committing the College in principle to a consolidation of the statutes, and on 1 March 1855 the Queen's Letter was issued.

The greater part of it is devoted to the repeal of obsolete clauses in the Caroline statutes, and the number of provisions stemming directly from the recommendations of the Commission is relatively small. The Board, in many cases subject to the consent of the Visitors, was given power to regulate admission to the Library, details of the examinations for Fellowship and Scholarship, and some other matters which hitherto had been precisely regulated by statute. The chairs of Greek and of Hebrew were no longer restricted to Senior Fellows, nor the office of Librarian to Fellows. And the number of lay Fellowships was increased from three to five.

(ix)

This last provision represented a very diluted version of the recommendation by the Commission that the obligation to take orders should be completely abolished. Even as little as fifteen years later this might well have been accepted by the main body of College opinion, but in making the recommendation in 1853 the Commissioners were too far in advance of their times to win much support. The Primate was strongly against the idea and many of the Fellows hesitant or lukewarm. The reaction of the College was merely an expression of the feeling, very widespread in mid-Victorian times, that the chief role in education should be entrusted to the clergy, and the suggestion that dissenters might prefer to entrust their sons to the tutorial care of laymen rather than clergy of the Established Church was easily refuted by a statistical analysis of the actual choice of tutor that had been made. The Commissioners realized, however, that even if the general obligation were to be removed there was a strong argument for having a clerical majority on the Board, since it controlled, *inter alia*, the affairs of the Divinity School, and they added a recommendation to this effect. But it was a clumsy compromise; one had only to envisage the situation when a lay Fellow was passed over for co-option to the Board because no lay place was vacant, and had to watch a clerical Fellow junior to him being co-opted instead, to realize that such a regulation would not be tolerated for long.

The limitation of the lay Fellowships to five in number was a compromise which represented fairly well the public opinion of the day. But many of the newly-elected Fellows appeared rather to favour the views of the Commissioners, for the two new lay places were rapidly snapped up and there still remained a demand for more, which could be met only by dispensations by the Crown. These dispensations were no new phenomenon; they had been granted on at least three occasions during the eighteenth century,[22] and as the nineteenth century progressed the applications gradually became more frequent. The Chief Secretary usually sought the Board's approval before issuing the dispensation, and this approval was usually given, though on some occasions grudgingly and with a dissentient minority. By 1855, although the Senior Fellows were all in orders, there were seven of the Juniors who were, and would remain laymen (Hart, Toleken,

McDowell, Michael Roberts, Ingram, Shaw and Williamson). By 1867 (when it was not yet a foregone conclusion that the ordination rule would be abolished) the number had risen to ten.

It soon became clear that new problems arose as a result of this shift. There were several offices, ranging from Senior Dean to lecturer in Divinity, for which only clerical Fellows were considered eligible; the Board found its choice limited, and the lay Fellows began to complain of being deprived of these possible supplements to their tutorial income. But more embarrassing was their tendency to seek remunerative employment outside the College in ways which their clerical colleagues (to whom most of these temptations were not available) held to be unsuitable for Fellows. The general attitude of the Board was that a Junior Fellowship in itself (rewarded as it was by only a minute salary) was compatible with any other respectable form of occupation, so long as the Fellow resided in Dublin and appeared regularly in the College; release from this obligation could be obtained only by leave of absence from the Crown. To such leave the Board usually consented; G.F. Shaw, for example, was permitted to take up the post of Professor of Physics in University College, Cork, and some years later John Gwynn was given leave of absence to act as Warden of St Columba's College. The trouble arose when a Fellow who was also a tutor tried to combine this with other occupations. At the same time as Shaw took the chair of Physics at Cork Michael Roberts was offered the chair of Mathematics, but when the Board refused him leave to hold this along with a tutorship he declined it. In 1853 the Board, with the consent of the Chancellor, ruled that a Fellow could not hold a tutorship and at the same time practise at the Bar; that did not prevent T.E. Webb ten years later from repeatedly seeking relief from the rule, but the Board stood firm. It had also ruled in 1848 that a lecturer or Professor in the University could not simultaneously hold a chair at one of the Queen's Colleges, but it abandoned this stand in 1859 by allowing Cairnes to be Professor of Political Economy in Galway as well as Dublin. The coming of the railway had made such an arrangement less objectionable, and as both posts were on any standard part-time ones the pluralism could be reasonably defended.

The real trouble, however, arose with George McDowell, elected Fellow in 1839 and given a dispensation from holy orders the following year on the grounds that he was reading for the Bar. It was against his double life as tutor and barrister that the regulation of 1853 was directed, and presumably he retired from the Bar. But by 1857 he was working for an insurance company, and Ingram, supported later by H.R. Poole and Humphrey Lloyd, complained to the Board that this was incompatible with a tutorship. McDowell replied that his insurance business occupied only 'two or three hours daily, after 3 o'clock', by which time he had finished his tutorial business. The Board declared itself satisfied, but J.K. Ingram, incensed on hearing that McDowell had added to his duties by taking on the post of receiver to the Tipperary Bank in liquidation, persisted and attacked on a broader front. The position was objectionable, he maintained, for three reasons. A tutor will take on very few pupils and will decline appointments as examiner or honor lecturer if he can earn higher rates of pay in business; the public will assume that College duties must be very light; and, above all, 'a Tutor should regard the care and instruction of his pupils and the cultivation and diffusion of science or literature as the business of his life'. The Board rather weakly indicated that it didn't like the situation but didn't know what it could do, but the threat of a visitation induced McDowell to give up his insurance business at the end of 1858. Next year, however, when the new offices of Senior Tutor came to be filled McDowell applied for one. The Board passed a resolution that the office was incompatible with McDowell's work for the bank, but he seems to have talked the Provost into acquiescence, for a week later he was elected Senior Tutor by the Provost's casting vote. An air of unreality was given to the argument by the fact that neither side could afford to admit openly that the office of Senior Tutor was a near-sinecure, and this enabled McDowell to take up his legal work again (apparently without censure) when the affairs of the bank had been settled.

This sordid little episode is worth recording because in Ingram's manifesto there emerges for the first time the concept of a full-time academic post, with the implication that whatever spare time a don may find within a reasonable ration of working hours should be devoted to 'the cultivation and diffusion of science or literature'. It is a concept which has gradually won acceptance, though the framing of rules to impose it equitably is a problem which plagues most universities to this day.

(x)

Soon after the issue of the Letters Patent of 1855 the Board was rewarded by a message from a former Chief Secretary congratulating the College on 'the judicious steps it has taken and by the wide extension it has given in many branches to the education which it affords', and on having 'met in a becoming spirit the requirements of the time'. Lulled by this flattery it turned its attention to other matters, and appeared to forget that there were still five fairly important recommendations of the Commission (as well as a few trivial ones) about which it had done no more than hold inconclusive discussions. These were the reorganization of tutorial finance; the foundation of Fellowships in Divinity of limited tenure; the appointment of an external auditor and publication of the College accounts; the payment of the Bursar, Proctors and other College officers by salary instead of by poundage and fees; and the abolition of the University Senate. For none of these did the Board manifest any enthusiasm, and to several they were frankly opposed.

It will be recalled that the tutorial system was extensively remodelled in 1834 in such a way as to apportion the lecturing on a rational basis and to make the tutor's emoluments depend not on the size of his chamber but on his seniority. In their evidence presented to the Commission the tutors stoutly defended these arrangements as working perfectly, but the Commissioners had two criticisms. In the first place they very fairly suggested that such an important matter should be regulated by statute and not, as for the past eighteen years, by a purely voluntary agreement. But they were also to some extent responsive to criticisms made by the Provost and some of the more elderly graduates, who said that the quasi-paternal relationship provided by the old system (whereby the individual tutor took his pupil's tutorial fee *in toto* and was responsible for the major part of his teaching) had now disappeared. It seemed that a financial incentive was necessary to call into being this 'quasi-paternal relationship'. The Commissioners recommended, therefore, that only three-quarters of each tutorial fee should be thrown into the common fund and the remaining quarter paid to the pupil's own tutor. After much hesitation the Board declared itself half-convinced; it adopted the recommendations, but cut the tutor's direct share of the fee from a quarter to an eighth.

The idea of seven-year Fellowships in Divinity originated with Longfield. It was designed to restore the 'healthy circulation' of Fellows going out to College livings, and to provide teachers in the Divinity School who would have a vocation for pastoral work, in place of mathematicians who had perhaps taken orders somewhat unwillingly. If it were adopted the non-tutor Fellowships were to be abolished. The idea had much to commend it, but the Chancellor, as well as the Board, was strongly opposed to having two types of Fellow, one appointed *ad vitam aut culpam* and the other for seven years only, and it was argued, perhaps rightly, that the new Fellows would, almost as much as the non-tutor Fellows whom they were to replace, form a 'nursery of discontent'. It was agreed that the idea could be pursued if the new recruits were to be called Divinity scholars, not Fellows, but in successive schemes the value of the proposed scholarships got more and more reduced and eventually all that happened was that in 1859 two theological exhibitions were founded which helped divinity students who had completed their course to stay on for another year or two to read for their B.D.

But although the theological aspect of the proposal was in this way drastically watered down, something like the original idea, but in secular terms, was agreed on in 1858. Two Studentships, free from any religious test, were to be filled each year from among those who had just taken Moderatorship; they were tenable for seven years and carried a salary of £100 a year. Although no explanation of their purpose was given it seems fairly clear that they were designed to support men working for Fellowship (or, in the case of dissenters, qualifying themselves for academic posts elsewhere), for the only condition attached to them was that they should be vacated on election to Fellowship. One was earmarked for mathematics and one for classics, but whatever marks might be won in a second Moderatorship were also to taken into account. They provided, therefore, a strong incentive for the aspiring Fellow to take a double Moderatorship.[23] Although this was criticized by a few of the Fellows as tending to frustrate real excellence in any one subject, there were more to welcome the incentive to a broad-based education. Mathematics and Experimental Science, Mathematics and Philosophy, Classics and Philosophy – these were the favourite combinations, but as the diversity of Moderatorship increased new combinations became possible; Classics was several times combined with History, and in 1878 William Wilkins was bold enough to combine Mathematics with Modern Literature and to do well in both. In 1889 the tenure of Studentship was reduced from seven years to five, but otherwise no change in the conditions was made until 1919, when the duty of giving some pass lectures was imposed on the student. In 1924 the tenure was reduced to a single year, and in 1948 Studentship lost its identity by being merged in a general reorganization of research awards given on graduation.

The new Studentships and theological exhibitions both left unsolved the problem of the non-tutor Fellows. Everybody was agreed that the experiment had been a failure, but it was very difficult to devise a scheme whereby they could be abolished without injuring the interests of the tutors, or of the Fellowship candidates, or of the non-tutor Fellows themselves. Eventually a statute was agreed on for their gradual elimination, and by 1871 they had been reduced to from six to two; thereafter the number oscillated between two and four until they were in effect abolished by the radical changes in the system of remunerating Fellows introduced in 1920. Although the Crown must take the blame for having invented the non-tutor Fellowships in the first place, it was greed on the part of successive generations of tutors and timidity on the part of successive Boards that prevented the nuisance from being eliminated much earlier.

To the remaining recommendations dealing with finance the Board displayed a vigorous and obstinate opposition. With regard to publication of the College accounts, the Commissioners had remarked that 'the Board have given such full information with respect to the College revenues in answer to our inquiries that the continuous publication would not lead to any greater disclosure of the affairs of the College'.[24] But the Board seemed to think that this argument might as well be used by a dentist in favour of a long series of extractions; in its opinion a distasteful operation had been rendered tolerable only by the thought that it would not be repeated. And the proposal that the College officers should commute their income from degree and other fees for fixed salaries was represented as preposterous, and indeed revolutionary; the Board believed that such a change would be 'a precedent for revolutionary measures of the most dangerous character', and would constitute an admission that the officers had hitherto acted illegally in receiving such fees, while one of its members (Todd) declared that he would sooner sacrifice any other part of his College emoluments rather than this. Such unreasonable opposition to reforms that were very much in the spirit of the age was to render the College wide open to attack a few years later, and, as we shall see, it had to some extent to retreat from its uncompromising position.

The last of the Commissioners' recommendations for statutory change which requires comment is the rather surprising one that the University Senate should be abolished. Admittedly the Senate had been for well over a century a purely ceremonial body, but to suggest its abolition for that reason was to ignore Macaulay's sapient advice to legislators: to think little of symmetry and much of convenience, and never to abolish an anomaly simply because it is an anomaly. Besides, the abolition of the Senate would mean the total reconstruction of the formulae and procedure for the conferring of degrees, and one did not need to be a very inflexible traditionalist to deplore this. The Board, therefore, rejected this piece of officious tidy-mindedness and at first proposed to strengthen the Senate by giving it power to elect the Chancellor (subject to veto by the Board) and to initiate addresses, and also to revise its constitution and rules of procedure so as to conform with current usage and to eliminate the many ambiguities and inconsistencies of its existing rules.[25] But this common-sense programme soon became eroded by an attitude expressed by Brady, the Lord Chancellor, when he declared that he 'would very much dread the Senate becoming a permanent debating body within the College' and by the Primate when he inquired whether his vote would count for no more than that of 'any country curate or dispensary doctor' who had acquired a master's or doctor's degree.[26] Democratic ideas were hastily abandoned, and the clauses forbidding the Senate to discuss any business except that brought before it by the Board were re-enacted in unambiguous terms. The Senate was still conceded the right to elect the Chancellor, but now only from a panel of three names chosen by the Board. This was a singularly inept decision, as the machinery thus proposed combined the disadvantages of oligarchy and of democracy without the merits of either, and was in practice a continuing source of embarrassment and confusion. At every vacancy in the Chancellorship the Board would write to Lords A, B and C asking their consent to be nominated, but it was usually an open secret that the Board favoured the election of A. B would hear this and decline nomination, so that D had to be found. C, in innocence, would declare that he was flattered and honoured, but a few days later would write an agitated letter saying that he had only just heard that his old friend Lord A was a candidate, and that he wouldn't think of opposing him. Eventually a panel would be patched up; there might be one genuine opposition candidate, who would receive at best a handful of votes, and a third who would assure the voters that he did not wish anybody to vote for him. This remarkable system of pseudo-democracy lasted till 1976.

But the Queen's Letter which finally appeared in 1857 contained an even more startling provision: the Senate was to be a corporate body with a seal, distinct from the College, with the right to own property and to sue and be sued. Where this idea originated cannot now be ascertained. If it was intended as an attempt to give the University an existence distinct from that of the College it was singularly half-hearted, as the new body thus incorporated was put firmly under the control of Trinity College. The incorporation served merely to raise false hopes among some members of the Senate, who imagined that if it could not implement or even initiate academic changes, it might at least discuss them. But this was firmly ruled out of order, except on the rare occasions when the Board, anxious to obtain the backing of a wide body of opinion for one of its decisions, invited the Senate to give it. Nor could the Senate even elect its own officers; at the first meeting of the new body Jellett was proposed as its Registrar, but the Board insisted that the Registrar of Trinity College must *ex officio* be Registrar of the Senate. After some rather tense discussion the question was adjourned, but later the Vice-Chancellor decided in favour of the Board. The incorporation was, therefore, a dead letter from the start, for a corporation with so little independence of action found no occasion on which it could use its corporate powers, and never acquired any property.

(xi)

The Government, as we have seen, had been quick enough to save itself £200 a year by accepting the Commissioners' recommendation that the Professors of modern languages should in future be appointed and paid by the College. The Board, however, hesitated before accepting this new responsibility, and it was not only on financial grounds. For one of the Professors concerned was at this time under a cloud.

Evasio Radice, who had been appointed Professor of Italian and Spanish in 1824, had been ill for some time in the mid-forties, and in any case had entered into other commitments which made it difficult for him to carry out his University duties. A Signor A.C. Marani was found to deputize for him, and when eventually Radice resigned in January 1849, Marani felt confident that he would be appointed Professor. The Board took no action until October, and then it nominated to the Lord-Lieutenant not Marani but Basilio Angeli, who appears to have been a protégé of MacDonnell. Marani immediately wrote to the Board impeaching the truth of several statements in Angeli's application, but the Board, satisfied apparently by Angeli's reply, dismissed the complaint as the malice of a disappointed rival. Two years later three of the Junior Fellows (Galbraith, Haughton and Ingram), convinced either by their experience of Angeli as a colleague or by Marani's insistence, asked the Board to suspend Angeli, pending investigation of Marani's charges. The Board refused. In February 1854, MacDonnell, now Provost, injudiciously proposed Angeli for an honorary LL.D., whereupon the three Fellows brought forward in their own name the charges against him. No action was taken until November 1855, when the Board heard the case. This rested principally on a translation into Italian made by Angeli in 1849 of Sir Robert Kane's inaugural address at Queen's College, Cork. It was claimed that the translation abounded in solecisms, and indeed illiteracies, and that Angeli was an adventurer, previously employed as a salesman of stucco figures, with only the merest smatterings of a literary education. The Board was convinced and asked Angeli to resign; he refused and appealed to the Visitors, who held, however, that as the appointment was made by the Crown they had no jurisdiction. The Board, therefore, asked the Lord-Lieutenant to dismiss him, but meanwhile Angeli had instituted proceedings for libel and slander against Galbraith. The case was heard in July 1856 at Athy, and for five days a jury of stolid

224

Kildare citizens had to listen to imported Italian witnesses swearing alternately that certain phrases were gross errors or legitimate Tuscan pleonasms. Not suprisingly the jury was unable to agree, and the case had to be re-tried in Dublin in November. After interminable bickering between counsel as to the admissibility of certain evidence the jury indicated that they thought that the plaintiff had made no case that required answer, and judgment was entered for Galbraith.[27] Angeli was, accordingly, dismissed by the Lord-Lieutenant in January 1857.

Fortunately for the defence it was not until after the case had closed that it transpired that a close parallel could be found in Manzoni's *I promessi sposi* for a phrase of Angeli's which had been singled out for especial ridicule – *signori di ambo i sessi*. But although some of the charges against him were exaggerated it seems clear that he was a plausible adventurer quite unsuited to his post, and that the *curriculum vitae* which he had supplied contained several false statements.

Against this background it is natural that the Board should feel little enthusiasm for the teaching of modern languages, and in 1855 they decided to continue for five years the salary of I.G. Abeltshauser, the respectable if uninspired Professor of French and German, but to make no provision for Italian and Spanish. After two years, however, the vacuum caused by Angeli's disappearance made itself felt, and in 1859 Marani was appointed as lecturer. In 1862 he was raised to the rank of Professor. No effective action to implement the recommendation of the Commissioners for separate chairs of French and German was taken until sixty years later, for although a separate chair of German had existed since 1866, French was no sooner freed from its link with German than it was tied up with Italian and Spanish in a chair of Romance Languages.

(xii)

If the Board imagined that with the establishment of the new Senate in 1857 it could forget about the Royal Commission and settle down once more to routine business it was soon to have a rude awakening. For the year 1858 was to prove as trying as 1848, not from threats of external revolution but from internal revolts, hostile press campaigns, attacks in Parliament, riot,[28] and financial distress.

At its first meeting in January the Board was faced with the problem of the Library roof, which had been declared to be unsound and even dangerous. Consultation disclosed a wide variety of views among the experts as to the best remedy, and it was only after a good deal of discussion that the proposals of Deane and Woodward were accepted.

These involved the complete reconstruction of the roof, bringing it externally above the line of the balustrade, and internally replacing the stucco ceiling with a much loftier, semi-cylindrical, wooden barrel-vault. By this means the height of the gallery was considerably increased and some much needed shelf-space was thereby gained. The reconstruction, which was not completed till 1862, provides a rare instance of a happy outcome resulting from Victorian insensitivity to the canons of Palladian taste. A room which had hitherto been elegant and splendid was invested with something of the mystery and majesty of a Gothic cathedral; and even the Georgian pundits of today are forced to admit, somewhat ruefully, the success of a reconstruction completely 'out of character'. But to the Board at the time it was just one more charge on an exchequer severely depleted by the economic distress which had followed the famine and the heavy expenses of building and equipping the Museum Building.[29]

But worse was to come. On 16 February, as we have seen, the new Senate held its first and rather contentious meeting. As the senators dispersed, doubtless arguing hotly the various constitutional points at issue, they noticed a gathering crowd in the south-east corner of the Library Square. The centre of attraction was the Revd Daniel Foley, Professor of Irish, who was delivering a spirited oration from his window on the first floor of the Rubrics, and those who came within earshot soon learnt that he was denouncing the Board with a vigour which he normally reserved for popish superstitions.

Foley had been appointed in 1852, despite misgivings on the part of some of the Senior Fellows, on the recommendation of Robert Daly, Bishop of Cashel, an extreme Evangelical and a patron of the Achill Mission. Although Foley had started life as a shop assistant in Tralee he was a man of some literary ability and probably a good teacher. He published an elegant and compact English–Irish dictionary, which certainly filled a need, and if it is to be criticized it can only be on the grounds of outrunning its ostensible purpose; for although the preface declares it to be based on Johnson's dictionary, omitting only such words 'as are of unusual occurrence in the English language, and therefore unnecessary for intercourse with the peasantry of Ireland', the words which Foley deemed to be necessary for this purpose included 'xerophagy' and 'apogee'. He also stimulated one of his pupils, C.H.H. Wright (later to become well known as an orientalist and a learned but controversial theologian in the Protestant interest), to publish while still an undergraduate a simple but clear grammar of modern Irish. Foley, however, like many Kerrymen before and since, seems to have found it difficult to temper his uninhibited eloquence to the dignity of academic life; 'whatever difference of opinion', his obituarist tells us,[30] 'might exist as to the correctness, no doubt could be felt as to the sincerity of his convictions, which were urged with a hearty zeal amounting to enthusiasm'. Only a month earlier he had been censured by the Board for criticizing it in the course of the sermon he had preached as one of the necessary acts for the degree of D.D. But this was only a premonitory tremor. In the harangue from his window he started with the familiar complaint of the inadequacy of his own salary, and then went on to accuse the Board of robbing the College, setting themselves up as a Venetian oligarchy and imitating the despotism and tyranny of the French Emperor. Nor did he confine himself to generalities; three Senior Fellows were denounced by name – Moore and Luby for their ignorance and Todd for his ritualism. When summoned before the Board for a more severe censure he skilfully raked up for his defence all the available scandal and got away with a very partial apology by threatening to publish the whole controversy in the press.[31]

In this threat he touched on a sensitive nerve, for the Board was already embarrassed by a hostile press campaign, which had started with rather scurrilous attacks in the provincial papers, but was soon to be taken up in polite but firm terms by the *Dublin Evening Mail*. The main charges were the maldistribution of the College income, with excessive emoluments going to the Senior Fellows and totally inadequate sums to the non-tutor Fellows and to some of the Professors, and also the secrecy with which the Board transacted its affairs, neither the accounts nor the changes in statutes made by Letters Patent being open to inspection by the public. The press attack culminated in a blistering, and in some respects unbalanced and malicious attack in the May issue of the *Dublin University Magazine*. Its tone was so wounding and its allegations so damaging that the Board was with difficulty dissuaded from taking an action for libel; it contented itself with informing Messrs Hodges and Smith that if they wished to retain their appointment as University booksellers they could no longer print the *Magazine*. The editors seem to have realized that they had gone rather too far, as two much more temperate articles of an explanatory nature appeared later in the summer.

Meanwhile, however, the Board found itself attacked from within the walls. Two of the very Junior Fellows, G. F. Shaw and R. B. B. Carmichael, contributed to the controversy in the *Evening Mail* by writing letters upholding the claims of the non-tutor Fellows. For this they were severely censured by the Board, on the grounds that, whatever might be the rights and wrongs, for a member of the College to discuss in the public press the propriety of his seniors' actions was a grave breach of discipline. Shaw and Carmichael appealed to the

Visitors against the censure, and the case was heard in public. It ended in a draw: the Visitors upheld the censure on Shaw but annulled that on Carmichael on the grounds that his letter was essentially a recital of facts which had been misrepresented in a leading article.[32]

By this time the Board felt itself besieged on all sides, for the Chancellor was making gentle but embarrassing inquiries, and the Government had begun to indicate that recommendations of the Commission which commanded such widespread support must be taken seriously. Accordingly it began to sue for peace. A long letter of self-justification was sent to the Chancellor, and a list of proposed reforms was drawn up and communicated to the Junior Fellows and to Lord Naas, the Chief Secretary. The resulting negotiations were intricate, tedious and somewhat unedifying, involving as they did arguments not only over proposed salaries, but also over compensation for loss of prospective rights. But at last agreement was reached, and the main heads were embodied in a decree of the Board and Visitors issued in December. The Junior Fellows were somewhat cynically bought off by the creation of two new offices to be known as Senior Tutorships. These were to carry a salary of £800 a year (approximately the maximum emolument of a tutor), but although they were to lecture and examine they were not to be burdened with pupils; they were instead, to 'supervise the tutorial lectures', a task which hitherto had been performed entirely satisfactorily by the tutors' committee.[33] The creation of these offices meant that everybody moved up two places and two of the non-tutor Fellowships could be abolished immediately. On the vexed question of the payment of officers by fees and poundage the Board reluctantly gave in, though it took care to point out that the Provost and Senior Fellows were voluntarily resigning 'a portion of their yearly income which has been pronounced by the tribunal to be their clear and undoubted right'.[34] Henceforth the degree fees were to be paid to the Cista Communis and the Proctors paid modest salaries proportioned to their duties; similarly the Bursar and Senior Lecturer were to be paid by salary instead of poundage. The delay of five years in assenting to these changes, and the fact that the assent was clearly given only under duress, cost the Board dear in its reputation with the public.

With regard to the publication of accounts and statutory changes, however, it rightly judged that public excitement on these issues would subside as quickly as it had arisen. Nothing was said about publication of Queen's Letters; the Board held, reasonably enough, that the Crown had the power and the right to publish them if it really seemed desirable. The accounts were to be open to inspection by the Junior Fellows, but no further. A second auditor, not a Fellow, was to be appointed by the Board and approved by the Visitors.[35]

Despite all these controversies the Board was able to find time to introduce in 1855 and subsequent years a number of changes in the academic courses, some of them, but not all, being in response to recommendations of the Commissioners. The scope of the entrance examination was enlarged so as to include arithmetic, history and geography. Foundation Scholarships were after 1855 no longer to be confined to Classics; a certain number were earmarked for 'Science', which was a combination of philosophy, mathematics and physics. The principle of choice in the pass course was in 1856 extended to a small extent into the Junior Sophister year, and at the same time a significant change was made in its title. Hitherto it had been 'the undergraduate course', implying that it was the norm, and that honor courses were unusual frills. It now became 'the ordinary course', indicating that it was only one option, though doubtless the most popular. And in fact the moderators were by this time forming 15 per cent of the total number of B.A.s.

This was in part due to an increase in the variety of the subjects in which Moderatorship could be taken. We have already seen that the original trio of 1834 – Mathematics, Classics and 'Ethics and Logics' – had been supplemented in 1849 by a Moderatorship in Experimental Physics. In 1858 its scope was greatly enlarged by the inclusion of a larger element of chemistry and of some geology, palaeontology, botany and zoology, and it was re-christened a Moderatorship in Experimental and Natural Sciences. In such a wide field the examiner could not probe very deeply, but before we condemn the course as superficial we might pause to consider whether the modern student of biology, saddled with fairly exacting requirements in biochemistry, statistics and computer programming, and expected to have a nodding acquaintance with tectonic plates and quaternary history, is really less widely stretched. At all events the polymath mid-Victorian world was satisfied with this arrangement for thirteen years, and it was not until 1871 that a division into separate courses in Experimental and Natural Science was thought necessary.

The only subject on the course in which there had hitherto been no teaching was zoology. Having no traditional connexion with medicine it was slow to win recognition as an academic subject, and although its teaching had been recommended by the Commissioners its inclusion in a moderatorship course as early as 1858 was due mainly to its place in the list of subjects which could be presented at the examination for the Indian Civil Service (of which more later). Whitehall evidently thought it desirable that some, at least, of its District Officers should know the difference between a leopard and a cheetah, and should use their leisure in collecting insects for museums at home. Robert Ball, the Director of the Museum, was the only man in College in 1855, when plans for an Indian Civil Service class were first mooted, with any wide knowledge of zoology, but he was far too busy to take on extra duties, and was, in fact heading for the sudden death in 1857 which his friends attributed to overwork. As a makeshift, Harrison, the Professor of Anatomy, was appointed lecturer in Zoology in 1856, but he died only a year after Ball so that it was possible to look around for somebody to do double duty as lecturer in Zoology and Curator of the Museum. The Board found such a man in E.P. Wright, who, though his academic training was in medicine, was a first-class naturalist with very wide interests.

At about the same time as the scope of honor teaching in the sciences was widened new opportunities were given to the student of humanities who found the classical tradition too narrow. The election to the Provostship of MacDonnell in 1852 left vacant the chair of Oratory which he had held for the past thirty-six years, but for the latter part of that time as a complete sinecure, no lectures having been delivered since 1833. He was succeeded by John Kells Ingram, a Fellow of only six years' standing, who had enough youthful enthusiasm to take the post seriously. He started lecturing, but in 1855, dissatisfied with the narrow field implied by the title of his chair, he enlarged the scope of his lectures with the approval of the Board to include English Literature, and was thereafter designated Professor of Oratory and English Literature. With surprisingly little opposition it was agreed that these lectures could be made the basis of a new moderatorship course, but English Literature alone being reckoned as too 'soft' for a degree course it was stiffened by the addition of Modern History, Jurisprudence and Economics (the last named being detached from the Ethics and Logics course, into which it had been inserted, presumably under Whately's influence). The prescribed reading in these varied subjects was not very adventurous: Smith, Mill and Senior in economics; in jurisprudence selections from Blackstone and Smith on contracts; the history of England and France up to 1789; English literature from Shakespeare and Bacon to Johnson and Goldsmith, with some simple philology. A few years later the *terminus ad quem* of Modern History was cautiously moved forward to the peace of Amiens, and Chaucer and Spenser were added to the literary course, but it was not until 1869 that, following Dowden's succession to the chair of English Literature, the Romantics were admitted. With Ingram, Anster and Cairnes as lecturers the course must have been quite a stimulating one. It persisted to 1873 before being broken up, and although some of the weaker candidates probably took it up as a soft option, more attractive than Ethics and Logic, the fact that the top men of its first two years were Peacocke, later Archbishop of Dublin, and Gibson, later (as Lord Ashbourne) Lord Chancellor of Ireland, shows that it attracted some talented students as well.

(xiv)

With so many new subjects crowding into Moderatorship it was natural that the Fellowship examination should also come under scrutiny from this point of view. The ascendancy of mathematics over all other subjects rested on no statutory basis, but had gradually been accepted as a convention which, being now about three-quarters of a century old, had almost the force of law. Several of the Fellows were dissatisfied with it, but the conservatives could argue that this was the field in which Dublin had won fame over the past generation, that if Oxford ignored mathematics Dublin had the right to cherish it, and that a system which produced scholars like Hincks and Wall in the Semitic languages, Kennedy in classics, Elrington and Lee in theology, Haughton in the natural sciences and Todd in Irish studies, despite their early mathematical training, could not be considered very constricting. Nevertheless, by 1855 the more far-seeing members of the College had begun to have some idea of the rate at which knowledge was growing and of the impact that this must have on academic courses; they were conscious of the fact that despite the occasional stars among the Fellows in a wide variety of subjects the majority were mediocre mathematicians. In consequence, many of the chairs had been filled by second-rate men. In 1855 the Professor of Philosophy (E.B. Moeran) could only be described as a clergyman with some interest in the subject; the Professor of Modern History (J.L. Moore) had just resigned, having been given the chair in 1850 as a consolation for having been eased out of the Regius Professorship of Laws, and having followed the example of Professors of History ever since 1778 in publishing nothing whatsoever on the subject; and when, in the same year, the Regius Professorship of Greek was reorganized and thrown open to Junior Fellows on the understanding that it would be a fulltime job, no better occupant could be found for it than Thomas Stack. The Board, therefore, decided that a change must be made, and after several discussions they agreed on a scheme which was to last for many years with only minor modifications. A definite scheme of maximum marks was now drawn up; there were to be 1,000 for mathematics and mathematical physics, 600 for philosophy, 400 for 'the sciences of experiment and observation' and 900 for classics. The scales were still weighted in favour of mathematics, but far less than before. At the same time it was agreed that Latin should not be used 'as a medium of communication' in any part of the examination, but a proposal in 1856 that the classical part of the examination be conducted entirely by written papers was defeated, and a significant part of the examination in all subjects was still conducted *viva voce*. The insistence on detailed knowledge of prescribed texts also lingered on, so that the examination still preserved some archaic features. Nevertheless, these changes had a profound effect in widening the scope of Trinity scholarship. Moderators in Classics and in Philosophy presented themselves at the Fellowship examination of 1859 for the first time for many years,[36] though without success, and the Fellows elected in 1859 and 1862 were both mathematical graduates, though the former (W.H. Ferrar) turned immediately to philology, and may well have won his Fellowship partly on prowess in classics. In 1863, however, the new Fellow was T.E. Webb, who had graduated in philosophy, and in 1864 Mahaffy, with a double Moderatorship in Classics and Philosophy. Thereafter it could be said that a reasonably equal balance was held between mathematics, classics and philosophy, and a supply of Fellows with a sound knowledge of these subjects was available for the next half-century.

(xv)

One more advance in the academic field during the eighteen-fifties deserves notice: this is the foundation of two new chairs of oriental languages.

Until quite recently readers with access to the gallery of the College Library would come across marble busts here and there, stuffed into alcoves or hidden behind piles of books, for the busts exceeded by half a dozen or more the pedestals in the Long Room below. Among them was one of a youngish man of rather prim aspect, in neat mid-Victorian dress, and bearing on its base the rather startling inscription 'Siegfried'. It is not, however, to be regarded as an eccentric aberration of Wagnerian culture, but as a by-product of Macaulay's reforms of the Indian administration. The committee of which he was the driving force had recommended that recruitment of the Indian Civil Service should be by competitive examination, and among the subjects recommended as suitable for the examination were Sanskrit, 'the great parent stock from which most of the vernacular languages are derived', and Arabic, which from its commanding position in the Moslem world had contributed to many of the languages of India, and which had a classical literature worth study for its own sake. And the first Professor of Sanskrit was Rudolf Thomas Siegfried.

17 Rudolf Thomas Siegfried. Lecturer in Sanskrit and Comparative
Philology, 1858–63. (J.R. Kirk, Trinity College.)

233

He was a product of the rapidly developing schools of comparative philology at Berlin and Tübingen, who had decided to come to Britain to study the Celtic languages. Todd had discovered him in Wales, and had brought him to Dublin with the promise of a post in the Library, where he did useful work in cataloguing some of the oriental manuscripts. In 1859 he was appointed as lecturer in Sanskrit, and was raised to the rank of Professor in 1862. But the following year he died in his early thirties, leaving behind only one paper, on the Gaulish inscriptions of Poitiers, to indicate the extent of his unfulfilled promise. Gentle, unassuming, and devoted to his subject, he seems to have inspired general affection, and a large part of the intellectual world of Dublin turned out to attend this young grammarian's funeral.

Meanwhile the chair of Arabic had been filled in 1855 by the appointment of William Wright, a graduate of St Andrew's who had studied in Berlin and Leyden, and who had an extensive knowledge of the Semitic languages. He got the teaching off to a good start, but after a few years wearied of his teaching duties[37] and departed, first to the library of the British Museum and later to the chair of Arabic at Cambridge. He was succeeded in 1861 by a more colourful figure in the form of Mir Alaud Ali, who held the chair for thirty-seven years and soon became, as 'the Mir', a well-known and well-liked member of Dublin society. A photograph survives showing him arrayed in a costume like a rich brocade dressing-gown, though doubtless his everyday wear was more sober. He was a native of Oudh, but married to an English wife. Although his mother-tongue was presumably Urdu he was judged to have the best knowledge of Arabic among the applicants for the post, and the addition of Hindustani in 1866 and Persian in 1873 to the title of the chair shows that his linguistic expertise was considerable. He had no pretensions to original scholarship but gave efficiently the type of teaching that was needed by the Indian Civil Service candidates.

The promptness with which the College responded to the new opportunity for its graduates by establishing chairs in these rather exotic tongues was due largely to the initiative shown by Haughton and Galbraith, two of the more active and outward-looking of the Junior Fellows. They were quick to see that the new category of 'competition-wallah', even if looked down on at first by the old hands nominated by personal influence, provided a new outlet for Dublin graduates seeking an employment that was at once adventurous and commensurate with their abilities and social status. It is thanks to their efforts that Trinity sent a steady stream of graduates to India as long as British rule lasted.[38] Too steady, indeed, for some, for one of the architects of the competitive system was dismayed to find that the service, instead of

18 Mir Alaud Ali. Professor of Arabic (and later also of Persian and Hindustani), 1861–98.

creaming off the best graduates of Oxford and Cambridge, was becoming filled up with 'crammed youths from the Irish universities or commercial schools'.[39] Trinity was unmoved by the ready assumption, made here neither for the first nor for the last time, that anybody but a graduate of Oxford or Cambridge must be crammed; it could retort that if unsuitable 'crammed youths' were accepted it was the fault of the examiners, and in any case its position was vindicated by its designation in 1877 as one of the institutions in which successful candidates were permitted to spend their probationary year and receive further instruction.

At about the same time as they set up the classes for the Indian Civil Service Haughton and Galbraith started another class, which, through no fault of theirs, was less successful. This was for commissions in the Royal Artillery or Engineers. The Crimean War revealed a serious shortage of officers with the necessary technical knowledge, and it was decided as a temporary measure to award commissions on the results of a competitive examination. Despite some efforts by the conservatives of the War Office to sabotage the scheme it worked well for a few years, and during the six years of its effective operation Trinity secured eighty-three commissions or cadetships. But when the emergency had passed the conditions were made less and less attractive for university graduates, and eventually the class was closed down.

(xvi)

In the course of the decade covered by this chapter two new buildings were erected in the College, the Museum Building and the Campanile, and although they are separated from each other by some two hundred yards there is a historical connexion between the two.

We have seen that in 1837 the red-brick range forming the west side of the Library Square had been demolished, thus uniting the Library and Front Squares. The effect was to give an unprecedented sense of space (for it was by far the largest academic enclosure in the British Isles) but also to some extent of bareness. Less than ten years after this change the Board was conscious of the necessity for a further building to provide space for the Engineering School, the rapidly growing Museum and various other academic needs. Naturally enough there was some dispute as to whether the new building should once more divide the Front from the Library Square or whether the new distant view from the front gate should be preserved. In 1849 Decimus Burton was asked for his views on the matter. He came out strongly against building on the line between the Front and Library Squares; he recommended the south side of the New Square as the best site, and his advice was taken.

Burton, however, did not envisage complete continuity between Front and Library Squares; he suggested that 'a small but highly architectural object with a central arched opening' should be erected on the line of division, 'connected north and south by an open colonnade or handsome piers and railings' to the two eastern corners of the Front Square. In 1852 this idea was realized in part. Primate Beresford, soon after his election as Chancellor in 1851, indicated that he would like to commemorate the occasion by a substantial gift to the College, and he fell in with the Provost's suggestion that it should take the form of a Campanile to house the College's bells, since the 1798 Chapel, unlike its predecessor, had no steeple. It was agreed that it should be sited where Burton had suggested for his 'object', and Lanyon's design was accepted. The foundation-stone was laid in December 1852 – a courageous date for an outdoor ceremony involving speeches, prayers and psalms. The building, perhaps inspired in part by the Roman mausoleum at St Remy in Provence, fits in well with its surroundings. The transition between the four square piers at the base and the cylindrical upper part is eased by four seated statues representing Divinity, Law, Medicine and Science; the keystones of the arches are formed by the masks of four worthies of ancient Greece; and the summit is surmounted by a cross. It rapidly became and has since remained the symbol – some might say the totem – of the College.

Before the Campanile had been completed, work on the Museum Building[40] was begun. The design was largely by Benjamin Woodward, and the building is celebrated for the praise it received from Ruskin in *Sesame and Lilies* as the first to embody his ideals, especially in the naturalistic but imaginative carvings of the O'Shea brothers.[41] It is by far the most daring building in College; it is also the most extravagant. If its exterior recalls a Venetian palazzo its interior, with its immensely spacious hall and staircase rich in marbles and polychrome tiles, suggests a more than usually sumptuous Pall Mall club, with at the same time a touch of a Moorish palace. How the Board was induced at a time of considerable financial stringency to sanction the plans is a matter on which records are silent. The contract price was £24,000, but in fact it cost a good deal more. But posterity can be grateful either to the negligence or to the imagination of the Board of 1853; for the building, after enduring a few decades of contempt, is now generally appreciated, and although most of the rooms, with their extraordinarily high ceilings, have had to submit to the indignity of horizontal division, the hall and staircase, as well as the exterior, remain in their original form.[42]

9

Shifting landmarks
1861–1880

(i)

To the educated middle-aged conservative alike in 1830 and in 1892 the world was full of disturbing portents of change. But the sphere within which the changes were operating or threatening differed at the two dates. In 1830 our conservative was still trying to swallow the bitter pill of Catholic emancipation, and wondering how soon popery would be enthroned in high places; he was increasingly apprehensive of the heavy artillery now being moved into position to bring about parliamentary reform ('falsely so called', he would say); if his ear was acute he could hear the democratic rumblings which were later to manifest themselves as Chartism; and in Ireland he was wondering anxiously from year to year whether his church would go bankrupt from non-payment of tithe. The world of politics and society was sadly out of joint, but in the realm of scholarship, philosophy and culture there was little to trouble him. The Romantic revival had been fairly well digested; Shelley and Byron were still rather distasteful, but one could always fall back on Scott. In the visual arts, classical canons were subject to no serious challenge, save by an odd madman like Turner. Classics, mathematics, logic, ethics, astronomy and Hebrew were the acknowledged staples of education, and the only arguments were about the order in which they should be studied. In philosophy one could still pin one's faith to empiricism and common sense; the mists of Hegelianism were still sunk beneath the eastern horizon. And the Bible was still the unchallenged word of God.

How different were his problems in 1892! In politics and social affairs there was little to worry about, and indeed the next twenty-two years were to show very little change. Parnell had got his deserts; Gladstone was at last an exhausted volcano; socialism was making little headway; and although France, Germany and Russia all needed watching, none of them presented an immediate menace. But the world of thought and culture was reduced to a misty and muddy whirlpool. The respect paid to George Eliot, Swinburne and now Hardy showed that

238

literature had lost all contact with morality. Tennyson was dying, and who was to succeed him? Not, at all events, moony creatures like Morris or Willie Yeats. Architecture was under control, but in painting and sculpture all rules had been thrown aside; the impressionists and pre-Raphaelites had been bad enough, but now critics who should surely know better were trying to tell us that Seurat's dots and Whistler's murky washes were to be taken seriously. In education new subjects were queuing up every year for admission to the curriculum. Religion seemed to be mostly a battle ground between ritualists and modernists, and first the Germans and now the French were reducing the Bible to the level of a folk-tale, while zoologists and geologists were presuming to tell us which bits of it we could still believe in. In philosophy you could choose what school you liked, and you had better choose quickly before all were swallowed up by scientific materialism.

The opening year, 1861, of the period to which this chapter is devoted, is equidistant between 1830, the last year in which the College could be said to be keeping the nineteenth century at bay, and 1892, when it received at its tercentenary celebrations, deservedly on the whole, the compliments of the learned world on its scholarly achievements and on the reputation of its graduates. It may conveniently be regarded, therefore, as the hinge which joins the intellectually stable, earlier part of the century to its restless end. Before 1861 the scholar, even in England, could, without wilfully shutting his eyes to the obvious, go on working within much the same framework of thought as his father had used. By 1861, with the Oxford meeting of the British Assocation and the publication of *Essays and Reviews* dominating not only the learned journals but even the daily press of the past few months, he could no longer do so. He could stop worrying about revolution, war, pestilence and famine, but he now had to start worrying about evolution, positivism, indifferentism and ultramontanism. The universities were, therefore, in the latter part of the nineteenth century nearer to the front line on which were fought the main battles of the age than they had been since the Renaissance. For Trinity, as we shall see, the battle ground shifted for several years from the board-room, lecture-room and library to the House of Commons, but it was a House discussing a subject familiar in common-room arguments, namely, the place of religion in higher education.

(ii)

We have spoken of battle, and for some years that was indeed the order of the day in Oxford, Cambridge and London. In Dublin the atmosphere was calmer, for in intellectual matters extreme conservatives were few and extreme radicals even fewer. There was nobody in Ireland of the calibre of Huxley on the one side nor of Pusey or Manning on the other. Intellectuals in Ireland with a taste for controversy were almost inevitably swept into the perennial fight between the Protestant churches and Rome. The English public had got this off its chest for the time being in the 'Papal Aggression' furore of 1851, which had subsided almost as quickly as it had arisen. But in Ireland, although all the arguments were now stale they had lost little of their fascination, and the growth of ultramontane views in the sixties and seventies made both sides more unyielding. The prominence of this controversy was a dissuasive to rationalists from pressing their attack on a broad front. To a militant rationalist in England the Established Church was the chief enemy; the Roman Church may have seemed even more preposterous, but it was much less powerful. But in Ireland the man of similar views felt compelled to some extent to side with the Protestants; as allies they were intellectually contemptible, but they were also fighting his most powerful enemy, and he felt some compulsion not to rock the boat.

Moreover, the Anglo-Irish had not entirely forgotten their past as frontiersmen, who might, according to circumstances, be governed either by their heads or by their hearts, but who could not afford to allow themselves to become a battlefield between the two. There may have been a few mute and unchronicled Robert Elsmeres in Ireland, but there were no prominent intellectuals to agonize in public about the receding tide of faith or the ethical problems facing a salaried agnostic in a Christian institution – nobody, at least, of the stature of Clough, Arnold, Sidgwick or Stephen. A spirit of independent self-confidence, which at times degenerated into provincial complacency, enabled even the most acute and scholarly minds in Trinity to ignore the controversies which were raging in England and to allow the new ideas to seep in so slowly as to cause no shock. It was not until Tyndall delivered his address to the British Association in Belfast in 1874 that Irish intellectuals were faced with a challenge on their doorstep to which they had to pay at least a little attention.

Furthermore, scholarship in Dublin in the period 1860–90 was mainly concerned with mathematics, physics and classics, subjects to which the contemporary controversies were largely irrelevant. The number of intellectuals who were concerned with biology, geology, philosophy, literary criticism or the fine arts was very small. Even biblical criticism attracted less attention than one might have expected. Lee in his Donnellan lectures of 1852[1] briefly dismissed recent critical work on the Bible, but did not in any sense controvert it, and nothing of substance was published in this field until Salmon's *Introduction to the New Testament* appeared in 1885. Its unaggressively conservative tone represented well the views of the more reflective members of the Church of Ireland.

There was, of course, an occasional squall. In 1856 James MacIvor, an ex-Fellow who had not allowed his intellect to slumber in his Ulster rectory, and who was later to fill for five years the still part-time chair of Moral Philosophy, was appointed as Donnellan lecturer. He chose as his subject 'The laws of religious progress'. The lectures were delivered without incident but when in 1859 he was invited to complete the course he got into trouble. In his first lecture he scandalized the orthodox, who accused him of denying the divine inspiration of the Old Testament prophets. The language was ambiguous, and MacIvor denied the charge, but when the matter came before the Board Todd, supported by the Provost and Hart, wanted to suspend him from the lecturership. The majority, however, led by Graves, thought it suf-ficient to admonish him and ask him to be more careful in his choice of language. In the same year J.W. Barlow, a Junior Fellow of nine years' standing, attacked the doctrine of eternal punishment as constituting a serious obstacle to the acceptance of Christianity by many modern minds. For this he incurred a rebuke from the Archbishop which was enough to deter him from ever officiating again as a clergyman, though he remained a faithful member of the Church of Ireland.[2]

Even those whose scepticism went much further than Barlow's were notable for their lack of clearly expressed hostility to Christianity. Caution, reinforced by a sense of loyalty to a still avowedly Christian institution, was in part responsible, but Lecky, who was independent financially and bound to the College by ties no stronger than that of a grateful graduate to his *alma mater*, showed the same restraint. He came up to Trinity in 1856 with the intention of preparing himself for a peaceful clerical life in a family living near Cork, and he actually completed the Divinity course and was awarded the testimonium; but in the meantime his systematic reading had turned his mind towards a firm but unmilitant rationalism, which found expression in 1865 in his *History of the rise of rationalism in Europe*. This was all the more telling for its total eschewing of Gibbonian malice, and its representation of medieval churchmen not as ridiculous but merely as misguided, and doing their best by their somewhat inadequate lights. Others were content to take their rationalism ready made in the form of positivism, which filled for the speculative undergraduate of the eighteen-sixties something of the same need as Communism supplied for his successor of the nineteen-thirties; like Communism it was embraced with very varying degrees of conviction and permanence. Positivism made one important convert, however, in John Kells Ingram, one of the most versatile and inquiring minds among the Fellows of the latter half of the century. Although he did not conceal his beliefs he did not parade them, and there were never any suggestions that he undermined the faith of his pupils.

On the biological and geological fronts there was little activity, for there were few people in Dublin competent to pronounce on these subjects, and fortunately few who felt impelled to follow Bishop Wilberforce in pronouncing without such competence. Harvey, the Professor of Botany, was not convinced by *The origin of species*, but his attitude was determined primarily by the cautious conservatism of a taxonomist whose life-work had assumed without question the fixity of species; he was a religious man, but had been brought up as a Quaker and was not inclined to dogmatism. He made gentle fun of the doctrine of evolution, and had to apologize to Darwin (whom he respected) for the annoyance caused by one of his squibs; but apart from his gentle, non-controversial temperament he was deterred from open opposition by the fact that two of his closest botanical friends, J.D. Hooker at Kew and Asa Gray at Harvard, emerged as the major botanical champions of Darwinism. The lecturer in Zoology, E.P. Wright, was a man of unspeculative mind, and if he had any views on evolution they did not emerge in his writings. Alexander Macalister, who succeeded him in 1869 when Wright moved to the chair of Botany, declared himself in 1871 prepared to accept the physical evolution of man from the lower animals so long as he was allowed to postulate the independent creation of the soul.[3]

But in 1861, although the Darwinian controversy was later to steal the limelight, the main attack on the literal interpretation of the Pentateuch came from the geologists. Once a uniformitarian outlook had been adopted the great age of the oldest rocks was almost impossible to deny, and more recently excavations in the caves of Aurignac and Les Eyzies had produced compelling evidence for measuring the antiquity of man not in thousands but in hundreds of thousands of years. Samuel Haughton, Professor of Geology, thought it impossible to date the origin of the older rocks with any certainty, but he was prepared to discuss the problem in terms of hundreds of millions of years; this implies that he accepted a metaphorical interpretation of the first chapter of Genesis, though he does not say so explicitly.[4] He regarded the creation of man, however, as a recent event (though not necessarily in 4004 B.C.) and pooh-poohed the stories of palaeolithic flint implements. Nor would he have any truck with evolution; there were successive creations of crustaceans, fishes, reptiles, mammals, and finally man. He regarded Macalister's compromise as untenable, as he apparently held it as axiomatic that a natural origin of man was incompatible with the prospect of supernatural life after death.

Haughton had a keen, versatile, and in some respects powerful mind, but it was neither philosophical nor imaginative, and his undisputed success in several diverse fields of science inclined him to complacency. He had, as early as 1859,[5] dismissed in a hasty and superficial judgment the theory of natural selection as put forward by Darwin and Wallace in their lecture to the Linnean Society, using the well-worn jibe that whatever in it that was new was not true and what was true was not new, and he was a man who did not readily admit that he had made a mistake. There is some evidence that towards the end of his life he began to feel uncomfortable in being in an obvious minority among geologists of repute, but he never made any formal retraction.

(iii)

If the average Fellow of Trinity in the sixties paid little attention to these controversies it was in part because he had other things to worry about. The immediate menace came not from the intellectual Left but from the intellectual Right, which the inescapable pressures of Irish politics had forced into alliance with the political Left. Ultramontanism became his bogy, not without good reason, and ultramontanism, however close its alliance with crowns and coronets in Paris or Vienna, was in Ireland allied to the forces which were soon to emerge as the Home Rule party.

Before he had completed half of his pontificate Pius IX had led the Catholic Church to a position of uncompromising rigour, such as had not been evident since the sixteenth century. The *Syllabus errorum* of 1864 made it clear that there was only one attitude possible for a Catholic menaced by liberalism, scepticism, destructive criticism or presumptuous science. No longer would the Church beg for concessions: it was going to fight for its rights – the rights of eternal truth against ephemeral error. Infallibility, which followed in 1870, caused more of a furore, but it formed merely the coping-stone to a structure which had developed during the preceding twenty years.

This new spirit found a ready response in Ireland, even if the Pope's references to liberalism had sometimes to be glossed by a suggestion that Mr Gladstone did not deserve *all* the anathemas hurled at Mazzini and Garibaldi. By 1861 it had become abundantly clear to politically conscious Catholics that emancipation in 1829 must be regarded, as the Tories had feared and the radicals had hoped, as the first step on a long road. Thirty years of parliamentary experience had shown that, although a large number of Irish constituencies returned Catholic Members to Westminster, they found themselves enmeshed in the English political system, and that these thirty years had not done much to satisfy Irish grievances. Irish Catholics, therefore, had begun to demand not the concessions appropriate to an oppressed minority, but the rights of a majority – the right to their fair share in positions of wealth, power and influence – and they found encouragement in the uncompromising (some would say intransigent) tone of recent pronouncements from Rome.

Their aspirations soon crystallized into three definite demands: for the improvement of the position of the (usually) Catholic tenant *vis-à-vis* his (usually) Protestant landlord, for the disestablishment of the Church of Ireland, and for the provision of university education acceptable to Catholics and endowed by the State.

The first issue, which was to dominate the political scene for more than a generation, does not greatly concern us here. The College was, of course, a landlord on a fairly large scale, and any threat to the value of its capital was disturbing. It could, in this connexion, complain with some justice that Maynooth received from a Treasury grant an income not very greatly inferior to the rent-roll of Trinity College and not subject to the same uncertainties. Furthermore the land question rapidly became tied up with Home Rule, which meant that the Fellows, although as individuals only a small minority came from land-owning families, were collectively forced into a political alliance with the landlords. The College, however, did not in its corporate capacity play a prominent part in the interminable debates on the land question.

(iv)

Disestablishment was another matter. Although the Act of Union had given the most explicit guarantees for the perpetual union of the Anglican churches of the two kingdoms as the United Church of England and Ireland, it soon became obvious that this was not a clause on which successive British governments were inclined to lay much stress. By the mid-sixties Disestablishment was being openly canvassed, and in the election campaign of 1868 it found a prominent place in the Liberal programme. When the Liberals were returned with a comfortable majority and Gladstone took office it was clear that the ecclesiastical aspect of the Union was in grave jeopardy.

In Trinity College the opposition was unanimous. The Provost's House was thrown open to a committee of laymen organized to fight Disestablishment, and eight Fellows or ex-Fellows wrote pamphlets in support of their Church. But as the issue was one on which the Liberal party was united, opposition was futile; the bill passed through Parliament rapidly without a hitch and received the Royal assent in July 1869.

After the lapse of a century we find it difficult to appreciate the intensity of the shock which Disestablishment administered to the world of which Trinity College was the intellectual centre. The worship of the Church went on in the familiar buildings with little change. The clergy continued to be trained in the Divinity School of Trinity College. The Church was to some extent disendowed, but much less harshly than had been originally expected, and the word 'spoliation', which was freely bandied around, was a serious exaggeration. With hindsight we can say that the shock to the Church was salutary in making it stand on its own feet.

But that was not how it seemed in 1869. Disestablishment was interpreted as a demonstration that the tacit alliance between the loyal world of the Irish landed gentry and the British government was, as far as the latter was concerned, a limited commitment. It showed that English Liberals no longer cared for the maintenance of religious truth, and were content to settle ecclesiastical questions by counting heads. And it suggested that even among the Conservatives the great absentee landlords cared more for their party than for their Church. The sense of disillusion and betrayal was profound and widespread, and it drove one of the Fellows, J.A. Galbraith, to join his fellow-Protestant Isaac Butt in founding the Home Rule party.

For the most part, however, the Fellows did not spend the years immediately following Disestablishment in profitless recrimination. The Church, deserted by the State, was befriended and supported by the University. Much of the credit for laying a firm foundation for the finances of the disestablished Church belongs to Fellows of Trinity. Among these Hart, Galbraith, Carson and Traill were foundation members of the Representative Church Body. Their mathematical training gave them a good head for figures; their loyalty ensured that they would devote much of their time to preparing the schemes; and they were all, and in particular Anthony Traill, good men of business. In the provinces, the dioceses of Armagh and Derry found in R.V. Dixon and John Gwynn respectively (both former Fellows) able architects of their new financial structure. In Dublin, Hart and Galbraith were members of the General Synod of the Church, as well as of the Representative Church Body; so also were Provost Lloyd and J.H. Jellett, who was later to succeed Lloyd in the provostship. But the dominant figure in the Synod was George Salmon, Regius Professor of Divinity. Disestablishment was viewed by the wilder evangelical laymen, who were in 1875 at about the height of their enthusiasm and numbers, as a God-sent opportunity to rid the Prayer Book of all its ritual and Catholic doctrine. To the serried ranks of Bible-thumping colonels from the midlands the leaders of the Church were unable to offer any effective opposition; the Primate, Marcus Beresford, was a rather feeble echo of his great cousin, and Richard Chenevix Trench, the Archbishop of Dublin (who was in any case suspected of a sympathy with ritualism), was more of a philologist than a statesman. But Salmon, with an assured reputation for opposition to Roman claims, but also with a sense of tradition, common sense, good taste, and an ability to appeal to the plain man in the pew, saved the day, partly by the respect given to his intellectual eminence, and partly by his instinct for judicious and timely compromise. Thanks to his efforts the revised Prayer Book of 1878, despite a generally low-church flavour, did not differ in essentials from that of 1662.

For Salmon's principal lieutenant in Trinity, however, these compromises were inadmissable. William Lee, Archbishop King's Lecturer in Divinity, a high churchman by Irish standards, was a warm-hearted man, but he had a cross-bench (some would say cross-grained) mind, which tended always to put him in a minority of one. He could not stand the prospect of membership of a church in which the clergy were to be bossed around by a largely lay synod, and he accordingly took advantage of a clause in the Disestablishment Act which enabled him, at the cost of forfeiting any right to direct the counsels of the new Church, to remain bound only by the canons of the United Church in which he had been brought up.[6]

(v)

Disestablishment gave the College a sharp and sudden shock, but its effects were largely indirect. The constitution, the personnel and the teaching of the College remained unaffected, and the only immediate consequence was the abolition of the ecclesiastical patronage. Although this was treated as a grievance and an affront,[7] we have seen earlier that the patronage had ceased to fulfil its original function, and there is no doubt that it was of less value to the College than the financial compensation which it received for its loss a few years later. But the prospect of an attempt by the Government to satisfy the third Catholic demand – for endowed university education acceptable to the tenderest Catholic conscience – implied for the College a far graver and more direct menace.

For the reader to appreciate the possible options open to those who wished to satisfy this demand, we must give a summary review of the history of the College in relation to religious tests. Although it was, up to the period which we are now considering, an unmistakably Anglican foundation, conformity was not enforced with anything like the same precision as was used at Oxford and Cambridge. In England a declaration of assent to the Thirty-nine Articles was required, the only difference being that at Oxford it was required at matriculation, but at Cambridge only at graduation. In either case, however, it ensured that all persons with any voice in the government of the university (and at Oxford also all the undergraduates) were committed, unless they lost or changed their faith, to the doctrines of the Established Church. In Dublin conformity among the Fellows was assured by the Fellow's oath, and also for most of them by the requirement to take orders, but for the undergraduates, including the Scholars on the foundation, and for most of the non-Fellow Professors there was no formal test. There was, however, an obligation for students residing in or near the College to attend Chapel regularly, and, as we have already seen, the conformity of candidates for foundation Scholarships was assessed by their willingness to receive the sacrament, at least occasionally. It seems fairly clear that in the early seventeenth century, when ecclesiastical allegiances were less precisely demarcated, the College was prepared to take in without question boys from Catholic or Presbyterian homes in the expectation that they would graduate as good Anglicans. But in the anti-Catholic reaction which followed the wars of 1689–91 Parliament imposed on candidates for degrees not only oaths of allegiance and anti-Jacobitism, but also an oath repudiating the doctrine of transubstantiation. This excluded from graduation anybody who was in any sense a practising Catholic, although a handful put in a few years as undergraduates, either by attending Chapel or by finding a plausible excuse not to do so. In 1794 the requirement for the anti-transubstantiation oath at graduation was abolished, and although there was no formal change in the statute requiring attendance at the College Chapel it was certainly not enforced against dissenters of any persuasion. The College thus became open to students of all creeds, and at first there was little or no opposition from the dissenting churches to their members receiving their education at Trinity, the prospects of increased influence apparently outweighing the risk to faith and morals. Nevertheless, the general pattern of Irish life was such that the great majority of students were still drawn from the Established Church. As the nineteenth century progressed the proportion of Protestant dissenters among the students rose steadily but very slowly, but the proportion of Catholics varied more irregularly, the effects of increased prosperity and ambition being to a large extent cancelled by the effect of increasing clerical disapproval (see Fig. 3, p. 504).

By the middle of the nineteenth century, then, the position had been reached that although the College was preponderantly Anglican, and its nucleus (the Provost, Fellows and Scholars) was maintained so by statute, no tests were applied to other teachers or to the students, and the minority of dissenting students was tending to increase. To the average Fellow this seemed an equitable and sensible arrangement. The original intention of the foundress had been preserved, but nobody was excluded from the benefits of higher education. But of course the Irish Catholic viewed the position differently. He saw his fellow-Catholics debarred from posts of value and esteem, and surrounded during their undergraduate years by the 'Protestant atmosphere', of which so much was to be made in the controversial literature. His tutor was likely to be a clergyman of the Established Church, and from the same type of man he would be lectured on philosophy or history; while the corporate worship of the College took one form only, in which he could not participate. The Protestant dissenter could echo some of these complaints, but his area of agreement with the Establishment was greater, and his grievances accordingly fewer; moreover he had had, since 1848, a tolerable alternative in Queen's College, Belfast. Nevertheless, he could not be ignored, as it was from his fellow-dissenters in England that the Liberal party drew so much of its support.

(vi)

We have already seen how Peel had twenty years earlier made an attempt to solve these problems by the establishment of the Queen's Colleges, and how it met with only limited success. Gladstone, when he came to power in 1868, resolved to tackle not only Disestablishment, but also the 'Irish University Question', as it had now come to be called. In this aim he had considerable support, even from Irish Protestants, but his supporters differed widely in their views on what would constitute an acceptable solution.

There were, it would seem, three possible lines of attack. The first was to remove from Trinity College its distinctively Anglican flavour and to make it equally acceptable to all creeds. The second was to leave its religious allegiance unchanged, but to unite it with a Catholic college, and perhaps one or more of the Queen's Colleges, into a federal university which, though some of its colleges would be sectarian, would itself be neutral. The third was to leave Trinity and the Queen's University unchanged and to set up a third university which should be as distinctively Catholic as Trinity was Anglican.

All were open to serious objection. The first was likely to alienate the Anglicans without satisfying the Catholics; only the Protestant dissenters were likely to find it satisfactory. Perhaps for this reason it was popular among English Liberals, many of whom found the Catholic objections unreasonable and were inclined to act on the principle of Mr Bumble that if you offer people something they don't want for long enough they will eventually go away. If it is difficult today it seemed impossible a hundred years ago to give a Christian tone to an institution without favouring one particular church, and so, quite apart from the now vocal pressure from Jews and freethinkers for equal treatment, the removal of the privileges of Anglicans from Trinity would lead merely to one more godless college. The dispassionate and fair-minded Catholic preferred a Protestant Trinity to a secular Trinity, and in one of the parliamentary debates the O'Conor Don voiced this sentiment when he said that Catholics had no desire to place members of the Established Church (who wanted their children brought up in a religious atmosphere) under the same disabilities as those imposed on the Catholics.

To the second solution the fundamental objection had already been voiced by Amos: 'Can two walk together unless they be agreed?' All Gladstone's ingenuity in 1873 failed to devise a satisfactory relationship between colleges and university in relation to the 'sensitive' subjects such as history, philosophy, biology and geology. Each college could teach them according to its tenets, but how could impartial examinations be devised? If there were to be no examinations, would it be a university worth the name? And if the colleges were to examine separately why join them in a university?

The third solution was the inverse of the first: it would satisfy the Catholics, but in a manner which the average English Liberal could not stomach. Even if a substantial part of the endowment of the Catholic University were to be derived from the expropriation of the assets of Trinity College some public money would be needed; but to charter and endow a university under episcopal control and unashamedly based on ultramontane principles was something which the British electorate would never agree to and which no British government dare risk.

It was, therefore, the principles of English Liberals rather than the claims of Irish Catholics which eventually broke the Anglican monopoly of Fellowships and Scholarships in Trinity College. To the average Fellow of the time none of the three solutions was attractive; the first threatened the religious traditions of his College, the second its academic independence, and the third, very probably, its endowments. He eventually opted for the first, not because he valued scholarship or money higher than his religion, but because it seemed more in accord with the spirit of the times, and because he realized that in his lifetime the changes would be small.[8]

(vii)

The campaign, which was reaching its climax in the late sixties, to break the much tighter control of the Established Church over Oxford and Cambridge was widened so as to include Dublin. Conservative and

Liberal governments alike preferred to regard Dublin as a less urgent issue, but this was not the view of Henry Fawcett. This remarkable man, who, though blinded in an accident at the age of twenty-five, rose to be Professor of Political Economy at Cambridge and Postmaster-General under Gladstone, campaigned with single-minded persistence for seven years to abolish religious tests in the University of Dublin, and was at last successful in 1873. His first motion on the subject, introduced in 1867 while the Conservatives were still in office, was opposed not only by the Government, but also by Irish Catholics. Nevertheless, it was lost only by the Speaker's casting vote. Next year he tried again, fortified by the recent failure of Disraeli to devise a constitution for a Catholic university which would satisfy both bishops and the House of Commons. A petition against his motion was organized, and was widely supported in the College, though the Board was prepared, as a compromise, to offer the opening of Scholarship to Catholics. This was not necessary, however, as the motion was withdrawn from lack of parliamentary time.

When Fawcett proposed his motion for the third time, in 1869, it was from the government side of the House. But there was another and more dramatic change in the situation. J.T. Ball, the senior Member for the University, rose to say that the Board of Trinity College had informed him that they did not wish him to oppose the motion. This decision had been taken by the Board on 29 July. The Provost was abroad on holiday, and may have been somewhat startled by the news, but although he had, only eighteen months earlier, described Fawcett's proposal as 'a dangerous experiment', he did nothing on his return to dissociate himself from the Board's policy. What had caused this sudden and surprising *volte-face*?

In the debate in the Commons, Ball ascribed it to Disestablishment; the Irish Church Act had received the Royal assent a few weeks earlier. The College, he asserted, had been founded by the Crown to provide 'an educational institution in connexion with the church which had a very short time before been established in Ireland'. Now that Parliament had severed the link between Church and State the College no longer felt itself bound by the same loyalties. A year later the same theme was developed further – perhaps with more eloquence than historical accuracy – by D.R. Plunket, Ball's junior colleague, who, declaring that he had been elected to repel 'aggressive ultramontane ambition', represented the College's attitude as 'no new idea on the part of her governing body but the proper and just consummation of the policy she had invariably pursued'.

If we discount the frills added for purposes of parliamentary debate, there was some truth in these explanations. The imminent prospect of Disestablishment had forced Irish Anglicans to reconsider the nature of their attitude to the State, and it had also forced them to recognize that they would shortly be robbed of one of their major debating points in defending the exclusive character of the Body Corporate of Trinity College. The status quo was becoming indefensible, and in looking for an alternative the Provost and Fellows favoured that which would cause least disruption; the majority of them also believed that it would be better for the country if the trickle of upper-class Catholics coming to Trinity could be increased to a larger stream. This point was clearly made by the Provost in a letter to the Chancellor, in which he maintained that the creation of a wholly Catholic college or university would, at this time, 'be fatal to freedom, in so much as it would subject Roman Catholics of the upper classes as well as those of the lower, to the domination of an ultramontane priesthood'.

But there were other factors too which favoured the rapid change. One was the death of Todd in June 1869. He might have been outvoted, but he would have fought for the maintenance of the Anglican establishment in Trinity, even if it was to vanish in the country, and he would have fought with determination and skill. After his death the more competent members of the Board (Luby, Hart and Carson) were all pragmatists – not without principles, but essentially men of affairs on the look-out for a practical solution. Another factor was the growing realization of the unpalatable nature of the alternatives that the Government was likely to propose. And finally, it seems clear that between 1867 and 1869 there had occurred one of those mysterious changes in public opinion (a change indicated and also helped on by the Liberal victory at the polls in 1868) which bring it about that what had seemed like an open question, debated between equal antagonists, suddenly becomes a matter on which all sensible men must think alike. It was during this brief period that the opposition to the removal of the religious tests at Oxford and Cambridge crumbled: in 1867 it seemed formidable, but in 1869 merely pathetic, and the tests were abolished in 1871. So it was also in Dublin. In 1868 a memorial had been signed by the Vice-Chancellor, six Senior Fellows and over six thousand graduates, praying that the Protestant character of Trinity College should be preserved, and the College followed this with an official petition deploring the proposed 'organic change' which 'would lead to the substitution of a new, untried system for one that has been confessedly successful'. In 1870 the Provost, all but four of the Fellows, and many of the Professors painted in glowing terms the advantages of a common education for men of all denominations, and in April of that year a meeting convened to protest against the change attracted an audience of only sixty graduates (mostly clergymen) and twenty-five ladies.

In these circumstances it might have been expected that Fawcett's proposals would have been carried. But he reckoned without his own Front Bench. Gladstone was more interested in satisfying Irish Catholics than in asserting Liberal principles, and he saw clearly enough that it was only a few Anglophile Catholics opposed to ultramontanism who would be satisfied by the abolition of tests in Trinity College. He was already considering the more far-reaching proposals which were to emerge in his abortive bill of 1873, and he did not wish his grand strategy to be prejudiced by piecemeal reform. After some manoeuvring Fawcett's proposal was defeated.

Undeterred, however, he came forward with new proposals in 1871. An obvious objection to equating the removal of the tests with the removal of the grievances of non-Anglicans was the constitution of the College, which concentrated all power in the hands of the Provost and Senior Fellows. This meant that even if a Catholic or Nonconformist were to be elected to Fellowship in 1872 he would be unlikely to have any voice in the government of the College until about 1905, and even the most sanguine estimate could not picture earlier than 1920 a Board which would not be dominated by members of the Church of Ireland. Fawcett, therefore, added to his draft bill some constitutional changes, providing for a generous representation of Junior Fellows on the Board, and for the creation of a mainly elective Council (not unlike that which actually came into being in 1875) to take charge of the more strictly academic side of the University's business. These proposals were drafted after consultation with the Board, and with at least its guarded approval; for Fawcett had by now convinced the Board that it was only by supporting the type of liberalism that he represented that they could hope to escape the sinister designs of the ultramontane party and more drastic interference on the part of the Government. His advice, in fact was:

> Always keep tight hold of Nurse
> For fear of finding something worse.

But he overestimated Nurse's protective powers, and very soon the College was to encounter something very much worse.

(viii)

For Fawcett's proposals of 1871, repeated almost unchanged in 1872, appeared to Gladstone as merely a further trespass on his territory and as an exasperating defiance of his authority. Fawcett's bill never got past a second reading, and in the following year it was Gladstone himself who took the initiative and introduced a bill designed to provide a comprehensive solution to the Irish University Question. It proposed the dismantling of the Queen's University and the enlargement of the University of Dublin so as to contain not only Trinity College, but also a number of other colleges to be designated in the schedule. This was still blank, but it was hoped, he explained, that they would include the Queen's Colleges of Cork and Belfast, Magee College in Londonderry (a Presbyterian foundation) and 'the college which is called the Catholic University'. This was the institution in St Stephen's Green which was later to serve as the germ of University College, Dublin, but which was then at the extreme nadir of its fortunes. Other colleges might be added to these, if the University so desired, but meanwhile University College, Galway, was to be closed down as uneconomic.[9] The new University was to be governed by a Council, which would consist of government nominees, Professors of the University, representatives of the Senate, and co-opted members. Twenty-eight members were to be nominated by the Government in the first instance. The University was to be financed by £12,000 per annum provided by Trinity College, £10,000 from the Treasury, an estimated £5,000 from fees, and about £23,000 from funds made available by Disestablishment. Each college could devise its own constitution, but the Queen's Colleges would be bound by the 'godless' clause in their charter, and Trinity College was to be required to abolish religious tests for all offices, and to hand over to the Church of Ireland its Divinity School, together with money to meet its running costs and to provide it with buildings. The University itself was to be neutral in matters of religion, and this meant that not only was it forbidden to examine or grant degrees in theology, but it was not even permitted to give any teaching in theology, modern history or mental or moral philosophy.[10] The colleges could teach these 'sensitive' subjects, and the University could examine in them, but only on condition that they were optional subjects in all examinations, and would not be even optional subjects for prizes, scholarships or fellowships of the University. University teaching must be of a nature not to give offence to the religious convictions of any student, and an examinee must not be penalized for 'adopting in Modern History, Mental and Moral Philosophy, Medicine, Law or any other branch of learning any particular theory in preference to any other received theory'.

The pathetic impracticality of these last two provisions shows the desperation with which Gladstone tried to cement over the cracks in a structure built of hopelessly discordant elements. Trinity College naturally resented its being placed on an equality with a college which was unendowed, unchartered, reduced to a mere handful of students and a few tired and discouraged professors, with tight clerical control and a disappearance of all the hopes and most of the ideals associated with Newman's period as Rector.[11] But Trinity need not have worried on this score; the bishops resented even more the idea of associating with 'the Protestant College' as they called it, and the godless colleges of Cork and Belfast. Moreover, Trinity had other things to worry about – the prospect of having to expel from its courts the oldest and most respected of its faculties, headed by George Salmon, already a medallist of the Royal Society and an honorary doctor of Oxford; the prospect of losing a substantial part of its endowment;[12] the prospect of hearing its philosophers lecture to classes from which all aspirants to university honors and prizes were excluded; and the prospect of forming part of a university in which free inquiry and free expression of opinion were to be severely curtailed.

The mood among the Fellows, therefore, was one of apprehension and gloom, for the speech with which Gladstone introduced his bill on 13 February 1873 was one which showed his greatness as an orator, combining as it did a broad sweep of principles with accurate mastery of intricate detail. Members hostile to the bill declared that he had put the House into a 'mesmeric trance', and that if the question had been then put it would have been carried almost unanimously. But it needed only a few days for criticism to make itself heard, and not only from the opposition. The Conservatives deplored the government-nominated element in the Senate; many Liberals were shocked by the 'gagging clauses' as they came to be called; and many of the Irish were inclined to follow their bishops in condemning as tainted with the principles of mixed education those very clauses which some Liberals deplored as too denominational. Gladstone had declared that his motive was to soothe and not to exasperate, but in this he was singularly unsuccessful, and it soon became apparent that a bill designed to please everybody was going to please nobody. Its only keen supporters were those Liberals who had no interest in the subject but were anxious to ensure the survival of the Government.

The Senate of the University of Dublin was convened on 25 February to consider the bill, and, after listening to a rather irrelevant lecture from the Vice-Chancellor (Sir Joseph Napier) on Gladstone's misinterpretation of the original relationship between the University and Trinity College, passed resolutions approving unanimously the principles of Fawcett's bill and, by a large majority, petitioning Parliament against the bill now before it. Compromise proposals supported by Haughton, Galbraith and Mahaffy were resolutely voted down. After the meeting three of the Fellows (Carson, Hart, and Traill) together with Mountiford Longfield, Professor of Feudal and English Law, who had for many years advised the Board on legal and parliamentary matters, were sent over to London to lobby Members of Parliament. They found

Plunket pessimistic, with his best hope that some of the more objectionable clauses could be improved in Committee. They addressed a group of Conservative Members at the Carlton Club, but were persuaded by Lord John Manners that they were wasting their time in preaching to the converted and would be better employed in talking to hesitant Liberals. They did so, but with inconclusive results. Vernon Harcourt was very friendly, but made light of their fears, assuring them that Trinity would be as influential in the new University as his own *alma mater* (another Trinity) was at Cambridge. Not for the first time did Irish Unionists have to deplore the sad ignorance of Irish affairs among their English friends.

Nevertheless, with increasing signs of restlessness among the Government's supporters, hopes began to rise. On 9 March, Paul Cullen, Archbishop of Dublin, ignoring an urgent appeal from his fellow-Cardinal Manning to support the bill, issued a pastoral denouncing it in such uncompromising terms as to make it difficult for any Catholic to support it, and at the same time to make many Protestants unwilling to offer any concessions to prelates of that temper. Meanwhile the debate on the second reading had begun. The very nature of the bill as a complex compromise meant that no section of the House was entirely solid in support or opposition; it was a debate in which speeches could win votes. Carson and his colleagues listened from the gallery. At first they were despondent; Liberal opposition seemed to be confined to details, and the attitude of many Members was still uncertain. But soon their hopes began to rise. The Cardinal's pastoral had its effect. Gladstone was obviously worried and reported to be very short-tempered. He tried to meet criticism by promises that many details could be amended in Committee, but could not persuade his opponents that such amendments would, in fact, be conceded. After five days' debate the division was at last taken in the small hours of 12 March, and the Government was defeated by three votes.[13]

The College was saved from the gravest threat to its future since the Jacobite occupation of 1690. But Gladstone was never to be forgiven. It seems probable that the opposition which the College would in any case have offered to the Home Rule proposals of 1886 and 1893 was given a sharper edge by memories of 1873.

(ix)

Despite their defeat the Liberals remained in office, and the way seemed clear, therefore, for Fawcett. His by now somewhat dog-eared bill came up for consideration by a sulky but chastened Cabinet. It had by this time acquired a rather complex appendix of proposals for changes in the academic constitution; the Government was unwilling to commit itself to these, but agreed that if the bill were to be reduced to its original simple provisions its passage would be facilitated. This was done, and Fawcett's Act, as it was hereafter to be called, came into operation on 26 May 1873, just in time to permit the election of two Roman Catholics to foundation Scholarships in that year. It provided simply that no religious test or declaration of faith was to be required for any post in the College or University, except in the Divinity School, that the obligation for Fellows to take orders should be abolished, and that no member of the College or University should be compelled to attend the public worship of any church to which he did not belong.

Fawcett's Act is rightly regarded as an important milestone in the history of the College, but its immediate effect was slight. The distinction between foundation and non-foundation Scholars disappeared, but to a hard-headed Presbyterian the distinction had not represented a very serious grievance, and neither this nor the opening of a pathway to Fellowship brought about the change in the composition of the student body that might have been expected. In the twenty years following the passing of the Act the proportion of Presbyterians among the entrants, which had been steadily rising, levelled off to a constant figure of 6 per cent, while the proportion of Roman Catholics over the same period showed a decline from 10 per cent to 7 per cent. Episcopal disapproval, the foundation of the Royal University in 1879, family tradition and various other social factors more than compensated for the new equality of status. Nor was the effect of the Act on the composition of the Fellowship body very noticeable at first. The years from 1873 to 1915 saw the election of thirty-nine Fellows, of whom six were Presbyterians (only two elected before 1900),[14] one a Moravian,[15] three Roman Catholics and two or three undoubted sceptics who might have been unwilling to take the former statutory oath; but the remaining two-thirds were members of the Church of Ireland, and only in a few cases was the membership nominal. It so happened that the tenure of all the Catholics was short,[16] and it was not till 1958 that a Catholic showed sufficient staying power to reach the Board as a Senior Fellow.[17]

Nevertheless, the symbolic effect of Fawcett's Act was considerable. It created in the College an atmosphere which none of the controversialists had accurately foreseen: an atmosphere that was religious but not clerical, tolerant but not indifferent, neither formally secular nor exclusively denominational. All posts were open to men of any creed or none, and this was true in fact, as well as in theory. But the Divinity School continued as an important and honoured part of the College; the

Chapel services were conducted according to the rites of the Church of Ireland and throughout the period covered by this history every Provost attended them regularly and willingly. These things meant that the College was in no way bound to the statutory 'godlessness' of the Queen's Colleges. The boast that in Trinity College, as nowhere else in Ireland, Orange and Green, Protestant and Catholic, believer and sceptic could meet and argue in a friendly atmosphere and on equal terms was made by after-dinner speakers with a repetitiveness which became tedious and with a complacency which was often embarrassing, but it was broadly speaking true. The conversion which the College underwent in 1869 was sudden, but it was genuine and lasting.

Haughton had written in 1869, 'Trinity College has never been, and never was intended to be, a national institution; her emoluments ... are the property of the Irish members of the English church.'[18] (In the same pamphlet he advocates the establishment and endowment of a Catholic university, which robs his words of the arrogance they suggest if quoted out of context.) Although his statement somewhat over-simplified the policy of the College during the first fifty years of its life, it is broadly speaking true, and it would have had the assent of most Catholics as well as of Protestants, the only point at issue being whether the ownership of the emoluments should remain unchanged. But after 1873 not only did such sentiments cease to be true for the present and the future, but the suggestion that they had been true in the past came to be regarded as being in the worst of taste. The doctrine that the College had always had an ecumenical concern for all Irishmen, of any creed or none, became a firmly established myth.[19] That it is true today does not justify its extrapolation into the past.

Nor did the adoption of this attitude do much to improve day-to-day relations with Catholics, except for the few who soon received from their co-religionists the contemptuous label of 'Trinity Catholics'. For the sole response of the Hierarchy to what the College saw as a generous change of front was to point out sourly that it merely added one to the number of godless colleges. Considering that much of the pressure in Ireland for Fawcett's Act had come from Catholic laymen, most Trinity men felt hurt at this response and came to the conclusion that there was no pleasing the Catholics.[20] They tended, therefore, to play down the religious aspect and to concentrate on Unionist politics. But the bishops were fortified by a last minor thunderbolt from the ageing Pius IX, who issued in 1875 a rescript forbidding absolution to parents who sent their children to non-Catholic schools or colleges without adequate safeguards – the adequacy to be assessed by the local ordinary in accordance with the instructions of the Holy See. What had hitherto been a somewhat indefinite disapproval thus became crystallized into what later came to be known as 'the ban', which will be further discussed in chapter twelve.

(x)

Fawcett had, of course, foreseen the long delay that the existing constitution of the College would impose on the arrival at any position of power of such non-Anglicans as might be elected to Fellowship, and had, as we have seen, won the consent of the Board to at least some of his proposals for constitutional changes designed to shorten this delay. None of these reached the Statute Book, and when the moment of crisis was past the Board began to have second thoughts. The proposals for Junior Fellows to sit on the Board or for the whole body of Fellows to take over some part of the government of the College were quietly dropped, but the Board was prepared to agree that the Junior Fellows and the non-Fellow Professors might be given a voice in the purely academic aspects of government. The number of peripheral subjects of study to which the Senior Fellows were strangers was steadily increasing,[21] and they were willing to hand over the management of these to their colleagues, subject to ultimate control by the Board. It was hoped that this might allay the restlessness of the non-Fellow Professors, who by this time numbered twenty-two and were beginning to complain that their influence was too nicely proportioned to their meagre salaries. At the same time, the constitution of the body on which these interests were to be represented could be designed so as to enable dissenters to be elected to it immediately.

It was agreed, therefore, that a University Council should be instituted, and the necessary Letters Patent were issued in November 1874. The Council was to nominate to most of the Professorships,[22] and to have an equal voice with the Board (the consent of both bodies being required for any change) in the regulation of lectures, courses and examinations, and also of the duties, qualifications and conditions of tenure of the Professors; the Divinity School was, however, excluded from its sphere of operations, as was the examination for Fellowship. In the case of nomination to Professorships the Board was bound to elect the Council's nominee unless it was prepared to justify its refusal to the Chancellor; this meant in practice that it would refuse only if the nomination procedure had been irregular or if new evidence were to come to light after it had been made.[23]

The constitution of the Council, which lasted unchanged until 1911, was simple. The Provost presided, and the remaining sixteen members were all to be elected from among members of the University Senate.

Four were to be elected by the Senior Fellows, four by the Junior Fellows, four by the non-Fellow Professors, and four by those members of the Senate who were neither Fellows nor Professors. Naturally enough the first three classes of electors tended to elect mainly from their own ranks, but both Senior and Junior Fellows seem to have sensed a moral obligation to include a Catholic graduate in their panel; the Seniors, accordingly, retained for over twenty-five years as one of their representatives D.R. Pigot, a well-known lawyer and son of the Chief Baron of the same name, while the Juniors elected Sir Robert Kane, former president of University College, Cork, and a pioneer of applied science in Ireland. Only the non-Fellow Professors stuck rigidly to electing from amongst their number, and were not deterred by the fact that the four most suitable men happened all to be members of the Church of Ireland.

The Council had no say in financial matters; it could veto the establishment of a new chair but it could not create one. For this and other reasons the Board remained for long the far more powerful body. But in its first few years some members of Council were reluctant to accept a subsidiary role and showed a spirit of sturdy independence which verged at times on truculence. They attempted to discuss questions relating to the election to Fellowship and its condition of tenure, which were clearly outside the competence of the Council, and several motions had to be ruled out of order by the Chairman. The most persistent originator of such motions was W.H.S. Monck, and he frequently failed to find a seconder. It says much for the tolerance of the Council that when Monck retired from it after three years in order to qualify himself for the chair of Moral Philosophy they agreed to nominate him for the post.[24]

After a few years, however, the Council accepted the limitations on its power and settled down to work harmoniously with the Board within its limited sphere, and for the time being it satisfied the desires of the Junior Fellows and the non-Fellow Professors for a share in the government of the College and University.

(xi)

This did not mean, however, that the Junior Fellows had no grievances against the Seniors; but the grievances related to money and work rather than to power. Most of the Junior Fellows were prepared to accept the tradition that government should be concentrated in the hands of the Provost and Senior Fellows; but during the mid-seventies a proviso began to win wide acceptance, namely that the Senior Fellows should not be too old, and the tenure of a Junior Fellowship not too long.

It was the latter clause that was the important one. For in 1874, when overt agitation on this issue began, the average age of the Senior Fellows was sixty-four, and only two were over seventy. They could be represented as elderly and set in their ways, but scarcely as senile. But Moore, the Vice-Provost, had enjoyed the *otium cum dignitate* of a Senior Fellowship for thirty years after serving for only fifteen years as a Junior, whereas William Roberts, at the head of the list of Junior Fellows, had already spent thirty-three years as a tutor, and at the age of fifty-six was still awaiting a vacancy among the Senior Fellows, who mostly looked all too hale and hearty. The basic bargain implied in a Fellowship – hard and mainly uninteresting work on a rather low salary in early life, followed by a choice of ease or administration on a generous salary later on – was still being kept, but the first part had become far too long and the second too short.

The philosophy of the age no doubt accepted the principle that every man's chosen career is subject to the hazards of social and economic changes, but few, even then, were prepared to apply these principles to themselves or to be backward in claiming from society some compensation for the disappointment of their hopes. The Junior Fellows felt that they had been tricked, and Traill used the actuarial skill which he had developed in calculating rectors' commutation for the Representative Church Body to demonstrate (with remarkable accuracy) that the situation would steadily become worse. The more percipient of them may have seen their problem as virtually insoluble, but in their mood of angry frustration they were prepared to press strongly for even the smallest palliative. The 'stagnation' of which they complained was, in fact, due mainly to the ill-judged terms of the Letters Patent of 1840, which terminated the celibacy rule. The creation of ten new Fellowships, designed to promote a 'healthy circulation' and to satisfy the hopes of Fellowship candidates, produced a blockage which could have been foreseen. In 1874 eleven out of the twelve most senior of the Junior Fellows were aged over fifty-one and under fifty-seven, and three of the Senior Fellows were under sixty.

Nothing but an epidemic could cure stagnation on this scale. It was in vain to point out that any man who sat for Fellowship after about 1852 should have been able to foresee his position thirty-five years later; it was in vain that Mahaffy urged the Fellows to regard themselves as 'a small aristocracy of letters holding emoluments which many have striven for in vain'. Most of the Junior Fellows felt that the rules should be changed, so as to give them in the latter half of their life less work and more pay.

The only palliatives which seemed practicable were to increase the number of Senior Fellows, and to devise some scheme for retirement, at least of those who could be deemed incapacitated for their work, and preferably at a fixed age. The first was rejected out of hand by the Board; it would merely mean, they said, paying ten men to do the work which had hitherto been accomplished quite satisfactorily by eight. They were prepared to consider a scheme of retirement which should be voluntary, or in consequence of incapacity certified by the Visitors. But they did not like the idea of compulsory retirement at seventy or even seventy-three and they were fortified in their opposition by the opinion of counsel, who held that the Crown could not, without the consent of all parties, convert to a limited tenure an office which the charter declared to be tenable *ad vitam aut culpam*.

Young men dependent on seniority for promotion are always in favour of a retiring age, but for most of them there comes a time in later middle age when they begin to wonder whether the arguments are quite as compelling as they had thought. As the controversy proceeded, with schemes and counter-schemes being handed to and fro, amended and rejected, some of the Junior Fellows with more than twenty-five years service began to suspect they might lose as much as they would gain by a rule for compulsory retirement. If, *per impossibile*, retirement at seventy had been enforced on everybody in 1875, it would have meant for the eight most senior of the Junior Fellows that Senior Fellowship would have come, on an average, only a year earlier, and would have been enjoyed for a year less. There must, therefore, have been several who shared Shaw's sentiments (even if they did not voice them with the same candour) when he declared that Fellows of his standing, having sacrificed for Fellowship their prospects in the learned professions, 'must play the part of barnacles and stick to the old ship whether they impede its progress or not'.[25]

In the early stages of the controversy a genuine difficulty in the way of any retirement scheme lay in the absence of funds: where was the money for pensions to come from? This was solved in 1874 by a *deus ex machina*. The College received under the terms of the Disestablishment Act a sum which, including a few years' accumulated interest, amounted to £140,000 as compensation for its loss of ecclesiastical patronage. The Board did not lack advice as to how this should be spent. The clerical Fellows claimed that the money was morally theirs, and were not deterred from pressing this claim by the fact that in the last days of the Establishment they had all refused a College living. The lay Fellows then pointed out that *their* promotion was held up by the absence of resignations among their clerical colleagues. The Divinity School put in its claim, while the non-Fellow Professors suggested that it might be used to give them pensions and security of the tenure. The last two claimants were easily brushed aside, and all the Fellows soon agreed that if any retiring pensions were to be instituted this compensation would be the source of funds. But no agreement on a precise scheme could be reached and, by June 1876, there was deadlock.

The Junior Fellows, over-confident, perhaps, of the justice of their claims, asked for a government inquiry, and although the Board refused to associate itself with this request a Royal Commission was appointed in March 1877, to advise on how best the advowson compensation should be spent. It heard some passionate oratory from various points of view, and eventually issued a very cautious report. It advised that a substantial part of the advowson fund should be spent in relieving 'stagnation', but instead of instituting retiring pensions for Fellows it recommended that the number of Senior Fellows be increased to nine, with a quorum of six for the transaction of Board business; this would allow for at least two Senior Fellows being retired in fact, if not in name, while drawing their full Senior Fellow's salary, though not, of course, any supplementary salary for offices. The Senior Fellows, however, objected successfully to this dilution of their ranks, and when the Letters Patent which settled the question for the time being were issued in April 1880 they merely permitted a sum of up to £5,000 per annum to be spent on retiring pensions for Fellows who were permanently incapacitated. They also stipulated that in future one Fellow and one only should be elected each year, irrespective of vacancies.

After so much waste of breath and ink the final settlement had something of the character of a *ridiculus mus*, and its effects were small. Two Fellows retired immediately under its terms: John Toleken, a Senior Fellow who was elderly and in poor health, and Benjamin Dickson, a Junior Fellow who had suffered a mental breakdown. Subsequent retirements took place in 1892, 1893, 1896, 1898, 1901, 1908 and 1915, but many of the elderly Fellows around the turn of the century held the same view as Barlow enunciated to the Royal Commission of 1906. 'I am seventy-nine years of age', he declared, 'but I am still quite competent to discharge the duties of a Senior Fellow.' The stagnation continued to 1913 (when Burnside was co-opted to Senior Fellowship after forty-two years as a Junior), and would have been even worse had not seven Fellows either resigned for other posts or died fairly young within the period 1898–1906. As for the annual election, this was of benefit to Fellowship candidates, but, once elected, it bore against them, for the number of Junior Fellows increased from twenty-five in 1881 to twenty-nine in 1896.

If the reader feels that we have strayed for too long from our main theme – the history of the College as a centre of education and scholarship – and devoted too much space to political, religious and constitutional issues, we can only plead that we have followed the example of the College itself, as for over a decade these themes were the major preoccupation of the Fellows, and to some extent of the Professors. Between 1867 and 1877 many of the pens which might have been busy with scholarly treatises were being sharpened for yet another trenchant pamphlet on denominational education or ecclesiastical finance. But there were a few, such as Haughton and Mahaffy, who had the energy and the versatility to be active on both fronts at once, and there were several, especially among the younger men, who gave the priority to scholarship. The troubled decade of 1867–77 saw the publication of treatises on screws by R.S. Ball and on friction by Jellett which soon came to be ranked as classics, of a pioneer work on the mechanics of animal musculature by Haughton, and of deservedly popular textbooks on the calculus by Williamson; editions of the *Heroides* by Arthur Palmer and of the *Bacchae* by R.Y. Tyrrell, Ferrar's essay on comparative grammar, and a flood of books on ancient history by J.P. Mahaffy; a translation of a commentary on Kant, also by Mahaffy, and a book on Plato's ethics by Maguire; Edward Dowden's assessment of Shakespeare, soon to run into a ninth edition; numerous and varied zoological works by Wright and Macalister; and a much needed exposition by Longfield of the law of land tenure. It is a record which needs no apology.

It was, indeed, the hectic year of 1873 that saw the launching of *Hermathena*, a scholarly journal intended primarily for contributions from graduates of the University, but occasionally extending the hospitality of its pages to others. It has continued in publication without a break since then, and although for a large part of its history it has been devoted primarily to classics, with a small admixture of philosophy and College history, in its early years its scope was much wider, and recently it has again diversified its subject-matter. The first two volumes contained articles on Romance philology, patristics, classics, algebra, geometry, dynamics, cystallography, Dravidian philology and the Ogham alphabet. Several of them, unfortunately, were marked by the violent and scornful tone which was in some degree characteristic of scholarly controversies of the day, but which *Hermathena* exhibited in an extreme form. The first fifty pages were devoted to a quite unprovoked diatribe by Robert Atkinson against an edition by Luard of a Norman-French poem. This was Atkinson's normal style of writing, but even milder men like Palmer and Ingram rent in pieces Paley's edition of Propertius and the new edition of Liddell and Scott. After this things were quieter for a while, but in 1884 a large part of two successive issues was occupied by a celebrated quarrel between Tyrrell and Maguire on the one side, and on the other side Sayce of Oxford with Mahaffy as his local ally.[26] It had the unfortunate result of polarizing classics in Dublin into two opposing camps. The severely literary approach was represented by Tyrrell, Palmer and Maguire, with R.C. Jebb and other Cambridge scholars as their allies, who regarded history as a spare-time amusement and excavation as mere manual labour; against them were ranged the historians led by Mahaffy and J.B. Bury, warmly supported by A.H. Sayce and others at Oxford. Nevertheless, if these controversies generated excessive heat they also produced some light and helped to make the Dublin classical school well known in the learned world.

Some of the credit for the considerable volume of the College's scholarly output belongs to Humphrey Lloyd, who succeeded to the provostship in 1867. He had been considered seriously as a candidate in 1851, although he was then only recently turned fifty, but was ruled out chiefly because he differed from the Government on the National Education question. By 1867 this was no longer an active controversy, and in any case Lloyd had changed his views. At that time Todd alone could rival him in scholarly reputation, but there were too many issues on which Todd held an inflexible minority view, and in any case his health was beginning to fail. Hart and Carson were perhaps Lloyd's equals in administrative competence, but their names were scarcely known outside Dublin. Furthermore, both in educational and in ecclesiastical affairs Lloyd was a centre-party man, anxious to make changes in any system which was working badly, but not wedded to change for its own sake.

His appointment is a landmark in College history, as he was the first Provost, at least since the seventeenth century, to have published a substantial corpus of original scholarship. He followed up his early demonstration of conical refraction by further important work in optics, and in the field of terrestrial magnetism he not only made valuable observations for many years in the observatory which had been built for him in the Fellows' garden, but successfully organized a team of other observers, some as far afield as India, to make measurements which would fit together into a co-ordinated whole. Although very conscious of the necessity of orderly administration and conscientious teaching, he struck an almost twentieth-century note in his emphasis of the importance to a university of the cultivation of scholarship and research, and was in full accord with such English colleagues as J.R. Seeley and Mark Pattison who were advocating similar ideals. He put forward this plea in a pamphlet,[27] printed privately and mainly for internal circulation soon after his appointment as Provost; it is anonymous, but the authorship was an open secret. It contains some other ideas which are suggestive more of twentieth- than of nineteenth-century thinking. Classics and mathematics should be optional after the first year, partly because variety and usefulness must be considered as well as mental training in deciding the choice of subjects; experience has shown in any case that classics and mathematics 'are studied by few or none except candidates for Fellowship'[28] and 'there are minds even of a high order which seem incapable of mathematical reasoning'. English Language and Literature and also Physical Science should be developed as elements of the pass course, and the course should be abbreviated so as to cover ten terms (as at Oxford and Cambridge) instead of twelve.

(xiii)

The increase in the diversity and the improvement in quality of scholarly production during the sixties and seventies must be attributed, however, not only to Lloyd's encouragement, but also to various changes which had taken place as a result of the Commission's report and the ensuing discussions. Pride of place must here be given to the renaissance of classical scholarship as a direct result of the changes in the Fellowship examination described in the last chapter. It was a few years before the best of the classical moderators could be persuaded that as an alternative to the Bar or the Indian Civil Service, which most of them had hitherto favoured,[29] Fellowship was a real possibility; and some able men, such as Ferrar, whose interests were mainly literary, had already committed themselves to mathematics before the new regulations were announced. But in 1859 for the first time for many years a classical moderator competed for Fellowship, and in 1864 Mahaffy, who had been narrowly defeated by a mathematician in 1862 and by a philosopher in 1863, was elected. His election was soon followed by that of Palmer in 1867 and of Tyrrell in 1868. By a strange and very fortunate chance these three men all turned out to be scholars of the first rank. By 1880 Mahaffy had published two of his very popular works on Greek social history, a massive, if somewhat controversial history of Greek classical literature, and a host of minor writings on topics ranging from Greek athletics to Greek cats; Palmer had established himself as an authority on Ovid and Propertius; and Tyrrell, equally at home in Greek and Latin, had edited the *Bacchae* and

19   John Pentland Mahaffy. Provost, 1914–19.

had produced the first volume of his *magnum opus* – the *Correspondence* of Cicero. Another fortunate chance decreed that between these men there should be a wide spread of interests: Mahaffy, though his mind was prepared to range into almost any corner, was primarily the social historian of the ancient world; Palmer had the rare talents required for a successful textual critic; and Tyrrell was above all else the stylist, translator and literary critic. The impact of their teaching, at least on the more able students, can be seen (apart from the tribute paid by Oscar Wilde to the inspiration he had received from Tyrrell and Mahaffy) in the roll of those who graduated in the decade 1868–77; they included Louis Claude Purser, who was soon to join them as a colleague, and seven others, with William Ridgeway as the most outstanding, who were later to fill classical chairs in other universities.

It was natural that this rapid recruitment of new talent should lead to the creation of new teaching offices in classics. Mahaffy had spontaneously started a course of lectures in ancient history in addition to his routine tutorial and honor lectures, and in 1869 the Board recognized its value by creating for him the post of lecturer in Ancient History and raising it to a Professorship in 1871. The salary was negligible, but for Mahaffy the right to be known as 'the Professor' at the age of thirty-two was sufficient reward. Meanwhile the chair of Latin, which had been stillborn in the financial squabbles of 1858, was finally instituted in 1870 as an attractive post, comparable to the Regius Professorship of Greek and the mathematical chairs. Ferrar, whose comparative grammar of the ancient languages had appeared in the previous year, was appointed as the first Professor, but unfortunately he died only a year later. Tyrrell succeeded him over the head of Palmer, who was a year senior, chiefly, it would appear, because Tyrrell had given evidence of his scholarly ability at an earlier age. In 1880, however, when Ingram became Librarian, Tyrrell transferred to the Regius Professorship of Greek, and Palmer's now substantial achievements were rewarded with the chair of Latin. There was also established at this time, in response to a request signed by nine of the Tutors, not all of them classical men, a new post with the rather quaint title of Professor Extraordinary of Classical Literature. It was given to T.J.B. Brady, a classical moderator of twelve years' standing who had collaborated with Tyrrell in bringing out *Hesperidum Susurri* (*Whispers from the far west*), an elegant little volume in the genre that was rapidly becoming fashionable among classical scholars – the rendering into unimpeachable Greek or Latin of English verses, in many cases of indifferent quality. Brady was certainly competent to instruct undergraduates in this art (in so far as it can be imparted by a teacher) and he had some years' experience as a successful private tutor. But he owed his appointment partly to an early exercise of what is now termed 'positive discrimination', for it was an open secret that the chair was made for him partly because he was a Catholic. In 1873, the year of his appointment, the College was committed to the support of Fawcett's Act, and was anxious to give visible proof that its non-sectarianism was genuine.[30] Brady resigned after seven years, however, to take up a career in the civil service; the chair was allowed to lapse, but Maguire, by then a Fellow, was appointed as lecturer in Classical Composition, with much the same duties.

(xiv)

Philosophy too might have been expected to benefit from the revised arrangements for the Fellowship examination, for although it carried less weight than either classics or mathematics it was a field to which most of the classical men and some of the mathematicians would look to pick up some extra marks. As it turned out, however, the harvest in philosophy was rather meagre. Of the twenty-four Fellows elected between 1860 and 1885 only eight were Moderators in Philosophy,[31] and of these only four showed any interest in the subject after their election to Fellowship. One of them, Thomas Maguire, may be said to have made his career in philosophy, and in the nine years for which he held a Fellowship he published some substantial contributions to Platonic studies. For Webb, Mahaffy and Bernard, however, philosophy was only one interest among many in their varied intellectual careers, and they never went beyond the role of translator, interpreter and commentator; no distinctive school of philosophers arose in Dublin. T.E. Webb was the most original of the three, though his career serves as a warning of how easily one who aspires to be a polymath may, from lack of discrimination and serious application, end up as a mere dilettante. The son of a dissenting minister in Cornwall (though surprisingly with a small private income), he came to Trinity after a few years as a schoolmaster. Although he won a scholarship in Classics and several prizes for classical and English composition, he graduated with a poor degree in philosophy in 1848. For the next nine years he seems to have had no fixed occupation, but in 1857 he was elected Professor of Moral Philosophy on the strength of an original and provocative but not entirely convincing reinterpretation and defence of Locke. In 1861 he was called to the Bar, and in 1863 was elected to Fellowship, defeating no less a competitor than Mahaffy.[32] After ten years as Professor of Moral Philosophy he exchanged his chair for the Regius Professorship of Laws, and no sooner was he established in that post than he imitated his predecessor, John Anster, by starting to translate

Faust.[33] In 1868 he stood unsuccessfully as a Whig candidate for one of the University seats in Parliament but a few years later was writing strong denunciations of Gladstone's Land Acts. Meanwhile, after having failed to persuade the Board to allow him to hold a tutorship while practising at the Bar, he acquiesced in 1871 in a reorganization of the terms of tenure of his chair, whereby it was assigned a salary of £500 but declared incompatible with Fellowship. Later still he filled successfully for nine years the post of Public Orator, where he showed that his early skill in classical composition had not deserted him. Finally, on his appointment as a County Court Judge in 1888, he severed all his ties with the College. At the end of the day it was found that the lawyers tended to admire his knowledge of philosophy, philosophers his literary skill and literary critics his ability as a lawyer. Significantly enough his last publication was a spirited but easily refuted defence of the Baconian authorship of Shakespeare's plays.

The remaining part-time philosophers, however, did some useful work in publishing a series of translations of and commentaries on Kant. When Mahaffy took his degree in 1859 the course was virtually confined to Plato and Aristotle, Bishop Butler, Descartes, the Scottish empiricists and Mill, though here and there a question might serve for a student enterprising and diligent enough to have read some Kant to display his knowledge. At this time, however, few of his works were available in translation. To Mahaffy, who had grown up partly in Germany, this presented no obstacle, but to the learned world in general, even at a time when a working knowledge of German was commoner among English speakers than it is today, it was a severe impediment, if only for the reason that Kant's style is to most readers so obscure that any additional obstacle makes it impenetrable. Mahaffy, though without a sustained interest in metaphysics, was attracted by Kant's view of the world, and his first publication after election to Fellowship was a translation, with some critical and indeed controversial notes, of Fischer's commentary on the *Critique of pure reason*. He followed it with a translation, also with critical notes, of some other writings, published in 1872–4 as *Kant's critical philosophy for English readers*, and some years later his elder colleague, T.K. Abbott, and his younger colleague, J.H. Bernard, translated respectively the ethical writings and the *Critique of judgment*. The new interest was soon reflected in the honor course; in 1867 Kant made his first tentative appearance among the recommended authors, and by 1880 he was well established as a major element in the course.

The failure of the university of Berkeley to foster any really original philosophic thought during the nineteenth century is in part attributable to the prevalence of a view which regarded philosophy as an elegant accomplishment rather than as a fundamental branch of scholarship. If a classicist interested himself more in Plato's thought than in his style; if a mathematician were to speculate about the basis of logic; if a theologian were to pursue the study of ethics outside the strict limits of the Christian revelation – all these would stand to their credit, but nobody expected them to abandon their primary studies in favour of these side-shows. This attitude was at once the result and the cause of the relatively poor calibre of moderators in philosophy compared with those in other subjects, and it expressed itself in the small importance which the Board seemed to attach to the chair of Moral Philosophy. Up till about 1840 Dublin made no worse a showing in philosophy than did Oxford or Cambridge, but in the middle and latter part of the century a comparison of the Dublin philosophers with Whewell, Grote and Sidgwick at Cambridge and with Green, Bosanquet and Bradley at Oxford became embarrassing. Yet it was just at the time when this disparity began that the Dublin chair was founded. Trinity in its early days had no Knightsbridge to provide a substantial endowment, and it is understandable that the chair should at first have carried a small salary and fairly light duties. But when the chairs of Latin and Greek were made into full-time posts comparable to those of Mathematics and of Physics there was no suggestion that the same thing might be done for Philosophy. We find, in consequence, that the ten men who occupied the chair from 1837 to the end of the century were a very mixed lot. Three were Fellows at the time of their election, one was an ex-Fellow, and one (Webb) was elected Fellow during his tenure of the chair; of the other five three were clergymen and one a lawyer. Butler (see p. 170) and Maguire died in office and might have continued their philosophical careers if they had lived longer, but all the others gave up the chair, in most cases willingly,[34] after a fairly short tenure. It would seem that in the eyes of Fellows and non-Fellows alike the responsibilities and duties of the chair outweighed the rewards and, paradoxically, it would seem that the fact that it was not restricted to Fellows depressed the average quality of its occupants. For the chair of Hebrew (restricted to Fellows by the terms of its foundation), though no better endowed, acquired a higher prestige, and its record for scholarship is considerably better.

(xv)

It was in 1870, nearly a century after the establishment of the Professorships of modern languages, that the first move was made to introduce these subjects into academic courses instead of maintaining them as 'fancy' embellishments which could be studied on an extra-curricular basis by those who had a taste for such things.[35] In January of that year Ingram proposed that the comprehensive (and in the eyes of some too comprehensive) Moderatorship in History, Jurisprudence, Economics and English Literature should be broken up, and it was easy enough to argue that a man might have a deep understanding of Shakespeare without much taste for Blackstone or Adam Smith. The Board accepted his case, and English Literature was detached from the complex and set up as as one half of a new Moderatorship in Modern Literature, of which the other half could consist of either French or German.[36] Ingram was, no doubt, motivated in part by the success of his protégé and successor in the chair of English literature, Edward Dowden, in popularizing the study of the subject and enlarging its scope; but the way had also been paved for him by changes among the Professors of Modern Languages. Abeltshauser, the Professor of French and German, had died in 1866. He was an Alsatian by birth and probably bilingual from childhood; presumably he had been baptized as a Lutheran or Huguenot, but he conformed to the Church of Ireland, took the testimonium in Trinity College and was ordained in 1842 at the age of thirty-five, the same year in which he was appointed Professor. On entrance to College he described himself as self-educated, but clearly the operation was successful, and as regards imparting a sound reading, writing and speaking knowledge of the languages he taught he seems to have given complete satisfaction; it was no part of his duties to teach literature and he did not attempt to do so.[37] But on his death in 1866 the Board, realizing the growing importance of language in competitive examinations, and of German in particular for serious students of almost any branch of scholarship, obtained powers to appoint separate Professors of French and German. A few months later it used these powers to appoint as Professor of German A.M. Selss, a Rhinelander who had studied in Berlin before coming to Dublin and taking a Moderatorship in Classics. He had qualified himself for the appointment by publishing in the previous year *A critical outline of the literature of Germany*, which was later to run through five editions, and during his forty-year tenure of the chair was to produce several more textbooks, primers and editions, all limited in scope but professional in tone. He was, in fact, the first Professor of a modern language in the twentieth-century use of the term, and although he had to supplement his modest salary by teaching also at Alexandra College he could almost be reckoned a full-time professor.

French seems to have been regarded as a matter of less urgency, and no appointment was made in 1866; nor is it not clear whether any instuction in the language was given for the next two years. There is, in fact, a curious lacuna in the official records in this whole sphere for the

271

years 1866–9. Marani, the Professor of Italian and Spanish, fades out without explanation; in June 1867, the Register records the appointment as lecturer in Italian (with no mention of Spanish) of Mr Edward Atkinson (though clearly Robert Atkinson was intended); in April 1869 there is a reference, *en passant*, to the Professor of Italian; finally, two months later, a decree declares that the Professor of Italian and Spanish shall henceforth be known as the Professor of Romance Languages, leaving one to infer that French has also been gathered up into his net.

At all events Robert Atkinson acted as Professor of the three Romance languages for nearly forty years, and was a good example of the precept that once you have learned six languages the rest come easily, for in 1871 he took on an additional chair – that of Sanskrit and Comparative Philology. His publications mainly concerned Old and Middle Irish but included brief forays into Welsh, Coptic and Old Russian, and in 1869, when Mir Alaud Ali, Professor of Arabic and Hindustani, obtained a year's leave of absence to polish up his Persian it was Atkinson who agreed to act as his substitute. He is said also to have spoken Chinese with an unusually perfect accent for a European and to have had a working knowledge of Tibetan, Tamil and Telegu.

It may well be doubted whether such a busy and versatile philologist could give very sensitive teaching on French literature; nevertheless the new Moderatorship in Modern Literature was launched in 1873 and soon became popular. In 1877 French and German were introduced also into the Sophister years of the pass course as optional alternatives to Greek and Latin, but the Professors did not have to bear the entire burden of the extra teaching as there were some of the Fellows such as Barlow and G.L. Cathcart who were, rightly or wrongly, considered capable of assisting them.

Italian and Spanish, however, languished for many years after this in an extra-curricular limbo; lectures were available, as before, for such students as cared to pay a fee for them, and prizes were offered at entrance and at two other stages in an undergraduate's career. The total number of prize-men, however, in the early seventies averaged only one or two a year in Italian and less than one in Spanish. In the light of this lack of interest the Board cannot be blamed for omitting these languages from the degree courses. Italian, which in early Victorian times had rivalled and sometimes even displaced French as an elegant accomplishment for well-educated people of either sex, had given place to German, partly under the influence of Carlyle, and partly by its usefulness as the key to so much contemporary scholarship. Spanish (perhaps because of memories of the Inquisition recently revived by Charles Kingsley) nowhere commanded much respect until well into the twentieth century.

Mathematics, meanwhile, though ousted from its complete predomin-ance at Fellowship, still remained a subject of primary importance, and of the fourteen men elected to Fellowship between 1860 and 1880 nine had graduated in mathematics (some of them also in experimental science). They were not, however, of the same calibre as their classical contemporaries, George Fitzgerald alone being of the first rank, though F.A. Tarleton and Frederick Purser had each a respectable corpus of publication to his credit. Salmon was still active in mathematics until his appointment to the Regius Professorship of Divinity in 1866 redirected his energies, and Michael Roberts, Jellett and Townsend, who held the mathematical chairs in the period under review, were all men of more than local renown and thoroughly well qualified for their posts. Experimental Physics under Galbraith and J.R. Leslie made less of a showing, and it was not until Fitzgerald was appointed to the chair in 1881 that a worthy successor to McCullagh and Humphrey Lloyd was found. Astronomy, however, had a sudden revival in 1865 after the death of Hamilton, who, it must be confessed, had let the observatory run down rather badly in his last few years. His successor was Franz Brünnow,[38] who had worked for a time in America as well as in his native Germany, and was the author of a widely used textbook. He immediately set about the reorganization of the observatory, and induced the Board to provide the money necessary for mounting in an equatorial telescope the excellent object-glass which had been pre-sented to the University a few years earlier by an English astronomer through the good offices of Lord Rosse. Not long afterwards he suc-ceeded in obtaining a new meridian circle, so that by 1873 the observatory could be considered well equipped and up to date. Brünnow made some important observations on the parallax of stars during his tenure of the chair, but in 1874 he retired and was succeeded by R.S. (later Sir Robert) Ball, son of the former Curator of the University Museum (p. 197) who, though he continued Brünnow's observations on parallax, was better known for his publications in dynamics and his successful books explaining astronomy to the layman.

The eighteen-sixties were years of rapid advance in almost all departments of natural science, and it is not surprising that this should have led to some pressure to enlarge and diversify their place in the curriculum. In 1871 the Moderatorship in Experimental and Natural Science established in 1851 was replaced by separate Moderatorships in Experimental Science (Physics, Chemistry and Mineralogy) and Natural Science (Zoology, Comparative Anatomy, Botany and Geology). Within each of these divisions a candidate had to cover the whole course, but at least the physicist was no longer plagued with botany or vice versa. Three years later the same groupings of subjects, in an abbreviated and simplifed form, were introduced as optional alternatives in the Sophister years of the pass course.

As with modern languages, so in the sciences these developments were accompanied by changes in the establishment and personnel of the teaching staff. In 1865 the health of Harvey, the Professor of Botany, which had always been rather precarious, finally broke down, and he died in the following year. His successor, Alexander Dickson, stayed in Dublin for only two years before returning to his native land as Professor at Glasgow, and in 1869 E.P. Wright, who for the past eleven years had been lecturer in Zoology, transferred to the chair of Botany. Alexander Macalister, an energetic medical man, succeeded him as lecturer in Zoology, and after two years he was given the title of Professor. Although he was later to publish textbooks on general zoology which, in spite of their severe and rigidly anatomical approach, ran through several editions, his interests lay mainly in the field of the comparative anatomy of vertebrates, and especially, perhaps under the influence of Haughton, of their muscular system. It was, therefore, appropriate enough that a new chair of Comparative Anatomy should be founded for him in 1872, but the fact that he continued to hold the chair of the very closely related subject, Zoology, and that the new chair was founded in response to an almost unanimous request from the tutors, suggests to anybody familiar with academic politics that there was a problem somewhere.

So indeed there was, and it took the form of the personality of Benjamin George McDowel, who had been Professor of Anatomy since 1858. McDowel was a brilliant and successful surgeon and a good teacher, but he was also absent-minded, ambitious, and apt to consider that regulations, no matter how well drawn up, did not apply to him. He had a large private practice; he acted for some years as joint secretary to the Zoological Society; he contributed to medical literature; he was physician to the workhouse hospitals; and as Professor of Anatomy he was *ex officio* clinical lecturer in Sir Patrick Dun's Hospital. 'This multiplicity of duties', wrote an admirer, 'would have proved too much for a less able man', but in fact it proved too much even for McDowel, who was able to hold all his posts only by giving scant attention to some of them. Complaints began to reach the Board of his irregular attendance, first at the dissecting room and later at Dun's Hospital, but he brushed them aside with excuses and promises for the future. Irregularity of attendance is not a fault which students condemn with great severity, and McDowel's lectures, relating as they did the dry facts of anatomy to some principles of physiology and to the practice of surgery, made him popular, so that one of the censures passed on him was followed by a complimentary address from his students, past and present. The Board was naturally annoyed and embarrassed; it declared that although it could not control the action of past students it could and did forbid present students from signing such an address and indicated to McDowel that to receive it would, in the Board's opinion, be an action in the worst of taste.

The chair of Anatomy was, by Act of Parliament, a renewable seven-year appointment. McDowel's renewal in 1865 passed without incident (although the complaints of his irregular attendance had been coming in since 1860), but in 1872 it was passed by only five votes to three, and was accompanied by an admonishment and by the appointment of Macalister to the chair of Comparative Anatomy and a share in the control (and the fees) of the dissecting room. Shortly afterwards the Board threatened to deprive McDowel of his chair for flouting the conditions which it had imposed, but he appealed to the Visitors and achieved at least a partial victory. But in 1879 the Board laid down quite clearly the conditions necessary for his reappointment and refused to modify them. McDowel did not stand for election; Macalister succeeded him, retaining also his chair of Comparative Anatomy but resigning that of Zoology.

The College was unfortunate in that two of its most brilliant Professors of Anatomy should have been such difficult men, and as with Macartney sixty years earlier, the Board was criticized for pedantic refusal to modify its rules to meet a 'special case'. Doubtless there were faults on both sides but the Board's quarrel with McDowel, as with his near-namesake George McDowell (p. 218),[39] represented a necessary, if perhaps unskilful move in the campaign to control the amount of time which academic officers gave to non-academic occupations.

Despite these tensions, however, the Medical School prospered during the period under review. Whereas from 1845 to 1860 the number of M.B. degrees awarded per annum averaged from nine to twelve, in 1860 it began to rise suddenly and rapidly, so that by 1870 it was averaging thirty-eight. From then up to 1911 it remained fairly constant, the five-year average over these forty years varying only between thirty-four and forty-five. Part of the rise is to be attributed, no doubt, to the legislation relating to registration; part to the administrative efficiency introduced by Haughton as Registrar of the school; part to the abandonment, except for a few formal purposes, of the dual control by Trinity College and the College of Physicians, so that the 'School of Physic in Dublin' became effectively the medical school of Trinity College; part to the steadily improving social status of the profession during the middle years of the nineteenth century; and part to the general improvement in quality of the Professors in the school.

For by 1865, with William Stokes still Regius Professor of Physic, and with J.T. Banks, Aquilla Smith and Fleetwood Churchill occupying three of the four King's Professorships, with Robert Adams Regius Professor of Surgery and McDowel, with all his faults, kindling enthusiasm for the study of anatomy, the school could confidently face comparison with any other in the British Isles. Ten years later it was to be further strengthened by the appointment of Bennett to the other chair of Surgery, of Emerson Reynolds to Chemistry and of J.M. Purser to the King's Professorship of the Institutes of Medicine. Purser was within a few years to revolutionize the functions of this post and to establish systematic and up-to-date teaching in physiology and histology. But a general assessment of his contribution to the school belongs more appropriately to the next chapter.

(xvii)

Before we bid good-bye to the world of mid-Victorian Trinity some mention must be made of one of its more outstanding and interesting figures, J.H. Todd, who died in 1869. Elected Fellow a month after Bartholomew Lloyd had been appointed Provost, he shows himself at first as a prim and starchy ultra-conservative. Disapproving of most of Lloyd's reforms but too junior to offer any effective opposition, he had to content himself with deploring the evils of the day: the Provost walking through the squares without cap or gown, the absence of Fellows from weekday Chapel, proposals that Fellows should be allowed to marry and that papists should be eligible for Scholarship. 'Discipline is laughed at, the office of College Tutor reduced to a cipher, the most dangerous revolutionary plans proposed'.[40] There seemed to be no hope or help for the College unless by Providential intervention C.R. Elrington should be made Provost. But although Todd preserved throughout his life many of his conservative principles (on the Board he was always quick to oppose an application for a dispensation for another lay Fellowship) he did not waste his time in grumbling or repining. Changes which could not be arrested must be endured, and some of them turned out to be less disastrous than he had feared; meanwhile he would stick to his principles and work hard. He was a devoted member of the small but resolute band of Irish high-churchmen (high in doctrine rather than ritual), and supported Elrington and later Lee in seeing that this attitude received at least some recognition in the Divinity School. In his Donnellan lectures, published in 1840, he demolished the doctrine, popular among evangelicals, that the Pope was the Antichrist of the Revelation, arguing that despite much corruption the Roman Church still maintained the essential truths of Christianity; but eight years later he attacked with equal vigour the rising doctrine of papal infallibility.

Todd held the chair of Hebrew for the last twenty years of his life, but his most substantial contribution to scholarship was in the field of Irish studies. He was assiduous in collecting Irish manuscripts for the Library, tracking them down in France and Germany as well as in Ireland, and buying them with his own money in the hope (often, but not always realized) of being repaid by the Board. He was equally assiduous in finding assistants to catalogue them, in editing several himself, and, as secretary to the Irish Archaeological Society, in encouraging others to the same task. His life of St Patrick, though open to attack on points of detail (like every other work on the subject), was a pioneer attempt to reconstruct Irish society of the fifth century. With the evangelical enthusiasm of the Achill Mission and the successive Professors of Irish in the University he shared no common ground, so his work on Irish studies was centred mainly on the Royal Irish Academy, of which in due course he became President.

He had other interests outside the College; as a keen supporter of the Church Educational Society; as Precentor of St Patrick's Cathedral; as the close friend, constant correspondent and at times influential counsellor of Primate Beresford; and as a key man in the foundation and guidance in its early years of St Columba's College, organized on public-school lines, and with a strong emphasis on churchmanship and the cultivation of the Irish language. But these outside interests did not prevent him from giving to the College more hours of devoted service than did many of his colleagues. He was a popular tutor and a conscientious lecturer. He was responsible for the launching of the University Calendar in 1833, and wrote for the first issue a long and valuable historical introduction, based partly on information accumulated by Barrett but also on his own researches. Near the end of his life he compiled the *Catalogue of graduates*, and although failing eyesight led to the passing of a rather large number of errors in the proofs, it is a most useful book, which has been kept up to date by supplements ever since.

But it is for his work in the Library that Todd deserves above all the gratitude of posterity, for more than any other one man he made of it the great library it is today. It was not till about 1835 that acquisitions under the Copyright Acts were put on a reasonably satisfactory basis, so that a copy of very nearly every book published in the United Kingdom (except for certain categories deliberately excluded as trivial, ephemeral or otherwise undesirable) actually found its way to the

Library. This meant that the annual intake went up to about two thousand a year,[41] and the shift from what had been a scholar's library to what we now call a deposit library had begun, with all its attendant problems of selection and cataloguing. It was fortunately at this juncture that Todd offered his services as unpaid assistant to the Librarian, though at first he concerned himself mainly with manuscripts. Only after his succession to the office of Librarian in 1852 did he have an opportunity of reforming the archaic cataloguing system by persuading the Board to appoint permanent Library clerks (instead of graduate scholars, who departed as soon as they had learned their job) and a further assistant, to be paid by a deduction from the Librarian's salary. He attracted foreign scholars like Siegfried and C.F. Lottner to double the teaching of Sanskrit with doing both skilled and semi-skilled work in the Library, and succeeded in making them happy. He supported the policy of opening the Library to as many readers as was compatible with security, granted the very small staff.[42] But his greatest monument is the printed catalogue, for although only the first volume was published in Todd's lifetime it was his achievement of an efficient and up-to-date slip-catalogue that made the printing of the remaining volumes possible within sixteen years of his death.

Todd's limitations are obvious; the rigidity with which he maintained as principles opinions which most other men regarded as negotiable disqualified him from statesmanship even on a small scale; as Provost he would have been disastrous. But men of this type, given the right niche, can do work of great value, and it is a tribute to the College and the Royal Irish Academy that they provided such niches, and to Todd himself that he worked so hard and so skilfully within their relatively narrow confines.[43].

10

The end of the Victorian age

1881–1900

(i)

Many of us are inclined to think of the last two decades of the nineteenth century, the decades of Queen Victoria's two jubilees, as a time of tranquillity: the golden sunset of the Victorian age. For much of the world this picture is valid, but in Ireland it was, at least up to 1893, a time of turmoil and tension. The years which compassed the Land War, the Phoenix Park murders, the fall and death of Parnell, and the introduction and defeat of two Home Rule bills may have seen the sunset of many hopes, but they can hardly be described as golden. Although the physical peace of the College squares was never disturbed or threatened it was natural that the Fellows and Professors should at times be diverted from academic studies by the double threat of an agrarian and a constitutional revolution. The Board conceded that 'the work of a university lies in general outside the field of politics, but . . .' and it needed little imagination to guess where the 'but' was leading. 'There are times when no loyal subject ought to be silent', and 1886 was one of them.[1]

The Land War and the Home Rule movement represented distinct aspirations, but they worked in close concert and reinforced each other. The attitude of the College to the former was simple: it did not mind what purchase schemes were devised so long as its own income from land (which represented about half the total income) was not sensibly reduced. During the various campaigns for the withholding of rents the College was in a relatively strong position, since it had used the enlargement of its leasing powers granted in 1851 to let most of its property in large blocks to perpetuity tenants; these were men of some substance, and when they asked the College for a scaling-down of rents the Board could give them a dusty answer without exposing itself to the charge of grinding the faces of the poor. Its refractory tenants in the fifties and sixties had included Lord Chief Justice Lefroy and the Earl of Leitrim. The latter was murdered in 1878 as a rack-renting landlord, but this did not prevent his nephew and heir from addressing the

279

House of Lords a few years later to plead the cause of distressed tenants against their flinty-hearted landlords (in his case Trinity College). Although the obduracy of the Board led to considerable arrears of rent its policy paid off well in the end, for when the College was bought out under the Wyndham Act the purchase price was based on the somewhat unrealistic rentals which the Board had insisted on maintaining. Although, therefore, most of the Fellows were sympathetic to the landlords' cause, it was only the Bursar who had to worry about the matter from day to day. But Home Rule was different: its menace was at once vaguer and more serious.

It is difficult after the lapse of a century – a century which has seen most of Ireland progress from a part of the United Kingdom to a dominion and then to a republic – to understand the intensity of the hopes and fears which were raised by Gladstone's modest Home Rule bills. It arose in part from the failure of those who have become embroiled in political debate to realize how much of the texture of daily life can survive unaltered after important constitutional changes.[2] It was due in part to the fact that both sides saw in the limited proposals of the Home Rule bills the first step towards a wider separation. But most of all its arose from a realization that Home Rule would mean a transfer to Catholics of part of the power hitherto held by Protestants, and to men who believed passionately in an infallible Church or an infallible Bible that must appear as the triumph of the forces of light or of darkness. There were, of course, some prominent Catholic Unionists (mainly landlords and professional men) and a few Protestant Home Rulers (mainly intellectuals), but their divided allegiance made them uneasy and they did little to blur the main line of cleavage. For the Protestant Anglo-Irishman and the Catholic of mainly Gaelic stock represented two different cultures; they differed in their accents, in the games they played and the songs they sang, in the schools they attended and the history they learnt at school, as well as in their religious practices and beliefs. Of all the differences, however, that of religion was the most conspicuous and the most important, and the belief on each side that the other was in the toils of a pernicious error accounts for the political intransigence of otherwise mild-mannered men.

It must be remembered also that it was these decades that saw the rise of liberal imperialism, a mood which persisted until 1914, and which permitted men who were keen supporters of free trade, an extended suffrage, prison reform and slum clearance to regard the maintenance and indeed the extension of the British Empire as part of the *summum bonum*, and to fasten on followers of the Gladstonian tradition the contemptuous label of Little Englanders.[3] Like most political attitudes it was not entirely free from self-deception and hypocrisy, but it was favoured by many undoubtedly high-minded and intelligent men, who believed without hesitation that the Virgilian injunction to Augustus applied to the colonial governors of Britain:

> Tu regere imperio populos, Romane, memento
> (Hae tibi erunt artes), pacisque imponere morem,
> Parcere subiectis et debellare superbos.

They were able to point out that in at least some places British rule had supplanted a squalid local tyranny, and to defend, at least in its earlier phases, the South African war, for even Lloyd George was unable to demonstrate convincingly that Paul Kruger was in the van of liberalism. Such men opposed Home Rule on the grounds that even if it were to bring benefits to Ireland it would endanger the cohesion and the safety of the Empire.

Unionism, therefore, provided a platform on which raucous jingoes, stodgy conservatives, earnest evangelicals, anti-clerical rationalists and liberal imperialists could sit together and for the time being forget their differences. Most of these groups were represented among the Fellows of Trinity, and the commitment to the Unionist cause was almost unanimous. There was no lack of young, and even middle-aged, Fellows and Professors who were promoting schemes for one reform or another and who on various issues did not hesitate to dissent from the orthodoxy of the day. But with the sole exception of Galbraith (who died in 1890) they voted against Home Rule because they saw in it not the realization but the frustration of their reforms and their hopes. When Lord Houghton arrived as Lord-Lieutenant in 1892 the Board, perhaps over-filled with self-confidence as a result of the Tercentenary celebrations, decided rather tactlessly that this was a moment 'when no loyal subject ought to be silent', and inserted among the usual platitudes of the loyal address from the Senate a clause indicating its hope that the Union would remain intact. As Houghton was the nominee of a government clearly pledged to Home Rule he returned the address, saying that he was unable to receive one phrased in these terms. The Board had to abandon its position of being *plus royaliste que le Viceroi* and removed the offending passage, but made it clear that its sentiments on the topic were unaltered.

At least a dozen of the Fellows, including most of those who were to play a prominent part in the College later, did not confine their Unionist zeal to voting, but sat on Unionist platforms and signed petitions and manifestos. There were moreover, one Fellow and one Professor whose enthusiasm for the cause carried them even further, and made them devote to it a large part of their leisure, at a time when the politically minded academic was a much rarer phenomenon than it is today. Thomas Maguire, the first Catholic non-foundation scholar and the first Catholic Fellow, was the son of a magistrate, and doubtless the respect for law and order to which he had been brought up was outraged by agrarian crime; his Catholicism may also have given to his Unionism a somewhat hectic and unbalanced quality. At all events he was foolish enough to act as intermediary in Paris in the sale by Pigott to *The Times* of the supposed letters by Parnell which were later shown to be forgeries. Maguire was almost certainly innocent of any deliberate deception, but he showed a strange lack of judgment in becoming involved in a squalid transaction, pardonable perhaps in a journalist, but scarcely in a Professor of Moral Philosophy. He died in London shortly after the fraud had been exposed and three days before Pigott shot himself in Madrid, and although this may have been a coincidence there were some who thought otherwise. The other active Unionist was, rather surprisingly, Edward Dowden, Professor of English Literature, whose sympathetic biography of Shelley appeared in the year of Gladstone's first Home Rule bill. But the radical rhetoric which he could forgive in Shelley he found unforgivable in his fellow-Irishmen. His explicit justification for his political activity, which involved much public speaking as well as committee work, and even the commissioning of Unionist songs from Swinburne and others among his fellow-poets in England, was that his literary criticism was 'imperial or cosmopolitan' and that the demand for Home Rule was provincial and isolationist. It is hard to believe, however, that this motive alone would impel a man who had confessed to a friend that 'politics do not penetrate to the individual centre of my life' to spend so much of his time in what must have been uncongenial company, for he admitted that the bad jokes which he made at meetings 'seem to have met the taste of the average Philistine very happily, and I have had to accept unexpected congratulations with an inward shrug of the shoulders of my spirit'.[4] Some stronger subconscious motive must surely have been at work.

Irish Unionists realized, of course, that they formed a minority in Ireland, and outside Ulster a small minority, and that even when all possible allowance had been made for the part played by the priests as political as well as spiritual directors of their flock, the majority of Irishmen were firmly wedded to the idea of Home Rule in some shape or form. But the Unionists believed that they constituted the *melior et sanior pars*, and that quality should not be beaten down by mere numbers. This tended unfortunately to encourage an attitude of complacency, and at times of arrogance, in men who in other contexts were modest and diffident, and by this means to widen the already considerable gap created by differences in class and religion between them and the majority. From the remote vantage-point of Hatfield, Lord Salisbury might compare the Irish to Hottentots in their incapacity for self-government. The Fellows of Trinity College realized that this was not really true of the gardeners, porters and tobacconists whom they met every day, but it is probably fair to say that they regarded them in much the same light as an Austrian official of the day would look on the traders of Ragusa or the peasants of Galicia. Nor was this attitude confined to the elderly and the established. The undergraduates (amongst whom the sons of really wealthy men formed only an insignificant minority) echoed the attitude of their elders, at times noisily. Among the very few of this period who took the opposite view, and who wished to get close to the common people and identify with them, the most celebrated in later life were Douglas Hyde and J.M. Synge. Neither carried away happy memories of his undergraduate days.

(ii)

But in spite of the constricting effects of·a growing siege mentality the texture of daily life was pleasant enough for most Irishmen who belonged to the world of Trinity College, for the country was reasonably prosperous, and to all but a few cynics the doctrine of inevitable, if at times interrupted progress seemed plausible. The near-unanimity of the Fellows and Professors on political issues,[5] and the absence, at least between 1880 and 1895, of any serious disputes over internal affairs meant that they could concentrate on their academic work. The two decades covered by this chapter saw the publication of a large part of the writings of Ingram, John Gwynn, Abbott, Mahaffy, Palmer, Tyrrell, Fitzgerald and Atkinson, while in the same period younger men such as L.C. Purser, Bernard and Bury were laying the foundations of their scholarly careers.

It was a period of quiet development and consolidation rather than of rapid change or dramatic conflict, and the aspect, activities and aspirations of the College in 1900 did not differ conspicuously from those of 1881. It provides therefore a convenient opportunity for us to attempt a general survey of the College, similar to that given in chapter five for the College of 1830. For this purpose the year 1892 is as suitable as any. Not only was it the year in which the College celebrated its Tercentenary, but it also comes near to the centre of this relatively static period, and it marks the beginning of the decade in which the reputation of the College was higher than ever before or since. For it can fairly be said that of the Fellows and Professors of the closing years of the century over a quarter were men whose scholarship was already, or was shortly to become, widely recognized outside Ireland,[6] while at least another quarter had (or were soon to have) substantial scholarly achievements which would make their names well known in Ireland to the general world of intellect, and outside it to men in their own field of learning. The College, indeed, lived for the first few decades of the twentieth century largely on the reputation it had acquired in the closing years of the nineteenth, and it was only around 1930 that the more perceptive of its members began to feel the chill of unfavourable comparisons and to become uncomfortably aware of the fact that their own fame fell considerably short of that of their predecessors.

To the modern mind the coexistence of so much brilliance with so little change is paradoxical; but in those days change was not regarded as an essential mark of vitality, and the stability of the College at this time does not imply stagnation. Some of the brilliant men of this period (and above all Fitzgerald) were busy, radical reformers, but scholarly excellence is quite compatible with academic conservatism, and men like John Gwynn, Tyrrell and Dowden were not anxious for any extensive changes in the curriculum. The conservatism of the period was based on deliberate choice rather than on negligence. Even though new textbooks were frequently substituted for old their scope remained largely unaltered; and this was true even in the sciences, where the changes indicated the incorporation of many new details of knowledge but not the opening up of totally new fields of investigation. We find that in 1900, as in 1881, *Maud* and *Past and Present* form the terminus of English Literature; Metaphysics and Ethics still end with Kant and the Scottish empirics; and Modern History has extended its compass from the peace of Amiens only to halt at Waterloo. The teaching given in 1900 was solid, sound, balanced, and here and there inspiring, but it was not particularly adventurous.

(iii)

Although our survey of the College will be based on the year 1892 we shall permit ourselves enough retrospects and anticipations over the preceding and the succeeding decades to be able to account for most of the relatively limited amount of change which they witnessed. There are two topics, however, which it would seem best to treat in isolation before we begin our survey; these are the provostship of Jellett and the controversy of 1895 between the Board and the Junior Fellows.

At the beginning of 1880 Provost Humphrey Lloyd was beginning to fail. He was in his eightieth year – an age which no former Provost except Baldwin had attained – and he was willing to retire, but there was no precedent for the retirement of a Provost, and it was not at all clear where his pension would come from. Most of the Fellows would have been content to let Lloyd live out his life, doing what he could and allowing the Vice-Provost (Hart, who was an efficient and businesslike man) to stand in for him on other occasions. There was, however, an ominous cloud on the horizon which rendered this policy perilous. Disraeli's government was in some difficulties; an early general election seemed all too likely; many were inclined to predict a Liberal victory; and if the Liberals won, the hero of last year's Midlothian campaign would be unlikely to persist in his by now somewhat unconvincing retirement from the leadership of the party. And if the appointment of the next Provost were to be in Gladstone's hands, who knew whom he would choose? A radical, probably, or even a Roman Catholic.

For most of the Fellows oppressed by these fears there seemed to be nothing to do except to pray that the Government would outlive the Provost. When this failed to happen and the victory of the Liberals became assured early in April all seemed lost. But not to Anthony Traill, who propounded to two Conservative M.P.s a dramatic rescue operation. Traill had a private income of £2,000 a year, which would suffice to pay Lloyd's pension; he would gladly devote it to that purpose (and as an M.D. he probably guessed shrewdly enough that he would not be out of his money for long), if the Conservative government in its last few weeks of office were to appoint him (Traill) as Provost. He had a good record of work for the party in Co. Antrim, and anyway 'a little new life and blood at the top' would be good for the College.[7]

The audacity of this exercise in academic simony is truly staggering if one realizes that there were twenty-five Fellows senior to Traill (many of them good Conservatives), and that Traill himself was only forty-one and had published nothing except a political speech. Whether the recipients of the proposal were inclined to take him seriously we do not know. In any case it came too late, for Gladstone took office on 23 April. Traill, with the remarkably unsnubbable resilience which was his most outstanding quality, probably dismissed the whole episode from his mind in a matter of weeks.

Lloyd lingered on for the best part of a year, but died in January 1881, whereupon Gladstone confounded the prophets of doom by appointing neither a radical nor a Catholic, but J.H. Jellett, a clergyman of the disestablished church and a right-wing Liberal in politics. He was the obvious choice from among the Senior Fellows. Ingram, although still a Junior Fellow, was the other name to receive serious consideration; his liberalism was more active than Jellett's, and he was favoured by the Lord-Lieutenant and the Attorney-General.[8] His positivism, however, though not flaunted, was an open secret and may have weighed against him, and he was also rated more of a recluse scholar and less of a man of the world than Jellett, who had been a prominent synodsman ever since Disestablishment.

Jellett held office for less than seven years, and does not seem to have made any great impact on College policy, but generally speaking he appears to have been a sound choice. His character is not easy to assess. On the one side we have the family tradition of a great and good man with scarcely a fault,[9] and an absence from his obituary tributes of those phrases which carefully wrap up implied criticism. Against this, however, we must set a few adverse judgments. Mahaffy's petulant outburst in 1886[10] – 'The Provost is getting all the vices of old age. He resents all reforms, is very rude and only thinks of maintaining the privileges of his rotten old Board' – may have been prompted merely by the rejection of some favourite scheme of Mahaffy's, but it suggests something less than universal satisfaction. Dickson is quoted as describing the Board as consisting of three capables, three incapables, and one man capable of anything, the last being Jellett.[11] This dates from a dispute over an examination in 1873, when Jellett was Senior Lecturer: Jellett was probably in the right, though he could have handled the matter in a less imperious spirit than he did. More revealing, perhaps, is Newport White's account of the impression Jellett made on undergraduates:

I was sitting in the Regent House at a Term Examination when the Chief Steward, flinging the door open, announced – 'Gentlemen, the Provost'; and we all rose as the Provost entered, 'pride in his port, defiance in his eye'. He was a very handsome man, with a fine presence and keen glance. He had a weighty and impressive utterance, which gave an air of importance to the most commonplace remark. If he said 'all that glitters is not gold', the hearers, for a moment, felt that a new revelation had been made to them. The grace of humility . . . was not the Provost's.[12]

When Jellett died in February 1888, the Conservatives were back in office and they had little difficulty in deciding to nominate Salmon as his successor. The only other possible names were those of Ingram (who was presumably rejected as a Liberal) and Haughton. The latter was at the time President of the Royal Irish Academy and had been honoured by three British universities, but his fame, considerable as it was, could not stand up against that of Salmon, who had by this time established himself as a leading man in theology as well as in mathematics. His appointment was generally welcomed both inside and outside the College.

(iv)

We have seen how the agitation in 1874–80 among the Junior Fellows about the problem of 'stagnation' in promotion petered out with only the slender gain of a scheme for providing pensions for a few Senior Fellows if they wished to retire. But, as might have been expected, such voluntary retirements were few. In the early eighties vacancies on the Board by death occurred regularly once a year, so that the rate of promotion seemed just tolerable. In 1884–90, however, there followed a period of over five years without a vacancy. This might have been expected to have led to a new agitation (the previous one having been sparked off largely by a similar blockage between 1870 and 1876), but the preparations for the Tercentenary gave the more active Junior Fellows something to busy themselves with, which suggests that their frustration arose as much from lack of power as from lack of money or leisure. By 1895, however, there were three Junior Fellows with more than forty years' service, and it began to look as though only a very lucky man would reach the Board before he was sixty-seven. Moreover, with the constitutional reforms of the Oxford and Cambridge colleges now vindicated by an experience of some twenty years, there was by this time added to personal frustration a more generalized dissatisfaction with an oligarchical rule which could be (and was) represented as indefensible in principle and reactionary in practice. Some of the Junior Fellows, with Bernard and E.J. Gwynn outstanding, had developed by 1895 a firm theoretical objection to the absolute rule of the Seniors.

In February 1895, therefore, the Junior Fellows met, and with only four abstentions[13] sent a communication to the Board asking for the establishment of four retiring pensions of £1,100 per annum, and that until these had been filled no Senior Fellow over seventy should be allowed to sit on the Board.[14] They declared that the existing state of affairs, with every member of the governing body over seventy,[15] constituted a scandal which invited governmental intervention, and they asked for a reply within a month.

It was in many respects a foolish document, corresponding to the sort of letter which most of us write in moments of irritation but rewrite the next morning if we have been prudent enough to sleep on the matter. The constitutional position of the Board was so strong that it was much more likely to be undermined by persuasion than by threats, and the peremptory imposition of a time-limit was bound to raise the hackles of elderly men. Furthermore, the implied threat of action by the Government was not to be taken very seriously. Even if a Queen's Letter were to be issued at the request of the Junior Fellows in defiance of the Board (an event which could be envisaged only if misgovernment had reached the proportions of a public scandal) it was very doubtful that the Crown had the power to compel the retirement on pension of any Fellow who had been elected *ad vitam aut culpam* unless he was clearly incapacitated for his duties; and the regular attendance at meetings of the Board and the orderly if unimaginative discharge of the duties of one of the smaller administrative offices were well within the powers of most septuagenarians. The Board, therefore, was able to send a crushing reply, lecturing the Junior Fellows on their manners and on their ignorance of the constitution of the body which they aspired to govern, pointing out that they were much better off than the professors of the Queen's Colleges and might, therefore, stand to gain little or nothing from a government inquiry, and concluding with an emotional appeal not to rock the boat at a time when the College had so many enemies outside.

The Junior Fellows sent a further request to the Board in which they tried to combine soothing words with insistence on the main issue, but this only elicited an even more spirited defence of the existing constitution. The history of the College over the past fifty years had been a continuous series of reforms by the Board; the duties of a Senior Fellow were such that experience and leisure were essential; all this talk of senility was nonsense; the fact that some of the Senior Fellows had pressed twenty years earlier for a change in the system showed merely that men can learn sense as they grow older; and finally, with a touch of inspired malice, the Board agreed that there *was* a problem of age – among the Junior Fellows. Some of them seemed to be too old for their heavy duties and the Board would investigate the possibility of devising a scheme for their retirement.[16]

The position of the Junior Fellows was further weakened at this point by a change of government. Whatever slender chance they might have had in inducing a weak Liberal government to put pressure on the Board in a matter which did not excite much public interest, the chance sank to zero when a strong Conservative government took office in August. Their angry disappointment was followed, as might have been predicted, by splits in their ranks. Several lost interest, preferring to devote their energies to less sterile causes. Others, notably J.I. Beare, became disgusted with the ill feeling generated by the controversy and frankly took the side of the Board. The more radical reformers dismissed the financial considerations as secondary and concentrated on a strategy for achieving a real redistribution of power. The remainder just continued to grumble, but their grumbling was muted by a sudden, if temporary, unblocking of the stream of promotion. Between December 1896 and June 1899 death or retirement produced six vacancies in the ranks of the Senior Fellows, so that by the latter date two members of the Board were under sixty-two, and only two were over seventy-two. By a curious irony Traill, co-opted in 1899, who had been the most persistent and vociferous exponent of the evils of stagnation, was the only man between 1870 and 1914 to become a Senior Fellow after less than thirty-five years' service as a Junior.[17]

(v)

As we turn now to sketch the College of 1892 we should first summarize the changes in its physical appearance since 1830. The original heart, comprising the Front and Library Squares, had been altered only by the removal of the red-brick range separating the squares, the erection of the Campanile, and the enclosure (completed just before 1892) of the ground floor of the Library, which had hitherto consisted (except in the pavilions at either end) of an open colonnade. The space was required for book storage, but the change has been usually represented as an act of vandalism. The colonnade, however, had been divided from the start by a longitudinal wall, so that there was no through view between the piers, and it is doubtful that the elegance of the building was much reduced, except by the choice of a very unsuitable style of window for the new ground floor. Further east the changes were more extensive. The New Square, including the Museum Building, had been added; the College Park had been effectively drained and its southern part was laid out as a cricket ground, of which part was used for football in winter; the wall separating the medical school from the rest of the College had been removed and a decent back gate had been built, leading into Park Street, now renamed Lincoln Place. The area east of the New Square was under rough grass and trees and was appropriately named the wilderness, but at the north-east corner of the Park were tennis courts and a gymnasium and rackets court. The most conspicuous change in the College Park was the addition of two large buildings in cut granite, built respectively in 1875–80 and 1885–7. The first, which today houses the departments of zoology, pharmacology and physiology, was originally built as an anatomical and zoological museum; a histological laboratory was added later. The building, though not distinguished, impresses a century after its construction by its massive solidity. The second building was designed to accommodate the Medical School and the departments of anatomy and chemistry, purposes which it still serves. Its main front is solid and dignified enough, but behind this is a rather chaotic complex of additions, some built before 1892 and others of later date, which link it on to the zoology block. For the erection of this building the old medical school of 1825 was largely, but not completely demolished.

(vi)

We turn next to the principal officers of the University and College. The fourth Earl of Rosse, who had been elected Chancellor on the death of Lord Cairns in 1885, was scarcely of the intellectual stature of his father, but he carried on the third Earl's work, both as a good landlord and as a practical and diligent astronomer. He inherited to the full his father's mechanical ingenuity (as did also his younger brother, the inventor of the steam turbine) and used it to perfect devices auxiliary to the great telescope; one of these enabled him to measure the heat reflected from the moon. As he spent most of his time in Ireland he was in close touch with the College, and his standing in the scientific world was of benefit to it when he gave his backing to the appeal launched in 1903 for the building of scientific laboratories. The Vice-Chancellor was Sir John Ball, who in earlier days had been a representative of the University in Parliament, and later Lord Chancellor of Ireland in Disraeli's last administration. His reputation rested chiefly on his efforts to reform the Church of Ireland before Disestablishment, to fight for it in the crisis, and to help in its reconstruction afterwards. By 1892, however, he was a semi-invalid, and was able to take little part in the Tercentenary celebrations.

As in 1830, so in 1892 the Board consisted of the Provost and the seven Senior Fellows; dilution of its ranks had been tentatively canvassed over the past two decades, but despite the reconstruction of the governing body of the College's Cambridge namesake the idea had made little progress, and it was not to win general assent until 1906 nor to be implemented until 1911. And the Board was still virtually all-powerful; the right of the Council to nominate to vacant professorships was the only effective diminution of its sovereignty.

Its members in 1892 were for the most part abler men than those which made up the Board of 1830, but they were also considerably older. Only one, Thomas Stack, aged seventy-eight, could fairly be described as past his work; he was to retire the following year. Joseph Carson, though nearly as old, was still vigorous and well able to discharge the duties of Vice-Provost. The Provost, George Salmon, was nearly seventy-three; the others, Samuel Haughton, John William Stubbs (Bursar), John Kells Ingram (Senior Lecturer), Hewitt Robert Poole, and George Ferdinand Shaw (Registrar) were all within a year of their seventieth birthday one way or the other. All except Stack were competent to carry out their duties, but clearly they belonged to a dying generation, and were unable to judge sympathetically or even objectively the aspirations and discontents of their juniors. The latter were at times importunate or tactless in their demands, and this led to a chronic state of tension, which is disclosed by the remarkably arrogant reply, sent by men who were individually not at all arrogant, to a protest made by a Professor and a Junior Fellow in 1894.[18] But if collectively these men formed a governing body open to criticism, the majority commanded respect as individuals. Only Stack and Poole can fairly be described as passengers; Salmon, Ingram and Haughton were scholars of great distinction; Carson and Stubbs were efficient administrators; and Shaw, whose energies were at this time devoted mainly to journalism, served at any rate to introduce a note of variety, and perhaps a less cloistered outlook to their deliberations. Shaw and Ingram were laymen; the other six were in orders.

The College was fortunate to have as its Provost in 1892 George Salmon, who was then at the height of his reputation. His fame as a mathematician, which was demonstrated, if by nothing else, by the large number of translations and foreign editions of his books, rested on four great treatises. Three of these (*Conic sections*, *Higher plane curves* and *Analytical geometry of three dimensions*) are, in the Dublin tradition, geometrical, but he moved into another field with his *Lessons introductory to the modern higher algebra*. All four are textbooks on the highest level, but they contain, nonchalantly embedded in expositions of received knowledge, original contributions of considerable value. Yet when he succeeded to a Professorship at the age of forty-seven it was not in mathematics,[19] but to the Regius Professorship of Divinity, and thereafter, although with the help of his colleagues he revised his textbooks for successive editions, he devoted himself mainly to theology. As a young man he had been influenced by Archbishop Whately, for whom he had acted as examining chaplain, and his attitude to religion was in some ways similar, combining as it did a sceptical and at times mocking temperament with a strong and simple underlying faith based on a devotion to the Bible, and equally opposed to sacerdotalism, emotional evangelicism and liberalism. In his attitude to biblical criticism Salmon was, as in other matters, conservative without lapsing into fundamentalism; he agreed with some reservations with the Cambridge school of Westcott and Lightfoot, and when, nearly twenty years after his appointment to the chair, he published his first substantial work in theology, *An introduction to the study of the New Testament*, it took the form of an extremely trenchant demolition of the Tübingen school of radical higher criticism, perhaps the most powerful in the English language. Four years later, in 1889, it was followed by *The infallibility of the Church*, a spirited and extremely readable, if not very profound refutation of ultramontane Roman claims, based on his lectures to the senior Divinity class. If in places the tone strikes a modern reader as slightly pert and cheap, it must be remembered that the conventions of religious controversy were different in those days.[20] Although these two books consist mainly of destructive criticism Salmon was not a mere controversialist in religious matters; his numerous published sermons illustrate the constructive side of his mind, as does his work on early Church history, to be found mainly in his contributions to the *Dictionary of Christian Biography*. And in the reconstruction of the Church after Disestablishment he played, as we have seen, an essentially conciliatory role, contriving by a combination of wit and wisdom to discredit and isolate extremists on both sides.

Although he was inclined in the preliminary discussions to play down the Tercentenary celebrations, when the time came he emerged (slightly to the mortification of some of his colleagues) as the undoubted star of the week, and many of the guests were to speak later of the impression that his combination of scholarship, modesty and direct and simple friendliness had made on them. Mahaffy might impress by his learning and wit, Traill by his energy, Ingram by his width of culture and Tyrrell by his urbanity and polish; Salmon impressed simply by his personality. When he crossed the square alone you saw only a short and rather ungainly figure with a shambling gait and a vacant stare, but if he stopped to speak to you all this was forgotten: the eyes became searching and quizzical and the features at once challenging and friendly. His strong conservatism in national and academic politics arose from a fundamental scepticism as to the value of most human effort in the sublunary world, but it expressed itself not in simple stone-walling, but in an uncanny gift for exposing the difficulties and inconsistencies in any proposed reform. This, combined with his great generosity,[21] prevented even the most ardent and frustrated reformer from bearing him personal ill will. Similarly, he was famous for his mordantly witty repartee without incurring the unpopularity which usually accompanies this gift, for he was able to puncture pretensions without in any way appearing to exalt himself.[22] More, perhaps, than any member of the College throughout its history he left with his contemporaries the impression of a great man, and posterity has seen no reason to reverse the verdict.

If Salmon impressed his contemporaries by his equal mastery of mathematics and theology, they had to admit that Ingram spread himself over an even wider field. His achievements were not, perhaps, quite as solid, but they were by no means superficial. Although his main interests lay in literature and in economics and social affairs, his presidential address to the Royal Irish Academy shows that in reviewing the Academy's work in mathematics and in Irish archaeology he was thoroughly *au fait* with his theme. By then he had published papers on geometry, medieval manuscripts, etymology, Shakespearean criticism and economics, and he rightly disdained the 'I am not competent to discuss' approach in which nearly every specialist takes refuge today. He was, as we have seen (p. 230), the founder of the study of English literature in the University. A selection from his lectures, which, although popular, were intellectually demanding, was published as *The afternoon lectures in English Literature* (London, 1863). In 1866 he transferred to the Regius Professorship of Greek, which he held till 1879, when he was appointed Librarian. Although he made no very substantial contribution to Greek studies he was the first Professor since Arthur Browne (d. 1805) to have made any at all, or to treat the post as anything more than a routine teaching office. As Librarian he put in seven years' efficient work, and after his co-option to the Board in 1884 he served for nine years as Senior Lecturer and three as Registrar. The neatness and accuracy of the College records during his tenure of office contrast strongly with the careless and slovenly work of even such able men as Jellett and Mahaffy, for Ingram was free alike from the impatience and the self-importance which prevent able men from carrying out routine tasks efficiently.

Ingram, though the son of a clergyman, developed religious doubts at an early age. This led him soon after his election to Fellowship in 1846 to study law, in the hopes that it would provide a plausible reason for a dispensation from the obligation to take orders. At about this time he met Auguste Comte and was immediately attracted to his creed of positivism, to which he remained faithful all his life. Though he scrupulously refrained from any writings hostile to Christianity while he held a Fellowship, in the years between his retirement in 1899 and his death in 1907 he wrote several books on positivism. Posterity regards Comte's metaphysical scepticism as his most valuable contribution to thought, but Ingram's temperament was essentially religious rather than sceptical. He concentrated therefore on the rather misty 'religion of humanity' which Comte in his later years tried to raise on the ruins of the theological religions which he had demolished; and Mahaffy used to tell a tale of calling on Dowden one evening and finding Ingram with him, conducting a positivist prayer-meeting and singing positivist hymns. It was his devotion to this positivist faith that led him to take a serious interest in social and economic problems. As a young man he took a prominent part in founding the Statistical and Social Enquiry Society under Whately's presidency. While he was active in the teaching of literature he published little in this field, but in 1878 he gave a long-remembered address to the British Association, which stressed the close links between economics and other social phenomena and urged economists to have respect for factual knowledge concerning a constantly changing society, as giving them the only sound basis for abstract generalizations. Ten years later he used his now relatively leisured position as Senior Lecturer to publish his *History of political economy*. This ran through many editions and was translated not only into the leading languages of Europe. but also into Swedish, Czech, Polish and Japanese.

As a student, Ingram, fired by the patriotic idealism of the Young Ireland group, published in *The Nation* a spirited ballad, 'The Memory of the Dead', which later found its way into every Irish anthology. In later years he did not support Home Rule, though he was in most other respects a Liberal; he held with Lecky that though the Union should never have been passed it should not now be repealed. But he never completely lost the idealism of youth; he befriended student societies and clubs, and on most political issues he was well to the left of his colleagues. This made him no enemies, however; even when he advocated agrarian reform or opposed imperial expansion in South Africa he did not become embroiled in angry controversy, for he was, to use his own description of Tennyson, 'a man of mild, humane and tolerant temper'.

Within the field of mathematical and natural sciences Haughton's versatility equalled that of Ingram in the humanities. A man who publishes papers on the musculature of the crocodile's leg, the pharmacology of nicotine and strychnine, the reflection of polarized light from polished surfaces and the distortion of fossils by slaty cleavage cannot be regarded as a narrow specialist. And as with Ingram these contributions, though most of them represented relatively minor advances in knowledge, were entirely satisfactory as far as they went, and were in no way amateurish. Only in the field of chemistry were his speculations somewhat fantastic; elsewhere his theories were founded on carefully observed fact. His career started with first place in mathematical moderatorship, and the following year he was elected to Fellowship at an age about three years below the average for those days. For a while he was interested mainly in dynamics, but from this he was led on to problems of the tides and to consideration of the earth as a planet and a solid body, and so to investigations in mineralogy. In 1851 the chair of Geology became vacant; Haughton was elected and held it for thirty years. His researches touched on almost every branch of the subject. He had too many ideas to pursue any one of them in depth, but although each paper is, in itself, relatively slight, together they add up to a substantial contribution to knowledge.

In the course of some investigations on fossils he became interested in wider aspects of vertebrate morphology, and especially the muscular system considered in relation to its mechanical efficiency, and his most original work appeared as a development of this theme in his *Principles of animal mechanics* (1873). It had two rather macabre by-products, for one of which he received the nickname of 'Hanging Haughton';[23] it was a calculation, based on entirely humane motives, of the height of the drop relative to a man's weight which was necessary to ensure the fracture of the axis vertebra in execution by hanging. Hitherto the drop had been too short and death was all too often by strangulation; Haughton persuaded the authorities to introduce a longer drop, which ensured virtually instantaneous death. Nor was his interest in prisons confined to the condemned cell; his chatty friendliness, reinforced by his clerical collar and liberal gifts of tobacco, won him the confidence of old lags and enabled him to learn from them how they used their muscles to the best advantage in turning the crank or operating the treadmill. Meanwhile he had started the publication, in collaboration with his colleague and contemporary J.A. Galbraith, of a series of elementary manuals on almost every aspect of mathematics and physics. They were deservedly popular, and won their authors both money and fame.

Haughton had originally intended to be a medical missionary in China. The practical idealism behind this resolve never entirely left him; aided by his interest in comparative anatomy, it prompted him to register as a medical student fifteen years after he had been elected Fellow, and to qualify in due course as M.B. He never practised, except informally among the sick poor, but in the cholera epidemic of 1866 he organized a student team of medical orderlies for nursing duties and took his turn himself. Less than a year after he had qualified he was appointed by the Board as Registrar of the Medical School. The school at that time included some brilliant professors but was somewhat deficient in organization, and since the passing of the 1858 Act for medical registration this was a defect which was full of danger. Haughton, who had the unusual advantage of combining the authority and maturity of judgment of a man in his forties with the recent acquaintance with medical teaching from the student's point of view, soon put things right, and it was largely due to his efforts that the Act of 1867, amending the 1800 School of Physic Act, was passed. He also played a leading part in bringing Sir Patrick Dun's Hospital up to date in several respects. As a sideline he devoted much time and attention to the affairs of the Zoological Society, improving its collections and its gardens and helping to steer it through a period of public neglect by delivering popular lectures on the animals. Many stories are told of his exploits at the Zoo – of how he operated successfully on the defective claw of a tiger; of how, when the hippopotamus died, he rushed up armed with saws and butcher's knives and dissected for forty-eight hours until the smell became too strong; of how he gave a lecture on the anthropoid apes with an orang-utan carefully combed and washed sitting on a chair beside him.

Every man has his defects; in Haughton's case these seem to have been a touch of Panglossian complacency, and perhaps some deviousness in pushing his innumerable schemes through the necessary committees. This must have been the basis for Salmon's remark – doubtless too severe, but probably with a basis of truth – on first seeing the portrait of Haughton by Sarah Purser (plate 20): 'Excellent! Excellent! You can just hear the lies trickling out of his mouth.' But his practical kindness combined with his genial manner and irrepressible flow of ideas and talk made him widely admired and liked by young and old, both in the College and outside it.[24].

We have had occasion to mention Carson earlier (p. 126) as an upholder at the end of the century of the examining methods by which he had been trained in his youth – the verification by *viva voce* methods of the detailed and accurate knowledge of a prescribed text. For many of Carson's examinations this text was the Bible, of which he knew large parts by heart, and divinity students had to be prepared for such questions as 'Who did what on a snowy day?' or 'Where is ink mentioned in the Bible?' It is for this devotion to the precise words of the Authorized Version that Carson is best remembered today, for in 1891 he endowed a prize 'for promoting among divinity students an accurate knowledge of the text of the English Bible'. But unlike the real terrors of the Examination Hall such as Stack, Cathcart and Wilkins, who seemed to view the failure of their victims with malicious glee, or at best with Olympian indifference, Carson distributed his zeros more in sorrow than in anger, distressed and worried that the young should be so ignorant, and urging them to try again. Behind a pietistic facade (he was nicknamed 'Holy Joe') he hid the mind of a shrewd man of affairs. He was Bursar for twelve years, and presented to the Board annual reports of an admirable clarity, which show considerable financial acumen. This, indeed, had been demonstrated soon after taking office, for he wrote a report to the Visitors demonstrating how much the duties of the Bursar had increased in recent years, and successfully claimed an increase in salary. But if Carson extracted in full what he thought was his due he gave the College good value. He had no talent for original scholarship, but such talents as he had he used devotedly in the interests of the College, which he is said to have loved 'as Pericles loved Athens'.

Stubbs had a less striking personality, and has left less vivid memories, but he also was an efficient Bursar, who had the difficult task of keeping within reasonable bounds the expenditure on the Tercen-

20   Samuel Haughton. Fellow, 1844—97. (Sarah Purser, Trinity College.)

tenary celebrations. Perhaps he was too cheeseparing, but he scarcely deserved to be pursued into his grave by a bitter complaint from Mahaffy.[25] In the field of mathematics he performed a modest but useful task in rewriting some chapters of Brinkley's *Astronomy* for a new edition, and he used his access to the College muniments as Bursar to write the first serious history of the College. In it he printed for the first time a number of important manuscripts relating to its early years, and despite its many imperfections as a history Stubbs takes his place in the not very long list of Fellows who have shown an interest in preserving, ordering and transcribing the College muniments.

Stack was remembered by the young men who met him at this time merely as a slovenly and disagreeable old man whose severity as an examiner had made him known as 'Stick, Stack, Stuck'.[26] Poole, on the other hand, was benign, if slightly pompous, and was interested mainly in promoting and supporting missionary work. He was at once the brother-in-law and the first cousin of Provost Jellett, and his niece was married to Fitzgerald, the Professor of Physics.

Shaw was something of a maverick among the Fellows. Like some of the other lay Fellows of his generation he used the College more as a base of operations than as the centre of his life and work. Soon after his election in 1848 he obtained a dispensation permitting him to go to Cork as Professor of Physics in the newly founded Queen's College. After his return six years later he devoted much of his energies to journalism; he was a constant contributor to the *Irish Times* and the *Dublin Evening Mail*, and for a while he edited *Saunders' Newsletter*. He gave 'novels, plays and operas' as his recreations in *Who's Who*, and he was, indeed, a man-about-town and the friend of Irving, Ellen Terry and other theatrical celebrities. Overflowing with tireless, if not clearly focused energy, he was never at a loss for an anecdote, wit and banter, and only a few days before his death he was to be seen chaffing pretty girls at the College Races. He contributed little, perhaps, to the education of Dublin, but a good deal to its entertainment.

(vii)

The Junior Fellows in 1892 numbered twenty-seven, of whom eight were in orders. Sixteen of them were tutors; of the remainder, six held 'protected' Professorships or lecturerships, which carried a salary equal to an average tutor's emoluments, the three most senior held the offices of Senior Tutor or Junior Bursar, and the two most junior were awaiting their turn to become tutors. Among the tutors the size of the chamber varied greatly; the most popular tutors, such as Gray, Traill, Culverwell, Russell and Beare had chambers five times the size of those of Abbott, Frederick Purser, Roberts or Bury. Whether these last did not wish to be encumbered with many pupils or failed to attract them it is difficult now to say, but there is, making allowance for a few exceptions, a clear and indeed natural negative correlation between scholarly productivity and tutorial activity. A few, such as Beare, shone in both fields, and a few, such as Roberts, were rather dim in both, but for the most part a Junior Fellow of this period concentrated his energies either on scholarship or on administration, of which tutorship formed an important part.

The most remarkable thing about the Junior Fellows of 1892 is that they included scarcely any dead wood, a compliment which could not be paid to their predecessors or successors without considerable reservation. With the exception of R.M. Conner, who seems to have been merely an amiable potterer, every one of the others published at least a little original work or else made his mark in administration or teaching.

In the second category we may put T.T. Gray, Anthony Traill and A.C. O'Sullivan. Gray is remembered above all as a famous and extremely successful Junior Dean, a post which he held for a total of seventeen years between 1866 and 1892. He was stern but fair, never losing his temper or his poise, and dealing out his punishments not as expressions of moral indignation but as the inescapable consequences of breaches of clearly defined rules. In consequence he soon gained among the more unruly undergraduates a reputation like that of Stalky's headmaster: a beast, but a just beast; and when a few years' absence had healed the wounds and mellowed the memories of College life, such a student on his return to College would probably put Gray first among those to be sought out for an exchange of reminiscences. After his co-option to the Board he devoted most of his energies to resisting with a tenacity which was as stubborn as it was usually misguided even the smallest change proposed in the teaching, administration or constitution of the College. The son of a country gentleman, he did not allow his natural conservatism to be troubled by any intellectual speculations, and he saw no reason why the agrarian conditions of Ireland and the educational and administrative systems of the College should not be permanently frozen in the state in which they existed in 1862, when he was elected a Fellow. In the last fifteen years of his life (he died at the age of ninety-two) he became, as often happens with a long-lived man of strong personality, an institution rather than a man. This, coupled with his integrity and his undoubted loyalty to the College as he conceived it, meant that his persistent obstruction (which rarely led to a delay of more than a year or so) came to be viewed even by his opponents as a virtuoso performance, to be enjoyed even as one voted against it. But one of his junior colleagues never forgave the frustration which Gray had inflicted on him as a young man; in the scrapbooks of Provost Bernard,[27] the obituaries of Gray are annotated with bitter and contemptuous comments, and on the day of the funeral of the by now almost legendary vice-Provost the Provost was 'unfortunately detained in London on business'.

A full sketch of Traill, who became Provost in 1904, must be reserved to chapter twelve. It suffices to say here that he was a very busy tutor,[28] an indefatigable committee man, a voluble member of Council, and a powerful and respected figure alike on the Representative Body of the Church of Ireland and among the landlords of Co. Antrim.

A.C. O'Sullivan was a more subtle character, difficult now to assess. At the time of the Tercentenary he was a Junior Fellow of six years' standing, but he was also a third-year medical student; having taken a brilliant double Moderatorship in Mathematics and Philosophy in 1881 and won Fellowship five years later, he was drifting intellectually with no real sense of purpose when a chance suggestion from a colleague made him take up medicine. By 1895 he had achieved his M.D. and was appointed to a new post of lecturer in Pathology, a subject which he had studied on the continent. He brought back up-to-date ideas and techniques, and established an efficient one-man department, in which he proved himself a popular teacher. In 1922, two years before his death, he was given the title of Professor, but it was a tribute to his seniority rather than to his researches, for he never published anything on the subject. This was due not to mental sloth, as he kept up a keen interest in mathematics and philosophy and was esteemed by Bernard (whose standards were high) as an intellectual companion, but to a strange indolence of the will, with which was associated a remarkable degree of absent-mindedness. The manner of his death was characteristic: he died of blood-poisoning incurred through a small cut on his finger when conducting a post-mortem examination, having neglected to take the precaution, hammered into the head of every student, of wearing rubber gloves.

At the head of the list of Junior Fellows in 1892 stood J.W. Barlow, and he is best considered in isolation as he fits into no category. Under a cloud in his younger days for a heterodoxy which verged on heresy (p. 241) and in his old age a defender of some of the more preposterous aspects of the status quo, he seems to have antagonized at least some of his colleagues by mere perversity. He could never resist the temptation, even when proposing quite sensible and commonplace motions, to coin epigrams and deploy far-fetched arguments. This was a pity, as he had in some respects an interesting and original mind. He was bullied mercilessly by Mahaffy and Traill,[29] but the fact that he was elected as a representative of the Junior Fellows on the Council from its foundation until he became a Senior Fellow, and was re-elected as its secretary annually for thirteen years, despite the opposition of Traill, shows that at least in his middle years he was not generally unpopular. He was, as we have seen, the first Professor of Modern History for many a long year to take his duties seriously, and he published two useful books on the medieval history of Italy, and another, more original, on the medical profession in seventeenth-century France. He had, however, more of a philosophical than a historical mind, and he meditated constantly on such problems as the nature of life after death and the possibility of evaluating human happiness and misery, for he rejected the hedonistic calculus of the Utilitarians and also the arguments for Schopenhauer's pessimism, although he groped unsuccessfully for answers to the problems which they had raised. His last book, published when he was well over eighty, was a stylish science-fiction fantasy of life on Venus, in which these problems are discussed, but with a light enough touch for them not to drown the narrative interest.[30]

If we turn to the more serious scholars among the Junior Fellows we find that the classicists steal the limelight. Mahaffy, Palmer and Tyrrell had gone from strength to strength during the preceding decade. Mahaffy had extended his survey of Greek social history into Hellenistic and Roman times, and by 1892 he was deeply involved in the work which formed his most widely acknowledged claim to scholarly renown: the decipherment and publication of the Flinders Petrie papyri. He had also made two forays into *belles-lettres* with booklets on preaching and on conversation (neither of them very successful) and had written in a very short space of time most of the historical chapters in *The book of Trinity College*, the souvenir volume presented to guests at the Tercentenary. In these he displayed, even more than in his Greek history, the characteristic blend of shrewd insights and fruitful generalizations with inapposite social and political prejudice dressed up as history.

Tyrrell, meanwhile, had made good progress with his *Correspondence* of Cicero, and had shown his versatility by producing in two successive years scholarly editions of a Greek and of a Latin play. Whereas Mahaffy strove for novelty and insight Tyrrell above all strove for elegance, and his dapper appearance, urbanity, and quiet, unobtrusive wit contrasted strongly with the more uncouth figure and the forceful apophthegms and social reminiscences of his great rival. Both were to some extent public men, but whereas Mahaffy (who would have looked quite at home laying down the law in a literary bar) was by now hot in pursuit of the dinner-tables and shooting-parties of the mighty, Tyrrell, despite the polish of his dress and manner, was to some extent a boon companion in the semi-bohemian literary circles of Dublin. Mahaffy made more noise in the world, but there is little doubt that among his classical colleagues Tyrrell was at this time more highly esteemed.

Compared with these two, Palmer, the remaining member of the original trio, was something of a recluse, although he enjoyed society and was a good conversationalist. This was partly because he lived outside Dublin, partly because the last ten years of his life were clouded by the ill health which was to kill him at the age of fifty-five, and partly because the austere and esoteric nature of his scholarship could be appreciated only by professionals. For he remained faithful to his particular forte, the editing and emendation of Latin texts, being attracted, as was Housman a few years later, more by the difficulties of the manuscripts than by a literary appreciation of the author. By 1892 he had added to his publications a very successful edition of the *Satires* of Horace, and also of one of the plays of Plautus.

By 1892 the original trio of classical Fellows had been reinforced by the election of five new recruits (apart from Maguire, who has been mentioned earlier, and who was dead by 1892). These were Louis Claude Purser, J. B. Bury, J. I. Beare, W. J. M. Starkie and George Wilkins. The first two were scholars of great distinction and neither needed to fear comparison with Tyrrell or Mahaffy. Purser joined Tyrrell, after the first two volumes had appeared, in editing the *Correspondence* of Cicero, and saw the work to its conclusion in 1901.[31] A fair number of minor writings also bore testimony to his scholarship, and they might have been more numerous had it not been for his quixotic generosity in spending much of his time in helping others. In many ways he was the archetypal bachelor scholar, who held that Christmas Day was the best day of the year for work, as nobody came to disturb you; but he was also an urbane and courteous host, a generous lender of his books, and a man who was able to fuse into one the roles of teacher and student. A vivid description has been given of his hunting up a word in his dictionary: 'How the pages used to fly under that lean, eager hand, while the bearded face craned over the book with the excitement of a terrier at a rabbit-hole.'[32] Modest, generous, hard-working, but a good 'College man' prepared to show up at any function which needed his support, he was for many years one of the best loved members of the College.

Bury spent only seventeen years as a Fellow before he left to fill the Regius chair of Modern History at Cambridge, but within that time he had collected four honorary degrees and Fellowship of the British Academy, and, apart from editing Pindar, had established himself as an unrivalled authority on Byzantine history, not least by his masterly edition of Gibbon's *Decline and fall*. In sheer erudition he stands head and shoulders above his contemporaries, and his knowledge ranged far from the domain of conventional scholarship into every by way of the history of Hungary and Bulgaria in the early Middle Ages. Having succeeded Barlow in the chair of Modern History in 1893, he was also made Regius Professor of Greek in 1898 in place of Tyrrell. Why Tyrrell should have resigned the chair is not now clear, but the esteem with which Bury was regarded by the Board is shown by his appointment to this second Professorship at the age of thirty-seven. Bury, like his favourite Gibbon, had a chilling, though as a rule courteously expressed contempt for Christianity, but it was only after he left Dublin that he wrote in defence of rationalism. It seems probable that, apart from the prestige of his new post, his resignation may have been prompted by a feeling that the atmosphere of King's College, Cambridge, would be less solidly conformist than that of Trinity College, Dublin.

Beare and Starkie were not quite of the stature of their seniors, but they were sound scholars of the second rank. Beare concentrated mainly on ancient philosophy. Starkie was chiefly known for his editions of Aristophanes' comedies, but only one of these appeared during his tenure of Fellowship, for he resigned in 1898 to become President of Queen's College, Galway, and later Resident Commissioner for Education. He maintained close links with the College, however, and for some years sat on the University Council.

Wilkins, the most junior of the classical Fellows, was also the least effective. His book on the Homeric problem was severely criticized as unoriginal and verging on plagiarism; his only other books were two small Hebrew texts for students. He is remembered chiefly for his disastrous tenure in November 1892 of the office of Junior Dean, which lasted for just a week. He had the misfortune to follow Gray, and he was as ill-suited to the post as Gray was well-suited. During his week of office anarchy rapidly got the upper hand and Wilkins went in fear of his life. The Provost eventually acceded to his piteous pleas for release, and he was replaced by O'Sullivan, who restored order within a month. This experience, coupled with what he must have seen as inadequate recognition of his scholarship, soured further the temperament of a naturally misanthropic man, and he is remembered also for his merciless judgments on most of his colleagues, which assorted ill with his clerical collar.

The eight classicists among the Junior Fellows were balanced by nine mathematicians, but this was the one subject in which the general level of ability was somewhat lower at the Tercentenary than it had been a generation earlier, and only the two most senior of the nine, Benjamin Williamson and F.A. Tarleton, effectively upheld the traditions of Salmon, Townsend and Michael Roberts. Although Williamson, like so many of his contemporaries, devoted much of his time to the writing of relatively elementary textbooks (his *Differential calculus* ran through nine editions in thirty years), his election to the Royal

Society in 1879 testifies to the value of some of his earlier papers. He was a layman and a bachelor, a genial and socially-minded clubman, and an indefatigable diner-out in professional, official and political circles, where he made friends with such public men as Lord Randolph Churchill, but the appearance as late as 1894 of his *Mathematical theory of elastic solids* showed that, despite his resignation from the chair of Natural Philosophy in 1890, his mathematics was not entirely sacrificed to his social activities.

Tarleton, who succeeded him, and who held the chair in 1892, was a man of lively and acute mind, with a curious mixture of liberal and conservative opinions. His *Introduction to the mathematical theory of attraction* (1899–1913) was a more solid piece of work than its title implies, and his other publications, which ranged from pure mathematics to physical chemistry, were sufficient to win him the presidency of the Royal Irish Academy in 1906. In philosophy a strict Kantian, his mathematical faith was firmly fixed on Euclid and Clerk Maxwell, and it was said that 'he had ... almost a physical aversion to any theory which seemed likely to upset the ordinary conceptions of space and time'.[33] Riemannian geometry and the special theory of relativity, therefore, were dismissed as perverse paradoxes. His colleague Frederick Purser, however, wrote a textbook of elementary geometry which was a manifesto directed against Tarleton's beliefs, for he was convinced of the unsoundness of Euclid's logic quite as strongly as Tarleton was convinced of his verbal inspiration.

W.S. Burnside held the chair of pure Mathematics, a subject for which he showed some real talent in his earlier years.[34] Unfortunately he had little taste for the other subjects (applied mathematics, physics and philosophy) which he had to master if he was to win a Fellowship, and in consequence he had to struggle for ten years before he was elected. This seems to have broken his spirit, for he spent much of his time in the hunting-field, and is remembered as the last man to arrive regularly in College on horeseback. The other four mathematical Fellows, though they all published something, were lightweights in the field of scholarship. Robert Russell and M.W.J. Fry were later to make their mark as administrators, but W. R. W. Roberts is remembered chiefly as a survival in the nineteen thirties of an older generation strolling benignly through the squares in the *otium cum dignitate* of the vice-provostship, and Cathcart as an extreme conservative and ferocious examiner. Even Cathcart, however, had his gentler side; he had a keen interest in gardening, and he gave some money to the College's botanic garden when it was sorely in need of it.

Of the Junior Fellows not so far mentioned T.K. Abbott, G.F. Fitzgerald and J.H. Bernard demand some notice. Abbott, though originally trained in mathematics, held successively the chairs of Moral Philosophy, Biblical Greek and Hebrew, and he was described by Mahaffy with characteristic but pardonable exaggeration as the most learned man in Europe. But he was better at absorbing knowledge than at diffusing it, and his publications, though numerous and varied, were not commensurate with his learning. His *Elements of logic*, however, won at least a local fame, as it was adopted (not without a struggle) to succeed Murray as the prescribed book for the Senior Freshman year of the ordinary course. Since the final examination of that year remained a compulsory hurdle for honor students long after they had emancipated themselves from the rest of the pass course, students of Literature, Natural Science or History could be seen as late as 1953 hastily turning the pages of Abbott as autumn approached, trying to familiarize themselves with the mysteries of connotation, *Barbara Celarent* and the undistributed middle. Of greater scholarly import were Abbott's translations of Kant's ethical works, an acute criticism of Berkeley's *Theory of vision*, and a new edition of Barrett's 'Codex Z' of St Matthew, with many additions and corrections. He succeeded Ingram as Librarian in 1887, and though he might well have been tempted to spend his old age merely rummaging among the beloved books and manuscripts which surrounded him, he worked steadily at the production of catalogues of coins, manuscripts and incunabula. By the standards of the modern bibliophile they leave a good deal to be desired, but they are indispensable, as they have not yet been replaced.

George Francis Fitzgerald, who graduated in experimental science as well as in mathematics, and who became Professor of Physics at the age of thirty-one, had undoubtedly a touch of genius; and in many ways he conformed to the popular stereotype. Impulsive, hot-tempered and totally unselfconscious, he alternated between abstracted meditation, highly individual experimentation (such as his famous attempt to fly with wings in the College Park) and passionate advocacy of his favourite causes. He possessed in remarkable degree the admirable quality of indifference to whether he or some other worker got credit for his ideas, so long as the ideas were publicized and made use of. His name is immortalized (coupled sometimes with that of his Dutch contemporary Lorentz) in the Fitzgerald contraction, the phenomenon which he postulated to explain the null result of the Michelson-Morley experiment to determine the velocity of the earth through the ether. (Lorentz, from a different angle, reached the same conclusion two years later, and elaborated the theory further.) It was to prove an important foundation-stone in the theory of relativity. Fitzgerald also predicted the possibility of Hertzian waves shortly before Hertz produced them experimentally, and collaborated with Hertz in their

21   George Francis Fitzgerald, Fellow, 1877–1901.

development. He published many other papers on radiation and electricity, mostly theoretical but some of them experimental, and their quality was sufficient to win him Fellowship of the Royal Society at the age of thirty-three and its Royal Medal a year before his premature death at the age of fifty. All this was achieved with minimal apparatus and in the cramped quarters in the Museum Building to which his department was confined; he managed, however, to get possession of a disused chemical laboratory in the medical school and used it to start for the first time practical classes (as distinct from demonstrations) for his students.

Although in one of his characteristic exaggerations he declared that it was the duty of the university to prosecute research and to give facilities for students to educate themselves, but not actually to teach,[35] he was in practice a conscientious teacher, and an inspiring one to senior students. Unfortunately he could not communicate his enthusiasm to the large elementary class of medical and engineering students, and during his tenure of the chair there was founded a tradition of wild disorder in these lectures which took many years to extinguish. He devoted much energy and eloquence to advocating the extension of scientific teaching, not only in the College but in the whole country, and he served as a Commissioner of National Education. Indeed, in another characteristic exaggeration in the opposite direction, he declared towards the end of his life that he was considering abandoning research to devote himself to educational organization: 'whether the human race got to know about the ether now or in fifty years hence was a small matter, but whether the present state of appalling scientific ignorance was to continue was another matter'.[36] He was also a pioneer in seeking recognition of educational theory as an academic subject, and in 1891 he proposed to the University Council that it should be included among the subjects of the Fellowship examination. Naturally he received no support, but it was largely as a result of his persistent pressure that examinations (leading to a diploma) in the theory and practice of education were instituted in 1896. When he died five years later the cause was taken up by his brother-in-law, E.P. Culverwell, six years his junior as a Fellow. He was originally a mathematician, but sooned turned to the propagation of Montessorian principles, and in 1905 became the University's first Professor of Education. He had the missionary zeal which is a frequent attribute of professors of this subject, and a passion for imparting information. If there was a fact to be ascertained, a phenomenon to be explained, or a theory to be expounded, Culverwell did not remain silent for long.

We have left Bernard to the last on our list of Junior Fellows, but he was certainly not the least; in the Tercentenary year, at the age of thirty-two, he was nearing the height of his powers. A graduate in mathematics and philosophy, he had published commentaries on and translations of the works of Kant, and had then turned to the editing of patristic writings; later on he was to be known chiefly as an acute and profound biblical commentator. But it was not only as a scholar that Bernard attracted attention; he was a gifted preacher, teacher and administrator, and seemed to be able to turn his hand to anything with an assurance of success. Tall, slim, handsome, serious but not solemn, radiating vitality and purpose, he was one of those young men who are fortunate enough to be respected and trusted alike by their seniors and their contemporaries. As a prominent member of the reform party in College he was keen and resolute, but never shrill and never too rigid to consider a possible compromise, and he made no enemies in controversy. He was appointed Archbishop King's Lecturer in Divinity in 1888, and during the twenty-three years of his tenure (the last five as Professor) he exercised a great influence on successive generations of ordinands by his incisive yet persuasive teaching, by his liberal high-churchmanship, and by his determination to counter the isolationist tendencies which the Church of Ireland had been showing since Disestablishment. The fact that only twelve years after 1892, when he was still in his early forties, he could be seriously discussed as a possible Provost showed the esteem in which both his character and his ability were held. When in fact he returned as Provost in 1919, the war, the Irish troubles and his eight years as bishop and archbishop had made him a different and a harder and less popular man, but in 1892 it would have been seldom that one would hear his name mentioned in anything but terms of praise.

A small pendant must be added to the roll of Fellows of 1892. Towards the end of October 1897 the great bell of College was heard tolling its muffled peal, announcing the death of a Fellow or former Fellow. Who was it: Carson, Haughton, Palmer? (All were to die within the next few months.) It was with a sense of anticlimax, coupled in some cases with irritation at having been duped into assuming a step up the ladder of seniority, that the Fellows learnt that the bell tolled for somebody whose existence they had all forgotten – James Byrne, who had graduated with a pass degree in 1841, and who, after six months as a Fellow in 1848, went out on a College living and had remained in his Ulster rectory for nearly fifty years.[37] He had a good mind, and he did not allow it to rust; his Donnellan lectures, an attack on contemporary naturalism, were followed by several pamphlets on church affairs, but most of his life was spent in preparation for his *magnum opus*, which was nothing less than a complete theory of language. The first two volumes (*General principles of the structure of language*) appeared in

1885; they were soon followed by *Origin of the Greek, Latin and Gothic roots*. The *Principles* consist of a comparative grammar of all languages, illustrated by ninety specific examples, including not only such commonplaces as Armenian, Amharic and Basque, but, with equal confidence and expertise, Choctaw, Samoyed and Yoruba. The display of erudition is staggering; references to Bopp, Zeuss or Zumpt appear on every other page, and for each of the ninety languages the standard grammar has been read, understood and summarized. Behind it all lie two grandiose theories; that the grammar of a people can be correlated with their mental attributes, especially quickness or slowness of thought; and also (in the *Origin*) that the roots of all words are to some extent onomatopoeic, or at least show a correlation between the idea and the physical movement of the lips and tongue. Both generalizations are, of course, far too wide and applied too uncritically; yet both may be held to enshrine a grain of truth. The result is a confusing mixture of sense and nonsense which is extremely difficult to evaluate. One German reviewer ranked Byrne with Humboldt, whereas J.S. Wilkins turned over the pages with 'a feeling of melancholy approaching to despair' and found his hypothesis baseless.[38]

Byrne was the last survivor of the ex-Fellows who had gone out on a College living, and he forms a fitting ending to the tradition to which we have earlier referred in the case of Hales, of immense learning and diligence pursued in complete isolation, sometimes, as in the case of Hincks, entirely vindicated by the results, but more often lapsing as a result of the isolation into the strangest by-ways of erudite eccentricity.

(viii)

The non-Fellow Professors constituted in 1892 a far more important element in the College than they had in 1830. For one thing their number had more than doubled; there were now twenty-eight instead of thirteen. This increase is accounted for by the creation of fourteen new chairs, and by the release of the Regius Professorship of Laws from its association with a Senior Fellowship. Of the new chairs twelve have already been mentioned in chapters six to nine; the remaining two, both of which were founded in 1888 as a result of bequests, were the Reid Professorship of Penal Legislation and the Professorship of Pastoral Theology. Both were very minor affairs, and one suspects that the Board, when accepting the bequests, wished that the testators had not defined their purposes so narrowly.

But the Professors had grown in prestige as well as in numbers. Some of the subjects which they taught had been gradually winning acceptance as essential to a university curriculum; their average salary, though still meagre enough, had been steadily increasing over the past twenty-five years or so; socially they had advanced by being now eligible for membership of the Common Room; and in their four seats on the University Council they had acquired a limited but fairly effective power-base.

Nevertheless they were on the whole a somewhat discontented, and in their own eyes a depressed class. The discontent did not find widespread expression for another ten years, but it was smouldering below the surface. It arose from a feeling that they were not only underpaid but also underestimated – that their salary, prospects, pension and influence on University policy were inferior to those of Fellows who did not appear to be obviously working harder or to be obviously their intellectual superiors. To this complaint most of the Fellows would reply that if the Professors wanted the status of Fellows they should have worked for the Fellowship examination; that expertise in surgery, Arabic or the law of real property was not a sufficient title to a share in the government of the College; that their statutory duties were in most cases small, and that there was no objection to their supplementing their incomes by other occupations which did not interfere with their academic duties. The College was run by the Fellows for the Fellows and students. If a Fellow can be found with a taste for teaching geology or English Literature so much the better; if not we hire a specialist for the job, and if he is dissatisfied with his conditions he can go elsewhere.

For a few of the chairs, such as those of Arabic or Biblical Greek, such an attitude was not entirely unreasonable; the only anomaly in the position of these peripheral chairs was that their occupants were given the title of Professor, partly for historical reasons, and partly so that a more exalted title could to some extent compensate for a small salary. If they had been called lecturers their position would have been clearer. But the trouble was that there was a smooth gradation, alike in salary, duties and general esteem, between posts such as these and the chairs of Engineering, Chemistry or Romance Languages, which involved lecturing several different classes, and in some cases looking after a laboratory. Salary was roughly proportioned to duties, but there was no break in the salary-scale large enough to form a clear-cut division between full-time and part-time posts. The formal regulations usually stated merely that a Professor must abandon any outside occupation which the Board considered incompatible with his duties; and in fact it was assumed that all non-Fellow Professors would (unless they had ample private means) undertake some outside work. The more highly paid were expected to give something like three-quarters of their time to the College; the lowest-paid perhaps not more than a tenth.

310

It is difficult to compute accurately the emoluments of the non-Fellow Professors in 1892, for in addition to their salary (which was fixed by a decree of the Board and Visitors) most of them also received capitation or examination fees and in several cases drew small additional salaries for minor administrative posts. The report of the Royal Commission of 1906, however, gives full figures for 1905, and by making a few adjustments to these the figures for 1892 can be estimated with fair accuracy. It would appear that the total emoluments from the College for fourteen of the Professors amounted to less than £250 per annum; six earned something between £250 and £550; four between £550 and £750; three between £750 and £1,000; and the Regius Professor of Divinity (who had, by statute, to be an ex-Fellow) about £1,230.[39] It was the second category that was ambiguous; a salary of £400 for a Professor of German or £250 for a Professor of Botany might have been considered adequate full-time remuneration for a young man holding such a post; but Selss and Wright had both spent over twenty-five years in the College service, and may have wondered at times whether it was fair that their contemporaries among the Fellows were earning about £950. These two men do not seem, in fact, to have complained, but it was round about 1892 that the Professors who managed to devote some time to research were beginning to feel that the College might pay them for this as well as for their lectures, and that it should be recognized that such research might redound to the credit of the College as much as publications in classics or mathematics. Moreover, they could fairly point out that they were no more 'specialists' than were many of the Fellows. Professors such as Atkinson, master of more than a dozen languages, or Wright, trained in ophthalmology but now working partly on corals and partly on microscopic algae, were much wider in their interest than Fellows such as Burnside or Palmer.

Among the non-Fellow Professors of the day Edward Dowden, Professor of English Literature, stands out pre-eminent, for his name was familiar not only to his fellow-critics, but to laymen of literary tastes throughout the British Isles. He was, by now, the acknowledged authority on Shelley and the most widely read interpreter of Shakespeare. His style of criticism has been out of fashion for over a generation, and it is doubtful that any of his books, had they appeared fifty years later, would have been kindly reviewed in *Scrutiny*. For Dowden was not an analyst of texts; he was always trying to get at the man behind the book, and to estimate the man and his writings as an individual whole. In the case of Shelley, this led to a celebrated controversy with Matthew Arnold, who resented, when reading 'Adonais' or the 'Ode to a Skylark', of being reminded of the elopement with

Mary Godwin. But other critics for the most part took Dowden's part against Arnold.

Paradoxically enough, however, he had many things in common with Leavis, for he saw literature and literary criticism in moral terms,[40] and, like Leavis, he greatly admired *Middlemarch*. Apart from his political commitment to the Unionist cause, books were his life, but they were valued above all as revelations of the minds and souls of their authors. The title of his best known work, *Shakespeare: a critical study of his mind and art*, is indicative of his approach; the art was valued chiefly as the key to the mind. He was drawn therefore, mainly to writers such as Wordsworth, Goethe and Shelley, who had a 'message' to impart, and in mere niceties of style he had no more than a passing interest.

Dowden's politics, which he justified, as we have seen, as stemming from his cosmopolitan approach to literature and his preference, therefore, for imperialism rather than small-scale nationalism, had in their turn an effect on his criticism. His attitude to Yeats and other figures of the Irish literary revival was not as hostile as has sometimes been suggested, for in Yeats's early years he and Dowden admired each other. But diverging politics led to irritation on both sides, and in 1895 Dowden wrote that 'If the Irish literary movement is to consist in flapping green banners ... I should prefer to stand quietly apart ... I am not ambitious of intensifying my intellectual and spiritual brogue.'[41] His belief that Ireland was dangerously small, and that a literature which refused to look outside its boundaries would be cramped by provincialism, is rational enough, though the work of Synge and Lady Gregory gives empirical proof that there is another side to the question. But at times it seems clear that his enunciation of this belief was only a cloak for his preference for his English over his Irish inheritance (he described himself as a 'half-breed').[42] He was not the first or the last person of mixed descent to prefer to live in Ireland but to give his allegiance to English values. There is nothing dishonourable in such an attitude, but it demands tact, forbearance and generosity; and sometimes Dowden, as when he declined membership of the committee to celebrate the centenary of Thomas Moore, presented an image which seemed chilling or churlish.

In any context free from politics, however, these are the last adjectives that anyone would have applied to him. He was a most successful lecturer, of the type who may impart information or help understanding, but who above all kindles enthusiasm. For many of his pupils he was the maestro at whose feet they were glad to sit. Apart from tutorial classes for his honor students, his lectures, delivered three times a week at one o'clock, constituted a survey of whole of English literature in a two-year cycle; all classes attended them, and they drew in many hearers from outside the College. H.O. White, his former pupil and later one of his successors in the chair, has given a vivid picture of the impact of these lectures on an impressionable youth:

I can still recall the distinguished presence; the noble brow; and the mellow, golden voice that took on a deeper resonance when he read from the poets ... Coming to that class-room as a callow Freshman, it seemed as though a new heaven and a new earth were unfolded before me. The history of human culture was revealed as a vast landscape shimmering with the divine colours of a Turner, and lit by a light that never was on sea or land.

To that voice one could listen forever.[43]

Victorian sentiment, some may say. But many besides White told much the same tale.

Of the other Professors in the field of language and literature, Mir Alaud Ali and Selss have been mentioned in the last chapter. So also has Atkinson, who still held the two chairs of Sanskrit and of Romance languages, but he deserves further notice here. By 1892 his main interests had moved into fields remote from the subjects covered by his Professorships, and he was working mostly on Coptic and on Old and Middle Irish. It was in the latter field that his reputation was chiefly made, and it would seem that it was his election to the council of the Royal Irish Academy (which had been for long the principal centre for Irish studies) that stimulated him to plunge suddenly and deeply into Celtic philology. Within a few years he had edited numerous important manuscripts and written introductions and glossaries to facsimile versions of others, his labours in this field culminating in 1901 in the editing of the fourth volume of the *Ancient laws of Ireland* and the production, as a fifth volume, of a glossary to the whole work. His reward was a blistering attack from Whitley Stokes,[44] which in the cold contempt of its language and its frank accusations of ignorance as well as carelessness outdid any abuse which Atkinson himself had directed against his fellow-scholars. The glossary, we are told, is not only incomplete, but 'swarms with non-existent or mis-spelt words or forms which ... some knowledge of Old and Middle Irish would have enabled him to avoid ... the meanings which he assigns are often wrong or vague, and his etymologies as a rule belong to the pre-scientific age'. Atkinson was not the only Irish scholar to come under Stokes's lash, for the whole edition of the *Laws* was declared to be 'almost worthless for philological purposes, with its inaccurate text, guesswork translations and pathetically feeble notes'. Atkinson, however, was an inspiring teacher for those with a taste for philology, and his most distinguished pupil, G.A. Grierson, author of the monumental

Linguistic survey of India, undertook the work at Atkinson's suggestion and with his encouragement.

The fact that the only work on the Irish language at this time was being done by the Professor of Romance languages is in itself a commentary on the chair of Irish, which at this time was held by the Reverend James Goodman. The heady days of the Achill Mission were long past, and there was no longer any realistic hope of spreading the doctrines of the Reformation in the west of Ireland by an Irish-speaking clergy; in any case the number of people who could not understand English was declining sharply and steadily. Although it belonged technically to the Divinity School the chair of Irish now lived in a sort of limbo, and the Professor, whose only literary monument appears to be a version in modern Irish of St Patrick's well-known hymn, lectured to a mere handful of students.

Before we turn to the scientists and the professional schools, we must mention C. F. Bastable, the Professor of Political Economy and Sir Robert Stewart, the Professor of Music. Bastable had broken with precedent in being elected to the chair for a second five-year term in 1887, and at the end of his sixth term, in 1912, he was given a life-tenure. This marks the development of the post from what was in modern terms a post-doctoral fellowship to something more like a real professorship. There was, however, no increase in pay, and Bastable was able to retain it only by virtue of the fact that he held also the chair of Jurisprudence and Political Economy at Queen's College, Galway. He had been called to the Bar, and was interested in jurisprudence as well as in economics, history and political science, and especially in the fields common to two or more of these subjects. His fame rests, however, on his publications in economics, and it was the Tercentenary year that saw the publication of his two most successful books: *The commerce of nations* and *Public finance*. The former was an immediate success and ran into nine editions, but the latter was probably the more original, as Bastable was almost alone in discerning so early the growing importance of the public sector.

Stewart was in 1892 nearing the end of his long tenure of the chair of Music (1862–94). Though a cultured man, he was scarcely a scholar, and his compositions find little favour today; but as an organist, a teacher, and a tireless stimulator of enthusiasm for music he was outstanding. He was organist to both Dublin cathedrals, a Professor in the Academy of Music, and conductor of the Philharmonic orchestra, so that for many years before the Tercentenary he had been the generally acknowledged doyen of the musical world of Ireland. His connexion with Trinity College dated back to some years before his election to the Professorship, as he had been conductor of the

University Choral Society since 1846, and had immediately made himself so popular there that when in 1851 he proceeded to his doctorate the Society presented him not only only with his robes, but also with a jewelled baton. His academic duties in Trinity were confined to examining candidates for musical degrees and arranging their syllabus. He introduced a rule that such candidates must first matriculate by passing a slightly modified version of the entrance examination (including a paper on elementary acoustics); and although as a test of general literacy this was not very demanding, it was better than nothing, for degrees in music enjoyed the anomalous status that, unlike all other degrees, they did not require the previous acquisition of a B.A.[45] There was as yet no teaching of either the theory or the practice of music, and the peripheral nature of the chair is indicated by the fact that although Stewart had been knighted in 1872, it was only twenty years later that the College (where he was generally esteemed and liked) expressed its appreciation (perhaps in return for his composing the music for the Tercentenary ode) by raising his salary from £100 to £125 a year.

Among the scientific Professors of 1892, Sir Robert Ball, Professor of Astronomy was the best known (p. 273), but in the Tercentenary week he was packing his bags for Cambridge, where he had been appointed some months previously to the Lowndean Professorship. After him the most widely known name was that of W.J. Sollas, Professor of Geology. He was a versatile worker; a monograph on the hexactinellid sponges, both living and fossil, was followed by collaboration with Huxley on the fossil Amphibia of the Kilkenny Carboniferous, and by petrological investigations on the Leinster granite, in the course of which he drew attention to the pleochroic haloes in the biotite, thus providing Joly with a clue (when the discovery of radioactivity had suggested the origin of the haloes) for the dating of the rocks. In 1891 Sollas had led the Royal Society's expedition to Funafuti, whose deep drilling in the atoll had furnished a confirmation of Darwin's theory of the origin of coral reefs. After leaving Dublin for Oxford he turned largely to anthropology, archaeology and the quaternary history of man, and his *Ancient hunters* (London, 1911) was a popular classic.

The Professor of Chemistry, James Emerson Reynolds, was also a man of some distinction. He is remembered mainly as the discoverer of thio-urea; that such a compound existed was fairly certain, but its preparation and isolation requred great technical skill, and Reynolds succeeded where Liebig and Hofmann had failed. He also did useful work on the chemistry of silicon, and assigned to beryllium (more, it would seem, by intuition than rigorous proof) its correct place in the periodic table. He held the chair from 1875 to 1903, and succeeding as

22   Sir Robert Ball. Professor of Astronomy, 1874–92. (*Vanity Fair*, April 1904.)

he did to the aged Apjohn he found plenty of scope for his drive and organizational ability in updating the teaching and improving the accommodation of his classes. In his lectures he was a pioneer in using the periodic table as their basis, and in his practical classes he stressed the importance – hitherto rather neglected – of quantitative work. He was something of a martinet, expecting his students to follow step by step the handbooks which he produced for them, and he kept his assistants (including Emil Werner, who was to succeed to the Professorship in 1922) mercilessly ground down to routine demonstrating, without giving them any encouragement to pursue their own researches. He felt with some justice that chemistry was undervalued in the University, but he lacked the diplomatic ability needed to improve its status, and his complaints of inadequate pay, which finally led to his resignation, must be viewed against his moves into successively more spacious upper-middle-class houses in the inner suburbs of Dublin.

E.P. Wright, the Professor of Botany, published relatively little on plants, but he was a first-rate, all-round naturalist, and by 1892, if anybody had a query about the Irish fauna or flora, Wright was the first man to consult. Though always interested in natural history as a hobby, he trained originally as an oculist, and had a year's study on the continent. But, as we have seen, on the death of Robert Ball the elder he took charge of the University Museum, and at the same time was appointed as lecturer in Zoology, a post which he held for eleven years before transferring to Botany in 1869. Had the zoological post been of professorial rank he might well have remained in it, as he kept up his zoological interests to the end, with the writing-up of the Alcyonaria of the *Challenger* expedition as his most important publication. He accepted fully, however, the responsibility of ordering and developing the important herbarium built up by Harvey, and with this end in view he accumulated at his own expense a fine library of Floras and other taxonomic works which, as he was in his later years a childless widower, he bequeathed to the College.

H.W. Mackintosh, who succeeded Macalister in the chairs of Zoology and Comparative Anatomy, was a dimmer figure. He followed Macalister's tradition by publishing a few papers on comparative musculature, but although he took his classes regularly and was an efficient, if not particularly dynamic Registrar of the Medical School for many years, his main interest in later life was the giving of evangelical addresses and the holding of children's services on the beach at Greystones. In consequence the state of zoological teaching and research when he retired in 1921 was not very different from what it had been in 1892.

Sixteen of the non-Fellow Professors held office in the professional schools (eight in Medicine, four in Divinity, three in Law and one in Engineering). A fair number of these were simply professional men who in return for a modest salary and the title of Professor came in to College to give two or three lectures a week, or else to supervise the final examinations. Among the medical men we may mention E.H. Bennett (University Professor of Surgery) and A.V. Macan (King's Professor of Midwifery) as the most outstanding accademically. Bennett was generally acknowledged as the leading authority on fractures, both in theory and in practice, and Macan, who had just completed his term as Master of the Rotunda Hospital, had added greatly to its reputation by subtracting greatly from its mortality figures. This had been achieved mainly by an obstinate insistence on antiseptic precautions at all stages, despite some obscurantist opposition. Here also we may rate G.T. Stokes, the Professor of Ecclesiastical History. He had no great profundity of scholarship, but he was an extremely able and successful popularizer of a subject which tends more often to the dry or esoteric. Stokes's talent lay partly in an instinct for selecting those facts which would make an interesting yet balanced narrative, and partly in a very felicitous prose style. His lectures were enjoyed by divinity students, but they also drew in a considerable audience from outside the walls, and his *Ireland and the Celtic Church*, based on these lectures and first published in 1886, was still being reprinted forty years later.

John Gwynn, the Regius Professor of Divinity, was, on the other hand, a scholar of great learning and distinction, but in a very specialized field which attracted few students. A kindly man, who was able to establish good relations with individual students, he was not a very effective teacher; White praises him for his *suaviter in modo*, but implies that he lacked *fortiter in re*.[46] His colleagues, however, made up for this deficiency, for, while Gwynn was Archbishop King's Lecturer, Salmon was Regius Professor, and after Gwynn succeeded to the chair in 1888 he was replaced in the Lecturership by Bernard. Gwynn's career in scholarship was unusual. Elected Fellow in 1853, he resigned on a College living (the last Fellow ever to do so) in 1864, having spent about half of his time as a Fellow on leave of absence, acting as Warden of St Columba's College. For nearly twenty years he led the life of a country parson, but soon after 1870 he began the study of Syriac to give himself an occupation during the long train journey between Co. Donegal and Dublin, where he had to attend the Synod and its committees. By 1892 he had as yet published little, but the next sixteen years saw the appearance of a large number of editions of and commentaries on important Syriac texts, as well as contributions to the *Dictionary of Christian Biography* relating to most of the early fathers who had

23   Officers of the College Theological Society, 1891. *Centre row*, left to right: John Gwynn, Regius Professor of Divinity, 1888–1917; George Salmon, Provost, 1888–1904; John Henry Bernard, Archbishop King's Lecturer in Divinity (later Provost). *Front row, centre*: E.H. Cornwall, later E.H. Lewis-Crosby, Dean of Christ Church Cathedral.

written in Syriac. At the age of about seventy he switched to the study of Irish, and taught himself the language (helped, no doubt by his son Edward, who was by then beginning to establish his reputation as a scholar in Celtic languages) well enough to produce, when he was well into his eighties, a meticulous and impressive edition of the *Book of Armagh*, one of the most important collections of biblical and hagiographical manuscripts of the early medieval period.

In the Medical School the two outstanding Professors were Daniel Cunningham, Professor of Anatomy, and J.M. Purser, King's Professor of the Institutes of Medicine and effectively, though he did not carry the title, the first Professor of Physiology.[47] Appointed respectively in 1874 and 1883, they transformed the school by introducing a scientific note into the pre-clinical courses, so as to supplement the clinical teaching which continued to flourish on the firm foundation laid by Graves and Stokes. Cunningham and Purser realized, however, that the days were now passed when 'walking the wards' was in itself enough to make a good doctor. Both of them made it clear to the Board that the accommodation for their subjects was totally inadequate, and their representations on this subject were sufficiently persuasive to induce the Board to sanction the extensive building programme of 1875–86 (see p. 289). Cunningham was a Scot who had done work of some importance in comparative as well as in human anatomy, especially notable being his work on the marsupials collected on the *Challenger* expedition. He was most widely known, however, for his *Manual of practical anatomy*, published in 1893–4, and still appearing in a tenth edition in 1940, and also for his only slightly less successful *Textbook of anatomy*. He was a very popular and effective teacher, possessing, it would seem, most of McDowel's talents without his defects, and he did much to foster the *esprit de corps* which is an important aspect of a medical school, and which was especially conspicuous in Trinity in the first half of the twentieth century.

Purser was a more austere figure; although he shared in the kindness and generosity of his classical brother, Louis Claude, he had a sharp tongue and was frightening (though not very severe) as an examiner. He published relatively little original work, but his *Manual of histology* was an excellent textbook in its day. The most original aspects of his teaching were a great faith in the *vis medicatrix naturae* and an opposition to the indiscriminate dosing with a multitude of drugs which was at that time popular; and also an insistence on careful experiment in place of an easy acceptance of *post hoc ergo propter hoc*. He retired from his Professorship in 1902, when he was still in his early sixties, but sixteen years later he was induced to take up the Regius Professorship of Physic, and he discharged the duties of the post with dignity and tact until his final retirement at the age of eighty-five.

Henry Brougham Leech, the Regius Professor of Laws, cannot easily be fitted into any category. Although definitely a part-time Professor (for a large part of his tenure of the chair he was, as registrar of deeds, the head of a fair-sized government department), he was a prominent figure in the College, never at a loss for an opinion on any matter of current controversy. He was a vigorous and active Unionist, and published not only a *Handbook for Unionist speakers* to meet the crisis of Asquith's Home Rule Bill, but also a long and detailed denunciation of the Home Rule movement and its supporters, and a constitutional study of the Boer republics, which must be regarded, however, rather as his contribution to the war effort than as a serious political study. But in University politics he was an iconoclastic radical; his suggestions to the Royal Commission of 1906 included the abolition of Fellowship, the appointment of a businessman as Bursar, and the assignment of the Senior Lecturer's duties to the Provost, whom he considered to be underemployed; the Provost's House could be made the nucleus of a women's college. His only substantial publication in the field of law was a passionate plea, undertaken at the request of the Irish Landlords' Association, for new arrangements for the registration of land-titles. Originally a graduate in classics and philosophy, he showed in his retirement that he had not let his classics rust, for he published when well over eighty his *Prolusiones emeriti*, a collection of Ovidian or Horatian versions of English poems, including, with a courage verging on foolhardiness, Housman's 'Epitaph on an Army of Mercenaries'.

The last name in our catalogue of the Professors is that of Thomas Alexander, Professor of Civil Engineering. He was a practical Scot of the type which dominated the engineering world of the day. A graduate of Glasgow, he had spent some years in Tokyo, introducing the Japanese to western technology. Author of some good elementary textbooks, he may be said to have preserved the traditions of the school, with its emphasis on constructional work and hydraulics, without notably adding to them; but under his rule it continued to send out efficient civil engineers into all parts of the Empire, and their reunion in 1921, on the occasion of Alexander's retirement, culminated in a banquet long remembered as 'Alexander's feast'.

(ix)

The Fellows and Professors still constituted in 1892 virtually the entire academic staff, for the concept of Lecturer as an established and more or less permanent grade had not yet arrived. There were, however, a few assistants to Professors. Some of these, as in the Divinity School, were mainly Fellows who added to their salary by taking a few classes over and above those required of them as tutors. In Physics and Chemistry, however, the assistants were young men devoted to their subject and willing to spend a few years in tedious routine demonstrating in the hope that a more attractive vacancy might present itself before too long. In Chemistry, as we have seen, one of the assistants was E.A. Werner, son of a German photographic pioneer who had settled in Dublin. He was doubtless brought up against a background of practical chemistry, but he was self-made in so far as his first and only degree was that of Sc.D., *honoris causa*, given in recognition of his work on the molecular structure of urea, with which his name will always be associated. In Physics, Fitzgerald had two assistants of even greater distinction – John Joly, an extremely versatile scientist who was to win fame for Trinity in the early years of the next century, and who was already experimenting on what turned out to be one of the most successful of the early methods of colour photography, and Frederick Trouton, who was to win his F.R.S. only five years later for his work in physics, and to succeed in 1902 to the chair of Physics in University College, London. The assistant to the Professor of Astronomy was in a rather different position; he did no teaching, and his assistance was given in the form of telescopic observations and computation. But it is worth recording that in 1892 the assistant was A.A. Rambaut, who was already designated as Ball's successor in the chair, and who was later to become Radcliffe Observer at Oxford.

(x)

We turn now from the seniors to the juniors, and attempt to review the students of 1892. The first fact to be noted is the rather surprising one that their numbers were lower than they had been for thirty-five years and were steadily falling. From 1887 to 1891 the number of annual matriculations had averaged only 273, whereas ten years earlier it had averaged 325, and in the years leading up to 1830 it had several times exceeded 400. But from 1886 to 1907 there was not to be a single year in which the annual intake exceeded 300. Admittedly the proportion of 'drop-outs' had somewhat decreased, but even so the student population of 1892 was less than three-quarters of that of 1830. The decline was to continue till 1904, when the intake began to rise again, mainly (though not entirely) as a result of the admission of women. But it was not until after 1945 that the number of male students rose once more to the figure which obtained in 1881.

This steady fall in numbers, at a time when the College enjoyed a prestige and esteem as high as at any period in its history, is hard to explain. The Protestant population of Ireland was, of course, declining, but no faster than in the sixties and seventies, which had seen a rise in student numbers. The Royal University doubtless drew off a few, if only because it was cheaper; and some of the possible recruits from Britain were diverted to the rapidly growing colleges of northern England, the Midlands and Wales. But it is as well to admit that university admissions are the resultant of a very large number of economic, social and intellectual variables, and any facile explanation of their fluctuations (except in catastrophic periods of war, famine or rebellion) is to be distrusted.[48]

In spite of the fact that Fawcett's Act had now been in operation for nearly twenty years, 81 per cent of the students were Anglicans. But this predominance, effective though it was, was less marked than it had been a generation earlier, for in 1855 over 91 per cent of the students belonged to the Established Church. The intervening years had seen a fairly steady increase in the proportion of Protestant dissenters, from less than 4 per cent in 1855 to 12 per cent in 1892. Nearly half of these were Presbyterians; the remainder were mostly Methodists, Baptists or Quakers. Less than 1 per cent of the students disclaimed affiliation to any Christian church.

The Catholics in 1892 numbered about 7 per cent, a figure significantly lower than the 9.5 per cent of 1830. Any effect which Fawcett's Act may have had in attracting those who aspired to Scholarship or Fellowship was more than neutralized by the much more specifically enunciated and more vigorously implemented episcopal disapproval which had been in force since 1875 (when the proportion had stood at almost 10 per cent). Of those who braved this disapproval a quarter were, perhaps rather surprisingly, the sons of business men, a third the sons of lawyers or doctors, and only a tenth came from the landed gentry. More than a quarter had been educated at English public schools (mainly at Beaumont or Stonyhurst); of the Irish Catholic schools which sent their sons to Trinity, Clongowes easily heads the list. More than half the Catholics came from the Dublin area, and nearly half of the remainder from Munster. Their age at entrance was lower than the average, and the proportion of those who did not proceed to a degree was much higher — 44 per cent among Catholics as against 27 per cent among Protestants. This may have been due to any of several causes: premature entry; schooling not so well geared to the Trinity examination system; delayed response to clerical pressure; or discontent with a community in which they did not feel completely at home. But for the episcopate it represented the worst of both worlds; every year seventeen boys entered the dread portals at the risk of their faith and morals, but only seven or eight emerged as a Catholic leavening of the Establishment.

The figures for geographical origin of the students show little change from the pattern of thirty years earlier. 79 per cent were born in Ireland, 16 per cent in Britain and 5 per cent abroad (in many cases of Irish parents, India accounting for more than half of this category). Dublin accounted for 29 per cent of the total and Ulster for 20 per cent. Comparison with the figures for 1830 shows that the chief changes were a doubling of the proportion born outside Ireland, and, within Ireland, a considerable falling-off in the numbers from Munster and an increase in those from Ulster. This last can be explained by the growth of the Belfast middle class and the fact that the Protestant population was declining less rapidly in Ulster than elsewhere. The increase in the numbers coming from outside Ireland can be explained largely by the railway and the steamboat; it was much less of an adventure to travel from Gloucester or Shrewsbury to Dublin in 1892 than it had been in 1830.[49] But the expense of the journey was still an important consideration, as may be seen from the fact that in 1892 just half of the entrants born in Great Britain came from Wales or the western counties of England.

The students educated in Britain were half as many again as those born there, indicating an increasing tendency for Irish boys to be sent to English public schools, a tendency almost as strongly marked among Catholics as among Protestants. In 1892 roughly one student in eight had been to an English public school. No longer, as in 1861, did Marlborough and Cheltenham have a big lead over the others, for Shrewsbury, Charterhouse, Clifton, Rossall and Haileybury were now as popular. Among Irish boarding schools Portora maintained its easy lead, and, as it had generally speaking a public-school atmosphere, it meant that the public-school men, although a minority, were numerous enough to set the tone for the College.

It was however, an upper-middle-class tone, for the Trinity of 1892 did not contain enough members of the upper class to influence it perceptibly. There was a handful of undergraduates related to peers or baronets, but they were too few (and in many cases too poor) to establish a focus like the Pitt Club or the Bullingdon, and they fitted in happily enough with the sons of prosperous professional men, whose leisure activities (fishing, shooting, occasional hunting) overlapped with their own more widely in Ireland than would have been the case in England. By 1892 the number of entrants who described their father as a 'gentleman' had sunk to 9 per cent of the total; and this elastic term covered, of course, not only the owner of 1,500 acres of good grazing land in Tipperary, but also the *rentier* living in Rathmines on £800 a year from Consols. All the term really meant was a man who did not have to get up in the morning if he did not want to. And in Ireland this implied neither great breeding nor very great wealth.

The professional class accounted by now for a clear majority of the students. 21 per cent were the sons of clergymen, 28 per cent the sons of lawyers, doctors, schoolmasters or other professional men; and for the purposes of social classification we may add to these the 11 per cent whose fathers were officers in the Army or Navy or higher civil servants. Of slightly more ambiguous status were the 12 per cent who were the sons of substantial businessmen. The City magnate who aspired to gentility on the strength of a fortune made by trading in figs had long been the butt of Victorian satirists and social commentators, but there were certain trades which did not draw down on themselves this disdain. In the late Victorian world of Dublin bankers, brewers, maltsters, millers and a few others were accepted on terms of near-equality by the professional men, especially if their business was an old-established one; and stockbrokers were on their way up to the same position. Between them these accounted for about half of the 12 per cent we have classified as 'substantial business men', so that it may be said that some 70 per cent of the students came from homes which were socially (though not always economically) on a par with those of Dublin professional men.

At the lower end of the social scale, 8 per cent were the sons of farmers, 9 per cent of clerks, retailers, craftsmen or labourers, and 2 per cent of fathers whose occupations defy our attempts at classification.

This virtual restriction of student recruitment to the middle and upper sectors of the middle class, which would arouse outraged protest today, invited little criticism at the time. Critics who wished to attack Trinity on religious grounds tended also to denounce it as a reserve for the rich. Admittedly its fees were a little higher than those of the Royal or the Catholic University, and the lifestyle of most of the students meant that only a boy of some determination and courage could pursue his studies from the traditional student's garret. But this difference could be (and was) exaggerated; the difference in cost between sending a boy to Trinity with an adequate allowance and sending him else-where in Ireland did not amount to more than £60 a year at most.[50] Nor was there any competition for university places; a rich idler was not keeping out a brilliant proletarian. Sizarships and other forms of financial assistance were sufficient to ensure that costs could be very substantially reduced for a really intelligent and hard-working boy, and although there was doubtless a case for enlarging such forms of financial assistance, society in general supported the policy of the College, which was that a student must pay for his education either in brains or in money. The number of bright boys who were kept out of Trinity by religious or political forces greatly exceeded those kept out by poverty, for even the most advanced social reformer of the day was demanding free or nearly free university places only for the intellectual élite; the idea that everybody who was more or less literate had a right to free university education still lay far in the future.

The average age at entry had been slowly rising through the nineteenth century, and by 1892 the median age at matriculation was as high as eighteen and a half. This was, however, largely due to an increase in the number of mature students (aged at least twenty at matriculation). They now amounted to 25 per cent of the total, as against 18 per cent in 1865 and 12 per cent in 1830. A fair number of these late entrants – perhaps a third – did not attend lectures, and kept all their terms by examination, but there were many others who had laboriously saved enough to register as full-time students, and had in some cases educated themselves up to the necessary standard. Sometimes this labour was in vain, but in many cases it was justified, for the proportion among the mature students of those who failed to stay the course was only slightly above the average for the student body as a whole.

It was the success of such men, who possessed the tenacity of Jude the Obscure without his unfortunate tendency to become entangled with two women at once, that justified in the eyes of many the persistence of the rule which permitted men to take a degree by examinations only. Their number had been declining, but still stood at about 11 per cent of the total.[51] This rule was regularly attacked by *a priori* educational reformers, and George Fitzgerald denounced as 'abominable' a system which gave to these men the same degree as those whose education was achieved 'by friction with their fellows and by contact with trained intellects'.[52] Whether he would have suffered with equanimity the cuts in the grants for physical apparatus which must have followed a disappearance of nearly 4 per cent of the College's income is not so clear. The economic motive, coupled with the genuine regard felt by many tutors for the moral worth of some of these men, who were usually pathetically grateful for the fleeting, and at times painful contacts they made with the great 'trained intellects' of the College in *viva voce* examinations, outweighed in the mind of the Board the ambiguity which they introduced into the significance of a Dublin degree. At all events, no serious effort was made to abolish this mode of graduating until it had dwindled almost to nothing.[53]

(xi)

It was, of course, only the pass B.A. that was open to these 'absentee' students; for a moderatorship, a degree in medicine or engineering, or a divinity testimonium attendance at classes was essential. But although the ordinary course in arts did not hold the virtual monopoly which it enjoyed in 1830, it was still the backbone of the University curriculum, and in its basic structure still accorded, despite many changes in detail, with the course devised in 1629. All students had to follow it in part, and about 40 per cent (all those who were neither reading medicine or engineering, nor studying for a moderatorship) had to follow it *in toto*.

Apart from frequent up-dating of textbooks, the chief change over the past sixty years was the introduction of a progressively wider choice of subjects in the Sophister years. Since the middle of the century it had been realized that although classics and mathematics each provided sound mental training it was not everyone who had a taste for both, and with many other subjects clamouring for attention it was reasonable to allow a student, at least in his later years, to drop either classics or mathematics. But as Astronomy, which was mathematics thinly disguised, was retained as a compulsory subject in the Junior Sophister year, it was classics which came off worst.

The Freshman years showed little change. English Composition had been introduced in 1877, but otherwise the traditional diet of Greek and Latin, Logic and Mathematics was preserved, with no element of choice. But in the Sophister years either or both of the classical languages could be replaced by French or German or both, and it was even possible to cut out languages altogether in favour of Experimental or Natural Sciences. The only subjects which were still compulsory were English Composition, Astronomy (including some mechanics and optics) and Ethics (with some additional logic).

Such a course represented, as might have been expected, a compromise. Reformers were busy pushing the claims of History, Economics or Education to be added to the list of options, while conservatives were deploring the disintegration of a tested and well-planned programme of mental training in a search for mere information. But most people accepted the compromise as a reasonable one. The change most frequently suggested was the abolition of Greek as a compulsory subject at entrance and in the Freshman years, and this topic aroused angry passions on both sides. But although there was no body in Dublin, as there was at Oxford and Cambridge, to which the country clergy could flock to vote for the preservation of Greek, an elderly Board was almost as effective, and it was only after persistent mining and sapping that the citadel fell at last in 1903.

One rather unexpected development since 1830 in relation to the ordinary course had been a progressive relaxation of the rules determining the assiduity with which it must be followed. In 1830 *all* the term examinations were in theory compulsory, though absence from an occasional one was punished only by a relatively small fine, but in

1835 the number that had to be passed was reduced to two a year. Without these, however, the student could not rise with his class. The Science and Greek lectures also were compulsory, but this was a disciplinary rather than an academic regulation, and applied only to those students who lived in College or in the city as bounded by the Circular Roads. The enforcement of attendance at tutorial lectures was left to the discretion of the individual tutor. In 1848, however, there had been a further concession. A pious exhortation in the Calendar informed the student that 'to gain the full advantage of a university education he should keep all terms by lectures and by examinations', but the minimum requirements to enable him to rise with his year were reduced to the passing of four examinations in all (two of them at specified times, the other two at the student's option) and also to keep by lectures a term in each year, or else to substitute for this the passing of a further term examination in each year. The compulsion for residents or near-residents to attend some lectures continued till 1875. Under these regulations a student who lived more than a mile and a half from the College could for one term in every year neglect his studies completely, and for another term could drop in merely to such lectures as he thought would help him to pass his coming examination. Attendance was, in fact, rather more regular than this might suggest, as the examinations in many subjects were cumulative, and as often as not they followed fairly closely the details of the lectures. But the general atmosphere was certainly easy-going, except for the minority who wished to qualify as Respondents – the name given to those who passed out with high marks at the degree examination.

There was simultaneously a relaxation of rigour in two further respects. From 1848 onwards a student who failed his 'Little-go' (the examination at the end of the Senior Freshman year, officially styled the Final Freshman examination, which was compulsory for all) was allowed to proceed, on probation as it were, as a Junior Sophister, with the chance of justifying himself by passing a supplemental Final Freshman examination in January. The supplementals gradually multiplied until by 1892 they were provided for many of the examinations, and in some cases second supplementals were devised to enable a candidate to have a third shot. The supplementals served the functions of a credit card; a student was able to proceed for a large part of his course on credit which could be paid off during the next nine months. This system, devised originally to provide for the occasional hard case, had been extended, thanks to steady pressure from the tutors, to an extent which meant that the Fellows had to conduct a larger and larger number of examinations, all of them including *viva voce* tests as well as papers, while the student was able to pick and choose, from an *à la carte* menu as it were, the timing of the comparatively small number which he had to sit. All this, however, seems to have been accepted as an inevitable part of the system, and it was not until well into the next century that the Fellows began to murmur against it.

There was also a progressive, and more easily justified, abbreviation of the arts course for professional students. Students of medicine or engineering had to take the full arts course in their Freshman years, but in the Sophister years the number of subjects required for each examination was considerably reduced. The course as a whole, however, was still of sufficient weight to justify the award of a B.A. for studies distinct from those leading to the M.B. or B.A.I.

Of the students who matriculated around 1892, 27 per cent would leave without obtaining a degree. This proportion, though surprisingly high, is rather lower than it had been earlier in the century, and is not much higher than the contemporary figures for Oxford and Cambridge. A few of these were 'abortive entries' who never (despite having paid their entrance fee) took up their places; a very few were sons of the nobility or gentry who never aspired to a degree; a handful had won a place in the Indian Civil Service as undergraduates and did not bother to proceed; doubtless some were victims of illness, death or financial disaster. But the majority were those who failed their examinations at one stage or another.

Of those who stayed the course and emerged with at least a B.A. degree some 37 per cent contented themselves with the ordinary course described above and did not proceed to a professional school or sit for Moderatorship. 27 per cent continued as students of divinity, while the medicals and the engineers, who studied their professional course concurrently with their somewhat abbreviated arts course, accounted for 21 per cent and 5 per cent respectively. Finally, there were 14 per cent who took a moderatorship; a few of these (perhaps a quarter) went on later to medicine or divinity.

The number of honor courses leading to moderatorships had not altered since the changes of 1870–1 (pp. 271–3). There were now seven; Mathematics; Classics; Philosophy; Experimental Science; Natural Science; History and Political Science (including Jurisprudence); Modern Languages. Only the first two, however, could be studied throughout the course; there were no honor lectures or examinations in Philosophy before the Senior Freshman year, and in the other subjects they were available only to Sophisters. The honor courses were not yet seen as alternatives to the pass course, but still as additions. In Classics (which could be studied throughout the pass course) this attitude was not unreasonable; a keen student, though still preoccupied with many subjects outside classics, could at least read more widely and be examined more searchingly in his favourite subject throughout his four-year course. But with History (which did not figure in the pass course) the student had to take on the burden of his honor course without any relief from or overlap with the pass course, for it was only in the same subject that honor lectures or examinations could be substituted for the ordinary ones.[54]

For the first-class student, of course, most of the pass examinations, even in subjects remote from his honor course, presented no great intellectual challenge, but they were an irritating distraction and (in the eyes of many) a waste of precious time. The Board would have replied to such criticism that a sound basis of general education was essential, and that it must not be jeopardized by excessive specialization. But there is little doubt that these restrictive rules kept down the number of moderators.

Within the honor schools the actual courses call for little comment, for they were well balanced, if somewhat conservative, by the standards of the day; nor does the course in the Divinity School, which preserved in its main outlines the structure which had been established in 1833. The other professional schools, however, deserve a little notice.

The structure of the medical curriculum was still remarkably lax. There were only two examinations, and the first, which covered physics, chemistry, botany, zoology, anatomy, physiology and histology could be taken piecemeal at any of the four occasions in the year at which examinations were held. Courses had to be attended in all these subjects, but again (subject only to their timing and to timetable clashes) in whatever order the student wished. The final examination was complicated by the fact that in theory it was divisible into three parts, qualifying for the Bachelor's degree in Medicine, Surgery and Obstetrics respectively. The student was able, therefore, to take it in instalments. Some order was, however, introduced to this rather chaotic system by an officially recommended sequence of lectures and examinations, occupying four years, and the majority of students probably followed this lead. Apart from the appearance of Surgery as early as the second year and, of course, the absence of Bacteriology and Immunology, this recommended sequence is in fair agreement with a modern course. Of the higher degrees in the School of Physic the M.D. was awarded either on a thesis or on the results of an examination; for the M. Ch. and M.A.O. an examination was compulsory.

The regulations of the Law School had been tidied up in 1889, and it now provided though only part, at least an essential part, of the education necessary to qualify for a call to the Irish Bar. During the eighties the number of Trinity graduates called to the Bar had averaged about fifteen a year, but by 1892 the number had sunk to ten. (The number who were admitted as solicitors averaged only about four a year, but their legal education was obtained primarily by apprenticeship and not many of them attended lectures in the Law School.) Students had to attend (over a period of two years) each of the courses given by the three Professors in the school, and to pass their examinations, but they also had to attend in their third year lectures at the King's Inns and to pass an examination organized by the Benchers. Students of the King's Inns who had not matriculated at Trinity were similarly compelled to attend the courses in the Law School of the College. The agreement between the University and the Benchers was one between equals, and to some extent represented a concession by the Benchers, as their control over the profession was tight enough for there to be no question of a 'registrable qualification' being awarded by the University. A student who took the University course alone was thereby (provided he had also obtained his B.A.) entitled to the degree of LL.B. This did nothing to help forward a legal career, but served as a recommendation for certain administrative posts. The LL.D. could be awarded on published work, on a thesis, or by examination.

Engineering provided, as before, a three-year course in which civil engineering was completely dominant, fitting its graduates for the construction of roads, railways, bridges and harbours, and to some extent giving them training also as mining engineers. Only minimal training in electrical and mechanical engineering was provided, but in view of the limitations in space and equipment this specialization was probably sound.[55]

One further duty imposed on the majority of students, though not strictly academic, also involved lectures and examinations. This was the Catechetical course, a system of religious education which was compulsory for Anglicans and Presbyterians in their Freshman years. Four terms had to be kept, either by lectures or examination, in these first two years; for the Anglicans, the College arranged the instruction and examination, but it deputed to the Dublin Presbytery the organization of the teaching and examination of its own students. Small prizes were available for 'students who exhibit peculiar merit, either at lectures or examination', and these were sufficient to induce even some avowed sceptics to follow the courses diligently. The lectures were held on Saturday mornings, but as the week-end habit had not yet begun and this was regarded as part of the working week it aroused no particular resentment. How strictly the rules relating to Catecheticals were enforced we cannot tell, but it was certainly impossible to ignore them or flout them completely.

(xii)

If we attempt to form an estimate of the beliefs, political attitudes, manners, recreations and general lifestyle of the students of 1892, the pages of *T.C.D.*, [56] the records of student societies and games clubs, the photographs of academic or sporting groups, and an occasional passage in an autobiography give us some clues, but much must remain guesswork. A few contrasts with 1830 and with the present day, however, emerge very clearly.

The student of 1892 was, generally speaking, contented and conformist. He did not want to set the world to rights or to change 'the system'; he was a stranger to what Trilling has called the 'adversary culture' which today dominates the thought of students and adult intellectuals alike. Here and there, of course, there was a socialist or a vegetarian, a positivist or an enthusiast for the Irish language, an admirer of Rimsky-Korsakov or Baudelaire, or a collector of Japanese prints. But such men were few, and they were mostly prepared to pursue their enthusiasms alone; they did not found societies or lead demonstrations. The majority was content with Gilbert and Sullivan, Lord Leighton and Conan Doyle, or, if they aspired to a higher cultural level, they followed their parents' tastes and relied on Mendelssohn, Franz Hals and *Idylls of the King*. The working philosophy of most of the undergraduates was that which Wells, writing in *The new Machiavelli* of the Cambridge of a few years later, aptly called Kiplingism. It was based not on the Kipling of crude, left-wing caricature, but on the Kipling revealed in *Recessional* and *The jungle book*, as well as in *Barrack-room ballads*. It comprised a set of values in which imperialism and racial pride went hand in hand with a strong sense of duty, an insistence on courage, a respect for efficiency, a reverence for law, and a tenderness for the weak so long as they did not challenge any of these values. It was a philosophy narrow but strong, representing the best of what Matthew Arnold regarded as the Hebraic streak in virtue – the determination to walk steadfastly by the light that we have – at the risk of ignoring the Hellenic element and of failing to inquire often enough whether the light that is within us be not darkness. It was an attitude which verged at times on arrogance and at times on philistinism but did not pass over completely into either (we are speaking of course of averages), being saved from the first by the elasticity of class-barriers in Ireland, and from the second by a limited but genuine respect for the intellect. The students of those days did not see Professors as enemies; they might occasionally curse them as doddering old curmudgeons, but they did not imagine that they themselves could run the College better than their elders, and their complaints were mostly confined to matters of detail which affected their own domestic comfort. They did not find it necessary to revolt against their fathers, and in many respects they imitated them. The 'perpetual student', who at the age of twenty-six is still sharing a disorderly flat, living off unprogrammed snacks and leading demonstrations, was then unknown; rather, if the satirist were looking for material, he would find it in the callow youth of twenty aping, with his cane, his stand-up collar and his heavy moustache, and with only very partial success, the manner of an experienced man of the world. Through this facade there appeared often enough the carelessness and the high spirits of youth, but this did not matter. The ideal was not a Soames Forsyte, but rather a pleasure-loving (though not dissipated) man-about-town. There was plenty of horse-play and of practical jokes, and there was an occasional gesture of deliberate casualness or nonconformity. The carefully contrived nonchalance with which the foreground figures lounged in many group photographs of this period fulfilled the same psychological need as do patched and faded denims today.

If we turn now to compare the students of 1892 with their predecessors of 1830, two changes stand out immediately. They were less preoccupied with religious issues, and they spent a large part of their time in sport.

The religious decline must not be exaggerated. The average student of 1892 went willingly enough to church on Sundays, and he led a life governed by moral principles which were broadly speaking Christian (with perhaps an occasional dispensation for Saturday nights). But the number of sceptics, openly avowed at least among their friends, though still a small minority, was growing, and for the most part ecclesiastical affairs were forgotten on weekdays. Even the earnest young men, discussing deep questions in the early hours of the morning, would be more likely to argue about Plato or Browning than about the nature of miracles or justification by faith. Christianity was a distinctive and conspicuous flavour in College life, but it was no longer a major ingredient of the dish.

In the matter of sport the transformation was more complete, for by 1892 organized games had very nearly reached the dominant position which they were to occupy for the next generation. Young men have always enjoyed exercising their muscles and pitting their strength or skill against that of their fellows. For many centuries this took the form mainly of races or of some kind of sham fight – boxing, wrestling, jousting or fencing. Why, within the compass of a few decades in the latter part of the nineteenth century, these activities should have been largely superceded by ball games (which had previously played only a minor role in exercise, especially for students) is a chapter of history which still invites exploration. At all events by 1892 'sport' had come to mean for most men no longer shooting, fishing and racing, but cricket, Rugby football and rowing, and to a lesser extent athletics and the minor ball games.[57] Clubs for the encouragement and organization of these sports had been in existence for some time, but up to about 1870 they had not formed a conspicuous feature of undergraduate life, except for the College Races, which were, however, of much more importance as a social than as an athletic event. But during the seventies and eighties the popularity and prestige of sport increased enormously, and by 1892 the student who did not participate in it was, though not exactly despised, regarded as peculiar. There was as yet no polarization into hearties and intellectuals; both types existed, of course, but they were not in conscious and open opposition. The figure who commanded almost universal admiration was the man who excelled both at work and at games, and these were plentiful enough. The best remembered were those who died young. Lucius Gwynn, who scored a century against Cambridge in 1895 and was for several years on the Irish Rugby team, was elected Fellow in 1899, but died of tuberculosis three years later. Andrew Marshall Porter, who won first place in classical Moderatorship in 1897 and captained Trinity in cricket and Ireland in hockey, was killed in the South African war. Such men, whose early triumphs could never be overshadowed by intellectual stagnation or middle-aged corpulence, formed the *beau idéal* for their generation. Even for a scholar whose athletic feats were much less distinguished, the sporting side of his undergraduate life was emphasized in after-dinner speeches and obituaries, and the river or the playing-field looms large in reminiscences of student days, even of those who never touched a bat, a ball or an oar once they left College.

For his remaining leisure hours the student could choose between the music-hall, a fair selection of mainly light theatrical performances, smoking-concerts, race-meetings, and restaurants which offered flashy, if perhaps rather insubstantial menus at astonishingly low prices. There were also the College societies, whose proceedings tended to be serious, but they did not exclude a flippant note now and then. The Historical Society, which held debates in the style of the Oxford and Cambridge Unions, and the Philosophical Society, at which a paper was read by a member and then discussed by anyone who cared to speak, were both flourishing at this time, and their Opening Meetings, addressed by distinguished men from outside, and often from across the Irish Sea, drew large crowds. The day of the specialist societies was only just beginning, but as well as the old-established Theological and Choral Societies there was a Chess Club, a Biological Association (which catered, despite its title, purely for medical students) and a recently formed Experimental Science Association. And if none of these attractions was sufficient to make the student leave his rooms there were, as in every generation, talks with one or two friends over a dying fire, with the teapot now drained of its second re-fill, on the spiritual regeneration of Ireland, the rights of women and the immortality of the soul.

(xiii)

Such were the structures, the personnel and the activities of the College which decided in 1891 to celebrate its Tercentenary in the following year. The date fell at a fortunate moment, as Trinity then stood very near the peak of its reputation for scholarship, and at the same time the achievement of its graduates over the past generation was generally acknowledged, as was the generally high level of its teaching. To the Protestant and Anglo-Irish world it was an essential pillar of society which was discharging its duties well. To Catholic and Nationalist Ireland it appeared, of course, in a rather different light, and, in attempting to pay a compliment to the College on the occasion of its Tercentenary without conceding any points in the perennial controversy over the 'Irish University Question', Archbishop Walsh became somewhat confused. Having been accustomed to dismiss the Trinity which followed Fawcett's Act as 'another godless college' he could not overlook the fact that the first item on the Tercentenary programme was a solemn service at St Patrick's Cathedral; and although he welcomed this, sincerely enough, as a sign that the College was withstanding the rising tide of secularism and infidelity, he could not resist the temptation to point out that it also demonstrated the College's incorrigible Protestantism. Having conceded that such Catholics as had received invitations could take part in the social junketings of the Tercentenary without sin, he went on to say that 'in the religious service in St Patrick's Cathedral no Roman Catholic should take part, although I acknowledge that there is no feature in the programme as to which Roman Catholics ought to feel more deeply satisfied'.[58] The schoolchildren whose prize-giving he had rather strangely selected as the occasion for these remarks must have gone away in some doubt as to whether they were expected to hiss or to cheer. The *Freeman's Journal* was more forthright, and simply gave the College its good wishes as serving well the needs of the Protestant community; it was only to be regretted that there was not another university doing the same for Catholics. The Nationalist politicians were too busy electioneering in an orgy of a fratricidal strife between Parnellite and anti-Parnellite factions to give the matter any attention, but the less fully engaged nationalist world had been wooed round to a position of benevolent neutrality by an imaginative gesture which the Board had taken five months earlier – the conferring of an honorary degree on the Lord Mayor of Dublin, to signify its recognition of the historic links which bound city and college closely together. The city responded generously by conferring on the Provost, shortly before the celebrations, the freedom of the city, and although this was an honour given primarily *ex officio* it was the more willingly given because of the high regard in which Salmon was held by the country as a whole.

There was naturally some divergence of views in the College as to the scale on which the celebrations should be planned, but the final programme seems to have given general satisfaction.[59] Nevertheless, there was at times a good deal of tension between the more active and ambitious members of the Tercentenary committee, headed by Mahaffy, and the Board, which was concerned to play down both ostentation and expense.[60] The celebration of centenaries and jubilees was a practice which had hitherto been relatively infrequent and was only then becoming general,[61] so that the Board had little in the way of precedent to guide it. The College celebrated its centenary in 1694[62] modestly but effectively, but there is no record of any commemoration a hundred years later. Mahaffy[63] uses this as the excuse for a scathing attack on his favourite target – the post-Hely-Hutchinson Fellows – and ascribed the omission to 'the creatures who were thinking of nothing but the loss of a step in their promotion, or the chances of succeeding to a lucrative post ... Had any of the three great Provosts been guiding the counsels of the College, this disgraceful omission of so honourable a commemoration would not have been tolerated.' Leaving aside the reflection that promotion was not an idea that was entirely absent from Mahaffy's own mind, the weak point of his attack is that in 1791 and 1792, the years in which a bicentenary celebration should have been planned, Hely-Hutchinson was fully in control of the College.

At all events the committee soon produced a fairly elaborate pro-gramme, which was agreed on, subsequent argument being confined to details. The committee, foreshadowing Edwardian sumptuousness, proposed champagne and claret-cup for the garden-party, but the Board preferred to stick to solid Victorian traditions and substituted sherry and claret, stipulating that they should be of good quality. It agreed that Mitchell's, the leading caterer, should provide the banquet, but insisted that details of the menu should be settled by the Bursar. When Traill, in an excess of exuberant hospitality, started assigning accommodation in the College to the wives of delegates he was sharply called to order. And against the suggestion supported by many under-graduates and some graduates that the occasion should be marked by excusing every undergraduate a term examination the Board stood firm, declaring reasonably enough that this would be a strange way in which to celebrate three hundred years of scholarship.

The selection from among the guests of those to be awarded honorary degrees also gave rise to some argument, and one name in particular was the subject of vehement debate, both at the Senate and at the Board. This was Burdon Saunderson, the Professor of Physiology at Oxford, who was opposed by an anti-vivisection lobby. They induced the Board to remove his name from the list, but Cunningham and J.M. Purser launched a powerful counter-attack on behalf of the Medical School and the Board changed its mind again, Carson, Ingram and Shaw dissenting.

In its final form the celebration was imaginatively conceived and executed with *panache*. It achieved a real festival atmosphere, in which solemn ritual, generous hospitality, sport and light entertainment all found their place. The participants included, in addition to the members of the College and the official and learned worlds of Dublin, a large number of guests invited from Britain and overseas; among these were over two hundred guests from some seventy universities or learned bodies distributed over the five continents. They provided as the main theme of the celebrations the international comity of learning; and Ingram struck the keynote when he spoke eloquently of

all the universities in the world which have responded to our call, from London to Melbourne and Calcutta, from Leyden to Bologna, from Yale and Harvard to Vienna and St Petersburg. Wherever such an institution has been established we ought to regard it as a stronghold founded for the defence of true science and sound learning and for carrying on the perennial warfare against ignorance, sciolism, prejudice and error.

A number of purely personal invitations were also sent out. Of the really great Victorians only Tennyson and Gladstone survived. The former was unfit to travel and died, in fact, a few months later; Gladstone sent a non-commital reply, saying that 'it would be very daring for a man on the stroke of eighty-two to enter into any engagement' for a date eight months ahead. But when July came it was not old age that kept him away; he was busy electioneering in Midlothian. Perhaps it was just as well, as, if the *Irish Independent* is to be trusted, the only recipient of an honorary degree whose name was greeted with silence instead of applause was a chemist who had the misfortune to be called Gladstone.

All the same, an impressive galaxy of talent was mustered; Dublin had never seen before and has not seen since so many men of real eminence gathered together. *Ex officio* guests included the Vice-Chancellors of Oxford and Cambridge, the Master of Trinity, Cambridge, the directors of the British Museum and National Gallery, and the President of the Royal Academy. Physics was especially well represented by Kelvin, Rayleigh, Sir George Stokes and J.J. Thompson,

337

as also was history by Stubbs, Creighton, Acton and Lecky. From the other guests we may pick out some names which are still remembered today: Verrall and Postgate in classics, Skeat and Max Müller in philology, Pollock in law, Edgeworth in economics, George Darwin in astronomy, Geikie and Judd in geology, Michael Foster in physiology, and Acland and Clark in medicine. Outside the traditional academic disciplines there were Lord Dufferin, W.H. Russell, the war correspondent, Parry and Stainer to represent music and, less happily perhaps, Leighton and Alma-Tadema for the fine arts. There was a strange absence of divines (no honorary D.D. being awarded), and literature was also without adequate representation, but this was because the great Victorian figures were dead or dying and none of their successors had as yet achieved general recognition. Two very minor literary men were present, both Dublin graduates, Aubrey de Vere and Bram Stoker, but the latter attended not in his capacity as the author of *Dracula* (which still lay four years in the future), but as secretary to the man whom the undergraduates, the press and much of the general public considered more worthy of honour than all the scholars put together. This was Henry Irving, who had in the past twenty years established himself as the idol of the theatre-going public, highbrows and lowbrows alike. His selection as one of the recipients of an honorary degree was primarily, perhaps, a tribute to his work as an indefatigable producer of Shakespeare, but it was the first occasion on which an actor had received such public and official acclaim and was certified, by implication, to be a respectable and honoured member of society. After Commencements the students chaired him across the Front Square and demanded a speech of him from the Dining Hall steps, and one of the few criticisms of the celebrations in the press was a complaint that at the banquet he was not seated at the High Table.

The guests were given a full programme for the four days in Dublin. The University provided a cathedral service, a garden-party, the performance of a choral Tercentenary ode, ceremonies for the conferring of honorary degrees[64] and for the presentation of complimentary addresses, a theatrical evening, a banquet, a ball, a cricket match and the College Races, the annual athletic meeting which, though its greatest glories lay in the past, was a still major social event for Dublin. To fill in the gaps the Lord-Lieutenant and the Commander of the Forces in Ireland each gave a garden-party, and the city another ball. All the functions were reported in long and loving detail, albeit somewhat solemnly, in the Unionist press; their Nationalist contemporaries, though friendly enough, allowed themselves a more flippant approach, as when a central European professor in his robes was described as looking like 'a cross between a Robert Emmet bandsman

and Count Arnheim from *The Bohemian Girl'*. The celebrations opened
with a procession of hosts and guests from the College to the Cathedral
through a mile of city streets, escorted by a military band in front and
another in the rear. The sight of several hundred costumes from a score
of countries must have been dazzling enough, but by general consent
the student delegates from Heidelberg stole the show with their green
velvet jackets, white breeches, high boots, swords and plumed hats. At
the garden party later that day the Provost's daughter planted a
mulberry tree with a silver spade bearing (so we are asked to believe)
on one side a facsimile in repoussé of a page from the Book of Kells,
while a choir sang a Sapphic ode in Latin. At the banquet there were
over 550 hosts and guests, the latter including, besides those specially
invited to the celebrations, anybody who was anybody in Dublin and a
few, such as Baron von Richthofen and the Thakore Sahib of Gondar,
who seem to have been gathered into the net at the last moment. At the
banquet, and on many subsequent occasions, speeches were delivered
by the dozen in a variety of languages; in some of them honorary
membership of the College was conferred by visitors who had not done
their homework well on such men as Robert Boyle and Laurence
Sterne. But everyone seems to have enjoyed themselves right up to the
small hours of the Saturday morning, when those of the guests whose
stamina had survived a long succession of Lancers, polkas, gavottes
and waltzes bade their adieux and set out for home with the strains of
'Tiddleywinks' and 'Ta-ra-ra-boom-de-ay' still ringing in their ears.[65]

(xiv)

The Tercentenary had a long-drawn-out epilogue. While the celebrations were being planned it was suggested that the occasion should
have a permanent memorial, and a committee appointed to consider
this suggested a building to house a Union on the general lines of those
of Oxford and Cambridge. The Board showed little enthusiasm for the
idea, and although subscriptions were collected from 1,600 graduates
they were mostly very small, so that the total amounted to only £7,500.
This was barely enough, and moreover there was no obviously suitable
site. The Board, therefore, stepped in and decided to demolish 'Rotten
Row', the red-brick range on the north side of Library Square, and to
erect in its place the Graduates' Memorial Building, which should
house the Union in its central block and provide at the two ends forty
sets of student rooms. Sir Thomas Drew was appointed architect, and
his building, completed in 1902, was described in a contemporary
appreciation[66] as coming 'under the broad category of Renaissance,
with decided French leanings'. It is not one of the glories of the College,

but it might, at that time, have been much worse. The idea of the Union, however, proved abortive; closer examination showed that the analogy with Oxford and Cambridge was misleading in several respects, and the long-established Historical and Philosophical Societies argued with some justice that they already provided between them all the amenities and activities which could be expected from a Union. After four years' bickering, therefore, the Board gave in, and the rooms intended for the Union were divided between the two societies.[67]

11

The admission of women

(i)

The campaign for the admission of women to Trinity College, its success in 1904, and the reduction after that date of successive bastions of male exclusiveness within the fortress is a story which extends over a century and would be difficult to accommodate in any one of our chapters, defined as they are by chronological limits. It is, moreover, a continuous story which would lose by division; accordingly we treat it here in its entirety in a separate chapter, poised between the history of those decades in which the campaign gained serious momentum and that in which the major victory was won. To complete the story we have strayed beyond our terminal date of 1952, for it may now be said with some assurance that the tale is told: even the most ardent feminist can scarcely claim in 1980 that, at least as far as formal regulations are concerned, women are at any disadvantage in College compared with men.

The recent lucrative trade in Victorian pornography has popularized, especially in radical circles, a belief that what we look on as the prudishness of the later nineteenth century was entirely hypocritical, and that Victorians were as lascivious as the keenest exploiters of permissiveness today. This may have been true of a limited smart set, but it was certainly not true of the Provost and Senior Fellows of Trinity College, Dublin, who, though they may have been apt to invest with the mantle of morality what should more truly be regarded as rules of social decorum, certainly believed in what they preached, and practised it as well. Throughout this period the College is completely free from any hint of sexual scandal among its senior members, and even Williamson, of whom it was said that his stories were as broad as they were long, was merely a tolerant clubman who led a blameless life and expected his colleagues and his pupils to do the same. Nor were the beliefs of the fighters for women's rights very different. Their view of morality coincided completely, and of social decorum largely, with that of the Board; where they differed was in their estimate of the

341

number of women seriously interested in intellectual matters or in a professional career, and of the power of such women to resist the temptations offered by a predominantly male society and to sit in the same lecture room as young men without forming a seriously disruptive element. Ardent reformers and dogged conservatives of those days would alike have been shocked and distressed if they could have envisaged the pattern of undergraduate life today, with men and women resident on adjacent staircases and rules about overnight guests lapsing into obsolescence. The conservatives, however, might be able to extract a little comfort by being able to say: 'I told you that it would lead to this.'

We ask the reader, therefore, to remember that in spite of the acute differences which divided the women's champions and their opponents round about 1900, they shared many assumptions which would be considered ridiculous today. And, granted these assumptions, there were difficulties in the idea of a mixed college which could not be lightly brushed aside. Much of the opposition to the admission of women came from unthinking conservatism, from an *a priori* view of the limitations of the female mind, from overemphasis on trivialities of masculine comfort, or from lack of the imagination needed to gauge the extent to which an institution can adapt itself to changed circumstances. But much of it also came from an apprehension of difficulties which were genuine enough at the time, and which have disappeared only because of a rapid change, which nobody can be blamed for not having foreseen, in the conventions governing social behaviour in mixed company.

So far we have spoken of the attitude of the seniors, but that of the undergraduates and would-be undergraduettes was not profoundly different. In Edwardian and late Victorian times young men of the professional class were not immune from sexual desire, nor did they disdain the pleasures of dancing and flirting with young women. But the desire was more often suppressed than indulged, and if indulged it was almost invariably in a milieu remote from their everyday world. If they boasted of their conquests they did so only among a narrow circle of close friends. And the more innocent pleasures of mixed company were valued as occasional treats, not, during term-time anyway, as a constant ingredient of life, or even of relaxation. A young man might spend a morning in romantic dreams of the girl he had met on the previous evening, but by midday he would be laughed out of this by his friends, and he would be happy to spend the rest of the week working, talking, idling, drinking and playing games in a purely male world. Even the most dissolute or susceptible undergraduate did not chafe unduly at the rules which society imposed on him; he might use ingenuity in evading them, but he did not call for their abolition. There was no demand for a return to the world of Petronius, or even of the Regency.

And the women undergraduates of the early years were, of course, stricter still. Most of them were genuine intellectuals, reluctant to be distracted from their books, and all regarded themselves as torch-bearers on trial under a searching public scrutiny; to become the occasion of scandal would be not only a personal disaster but also the betrayal of a cause. Before very long, of course, their ranks were infiltrated by a few who were seeking primarily a good time and a suitable husband, but it was not until after the First World War that this attitude came out into the open. Although in the inter-war period the austere rules of Edwardian days were in many respects relaxed, it was still true of the average male undergraduate that 'man's love is of man's life a thing apart'. Two or three terms of his twelve might, perhaps, be disrupted by love-affairs; once or twice a week he might take a girl out to lunch or to the pictures, and twice or three times a term invite her to a dance. For the rest, he would talk to girls between lectures, but the greater part of the day he would spend in exclusively male company, and he would accept, and often, indeed applaud the rule which banished women from the College after 6 p.m.

In the earliest stages of the campaign Dublin was ahead of Oxford and Cambridge in the educational privileges which it afforded to women; later it lagged behind them; and later still it took the lead by being the first to give them full degrees. But in the period in which it lagged behind – the period in which the women's colleges at Oxford and Cambridge were finding their feet – the delay at Dublin was due not so much to inordinate conservatism as to the fact that the structure of the University did not permit of advance along the same lines as in England. Girls could go to Girton or Lady Margaret Hall, live in a purely female environment, be taught mainly by women, and sit for examinations organized by the university, without impinging notice-ably on the traditional pattern of life in the men's colleges. In them dons and undergraduates alike could forget about women students for nine-tenths of the day, unless they cared to seek them out, for it was only in the laboratories or at professorial lectures that they met them willy-nilly. But in Dublin the Library, the laboratories and the lecture-rooms of the University were situated in the grounds of Trinity College and belonged to its governing body, so that the solution of separate colleges for women and men was never really viable. Various fumbling attempts were made to find a way round this difficulty, but they made little progress, and for this reason the capitulation at Dublin, when it came, was more or less complete.

Alexandra College, founded in 1869, was the centre of higher education for women. It was modelled on Queen's College, Harley Street, and was designed as a finishing school, but giving a finish much less frivolous than the term usually implied. Its pupils were mostly in their late teens, and many of them were working, from 1879 onwards, for examinations of the Royal University. They were taught partly by women, but partly also by men, including several of the Fellows and Professors from Trinity College; notable among these was J.H. Bernard, the future Provost, who taught mathematics there from 1885 onwards and became Warden of the College in 1903.[1] As the college found its feet it was able to invite distinguished scholars from England to give an occasional lecture, and it thus became a centre of some importance in Dublin of literary and artistic culture.[2] Not without justification it set itself the aim of becoming the Girton of Dublin, and its efforts to develop and maintain the necessary standards were assisted by the remarkably intense *esprit de corps* of its teachers, pupils and alumnae, who centred on the college all the intellectual dedication, public spirit and self-reliance characteristic of the women of late-Victorian times who were engaged in the educational battle.

But to become a Dublin Girton some recognition and some help from the University was needed. In 1869 (even before Girton had been founded) Cambridge agreed to hold annual examinations for women, of a standard intermediate between those of the pass degree and the tripos. Alexandra immediately requested Trinity to organize something similar. Within a few months the Board had agreed: examinations could be held wherever a ladies' committee had been constituted, so long as there were at least ten candidates, and certificates of proficiency would be issued on the results. There were to be two examinations, the junior at about the level of College entrance, the senior at Senior Freshman level. For a few years they were popular, but soon the numbers began to fall off, especially after 1878, when London University and the Royal University of Ireland simultaneously opened their doors to women; and the counter-attractions were further increased when Cambridge in 1881 and Oxford in 1884, though giving no degrees, enabled women to participate in much of the teaching and most of the examinations provided for men. As early as 1873 the governors of the Queen's Institute had indicated to the Board, somewhat ungratefully perhaps, that in their opinion the Trinity examinations for ladies had not won public confidence nor raised the status of the teaching profession, and they pressed for admission to the University, where they could have access to the same teaching and the same testing as men. They justified their plea, either very subtly or very naively, by claiming that the women so admitted would within twenty years or so be competent to found and govern women's colleges affiliated to the University, but whether they really imagined that women, having once got their foot inside the door of Trinity College, would consent to withdraw to these affiliated colleges must remain doubtful. In any case the Board was not convinced, and after a long discussion the request was rejected, Jellett, its most junior member, alone dissenting.

But if he was alone on the Board, Jellett had some support among his juniors, notably Traill and Tarleton. In 1880 a fair number of Junior Fellows and Professors signed a memorial asking the Board to follow the lead of the Royal University by admitting women to degrees in arts; and as the University Council had been established since the last attempt it was here that the reformers waged their next campaign. The Council was reasonably representative of the College, and it indicated well the wide diversity of views on the question by refusing to give a definite opinion. A motion proposed in 1880 that degrees in arts should be open to women was countered by an amendment to the effect that this would not be desirable. The amendment was lost by ten votes to six; whereupon the motion was also defeated, by eleven votes to five. Agnosticism, not only in Professor Huxley's sense, was the order of the day. Two years later another attempt was more successful, for a similar motion proposed by Traill was carried by a small majority. But the vote carried little moral authority; three members of the Council (including Carson, an inflexible opponent of mixed education) were absent, and there were two abstentions, so that only seven members out of seventeen had actually declared themselves in favour. In consequence when, a few months later, Traill proposed the appointment of a committee to consider the best way of implementing the resolution, Carson was able to carry an amendment directing the committee to consider not merely how, but also whether it should be implemented. Half the Council was put on the committee, as well as two other Professors; every shade of opinion was represented on it, and, as might have been expected (and as no doubt Carson wished), it was unable to agree on a report.

So matters rested for another ten years, till the Tercentenary shed a bright light of publicity on the College, giving the occasion for many compliments but also some criticisms. On the surface the outlook was still rather bleak for the women's party, for Salmon had succeeded Jellett as Provost, and Salmon was its uncompromising foe, whose opposition was strengthened by the near-universal respect and affection which he commanded. But beneath the surface things were changing; the women's friends among the Junior Fellows and Professors were gaining both in numbers and in authority, so that when the Board received in June 1892 four separate memorials for the women's cause (one from professional men, one from Irish women, one from a majority of the Fellows and Professors, and one from the medical Professors alone) it looked as if the walls of Jericho might show at least some local crumbling. But the Board sat tight, and nine months later the reformers tried their luck again with the Council. The resolution of 1882 was again carried, this time with a convincing majority, and the committee appointed to work out plans consisted of four keen reformers and one centre-party man (Ingram). One of the reformers on it was Bernard, so that it started by examining the role which Alexandra College might play. But the practical difficulties in making it the main centre for the women students of the University appeared so great, that the committee decided (Ingram dissenting) that women should be admitted to lectures in Trinity. Some concessions were made to the fears of conservatives. Women should be lectured in public rooms, and not in the rooms which were attached to the chambers of many of the Fellows; for classical examinations in the pass course alternative books might be prescribed, to avoid the embarrassment of expounding Juvenal to a mixed class; and for pass lectures in the Junior Freshman year (where, it was assumed, the standards of chivalry of the male student might leave something to be desired) separate lectures should be arranged for women. The Council accepted the report, though only by a narrow majority, and sent it on to the Board, which marked it as 'read'.

Finding itself under considerable pressure, however, from various groups interested in women's education, the Board suggested to the Central Association of Irish Schoolmistresses that it might propose some less revolutionary scheme. The Association, always ready to insert the thin end of the wedge, suggested that degrees, examinations and honor lectures should be open to women. The Board promised to consider the plan, but explained that in considering a course of action which would 'produce a fundamental change in an ancient and important institution' it must consider law as well as expediency. Accordingly, it played its last trump by asking for counsel's opinion, and by choosing as counsel, Serjeant Jellett (who was not tainted by the liberalism of his brother, the late Provost) and Piers White. Both were eminent silks, but both were over seventy, and their opinion did not come as a great surprise. It was clear from the charter, they averred, that Trinity College was founded for male students only, and the change made by admitting women would alter its constitution so profoundly that it was doubtful whether the Crown could do this even with the consent of the majority of the corporation. Any dissentient Fellow or Scholar could apply for an injunction to restrain the Board from petitioning for such a Queen's Letter, or from accepting it if issued.[3] Only by an Act of Parliament could women enter – and, they added, to rally the waverers, such an Act would inevitably open to women *all* offices in the College and University: Fellowship, Provostship, nay the office of Chancellor itself.

Armed with this document, the Board declared to the schoolmistresses that, no matter how willing, it was powerless to act, and when it was suggested that it might promote legislation to solve the problem it declared that it had no intention of doing so, and if a bill was introduced providing for the admission of women to degrees in Dublin but not at Oxford and Cambridge it would oppose it. It reiterated some of its objections to mixed education in the College. Once a woman was in College it would be impossible to know where she went and how long she stayed, or, indeed, whether she ever came out at all. As to chaperonage, it would be impossible for the porters to decide whether, when two women entered together, one was old enough to act as guardian of the other. It was not to a college of this kind that parents sent their sons. Granted that most undergraduates of both sexes would behave well, an occasional scandal was bound to occur, and in any case many a susceptible boy would become entangled in an imprudent marriage. From such *liaisons dangereuses* and fortune-hunters the Board had a duty to protect its students.

All the same, the Board was beginning to feel uncomfortably isolated. With the defection of Durham in 1895, Dublin was now the only university in the British Isles which offered to women neither degrees nor a comprehensive scheme of examinations and teaching comparable to that which it gave to men. At this time the Conservative government was building harbours and light railways in improbable parts of Ireland as part of its programme of 'killing Home Rule by kindness', and the Board decided to take a leaf out of its book. Various schemes for a more extensive examination programme were suggested, but whatever conciliatory effect they might have produced was destroyed by the revelation at about the same time that what the Board really favoured was a separate university for women in Ireland, which would not only avoid all the social embarrassments of mixed education, but would also be able to devise a course suited to the needs and talents of women, and 'would perhaps be able to find some more suitable title than bachelor to designate a well-educated woman'.[4]

The dogged obstinacy with which the Board attempted to swim against the tide was due in part to the fact that it included at least two strong conservatives of great ability (Salmon and Carson), but even more to the fact that it was composed of very old men. For it was just at this time that the average age of the Board attained its all-time record.

In December 1896, Graves's prediction (p. 211) had been more than fulfilled, for there was then no member of the Board under seventy; most of them were over seventy-five and the aggregate of the ages of the eight members was just 600. Men like Haughton and Ingram, who twenty years earlier had been fertile with ideas for enabling the College to move with the times and prodigal of their time and energy in securing the acceptance of these ideas and in putting them into practice, still favoured higher education for women, but could not now face the disruption to the College which they thought it must cause, and voted, therefore, with colleagues who were convinced that women should not stray outside the drawing-room.

But if these men possessed great staying-power, they were not immortal, and among the more senior of the Junior Fellows there were several committed to the women's cause. The question was, therefore, whether they would move up to the Board before they in their turn lost their reforming zeal. There were, in consequence, several years in which public-spirited women, as well as Junior Fellows impatient with 'stagnation', were tempted to follow with more interest than could be ascribed to friendly solicitude reports on the health of the frailer Senior Fellows.

Poole retired in December 1896, and was replaced by Conner, of whom little is remembered except that he was a kindly old man who went around with a dog at his heels; he was certainly not a radical. After this, however, the seniors began to go down like ninepins. Stubbs died in January 1897, and Haughton nine months later; they were replaced by Williamson and Abbott, the former a vigorous campaigner for the women's cause, the latter less committed, but likely to vote on the right side. The next to go was Carson, in February 1898, but in this case indeed Amurath to Amurath succeeded, for he was replaced by Gray, whose conservatism was so strong and consistent that Carson in comparison seemed a mere trimmer. In 1899, however, Ingram retired and Shaw died, to be replaced by Mahaffy and Traill. The Board was now evenly balanced, and there was a tantalizing wait of two and a half years for another vacancy. At last, in December 1901, Conner retired and was succeeded by Tarleton, giving the women's party a clear majority. Mahaffy immediately proposed a motion that it was expedient to admit women students and to award them degrees, and it was passed by five votes to three. Similar motions were brought before the Council and the Senate and passed with substantial majorities, and in December 1902 a draft of a King's Letter was forwarded to the Government, the Provost and Gray dissenting.[5]

The law officers of the Crown accepted the view that the change could be made by means of a King's Letter, but there remained one final obstacle. The Crown was advised that a modification of the charter required the assent not merely of the Board, but also of the Provost, as head of the corporation. This put Salmon in an awkward position. He was still as certain as ever that the admission of women would be a mistake, but even his great popularity would hardly weather a situation in which, thanks to a technical prerogative, he would thwart the will of at least four-fifths of his colleagues. Prompted in part by a sense of responsibility and in part by weariness (for he was by now eighty-three) and the knowledge that whoever would succeed him would almost certainly hold the opposite view, he wrote to the Lord-Lieutenant in July 1903, withdrawing his 'official' opposition, though making it clear that his views were unchanged.[6] In December, the King's Letter was issued, and the following month Salmon died. His defeated supporters had to console themselves by hinting that he had died of a broken heart, caused by the impending ruin of the College he had loved and served so well.

(iii)

The first woman student was admitted in January 1904, and before the year had ended forty-five others had followed her. Many of these had been awaiting their chance for months or even years, and several (including the youngest daughter of Provost Jellett) transferred from the Royal University, even though it meant the loss of an academic year. It was natural enough, therefore, that the rate of enrolment in 1905–7 should be somewhat smaller (averaging twenty-six a year), but soon the numbers began to pick up, and shortly before the outbreak of war in 1914 women were forming about 15 per cent of the annual intake. Although the extremely high intellectual standard of the first entrants was not maintained, the academic success of the women in their early years was out of proportion to their numbers: of the 160 who entered up to the end of 1908 over half won honours of some kind at graduation. Naturally enough they scored most consistently in those subjects traditionally considered appropriate for women – Modern Languages and History – and it was in these subjects that their first gold medals were won. But male complacency was somewhat jolted when a gold medal in Natural Science went to a woman in 1910 and again in 1912, and even more so when the same thing happened in Philosophy in 1913 and in Experimental Science in 1916.[7]

The women students were at first subjected to rather stringent rules; they had to wear cap and gown at all times in the College squares; they could not visit any chambers in College – even of the most senior of the Fellows – unless accompanied by a chaperon; and they had to be out of

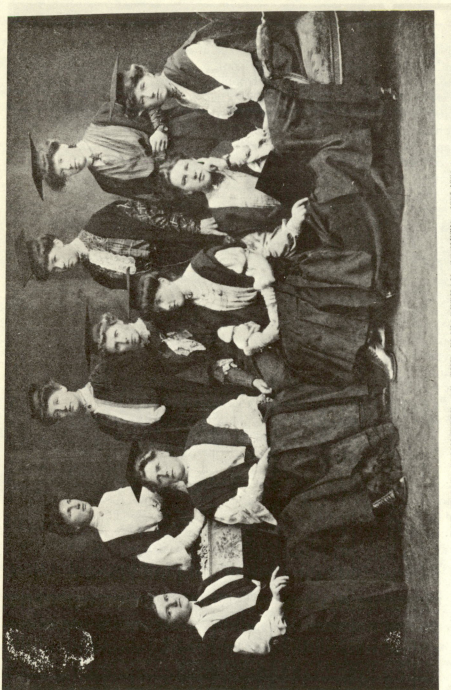

THE FIRST COMMITTEE OF THE ELIZABETHAN SOCIETY, 1905-1906

Standing. L. Craig. R. Fitzgerald (*Hon. Librarian*). O. Purser (*Hon. Record Secretary*). S. Auchinleck (*Hon. Treasurer*).
Seated. B. Stafford. Mrs. Finegan. E. Tuckey. M. Weir Johnston (*Hon. Correspondence Secretary*). E. Maxwell. I. Shegog.

24 The Elizabethan Society.

College by 6 p.m. At first these rules created no resentment. The cap and gown was an honourable uniform, and served also to protect them from inquiries as to their business by officious porters. The other rules might cause occasional inconvenience, but were recognized as reflecting the conventions of Edwardian society; it was not until after 1918 that they were criticized, and in some small degree evaded. A Lady Registrar was appointed to act as their guide, philosopher and friend (and, occasionally, policeman), and a hall of residence (Trinity Hall) was soon provided, which, thanks to the personality of its first warden, Miss Margery Cunningham, took on something of the atmosphere, if not the formal structure or function, of a women's college.

We have seen that it was difficult, if not impossible, to admit women to membership of the University of Dublin without at the same time admitting them as members of Trinity College, even if the latter membership was hedged in by restrictions. This was of course a severe blow to Alexandra College, and a last-minute effort was made in the suggestions put to the Royal Commission of 1906 to build it somehow or other into the structure of the University. But every circumstance was against such an integration, for even the most demure and loyal student of Alexandra was bound to be attracted to the busier and more varied world of Trinity. At all events the ladies voted with their feet, and Alexandra College had to content itself with the role of the leading Protestant girls' school in Dublin, supplemented by classes in such subjects as domestic economy and secretarial training, which in those distant days were believed to lie outside the scope of university curricula.

In the first few years after 1904 the Board, reasonably enough, allowed some academic credit to such newly enrolled students as had already passed examinations of university standard, whether those organized by Trinity or those of the Royal University. And it was in keeping with an old tradition of reciprocal recognition of the examination and tuition provided by Oxford and Cambridge that women who had studied there for two years should be allowed to enter as Junior Sophisters. But what of those who had performed at Oxford and Cambridge all the exercises which, had they been men, would have entitled them to a degree? For Oxford and Cambridge, though liberal in providing facilities for the tuition and examination of women, were not yet prepared even to consider the idea of giving them degrees, because if this were done they could vote in the Senate or Convocation, and where would we all be then? It was not till 1920 that Oxford yielded on this point, while Cambridge held out till 1947;[8] concession was then easy, as Convocation and the Cambridge Senate had by this time been shorn of much of their powers. Meanwhile there were women, and some of them Irish, who were as well educated as any Dublin B.A., but lacked the magic letters after their names. Should not Dublin admit them on an *ad eundem* basis as Candidate Bachelors and allow them to graduate without further examination? Such a concession for a few Irishwomen seemed reasonable enough, and the first of them came to claim their degrees in December 1904. But what was intended for Irishwomen seemed attractive also to Englishwomen, so that first a trickle but soon a stampede of alumnae of the women's colleges at Oxford and Cambridge[9] took their places on the mailboat to pay their first visit to Dublin and return with a Dublin degree. Fortunately the Board, in announcing these concessions, had a fixed a *terminus ad quem* at December 1907, but in the four years leading up to that date some 750 women had been added to the roll of Dublin graduates, of whom only 30 had studied in Trinity College.

The College naturally incurred some ridicule and some criticism for selling its degrees to strangers in this way. But it could reply that there was no depreciation of the academic currency, for all the new graduates had impeccable credentials, and that there was nothing wrong in selling to willing buyers if the commodity were accurately described. It would doubtless have been better if Oxford and Cambridge had been liberal enough to give to these women the recognition they deserved, but as they did not,should not Dublin step into the breach? At all events Provost Traill, whose thick skin stood him in good stead on such occasions, shrugged off the ridicule and pocketed the fees, forestalling criticism by devoting them towards the equipment of Trinity Hall.

In 1909, Constantia Maxwell, who had graduated with a gold medal the previous year, was appointed as lecturer in Modern History – the first woman on the academic staff. It was the beginning of a lifetime's career: she was given a personal chair in 1939, and in 1945 succeeded to the Lecky Professorship as the first woman to hold an established full-time chair.[10] But there have been few to follow her example: two other women have been appointed to established full-time chairs, and personal chairs have been created for two others, but for the most part they have held only junior posts, and usually for only a few years. This may in some small part be due to their exclusion from Fellowship until recently, but the main explanation must lie elsewhere.

The women students, however, have, with scarcely a setback, played a steadily increasing role in the College. Their relative numbers naturally increased in 1914–18 when the College was denuded of men, but for the first few years of peacetime they continued to form over 25 per cent of the student body. The figure dropped to 21 per cent in the thirties, but picked up again in the Second World War and, save for a mysterious drop in the late fifties, continued to increase until, at the time of writing, the figure stands at over 40 per cent and is fast heading towards parity, if not indeed beyond it (see appendix 2). Meanwhile the restrictions of the earlier part of the century have one by one been removed. The 'six 'o'clock rule' for the barring-out of women was first eroded by various exceptions, and then the hour was pushed through 7, 7.30 p.m., 11 and 11.30 p.m. finally to midnight. By about 1950 the increase in the number of women lecturers and the inadequacy of their accommodation led to a demand for their admission to the Common Room. This was skilfully parried for some years by the plea that no space could be found for a second lavatory, but that barrier fell in 1958 before the ingenuity of an architect, and eight years later women were admitted also to the High Table.

At about the same time the question of the eligibility of women for Scholarships on the foundation and for Fellowship was discussed from time to time. Counsel had recently ruled that it was inconsistent with the charter, but impious voices began to mutter that counsel had been proved wrong in the past and might be wrong on this point too. In the case of Scholarship the only issue at stake was that of prestige, for the non-foundation scholarships instituted for women in 1905 were materially as valuable as those on the foundation. But Fellowship was a different matter. A meeting of the Fellows was held in 1964 to debate the matter. It soon became apparent that a substantial majority was in favour of opening Fellowship to women if such legal obstacles as might exist could be overcome. A.A. Luce led the opposition, stressing the undoubtedly valid point that for a married woman domestic duties were apt to increase gradually but insidiously, until they were sufficient to prevent her from conscientiously carrying out the duties of a full-time post. But his characteristic peroration, 'Can you imagine it, Mr Provost – Mrs Quiverful, F.T.C.D.?', though it brought the house down, did little to change opinions. After some argument it was admitted that the legal objections had no real substance; women have been elected to foundation Scholarship since 1968, and in the same year four women were elected to Fellowship. A few months later, as a natural corollary, women students were allowed to dine on Commons, and in 1972 they were admitted to residence in College rooms.[11]

12

The last days of the Ascendancy
1901–1919

(i)

The opening of the twentieth century was darkened by the shadow of the South African war. The average Irishman knew little about Kruger or Rhodes and, had he known more, would have found them equally distasteful. Even in Trinity there must have been a few who saw the conflict in this spirit. But most of the students responded with a simple, unquestioning loyalty; and the number who volunteered, partly because their Queen called them, and partly because the idea of 'a bit of a scrap' (and with luck on horseback) appealed to their adventurous instincts, was sufficient to make a small but noticeable dent in student numbers. A few were killed, and to their friends who remained behind their deaths gave an unfamiliar kind of shock, inspiring some elegiac verses in *T.C.D.* which still can move the reader. In retrospect Lindley can be seen as a small-scale dress-rehearsal for Gallipoli and the Somme.

In its official capacity the College left no opening for doubt about its attitude to the war, by conferring honorary degrees on Joseph Chamberlain in 1899 and on Lord Roberts in 1903. The first was the occasion of demonstrations and counter-demonstrations, leading to a minor riot. Roberts had already received an honorary LL.D. in 1880 as the victor of Kandahar, but the Board ingeniously decided in 1903 that his reminiscences of Indian life and service, which had appeared six years earlier, entitled him to a Doctorate of Literature.

The beginning of the new century coincided also with the death of the old Queen; and the removal of the familiar mother-figure produced a sense of unease and a realization that the twentieth century was going to be very different from the nineteenth. Provost Salmon, who was four months younger than the Queen, survived her by just three years, and it is not altogether fanciful to suggest that his death in January 1904 produced something of the same feelings in Trinity. For sixty-two years he had been a familiar figure in the squares, and for the sixteen years of his provostship he had filled the role of father of the College family, respected and to a large extent loved even by those who were exasperated by his rigid conservatism on many issues. But there was one great difference between the two deaths. The successor to the Queen was predetermined and accepted by all; the successor to Salmon remained to be determined by the Prime Minister in the name of the Crown.

(ii)

Salmon, though obviously ageing, was active to within a few weeks of his death; but when he had passed his eighty-fourth birthday there could be little doubt that a struggle for the succession lay not far ahead. And it was clear that it would indeed be a hard-fought struggle, as there was no candidate who commanded the general support of the Fellows. Among the Senior Fellows, two stood out alike by their ability and their determination to become Provost; these were Mahaffy and Traill. Although, as we shall see, two ex-Fellows were also to receive serious consideration, it was as a struggle between Mahaffy and Traill that Dublin as a whole saw the fight for the succession. The ageing Salmon seems to have seen it also in these terms, as is shown by a story which, even if apocryphal, has the authentic sardonic note. Salmon is said to have told a group of Fellows of a curious dream he had had the previous night. He was dead, and preparations for his funeral were in progress. He was carried across the Front Square to the Chapel in an open coffin, escorted by the Fellows and Scholars, many of them weeping and sobbing. His coffin was laid in the Chapel, 'and then,' he concluded, 'I sat up in my coffin and Mahaffy and Traill wept louder than ever'.

The contest between these two men would make the basis of a good novel, a subtler version of Snow's *The Masters*, for Mahaffy and Traill, though poles apart in some respects, were in others very similar. Both saw themselves as country gentlemen, born to command; both had immense and brazen self-confidence; both embraced a rather curious mixture of conservative and liberal ideas, and had voted on the same side on many issues before the Board; both were devoted to the College, but had wide contacts outside it; both were big, strong men with impressive athletic records and a taste for sport which lasted well into middle age. Both prided themselves on intellectual versatility, wit-nessed in Mahaffy's case by the very wide range of his publications, and for Traill by the fact that after winning his Moderatorships in Mathematics and Experimental Science he had gone on to qualify as Doctor alike in Medicine and in Laws. And each regarded himself as uniquely fitted for the provostship by virtue of being able to con-tribute a quality which his colleagues, good fellows though they were, completely lacked. But the roles which they envisaged for themselves

355

differed widely. Mahaffy saw himself as a twentieth-century Lord Holland, presiding over a *salon* in which literary brilliance mixed easily with high society; Traill saw the Provost's House rather as a series of smoke-filled committee-rooms, in which compromises were hammered out and the right men found to fill key jobs.

For the differences between the two men were as striking as their resemblances. Mahaffy was famous for his classical writings in most of the universities of Europe (and notorious in some of them); Traill's publications were limited to a few speeches and pamphlets on church finance or the landlord's rights. Traill, though a layman, was a dominant figure in the General Synod of the Church of Ireland and on the finance committee of its Representative Body; Mahaffy viewed ecclesiastical affairs in terms of elegance of preaching, and described himself as 'a clergyman, but not in the offensive sense of the word'. Mahaffy was on visiting terms with marquesses and rubbed shoulders with royalty; Traill was content with the company of Ulster landlords, archdeacons and back-bench M.P.s. Mahaffy had a ponderous, if at times pompous dignity; Traill did not know the meaning of the word. Both men were often rude, but with Traill it was the rudeness of indifference; with Mahaffy it arose from a desire to put a critic or a rival in his place. Mahaffy had reserves of charm, which he displayed not only to his social superiors, but also, united with real kindness, to the young who took his fancy and to others whose competition he need not fear; 'charm' was a word rarely used in connexion with Traill. Most important of all, perhaps, was the fact that Traill had the strength which came from a quite extraordinary insensitivity. He often trod on people's toes, but he did not mind much if they trod back; it was impossible to snub him and almost impossible to insult him; he never sulked or bore rancour; and if he was justified in his own eyes he cared little what others might think. Mahaffy, on the other hand, was beneath his facade of self-confidence a very sensitive man; he had a great need of praise and appreciation, and he was slow to forget an injury. The consequence was that Mahaffy, although widely admired and loved by a few, made many enemies; Traill caused constant but short-lived exasperation, and was generally laughed at, but nobody hated him.

In these circumstances it was natural that other names should come up for consideration, and those of two ex-Fellows began to be canvassed: Bury and Bernard. Both were young men, still in their early forties, but had already made for themselves impressive reputations, which in the judgment of outsiders, though perhaps not of the seniors in College, compensated for their youth. Bury, who had very recently resigned his Fellowship to take up the post of Regius Professor of

Modern History at Cambridge, was widely recognized as a man of quite remarkable intellectual powers, and as a prolific author of works of impeccable scholarship. Bernard, with a less dazzling but nevertheless solid reputation for scholarship, was also regarded as a man of affairs and of sound judgment, and had been elected as Dean of St Patrick's Cathedral at the age of forty-one by a chapter consisting almost entirely of much older men. Whether Bury would have accepted the Provostship, if offered it, is perhaps doubtful; he had left Dublin to enjoy the freer intellectual atmosphere and the better library facilities of Cambridge, and a return to an administrative post in Dublin would have cramped both his rationalist beliefs and his devotion to scholarship. In any case he lacked any taste or obvious talent for administration, and for that reason he was ruled out at a fairly early stage. Bernard would probably have accepted; he would doubtless have been criticized for abandoning his deanery so hastily, but he was prepared to face similar criticism fifteen years later when he resigned his archbishopric after only four years' tenure.

When Salmon died the manoeuvring took a rather unexpected turn. Traill left for London that night, and Mahaffy doubtless lost no time in calling at the Chief Secretary's Lodge. But among the Fellows and Professors there were no cabals in favour of this candidate or that, discussing whose vote they might win. For although College opinion was a consideration that would be bound to weigh with the Prime Minister it was not necessarily decisive unless it was almost unanimous. In contrast, therefore, to the conditions obtaining in Snow's imaginary college, where one vote might sway the result, there arose instead a series of meetings whose resolutions had the effect of votes *against* specific candidates.

Mahaffy and Bernard both fell victims to these, and in each case the resolution was made on grounds of public policy and wrapped up in terms which meant that no names need be mentioned. Mahaffy had in the eyes of his colleagues blotted his copy-book badly by supporting in his evidence before the Robertson Commission of 1901 (of which more hereafter) the idea favoured by his friend Wyndham, the Chief Secretary, of including Trinity as one of four or five colleges in a new federal university. Mahaffy's statements to the Robertson Commission (as also to the Fry Commission of 1906) suggest that he had not given much serious thought to the Irish University Question, and it may well be that it was loyalty to Wyndham rather than deep conviction that made him persist in a policy condemned by nearly all his colleagues. He was, however, branded as a supporter of a most unpopular scheme, and twenty-three of his colleagues signed a resolution requesting that the new Provost should be a man who did *not* hold such views.

There were two arguments against Bernard's appointment. The first, easy to understand but difficult to avow gracefully in public, was that he was no longer a Fellow, and this meant that nobody would rise a step on the ladder of promotion if he were to be appointed. Bernard's position was closely parallel to that of Salmon at the time of the latter's appointment as Provost. Salmon had been an ex-Fellow and Regius Professor of Divinity; Bernard was an ex-Fellow and Archbishop King's Lecturer in Divinity, a post widely regarded as of professorial rank and raised formally to that status two years later. But the closeness of the parallel was the basis for the other argument against Bernard: there was a widespread, though by no means unanimous feeling that the new Provost should *not* be another Church of Ireland clergyman closely associated with the Divinity School. For the past forty years opinion in College had oscillated between defiance of Catholic claims and appeasement, and in 1904 appeasement was the dominant note. The various schemes to defuse Catholic hostility to Trinity College which were to be aired before the Fry Commission in 1906 would obviously have a better chance of success if the Provost were to be a layman. Of the Senior Fellows three were laymen and two (Barlow and Mahaffy) very unclerical clergymen, so that it is not surprising that they passed a resolution in favour of a lay Provost.

By these resolutions the College, almost it would seem by inadvertence, implicitly declared its support for Traill. Balfour, who gave a good deal of thought to the matter, was, it would seem, largely influenced by two very judicious letters he received from D.H. Madden, Vice-Chancellor of the University,[1] who had the advantage of knowing all the candidates and also of being above the fray. He was the only correspondent from Dublin to offer a balanced appraisal, as Dudley, the Lord-Lieutenant, was as fiercely opposed to Mahaffy as Wyndham was devoted to him. Madden personally favoured Bernard, but he summarized very fairly the arguments raised against him. Accordingly Balfour, although he had started by describing Traill as 'impossible', was led reluctantly to rule out Mahaffy both on personal grounds and because of his policy; and then equally reluctantly to rule out Bernard, chiefly because he was no longer a Fellow. This left only Traill, and Balfour recommended him for appointment, justifying his choice partly on the grounds that he was a Fellow, partly because he was energetic and businesslike, and partly for the curious reason that he had a private income.[2]

After two months' suspense, therefore, Dublin was startled to hear of Traill's appointment. It soon became clear that he made a much better Provost than his detractors had believed possible. His lack of dignity and culture were at times disconcerting or embarrassing, and his transparent egoism made him the butt of some ridicule,[3] but he soon won a grudging respect for his energy, his fair-mindedness, his skill in pushing the Board gently along the path of progress and moderate reform, and his common sense and good judgment, except on a few issues in which the instincts of an Ulster Unionist proved too strong. Mahaffy was naturally a bitterly disappointed man, and he never let slip an opportunity for a jibe at the Provost, but he did not refuse co-operation and did not attempt to form an anti-Traill party; indeed he was nearly always among the Provost's supporters in his clashes with the rigid conservatives of the Board.

From the day of his appointment Traill had his hands full in dealing with four important issues in addition to the normal academic routine of new courses and new appointments. These were the Irish University Question, which was on the boil again, the future of the Divinity School, the demands for constitutional reform in the College, and the financial problems posed by a campaign for the expansion of scientific teaching and research. To the first of these we must now turn our attention.

(iii)

We have already seen how successive British governments had made three attempts to meet the Catholic demands for a university acceptable to their religious principles. All the proffered solutions were, however, rejected as inadequate. The Queen's Colleges were denounced as godless; Gladstone's offer of a Catholic college in a mixed, federal university was rejected as financially unfair and tainted with the principles of mixed education; and Fawcett's Act was dismissed as misleading window-dressing designed to divert public attention from the real problem. Neither Trinity College nor the Queen's Colleges could be made acceptable by minor changes in their constitution, so the demand continued for the endowment by the government of a purely Catholic university broadly similar to Louvain, or of a purely Catholic college with a sufficiently powerful voice in the management of the university of which it formed part to prevent its teaching, examinations or courses being contaminated with Protestantism or indifferentism.

The opposition was, of course, to some extent based on ancient memories; if Guy Fawkes had never lived and if the fires of Smithfield had never been kindled, Catholic claims might have been viewed with more indulgence. But apart from this, a dislike of denominational endowment in any form had become a fixed article in the creed of most Liberals, while Conservatives (who mostly favoured denominational schools in England, and could not therefore condemn the claim on principle), saw no reason to inconvenience themselves for the sake of a community 90 per cent of whose members were striving to disrupt the United Kingdom. Neither party could see why the Catholics could not accept the existing colleges if a few guarantees for their religious instruction and protection from proselytization or attacks on their faith were provided.

There was, consequently, a stalemate for some twenty years. The question was regularly aired in Parliament and was dismissed with evasive phrases. From 1885 onwards, however, the campaign acquired a new impetus from the appointment of William Walsh as Archbishop of Dublin. He devoted himself to this more assiduously than to any other cause, and showed himself to be a skilful and tireless (if at times tiring)[4] advocate of the Catholic case. Nobody could mention the word 'university' in connexion with Ireland without a column or two being filled the next day on the correspondence page of *The Times* or the *Dublin Evening Mail* by the Archbishop, correcting misunderstandings, denouncing misrepresentations, nailing lies, dismissing false analogies, summarizing history and reiterating claims.[5] He gave these claims a new twist by insisting that the Catholic college or university should have an endowment and a constitutional position which would give it absolute equality with Trinity College, and if 'absolute equality' was italicized once it was italicized twenty times.[6]

Walsh's insistence certainly played a part in breaking the deadlock and in convincing the Government that something had to be done. The first move was made in 1889 by Arthur Balfour, who was then Chief Secretary and was busy implementing his policy of 'killing Home Rule by kindness'. He hinted, therefore, in a speech at Partick that if the bishops were to couch their demands in less imperious terms, to exercise some further patience, and to compromise on what he hoped might be regarded as minor issues the substance of their claim might one day be met.

Archbishop Walsh took the hint, and spoke in terms of respect, and even of admiration, of the man who was still generally known in nationalist circles as 'Bloody Balfour'. The Catholic demands were gradually and inconspicuously toned down, partly because of the increasing prospect of success, and partly to accord with the changing temper of the times. The bishops' statement of 1871, signed by Cardinal Cullen, had a definite commitment to denominational education without qualification; it condemned mixed education as 'intrinsically and grievously dangerous to faith and morals'; it declared that 'we shall never cease to oppose to the utmost of our power ... the Queen's Colleges, Trinity College and all other similar institutions'; and it concluded by observing 'the melancholy wreck in other countries of all order, moral and social, mainly caused by the wide diffusion of a literature immoral and hostile to religion'. Allowance must be made for the fact that this was written shortly after the loss of the temporal power, but even as late as 1889 (just before Balfour's overture) the bishops were still demanding 'an exclusively Catholic university, or one or more Colleges conducted on purely Catholic principles'. By 1895, however, Walsh was denouncing as a 'mischievous misrepresentation' and a 'silly fable' the idea that the bishops demanded a clerical majority on the controlling board of the new institution.[7] Finally, the statement issued by the Hierarchy in 1897 made an even more significant concession: the principles of Fawcett's Act could be applied to the new Catholic college or university.[8] An exegesis of this statement by accredited Catholic spokesmen before the Royal Commission of 1901 made it clear that provided the general atmosphere was sufficiently Catholic to reassure the bishops that there was no danger to faith or morals, the presence of a few Protestants among the students, the Professors, and even the governing body or the Visitors could be tolerated. The statement of 1897 was a sensible and statesmanlike compromise, and served as the foundation of the final settlement of 1908, but there must have been some who imagined that they could hear from the grave of Cardinal Cullen sounds indicative of rapid rotation.

The reader may ask what relevance do these theological distinctions and political manoeuvrings have for the history of Trinity College. Most members of the College hoped that the relevance would be slight; they were in the main anxious to see a settlement that would be acceptable at least to the more reasonable Catholics, but they hoped that it would leave the position of Trinity unchanged. A few were dismayed at the thought of the expansion of university education in Ireland being subjected to clerical control, and a few were unhappy at the prospect of the cleavage between the two nations in Ireland being further deepened by strictly segregated higher education. It was these men who looked around, in vain as we shall see, for devices to make Trinity more attractive to Catholics. But there were three further considerations which kept Trinity continuously on her guard throughout these controversies and negotiations. One was the fact that competition in any form was bound to be somewhat distasteful, and in the period 1900–4, when the student numbers in Trinity had sunk to a minimum unparalleled since 1810, the possibility that some potential students, both Catholic and Protestant, might be drained off elsewhere was unwelcome from the point of view of prestige and of finance alike. The other fears were more widespread, and probably more justified, and both were fired by memories of Gladstone's abortive bill of 1873. The first lay in the suggestion that although a separate Catholic university would have satisfied the Hierarchy it was not very likely to be granted; whereas a Catholic college in a federal university would satisfy them only if Trinity were to be included as well. For much was made of the perfectly valid point that even if the University of Dublin were to be regarded as a corporation distinct from Trinity College[9] it was completely controlled by the College; no questions could arise as to fair representation of colleges on a university senate or squabbles over the method of appointing examiners. And if 'absolute equality' were to be obtained Trinity must be subjected to the same constraints as a Catholic college might have to face. The other danger lay in the threat to her endowments. If a Catholic college or university were to be endowed the opposition from Scottish and Ulster Presbyterians might be lulled into acquiescence if part of the endowment were to come, not from public funds, but from the endowment of Trinity College – an institution which at this time commanded little respect from the more sectarian-minded type of Presbyterian, despite (or perhaps because of) the steady increase in the number of Presbyterian students since 1894. Alternatively, the argument might be used that part of her endowments belonged morally to the University of Dublin and might be diverted in that direction.[10] The threat to the complete independence of Trinity was, in fact, to become very real in 1902–7 (and secured, as we have mentioned, the acquiescence of Mahaffy). The threat to the endowments was more remote, but nevertheless vaguely menacing. These fears were increased by some ominous words from Archbishop Walsh, repeated more than once. He hoped, he said, that his claim to 'absolute equality' could be met by a process of levelling-up, but if not, it must be by a process of levelling-down; Trinity, in other words, must be stripped of its university privileges and of much of its endowments. There was probably not very wide support for this attitude, but it was expressed very clearly and forcibly on more than one occasion. A memorandum[11] circulated in College in 1893 on the occasion of Gladstone's second Home Rule Bill pointed out that it was all very well for the *Freeman's Journal* to say that 'it is absolutely false to assert that the spoiling of Trinity is the object of any section of the Catholics of Ireland', but that nobody had disavowed Archbishop Walsh's statement made seven years earlier that 'so long as that central fortress of the education that is not Catholic is allowed to ... occupy the most glorious site in our Catholic city of Dublin, so long will it be impossible for any statesman ... to deal with this great question on the open and level ground of full and absolute equality for the Catholics of Ireland'.[12]

(iv)

There was another factor which tended to weaken the position of Trinity College in Ireland during the closing years of the century; this was the rise of a romantic and literary-inclined nationalism. Soon after 1890 the rights of the small tenant-farmer against his landlord ceased to be the driving force of the movement towards partial or complete independence, and their place was taken by a feeling of national pride, a desire for independence for its own sake, and for the fostering of a distinctive Irish culture based above all on the revival of the Irish language as a vernacular for the whole country. The 'grass-roots' aspect of the movement had already been embodied in the Gaelic Athletic Association, which was founded in 1884. This was a great success, and had much influence in the provinces, but in literary and educational circles the most important event was the foundation of the Gaelic League in 1893. Its first president was Douglas Hyde, a Trinity graduate and son of a country rector, and although he was severely critical of some parts of the intellectual orientation of his *alma mater* he was not embittered or fundamentally hostile. He had little interest in politics, and, mainly at his insistence, the League in its early years remained strictly non-political. The language movement, nevertheless, if not the League itself, became identified in the public mind with a fairly advanced nationalism, and, largely because of this identification, it received a frosty reception in Trinity College. It was unfortunate, however, that the first public manifestation of the College's attitude to the movement should have taken the form of the evidence given by Mahaffy and Atkinson before the inquiry into Intermediate Education of 1898, appointed to investigate the suggestion of the Gaelic League that Irish should be given a prominent place in the school curriculum. Mahaffy, while conceding that Irish had some philological interest, denied that the study of the contemporary language had any cultural, literary or educational value. With a dogmatism untrammelled (and perhaps fuelled) by the fact that all his knowledge was second-hand, he declared that, except for some religious works, all writings in modern Irish were either silly or indecent. His sole concession, that a few words of Irish might be serviceable to a man shooting grouse or fishing for salmon in the west, was so patronizing as to be even more infuriating than his opposition. Atkinson was no more conciliatory. He dismissed the spoken language as a series of local patois without standardized spelling or grammar and most of the modern literature as 'folk-lore untouched by the movements of the great literatures' and 'incredibly low in tone'. E.J. Gwynn also put in a statement in much more temperate terms, and with the advantage of a thorough knowledge of the language in all its periods. He declared, however, that modern Irish was spoken by few and had no developed syntax, while its literature 'certainly possesses no general interest of any significance in the history of European thought.'[13]

Since the subject under discussion was the teaching of Irish in schools it was quite proper that anybody who thought that this would do more harm than good should say so; and there were many Catholics (not least among the bishops) who were very lukewarm in their support of the revival movement. But it would have been wiser if the spokesmen for Trinity had based their opposition, as Salmon was to do a few years later,[14] on the impracticability of bilingualism and the uselessness of mouthing a few ritual phrases of Irish by those who would for the most part be unable to sustain an intelligent conversation in the language. All this would have been quite compatible with a belief that the study of Irish was a legitimate occupation for those who had a taste for it, and should receive some encouragement without being forced down anybody's throat.

At all events this attitude did not go unnoticed by those who were hostile to Trinity on other grounds. Up to about 1870 the College had been criticized mainly for its religious exclusiveness, but apart from that it was an institution of which Ireland could be proud. From 1870 to 1900 it was mainly its effectively monopolistic position that was under attack, but although there is a political undertone in some of Archbishop Walsh's remarks, on the whole the College and its members were still given intellectual respect. By 1900, however, the hostility was showing itself on a much wider front: Trinity was denounced on all sides not only as irredeemably Protestant but as 'anti-national', a preserve of the wealthy ascendancy, living on a prestige which it no longer deserved and teaching an outmoded curriculum which gave no heed to the practical needs of contemporary Ireland. The fact that many of the critics enjoyed an income as great as that of the rectors or schoolmasters whose sons still formed a large part of the student body, and that demands for utilitarian education came strangely from those who were also advocating compulsory instruction in Irish made little difference; all the issues which divided Ireland were united in a common package, and Trinity was seen as representing one side of the divide and the plain people of Ireland the other. Of course there were some Catholics, some nationalists, some social reformers and some Irish language enthusiasts who declined to see the matter in such simple terms, but it is fair to say that the two decades preceding the outbreak of the First World War found Trinity at the nadir of its popularity in Ireland. Even James Joyce, who had no enthusiasm for the Gaelic League and less for the bishops, was to refer in *Ulysses* to the 'surly front' of Trinity College,[15] and in the *Portrait of the artist as a young man* his description of 'the grey block of Trinity . . . set heavily in the city's ignorance like a dull stone set in a cumbrous ring',[16] though more severe on Dublin is scarcely complimentary to the College.

(v)

It is against the background sketched in the last few pages that we must view the Royal Commissions of 1901 and 1906. The former, under the chairmanship of Lord Robertson, a retired judge of some distinction, was appointed in response to a deputation from the Senate of the Royal University.[17] Its terms of reference were to inquire into the facilities for higher education in Ireland and to suggest how they might be improved, but Trinity College was excluded from the scope of its inquiry. The exclusion was the result of the indulgent view taken by a Conservative government of the College's natural desire not to be dragged into a complex controversy involving the Queen's Colleges, the Catholic University and various minor educational establishments, for most of its members cared little how these were to be rearranged so long as Trinity was left alone.[18]

In spite of its exclusion, however, several prominent members of the College gave evidence before the Commission, and there are relatively few pages in its voluminous report on which the name of Trinity is not mentioned. This was inevitable, as its unacceptability to Catholics had to be demonstrated and justified for their claims to be considered. The spokesman for the bishops, O'Dwyer of Limerick, presented his case well, and, claiming that he was speaking for the Hierarchy as a whole, effectively repudiated Archbishop Walsh when he said that the bishops had the greatest admiration for the work of Trinity College and of Queen's College, Belfast, and that 'we should have no desire what-soever to see any measure taken that would in the least lower their status or impair their efficiency', adding that he personally 'would view the wrecking of Trinity with absolute horror'.[19] He gave a convincing sketch of the nature of a college which would be *de facto* Catholic but *de jure* non-denominational and emphasized the freedom of teaching and discussion that would prevail, so long as nothing was taught specifically contrary to the doctrines of the church. A professor of geology would be perfectly free to expound the scientific reasons for attributing to the earth an age to be measured in hundreds of thousands of years, so long as he did not add that this showed the Mosaic cosmogony to be false. The Bishop was, however, unable to extricate himself convincingly from the difficulty posed by one member of the Commission, who asked him what the professor should say if a student were to ask, 'But, please Sir, does not that contradict the Mosaic cosmogony?'[20] It was a small debating point, but it illuminated the essential difficulty as it appeared to most liberals: on matters of faith it is the bishops who must decide what may be taught, and if there is a dispute as to where faith ends and licensed speculation begins it is the bishops who define the boundary.

The Commission heard a great deal of varied, and of course largely contradictory evidence through the autumn of 1901 and the greater part of 1902, and it published its report in February 1903. It accepted the fact that the attitude of the Hierarchy in discouraging[21] Catholics from entering Trinity or the Queen's Colleges was unlikely to change or to become less effective, and it therefore recommended the establishment and endowment of a college in Dublin to replace the existing University College; the new college was to be so organized that, although not under clerical control, none of its teaching should be objectionable to Catholics, and that it should be affiliated to the Royal University. This somewhat predictable and not very sensational recommendation was, however, robbed of most of its effect by the fact that one member of the Commission (an Ulster Presbyterian) dissented from it, and nearly all the others made reservations on one point or another. Some of them were doubtful as to the propriety of denominational endowment, but of greater import to Trinity was the fact that three members (including W.J.M. Starkie, an ex-Fellow) made it clear that they would have preferred (had their terms of reference allowed them to make such a recommendation) that the new Catholic college should be associated with Trinity in the University of Dublin.

The motives for this preference were very varied. Some saw it as the only practicable means of achieving Archbishop Walsh's 'absolute equality'. Others on the Catholic side wanted, naturally enough, to say that their College belonged to the University of Dublin (or, as it was more sourly expressed from the Trinity side, 'they want to steal our trademark'). Some friends of Trinity thought that it would otherwise suffer from isolation, both in prestige and in resources. Some thought it absurd to have two separate universities less than a mile apart. The most widespread argument, however, for the incorporation of Trinity into the scheme was also the least precise: it was a feeling that there should be 'a great national university' in which all creeds and classes could find a place, in which the colleges would have their different traditions and loyalties but would be united by a friendly rivalry in the examination hall and on the football field, and whose students would find opportunities for meeting each other in debating societies, choirs and other recreational activities. This feeling found its widest expression among English Liberals (who did not know enough about Irish life to see the numerous practical difficulties) and Trinity Catholics (who wished at almost any cost to reconcile their two loyalties). But subsequent experience, not only in Ireland, has shown that 'friendly rivalry' is one of the most overworked of after-dinner clichés to describe a rivalry that is often hostile, or at best based on armed neutrality. Nor was it clear why 'friendly rivalry' could not equally well exist between neighbouring universities. It would be difficult to find a better example of genuinely friendly rivalry than the Oxford and Cambridge boat-race, and the sporting encounters in Dublin would be more likely to prove friendly if they did not have as their background constitutional wrangles in the University Senate. And the more hard-headed of the bishops were, of course, anxious to minimize contacts between Catholic students and others, for if the rivalry were to become too friendly it might well lead to indifferentism. Moreover, federal universities were by now beginning to be viewed mainly as temporary expedients, and the Victoria University had been dissolved as soon as Manchester, Liverpool and Leeds were strong enough to stand on their own feet. Galway and Cork, it was true, still needed to be sustained by a federal structure, but neither for Trinity nor for the new Catholic college in Dublin was this likely to be true.

Nevertheless, the expression of these sentiments in the minority reports of the Robertson Commission put Trinity on the alert. As often happens in moments of danger, a division soon became apparent between hedgers and ditchers. The ditchers believed that Catholics who came to Trinity must take it as they found it; Fawcett's Act would be observed in letter and in spirit, but the Catholic student would have to put up with the Protestant traditions and 'Protestant atmosphere' or take whatever individual precautions he thought best to isolate himself from them. The hedgers, however, who were at least temporarily in the majority, were in favour of going some considerable way to make Trinity more attractive to Catholics. The Board agreed that a site should be made available for a Catholic chapel, Catholic chaplains should be recognized, and religious instruction for Catholics should be organized on the same lines as the catechetical lectures for Anglicans. (Similar arrangements were to be made for Presbyterians.) On 14 November 1903 the Registrar was instructed to write to Cardinal Logue, Archbishop of Armagh, to inform him of these proposals. The Cardinal's reply came by return of post, and was unique among episcopal pronouncements of the period in a conciseness which, though it perhaps verged on discourtesy, allows it to be quoted in full:

Dear Sir,

I beg to acknowledge the receipt of your letter of yesterday's date, and to say I can be no party to the arrangements proposed therein.

I am, dear Sir,
Yours faithfully,
✠ Michael Card. Logue.

(vi)

Meanwhile, however, Wyndham was still urging on Balfour the desirability of including as a prominent feature in the Government's programme a solution of the Irish University Question. But, early in 1905,
Wyndham was forced to resign on a political issue unconnected with
education; he was succeeded by the solid and unadventurous Walter
Long, and it looked as though Trinity could relax its vigilance. But not
for long, for at the end of the year Balfour himself resigned, and the
ensuing election of January 1906 produced the celebrated landslide
which returned the Liberals to power with a very large majority. The
new Chief Secretary was James Bryce, a Belfast Presbyterian of great
ability and enormous energy, best known, perhaps, as the author of
The Holy Roman Empire and *The American Commonwealth*. A man who
in his middle sixties kept his Castle officials on their toes by running
them up the higher mountains of Co. Mayo was not likely to waste
much time in his search for a solution to the problem on which the
Conservatives had made no progress. His first step was to fill the gap in
the inquiries made by the Robertson Commission by recommending
the appointment of a further Royal Commission, devoted this time to
Trinity College alone. It was to report not only on its present state but
also on its potential usefulness to the country. The Irish University
Question was wide open once more.

The Commissioners were on the whole well chosen. Once more a
distinguished judge – this time Sir Edward Fry – was appointed as
chairman. He was a staunch upholder of the Quaker traditions of his
family. The other members were Sir Thomas Raleigh, an academic
lawyer, Fellow of All Souls and formerly legal adviser to the Viceroy of
India; Sir Arthur Rücker, a chemist who had recently been appointed
Principal of London University and had served as Secretary of the
Royal Society; Henry Jackson, who had in the previous year succeeded
Jebb as Regius Professor of Greek at Cambridge (and was, in contrast to
Jebb, well disposed towards Mahaffy); S.H. Butcher, another classical
man, widely known for his collaboration with Lang in the translation
of Homer, and with academic experience at Oxford, Cambridge and
Edinburgh (and with some knowledge of Dublin, for his father had
been a Fellow of Trinity from 1837 to 1852); Christopher Palles, Chief
Baron of the Exchequer in Ireland, a lawyer of considerable eminence,
at once a keen Catholic and a loyal graduate of Trinity College, D.J.
Coffey, Professor of Physiology in the medical school of the Catholic
University, and soon to became President of University College;
Douglas Hyde, President of the Gaelic League; and S.B. Kelleher, a
Catholic who had very recently been elected to a Fellowship in Trinity

College. The Government had invited the Board to nominate one Commissioner, and the choice of Kelleher gave rise to some controversy, Mahaffy denouncing him as a 'mere peasant' and put in by Traill because he thought that Kelleher would faithfully mirror his views.[22] Kelleher contributed little to the work of the Commission, and was, in fact, representative of no substantial group among the Fellows; it would have been better if a more typical Fellow, such as Russell, Fry or O'Sullivan had been appointed.

But in its general composition the Commission was such as to give the College no serious cause for alarm. Three of its members were Dublin graduates and a fourth the son of a former Fellow. At least three of the nine were Unionists; five were Anglicans, three Catholics and one a Quaker. Only two could be regarded as potentially hostile: Hyde and Coffey. But Coffey, although he represented fairly enough the standpoint of the Catholic University, was a man well known (and in some circles criticized) for his caution, moderation and courtesy, while Hyde, though severely critical of the College for its lack of support for the Irish language and its lack of interest in aspects of higher education which had a particular importance for Ireland, did not allow this to drown his affection and respect for other aspects of the teaching of his *alma mater*, and in one of his most angry publications he paid a generous tribute to Mahaffy, one of his most provocative opponents.[23]

The Commission got to work quickly, and although it heard a lot of evidence and examined numerous written submissions it brought out its report less than eight months after its appointment.[24] Its principal fields of inquiry were three: the existing and potential relationship of Trinity College to the Catholic and Presbyterian churches and to other Irish institutions of university standing; the status and future of the Divinity School; and the internal constitution of the College, including its method for recruiting its Fellows. For the moment we shall consider only its deliberations on the first of these topics and return to the others after we have shown how the Irish University Question received at last its final answer.

A great deal of the evidence on this topic was, naturally enough, a repetition of that which had been offered to the Robertson Commission; for the Fry Commission could not decide on Trinity's place in the university system of Ireland without considering in some detail the constitution, prospects and alleged defects of the Royal University. There were, however, a few significant differences in the evidence offered to the two Commissions. In the first place the fact that Trinity was now the main object of inquiry meant that it could be attacked more directly and more forcibly. In most cases the attacks, even when involving harsh judgments, were couched in temperate language, but there were two notable exceptions. The representatives of the Gaelic League, and of a somewhat obscure body known as the Catholic Graduates' and Undergraduates' Association saw no reason to mince their words. The attack made by the Gaelic League was nominally only on the limited front of the College's neglect of Irish literary culture, but it had strongly political overtones, and it so abounded in such phrases as 'frigid and unsympathetic', 'squalid and barren', 'a primitive spirit of racial antagonism', 'held sullenly aloof' as to disclose the bitterness that had been festering in the breast of its main spokesman Eoin (or John, as he then was) MacNeill. The attack made by the spokesmen of the Catholic Graduates' and Undergraduates' Association was more remarkable in that, while most other critics had, in the course of pointing out grave defects in the College, allowed its other aspects an occasional word of praise, these men pictured it in terms of total and unrelieved depravity and corruption. Apart from its incorrigible Protestantism it was 'hopelessly out of touch with the national life of the country'; it was 'antique and narrow', 'unprogressive', and had 'done nothing towards the development of Experimental Sciences on university lines' (one wonders whether they had heard of George Fitzgerald). Its organization of studies was that of a high school, not a university; it had no faculty of philosophy; its fellowship system was ludicrous, its facilities for residence were totally inadequate, and its fees were excessive. The document in which these views were expressed was signed by the President, William Magennis (who elaborated them with gusto in his verbal evidence), and one of the Secretaries, Thomas Kettle. One is surprised to see the latter name associated with the document, for Tom Kettle, who was killed fighting in France in 1916, left behind him the memory of a chivalrous and generous man, impulsive in controversy but not given to needless persecution of his opponents. The name of Magennis causes less surprise in this context. A Belfast Catholic, he brought with him southwards that extreme bitterness which has been an unfortunate (if understandable) contribution of Ulstermen to Irish public life. Though he extolled so forcibly the 'philosophical system' in University College as immeasurably superior to the merely historical teaching of the subject in Trinity, one searches library catalogues in vain for any contribution which he made to the 'system' during his tenure of the chair of Metaphysics for over thirty years. He was undoubtedly a well-read man, a popular lecturer and a good talker, but outside his own College he is remembered chiefly as an active member of, and public apologist for, the Censorship of Publications Board during its most illiberal phase.

Another difference in the evidence from that given to the Robertson

Commission was in the more independent attitude of the Catholic laity. A document signed by nearly five hundred Catholic laymen, predominantly but by no means exclusively of the professional class, was presented to the Commission. It took the form of a negative declaration – that Trinity would not provide satisfactory university education for Catholics unless certain conditions were fulfilled; but the implication, though not spelt out in words, was perfectly clear: that if these conditions were to be fulfilled Trinity would be satisfactory, or at least acceptable. The conditions were an adequate representation on the governing body, the duplication of the chairs of Philosophy and Modern History, the provision of a Catholic chapel, a Catholic faculty of theology and religious instruction for Catholic students, and a council to see that these conditions were adequately observed. Two of these had already been offered to the Hierarchy in 1903 and peremptorily rejected; it is doubtful whether Cardinal Logue's reply would have been any more discursive if the other three had been included. At any rate it was clear that the laymen had ignored or dismissed the statements repeatedly made by the bishops and other clergy that no conceivable modification of the constitution of Trinity could render it acceptable. For the demand of the bishops was not for equality within the College but for a guaranteed predominance, if not in a university then at least in a college, and inside Trinity College this predominance would always be threatened by its Protestant traditions, no matter how radically its constitution were to be rewritten.

The Catholic laity were, no doubt, motivated in part by impatience, for the number of Catholics who aspired to a university education of the type that Trinity provided was increasing rapidly, and they did not want to wait for ever while the stately minuet performed by the bishops and the Government, which had already been in progress for sixty years, proceeded to its still invisible conclusion. They were also, no doubt, puzzled by some of the apparent inconsistencies in the attitude of the bishops. For eleven years now Catholics had been permitted to go to Oxford and Cambridge, apparently without very dire results; one was tempted to wonder whether the atmosphere of Christ Church, Oxford, where the chapel was also the Anglican cathedral of the diocese, could be all that much less dangerous than that of T.C.D. And why had 'mixed education' at the Royal College of Science in Dublin, where about half the students and nearly all the Professors were Protestants, never been the subject of adverse comment? Again, if Trinity was so dangerous to faith and morals why had the number of Catholic students increased significantly since 1900? Why were they not positively forbidden to enter, instead of being merely warned and then looked on with disapproval or contempt as 'Trinity Catholics';

after all the *Index librorum prohibitorum* itemized books which the faithful were not merely counselled not to read, but positively forbidden to read except under licence. And why, when Trinity had been denounced as godless for accepting Fawcett's Act, were the bishops prepared to accept for the new Catholic college the provisions of that Act?

To each of these questions the bishops could, of course, offer a ready reply. Ireland is different from England; the English bishops doubtless know their own business best, but we are not bound to follow them; decisions must be made in the light of what developments are seen as probable or possible; concern for individuals must be weighed against the giving of scandal, and so on. Inevitably such arguments fall under the head of casuistry – the application of eternal principles to individual cases and changing conditions – but however logical and necessary casuistry may be it is a science that has little appeal to the average layman, who finds the intervention of political and prudential calculations in matters allegedly relating to the eternal welfare of souls both confusing and distasteful.

To the English, whether cabinet ministers or members of a Royal Commission, such arguments were of little interest; even if they thought the bishops were entirely unreasonable they had long ago concluded that they could do nothing without them, and that their unreasonableness was incorrigible. But to the Irish liberal, whether Catholic or Protestant, these signs of divergence between the clergy and the laity suggested the misleading (and, as it turned out, almost entirely false) idea that the bishops were bluffing, and that their bluff could be called. Some of the Fellows of Trinity who could reasonably be described as liberal, and notably Bernard, were not so deceived. But at a meeting of Fellows and Professors convened in July 1906, the idea of devising a scheme to make the College acceptable to Catholics won considerable support, and a committee was appointed to confer with the Catholic Laymen's committee with the object of presenting parallel and substantially similar memoranda to the Commission. The proposals from the Trinity side covered all the points made by the Catholic Laymen's committee, though in places its language is somewhat guarded. In the end, however, it secured the signatures of only twelve out of thirty-one Fellows, one ex-Fellow (Starkie) and eight non-Fellow Professors (of whom only four were full-time) out of thirty.[25] The signatories were a curiously mixed bunch, including one strong Conservative (Beare), two busy reformers prepared to sign almost anything (Russell and Culverwell), and a few devoted scholars remote from controversy and primarily seeking peace. Seven of the twenty-one signatories were relative newcomers, having held their Fellowship or Professorship for less than five years, and in general the list was not one which carried much weight. E.J. Gwynn, however, although he disagreed with some details and for this reason sent in a separate statement, was in broad agreement with the proposals, and his opinion was not so easily dismissed, as he combined (as did also Bernard) reforming zeal with constructive criticism, a command of forcible argument expressed in temperate language, and a sense of proportion which allowed him to concentrate on the main issues and not waste time (as did several of his colleagues) in riding a purely individual hobby-horse.

The most controversial proposal (to which Gwynn also assented, albeit reluctantly) was one designed to give Catholics an immediate and substantial representation on the Board. This was to be done by specifying that as a temporary arrangement, with a maximum life of twenty-five years, a quarter of the members of the Board should be elected by a nominated body of electors, drawn mainly from among the graduates, who would, it was implied, be wholly or at least largely Catholic. To liberals this idea was distasteful because it meant a very thinly disguised system of appointment on the basis of religious affiliation rather than merit; to conservatives it was equally distasteful because it completely upset the traditional composition of the Board. On both sides it was accepted as a desperate expedient, accepted after hours of argument, to solve what was otherwise a certain and complete deadlock, and one wonders how many of the signatories slept easily while the memorial was being examined by the Commission. Even if it had been accepted by the bishops it is very doubtful that it would have received the assent of the Board. The memorial was, in fact, immediately rejected by the bishops, and even dismissed as inadequate by some of the Catholic Laymen; and the fact that as clear-sighted a man as Gwynn should have brought himself to assent to proposals which were at once impracticable and objectionable demands some explanation. It may, in part, have been a mere manoeuvre: a device to enable him to say, 'Since they refuse such a generous offer as this, there is nothing more to be done, and we have a right to be left alone.' In part it arose from the fear of a very convinced Unionist that a new Catholic college would serve as a nursery of extreme nationalism (as in fact it did). In part it may have been because he, like Bernard, seems to have been rather alarmed at the low level of student numbers in Trinity, and wished to cast the net as widely as possible. But chiefly it would seem that, like many Protestants, he underestimated the growing demand for university education among lower middle-class Catholics, and believed that to increase the numbers in Trinity of Catholics from the lesser landed gentry and the professional classes[26] would relieve the greater part of the strains which were so distressingly polarizing Irish intellectual life. He must have been sadly disappointed when Chief Baron Palles, who represented exactly the type of Catholic which Gwynn was hoping to attract to Trinity in larger numbers, came out so strongly in favour of what was to Gwynn the worst possible solution of the Irish University Question.

At any rate the bishops lost no time in issuing a statement reiterating their objection to Trinity College as a fit place for the education of Catholics, whatever changes might be made in its constitution; and, stepping for the first time (perhaps rather injudiciously) outside the sphere of faith and morals, where their authority could not be questioned, into the social and political sphere, where their opinions were, at least in theory,[27] only those of ordinary citizens, they denounced the College not merely as Protestant, but also as expensive, snobbish, out of date and anti-national.

We have devoted some space to this abortive side-issue, which the Commissioners rightly ignored, because although in 1906 the independence of the laity was far too slender a prop on which to rest any proposals for their whole-hearted support of Trinity, nevertheless, the fact that the number of Catholics matriculating in Trinity each year showed a fairly steady increase, even after the establishment of the National University had given them an officially approved alternative, shows that this independence was tending to grow. There was to be no open defiance of the Hierarchy, but the pressure on them was steadily increased.

Several other Fellows and Professors aired before the Commission their views on the relationship of Trinity to the Catholic church and to the other institutions of higher education in Ireland, but the mind of the College as a whole was clearly expressed in two parallel resolutions, one or other of which was signed by the vast majority of the Fellows and Professors. The original resolution, supported by the Board, declared that the signatories 'are strongly opposed to the proposals which have been made to introduce into the University of Dublin a separate foundation intended for the special benefit of one religious denomination'. There followed some 500 words of explanation and justification. This resolution was signed by nearly two-thirds of the Junior Fellows and non-Fellow Professors, but there was a group of sixteen who were dissatisfied with the wording of the explanatory matter, and therefore signed a separate resolution in the same words but with no explanation. In all, the Provost, all but four of the Fellows, and all but three of the non-Fellow Professors committed themselves to the resolution in one or other of its forms. The Fellows who refused to sign were Mahaffy, Cathcart, Wilkins and Mooney; the non-Fellow

374

Professors were Atkinson, Whittaker and Prout. Apart from Mahaffy none of them carried much weight.

On this point, therefore, the College spoke with a virtually undivided voice, and E.J. Gwynn, in his memorandum to the Commission, set out at considerable length the arguments against a new Catholic college in the University, demonstrating lucidly and persuasively that it would be far more likely to create new enmities than to heal old ones. Some support for this attitude came from rather unexpected quarters, for Delany, the President of University College, made it clear that although he would accept the incorporation of his College into the University of Dublin, he would very greatly prefer, if there could not be an independent Catholic university, that it should be incorporated in the Royal University. Referring to a proposal that the new 'great national university' should embrace five colleges he remarked that 'Dr Traill and I are friends, but we should not embrace on that'. Sir Bertram Windle, President of Queen's College, Cork, who regarded federalism in universities as at best a necessary evil, declared that 'it would be a great mistake to federate colleges differing in age, in wealth, and in religious ideals'. Mgr Molloy, Rector of the Catholic University, in a far-sighted statement pleading for the independence of the new Catholic foundation, said that he wished to see it not as a graft on an old stock, but rather as a sturdy sapling on its own roots, which would in time generate its own traditions.[28] He was prepared to sacrifice the shadow of Archbishop Walsh's hankering after a share in the name 'University of Dublin' for the substance of genuine independence, and we do not believe that any member of University College today would hold that he was wrong. There were, however, a few on the Catholic side who argued the opposite case, while the bishops left the question open.

Although on all other matters the Commission was able to reach unanimous conclusions, on the position of Trinity in the University structure of Ireland they were hopelessly divided. They agreed that the attitude of the Hierarchy made useless any drastic steps to 'catholicize' Trinity College, but at this point their agreement ceased. All but one recommended that a Catholic college of a nature acceptable to the bishops should be established in Dublin, chartered and endowed; Kelleher alone dissented from this, holding that it would be a disservice to lay Catholics and a danger to the peace of the country. But the problem of where the Catholic college was to be fitted in to existing structures divided the Commissioners almost equally. Three – Fry, Butcher and Rücker – recommended that it should be affiliated to the Royal University, and that Trinity College and the University of Dublin should, in this respect, remain unaltered. Presumably they were impressed by the widespread opposition in both the Colleges which would be involved in the alternative scheme. But the remaining five Commissioners (three of them Irish) brushed these objections aside and held that all the colleges of Ireland should be united in a 'great national university' which, rather oddly in view of the geographical scatter of its constituent parts, should be known as the University of Dublin. Palles was probably the driving force behind this decision: he wished above all to put an end to the strain from which he had suffered all his life by his divided loyalties as a good Trinity man and a good Catholic. But although five Commissioners believed this to be the best solution, only four recommended it, for Jackson was sufficiently impressed by its unpopularity to prevent him from recommending *any* immediate action. Raleigh, one must suppose, was impelled by his Indian experience to a belief that faction fights are often best settled by *force majeure* applied impartially by an indifferent government, and doubtless from the standpoint of All Souls he could not see the material in Ireland sufficing for more than one university. Palles, Coffey and Hyde justified their decision in an extremely lengthy memorandum; much of it was an elaboration of the current rather woolly idealism, with plenty of 'friendly rivalry' and visions of the youth of the country fraternizing on the playing-fields, supported by the curious assertion that three strings on the same instrument would vibrate in harmony, but separately they would create a discord. Hyde, of course, was also concerned to 'bring Trinity into the main stream of Irish life', but why Coffey should have paid so little attention to the opinions of his Rector and the Principal of the College to which his school was so closely tied is not clear. Perhaps he simply believed that everybody would act with the gentlemanly tolerance which he himself showed to his opponents.

(vii)

The Commissioners published their report on 21 January 1907, but although it presented a lot of valuable evidence, and its recommendations on all other matters were lucid and concise, on this one vital issue it cannot be said to have given the Government any clear guidance. This was, however, of small consequence, as Bryce had already made up his mind what should be done. Having had his scheme approved by a perhaps somewhat bemused Cabinet preoccupied with other matters, he announced it four days after the Commission had reported. It approximated to the recommendation of four (or perhaps one should say four and a half) of the Commissioners in that it was an all-inclusive, single-university scheme. A new college was to be established in Dublin, adequately endowed, with an 'atmosphere' and personnel sufficiently Catholic to be acceptable to the bishops, but without any religious tests for offices or awards. It would incorporate the laboratories of the College of Science, and was to be included, with Trinity College and the Queen's College of Belfast and Cork, in a reconstituted University of Dublin; Galway was to be an affiliated college, under a sort of Crown Colony government. Alternative examinations and dual Professorships were to be provided in such subjects as philosophy and modern history. From the point of view of Trinity it was marginally better than Gladstone's scheme of 1873 (there was to be no disendowment and no expulsion of the Divinity School), but it was still exceedingly objectionable, all the more so as Bryce concluded with a brutal assurance that there was no hope of any other scheme being approved by the present Government.

Here, however, his self-confidence had run away with him. For the great weakness of his scheme was that when he announced it he had already been appointed as Ambassador to the United States, and he left Ireland a few days later. As Balfour was to comment sardonically, he retired from the fighting line, shouting 'No surrender!' at the top of his voice, having nailed his colours to another man's mast. There was some substance in the plea that swift action was necessary to put an end to the long-drawn-out uncertainty on this important issue; but it was too much to expect the new Chief Secretary to implement the plan immediately, without taking soundings in Ireland and at least investigating how the opposition to it might be overcome. And as the new Chief Secretary was Augustine Birrell, another literary man, but with something of Balfour's attitude of 'philosophic doubt' and none of Bryce's hustle, there was a chance for reconsideration.

Trinity College seized this chance boldly. A Trinity College Defence Committee was set up, with the Provost as chairman and Culverwell and E.J. Gwynn as secretaries, and with 'Hands off Trinity!' as its rallying-cry. Gwynn republished as a penny pamphlet part of his evidence given before the Commission, prefaced by a reply to the arguments which Bryce had used in recommending his scheme. Subscriptions were requested, and came in in good numbers, pamphlets were circulated, meetings were held, in Oxford, Cambridge and London as well as in Dublin, and influential bodies were lobbied for their support. A number of universities sent memorials to the Government, as did the Royal Society in a document signed by 200 of its members. In view of the fact that the welcome given to Bryce's proposals elsewhere in Ireland had been little more than tepid, Birrell had an ample excuse for exploring other possibilities. An alternative plan was suggested by Haldane, who, more than any other member of the Cabinet, had an interest in and an understanding of the problems of university education. Both Haldane and Birrell were admirers of Trinity: the former told the House of Commons in 1901 that 'T.C.D. is the ark of the covenant, and any Englishman who touches it will surely perish', while Birrell appealed to the sympathy of his fellow M.P.s by declaring in 1908 that 'I do not suppose there is any man in this House who has not been preached to, prescribed for, or . . . cross-examined as to character by some member of Trinity College, Dublin.'

Haldane's plan was simple and straightforward, and had been suggested by him as long ago as 1898. He does not seem to have pressed it on Bryce, partly because Bryce was a better talker than listener, and partly because Haldane was at that time extremely preoccupied as Minister for War with Army reorganization and the founding of the Territorials. After a few weeks of inquiry here and there in Ireland, including an interview with Traill, Birrell declared himself satisfied with Haldane's plan, and began to work out details. By December 1907 Traill was able to reassure Trinity and its friends that the situation was saved; T.C.D. and its endowments were not to be touched in the forthcoming bill. There was general relief and jubilation, the only sour note being struck by T.T. Gray, who seemed doubtful that even the salvation of the College justified the degrading sight of the Provost hobnobbing with Liberal politicians.

The Irish Universities Bill was introduced into Parliament in March 1908, and received the Royal assent in August. There were to be three universities: Queen's College, Belfast, was to receive university status as The Queen's University; Trinity College and the University of Dublin were to remain as they were; the Royal University was to be dissolved, and in its place the National University of Ireland was to be established, with constituent University Colleges in Dublin,[29] Cork and Galway. University College, Dublin, was to be endowed much as in Bryce's scheme, and was to take in the Cecilia Street medical school, but not the College of Science.[30] The relationship of the National University and its colleges to the Catholic church were to be such as would satisfy the bishops, but without any formal religious tests.

The Irish University Question had at last been answered. Although the bill received a good deal of detailed criticism the great majority of Irishmen of all persuasions were satisfied that it represented a reasonable compromise between the many differing points of view and the best hope for peace and development. The subsequent history of the three universities has justified this view. The problem of just how the National University was to be maintained *de facto* but not *de jure* Catholic had received curiously little discussion at the hearings of either the Robertson or the Fry Commission, and it represented a possible source of trouble. Lecky, an agnostic with a Protestant background, had argued to the former that it would be preferable to have a university that was frankly and constitutionally Catholic, but there were not many to agree with him. Delany was asked a few questions on this point; he declared that the appointment of professors would always be on merit, but that merit included other things than scholarly eminence; a man must 'fit in', be acceptable to his students, and so on. One can almost imagine him venturing a wink in the direction of Palles or Coffey. But in fact all went smoothly. There were a few Protestant professors, mainly in peripheral subjects,[31] and there were no controversies over a Protestant applicant being turned down in favour of an inferior Catholic, if only, of course, for the reason that Protestant applicants for posts in such a strongly Catholic institution were bound to be few. And although fifty years later the bishops were still continuing to make annually their ritual complaint that the National University represented only an acceptable compromise and fell far short of the ideal of Catholic education, nobody took this very seriously. The only complaints to be voiced with conviction were on a topic common to most universities – the inadequacy of the endowment.

Trinity continued to draw in a slowly increasing proportion of Catholic students, though not as many as some of its members would have wished.[32] It also found that many Ulstermen still preferred to send their sons south to Dublin rather than to Queen's, Belfast. But it had to reconcile itself to the fact that, although it had preserved its independence, it had lost its virtual monopoly in Ireland of university education in the fullest sense of the word, and that it now had two powerful competitors for students, for professorial talent, and for scholarly prestige. Many of the Fellows were slow to realize this, for relations between the three universities were to remain for many years neither friendly nor hostile, but virtually non-existent. Trinity had still, undoubtedly, the greatest prestige of the three, but it was easy to exaggerate the extent of this, and to assume that it was bound to last for ever. The first warning of a new, competitive atmosphere was given in 1915, when R.A. Williams resigned the chair of German in T.C.D to take up the chair in Belfast; only thirteen years earlier the traffic had been going the other way.[33]

(viii)

The problem of the status of the Divinity School in Trinity College, though it cropped up occasionally in the controversies which we have been discussing, did so mainly as a debating point, for it was in its essence a question which involved only the College and the Church of

Ireland. Fawcett's Act had barely reached the statute-book when the alarm was raised in some Church of Ireland circles as to the fate of the Divinity School, now that Fellowship, and eventually, therefore, membership of the Board, had been thrown open to Jews, Turks, heretics and infidels. It was not long before the Church began to press for two guarantees: that the teaching staff of the school would always be orthodox members of the Church, and that the scale on which the school was financed would not be reduced.

On these two issues, and on some minor ones arising from them, a desultory controversy between the Church and the College continued for almost forty years.[34] The attitude of the Church (as represented by its General Synod, for the bishops were usually more moderate) was simple: it started by demanding complete transfer of the school from the University to the Church and the payment of a capital sum adequate to ensure its maintenance. These demands were modified only gradually and reluctantly when it became clear that they would not be granted. The attitude of the University, however, was more complex, and shifted rather confusingly between appeasement and defiance.

Logically the Church had a fairly good case, although it could be (and was) argued that the disaster which its spokesmen feared lay in the distant future, and the truth of this contention was shown by the fact that it was not until after 1952 that a Board which could be described as in any way hostile to the Divinity School came into being. Nevertheless, a demand for some guarantee of stability in a school which supplied the Church with most of its clergy could not be lightly dismissed. On the other hand there were many in the College who shared a natural and defensible reluctance to hand over to another body its rights of management and the material resources needed for this management of a school which was running satisfactorily, which sent many clergy to England and the colonies as well as to Ireland, and which served also as the theological faculty of the University and included its most senior Professorship.

Provost Humphrey Lloyd, however, was inclined to grant the Synod's demands almost *in toto*, and he carried a majority of the Board with him in January 1876. The explanation of his attitude is not at all clear, but it may be that his enthusiasm for the changes rendered likely by the operation of Fawcett's Act was rather half-hearted (it will be remembered that he was not present when the Board underwent its sudden conversion in favour of the bill), and that he reacted to the Synod's demands more as a churchman than as Provost. He did not, however, have the unanimous support of the College, and the opposition showed itself when the Royal Commission of 1877, set up at the request of the Junior Fellows (see p. 262) to determine the proper use of the money paid to the College in compensation for its loss of advowsons after Disestablishment, turned its attention to the Divinity School. A group of nine Fellows, including Carson, Haughton, Stubbs, Barlow, Abbott and Gray, sent in to the Commission a statement deprecating any drastic change in the position of the school. They were actuated not only by conservatism, but also by the fear that under the control of the Synod the school might pass into the hands of the extreme low-church party.

The majority report of the Commission, however, recommended that the initial demand of the Synod be met: that the school should be governed by a council appointed by the Church, and that a liberal provision for its support should be made over by the College to the Representative Body. The driving force behind these recommendations was undoubtedly Lord Belmore, chairman of the Commission, and he lost no time in introducing in the House of Lords a bill to give effect to them. The Government, however, was unenthusiastic, and Lord Cairns, who was Chancellor of the University as well as Lord Chancellor of England, thought that the proposals should be more widely discussed before any action was taken; he suggested that they should at least be brought before the Senate of the University and a plenary meeting of the Synod (the proposals having come from one of the Synod's committees). In May 1879 they were debated at a crowded meeting of the University Senate, and rejected by a substantial majority, which declined to make any counter-proposals, and despite the annoyance voiced by Cairns (who wanted a speedy and generally agreed solution of the question), the Board declined to summon a further meeting of the Senate to consider such proposals. Meanwhile the University Council had debated the matter at several meetings from March to June, and, while repudiating any proposals to sever completely the connexion between the Divinity School and the University or to alienate any of the College's funds, it took the first steps towards a compromise by suggesting that the College's financial support should in some way be guaranteed, and that the management of the school should be entrusted to a council analogous to the University Council, on which the bishops of the Church of Ireland should be represented. Encouraged by this, the Synod put forward a new series of proposals, which left the school as part of the College, with its endowment guaranteed though not handed over, but with the bishops empowered to determine its course of instruction, to ensure the orthodoxy of its teaching, and to nominate, for appointment by the Board, all its Professors and Lecturers. The Board was prepared to agree in principle to all of this except the last clause, and when asked for an alternative proposal began to backtrack, stressing once more the lack of urgency, and delicately hinting that, far from being inclined to hand over any money, the Board would be more inclined to favour some system of dual control of the school if the Church of Ireland were to provide some funds for its expansion and improvement. This suggestion (which was to be repeated ten years later by Traill, in his characteristically more direct language)[35] was of course repudiated by the Church; both sides dug themselves in, and after the exchange of a few more salvoes the controversy petered out in 1881 for more than twenty years.

In 1902, in the atmosphere of general unease produced by the sitting of the Robertson Commission, the Synod made another attempt to reopen the question, but it found the Board in an unaccommodating mood. The Synod, therefore, had to wait till 1906, when the Fry Commission offered it another chance, and it sent in a long statement, giving the entire history of the controversy and repeating its claims. The Commission recommended a solution very similar to that which Salmon, with his characteristic common sense, had proposed as long ago as 1877, but to which he had been unable to secure the assent of either the Board or the Synod. The Commission's recommendation was agreed to by the Board and the Junior Fellows after some adjustment of details, and also by the Synod, reluctantly and with rather a bad grace, as representing the best terms it was likely to obtain. As finally enacted in the Letters Patent of 1911 it provided that the management of the school should be entrusted to a Council consisting of representatives of the Board, of the teaching staff of the school, and of the bishops. All were to be members of the Church of Ireland or a church in communion with it. This Council was to nominate to all appointments in the school, but since no money was to be transferred, and the Board remained the paymaster, the formal appointments were to be made by the Board; it could not, however, refuse the nomination of the Divinity School Council unless it was prepared to justify its refusal before the Chancellor. Subject to the same proviso the Board would approve all regulations regarding teaching and examination in the school made by its Council. Finally, as a guarantee of the stability of these arrangements, the powers and constitution of the Divinity School Council were made an 'entrenched clause'; they could not, like most other statutes from 1911 on, be changed with the consent only of the Board, the Fellows and the Visitors, but only on the initiative of the Crown, which would presumably satisfy itself that any proposed change was agreeable both to the College and to the Church of Ireland. In spite of its initially cool welcome from the Church, it was generally agreed after a few years that this solution was a satisfactory one, and it was not until after our history closes in 1952 that any desire to modify it was expressed by either side.

(ix)

In 1906, however, the Divinity School found itself attacked from another and somewhat unexpected quarter. On the varying occasions on which a chapel and a theological faculty had been offered to the Catholics a corresponding offer had been made to the Presbyterians, more for the sake of symmetry than from a consciousness of any real demand for them. And in fact there was no such demand, for the Assembly's College in Belfast was adequate for the training for the ministry, and the Presbyterian students in Trinity (who were fewer than the Catholics) could be easily looked after from the churches in the city. But the General Assembly's committee on higher education decided that they must imitate Archbishop Walsh in demanding 'absolute equality' and sent in to the Fry Commission a singularly sour document demanding that in the interests of such equality the Divinity School should be removed from the College and that the Chapel should cease to be used for Anglican worship. Since levelling up was not desired, there must be levelling down. This dog-in-the-manger attitude, which would certainly have been repudiated by the Presbyterian Fellows, and probably by most Presbyterians in Dublin, failed to impress the Commissioners.

The manifesto of the General Assembly's committee must have been particularly distasteful to Traill, as he had got into trouble with his colleagues in the Divinity School only a year earlier for appointing a Presbyterian minister as one of the select preachers in the College Chapel. The Divinity Professors protested to the Board and asked for the decision to be reversed, but the Board denied any responsibility in the matter, pointing out that the Provost alone appointed the preachers. Eight years later, however, there was a more serious dispute on a somewhat wider issue. The Board, at the Provost's instigation, decided that the Chapel could be used occasionally for Presbyterian services. The Divinity Professors once more protested, and A.A. Luce, then a very junior Fellow, associated himself with the protest. The Archbishop of Dublin, in a letter to Bernard in December 1913, wrote that 'it is a lamentable business and all arising out of the perverse self-assertion of the Provost',[36] but the Provost had the Board fairly solidly behind him, and maintained that, as long as he was a member of the Church of Ireland he was Ordinary of the Chapel, and could make whatever arrangements for services he thought fit, whatever the Regius Professor or the Archbishop might think. The Divinity Professors replied with a counsel's opinion which denied this claim and stressed the fact that the consecration of the Chapel constituted a deed of trust and limited the uses to which it could be put. The Board was not impressed; it resolved that the Chapel was the property of the College and that no external body could interfere with the services to be held there; it also resolved that Presbyterian services did not come under the head of 'common and profane usages', which were forbidden by the deed of consecration. And there the matter was allowed to drop.

(x)

The days of ecumenicism still lay far ahead, and sober and level-headed members of the Church of Ireland still viewed Presbyterianism in a spirit which today would appear narrow and uncharitable. But behind the purely sectarian aspect of this squabble there lay a feeling of unease among the Church of Ireland clergy (and a few of the older laity) that they were threatened by a slow but stealthy increase of a secular and mildly anti-clerical spirit. Up to 1900 Fawcett's Act was interpreted in the letter, but as the years went by there was an increasing tendency to query various religious practices or regulations as 'contrary to the spirit of Fawcett's Act'. Newport White (who was by then acting as deputy for John Gwynn, retired in all but name from the Regius Professorship of Divinity),[37] in a general lament to Bernard in 1914, wrote that the Board was determined to do what they liked with the Chapel:

the Provost cannot last long ... and he is certain to be succeeded by someone more hostile to the Church ... already the Donnellan endowment[38] has gone; J.P.M.[39] has told me that he intends the lectures at times to be on quite secular subjects ... a junior lecturership in Divinity has been abolished; when I said the money was earmarked for the Divinity School J.P.M. laughed ...[40]

Up to 1869 the educational ideals of the College remained unchanged in fundamentals from what they had been at the beginning: sound learning and Anglican piety were of equal importance. But Disestablishment and Fawcett's Act upset the balance, and it gradually became apparent that if the pursuit of the piety were to interfere with the acquisition of sound learning, even by a small minority of the students, then it was the former that must yield. Over the years, therefore, religious practice ceased gradually to be something governed by regulations and enforced by penalties, and became something to be left to the individual conscience. An inevitable process of *aggiornamento* went on, and gathered speed in mid-century; and although even today the College is far from being godless in the sense that the Queen's Colleges were, it is, despite the fact that Catholics are now allowed to enter it freely without any dissuasive,[41] much nearer to that condition than in the days when it was the target for Cardinal Cullen's thunder-bolts, shortly after the passing of Fawcett's Act.

The two main fields in which this process of secularization showed itself during the first two decades of the century were the enforcement of Chapel attendance and the regulations for catechetical lectures and examinations. In both cases the changes were gradual and the arguments conducted with moderation, and neither gave rise to a serious controversy, but the process of change is worth chronicling as giving particular examples of the tendency described above.

In the early years of the College daily attendance at Chapel was compulsory, not only for the students, but also for the Fellows, as was the case in almost all colleges at that time, and this requirement was incorporated in the Laudian statutes. It would seem probable that the rule was enforced fairly strictly up to the middle of the eighteenth century, at any rate for those living within the walls. In a matter of this kind it is virtually impossible to know how closely practice accorded with precept, but we may suspect that under Andrews and Hely-Hutchinson enforcement may well have been less strict. But although the early nineteenth century probably saw a reaction, it was not long before the average Irish Protestant, no matter how deep his commitment to evangelical religion, adopted the opinion of Mrs Proudie that there was something popish about weekday services (if only because they did not include a sermon) and that the enforced Sabbath rest implied hard work on weekdays uninterrupted by ecclesiastical distractions. It is doubtful, therefore, that more than a minority attended weekday Chapel during any part of the nineteenth century, although it was enjoined by statute up to 1855 and enjoined in the Calendar as part of the duty of resident students up to 1905. Barlow, writing in 1871,[42] with a characteristic mixture of acute comment and malicious irony, pointed out that the average attendance at weekday services (deducting those who were paid to attend and perform specific duties) amounted to 2.78378 students and 0.29729 Fellows.

Although a good deal of statutory revision was carried out in the years following the Royal Commission of 1851 no change was made in the matter of Chapel attendance on Sundays and feast-days, probably on account of the feeling, so frequent among conservatives who are unwillingly and uneasily accommodating themselves to a changed world, that even when a regulation cannot be enforced its repeal represents a surrender of principle. This was felt even though nobody seriously proposed that the rule should be applied to the Catholics, who had been admitted in 1794, and to the Protestant nonconformists, who were slowly increasing in numbers during the early part of the century. The fact that the statute was by general consent not applied to dissenters made it less easy for it to be applied in its full rigour to Anglicans.

The passing of Fawcett's Act in 1873, however, with its provision that nobody should be compelled to attend the services of a denomination to which he did not belong, meant that the wording of the statutes had to be altered. The Act quite clearly implied that there was no objection to enforcing attendance at services of a denomination to which the student *did* belong, but the Letters Patent of 1874, though reaffirming that it was the duty of Anglican students to attend on Sundays (feast-days were dropped) removed from the Board and the Deans the duty of enforcing this, and left its execution to a mysterious body of persons described as 'those whose duty it is'.

These revisions left the practical position unchanged until 1909, when five tutors challenged on behalf of their pupils the right of the Board to enforce Chapel attendance on Anglican students by means of fines, and the case went to the Visitors for decision. Their very lengthy and in places rather misty judgment reaffirmed the duty, imposed by statute, of such students to attend Chapel on Sundays; they found that the Board had the power to levy fines for breaches of discipline, but that as neither the Board nor the Deans had now the duty of imposing penalties for this particular breach, neither apparently had they the power, and that the enforcement of attendance must be left to 'those whose duty it is', which the Visitors identified, rather strangely, as the chaplains – strangely, because there were no chaplains in 1874. The chaplains, of course, had no coercive powers, so they were expected to carry out their duty 'by precept and example'. The Visitors, however, held that the Provost, had the right, if he thought fit, to deprive a resident student of his rooms for a breach of this, as of any other College rule, the occupation of rooms being regarded, reasonably enough, as a privilege and not a right.

In its slightly muddled way the judgment gave expression to the general feeling of the age: a student should be strongly encouraged to attend church regularly on Sundays, but he should not be coerced by penalties. For the majority of students the compromise worked well enough; anyone who repeatedly absented himself from Sunday matins received a warning from the Junior Dean, with perhaps a hint as to the ultimate sanction of the Provost's powers, though we cannot trace any instance of these powers actually being used as a penalty for non-attendance. But in most cases a prudent student realized that to put himself on the wrong side of the law in this matter might lead to a more serious sentence for another offence. The number of attendances required to escape a rebuke very gradually declined, and with it the numbers in Chapel, but it was not till about 1957 that all attempts to enforce attendance were quietly dropped, and it was not till eight years later that the relevant section in the College Calendar, which still repeated the *ipsissima verba* of 1905, was finally deleted.

The history of the regulations for religious instruction (known as catechetical lectures and examinations, and regulated by one of the Senior Fellows, who bore the title of Catechist) is not very different, though here the changes were made in a more orderly fashion, and practice was never so completely divorced from formal regulations. The statutes did not include detailed regulations for attendance at the lectures or success in the examinations, but throughout the middle part of the nineteenth century the Board decreed that students (other than Catholics) were required to keep, either by examination or by lectures, two catechetical terms in each of their Freshman years. This was an academic rather than a disciplinary requirement, and the penalty for non-compliance was failure to rise to the next academic year. From 1886 onwards separate lectures and examinations were arranged for Presbyterian students, but otherwise the system continued unaltered.

In 1901–2 there was a very involved exchange of schemes between Board and Council, in which proposals for the removal of compulsion became complicated by proposals to make the catechetical course an integral but optional part of the ordinary course in arts (English being proposed as the alternative). The Board oscillated unpredictably between freedom and compulsion, while on the Council an instinctive suspicion of any change on the part of conservatives was reinforced by a dislike on the part of the more extreme liberals of countenancing the course at all, even as an option; this meant that no agreement could be reached. In 1904, however, Traill, soon after he became Provost, cut through the tangle of rival schemes with a simple proposal that the system should remain unchanged except that students over twenty-one, or the parents of younger students, could 'opt out' on conscientious grounds. This was accepted by a narrow majority on the Council. Twelve years later the most significant change was made: it was now up to a student or his parents to 'opt in' to the course, and a statement as to the student's performance would be sent to the parents. Such small element of compulsion as remained was in this way transferred from the College to the home. On this voluntary basis the system continued, being kept alive by the fact that intending students of Divinity were excused certain parts of their Divinity course if they had kept their catechetical terms. It was not until 1972 that the course and the office of Catechist were finally abolished.

(xi)

The sectarian disputes and ecclesiastical problems which have so far filled the greater part of this chapter are issues which, no matter how remote or futile they may appear to some of our readers today, no historian of the early twentieth century in Ireland can afford to neglect. But in Trinity College, although many of its members became deeply involved in one or more of them, there was also widespread interest in several important questions in the purely secular sphere. Amongst these pride of place during the first decade of the century must be given to the problem of internal constitutional reform.

In practice this meant proposals for changes in the composition of the Board. With a very few exceptions the Fellows and non-Fellow Professors[43] were content to continue with a small and more or less omnicompetent governing body, its powers limited only by those already possessed by the University Council (and in a few unimportant matters by the University Senate). But the statute which had been in operation since 1637, specifying that the Board should consist of the Provost and the seven Senior Fellows, came in for more and more criticism. During the last quarter of the nineteenth century there had been, as we have seen, some grumbling and agitation on the part of the Junior Fellows about 'stagnation', which meant simply the slow rate at which promotion proceeded, and in the rather desperate search for a means whereby this could be relieved an increase in the number of Senior Fellows and their retirement at the age of seventy had both been canvassed, but the principle of seniority (within limits) as the passport to power had not been directly challenged or even queried. It was not until 1896, when the preposterous situation was reached in which the youngest member of the Board (Barlow) was sixty-nine, that gerontocracy as such was openly questioned. A more radical approach was canvassed by some of the Junior Fellows, notably Bernard and E.J. Gwynn, who began to argue that the Board should be chosen by election rather than by the lottery of survival.

The Board was not likely to be moved by resolutions or protests unless they were moderate, persistent and virtually unanimous. Any such approach to unanimity was almost impossible to achieve, for like most groups of academic men the Junior Fellows included some conservatives, some hair-splitters who would drag out *ad infinitum* discussions on amendments to amendments, some cantankerous non-signers on principle, and always a few at the top who were reluctant to destroy a system whose fruits they expected to enjoy in a few years' time.

The Professors were more solidly in favour of reform, for they had no terrestrial nirvana to look forward to, no matter how long they lived, and meanwhile most of them suffered under a system which gave them no security of tenure, at least in their early years, an inadequate salary and no secure pension rights. But their great weakness (for which they cannot individually be blamed) was the fact that they tailed off by a gradual transition from chairs like those of Chemistry, English and Engineering, which were obviously of primary importance in any overall view of the College's activities and responsibilities, to those of Music, Arabic and Pastoral Theology, which could reasonably be regarded as non-essential; the opinions of the occupants of these latter on the constitution of the College carried, therefore, little weight. The body as a whole oscillated between solidarity and a policy of claiming rights only for the more important chairs, and this inconstancy deprived them, as we shall see, of substantial gains which might have been achieved if the leaders had been able to follow the latter policy consistently.

The atmosphere of general deadlock was, however, broken by the appointment of the Royal Commission of 1906, which gave the reform party a chance to publicize their demands and their grievances, and to do so before a body whose opinions could not be completely flouted, and which was unlikely to approve the existing constitution *in toto*. Among the memoranda presented to the Commission, therefore, was one on behalf of the reform party, which proposed that in future the Board should consist of ten members, all except the Provost elected from among the Fellows, the ranks of the Fellows, however, having been strengthened by the election to Fellowship of those occupants of the 'principal chairs' who were not already Fellows. The memorandum was signed by seven Junior Fellows (L.C. Purser, Culverwell, O'Sullivan, Russell, E.J. Gwynn, Thrift and Rogers) and thirteen Professors, of whom eight can be regarded as occupying important and more or less full-time chairs. The signature of W.J.M. Starkie was also added, rather imprudently, perhaps, as it was now eight years since he had resigned his Fellowship. The proposed reforms were set out in considerable detail, with compulsory retirement, probationary Fellowships, a faculty structure and various other novelties, all sensible enough and readily defensible in argument, but together offering a wide variety of possible sources of objection, even by men who were in favour of a considerable measure of reform. And it soon became clear that the signatories had made a great mistake in producing such a cut-and-dried scheme, for another memorandum was sent in to the Commission, signed by fourteen Junior Fellows, stating tersely that 'while heartily agreeing to any proposal for real reform' they were 'opposed to schemes of change which may upset our constitution without doing any equivalent good', and objecting specifically 'to many of the features embodied in the scheme proposed in Document No. 5' (the reform proposals summarized above). Some of the signatories were conservatives who wanted only the minimum of change, but others would seem to have been reformers irritated by what they saw as officious and cliquish behaviour on the part of some of their colleagues and the over-simplification of complex problems which required careful discussion if injustice was not to be done to individuals.

The Provost and Senior Fellows expressed no collective opinion on the matter, but the Provost, Mahaffy and Gray gave verbal evidence, and Barlow, Tarleton and Gray submitted statements. As one might have expected, the general tone was conservative. Traill was prepared to advocate a little reform on account of the alarming rise in the average age of the Senior Fellows, and he was coaxed by the Commissioners' questions into a slight enlargement of his original proposals, but reasonably enough he was impressed with the financial costs of compensating the vested interests in any sweeping change. Tarleton, who was Bursar at the time, produced an intelligent and well-worked-out scheme involving a Board recruited half by election and half by seniority. But when Mahaffy, who had volunteered no opinion on the subject, was asked whether he was satisfied with the present constitution, he sulkily replied that 'if anyone will show me a reformed system that is likely to be as good . . . I should be willing to adopt it, but all the proposals appear to me so perfectly rotten that they had better be left alone'. The snappish tone was probably dictated by a guilty knowledge that he had advocated reform not many years since, while still a Junior Fellow, and that his intellectual disposition towards it was now negated by his dislike of the reformers. Barlow struck the same note. After having declared that although seventy-nine years old he was still quite competent to discharge the duties of a Senior Fellow, he went on to point out that if, like a civil servant, he had retired at sixty-five it would have cost the College £15,000. As regards schemes of reform, he repeated Mahaffy's point with greater urbanity, citing Fitzgerald, a keen reformer, as having admitted that of the twenty different constitutions which he had at one time invented, none of them pleased him. (The shade of Fitzgerald might have replied that the present system pleased him even less.) He also made much of the argument that the Professors, being specialists, were not fitted to sit on the governing body, the motto of the average Professor being '*Fiat* my special work, *ruat* everything else'. Gray threw himself with zest into the role of *Athanasius contra mundum*, and even persistent cross-questioning by the Commissioners did not wring from him the smallest doubt as to government by the Provost and Senior Fellows being the best that the wit of man could devise.

Even from the Junior Fellows came opinions scarcely more enthusiastic for constitutional reform. Beare and W.R.W. Roberts in particular appear as strong conservatives, although Roberts was six and Beare ten places away from co-option to Senior Fellowship. Beare was much the abler man of the two; his conservatism was highly articulate and clearly expounded, and may be explained in part as arising from disgust at the ill feeling caused by the noisier members of the reform party, both at this time and ten years earlier. His anxiety to solve the Catholic problem had, however, led him against all his instincts to support the scheme to which we have referred above (p. 373) involving the election of 'outsiders' to the Board. Roberts, on the other hand, thought that Catholics should take the College as they found it, but was prepared to concede that the retirement of elderly Senior Fellows might be somewhat accelerated – an opinion which he seems to have abandoned twenty-five years later.

Faced with this heavy weight of conservatism and with a wide division of opinion among the Junior Fellows as to which of the suggested reforms were desirable the Commissioners might well have refrained from making any firm proposals for constitutional change. But those from Oxford and Cambridge had seen systems similar to that which still survived in Dublin abolished some thirty years ago and replaced by elected governing bodies which had been subject to no serious criticism; Kelleher had not been in the College long enough to be mesmerized by the mystique of Senior Fellowship; and the others had seen, if only from a distance, the performance of an elderly Board, and had not been impressed. At all events the Commissioners unanimously recommended a Board whose members (apart from the Provost) would all be elected, and on which Professors would sit as well as Fellows. But on the difficult problems of the extinction of vested interests and the presence on the Board of persons who might not be members of the Corporation they did not touch.

For the best part of a year after the publication of the report the Fellows, and to a large extent the Professors, were too busy with the fight against the Bryce proposals to give much thought to the question of the composition of the Board, and anybody who felt inclined to give it priority was easily silenced by the plea that a united front against the external enemy was essential, and that this was not the time to raise controversial issues. Furthermore, it was at this time, as we shall see in a later section, that the problem of whether (and, if so, how) the nature of the Fellowship examination should be changed became particularly pressing. By the end of 1907, however, the Bryce scheme had been publicly interred, and in December a meeting of Fellows, Professors and members of the University Council resolved that the principle of representative government should be introduced to the Board, and that its members should include elected representatives of the whole body of Fellows and of the Professors, the number of such representatives being left undetermined. It was also agreed that a joint committee of four Junior Fellows and four Professors should draw up more detailed plans for reform.[44]

The Junior Fellows chose Beare, Roberts, Fry and W.E. Thrift as their delegation, and left them unfettered by any instructions or limitations. Beare could be regarded as belonging to the extreme (but not entirely inflexible) right, Roberts to the moderate right, Fry to slightly left of centre and Thrift to the left. The Professors selected Joly, Dowden, Bastable and A.F. Dixon; three were distinguished scholars, of whom the first two were well trained in committee work, and the fourth was the most active man in the teaching and organization of the Medical School. The meetings of the joint committee were unexpectedly amicable if one considers the wide spread of opinion among the participants. Even Beare was led by argument and by an uneasy feeling that the *Zeitgeist* was working against him to agree that 'mere specialists' might in some cases be fit to sit on the Board, and the Professors were careful not to urge their grievances too energetically. The chief problem was that of the best method of arranging for the representation of the Professors on the Board. Which Professors were eligible, and which should elect? Could they sit on the Board and take part in the disposition of corporate funds if they were not members of the Corporation? And if they were to be made members of the Corporation would this best be done by introducing them as a new element or by electing them to Fellowship?

By May 1908, agreement had been reached, and a new constitution was recommended by the joint committee. Full-time Professors[45] were to be declared members of the Corporation (but not elected to Fellowship), and from the enlarged Corporation the Junior Fellows and the whole body of Professors would each elect three members to the Board. To these would be added the Provost; a Bursar and an Auditor elected from the Corporation by the Fellows; a Senior Dean, Senior Lecturer and Senior Proctor elected from the Fellows by the nine most Senior Fellows (and presumably from among their own ranks); and a Registrar, appointed by the Board. The University Council was to be reorganized on a faculty basis.

The next month this scheme was submitted to the Junior Fellows and the Professors for their approval. The former, despite the distinctly radical tone of the proposals, approved them by twenty votes to one. The Professors were much less enthusiastic, and the lack of clear definition between full-time and part-time led them to query what could be represented as an arbitrary division by the joint committee. That there was an intermediate 'grey area' was apparent from the fact that the Professors themselves in their memorandum to the Royal Commission had identified eleven chairs (not at the time held by

Fellows) which could be described as 'principal' or full-time; but only two years later the number had been raised to thirteen by the inclusion of the Professors of German and Astronomy. The trouble was that whether a Professor devoted all his time to his College duties depended partly on the chair, but partly on its occupant. It is difficult to believe that Professor Alexander (Engineering) was not receiving an occasional fee as a consultant. And if Emil Werner, Professor of Applied Chemistry, was rated as full-time it was chiefly because he was a modest and conscientious man; his salary was almost identical with that of the Regius Professor of Feudal and English Law, who spent a large part of his time at the Bar. But who knew whether the next Professor of Applied Chemistry might not wish to supplement his modest salary by consultancy work?

Moreover, some of the Professors who were quite indisputably part-time were not the sort of men to play second fiddle to anyone contentedly. Leech thought he knew more about how to run a College than the whole of the Fellows put together. Sir Charles Ball, the Regius Professor of Surgery, had his eminence as a surgeon certified by a knighthood and was an active member of the University Council; this certainly compensated, if only in his own eyes, for the fact that he did no teaching. J.H. Wardell doubtless thought, and with considerable justification, that the chair of Modern History *ought* to be one of the 'principal' chairs, even though the minute salary which it then carried prevented it from being ranked with them. So the part-timers refused to accept the proposed principle of division, and the full-timers, whether from chivalry or because they wished for a united front from the Professors on other issues such as security of tenure, resisted the temptation to throw their part-time colleagues to the wolves. The Professors, therefore, rejected the proposals, and asked that all Professors should be made members of the Corporation, or, if this was not acceptable, that the number to be incorporated should be at least two-thirds of the number of Fellows (which would, as numbers then stood, have meant all the non-Fellow Professors except two), and that they should be chosen by the Professors themselves.

The reaction of the Junior Fellows to this demand was one of irritation. Against their deep convictions they had gone out of their way to conciliate the Professors, and in a moment of unity-seeking euphoria had committed themselves to a scheme which now looked alarmingly radical, and this was all the thanks they got. They refused the Professors' demand, and even expressed doubts as to whether adding any Professors to the Corporation was the best way of achieving reform. The Professors then began to backtrack, but it was too late, and though Joly did his best to patch things up the distrust which each

393

body felt for the other now came out into the open, and the joint committee ceased to meet after February 1909.

This left the initiative to the Board, which, after rather unsatisfactory conferences with each of the disputing bodies, decided to produce its own scheme. Although the temper of the Board was still generally conservative, two of its members, Traill and Tarleton, wanted to promote a measure of moderate reform, while Williamson, Mahaffy and Tyrrell were at least not hostile, and were prepared to yield to the steady pressure exercised by Traill in favour of the proposals he had agreed to in his evidence before the Fry Commission. It was proposed, therefore, that although the Professors should not become members of the Corporation they should elect two representatives to sit on the Board, as should also the Junior Fellows; the hard core of the Board, however, consisting of the Provost and Senior Fellows, was to remain.[46] There was, however, to be a provision that Junior, as well as Senior Fellows were to be eligible for the offices of Bursar, Senior Lecturer and Registrar, and if elected would sit on the Board; this gave the possibility of more than two Junior Fellows. The problem of having non-corporators sitting on the Board was neatly solved by providing that the representatives of the Professors should be members of the Corporation so long as they sat on the Board, but no longer.

Although this rather modest reform aroused no great enthusiasm anywhere it was eventually accepted by both Junior Fellows and Professors. The Board emphasised that the discussion had gone on long enough (it was by now June 1909) and that if nothing was done the possibility of a Statutory Commission, similar to those which had forced constitutional reforms on their unwilling sister-universities in England, was not to be excluded. Accordingly the settlement was accepted in much the same spirit as was the Anglo-Irish treaty of 1921: by the conservatives as a concession which, disastrous though it might be, was the minimum which seemed acceptable to the radicals, and which at least preserved something of the old regime; by the rebels as a limited but useful advance which would serve as a springboard for further progress at a suitable moment. The Junior Fellows assented to the Board's proposals, hoping that the reconstructed Board might proceed to the implementation of the joint committee's proposals or something like them. It was a misguided hope, as no further change in the composition of the Board took place till 1958, and although from 1927 onwards the Registrar was chosen from among the Junior Fellows, it was not until 1952 that more than three Junior Fellows sat on the Board. The Professors consented more reluctantly, declaring that they preferred the scheme of the joint committee; they were in this way taught the painful lesson of the Sibylline books, as it was they themselves who had rejected the joint committee's scheme only a year earlier.

In July, therefore, counsel was asked to prepare a draft of the relevant section of the King's Letter. But there remained one further hurdle to be surmounted. Gray and Cathcart, defeated on the Board, applied to the High Court for an injunction to restrain the College from applying for or accepting a King's Letter embodying these changes. The Board, badly advised by its counsel, attempted one line of defence which was easily dismissed – that the Crown had reserved power to alter the Charter without the consent of the Corporation – but in its second line it was successful, for the Court held firstly that it had no power to restrain any subject or group of subjects from petitioning the King about anything, and secondly that the consent of the Corporation could be given by a majority of its members and did not require unanimity. Somewhat to the Provost's disgust the Court recommended that the costs of the petitioners as well as of the defence be paid from College funds. Even so, Gray and Cathcart did not consider themselves beaten. They appealed directly to the Crown not to issue a King's Letter which purported to change the constitution of the College in the manner requested by the Board. They complained of loss of prestige, privilege and power (not to mention financial pickings) by the throwing open of three senior offices to Junior as well as Senior Fellows. Moreover, the Provost had been vindictive and unjust in the assignment of offices for 1910–11; Gray had been turned out of the Senior Lecturership and Cathcart had not been made Bursar. Traill, provoked beyond endurance, replied: 'What else could you expect after all the worry and expense you have caused?'[47] Next year harmony was restored to the Board, at the expense perhaps of some administrative efficiency, by appointing the 80-year-old Gray as Registrar and Cathcart as Bursar. But the Provost also drew public attention to the unrepresentative quality of their obstruction by calling the Corporation together and securing the assent to the acceptance of the King's Letter of twenty-seven out of thirty-three Fellows and sixty-eight out of seventy Scholars. The dissentient Fellows comprised five unyielding conservatives – Gray, Cathcart, Burnside, Wilkins and Mooney – and one disillusioned and disgusted radical who considered the reforms totally inadequate. This was E.J. Gwynn.

The Letters Patent of 1911, besides effecting these changes in the constitution of the Corporation and the Board and setting up the Divinity School Council as we have already described, made a partial concession to those who wished the University Council to be reorganized on a faculty basis. Its membership was increased from seventeen to nineteen; the Provost, Senior Lecturer and Registrar sat *ex officio*; four members represented the professional schools other than Divinity (one each for Law and Engineering and two for Medicine); six members represented the 'Schools in Arts' (which of course included pure science); but some continuity with the old system was maintained by having two members appointed by the Board and four elected by the Senate. The electorate for the last category was, however, the whole Senate, and not, as before, the Senate less Fellows and Professors. As a result of this the Senate seats tended to go to Fellows or Professors who had failed to secure election under other heads, and the number of outsiders sharply diminished. The faculty structure was further emphasized by the setting up of School Committees (eighteen in all) which reported to the Council and relieved it of a fair amount of detailed routine work.

(xii)

The contrast between Fellows and non-Fellow Professors which was repeatedly emphasized in these constitutional arguments rested ultimately on the method by which the members of the two classes were recruited. For the Professors the procedure was not so very different from that of today: in most cases the chairs were advertised, references were scrutinized, occasionally outside opinion was consulted, and the Council then proceeded to a nomination. Sometimes, admittedly, a Fellow was appointed to a vacant chair to which he was suited without any advertisement of the post, but this could fairly be justified on the grounds that the resources of the College could seldom afford the luxury of two highly qualified men in a specialized subject, and there had been for over half a century no appointment of a Fellow to a chair which invited serious criticism.[48] The election of Fellows, however, still followed the old pattern of an open examination (now almost entirely by written papers instead of *viva voce*, but that was the only change) in a limited range of subjects – Mathematics, Physics (with a little Chemistry), Philosophy, Classics, Hebrew – and the claim that the Fellow had a broader education and was less of a specialist than the Professor rested partly on the traditional respect given to Classics and Mathematics (which carried the greatest number of marks in the examination) but also, with greater justification, on the fact that a candidate had to perform reasonably well in at least two subjects to succeed.

Although it was beginning to appear somewhat archaic by the latter part of the nineteenth century the system enjoyed general confidence and approval until about 1900, firstly because it passed the pragmatic test and had been producing for several decades a stream of Fellows of whom the great majority were good and productive scholars, and secondly because it was generally agreed that it was completely objective, an important recommendation in a country perpetually rent with charges and counter-charges of favouritism in appointments.[49] But soon after the turn of the century it began to incur criticism, and many of the Fellows who gave evidence before the Fry Commission, including some strong conservatives, suggested that the system should be overhauled. These suggestions came, naturally enough, mainly from the older men, as it was too much to expect a Fellow elected during the past ten years to complain that the system by which he had been elected was a bad one.

Critics of the traditional Fellowship examination attacked it on three different grounds. The first was that the subjects which it covered, although a century ago they had made up virtually the whole undergraduate curriculum, now amounted to only a small part. Why should not Fellows be elected for their excellence in Natural Science, History, Modern Literature or Economics? The second rested on an uneasy feeling that a system which selected the best examinee could not be guaranteed to produce the best scholar or teacher; it set a premium on accuracy and a mind well-stored with remembered facts, but it tended, if anything, to discourage originality and creative imagination. And as regards teaching, although at least half the Fellows were reasonably competent, there was none elected between Macran (1892) and Fearon (1921) who was generally regarded as a brilliant or inspiring lecturer. Finally, there was a growing feeling that the steadily increasing prestige of Fellowship during the latter part of the nineteenth century had been self-destructive, for it increased the number of candidates and hence the number of unsuccessful attempts before the prize was won, so that the newly elected Fellow was all too often worn out by years of hard and monotonous work, drained of much of his energy and all of his creative impulse, and inclined merely to rest on his oars and bask in the glory of his great achievement. This last argument was widely held outside the College as well as inside. George A. Birmingham, for example who often fell back on his College memories for incidental décor for his novels, wrote in 1912 that:

It is generally believed that the examination for Fellowship in Trinity College, Dublin is so severe that no one who is successful in it is ever good for anything afterwards. Having once passed the examination men are said to settle down into a condition of exhausted mediocrity.[50]

This opinion was so widely expressed that there must have been some truth in it, but it is difficult to point to any great difference in the ordeal suffered by the candidates of 1895–1910 from those of 1880–

1894, the generation that had included L.C. Purser, Bernard, Bury, E.J. Gwynn and C.J. Joly, all scholars of the first rank. The average interval between graduation and Fellowship admittedly had risen by nearly a year, and the average number of unsuccessful candidatures from two and a half to a little over three. But these were not catastrophic changes. C.J. Joly (1894) was elected at the fifth attempt and J.G. Smyly (1897) at the sixth, both eight years after graduation; yet Joly was elected Fellow of the Royal Society ten years later and Smyly settled down immediately to continue, effectively enough, Mahaffy's work on papyri. Smyly, however, was the last Fellow for fifteen years to win anything but local recognition for his publications. Admittedly there was a bad blockage from 1897 to 1903, when the number of candidates multiplied unprecedentedly, and in this period nobody was elected after less than four attempts, while Goligher and Fraser each needed seven. It was mainly this short period that focused attention on the problem and helped to give the examination a bad name; nor was its reputation helped when one of the candidates in 1903 went mad under the strain. But the idea that the newly elected Fellow was physically worn out to an extent that could not be cured by a few months' rest was certainly an exaggeration. Admittedly Mooney and Kennedy looked old before their time, but Smyly, Fraser, Alton and R.M. Gwynn all lived on into their late seventies or early eighties with plenty of energy left. It was to be said of this generation, with only a touch of romantic exaggeration, by one who had sat under them as an undergraduate:

Some feet of clay, if you like, and not all hearts of gold. But there was salt, and sinew. They were tough – you had to be tough to survive the old Fellowship examination. Not one of them would have taken an opinion at second hand. Not one but would fight like a Tasmanian devil for his opinion or for a friend or even for a pupil (and in some cases with equal ferocity for an increase in private emoluments).[51]

But why did so little of this energy emerge on the printed page? No single explanation suffices, but a few contributory factors may be noted. The real trouble was not so much the nature of the examination as the excessive reputation which Fellowship had acquired. There was dangled before the eyes of a good examinee a 'glittering prize' which was hard to dismiss, but a prize which led on to a career for which some of those tempted were quite unsuited. In the old days such men went out to a country living after a few years, and if they were equally unsuited to that – well it was the Church's problem not the College's. But this way of escape was no longer open. So the College was saddled with men who had no talent for either teaching or scholarship. They included a few open and unashamed philistines like John Fraser and Harry Thrift, who had quick minds but none of the other mental qualities one looks for in a don, for they were perfunctory lecturers and not conspicuously diligent as tutors. Fraser was far less at home in the Common Room than at a cattle fair or a race-meeting in Mayo, or in his arm chair at the University Club, laying down the law on how the College had gone to the dogs since his young days. He would have served the community much better as a cattle breeder or a race-course steward. Thrift's spiritual home was the selectors' box at a Rugby international; he had also some talent for the minutiae of finance and might have made a good stockbroker. Others, more pathetically, pursued culture as they saw it, but their vision was sadly provincial or muddled. Here we may class Sir Robert Tate, who devoted the intellectual energy of his entire lifetime to polishing and repolishing the skills he had learnt at Shrewsbury of turning trivial English verses into convincing pastiches of the Latin poets of the golden age. He enjoyed the company of students and was very popular with them, but although in his lectures he hammered grammatical rules into them with much strength if little subtlety, his extra-curricular activities, if they helped to strengthen a feeling of collegiate loyalty, did little to broaden their cultural horizons. He presided over their dramatic society for years without once suggesting that they should deviate from their tradition of fashionable drawing-room comedies, and he entertained them after dinner with tap-dancing or recitations from Kipling. He was a man of great integrity and generosity of spirit, but his talents were those of a schoolmaster or an army officer rather than of a don. J.M. Henry, on the other hand (who had won first place in the Civil Service examination, but threw it over to compete for Fellowship), took such a wide view of culture that he tried to combine all elements of it together. Mathematics, psychology, philosophy, comparative religion, education, dietetics, fringe medicine – all were grist to his mill, and ignoring the warning he had received from Provost Bernard in 1922,[52] he boiled them all down into *A new fundamentalism* (1934), a credo of an eccentricity which places it in the outer fringe of the curiosities of academic literature. His power of judgment may be assessed by his genuine surprise at the indignation caused by an implication, tossed off incidentally in his book, that the Virgin Mary was a respectable temple prostitute. It is difficult to see what niche would have suited him in his lifetime, but had he survived into old age he would have made an admirable guru in a Californian commune, for he too was a kindly man with a passion for imparting information and ideas. R.M. Gwynn, one of the few Fellows of this period to take orders, was as near to a saint as any Fellow has been. He devoted an immense amount of time and energy to missionary societies, to acting as chaplain before the post was officially established, to founding and superintending societies for social service, and to publicizing and helping to alleviate the lot of the Dublin poor in the dark days of 1912–14. He had also a wide and balanced culture, and was held in universal respect and admiration as a man. But not always as a Fellow, for as a teacher, an administrator and a scholar he left much to be desired. His published works amounted to two or three short papers and an edition of Amos for schools. He was handicapped by severe deafness; his speech was a mumble almost as hard to interpret as his atrocious handwriting; his total inability to operate any mechanical device forbade him the use of a typewriter; he was naturally untidy, and the state of his office when he held the post of Senior Lecturer, with gum-boots, ear-trumpets and grey woollen mufflers jumbled together with dog-eared volumes of College records, was an embarrassment even to his best friends.

Such anomalies were by no means unknown at Oxford and Cambridge at this time, but they were becoming disproportionately numerous in Dublin, and it was impossible to get rid of them, as all Fellows still held their posts *ad vitam aut culpam*, a state of affairs which was being progressively abandoned elsewhere. But what was equally disturbing was that most of the Fellows elected in this period who were *not* misfits, who seemed well suited to academic life, who were men of genuine culture and could have held their own in conversation at any High Table, were producing little or nothing in the way of original scholarship. Some of them were still too young to be fairly judged in this respect in 1906, but the disquiet then voiced on this phenomenon was justified by subsequent events, for of the eighteen Fellows who were elected from 1896 to 1915 (L.H. Gwynn and S.A. Stewart, who died young, being excluded from the count) Smyly and A.A. Luce alone produced original work of any substance and distinction. G.W. Mooney edited three classical texts with reasonable efficiency;[53] R.A.P. Rogers wrote a good textbook of ethics and sufficient articles on logic, mathematics and their meeting-point to suggest that his death at the age of forty-eight may have deprived the College of a respectable scholar of the second rank; and Joseph Johnston was prolific in the field of economics, even if he made few converts to his somewhat heterodox views. E.H. Alton's early articles on the complex question of the text of Ovid's *Fasti* gave promise of a mastery of the subject, but it was a promise not to be fulfilled in his lifetime. But the remainder – W.E. Thrift, Kennedy, Goligher, Fraser, Kelleher, R.M. Gwynn, G.R. Webb, Tate, H. Thrift, Canning, Henry and Godfrey – left behind as their literary monuments only a few scattered articles, some high-class hack-work, or in several cases nothing at all. We have already classified Fraser, Gwynn, Tate, H. Thrift and Henry as not at home in the academic world. Of the others W.E. Thrift, W.A. Goligher, G.R. Webb and F. la T. Godfrey justified themselves to some extent as administrators. Thrift will be mentioned later as Provost. Goligher had the reputation of running the College from about 1933 to 1940, first as Registrar and later as Vice-Provost; certainly he was the first man to bring any sort of order into the Registrar's Office. Webb, had he lived longer, might have made a good Bursar, for he had a keen analytical mind and was not easily mesmerized by tradition; as Junior Bursar his rigid enforcement of the letter of the law created some unnecessary friction with students, but he worked deliberately to rationalize the office out of existence, and on his death in 1929 it was abolished as he would have wished. Godfrey did not believe in such radical changes, but he was an excellent tutor and secretary of innumerable committees; he was, as it were, the skilled mechanic who loved his machine and went round with an oil-can and a spanner making small adjustments as they were needed, but the idea of replacing the machine by a more up-to-date model filled him with horror. Of the others Alton did useful work representing the College first in the Dail and later in the Senate, where his capacity for warm personal friendship helped to break down ideological barriers; William Kennedy was a kindly old man with solid, but conventional culture; Hugh Canning was a very good talker and a popular secretary of the Common Room; Kelleher has left no memory save that of failing to fulfil his initial brilliant promise as a mathematician, for when a mathematician (of all men) dies at forty-two and is still described in his obituary as 'a mathematician of promise' it shows that something has gone wrong.[54]

If we look for an explanation of this paradox of talented and cultured men willing to hand on to posterity so little of their knowledge or insights we must realize that it was not entirely confined to Dublin. The early twentieth century was, *par excellence*, the age of the Oxbridge tutor who, while his pupils droned out their essays on Plato or Ricardo, did little but suck on his pipe, grunt, and eventually decide to award them a mark of beta plus query plus. But they were leavened with an occasional genius and a fair sprinkling of talented writers. Dublin was, in Joyce's phrase, the centre of paralysis. A few contributory factors may be suggested. In the first place 1901–25 probably saw the peak of the social pressure, not merely on students but also on adults up to early middle age, to take part in sport, and later to watch it. Many, therefore, who had little aptitude or liking for it were drawn in to keep up with their friends, so that on certain days Donnybrook Tennis Club or Rathfarnham Golf Club seemed almost like extensions to the Common Room, and the most unlikely of intellectuals would be seen clinging on to the rail of an outside car on his way to a Rugby international. It was at this time too that the advent of the motor car as a normal means of transport made the week-end cottage practicable, as well as demanding many hours of tinkering to keep in running order the temperamental machines of those days. There was also a general feeling that fathers should spend more time with their children than had been usual in the past, and after 1918, with reduced domestic staff, this pressure grew. The cult of fresh air and sunshine was beginning to spread, so that the wife who adjured her husband to 'take his nose out of those frowsty old books' and cut the grass or take the children to the zoo had more moral force at her command than had her predecessor of late Victorian times. And finally, though we may condemn the generation we can excuse the individuals, for neither in their own eyes nor those of their contemporaries was their failure to publish original work a serious charge. Such work was laudable, but it was a work of supererogation; until after 1920 it was held that if a man lectured well, looked after his pupils conscientiously and did his share of minor administrative jobs he was earning his salary. It was realized that if the College were to maintain its renown it must continue to produce some first-class scholars; but it was not the business of anybody in particular to see to this, and meanwhile the temptation to live on capital, as far as reputation was concerned, was considerable. This viewpoint was made more plausible by the fact that during term-time the hours of a tutor-Fellow were fairly well filled by lectures, examinations and tutorial correspondence and interviews; he had a little time and energy to spare for other work, but not much. But even at a generous estimate this took up only half the year; six weeks pure holiday could reasonably be granted, but there remained twenty weeks in the year unaccounted for. Some of it went on exhausting money-making activities such as correcting Intermediate Certificate papers; some on pottering rather inefficiently with small items of College business; but the greater part, apparently, went on pure recreation, which, unless it took a flashy or dissipated form, incurred no censure.

It was not, however, these broad considerations that first brought the problem of the Fellowship examination to the notice of the Board, but a sudden crisis which arose in 1904 and rapidly became worse over the next two or three years. The decision of the Board and Council in 1903 to allow French and German to be substituted for Greek in the Freshman years of the pass course led to a sudden increase in the number of students opting to study French (or, to a much smaller extent, German) at pass level, and this increase was greatly reinforced by the advent of women in 1904, for most of them had learnt no Greek at school. Who was to give all this teaching in French and German? The tutors, of course, said the Board. The tutors demurred; they were under no legal obligation to teach subjects in which they had not been examined. Nevertheless they were prepared to lend a hand, and they agreed that E.J. Gwynn and Macran, who had already a good working knowledge of French and German respectively, should be sent abroad on subsidized leave of absence to brush up their knowledge of the spoken languages. The situation was complicated soon after this by the fact that Selss, the Professor of German, died, and Atkinson, Professor of Romance Languages (who was by then an elderly man) prudently retired; this meant a crisis in the teaching of honor as well as pass students. But they were replaced without delay: Selss by R.A. Williams, probably the best German scholar to hold the chair during the period covered by this history, though not without a touch of the stodginess to which professors of German seem more prone than those of other subjects, and Atkinson by Maurice Gerothwohl, who had been appointed as his assistant the previous year. Gerothwohl can be described either as a cultured and versatile *littérateur* with a cosmopolitan background, or as an adventurer in the academic world who eventually found his proper niche as a journalist.[55] At any rate he filled the gap for a couple of years, and for some time Gwynn and Macran looked after some of the teaching and most of the examining of pass students, aided to some extent by other Fellows such as Smyly, Alton and even Roberts. The arrangement seems very amateurish today, but Macran had taken a good degree in Modern Literature before turning to philosophy, and Gwynn, though his training was in classics and philosophy and his current interest in Old Irish, was a well-read man with an aptitude for languages. All they were expected to do was to instil into their pupils a reasonable vocabulary, a sound knowledge of grammar and an acquaintance with two or three literary classics, and for this their skill was quite adequate. Any deficiencies in their accent or their familiarity with contemporary idiom could be overlooked; those were matters which concerned only honor students.

Meanwhile the Board continued to mull over the problems of bringing the Fellowship examination up to date. All sorts of schemes were suggested: including modern languages as an extra subject;[56] varying the subjects from year to year at the Board's discretion; supplementing the examination with estimates of dissertations submitted; taking performance at Moderatorship into account; instituting probationary Fellowships, of which only a proportion would be confirmed in permanent places; an upper age-limit for candidates (to put an end to an excessive number of attempts); and every possible combination of these proposals. Although some distinction between reformers and conservatives soon became apparent the issue was not fought out on party lines, for every reformer was pushing a different nostrum, and every conservative was prepared to yield on some point. Some rather unexpected difficulties arose. One was the fact that the Board's first set of proposals, giving to themselves power to vary the timing, nature and subject-matter of the examination in accordance with the needs of the College, was decisively rejected by the Junior Fellows, who declared that such discretionary powers might well be given to a Board elected on rational principles, but not to one based on the present anachronistic and oligarchical constitution.[57] Another difficulty lay in the fact that the Fellows, having no first-hand acquaintance with contemporary studies in modern literature or any knowledge of contemporary philological studies of living languages, found it difficult to picture clearly the nature of the examination which was proposed. It gradually became evident, therefore, that it was impossible to graft new subjects on to the old system; either the examination remained unchanged except in small details, or else the whole system was scrapped and a new start made.

The second alternative was eventually adopted, but it needed a further twelve years or so of argument before the College could steel itself to such a drastic change. An even longer period might have been needed had not the advent of war in 1914 on the one hand convinced the doubters that they were indeed launched willy-nilly into a new age, and on the other hand, by giving a good reason for suspending the examination in the interests of fairness to possible candidates who were absent in the trenches or on other forms of war-work, removed the difficulty of the vested interest of candidates who had been preparing for the examination under the old conditions. A further complication arose in a form which often plagues institutions: no sooner had the Board decided that the long queue of candidates and the eventual election of a weary and relatively elderly Fellow was a problem that called for action than the queue melted away, and by 1907 speculation was afoot as to whether 1908 would produce *any* candidates of the requisite calibre. Beare, rationalizing in 1906 his emotional preference for classics and mathematics, had argued that no matter how high a maximum of marks was assigned to modern languages or experimental science[58] there was no assurance that a first-class teacher in either of these subjects would come forward. He overlooked the fact that the corresponding assurance with respect to classics and mathematics was not entirely well founded. Moreover, the Board's hasty, and at times perhaps rather blundering attempts to solve the short-term problem met with little sympathy from the Visitor (D.H. Madden), who twice declined to sign a decree sent up to him, because he held that the proposals for patchwork reform were in certain respects ambiguous or inequitable.

It followed, therefore, that when the time came for the drafting of the

King's Letter of 1911, the changes that had been agreed on were small. External examiners could be appointed for the Fellowship examination; the Board (with the Visitors' consent) could omit the examination in any year on giving due notice, or decline to elect if insufficient merit had been shown; and, more important perhaps, the Board could, with the assent of a majority of the Fellows, elect a Professor to Fellowship without examination. None of these powers was exercised for four years, but in 1915 the Board declared that there would be no Fellowship examination in 1916 (and followed this up with similar declarations for the years 1917–19), and in 1918 they proposed to elect Bastable and Joly to Fellowship, as representing the most distinguished of the non-Fellow Professors in the humanities and science respectively. Joly accepted, and was duly elected; Bastable refused, presumably from a feeling of injured pride and a reluctance (which Joly was big enough to overcome) to see his name at the bottom of a list of men by many years his junior.

(xiii)

In the midst of all the *Sturm und Drang* of these external and constitutional campaigns and disputes the provostship of Traill saw also a considerable amount of quiet and normal academic development. The most important element in this was the improvement of the sadly inadequate laboratory facilities for the sciences.

Between 1860 and 1900 the intellectual prestige of the experimental and natural sciences had increased enormously. Darwin had provided a theoretical framework to which the collection of isolated facts of almost any kind from the immense diversity of the organic world could claim to be relevant; the discovery of the aniline dyes had given a tremendous boost to organic chemistry, both in its pure and its applied aspects; and the discovery of radium and the first steps taken at Cambridge to reveal the structure of the atom had changed physics from one of the more dreary to one of the most exciting of the sciences. This naturally led to a demand for the provision of more extensive laboratory facilities in the universities. They were demanded alike for teaching and for research, and they needed new apparatus to fill them (the microscope of 1875, for example, was sadly out of date by 1900) and new staff, both academic and technical, to teach and to look after the increasing flow of students. The institutions which were at this time developing into the first of the English redbrick universities had for the most part started from a technological base, so that scientific facilities were given a high priority in the carve-up of public funds and of industrial donations on which they largely subsisted. At Oxford and Cambridge private bene-

factors, with Cavendish and the Clarendon trustees in the lead, helped
to get things going in a way that the colleges, left to themselves, would
never have done. Trinity, it would seem, had none of these resources at
its disposal, and in consequence a rather severe crisis was looming by
1900. It is true that by devoting to scientific development a thousand or
two in any year in which the accounts showed a surplus some small-
scale relief for the congestion and lack of equipment was obtained, but
this was devoted mainly to the Medical School, where there was a
widely admired asset to be saved, whereas in pure science there was
merely a new field, not highly esteemed by all, to be developed.

The first step in what was to develop into a large-scale campaign to
remedy this deficiency was a small committee appointed by the Board
in 1899 to investigate the possibility of widening the course in
Engineering by adding some instruction in the electrical and mechanical aspects of the subject. Professor Alexander was not interested in
developing the school in this direction, and the driving force was
obviously Traill, who had played a large part in his brother's project of
launching the first electric passenger tramway in the British Isles. It ran
from Bushmills (the village nearest the Traill family seat) to Portrush,
the nearest town, and for over sixty years it was a popular feature of the
north Antrim coast and paid its way. Traill rightly enough saw that
there was a big future in electrical engineering; the problem was
whether the College could afford the plant needed to teach it. Fitzgerald
supported the idea enthusiastically, and since, as we have seen, he was
a passionate advocate of the promotion of education in all branches
of science, he secured the enlargement of the committee by including
the Professors of Engineering, Chemistry, Botany, Zoology, Geology,
Anatomy and Physiology, together with some of their assistants, and
Mahaffy (representing the Board) as chairman. The committee reported
not only within its original terms of reference, but on the general
question of what was needed for the promotion of efficient teaching
and research in all the scientific departments. It found that Anatomy,
Chemistry and Pathology were reasonably provided for as regards
space and equipment (though each had a small deficiency which called
for attention); that Physiology, Geology and Zoology were accommodated in severely cramped quarters and under-equipped, while
Physics and Botany were working under conditions which could only
be described as makeshift and quite unworthy of the University. All
departments required further junior staff and technical assistance. The
minimum sum needed to put things right was £57,000 for capital
expenditure and an endowment sufficient to yield £4,000 a year.

To the Board, accustomed to think in terms of hundreds of pounds,
this response to a modest inquiry about electrical engineering seemed

25 Thomas Thompson Gray. Fellow, 1862–1924. (Sir William Orpen, Friendly Brothers' House, Dublin.)

to lie completely in the realm of fantasy, especially as it had provided over the past three years, in a period of declining income from fees, some £9,000 for the building and equipment of a pathological laboratory. It contented itself, however, by asking the committee to reconsider its figures with a view to making all possible economies, and to separate the expenses necessary for the immediate teaching of students from those proposed for 'mere research'.

The word 'mere' (which was probably put in by Salmon, whose

educational views, despite his own reputation as a scholar, lay closer to Jowett's than to those of Mark Pattison) was not calculated to produce a conciliatory reply from scientists, least of all from Fitzgerald, and it did not do so. Fitzgerald's reply was to revise his figure upwards, to insist that no sum less than £250,000 would suffice to ensure that the University should remain in the first rank as far as science was concerned, and that the Board should not be content with anything less until it had tried for this sum and failed. His attitude, unrealistic though it might be, at least encouraged his colleagues to lift their sights higher than they might otherwise have done. Most of them, however, thinking that a fraction of a loaf now was better than the starvation to be endured before Fitzgerald's dream could be realized, consented to draw up a list of priorities in financial terms which, though still far beyond the means of the College itself, were much more modest.

At this stage the situation was transformed by Fitzgerald's sudden and premature death early in 1901. Naturally enough it was proposed that his work and aspirations should be perpetuated by a memorial, and that this should take the form of what was dearest to his heart – the encouragement of research in physics. For a while this project became confused with the larger scheme, but as experience had shown that funds subscribed as memorials to even the most popular or respected of Fellows had never been large, the two were prudently separated. Some £1,600 was, in fact, subscribed for the Fitzgerald memorial, and this was enough to endow a modest scholarship in physics, sufficient, at any rate, to enable a student to spend a year in post-graduate research if he had a foundation Scholarship or some other support to supplement it. It obviously did not touch the real problem.

The leadership of the campaign for scientific expansion passed naturally to John Joly, who, if he lacked some of Fitzgerald's fire, had a sounder judgment and a more even temper. He was a remarkable man: certainly the most versatile and productive, and perhaps the greatest of the scientists that the College has ever produced. He had been elected to the chair of Geology in 1897, though he was equally well fitted to have been a Professor of Physics or of Engineering. In his younger days he had much of the appearance of a professor in a comic strip, with his unstable-looking pince-nez and his motor-bicycle festooned with home-made gadgets. But he was, in fact, a man of cosmopolitan culture and of shrewd business sense; he was a good committee man and mediator, and although devoted to the advancement of physical science did not despise the other departments of College or unduly ruffle the susceptibilities of his colleagues in the humanities. He was a man of extremely ingenious and inventive mind who kept tossing off

26   John Joly. Professor of Geology, 1897–1933.

ideas, of which the majority were well-founded, but he tended to leave
the elaboration of them to others. He had, perhaps, more in common
with Edison than with Einstein. In his young days he invented several
simple, but very effective and useful, instruments, such as the meldo-
meter and the steam calorimeter, and his stream of inventions never
dried up; in later years they related mainly to navigation, and during
the war of 1914–18 he bombarded a mainly unresponsive Admiralty

with a long series of proposals for the detection of submarines and many other purposes. As early as 1896 he had devised and brought to a high level of efficiency a system of colour photography, and although later developments were based on a different principle from Joly's he undoubtedly stimulated research in the subject, and those of his photographs which survive today, if a little coarse in grain, are as true in the reproduction of tone as many modern examples. Although he left it to H.H. Dixon to work out all the details and the implications for the living plant, he was probably the principal originator of the basic idea of the Dixon-Joly theory of the ascent of sap (now universally accepted), namely the cohesive strength of water. His estimate of the age of the oceans based on measuring the rate at which salt was fed into them by the rivers is still quoted in the textbooks, though the figure has had to be drastically revised. He was quick to seize on the many implications involved in the discovery of radioactivity, and not only did he collaborate with medical colleagues in devising radium needles which enabled a controlled dosage of radiation to be diffused through a considerable body of tissue, but he also recognized that thorium was as important as radium in releasing energy in the earth's crust, and that this energy, released as heat, must eventually melt the deeper layers of the earth's crust, allowing the lighter continents to float freely for a while until the escape of heat from the underlying basalt froze it into solidity again. This theory of thermal cycles, elaborated in his *Surface history of the earth* (Oxford 1925), did not escape criticism, but, suitably modified, it served as the starting-point for the modern revival of theories of continental drift.[59]

Well-suited though he was to lead the renewed campaign for putting science on a sound basis in Trinity, Joly might not have achieved much if he had not found a powerful ally in Lord Rosse, Chancellor of the University, who was both an important figure in Irish public life and also an astronomer of considerable repute. The events of the past twenty years had made him desert the liberal traditions of his family for a pessimistic and disillusioned Toryism; he was prepared to describe Lord Salisbury's government as 'republican' because it had passed the Local Government Act of 1898, and regretted that the Balfour brothers had apparently set their hearts 'on making friends with the Nationalist ecclesiastics'.[60] He felt, therefore that there was no hope of any help from the Government, and not very much from the (as he saw them) impoverished and discouraged Protestants of Ireland. Nevertheless he agreed to do what he could, and in 1903 the committee, under his guidance, decided to launch a public appeal. The College, in the meanwhile, had managed from its own resources to find a solution for the *fons et origo* of the whole campaign by building on the north side of the College Park a somewhat bleak but adequate building in which elementary tuition in mechanical and electrical engineering could be given; it had also made small improvements in the physiological and pathological laboratories. The committee therefore framed its appeal as a request for funds to provide Physics, Botany and Geology with at least such accommodation and facilities as would give the University a chance to hold its own in these subjects. It was estimated that £34,000 was needed for capital expenditure, and an endowment sufficient to give an annual income of £2,730. The chances of success seemed minimal, but just as the appeal was launched a good fairy appeared unexpectedly from the wings. Lord Iveagh, chairman of Guinness's brewery and one of the richest men in Ireland, who had already shown himself to be a generous and discriminating philanthropist, had been approached by Lord Rosse, and came forward with an offer to meet the capital costs if the appeal for endowment were successful. This gave the appeal the necessary impetus, and a sum of £19,000 came in.[61] Although this was very far short of the target it was decided that it would suffice to pay the running costs of a Physical and a Botanical Laboratory, and Iveagh, overlooking the somewhat sympathetic accountancy by which these conclusions had been reached, made over £24,000 for the erection of the buildings. They were sited in the northeast corner of the College Park, and both served their purposes well for half a century, till expansion in numbers of staff and students made them too small, though the lecture theatre in the School of Botany still remains after seventy-five years by far the best medium-sized theatre in the College. Sadly for Joly, Geology, which was given the lowest priority because it already had tolerable accommodation in the Museum Building, got nothing, but a few years later, thanks to some tactful diplomacy by Williamson and his friend Lord Rathmore, Iveagh agreed to hand over the remaining £10,000 of his original guarantee to pay for apparatus and assistants to promote Joly's researches in geology.[62]

(xiv)

Development in other academic disciplines was fortunately not so immediately dependent on large sums of money, though the small margin in the annual accounts of most years meant that even the two or three hundred pounds a year required to bring up the salaries of some of the Professorships to a living wage could not always be found – or at least was represented as a preposterous extravagance by those members of the Board who were suspicious of any development of peripheral subjects. This especially affected Modern History. From 1860 to

1903 the College had been well enough served by Barlow and Bury, who were Fellows and were therefore content to lecture for an extra pittance on a subject in which they had a real interest. But when Bury resigned there was no Fellow who could be considered competent to replace him, and the Council had to advertise the chair as an obviously part-time post on a very meagre salary. The successful applicant was J.H. Wardell, who already held the chair of Economics at Galway, but as History and Economics were still bound together in Trinity, along with Political Science, in a joint Moderatorship course,[63] this was, if anything, a recommendation. With his two chairs and some odds and ends of other work in Trinity he managed to patch together enough money to live on, but in his evidence before the Fry Commission he made an eloquent case for better treatment of the subject. He was a vigorous young man who had graduated in Modern History with a gold medal only four years earlier. His main interest was in military history, but he broke new ground by lecturing on Irish history, a topic whose complete neglect by the College hitherto had been the subject of much barbed comment in the evidence given before the Fry Commission. Barlow doubtless took refuge behind the principle which he had enunciated in 1873[64] that a lecture on modern Irish history must be regarded as an extremely hazardous undertaking; and Bury, whose active interest in Irish history was confined to the fifth century, was probably content to adopt the course as he found it. Wardell's campaign for the better recognition of his subject was successful in two respects: a post of assistant to the Professor was established, and the honor course in History was extended backwards into the Freshman years, so as to cover four years instead of two. The first assistant was H. L. Murphy, who later turned to the law, but his abilities as a historian can be deduced from his study of the early years of the College, written at this time, although it was not published until 1951. His successor in the assistantship was Constantia Maxwell, the first woman to be appointed to an academic post, who made her career in the College and was eventually given a personal chair in 1939. Unfortunately Wardell suffered a severe breakdown in 1910, and never recovered sufficiently to resume his duties. He was replaced by Weaver, an Oxford man, who returned to Oxford, however, three years later, to end his career as President of Trinity College. Weaver's successor in the chair was Edmund Curtis, who was to become a devoted student of medieval Irish history, and who brought to the school – albeit at the cost of a certain dryness – a severe professionalism which it had hitherto lacked. Meanwhile, however, there had been an unexpected windfall. Lecky's widow, who died in 1912, left to the College a substantial sum to endow a new chair in Modern History, which should bear her husband's name. The first Lecky Professor was appointed in 1914; he was Walter Alison Phillips, who formed a good complement to Curtis, as his interests lay mainly in recent European history. If some of his writings can be categorized as high-class journalism, he was undoubtedly a stylist. Widely travelled and well read in French and German, his outlook was in many ways international, but he did not extend his catholicity in this respect to Ireland; he remained the undisguised and unashamed Englishman doing a job in a foreign land, and spending in Dublin only the minimum period needed for his lectures and examinations.

Within ten years, then, Modern History had been transformed from the stepchild of the humanities into an effective school with three well-qualified, full-time teachers. An attempt was made to do something of the same kind for Law, but it was much less successful. Around 1900, whereas the Divinity School (which could boast of eminent scholars even among its part-time teachers)[65] and the Medical School (where Cunningham and J.M. Purser were still active) could challenge comparison with those of any other university, the Law School made a sad and sorry third, and was often the target of well-justified criticism. We have already mentioned Leech, the Regius Professor, who spent two-thirds of his time in an administrative post unconnected with the University, and Hart, the Regius Professor of Feudal and English Law, who never pretended to be anything more than an efficient barrister lecturing on the practical aspects of law, especially in relation to property, as it was met with in the courts. A third chair, of Jurisprudence and International Law, had been created in 1877, and it was to this chair that Leech had first been appointed, but when Webb finally departed to take up his post as County Court Judge Leech succeeded him as Regius Professor and the other chair was allowed to lapse. The staff included also the Reid Professor, who was concerned mainly with criminal law, but this was a post to which the professorial title had been riveted by a legal accident, and was held for a period of five years by a young barrister who wanted to make a name for himself and to earn two or three hundred pounds at a time when the briefs might still be slow in coming in.

The obvious defect of this structure was that there was no full-time teacher, and that all teaching was delivered from a practical angle: the school trained lawyers, not jurists. In 1901 the Board appointed a committee to report on the school; it consisted of two judges, a chancery lawyer, a Senior and a Junior Fellow, and the two senior Professors of Law. The committee found that the teaching was too restricted and elementary; that the school should, in addition to training barristers, contribute to the general educational system of the University;

that the scientific and historical aspects of the subject should receive more attention; and that a Moderatorship in Legal and Political Science should be instituted. Needless to say the Professors dissented from this report, and Leech elaborated his dissent in a 8,000-word memorandum. But the new moderatorship was nevertheless set up without delay, and to provide some teaching in the more theoretical aspects of legal science the chair of Civil Law and General Jurisprudence was revived and given to Bastable, who was already Professor of Jurisprudence in Galway as well as Professor of Political Economy in Dublin. For a few months he had the distinction of holding three professorships, but he soon resigned from the Galway post. Although he was interested in jurisprudence, and doubtless delivered some good lectures on the subject, he never published anything on it, his interest in economics being far stronger, and he must be reckoned as one more part-timer as far as the School of Law was concerned.

In 1908 Leech resigned and Bastable succeeded to the Regius Professorship. The chair of Jurisprudence and International Law lapsed once more, but almost at once arose, phoenix-like, with a new title, the Chair of Civil Law and General Jurisprudence,. The new Professor, J.S. Baxter, was a Belfast man, and since 1900 he had held the chair of English Law in Belfast. Next year the pack was shuffled once more in consequence of Hart's resignation. Baxter moved to Hart's chair, and held it for twenty-four years along with his Belfast post, so that the Great Northern Railway must have seen almost as much of him as either of the universities at which he taught between train journeys. He was an industrious man, but thoroughly down-to-earth, and his editorial work and occasional articles represented no break in the traditions of the school. The Professorship of Civil Law and General Jurisprudence was given to Charles Maturin, a member of the Irish Bar esteemed for his good conversation and his great knowledge of international law. But he had apparently no desire to put this knowledge to any use, either in the courts or in publications. When he died in 1915 his chair was allowed to lapse, so that all the general post in chairs and the juggling around with high-sounding titles left the school in 1915 in much the same position as it had been in 1900, save only that there was a moderatorship in the subject, and that Bastable made a more responsible and erudite head than Leech. The moral – that no serious improvement could be achieved until a full-time academic teacher was appointed – was not taken to heart until 1935.

(xv)

The other academic developments during this period can be dealt with more briefly. In 1907 a Moderatorship in Celtic languages was instituted, thanks partly to E.J. Gwynn's enthusiasm for the subject and partly as a reply to the criticisms voiced before the Fry Commission of the College's neglect of the Irish language. It was viewed with suspicion by some; Dowden and Mahaffy voted against it on the Council, and in 1914 Gray proposed that it be abolished, or at least merged with the Moderatorship in Modern Languages. Gwynn made a crushing reply, and no more was heard of Gray's proposal. The course, which was a fairly stiff one, comprising Welsh as well as Old, Middle and Modern Irish, never attracted many students, but it has provided over the years a nucleus around which could develop a continuous tradition of serious scholarship in Celtic philology.

Although it was short-lived another and very different school set up during Traill's provostship deserves mention. This was the Army School. In 1901 a committee of the War Office sent out feelers to the universities about courses designed to fit students to be commissioned in the Army. Mahaffy replied with even more than his usual exuberance that the B.A. degree of Dublin gave 'a complete general education for the Army'; the College could, if required provide instruction in military subjects, and 'we have all the necessary games, cricket and football and all that sort of thing . . . we could train them not only in military riding but to follow the hounds.'[66] But his vision of himself as Hely-Hutchinson *redivivus* gave way to a more prosaic curriculum. The Army School, set up in 1904, gave instruction in tactics, strategy, military history, engineering and military law, and those who passed an examination on this course were eligible for commissions. A few years later an Officers Training Corps was set up and, providing as it did an atmosphere much like that of an athletic club with the additional panoply of uniforms and a pipe-and-drum band, proved very popular, even with many who did not envisage for themselves a military career. But *dis aliter visum*, and in 1914 the Corps fulfilled its grimmer purpose.

The Army School stood outside the range of normal academic studies, but its justification was clear enough. During the earlier years of the twentieth century the College experimented with teaching in subjects which the more conservative members of the Board viewed with suspicion as based on ephemeral enthusiasms – 'trendy' they would have called them had the word been invented. These comprised agriculture, commerce and education.

The lack of an agricultural school had been prominent among the charges brought against Trinity in 1906 by those critics who complained of the irrelevance of its curriculum to the practical needs of Ireland, and as Cambridge and Reading had already started courses and Oxford was just about to do so, the Board rather hastily fudged up a course which was to lead to a diploma, though if it was combined with the B.A. course a degree of Bachelor in Agriculture could be conferred. The first year was devoted to elementary science, and the second to its applications in agriculture. Students were to spend part of each vacation living and working on a large farm in Co. Meath owned by W.A. Barnes, a contemporary and friend of Provost Traill; in return for looking after them he was, probably rather to his surprise, given in his middle sixties the title of Professor of Agriculture. For six years this modest structure jolted along, attracting one or two students each year, but with Barnes's death in 1912 it collapsed. A rescue operation was organized in conjunction with the College of Science, whereby the basic science, combined with the Freshman course in Arts, was spread over two years; after Little-go the student migrated to the College of Science for his more technical instruction. But if he managed at the same time to pursue the Sophister Arts course in Trinity (abbreviated by 'professional privileges', as for medical students) he emerged with his B.Agr.Sci. as well as his B.A. The professional instruction was better organized than under Barnes, but the course still attracted very few pupils, although it carried on in the same form until 1968 (University College, Dublin, replacing the College of Science after 1926). The School of Agriculture, however, received support in 1914 from one unexpected quarter. Writing to Alton about the prospects of the college during the war, George Wilkins (p. 303), who was not normally sympathetic to educational experiments, said:

the number of pupils entering [the College] will probably be few, therefore it is most desirable to whip up any boys who show any inclination whatsoever for a college career. It might be possible to attract some *dunderheads* who are fit for neither classics or mathematics to the Agricultural School and so to college and thus prevent them rotting idly through the country or graduating in a taproom ... Schoolmasters are always burdened with *healthy boys who are fit for nothing*, to occupy whom carpentry was introduced.[67]

So much for vocational education.

The diploma in commerce, set up at about the same time as that in agriculture did not prove any more popular, but was less embarrassing to the College, for it consisted solely of an examination, for which candidates had to prepare themselves by private reading. The course was a wide one and the recommended books well selected, but although it lingered on until 1939, during its life of thirty-three years only fifty-three diplomas were granted.

The courses in Agriculture and Commerce were instituted primarily as a response to outside pressure, and pressure not merely from outside the College, but outside the world from which it drew its students. Protestants, even of the lower middle class, who wanted their sons to farm or to go into business did not expect them to gain the necessary expertise at a university; they would get it on the farm or behind the counter. If they sent them to a university it was to train them for a profession, or to give them some polish and the chance of making the right kind of friend. For this reason the courses failed. The School of Education, however, was even in its early days (when to some it looked just as sickly a plant as the other two) sustained by enthusiasm from within the walls. We have already seen how George Fitzgerald repeatedly pleaded its cause at the University Council, and soon after Culverwell's appointment as Professor, Education was introduced as a subject in the pass course. But when Culverwell resigned the chair on co-option to a Senior Fellowship in 1915 the Council decided not to fill it at once. A minority wanted to take advantage of the vacancy to wind up the subject, but a compromise was agreed on whereby Education was taught for only four instead of six terms in the Arts course, the diploma was maintained, and J.M. Henry, who had dabbled in educational theory perhaps rather more deeply than in some of his other subjects, was appointed to run the School temporarily as lecturer. It was not until the chair had been filled by the appointment of R.J. Fynne in 1922 that it began on a further course of expansion.

One further academic development of a very different kind requires brief notice. On the dissolution of the Royal University in 1908 one of its constituent colleges was left stranded. This was Magee College, Londonderry, which trained students for the Presbyterian ministry, but also provided teaching in a limited number of arts subjects to students who were mainly but not exclusively Presbyterian. In 1909 an arrangement was come to whereby students who had kept their first two years at Magee could, if they attended lectures in Trinity for one term of their Junior Sophister year and all three terms of their Senior Sophister year, present themselves at the degree examination and qualify for a Dublin B.A. The students from Magee formed an industrious, if inconspicuous and for the most part unexciting addition to College life, but they gave to Trinity a more intimate contact with the Presbyterian world of Ulster than it would otherwise have had. The arrangement which, at first confined to pass degrees, was later extended to moderatorship in certain subjects, lasted until 1968, when Magee College was, somewhat reluctantly, taken under the wing of the New University of Ulster. The chief criticism that can be made of the scheme is that, just about the time when the 'steamboat man', who kept all his terms by examination and not by lectures, was heading for extinction, it revived in a different form the doubt as to just how much contact with the cobble-stones of the Front Square of Trinity College was implied by the letters B.A. (*Dubl.*).

To say that the war of 1914–18 took most of Europe by surprise is a commonplace. In Dublin, as elsewhere, the events in Sarajevo had little immediate impact, but this was largely because there was plenty to worry about nearer home. The Home Rule Bill was looming; volunteers were arming both in north and south; the Curragh 'mutiny' put a large question mark over the Government's intentions; blood had been spilt on Bachelor's Walk; and the great lock-out of 1913 had left a bitter aftermath.

Although many of its members must have been worried as individuals, the College did not in its official capacity react to the third Home Rule Bill as strongly as it had to the first and second, perhaps because it was generally felt that the Ulster resistance was strong enough to force a last-minute reprieve. But it had to be prepared for the worst, and the worst was seen as a hostile Dublin parliament, which would have scant respect for the constitution and the property of Trinity College. A meeting of Fellows and Professors pressed successfully on the Government an amendment to the Home Rule Bill, specifying that the property and constitution of the College should not be interfered with without its consent. The attitude of the Free State Government after 1921 could be cited as showing that these fears were groundless, but the tolerance and understanding shown to a weak minority in 1921 might not have been extended to a much stronger one in 1914.

The labour disputes touched the College less closely; only R.M. Gwynn, now a Fellow of some seven years' standing, played a prominent part. He showed great sympathy with the workers' claims, though he did not behave like the political priest of today, for he rejected the concept of class war and was always conciliatory in his tone. A 'peace committee' of which he was a prominent member, developed (some say in Gwynn's rooms in college) into the Citizen Army. Gwynn's support of the 'army' concept was based simply on the idea that military-style discipline would keep unemployed men fit and give them self-respect. *Sancta simplicitas*! The Citizen Army under James Conolly was second only to Pearse's Volunteers in leading the insurrection[68] in 1916. On one occasion, however, the students became involved in the politics of the labour dispute. In November 1913, at a meeting of the College Gaelic Society, one of the speakers was Captain White, an eccentric Ulster Home Ruler, who tended to become a hanger-on of whatever extreme movement took his fancy. In an almost uncanny foreshadowing of Mr Tariq Ali he urged the students to strike: to tell their professors to close the College as they had more important duties elsewhere. He ended by urging them to attend a meeting at the Antient Concert Rooms on the following night, when the conduct of the police was to be discussed. Had there been no follow-up a dozen students might have attended, but Provost Traill, who was by now an ailing man and had less than a year to live, allowed his political sympathies to override his common sense and let it be known that any resident student who attended the meeting would lose his rooms. The result was that a hundred students marched to the meeting in procession, mocking the Provost by singing a ditty of the day of which the refrain was 'Oh, oh Antonio!' Having let off steam in this way they returned contentedly to bourgeois life in College.[69]

In 1913 Williamson, by now eighty-five and beginning to fail, stung by the criticism of an outspoken Junior Fellow, made history by resigning the Vice-Provostship but remaining a Senior Fellow. Whereupon Traill also made history by passing over not only the next senior (Abbott, who was virtually on his death-bed) but also Gray, who had not yet been forgiven for bringing the College into the courts in 1911. Next in order came Mahaffy, and it was he who was appointed Vice-Provost.[70] Not long afterwards Traill's health began to go from bad to worse, so that Mahaffy had in practice most of the powers of the Provost throughout 1914. On one occasion his exercise of them was rather maladroit. Very shortly after Traill's death, when the Provostship was still vacant, the College Gaelic Society made itself troublesome once more by inviting Patrick Pearse to speak at its inaugural meeting. It was a natural enough thing to do, but by this time Pearse was no longer simply an educationalist and a Gaelic Leaguer; he had become an active politician and was busy making anti-recruiting speeches. It was an activity which lay rather on the border-line between the exercise of democratic rights and the giving of comfort to the King's enemies. As he had not been charged with any offence he might have been given the benefit of the doubt, but Mahaffy's anti-Gaelic prejudice was too strong to allow this, and he forbade Pearse to speak within the walls. The meeting was held elsewhere, and the matter might have soon been forgotten, had not Mahaffy, in a characteristic flourish, referred in his letter to the Society to 'a man called Pearse'. Pearse was not, of course, at that time the household word he was later to become, but Mahaffy must have known his name and something about him, and this needless piece of contempt for the sake of rhetoric was not quickly forgotten.

When Traill died in October 1914 there was little doubt as to who should succeed him. Mahaffy, though seventy-five, was still vigorous, and there was nobody among the Senior Fellows, or even among the more senior of the Junior Fellows, who could be seriously represented as likely to make a better Provost. The earlier objection to his appointment (his 'unsoundness' on the Irish University Question) was now irrelevant; his capacity for giving needless offence, though it had not vanished, had diminished with the years; and most people thought that, having purged his contempt by ten years' service under Traill, he deserved the final accolade. And it is as Provost that he survives in the communal memory of the College, although he was to fill the post for only four and a half years.

It was, of course, his tragedy (nemesis if you like) that his opportunities as Provost were severely curtailed, not only by old age, but even more by the stringencies of wartime. He was appointed three months after the outbreak of war; he survived to see the Armistice, but not the Peace Treaty. During his provostship all the big dinners and other major festivities of College were suspended; in the years 1915–18 only six honorary degrees were conferred; academic development was arrested, and in many schools the teaching took on a utilitarian flavour dictated by the necessities of war; sheep were pastured on the football field and part of the College Park was dug up and planted in potatoes; and gradually but steadily the student numbers dropped. Although the depopulation of the College squares tends to be somewhat exaggerated in reminiscences of the period, the number of students on the books fell from over 1,250 in 1914 to scarcely over 700 in the last year or two of the war. In all, 869 students interrupted or terminated their university course to join the forces; and a large number of potential students never reached the College at all. There were gaps also in the teaching staff. Three of the Junior Fellows (Luce, Godfrey and Stewart) fought in France, Luce, despite his orders, disdaining the role of chaplain and insisting on membership of the combatant forces, and O'Sullivan helped with the organization of medical services in the Mediterranean. Several other junior members of the academic and administrative staffs went to civil service posts in England, and many of the staff who remained in Dublin spent much of their time on war-work of one kind or another, Joly, for example, having organized the use of the Engineering workshops for the manufacture of munitions during the vacations, braved the Atlantic crossing in 1918 as a member of the Balfour mission to the United States. Early in October 1918, when victory and peace were in sight, it seemed that all these men would return, but by a cruel blow of fate two of them lost their lives within a month of the Armistice. Sir William Thompson, who had come from Belfast in 1902 to succeed J.M. Purser as Professor of Physiology, and had made a considerable name for himself in the field of digestion, nutrition and dietetics, crossed frequently to London in his capacity as scientific adviser to the Ministry of Food, but his last crossing was on the *Leinster*, which was torpedoed on 11 October 1918. Less than three weeks later came the news of Stewart's death in action in France.

Apart from the casualty lists the immediate impact of the war was not so inescapable in Ireland as it was in England. There were no Zeppelin raids, no invasion scares, and rationing was less severe; conscription was threatened, but never enforced. But for a week in 1916 Dublin experienced a short-lived and localized but alarming civil war. Whether the Volunteers had intended to make Trinity one of their strong points is extremely doubtful, for its excellent strategic position would have been seriously offset by the resistance to be expected from its occupants. But the shutting of the gates and the manning of the perimeter by the Officers Training Corps were obvious and necessary precautions before regular troops arrived after two days' fighting. The story of life in the College during that week has often been told, most vividly by John Joly.[71] An attempt was made to keep the academic machine going, and it was only when candidates emerging from an examination found that they had to pick their way down the steps over the bodies of sleeping soldiers that the Provost, having given them lunch, declared the rest of the examination suspended. Opinion in College was of course entirely against the insurgents (as was, at first, the opinion of most of the population of Dublin), and all its members did what they could to help the forces of the Crown in bringing it to a rapid end. But the general opinion among the students was well summed up in an editorial in *T.C.D.*[72] by T.C. Kingsmill Moore (later a judge of the Supreme Court and for many years Visitor of the College and University). 'Trinity College, true to her traditions, has played a worthy, if an unacceptable part. To be called upon to defend our University against the attack of Irishmen, to be forced in self-defence to shoot down our countrymen – these are things which even the knowledge of duty well fulfilled cannot render anything but sad and distasteful.' The attitude of many of the seniors may have been somewhat sterner, but it was from the Archbishop's Palace and not from the Provost's House that there went out the call for swift retributive justice untempered by mercy.[73]

Throughout all these trials and handicaps Mahaffy did his best to keep the flag of culture and scholarship flying, and to make the College as pleasant a place as circumstances would permit. He entertained generously, if plainly, and he was always available to welcome a member of the College back on leave. He invited the abortive Convention of 1917 to meet in the College, and played a prominent, if not entirely judicious part in its proceedings. Since the College silver could not be used for dinners, Mahaffy had it catalogued, and brought out a handsome illustrated volume based on the catalogue with much historical information added by himself. He would not have been Mahaffy if he had not made a number of unauthorized changes in the catalogue in defence of a highly idiosyncratic explanation of the historical problems presented by some of the cups. Up to his death he was writing notes on byways of College history, diversified by a paper on the introduction of the ass into Ireland. He exercised steady and effective pressure on the Fellows to bring their endless discussions on the best procedure for Fellowship elections to an end, and to agree on something; this led to the effective ordinances of 1919 and 1920 which will be examined in the next chapter. When he died in April 1919, a few months after his eightieth birthday, he may be said to have earned in his smaller sphere the epitaph that Pope John III had inscribed for himself in the Church of the Holy Apostles in Rome, which he had built while the Lombards were ravaging the surrounding country:

> Largior exsistens angusto in tempore praesul
> Despexit mundo deficiente premi.[74]

13

Low profile

1919–1947

(i)

When Mahaffy died Lloyd George was hard at work peace-making in Paris, and the selection of the new Provost devolved on Bonar Law. The field was not at first sight promising. Among the Senior Fellows Gray and Tarleton were too old; O'Sullivan was too indolent and absent-minded; Culverwell was too full of notions; Roberts was lacking in drive and lived too much in the past; and Cathcart was too reactionary and cantankerous. This left only Louis Claude Purser, scholarly, gentle, loyal and conscientious, and without an enemy in the College. But as an administrator he was incapable of delegation, and he hated and feared responsibility. As Vice-Provost a few years later he fretted and worried on the few occasions when he had to act for the Provost; as Provost he would have been miserable, and for that reason ineffective, so that it was only temporarily and most reluctantly that he allowed his name to be mentioned as a candidate.[1] Nor was there any obvious talent in the upper ranks of the Junior Fellows. At the bottom of the list, however, stood the name of John Joly, who had been elected to Fellowship only a few months earlier in a tardy response by the Board to the powers granted it in 1911 to elect any Professor to a Fellowship. He was distinguished as a scientist; he was no stranger to public affairs; as a reformer he tempered zeal with discretion; and he was well liked by most of his colleagues. A few of the other scientific Professors, headed by his devoted friend and disciple, H.H. Dixon, organized a campaign on his behalf, but although Joly would probably have made a good Provost they won few converts. Most of the Fellows were not yet used to regarding as one of themselves a man who had so often acted as the spokesman of the non-Fellow Professors, and several of the teachers in the humanities were afraid that Joly's enthusiasm for science would make him a biased partisan in the allocation of the College's resources.

If one turned to the ex-Fellows the only possible name was that of Bernard. Fifteen years earlier he had been for a while the favourite

423

runner, only ousted by Traill at the last moment (p. 358), and in 1919 he was still in the prime of life. But the Bernard of 1919 was very different from the Bernard of 1892 whom we sketched on pp. 307–8. The eager, intellectual divine and the keen but conciliatory reformer had now become Archbishop of Dublin, Privy Councillor, and joint leader with Lord Midleton of the more realistic wing of the southern Unionists. The slim and handsome young man had become a solid and somewhat stony-faced prelate. That he should have gained weight in the figurative as well as in the literal sense was natural enough. But he had also gained what is a synonym in the literal but not in the figurative sense – heaviness; and with heaviness of touch and manner went a hardness which made him more respected than loved. It was he who as President had pressed strongly and successfully for the expulsion from the Royal Irish Academy of Eoin MacNeill in 1916;[2] and it was he who, in the letter to *The Times* mentioned on p. 553, had called on the Government for stern punishment, untempered by mercy, for those who had taken part in the insurrection. But there was a widespread feeling that Trinity needed a strong man to see it through the difficult days which lay ahead, and Bernard certainly was strong. Bonar Law was more likely to be impressed by Bernard's qualities than by his defects, and when his name was recommended by James Campbell (later Lord Glenavy), M.P. for the University, and supported by Sir Edward Carson and Lord Iveagh,[3] Law did not hesitate for long.

Numerous Provosts up to 1831 had left the Provost's House for the episcopal Bench, and there was a widespread feeling that there was something preposterous in a journey in the opposite direction. There were several churchmen, including Gregg, who was very soon to become Archbishop of Dublin himself, who thought that to forsake the pastoral office for a secular one was a profanation of episcopal orders. Others, more cynically, pointed out that times had changed; episcopal salaries had gone down since 1831 but the Provost's salary had not. It was an ill-founded jibe, as Bernard was never an avaricious man; he may have been hungry for power, but not for money. At all events he accepted the nomination, and was admitted as Provost just before Trinity Sunday, 1919.

The appointment was received in College without great enthusiasm; before long it was clear that although he was given a somewhat grudging respect he was not going to be a generally popular Provost, and although he had his defenders he disappointed many, not least his closest friends and former admirers.[4] Bernard was a perfectionist, reluctant to delegate; he interfered too often in small details of College administration and soon came to be regarded as an over-meticulous disciplinarian. His first public duty as Provost was on Trinity Monday, and when he appeared with the rest of the Board on the steps of the Examination Hall to read out in the accustomed ritual the names of the new Scholars, some students threw pennies at his feet to mock his supposed quest of a higher salary. The same evening he presided for the first time at the High Table, and although the ceremonial Trinity Monday dinners of pre-war years had not yet been resumed it was a formal occasion, with the new Scholars and many of the Fellows present. Towards the end of the meal there was a disturbance and an irruption of noisy students. The Junior Dean went to the door to investigate, and found that Alcock and Brown, the first men to fly the Atlantic, who had landed on Saturday in a Connemara bog, had reached Dublin that evening. A body of students had met their trains, brought Alcock down in triumph to the College (Brown had prudently escaped), and escorted him in to the dinner. The legend has grown up that Bernard tried to ignore him and when he could no longer do so received him coldly, but the account given by an eye-witness suggests that this is unfair.[5] Doubtless the Provost was confused and may have taken some time to understand what was happening, but he certainly asked Alcock to sit beside him and gave him a glass of wine. At the worst he can only be charged with slow and slightly reluctant accommodation to an unexpected interruption of the orderly routine; but one feels that any of his three predecessors might have contrived a warmer and more spontaneous welcome.

In spite of these defects, however, Bernard gave of his best to the College. He worked hard for it and used all his influence on its behalf; he was stern, but did his best to be just; and he behaved steadily and responsibly when the events of 1921 destroyed at once the political ideals for which he had fought and also, as we shall see, his hopes of financial prosperity for the College. Moreover, it was during his years as Provost that he did most of the work on his commentary on St John's Gospel, the book on which his reputation as a theologian largely rests.

(ii)

The first question to face the new Provost was the serious financial plight of the College. Prices had risen enormously since 1914, and the falling-off in the number of students during the war had caused a serious drop in the receipts from fees. By the time the war ended it was clear that the only hope of solvency lay with the Government, and as Oxford and Cambridge had come to the same conclusion it was no surprise for Fisher, President of the Board of Education, to find on his doorstep soon after the Armistice representatives of three universities which had never before received state aid on any substantial scale.[6] Royal Commissions were accordingly appointed early in 1920, one for Oxford and Cambridge, and another for Dublin. The Commissioners for the University of Dublin were, thanks probably to Bernard's influence, men who were extremely well disposed towards it. The chairman was Sir Archibald Geikie, doyen of British geologists and an old friend and admirer of the College.[7] The other four were John Joly, as representative of the University, Sir Arthur Shipley, biologist and Master of Christ's College, Cambridge, J.S.E. Townsend, an Oxford physicist but originally a graduate of Dublin, and Sir John Ross, a High Court judge and also a loyal son of the house. The Commission declared itself favourably impressed by what the College was doing, made some helpful and not very radical suggestions for administrative reform, recommended an all-round increase in salaries, better buildings and equipment for the scientific departments, and scope for development in Economics and in Agriculture. The University's requirements were assessed as a capital grant of £113,000 and an annual grant of £49,000.

The brilliant future which this promised was, however, already darkened by a shadow. Before the Geikie report had been published the Government of Ireland Bill[8] had been introduced in Parliament, and under its terms education was one of the subjects transferred to the Irish Parliaments. Bernard pointed out that there was a grave risk that an Irish parliament would be unwilling to implement the report, and his strenuous efforts succeeded in adding to the bill a clause assuring an annual grant to the College of £30,000, chargeable on the exchequer of Southern Ireland. This was a bit of a come-down from the £49,000 which had been recommended, but it was something. The next urgent problem was to secure payment of the capital grant, but the Government was reluctant to sanction this until the grants to Oxford and Cambridge had been agreed on, and the report of their Commission was not yet published. Various ways of circumventing the delay were explored, but all ran into legal difficulties or administrative objections, and by the beginning of 1921 it would have been clear to an impartial observer that the capital grant would be entirely at the mercy of the parliament of Southern Ireland, or whatever replaced it. But Bernard refused to give up. Although some of his statements over the next eighteen months betray the emotional frustration and indignation common to all southern Unionists of the time, who felt that they had been first thrown to the wolves by the northern Unionists and then let down by a predominantly Conservative government in England, he preserved a cool head and a dignified demeanour in his interviews with politicians and civil servants. In private he might lament that 'inasmuch as we are only loyal people who have given the Empire all in war and peace, we get nothing and are faced with academic bankruptcy because the pledges of an act of parliament are not carried out',[9] but he impressed favourably men like John Anderson, Hamar Greenwood and Stanley Baldwin, and made them feel that they should look round and try to find a little money to soften the blow to Trinity's hopes. The result was that, although the Geddes axe was cutting estimates along the whole length of Whitehall, Trinity received from the British government a series of *ad hoc*, non-recurrent grants which totalled £56,000 over the years 1919–23. This was almost half the capital sum recommended by the Geikie Commission, but it had to be spent, not on development, but on plugging some of the holes in the annual budget.

The chance of actually receiving the annual grant took a turn for the worse when in the autumn of 1921 discussions began in London which were eventually to lead to the Anglo-Irish treaty, signed in December and ratified in January 1922. Before long it became clear that the Government of Ireland Act would have to be replaced, as far as the south was concerned, by a new settlement. In November 1921, the Prime Minister received a deputation of southern Unionists and assured them that the Government was willing to include in the treaty guarantees regarding church property and educational institutions, and the following day Arthur Griffith, on behalf of the Sinn Fein delegation, told Bernard that he had no objection to the retention in the treaty of the clause from the Government of Ireland Act which assured Trinity of its annual grant. But when the treaty was signed on 6 December it contained no such clause. Bernard immediately protested to Lloyd George, who 'after reflection admitted that he had not appreciated this point, for which he was sorry, but he did not doubt that Sinn Fein would act on the repeated promises they had made to deal impartially with all classes in Ireland'.[10]

In the early months of 1922 Bernard was still preoccupied with lobbying the British Government, and from April onwards the threat of civil war in Ireland, soon to be followed by the reality, ruled out any chance of conversations with the Provisional Government in Dublin. It was not, therefore, until May 1923 that there was a chance to put to what was now the Government of the Irish Free State the College's case for financial assistance. The fact that Griffith was now dead constituted a fresh handicap, for his assurance had never been put down on paper. It was not altogether surprising, therefore, that the reply sent by the Department of Finance was cool and discouraging. It demanded, before any question of a grant could be considered, detailed information on the remuneration and duties of the various members of the staff, and it queried the justification of financial support for student activities such as athletic clubs. The Board replied, protesting at the apparent intention of the Government to treat 'in so illiberal a manner ... an institution of national importance', which was now the only university in the British Isles not in receipt of a grant from public funds. This elicited a reply which was not only cool but severe, pointing out that the Free State was a poor country and that the amount of money available for the universities was very small, that from many points of view University College, Dublin, had a better claim on it, and that Trinity College was not using its resources in the most equitable or efficient manner. The Government was prepared to make a non-recurrent grant of £5,000 to relieve hardship in individual cases, but on conditions which were so detailed and searching as to be positively humiliating. This was a somewhat crude foretaste of what all universities have had to stomach since – that governments do not pay pipers, at any rate for long, without demanding some say in the choice of tune – but to the Board of Trinity College, whose recent grants from the British Treasury had been without strings, it seemed an outrage. Its members could not at once adjust themselves to two distasteful facts: that they were now members of a much poorer community than heretofore, and that, as a displaced ascendancy, the best they could hope for from their successors in the saddle was a grudging equity – certainly not generosity. But although prompted by a sense of outrage the reaction of the Board was adroit. It expressed surprise at the tone of the letter and declared that it would be impossible for any academic authority to accede to its terms; it went on to suggest 'that the matter should be further considered by the Government before publicity is given to the correspondence'. The threat was successful and the Government backed down; the conditions were modified sufficiently to make them acceptable, and the £5,000 was paid.[11]

Shortly afterwards the Government made a reasonable settlement with the College in relation to a complex financial liability arising from the Land Act of 1903. The Government agreed to make over to the College for investment a balance of £76,000 in the hands of the Public Trustee, representing money which might have been payable to the College if its loss of income resulting from compulsory land purchase had been greater than in fact it had been. In return, the College agreed to accept an annual grant of £3,000 on the understanding that it would abandon all further claims in connexion with land purchase. By this means the College secured an immediate increase of about £4,000 in its annual cash income, though much of it was to be later eroded by land purchase on relatively unfavourable terms. The Government, on its side, released itself from a rather tiresome contingent liability.

(iii)

There was to be no further communication for twenty-three years between the College and the Government on the subject of financial assistance. At first sight it would seem that the College had been the victim of a particularly unlucky piece of timing, and that, had the report of the Commission appeared a year earlier or the treaty been signed a year later, all would have been well. But it is very doubtful if the College would have benefited in the long run from being the beneficiary of a grant unwillingly paid by the Irish government as part of a bargain for independence. It would not have been long before the figure thirty became associated not with thousands of pounds, but with pieces of silver. It was natural for Bernard to strive in every way to grasp the prize that had so narrowly eluded him, but one of the Junior Fellows (Alton) had the perspicacity to see the disadvantages of an imposed settlement, and wrote to Bernard, advising him against pressing for a guarantee either of financial support or of freedom from constitutional interference.[12] As things turned out, although the College was baulked in most of its plans for expansion it was just able to tide over the crisis without going into debt, and by 1923 prices were beginning to fall again. The inter-war years thereafter were marked by a moderate but not acute atmosphere of financial stringency. Attempts to obtain a grant for the Library from the Carnegie foundation and for the medical school from the Rockefeller foundation were both unsuccessful. The campaigns may not have been very skilfully conducted, but it is probably fair to say that, for any cautious member of the board of a charitable foundation, a university so closely identified with a recently dispossessed regime, with its survival, but little else, assured by the Government, was not an attractive field for expenditure. With prudent management, however, the College was able to balance its budget well enough to avoid the need for risking a further rebuff from the Government, and by dropping out of its consciousness from 1923 to 1946 it facilitated the first stage of the relaxation of the tensions between the two which had been imposed by the course of history.

This policy of inconspicuousness was in part dictated by the logic of facts, but it was to some extent followed deliberately, and the title which we have given to this chapter is meant to suggest that it was the guiding principle of College policy up to 1946. It had its craven side; at times the College was afraid to request some trivial and technical concession from a government department for fear of focusing attention on itself and provoking a debate in the Dail. Another aspect of the somewhat over-assiduous, low-profile policy was the active discourage-

ment by the Board of the expression in the public press by members of
the College of views on religious or political matters which could be
described as controversial. Not unreasonably they were forbidden to
use the College as an address on such occasions, but the private
addresses of such indefatigable correspondents as Luce and Rudmose-
Brown soon ceased to serve as a convincing disguise, and a mildly anti-
clerical letter from the latter in 1937 called forth a stern admonition for
greater restraint, even in letters written from Killiney. But if at times
the low-profile policy was carried to excess it was on the whole a wise
one, if only for the reason that it gave the former Unionists, who
constituted the great majority of the academic staff, time and privacy in
which to lick their wounds and to determine to what extent they would
accommodate themselves to new conditions.

The extent to which they did this and the speed with which they did
it varied greatly. A few days after the treaty had been signed the Board
passed a resolution expressing the hope that the University's representatives in Parliament would support the settlement, since 'the
true interests of Trinity College can only be furthered by Irish peace,
and in building up happier conditions in Ireland the Board believes
that Trinity men should take an active and sympathetic part'. It was a
well-drafted resolution, constructive but restrained, and without any
note of hypocrisy. But it was passed only by nine votes to three. Two of
the dissentients were, all too predictably, Gray and Cathcart; the third
was H.H. Dixon, one of the elected representatives of the non-Fellow
Professors, who on most issues could not be regarded as an extreme
conservative. It is worth while pausing to attempt an analysis of the
feelings, prejudices and loyalties which impelled a rational and normally moderate man, who had little real interest in politics, to dissociate
himself from the only alternative to renewed civil war, and virtually to
refuse recognition to the *de facto* government of his country, which,
however distasteful it might be, could not be regarded as a temporary
usurpation, soon to be displaced. For Dixon was by no means unique.

There was, in the first place, the confusion and consequent indignation which follows a settlement that can be interpreted as a betrayal
by those in whom one has trusted. One could put most of the blame
on the tricky little Welsh attorney, but there was no denying the fact
that Unionists as orthodox as Austen Chamberlain and as militant as
Birkenhead had also signed the treaty, and they were no more popular
among Unionists in Dublin than were General De Gaulle among the
pieds noirs of Algeria or Mrs Thatcher among Rhodesian farmers in
more recent times. The second element in their attitude is less easily
apprehended by those who have lived through the mid-twentieth
century than it was sixty years ago, for the Anglo-Irish struggle of

1919–21 and the manner of its settlement, which have served as models for so many later episodes of decolonization, were novelties at the time. If any government today proclaims that it refuses to shake hands with murderers, memories of Makarios, Kenyatta and Mugabe being ceremonially installed in power by members of the Royal family raise a wry smile. But in 1921 this attitude could be struck with more conviction. And finally, there was the potent influence of religious division. There were, of course, some Catholic Unionists, and some of them were prominent in public life, especially at the Bar, but they were not numerous enough to blur seriously the identification by the plain man of Unionist with Protestant and Nationalist with Catholic. Dixon was a firm rationalist, but a rationalist brought up against a Protestant background was at one with a fervent Evangelical in deploring the fact that 'they' were now going to be top dogs, the only difference being that the militant Protestant saw 'them' mainly as scheming Jesuits and luxury-loving Cardinals, whereas the liberal agnostic tended to see them rather as serried ranks of red-faced priests for ever chomping on bacon and cabbage and pausing only to denounce mixed bathing.

The result of this identification of religious difference with political distaste meant that the ex-Unionist tended to be driven back into defending in the name of Protestant rights causes for which he really cared little. The number of Protestants in the Free State who wished for a divorce was extremely small, but even the most contentedly married did not like being told by Catholics that he could not have one, and the sentiments of Yeats's famous speech in the Senate, in which he declared that the Protestants of Ireland were 'no petty people', but the heirs of Swift, Berkeley and Grattan, were echoed in less sonorous phrases by the University representatives in the Dail. When the Censorship of Publications Act followed, even the most prudish Protestant found himself manoeuvred into defending erotic literature and contraception, and it was only the idiocy of the Censorship Board (which in its prime banned at least one work of most of the contemporary writers in English of any merit) which gave him an opportunity to attack it without feeling uncomfortable.

This polarization was not lessened by such publications as the *Catholic Bulletin*, one of the journalistic curiosities of the inter-war period. Its combination of mawkish piety, extravagantly chauvinistic politics and crude sectarian abuse, conducted mainly in terms of personal vilification, was well calculated to stiffen the morale of any Trinity man who might feel that his Protestant and ex-Unionist loyalties were becoming a little *démodé*. Its sharpest barbs were reserved for Trinity College, and especially for the few Catholics on its staff. The College was referred to as 'the Elizabethan rat-pit' and the Vice-

Chancellor (Sir Thomas Molony) as 'the Provost's pet penguin'; the supposed amatory adventures retailed by Walter Starkie ('Don Gualtero') in his books (some of them rumoured to have been inserted by his wife to liven up the narrative) were reprobated with pious horror; Broderick, on whom it was difficult to fix any specific vice, was dismissed as being permanently absorbed in the contemplation of the square root of minus one. Every cause is apt to generate its gutter press, but the title of this particular journal, suggesting that it had some form of ecclesiastical imprimatur, misled many; and although no respectable Catholic would openly defend it the fact that the bishops neither asked it to change its title or to moderate its language suggested that their disapproval of controversy of this type may not have been very heartfelt.

Faced with these distasteful aspects of the new regime, the ex-Unionist could do one of four things. He could emigrate to Britain; he could remain physically in Ireland but emigrate mentally, recognizing contemporary Ireland only in so far as was necessary for the purchase of stamps or the payment of income tax; he could do nothing in particular, accepting the new order with a distaste which time gradually eroded, and remembering the good old days, but a little less vividly each year; or he could make a conscious effort to re-orient his loyalties towards the new Ireland and to do what he could to serve it. Only two members of the academic staff seem to have followed the first course; Plummer (an Oxford graduate) resigned the chair of Astronomy in 1921 to become Professor of Mathematics at Woolwich, and Sir Lucas White King, Professor of Arabic, who was nearing retiring age anyway, although brought up in Ireland elected to retire to Scotland. There were a fair number who followed the second course; like the early Christians they submitted themselves to the powers that God had in his inscrutable providence ordained, but they made it clear that their abiding city was not in the Irish Free State, but rather in Britain or in the Ireland of the past. Smyly, Godfrey and Miss Maxwell can serve as examples of this attitude. The third course probably represented the attitude of most of the Fellows and Professors; they made no deliberate readjustment, but they made no attempt to delay its natural progress. They had a genuine, but in its early days a tepid loyalty to the Irish government. The fourth attitude was adopted by a few of the younger men and one or two others who were involved in public life. They did not totally abandon their traditional loyalties, but the ambiguities inherent in Dominion status and the Commonwealth concept during the twenties made a double loyalty easy and indeed logical. W.E. Thrift, who represented the University in the Dail, and who had been born in England and came to Ireland as a boy, declared in the Dail as early as 22 September 1922, that he had been a convinced Unionist and was not ashamed of the fact, but that he recognized that the days of Unionism were over and had turned the page completely. He spoke rarely on controversial political issues, but showed himself, in the Dail as elsewhere, to be a hard-working committee man, and he served Ireland, while remaining English, in much the same spirit as that which enabled Glubb Pasha to be loyal at once to Britain and to Jordan. Alton, in his more confused way, had similar sentiments; passionately loyal to Trinity, he was determined to retain its traditions, but he was also anxious to have its merits and status appreciated by all Irishmen, and by ignoring the great difficulties which lay in the path of this ideal he had some success in promoting it.

(iv)

Apart from religious squabbles there were few issues in the politics of the twenties and thirties on which ex-Unionists were tempted to take a distinctive stand, except for the interpretation of Dominion status. One or two practical issues were at stake in this connexion, as in 1924, when there was a sudden scare that the introduction of an independent medical register for the Free State might jeopardize the rights of medical graduates of Trinity to practise in Britain. But this alarm was short-lived. It was reasonable for Trinity men, like other ex-Unionists, to interpret the Commonwealth connexion (which was, before the Statute of Westminster in 1931, distinctly ambiguous) as closely as possible; it was equally reasonable for the Government to play it down as far as it could without causing a crisis in Anglo-Irish relations. But within the Free State the battle had to be fought out on the rather sterile ground of symbolism – flags, anthems and toasts, all of them issues which, because their purely symbolic nature and lack of intrinsic importance allow little scope for rational argument, bring out the fiercest and most intransigent of political emotions.

In 1922 Trinity toyed briefly with the idea of flying the crowned harp, but this was soon abandoned in favour of the Union Jack. Soon, however, some of the Junior Fellows convinced the Board that it was foolish to ignore completely the Irish tricolour, and a generally agreed policy was devised of flying the tricolour on one pavilion of the West Front, the Union Jack on the other, and the College flag in the middle. It was not a bad compromise, at any rate up to the middle thirties, but by that time De Valera's steady and skilful erosion of the Commonwealth connexion had made the arguments justifying the use of the Union Jack more and more difficult to sustain. It was interpreted no longer as an anachronism, but as a symbol of provocation and defiance, so that it

433

flew for the last time in 1935, on the occasion of the Jubilee of King George V. When the King died eight months later the Vice-Provost (Thrift) had what he thought was the brilliant idea of flying the Royal Standard at half-mast.[13] The Dublin populace took no exception, and probably welcomed the sight of such novel heraldic splendour, but the College soon found that it had given offence elsewhere: the experts in protocol were sadly shocked, and a letter from the Deputy Ulster King at Arms, though politely expressed, set out the reasons for regarding the action as a double solecism.[14]

In the matter of toasts, it was difficult to fault the drinking of the King's health up to 1936, when, in the legislation necessary to give effect to the abdication of Edward VIII, the King's position in the constitution was made much more shadowy. In 1930 Eoin O'Mahony, an exuberant eccentric who was Auditor of the College Historical Society, caused a storm by toasting Ireland instead of the King at the supper following the Society's opening meeting. Loyalists walked out, and the Society was forbidden the use of the Common Room premises until it had purged its contempt. But it was only a few years later that it became customary at College dinners to follow the royal toast, after thirty seconds' embarrassed silence, with the toast of 'Ireland', and at the end of the war it was agreed that the King should be toasted in June 1945, but never again.

And finally, anthems. The same ambiguity as with flags reigned here: was 'God save the King' the anthem of the Commonwealth or of Great Britain alone? Either interpretation was possible. The determination of the College to adhere to its tradition of playing it at the College Races led in 1929 to a brush with the Governor-General (James MacNeill), who, presumably on the advice of the Government, refused to attend the races if he was to be greeted with this tune. The Board said that they would defer to His Excellency's wishes, but made it so clear in the same letter that they thought His Excellency to be wrongly advised that MacNeill decided that it would be better not to attend. As there was nobody to greet, 'God save the King' was triumphantly played at the conclusion of the races. It was also played at the conclusion of every Commencements as late as 1939.

(v)

No matter how remote these political and religious issues may seem from the academic work and development of the university, its future fortunes and reputation depended on a reasonable settlement of them, for if it was to prosper and retain respect it had to face the difficult task of preserving its traditions without losing touch with reality. This said, however, we can say goodbye for twenty years or so to political issues and concentrate on the truly academic world. In this sphere the most important topic is the changes in 1910–20 in the statutes governing the method of election to Fellowship, and the financial conditions of its tenure.

We have seen that during Traill's provostship the debate on possible modifications of the Fellowship examination had proved entirely inconclusive, except for a few small changes sanctioned by the Letters Patent of 1911 (p. 405). The debate was resumed again in 1914, and went on throughout the war years. But it was very difficult to secure the agreement of Senior and Junior Fellows alike to any of the suggested modifications which were constantly proposed. Whether a written examination, as distinct from an assessment of original work with perhaps a *viva voce* examination as well, should be the normal method of selection, or an occasional method, or should be abandoned altogether, was a question on which opinion seemed to be permanently divided. So also were the questions of whether Fellows should be selected exclusively or mainly from those who had served as lecturers, or at least from graduates of the University,[15] or whether competition should be thrown open to the world, and whether Fellowships should be offered mainly or entirely in the traditional subjects or should be extended to those subjects which had hitherto been taught mainly by non-Fellow Professors. Eventually, however, thanks to some fairly firm guidance by Mahaffy, these questions were dodged rather than solved by the passage of an Ordinance in 1919 giving wide discretionary powers to the Board, which, now that it was at least in part democratized, was entrusted with a discretion which had been refused to the Provost and Senior Fellows alone. The Board could decide whether in any given year an election should be held or not; they could decide on the method of examination; and they could determine the qualifications required for candidature and the subject or subjects to be presented.

This certainly gave a welcome flexibility to the system, but at times it seemed that the flexibility might be too great. Most of the elections from 1920 to 1939 fell rather embarrassingly half-way between two methods which were perfectly respectable if considered as alternatives, but of which the mixture gave a bad impression. If there was a young lecturer or recent graduate who showed evidence of unusual intellectual promise and had the other qualities which were thought to be needed in a Fellow, then it would be quite reasonable to elect him to a Fellowship without further ado. There were, however, few of the younger Fellows who were prepared to allow the Board such an unfettered exercise of judgment. If, on the other hand, the Board were to decide that the staff in a particular subject needed to be strengthened by the addition of a Fellow, then it would be reasonable to hold an open competition and appoint the best among the candidates who came forward. What usually happened, however, was that the Board would announce a competition in a given subject, but by the timing, the choice of subject and the restrictions on candidature it gave the impression (sometimes justified, sometimes not) that it was hoping to secure the election of a particular candidate. This tended to scare off outside competitors, who were apt to conclude that the whole thing had been fixed in advance. In one sense this was unfair, as it is impossible to point to a single election in which it can be said that a 'favourite son' was elected in preference to a more able outsider. But there is no doubt that on a few occasions the qualifications were so framed that it was unlikely that more than one candidate would materialize; in 1924, when Walter Starkie (who was a competent violinist) was elected to the Fellowship in Modern Languages, a cynical commentator suggested that the only qualification for candidature that had been omitted was 'must be able to play the fiddle'. Again, when a Fellowship in Mathematics was announced in 1930 the conditions allowed for the candidature of outsiders, if approved by the Board, but when Louis Rosenhead (whose subsequent career showed that intellectually he was well up to Fellowship standard) offered himself as a candidate he was refused permission to compete, and even an indignant protest from J.L. Synge, who was at that time Professor of Applied Mathematics, did not make the Board reverse its decision. The 'favourite son', on this occasion was A.J. McConnell, the most brilliant graduate in mathematics for some years past, and although it was perfectly reasonable to make a niche to secure him for the College, this was not the most dignified way of doing it.

In the years 1920–39 fifteen Fellows were elected. One of these was E.T.S. Walton (1934), who, rather tardily, was the first to be elected under the Ordinance of 1916, which allowed for the occasional election without examination for 'distinguished merit as shown primarily by published work'. Only one other Fellow was ever elected under this clause (R.A.Q. O'Meara in 1941), and although Walton's work on atomic fission and O'Meara's on the immunology of diphtheria were without question of 'distinguished merit' it is rather a sad commentary on the Board's methods of search that in both cases the proposal to elect them to Fellowship followed close on the appearance of their names in headlines on the front page of a daily newspaper.

Of the remaining elections of this period it may be said that those of 1924, 1925, 1930 (both mathematics and economics) and 1935 were tailored, either in their timing or in the conditions of candidature, to suit specific graduates,[16] those of 1921, 1926 and 1934 were seen as contests between two well-matched local candidates;[17] and those of 1920, 1928, 1929 and 1939 (both classics and history) were dictated by the needs of the College and were genuinely open competitions, without a favoured internal candidate.[18]

Apart from the exclusion of the external candidate in 1930, only one other election caused any controversy or ill feeling; this was the election of Fearon in 1921. W.R. Fearon, originally a graduate in experimental science, had studied biochemistry under Hopkins in Cambridge, and, apart from those who esteemed his obvious originality and versatility, was backed by some members of the Medical School who thought it was time that the teaching of biochemistry was established on a firm footing in College. But J.H.J. Poole, a nephew of George Fitzgerald and a pupil and protégé of Joly, whom he had assisted in his work on radio-activity in rocks, had the backing of Joly and the Dixon brothers. There was, in consequence, much manoeuvring for position when the subject in which the Fellowship was to be offered came up for decision, and many formulae were suggested, either to exclude biochemistry or to tip the balance in its favour. The candidates, exact contemporaries, were well matched intellectually, but Fearon made a much better impression in the interview and was recommended by the majority of the examiners. The Board probably made the right choice, but its indecision and subterfuges exposed it to the charge of double-dealing, for which it was taken to task in an angry protest by H.H. Dixon.

But despite some clumsiness on the part of the Board the new methods for selecting Fellows were an undoubted improvement on the old. Original work had now become the main criterion of judgment, the Fellowship in Classics in 1934 being the only occasion on which the candidates were judged purely on the results of a written examination and a prelection. In consequence we find that of the fourteen Fellows we have been considering all published some original work, and at least half of them a very respectable corpus. Most of them, moreover, were efficient as administrators, departmental heads or tutors, while Fearon, Walton and Duncan were deservedly admired as lecturers.

The subjects chosen for Fellowship in this period represented a somewhat uneasy compromise between an adherence to those required for the examination in earlier days and an attempt to spread Fellowship over the whole range of contemporary scholarship. Eight out of fourteen were awarded in the traditional subjects – classics, mathematics and physics – the remaining six being equally divided between the humanities (modern languages, economics and history) and the natural sciences (chemistry, biochemistry and physiology). It was not mere conservatism that favoured the first group so strongly, for the Professorships in these subjects were restricted to Fellows either by statute or custom, and if the Board is to be criticized here it is not so much for an excessive award of Fellowships in the traditional subjects as for postponing the elections for too long. This led to the appointment of very young and largely untried men to chairs in these subjects. Another effect of the dilatoriness of the Board in electing to Fellowship was a decline in the number of Fellows. To some small extent this may have been motivated by financial stringency, but it was due largely to indecisiveness or to a stalemate produced by rival factions. In 1919 there were thirty-one Fellows, which was a little below the average of pre-war years (about thirty-three). But death and retirement took their toll more rapidly than the Board could bring itself to organize elections, so that by 1928 the number was down to twenty-eight and by 1938 to twenty-four. This was all the more surprising as a statute enacted in 1926 decreed that the number of Fellows should not be allowed to fall permanently below twenty-seven but from 1936 to 1951 this statute was blandly ignored. The effect of this policy was something which the Board cannot have desired – a gradual lowering of the significance of Fellowship in the academic system. Tutorship and the senior administrative offices were still confined to Fellows, but a decline in their numbers at a time when the number of lecturers was rapidly increasing undoubtedly paved the way for the arguments based on numerical democracy which succeeded in the sixties and seventies in producing a striking reduction in the importance and prestige of Fellowship.

The Ordinance of 1919, which altered fairly drastically the method of election to Fellowship, was followed by another in 1920, which altered equally drastically the financial conditions of tenure. As a result of the reduction in the income of the tutors which followed the fall in student numbers in 1915–18 a committee was appointed to report on the administrative and financial aspects of the tutorial system, which had remained virtually unchanged since 1859. Its report was devastating.[19] It demonstrated with great lucidity that under twentieth-century conditions the system led to great waste of labour and to an inequitable division of fees. An alternative scheme was proposed, which, after some amendment, formed the basis of the Ordinance of 1920.

In future a newly elected Fellow would not need to starve until a tutorship became vacant; instead of £40 Irish he would receive on election, simply as Fellow, a salary of £440 a year, in return for which he must perform specified teaching and examining duties, though these could be to some extent tailored to suit individual cases. His salary would increase by small increments up to £690, and meanwhile he might expect to earn after a while an extra £250 or so by taking on a tutorship if one was offered to him (for which he received £1 for every pupil), and in some cases by doing more examining than his statutory duties required of him. But to counterbalance this relative prosperity in his early years his expectations as Senior Fellow were considerably less than they had been in the past. His basic salary went up to £892, but he would have to resign his tutorship and (with occasional exceptions, which gradually grew more frequent) his Professorship if he held one. On the other hand he would, unless he was particularly incompetent (and perhaps even then), hold for a large part of his tenure of Senior Fellowship one of the administrative offices which were, either by statute or custom, reserved to Senior Fellows, and by this means he would earn a further £100 to £400 a year, so that he could expect in his riper years an average income of about £1,150, and in his final decline a reasonably generous non-contributory pension.

It was a well-thought-out scheme, which never met with any serious criticism, and it remained intact, with only minor changes, until postwar inflation required an increase in the figures. But it could not, of course, be applied retrospectively, all Fellows elected before 1920 remaining under the old system. This had the unfortunate result of polarizing the Fellows into pre-1920 and post-1920,[20] and before long this came very largely to replace the previous antagonism between Seniors and Juniors. Men elected in the period 1908–15 began soon after 1920 to look on themselves as prospective Senior Fellows of the old dispensation, and this, combined with the fortuitous fact that most members of this particular group – Tate, Harry Thrift, Luce and Godfrey – were men of conservative temperament, meant that they tended to vote with the Senior Fellows and to be suspicious of any move towards constitutional reform. It is perhaps significant that 1949, the year that saw the last of the pre-1920 Fellows co-opted to Senior Fellowship, and the Junior Fellows thereby freed from dissidents within their ranks, was the year which saw the outbreak of more or less open warfare between the Junior Fellows and the Board.

(vi)

Bernard died in 1927 and was succeeded as Provost by E.J. Gwynn, who had been co-opted to a Senior Fellowship only a few months earlier. The names of Russell and W.E. Thrift were also mentioned at the time, but there is little doubt that Gwynn had the support of the majority of the Fellows and Professors. He was, however, no longer the pertinacious and radical reformer of pre-war days. Increasing years and the eclipse of his political ideals had taken the fight out of him, and

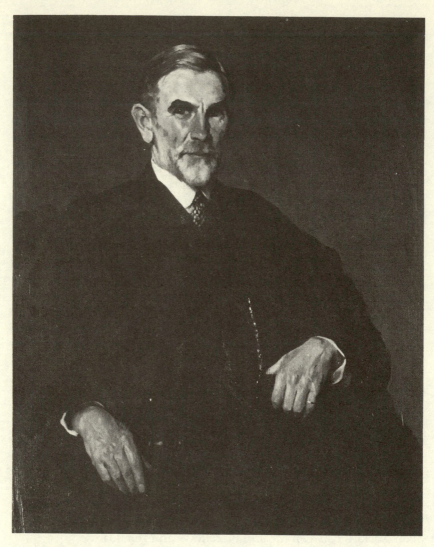

27   Edward John Gwynn. Provost, 1927–37. (Leo Whelan, Trinity College.)

as Provost his influence on policy consisted more in steering the Board in the direction of common sense and civilized values than towards anything that could be called reform. But he suited well the needs of the College in its low-profile period. A small man, he had none of the self-assertiveness that often accompanies low stature, but he had a remarkable natural dignity which, fortified as it was by his very neat appearance and manner and his steady, cold eye (which could twinkle engagingly, but not very often), could make the burliest under-graduate quail and the most quarrelsome Fellow hold his tongue. He was a master of the felicitous phrase, based often on understatement, which made him an excellent, and mercifully brief, after-dinner speaker. He had achieved considerable eminence as a scholar in Old Irish, and although his dislike of the revival of the modern language remained unaltered his academic reputation served to some extent as a lightning-conductor against attacks on the College as 'un-Irish'. He would probably have achieved more if he had not been handicapped by periodic recurrence of the tubercular trouble which had dogged him for much of his life, and which finally forced his retirement in 1937.

When L.C. Purser resigned the Vice-Provostship soon after Gwynn's appointment the Provost found the pressure of tradition powerful enough to make him appoint as Vice-Provost Roberts, the most senior of the Fellows. Roberts could deputize adequately for a few weeks if the Provost was ill or absent, but he was by now very elderly and was in no way suited to help the Provost on a day-to-day basis. It was only after his death in 1935 that a new departure was made by appointing W.E. Thrift as a 'working' Vice-Provost, a policy which, apart from the years 1942−6, has been followed ever since.

Gwynn also acted wisely in appointing Fry as Senior Lecturer in 1927 and Goligher as Registrar in 1930. Fry, a mathematician of only moderate talent and with few pretensions to general culture, had two saving graces: plenty of common sense, and a passion for accuracy and order in detail. The latter was occasionally pressed to ludicrous extremes, as when he published the percentages in examination results to the second place of decimals, or gave to a paper which he contributed in 1907 to the *Proceedings of the Royal Irish Academy* the remarkable title:

The centre of gravity and the principal axes of any surface of equal pressure in a heterogeneous liquid covering a heterogeneous solid composed of nearly spherical shells of equal density, when the whole mass is rotating with a small angular velocity in relative equilibrium under its own attraction.

No shallow or risky generalizations there! But he kept in a single book, by an ingenious but obscure notation which he alone could interpret, the entire academic record of every student, and he ran the by now very complex examination system with the care that an enthusiast devotes to compiling a railway time-table. He claimed an absolute right to determine who should set each particular paper, and though the summons arrived in the form 'Dear X, I should be obliged if you would set . . .' woe betide the man who did not set the paper, collect it from the Press, turn up at the hall to lay it down, take his turn at invigilation, collect the scripts and return the marks on time. No second thoughts by examiners were allowed, and tutors who queried the justice of the failure of their pupils were given short shrift.[21]

Goligher, as Registrar from 1930 to 1937 and then Vice-Provost until his death in 1941, was held by many to be the man who really ran the College. He certainly got his way on many issues, if only because he always knew his own mind and could state his case incisively, if at times brutally. The amount of power that was conceded to him was all the more remarkable in that less than ten years earlier he had been censured for an indiscretion with a female pupil (relatively innocent, but reprehensible by the standards of the day) and had been deprived of his tutorship. He had no grace of manner, and his harsh Derry accent added force to his frequently caustic or cynical comments, but he commanded respect as the man who cut through the fine-spun complexities of academic debate and forced his colleagues to a decision. He enjoyed the substance of power rather than its trappings, a Bismarckian attitude which was reinforced by his fondness for cigars. Well read in French and Spanish as well as in classics and ancient history, he displayed to the world little of his literary interest, and most of his publications fall under the head of high-class hack-work: a skilful scissors-and-paste job in compiling the section on Roman society in Herbert Spencer's monumental *Descriptive sociology*, and an index to the speeches of Isaeus, a Greek orator of little distinction, but who had not been indexed before. But he was the first Registrar to give to the office some significance and to file correspondence and records in an orderly way; the filing system was primitive, but it gave a start on which his successors could build. Apart from Thrift, to whom we shall turn shortly, the only other administrator of this period who requires notice is Russell, who was Bursar from 1921 to 1938. As a mathematician he excelled in setting tricky problems and devising neat solutions, but he had little real creative talent. As Bursar his only consistent policy was cheeseparing, but although he was now and then successfully over-ruled, the policy was not altogether out of step with the times. He was something of a bully, and not generally popular, but at least one of his actions earned him some posthumous gratitude. He took seriously his duties of wine-purchase for the College cellars, and shortly before his powers began to fail he seized the opportunity of an exceptionally favourable offer to purchase a fairly large quantity of Haut Brion and of Yquem, both of 1934.[22] Many of the good burgundies he had bought earlier were dissipated by his successor, Harry Thrift, at Rugby Club dinners, where many of the diners arrived in no condition to distinguish Vosne-Romanée from Guinness, but Russell's two 1934 vintages brightened the dark days of 1943–7, when good wine was hard to come by, and by judicious rationing the last of the Yquem was spun out to the middle sixties.

When Provost Gwynn retired a new initiative was taken in informing the Government of the wishes of the College with regard to his successor. The Junior Fellows, who at this time met at irregular intervals to discuss matters of College policy, invited the non-Fellow Professors to join them in proposing a candidate for the Provostship. W.E. Thrift was proposed, seconded and adopted, *nem. con.*, and was duly appointed by the Government. He held office for less than five years, and for more than half of his term Europe was at war. He was that rarity among academics, a first-rate committee man (it was in recognition of his abilities in this field that he was, despite his English birth, appointed Deputy Speaker of the Dail), and as he was completely honest and straightforward he was generally trusted. But he had no talent for leadership. His physical presence was against him, and the casual acquaintance saw only a shabby, apologetic little man, anxious to agree with everybody, without any signs of wide culture, wit or originality. Those who knew him better realized that behind this lay a firm determination and a shrewd analytical mind. But the office of Provost did not suit him, and his portrait by Leo Whelan, though not a great work of art, shows aptly enough a sad, tired little figure enveloped in a doctor's gown too big for him. It would have been a happier solution if Alton had been made Provost and Thrift continued as Vice-Provost to guide, support, advise and check.

The reader may wonder whether this sketch of the academic administrators of the College overestimates their role; what about the professional administrators? The answer is that they scarcely existed; the work of administration was carried on almost entirely by the officers we have named and the tutors. The isolation of the College from the Government made this easier; there were no applications for grants to be prepared, and none of the questionnaires to be answered which nowadays rain down on universities in such enormous numbers. The College was a self-sufficient family business. Even so, visitors from outside must sometimes have been startled at the paucity of telephones, typewriters and secretaries. Up to the First World War there were no established administrative posts except for two or three library assistants, an accountant, and the registrar of university electors who also discharged some of the duties of a chief clerk. Such secretarial assistance as may have existed was part-time, temporary, and arranged at least in part on a personal basis. Even in 1939 the Calendar lists (in addition to the library staff, which had by now grown to eight) only ten persons employed full-time on administration; of these five can be classified as secretaries and five as middle-grade administrators. No Provost had a private secretary until Alton with some difficulty managed to get a grudging consent from the Bursar. It was an archaic, and in many respects an inefficient system, but it represented one horn of the dilemma which faces universities – to employ scholars in administrative work, or to employ professional administrators who are liable eventually to dictate policy. And the first alternative, favoured in Trinity, was on the whole accepted without complaint. By the thirties some of the Junior Fellows were beginning to mutter, but demands for secretarial help were not to become a controversial issue until after the war.

A related aspect of the administration was its great centralization. Reading the minutes of the Board as late as 1950 one is struck by the enormous amount of petty detail which they contain. There were no departmental budgets, no committees with power to act independently, subject only to reporting to the Board, little discretion allowed to individual officers. In consequence the Board is asked, term after term, to vote a small sum to the Professor of Geology for demonstrators, to sanction the use of such and such a hall by some outside body or to approve or veto the list of topics on which the Historical Society proposed to hold debates. Critics of this procedure were silenced with the reply that centralization of decision-making saved time, and that the alternative was proliferation of committees. This reply dodged some of the issues, but on the whole it was accepted, and there was no sustained campaign during the inter-war period to change either the constitution of the College or its methods of administration.

(vii)

This is just one aspect of perhaps the most striking feature of the College in the years from 1924 to 1939 – that it was a very contented community. And this applied to the students as well as to the staff. Of course there were grumbles about food and about some minor regulations, but nobody devoted much time to them; there were no professional agitators and no student imagined that he could run the College (except in a detail here and there) better than the Board. For a few years after 1921 there was a small group of noisy southern ex-Unionists who staged occasional provocative demonstrations, but before long they lost support and dwindled away, while the considerable body of undergraduates from the north with Unionist sympathies had for the most part (at least when sober) the good sense to keep their opinions to themselves while they were in Dublin. The advent of De Valera to power in 1932 caused a tremor, but it was not long before it was discovered that he presented a greater threat to cattle-farmers than to the universities, and he was soon asked in to speak at meetings. Otherwise Irish politics was ignored, or followed as an intellectual game without any commitment. One could laugh with equal ease at Mr

Blythe's cutting a shilling off the old-age pension, De Valera's sudden conversion from a homburg to a top-hat, or the latest oration from Stormont in which the Battle of the Boyne was fought once more. The Italo-Abyssinian war produced some mild enthusiasm either for pacifism or for collective security. The Spanish Civil War had curiously little impact; most students were inclined to favour the Republic, but critically, and totally without the feeling so widespread in the English universities that the bell was tolling for them. Meanwhile life in College was pleasant; one could play games, learn the art of politics in the College societies, take advantage of the first-rate theatrical fare which Dublin provided in those days, not to mention its myriad cinemas, have an occasional good steak at the Dolphin, do some work either in term or in the vacation as seemed most convenient, and above all talk, while walking round the squares or through the Wicklow mountains, or indoors over innumerable cups of tea – for alcohol was produced only for a birthday, an election to scholarship or society office or some similar occasion. In this way, and aided by the low prices consequent on the depression, most of the students were able to enjoy an upper middle-class way of life on a lower middle-class income.

Contentment can, of course, slide into complacency, and it would be rash to maintain that this was entirely absent from the Trinity College of the thirties. But it was by no means general, nor was it offensively conspicuous. Some Professors in the medical school needed to be reminded that its great reputation would not last for ever unless they in their turn performed as well as their predecessors, but such reminders were voiced now and then. In 1940 the College received a rather ill-considered broadside from J.L. Synge,[23] who had resigned his Fellowship ten years earlier. He accused it of neglecting research, and declared that, as seen from Toronto, Trinity did not shine – it glimmered. He was answered easily enough, but one of the replies, from K.C. Bailey, which enumerated publications and Ph.D. theses, leaves one with a feeling that enumeration is not enough. There is a suggestion that quantity might be confused with quality, and the second-rate too easily praised as first-rate. But all in all, though one can point to corners here and there where the College might have done more, its educational and scholarly achievement in this period does not, if regard be paid to the limitations of its resources, need any apology.

(viii)

If we turn now to consider the changes in academic courses during the inter-war period we find that they were mainly at the periphery. Neither the pass course nor the old-established moderatorships were extensively remodelled. In the pass course the chief change was yet a further increase in the choice of subjects permitted. In the Freshman years from 1932 onwards Additional Mathematics was permitted as an alternative to Latin, and Physics and Chemistry in place of Mechanics. In the Sophister years the already lengthy list of optional subjects was further swollen by the addition of Italian and Spanish (1925), Geography and History (1930), Music (1935) and Hebrew (1936).

More important, however, than changes in content was a change in the prestige and reputation of the course over this period. In 1919 a pass student, if asked what course he was reading, could reply 'Pass Arts' without embarrassment; in 1939 he would be more likely to say 'Well, actually I'm just doing Pass Arts', and perhaps provide an explanation. This fall in prestige was helped by the enlargement of choice just mentioned; more than one subject got the reputation of being a 'soft option', and some of the combinations chosen were bizarre without providing what could reasonably be called a balanced education. The course came to be despised more and more by teachers and pupils alike. In scientific subjects the course provided was (from lack of man-power to provide special lectures) that given to honor students one or two years junior. In the humanities special lectures were given, but their delivery was regarded as a form of slumming.

The reputation of the course suffered also from the way in which it was steadily eroded as far as students of medicine, engineering and, later, agriculture and commerce were concerned. The principle remained intact whereby degrees in medicine, engineering, commerce and agriculture could be conferred only on those who already possessed a B.A. But the same Professors who protested that they wished their pupils to have a liberal education and fought tenaciously to ensure that they would be graduates in arts as well as in a professional subject, filled up the pupils' week with so many professional classes that the arts course was cut down to a fragment which scarcely merited a B.A.

Attempts to reconcile the claims of specialization and of a broad-based culture form, of course, one of the most familiar topics of educational controversy, and it was a distrust of excessive specialization as well as mere conservatism that made the Board persist for so long in maintaining that the pass course was the central core of University education, and that other courses were additions, not alternatives. As we have just seen, this gradually became something close to a formality as far as the professional schools were concerned, but 'honor privileges' with respect to the pass course were granted more slowly and more grudgingly than 'professional privileges'. It was not until 1952, when we end our story, that the honors man became completely emancipated from the requirements of the pass course, but since 1928 his involvement had been reduced to one single hurdle – the Final Freshman examination, universally known as Little-go, which every student, no matter what his course, had to pass before he could call himself a Sophister.

There was some choice of subjects, but for most candidates it meant Latin, French, Mathematics, Mechanics, Logic and English Composition. The Latin required some knowledge of books four and six of the *Aeneid*, and it was wise to have at least a nodding acquaintance with these. The Logic owed nothing to Keynes or Russell, nor even to Mill or Locke; it was Aristotle undiluted, mediated through Abbott's *Handbook*. In none of the subjects was the standard high, and for an intelligent honors student two or three weeks' work on the subjects with which he was not familiar would be enough to see him through; moreover, one of his honor privileges was that he could take the examination in parts, though not all had the foresight and will-power to do this. The *viva voce* part was in several subjects as important as the papers, and the hall would ring with cries of 'Any more for logic?', Fraser's snorts as a candidate offered him a demonstration from a modern geometry and not from Euclid, or Sir Robert Tate's exasperated 'Speak up, woman; I can't hear you', followed soon afterwards by 'Don't shout, woman; I'm not deaf'. By some Little-go was regarded as an ordeal, by others as an insult, by others again as a joke. Its final abolition in 1952, though long overdue, was attended with some sentimental regrets. But no words of ours can convey as felicitously the way in which it was regarded by the average honors student as was done by R.B.D. French in a poem 'Breakfast before an exam.', based on recent experience and published in *T.C.D.* on 5 November 1925.

Nine o'clock, the bell is tolling! Only half an hour to go!
Put the pan upon the Primus, take the kettle off and throw
On a piece or two of bacon, then we'll tackle Little-go.

Just a glance or two through Abbott, Barbara and Darii,
Fallacy of many questions – what *is* Logic, by the bye?
'Science of the form of thinking.' Here the bacon starts to fry.

Fill the teapot! Where's the kettle? Virgil, *Liber* number six,
Here's a bit they're fond of setting – Charon's boat upon the Styx –
Note the place he meets with Dido – '*Ergo mihi infelix* . . .'

'*Regere*' – we're out of sugar – '*populos imperio*';
Here's the crib – 'To spare the conquered', that's a bit we ought to know.
Where's the milk? '*Heu prisca fides* . . .' should have been here hours ago.

No more marmalade? Confound it! Can't do Euclid, haven't time –
Just a final glance at Dido – 'By this name she veils her crime,
Sitting *stratisque relictis*, nourishing a youth sublime.'

Classon's notes upon the poundal – lifts in motion up and down –
There's the bell – O Asof! Apnu! may the gods avert their frown!
Curse on all examinations! Where the dickens is my gown?[24]

By 1930 at any rate Little-go had come to be regarded by most honors students as a gratuitous obstacle *sui generis*; it was only the unusually well-informed who realized that it was a sort of dinosaur, the sole survivor of the days when all students were subject to the discipline of 'the undergraduate course', whatever else they might study as well. And thus the pass course dropped completely out of the consciousness of the honor or professional student. But there were some who still revered it. One of the authors, as a very junior lecturer in Botany found himself, at a tea-party given by a colleague, next to the by then almost legendary Senior Lecturer, M.W.J. Fry. Fry began the conversation by remarking, 'Well, this is a very important day for a large number of people.' It was in early November 1940, when the American voters were going to the poll to elect (as it turned out) Roosevelt for his third term as President. The young man tried to string together a few platitudes about American politics, but he was soon cut short. That was not what Fry meant; he thumped his stick impatiently on the floor and said, 'It's the re-examination for all classes!'[25] First things first.

Few of the post-1920 Fellows, however, shared this view; the pass course was the subject of constant criticism, and the Junior Fellows devoted several meetings during the war to earnest and agonized debates on the subject without reaching any clear conclusion. It was formally abolished in 1957, and for it was substituted a course entitled 'General Studies', designed as an unspecialized but 'serious' alternative to a Moderatorship. Cynics, however, declared that they saw little difference, and it soon sank in general esteem almost to the level of its predecessor. The real difficulty was that by this time it seemed to be virtually impossible to find university teachers prepared to devote themselves to conscientious and thorough teaching at a fairly elementary level.

(ix)

Most of the Moderatorship courses received some updating during the period covered by this chapter, but none of them to an extent that needs detailed scrutiny. Italian and Spanish were added to the Modern Languages course in 1921, and Irish in 1927. In 1922 a curiously ambitious Moderatorship in Oriental Languages was instituted; the languages which could be offered (though only in certain specified combinations) included not only Hebrew, Arabic, Persian, Sanskrit and Hindustani, for which there was some tradition of teaching, but also Aramaic, Syriac, Assyrian, Pali and classical Tamil, the last being added in response to an earnest plea from Pope, the Professor of Modern East Indian Languages. But only a year later the Board terminated Pope's appointment, presumably for reasons of economy, and in 1926 there was a sad change for the worse in the Professorship of Arabic, Persian and Hindustani. Ever since 1898 the College had been fortunate enough to secure the services of men of scholarly distinction – Lane-Poole, who had catalogued the Oriental coins in the British Museum, Sir Lucas White King, who had edited and translated Persian poems, and Sir Thomas Wolseley Haig, who had written extensively on Indian history. Haig was followed in 1926 by E.G. Hart, a typical Indian Army eccentric, who dabbled in mysticism and Yoga, but whose writings did not rise above the level of *Examinations and how to pass them* and *The art and science of organization*.[26] During the fifties and sixties the more exotic languages were progressively pared away, and the final transformation of the course into a Moderatorship in Hebrew and Semitic Languages was simply a recognition that save for a single student who took Sanskrit and Pali in 1946, Hebrew, backed up by Aramaic, Syriac, or occasionally Arabic, had always represented the reality of the course. A more realistic Moderatorship was instituted in 1932, in Economics and Political Science. This was made possible by the retirement of Bastable after a fifty-year tenure, and the appointment of a young, vigorous and full-time Professor (G.A. Duncan).

A new professional school was added in 1925 in the form of the School of Commerce (we call it 'professional', although it was intended for the training of business men, as its students were given professional privileges with respect to the pass course in arts). It was founded largely at the instigation of John Good, a Dublin business man, who later left a legacy to endow some prizes in the School. It was a fairly humdrum affair; service teaching in economics and modern languages, and in relevant aspects of geography, history and law was given by slotting the commerce students into appropriate classes, while part-time lecturers from the business world of Dublin came in to instruct them in strictly commercial matters. Successful candidates emerged with a B. Comm. as well as a B.A. The School pottered along until 1962, when it was replaced by a School of Business Studies. It did not add much to the lustre of the College, but at least it induced a few commercially minded fathers to give their sons a university education without feeling that they were completely wasting their time.

Other developments during this period are so numerous that they cannot easily be grouped; they must merely be catalogued. Courses were arranged for diplomas in religious knowledge for women (1919), geography (1930), the history of European painting (1934), social

Low profile

studies (1934), biblical studies (1936) and public administration (1941). The diploma in geography was the first step in the development of what is now a popular and important department in the School of Natural Sciences; for this much of the credit must go to T.W. Freeman, lecturer and later reader in Geography from 1936 to 1949, who, initially in the teeth of some ridicule, eventually persuaded the College that a subject taken seriously at Manchester and Leeds should also be taken seriously in Dublin. The diplomas in public administration and social science were later incorporated into the degree course in Social Science (1962), but especially in its first few years, when the public administration classes were given mainly in the evening, this diploma served to bring into the College many junior civil servants who would otherwise have had no occasion to cross its threshold, and to convince them that it was a much less terrifying and dangerous place than they had been led to believe.

When the School of Education was revived after five years of dormancy by the appointment of Professor Fynne in 1922 its scope was enlarged so as not only to train graduates as secondary teachers, but also to co-operate with the Church of Ireland Training College (the successor of the Church Education Society which had been the subject of some controversy three-quarters of a century earlier) in giving some of the lectures for would-be primary teachers, and to enable them, on taking some extra courses, to obtain a degree.

1945 saw the germ of a veterinary school, in an arrangement similar to that made for the School of Agriculture, with the students attending in Trinity lectures in pure science and in an abbreviated arts course and going to University College for technical instruction. An attempt was made later to establish a veterinary school in which the whole course should be at least partly under the control of Trinity College, but its full realization was frustrated first by ecclesiastical and later by political prejudice. Fortunately, however, the chronicle of these events lies outside our period.

(x)

This rather meagre record of development was conditioned in part by financial stringency. But few universities except the newest were developing much faster, for the idea that stability implied stagnation had not yet won the day. By dint of careful economies elsewhere the College was able during these years not only to invest annually a surplus sufficient to compensate for falling interest rates and compulsory land purchase but also to edge up slowly the sum devoted to academic salaries.[27] Some of this increase is to be attributed to bargains struck with individual Professors who alleged that they had been offered better-paid jobs elsewhere, but most of it was the result of a steady growth in the number of lecturers and assistants on salaries ranging from £150 to £300 a year. The Calendar for 1919–20 lists 31 Fellows, 31 non-Fellow Professors (of whom 18 were full-time) and 26 lecturers and assistants. Twenty years later the figures were 26 Fellows, 32 non-Fellow Professors (20 full-time) and 67 assistants and lecturers. A very gradual transformation was taking place whereby the Professors ceased to be completely maids-of-all-work in their departments, so that the subjects taught were covered more completely, with at least a little scope for specialization.

Broadly speaking it may be said that between the wars most departments were reasonably efficient; few were really distinguished, but few were occasions of shame. For the most part the education imparted was sound, if somewhat stodgy. As late as 1939 English literature ended with Matthew Arnold and Browning and European history with the treaty of Berlin; the word 'ecology' was never mentioned to students of botany, nor were students of zoology given any indication that comparative physiology was a respectable and expanding field. But despite its obvious disadvantages this conservatism had some compensating advantages; a sound and widely based knowledge of essentials fitted in better with the traditional reputation of the T.C.D. man, prepared to 'go anywhere, do anything' than would a more sophisticated and specialized training. A graduate who went to Oxford or Cambridge for post-graduate study was apt to be alarmed at first at the cultured chatter he heard from the lips of men not obviously more intelligent than himself and to conclude that he must be a provincial ignoramus, but later on, when he found that when he imparted what he thought were pieces of standard textbook knowledge he was listened to with interest and respect, the perspective altered.

A hasty review of the main schools will serve to give some idea of the teaching and research between 1919 and 1947 and to introduce the more striking personalities.

We begin with Divinity, as befits its seniority. A striking feature of this school was that, having gone into a considerable decline in the first quarter of the century in respect of the number of its students, it showed a remarkable recovery during the thirties, not only in their number, but in their intellectual quality and general liveliness. The Divinity School had not shared in the post-war boom enjoyed by the doctors and engineers, but around 1925 the annual number of testimoniums began to increase from its low level of twelve, till in 1938 the figure was up to forty-two, with men of the calibre of George Simms, Michael Ferrar and the Hanson twins among its present or recent members. Its professoriate maintained well enough the traditions of the previous half-century of intellectual rigour and very moderate high-churchmanship – a tradition which had been reinforced by the appointment of two Cambridge men to chairs: J.A.F. Gregg (later Primate), who was Archbishop King's Professor from 1911 to 1916, and H.A. McNeile, who succeeded the aged John Gwynn as Regius Professor in 1917. But Gregg's *métier* was that of ecclesiastical statesman, and he was soon promoted to the Bench, while McNeile, although he produced during his Dublin years some biblical studies which were well received, was handicapped from 1925 onwards by the ill heath which was to force his retirement. The leading figure during the period under review was Newport White, who, after serving for nine years as deputy to John Gwynn, became Archbishop King's Professor in 1916 and succeeded to McNeile's chair on his retirement. Although he was not a great scholar, his diligence and erudition, his precision and Kantian punctuality, his felicity of phrase and salty academic wit, and the assurance of his speech which contrasted strangely with his faltering gait (due to extreme short sight) made him one of the best-known personalities in the College. He was followed in both his chairs by J.E.L. Oulton, a sound patristic scholar, too shy to be in this sense a personality, but with a lucid and elegant mind well displayed in his sermons. On his promotion to the Regius chair he was succeeded after a short interval as Archbishop King's Professor by R.R. Hartford. The appointment was made under strong pressure from Gregg (by now Archbishop of Dublin, and the effective leader of the Church of Ireland), and was a curious one. Hartford had won a gold medal at his Moderatorship in Philosophy, but he had won no prizes in the Divinity School and had published little of consequence. He did not even possess the degree of B.D., a statutory requirement for the chair, so he could only be appointed as acting Professor, with a promise of confirmation if he got the degree within a year. Against these limitations were to be set his record as a successful and generally popular College chaplain for some years, and his obviously versatile and inquiring, if not very profound intelligence. But there were many ways in which he could have served his church better than as a professor of divinity, and even his friends came to see that Gregg's judgment had been faulty.

One other figure in the Divinity School deserves mention – G.V. Jourdan, who was Professor of Ecclesiastical History from 1933 until his death in 1955. His field of study was the Reformation and the succeeding century, and he published from his parish in Cork many substantial and well-planned books and articles on this period. He was a pugnacious cock-sparrow of a man who loved argument – especially if it was against a bishop – but although his wording was vigorous his kindliness shone through, and he never gave offence. His enthusiasm for scholarship and controversy kept him working until long after his eightieth birthday, and as his lectures were liberally spiced with reminiscences of his confutation of eminent historians or theologians with whom he had disagreed they became a sort of intellectual variety turn, the applause being led by engineering students and others who had strayed in to hear the fun. Whatever the faults of the Divinity School it could not be called dry or dull while Jourdan was there.

The Law School continued in the rather sad state in which it stood when we last reviewed it, with Bastable as an impressive but very part-time Regius Professor, giving a few lectures on jurisprudence, and the rest of the teaching given by busy working barristers, or by Baxter on his visits from Belfast. In 1932 Bastable retired, and the following year Baxter died. After some months of unprofitable brooding the Board and Council appointed to the Regius chair an elderly K.C., S.L. Brown, on the understanding that his duties would be little more than ceremonial. Tired of switching round titles to indicate different aspects of the law, they abolished Baxter's chair of Feudal and English Law, and appointed, under the non-committal title of Professor of Laws, Frances Moran as the effective head of the school. (A motion to advertise the chair publicly was narrowly defeated at the Council.) Miss Moran was a strange mixture of progressive feminism and strong conservatism in the fields of politics, morality and social behaviour. She dressed and talked with style, and her conversation was full of well-informed gossip, pithily expressed, so that she was a popular luncheon guest. She moved as a queen in the world of women graduates, and in due time became President of their world federation. But she had no claims to serious consideration as an academic lawyer. Her lectures were businesslike, but they were essentially dictation exercises, and she never manifested any interest in the speculative, philosophical or social aspects of law.

The following year, however, the Board took the step that should have been taken much earlier; it appointed O.H. Phillips as a full-time lecturer in Law, and this permitted the extension of lectures for the Moderatorship in Legal Science downwards into the Freshman years. Phillips (who later became Professor at Birmingham) stayed only for two years, but he was replaced by another full-time academic lawyer, J.A. Coutts, who was efficient enough not only in this post but also in cognate spheres such as the diploma in public administration that he was with general consent elected to Fellowship in 1944, and soon afterwards to the chair of Laws, while Miss Moran stepped up to the Regius Professorship. Unfortunately Coutts left in 1952 to become

Professor at Bristol, and it was not until 1960 that there was more than one full-time teacher in the school, and not until 1962 that there was a full-time Professor. Since then, however, progress has been satisfactory and rapid.

In the Medical School the number of students fluctuated rather hectically, giving rise to some difficult practical problems. An immense post-war boom (in which students from South Africa were prominent) was followed by a sharp decline; later there was a recovery, followed by a lesser decline during the war of 1939–45 (see Fig. 2, p. 502). Under the fatherly guidance of A.F. Dixon as Dean until his death in 1936 it prospered well enough, but there were signs that it was living too much on its former reputation. Dixon was followed as Professor of Anatomy by Jamieson, a genial Shetlander who ran his department well but was too old to initiate far-reaching changes, for he came to Dublin only after his retirement from the chair at Leeds at the age of sixty-five. The department of Physiology showed little life during this period; Harold Pringle, Professor from 1919 to 1936, was a sad comedown after Sir William Thompson, for he was dull, conservative and unproductive. His successor, David Torrens, was popular with students and a fair teacher, but although he tried to make an entry into the world of research by assisting Barcroft at Cambridge in successive long vacations, he was not really a big enough man for the post. Pathology was equally dead, for J.T. Wigham, Professor from 1924 to 1945, gave the impression that he was more interested in sailing and in the Society of Friends, of which he was a prominent and loyal member, than in pathology.

The two most lively departments were those of Biochemistry and Bacteriology. Fearon, the first Professor of Biochemistry, was a remarkable man who only partly realized his great potentialities. Author of an excellent textbook and a small monograph, he knew his subject well, but he was not content with that. At an early age he fell, rather unfortunately, under the influence of Oliver Gogarty, and tried, as Gogarty did with some success, to become a complete Renaissance man. But Fearon was shy and timid, and would not have lasted long in the world of Rabelais and Machiavelli. He would have been more at home in the seventeenth century with Sir Thomas Browne or the early members of the Royal Society. So he dabbled in mysticism, wrote a play about Parnell, and speculated endlessly on this and that. In his work he was forever looking for neat, new colour-tests, but could not settle down to any serious continuous work with a burette or a balance. His lectures, however, were the best in the school; spiced with titbits of curious erudition, they nevertheless imparted an understanding of the fundamentals of biochemistry, and were remembered long afterwards with nostalgic affection by many of his students.

The chair of Bacteriology was instituted in 1919 for Adrian Stokes, the last really brilliant member of the family whose connexion with the College started with the election of John Stokes as Fellow in 1746. But after three years he left for London, and not long afterwards added his name to the roll of medical martyrs by dying of yellow fever in West Africa while investigating its cause, prevention and cure. After a two-year interval he was succeeded by J.W. Bigger, whose personality and achievements will be discussed more fully later (p. 492). It is sufficient here to say that he did more than anyone else in the thirties and forties to infuse some dynamism into the school and to focus attention on the problems that faced it.

What the school prided itself on at this time, and with some justice, was the turning out of efficient and resourceful general practitioners, suitable men for the Army and the colonial service as well as for busy suburban practices. The concentration on this aim meant the encouragement of efficient all-round teaching at the cost of research, and there were few medical graduates of the period who took up research posts. The policy was energetically supported by T.G. Moorhead, a very influential figure in the school from 1925 onwards, the year in which his enormous practice as one of the leading physicians of Dublin was drastically reduced by the onset of total blindness. Thereafter he became perforce a medical statesman, and was appointed Regius Professor in the same year. Although he was ready to recognize talent wherever he found it, his instincts were essentially conservative, and he ruled the school committee somewhat as an autocrat. When Bigger became Dean he very injudiciously (and unsuccessfully) tried to oust Moorhead from the chairmanship, and the ensuing bad blood only intensified Moorhead's suspicions of Bigger's reforms.

The clinical Professors were still all part-time; they included some nonentities, some public figures, and some excellent clinicians who published occasional papers, such as Micks, Synge and O'Donel Browne. But none was outstanding for his publications. William Pearson, who held the chair of Surgery from 1929 onwards, was a first-rate surgeon and a good teacher, but he forfeited the respect of his students by his extreme partiality as an examiner. If you were a Corkman, a rugby player or the son of a Freemason, then your prospects were good, but if you had other affiliations or too heavily pigmented a skin you needed to know your surgery very well indeed.

Of the Engineering School little need be said except that it carried on its traditions. Alexander was succeeded in 1921 by David Clark, a silent and efficient Scot, and he in his turn by John Purser (a nephew of the Professors of Latin and Physiology) in 1933. Purser was not a revolutionary, and made few changes. He was unpopular with the more progressive element among the Fellows for his entrenched conservatism on the Board, where he sat for many years as a representative of the non-Fellow Professors, but he was well liked by his staff and his students. The numbers in the school were subject to booms and slumps rather similar to those in medicine, but they showed no decline in 1939, and from an average of something like thirteen B.A.I. degrees a year in the thirties they rose to double that figure in 1945.

Turning now to the non-medical sciences we find that in Chemistry, Botany and Zoology the pattern was very similar – a Professor of long standing, with an international reputation in a narrow field, but not venturing (at any rate with much success) outside its boundaries. Werner was in charge of Chemistry from 1928 to 1946,[28] Dixon of Botany from 1904 to 1949, and J.B. Gatenby of Zoology from 1921 to 1957; and to anyone working on urea, the ascent of sap or the Golgi apparatus the writings of these men were essential reading. But to workers in other aspects of these same sciences their names were not necessarily well known. Temperamentally they were very different. Werner was modest and amiable, and for years a popular secretary of the Common Room; Dixon was courteous but reserved, and mixed little with non-scientific colleagues; Gatenby was a perpetual storm-centre, diversifying his attacks on cytological heretics in Oxford or Paris by quarrelling with his assistants, none of whom he was able to keep for very long. In Geology, the great John Joly lasted on until 1933, but his final years were pathetic; his lectures were muddled and unappreciated, and he should have retired at least five years before he died. He was succeeded by L.B. Smyth, a quiet, conscientious and methodical palaeontologist who had been keeping the department going during Joly's decline. His lectures were not inspiring, but they were models of clarity, and his publications on the Irish Carboniferous were careful and thorough.

Physics presents a more complex picture. With W.E. Thrift as Professor and his brother Harry as his lieutenant the department can best be described as stagnant. Its only member with a lively mind was Jack Poole, but he was so idiosyncratic and often contrary that he was not in a position to influence policy. By 1926 the elder Thrift was second in line for co-option to a Senior Fellowship, and this stirred the Board rather tardily into offering a Fellowship in Physics in 1928. At least some members of the Board had their eye on Poole as the likely Fellow and the next Professor. But R.W. Ditchburn, a research student at Cambridge, believing that he had little chance of the Fellowship, thought nevertheless that the Madden Prize was well worth competing for. He was elected Fellow to his own and everybody else's astonishment.

What was to happen now? Thrift had become a Senior Fellow nine months earlier, and although there was no longer a statutory bar on his combining this with the chair it was clearly most undesirable that a man already well immersed in committees and likely to become more so should be in charge of a large laboratory. Poole could not succeed him, because the statutes required that the Professor be chosen from the Fellows. But the idea that this very young *arriviste* from England, who was, in addition, an archetypal *New Statesman* reader with the correct radical views on every question, was to be put in over the heads of his seniors and allowed to turn the department upside down was too much for many to stomach. For a while the Board did nothing, and in November Ditchburn wrote to say that he was dissatisfied with his position and wondered whether he had made a mistake in coming to Dublin. The Provost asked him to exercise a little patience, and meanwhile to send in a report on the teaching of physics as he saw it. The report, when it came, was rather trenchant, and on first reading caused some indignation. But reflection convinced many members of the Board that most of its recommendations were sound, and after a flurry of recriminations, apologies and explanations Thrift resigned from the chair a few months later and Ditchburn was elected in his place. Within a few years he made good progress in modernizing the department, which after 1934 was further strengthened by the accession of Walton.

Among the humanities, Modern Languages led the field in the number of its students. W.F. Trench, who succeeded Dowden as Professor of English in 1914, was in a sense a minor Dowden. His book on Shakespeare reveals a sensitive and original mind, but he found extraordinary difficulty in clothing his thoughts with words. His lectures and much of his conversation were filled with agonized pauses during which his limbs and his body went through strange contortions in the search for the right word, and presumably a similar blockage impeded his pen. On his death in 1939 he was succeeded by H.O. White. It was a curious appointment, and one much criticized at the time by academic purists, as at least two other applicants had far better qualifications on paper. White was a T.C.D. man who had kept in close touch with the College, and there is little doubt that he was elected on what may be called an 'old boy vote'. But although negligible as an author and only fair as a teacher of undergraduates, he justified his appointment by building up immediately after the war a very successful post-graduate school of Anglo-Irish literature, and the fact that he had sat at the feet of AE (George Russell) and had many first-hand anecdotes of the leading figures of the literary revival gave him a god-like status in the eyes of young Americans, whose studies he directed with sympathy and skill. He was for many years the best known personality in College, hiding behind a screen of eccentric and assiduously cultivated mannerisms a personality which combined timidity, great kindness and surprising touches of Ulster shrewdness.

French, which attracted even more students than English (a large majority of them women),[29] was for long in the charge of T.B. Rudmose-Brown, who had succeeded to the chair of Romance Languages in 1909. He never laid claim to any deep knowledge of languages other than French and Provençal, and the change in the title of his chair to that of French in 1937 was long overdue. He is a difficult man to estimate, for his undoubted literary sensitivity and awareness of contemporary French poetry was masked by a partly assumed cynicism and an all too genuine laziness. In his later years much of his energy was devoted to a guerilla war with Walter Starkie, Professor of Spanish since 1926. Neither had much respect for the other, but the campaign was waged without real malice.

Starkie himself is even more difficult to evaluate. Full of energy, bonhomie, gossip and wide, if disorganized literary culture, he was a stimulating lecturer – when he lectured, for his absences were frequent and at times prolonged; nor was criticism entirely stilled when, having obtained permission from the Board to appoint as his temporary deputy a 'native woman speaker', this turned out to be his wife. He wrote little of real scholarly value, but his accounts of his travels in search of gypsy lore sold widely, and these, together with his directorship of the Abbey Theatre, made him a central figure in literary Dublin. He was the sort of professor of which every university should have one, but not more than one.

In History, Curtis and Alison Phillips continued on their established courses, assisted by Constantia Maxwell, who was given a personal chair of Economic History in 1945, though her most successful work lay in her semi-popular accounts of social life in eighteenth-century Ireland. In 1939 Phillips retired and was succeeded by T.W. Moody, recently elected Fellow. He was already one of the editors of *Irish historical studies*, and the detailed and devoted care which he gave to this task served as an apprenticeship for his major achievement, the planning and editing of the *New history of Ireland*. He revised the course so as to give Sophister students an opportunity for greater specialization, and under his meticuluous, but nevertheless stimulating guidance his post-graduate students produced some notable work in Irish history of the nineteenth century.

In Philosophy there were two big names: Macran and A.A. Luce. Macran had taken his degree in Classics and Modern Languages, and his first writings were on Greek music. But in 1901 he was elected Professor of Moral Philosophy, and under him it developed into a permanent, instead of, as hitherto, a temporary post. About the same time he fell under the spell of Hegel, whose philosophy soon became with him a positive obsession. 'Philosophy', he would say to his class, 'begins with Thales and ends with Hegel.' And he believed it. He published translations with commentary of two of Hegel's works, but he did not join the neo-Hegelians of Oxford in developing the master's ideas. He certainly understood Hegel, and in his widely admired lectures he persuaded some of his students (dangerously perhaps) that they understood him too. He was a popular member of a circle of semi-bohemian literary figures including Gogarty, and perhaps that was one reason why he did not achieve more, for the fatal connexion between Irish literary talent and alcohol had by then been formed, and Macran spent much of his later life in a battle against alcoholism.

He was succeeded in the Professorship by A.A. Luce in 1934, and although two men could not have been more different in temperament and way of life, Luce too succumbed to an obsession. After a brief flirtation with Bergsonianism he took up the study of Berkeley, and for the rest of his life he gave the impression that he ate, drank, dreamed and lived Berkeley. Although, like Macran, he did some valuable exposition and editing, and in later years devoted much study to Berkeley's life, he remained a Berkeleian, not a neo-Berkeleian. What the master had said, if properly interpreted, was sufficient.

In Classics, Smyly and Mooney, followed by Goligher and Alton, carried on along the lines which we have already indicated, but there was a welcome infusion of new blood into a school which had perhaps become too inbred, by the election of H.W. Parke to Fellowship in 1929 and D.E.W. Wormell in 1939. They brought with them the more professional standards of Oxford and Cambridge respectively. Parke soon made a name for himself in Ancient History (of which he became Professor in 1934), while Wormell, although originally his interests were mostly in Greek, was steered towards the impending vacancy in the chair of Latin, and settled down to what was nearly a lifetime's work in ordering and completing Alton's inchoate work on Ovid. Meanwhile W.B. Stanford, elected Fellow in 1934 and Regius Professor of Greek in 1940, although an 'insider', struck a new note by ignoring alike textual criticism and history and treating the classics as subjects for literary criticism. Although they lie outside our time-span some mention must also be made of his work on Homer and his capitalization of what is probably his greatest gift – the highest level of popularization – in his widely appreciated lectures before cultured but unspecialized audiences.

The mathematical school had been rescued from the rather low ebb to which it had sunk in the early part of the century by the accession of

C.H. Rowe (1920), J.L. Synge (1925) and A.J. McConnell (1930) to Fellowship. It was unfortunate that Synge, the most distinguished and productive of the three, should have found Ireland too slow for his restless spirit and resigned in 1930 to make his name in the New World. Rowe and McConnell, however, did useful work in their earlier years, and reminded the world that the mathematical traditions of Dublin still had some life in them.

Economics was transformed in 1932 from a peripheral to a central subject by the replacement of Bastable by a full-time Professor in the form of G.A. Duncan. He had as acutely critical a brain as any of his generation in the College, and he used it to good effect in his lectures, in which his demolition with surgical skill of the theories of some of his fellow-economists delighted at least the first-class men in his audience. His planning of the course showed a professional touch, and it was, up to 1952, well up to date. But he seems to have turned in on himself the same unsparing criticism which he applied to others, for his writings were not commensurate with his ability, and apart from an interesting appendix to the Report of the Banking Commission of 1934, are for the most part 'occasional papers'. His only senior colleague in the school was Joseph Johnston, who, having studied both Ancient History and Economics fell badly between the two stools, for he saw junior colleagues appointed to the Professorships in both subjects. He then took up farming in his spare time and wrote extensively, if somewhat idiosyncratically on agricultural economics with special reference to Irish problems.

(xi)

A word must be added here on the subject of higher degrees, and on the proliferation of primary degrees. Up to the middle of the nineteenth century there were, as in Oxford and Cambridge, only ten degrees: a man could be a Bachelor or Master of Arts, or a Bachelor or Doctor of Divinity, Law, Medicine or Music. We have seen how the emergence of surgery and engineering as distinct professions led to the establishment of Bachelor's and Master's degrees in those subjects within the period 1858–72 (pp. 184, 188). Similar motives led to the establishment of Master's and Bachelor's degrees in Obstetric Science in 1877 and 1887 respectively. 1891 saw the institution of Doctorates in Literature and Science. The immediate stimulus was the need for appropriate honorary degrees for conferment at the Tercentenary celebrations, but the change was also a delayed reaction to the disappearance of clerical Fellows, and was, significantly enough, accompanied by a tightening up of the regulations for the degree of D.D. (This had hitherto been merely a badge of seniority and respectability, achieved by formal exercises; henceforth it was to require a thesis or published work in theology.) Mahaffy might be content with his D.D. and Dowden with his LL.D., but there was a general feeling that scholarship which lay outside the scope of the old-established professions should in future be given a more appropriately descriptive accolade, and one which implied the publication of some scholarly work.

Early in the twentieth century the claim for dentistry to be regarded as a profession distinct from surgery was conceded by the institution of Master's (1904) and Bachelor's (1911) degrees in Dental Science. 1911 saw also a more significant development in the institution for the first time of a research degree in the modern sense. The degree of Bachelor in Science could be achieved by a moderator in mathematics or science who had spent a year in 'advanced study and research'. In 1918 M.Sc. and M.Litt. were instituted as similar but more advanced degrees, requiring two years' research, but they had a short life for in 1920 Dublin agreed with the other universities of the United Kingdom to offer instead the degree of Doctor of Philosophy. This decision was taken in response to American pressure, as it was made clear that American graduates who came over for research would not willingly return unless the magic letters of Ph.D. had been attached to their names.

Soon afterwards a number of degrees of rather dubious utility were instituted, for which some elementary preliminary instruction (and also the concurrent, though abbreviated, course in Arts) was given in Trinity College, while the main part of the technical instruction was given in University College (or, up to 1926, the College of Science). These included Bachelor's degrees in Agriculture and Forestry (agreed in 1914, but not formally instituted until 1918), a degree of Sc.B.(Tech.) which in practice meant applied chemistry, and diversifications of the primary Engineering degree under the names of B.A.I.(Mech.) and B.A.I.(Elec.), though after a few years these last two were amalgamated. None of these degrees can be considered a success; they attracted few students, and fewer and fewer as the years went by, although they survived until after 1952. They are of some interest, however as representing the first manifestation of a tendency (later to run riot in the fields of engineering, business studies and social science) of indicating by separate degrees small variations in the specialization of the field of study, ignoring the tradition (with which nobody seemed very dissatisfied) whereby the degree of B.A. might represent equally well a knowledge of zoology, Semitic languages or economics.

Meanwhile the Dublin B.Sc. had been coming to appear rather anomalous, for this degree was now used by many universities to

461

indicate a primary degree in scientific subjects, parallel and not superior to B.A. In 1928, therefore, the M.Sc. was resurrected to replace it,
and all holders of the old B.Sc. were entitled to claim an M.Sc. This gave
an opening to those who wished to emphasize the difference between
science and the humanities, so that from 1928 onwards, although
Moderators in science graduated as B.A., a pass course in science was
devised, leading to a B.Sc. For this course Latin was not required at
entrance, and optimistic but mainly unsuccessful attempts were made
to ensure a working knowledge of French and German instead. This
degree also was a failure; it attracted mainly the type of student which
Wilkins (p. 416) had characterized as 'dunderheads', and its reputation
was low, almost from the start. The School of Commerce, described
earlier (p. 449), generated the degrees of B.Comm. (1926) and M.Comm.
(1930). In 1936 the humanities decided that they needed a one-year
research degree parallel to the M.Sc., so the B.Litt. (changed in 1958 to
M.Litt.) was instituted. Finally, the first attempt to start a veterinary
school was signalized in 1945 by the appearance of B.Sc.(Vet.) among
the degrees, now numbering thirty-one, to which the incoming
student might aspire.

So much for the formalities; what of the realities that lay behind
them? The research degrees were well administered from the start, and
although the Ph.D. found few takers at first (only five were awarded up
to 1927), the numbers began slowly to increase until by the end of the
war there were about ten a year. The Americans, for whom the degree
was instituted, were conspicuous by their absence; Indians at first
predominated, and later Irish, with a sprinkling of candidates from
Britain and a few from overseas. The growing popularity of the Ph.D.
tended to raise the standard required for the other doctorates (which
previously had been awarded for work not much higher than that
which we would now regard as Ph.D. level). But two qualifications
must be made to this statement. Law, as in the staffing of its school,
lagged sadly behind, and up to 1930 the LL.D. could be (and usually
was) secured by passing an examination, which, though by no means a
formality, demanded from an intelligent graduate not more than a
year's hard reading. Since 1931 it has required a thesis or published
work, and in consequence, whereas the fifteen years up to 1931 saw the
award of fifty-seven doctorates of laws, there were only eight in the
next fifteen years. The second qualification is more embarrassing, but
it cannot be denied that there was a distressing tendency to require
from senior members of the academic staff a lower standard than that
which a higher doctorate implied to most men. Sometimes this was
secured by the careful choice of a sympathetic examiner, but for many
years it was held that a Senior Fellow who sought a higher doctorate

need not be subjected to the indignity of submitting his publications for examination: he could be judged by his peers. Such degrees were in some cases certainly well-deserved, but in others it is equally certain that they were not; and it was not until about 1950 that the College could be confident that none of its higher degrees were being awarded on standards that were seriously out of step with those of other universities.

(xii)

When war broke out in September 1939, De Valera's announcement of Irish neutrality surprised nobody. Apart from the prudential considerations which led all the small powers of Europe to remain neutral unless and until they were invaded, neutrality formed the most unambiguous demonstration of the reality of independence from Britain. There is no doubt that it was approved by the overwhelming majority of the electorate, though there was a small minority, composed partly of unrepentant ex-Unionists and partly of particularly strongly committed anti-fascists, which would have preferred belligerence, and there was a minute, but inevitably conspicuous pro-German faction, with whom hatred of England overrode other considerations, and who naively believed that a victorious Germany would reunite Ireland and then go away. Among the supporters of neutrality, however, one can distinguish three different strains of thought. A substantial minority accepted it as inevitable and defensible, but wished to see it shaded and even strained in favour of Britain as far as possible. A second attitude, that of the majority through the country, was somewhat detached: a British victory was certainly to be preferred to a German one, but meanwhile a little twisting of the lion's tail would do no harm, and perhaps a negotiated peace might be best of all. Finally a handful of pacifists and cynics called indifferently for a plague on both the warring houses.

All these attitudes were represented in Trinity, but in very different proportions from those in the country as a whole. There may have been among the students one or two pro-German sympathizers who had links with the I.R.A., but they kept very quiet. Interventionists were in a minority, but a fairly substantial one; many of them had been brought up in the north (which was, of course, at war) and still had strong links with it. The majority of staff and students alike adopted the attitude of heart-felt and anxious, but somewhat impotent, sympathy with the allied cause. Those with genuine but cautious and limited sympathies in the same direction were represented, though not in very large numbers; they tended to oscillate between two poles, being pushed in one direction by the naivety and noisiness of some of their colleagues' belief in the verbal inerrancy of the B.B.C., only to be pushed in the other by some particularly needless and clumsy piece of censorship imposed by Mr Aiken on the plea of military security. The third, completely neutral group had a few adherents among the students, but scarcely any among the staff.

In spite of these divergent views there were few quarrels over political issues. Most members of the College realized that some tact and forbearance was necessary, but though the atmosphere was fairly peaceful it was claustrophobic and tense. Differences which were not expressed began to fester. It was not easy to get permission to visit Britain except for war-work or to visit relatives, and as the war went on fuel shortage made travel even within Ireland uncomfortable and difficult. That most effective restorer of low morale – a hot bath – was virtually unobtainable in College for a year or two, and even in the suburbs was a comparatively rare luxury. It is not surprising that it was during the war that the atmosphere of contentment which we have mentioned as characterizing the preceding years broke down, and vigorous, and at times bitter debates on the constitution and adminis-tration of the College began to recur.

It was, paradoxically enough, the coming of peace rather than any incident during the war which produced the only political crisis in which the College was involved. When the news came through on the morning of 7 May 1945 of the final German surrender there was naturally a good deal of excitement in Dublin, with people walking the streets vaguely expecting something to happen. In the early after-noon a group of undergraduates, taking advantage of the fact that fire-watching drill had made access to the roofs easy, began hoisting on the main flag-pole of the West Front whatever flags they could lay their hands on. The Union Jack was prominent, but it was by no means alone; the Irish tricolour also appeared, as did the Soviet flag and, later on, the Stars and Stripes. The hoisting of the Russian flag did not take place without protest; a Hungarian lady of right-wing sympathies tried to pull down the student who was hoisting it, and finding her strength insufficient sank her teeth in his calf until she herself was pulled away. So far all was in the spirit of a normal student rag, but like so many rags it went on too long. It is said that the first hostile reaction from the crowd below was set off by the Irish tricolour appearing, in one of the numerous permutations of bunting, below the Union Jack, and unfor-tunately just at this moment there arrived a procession of members of Ailtiri na hAiseirghe, one of the nastier of the minute extremist splinter groups which regularly appear on the Irish political scene and equally regularly die after a few years. It combined extreme nationalism with noisy Catholicism and a large admixture of fascist principles. Its members staged an anti-Trinity demonstration in the street, in the course of which a Union Jack was burnt. Some of the students on the roof retaliated, perhaps understandably, but most imprudently, by burning an Irish tricolour. Then things got really out of hand. The roof was belatedly cleared of students and the flag-pole of flags, but for the next two days the College was virtually in a state of siege, and corner-boys from the back streets had the fun of being able to throw stones at the windows of Botany Bay and being regarded as heroes and patriots instead of being cuffed on the head.

Much of the blame must be laid on the Junior Dean (J.M. Henry), though in fairness it must be allowed that he was a somewhat unwilling conscript for the post. He was relieved of the office a few months later. The Provost sent a note to the Taoiseach apologizing for the provocation, and was rewarded by receiving abusive letters from indignant Unionists in addition to those from indignant Republicans which had been coming in for some days.[30] But although the situation was tense and unpleasant for a week or so, things calmed down remarkably quickly and the whole episode was forgotten quicker than one might have imagined possible. It served, in fact, the function of a bloodletting; the tension to which we have referred was now relieved, and both the College and the country settled down to face a new world in which neutrality no longer shielded them from the rest of Europe.

The main effect of war on the College was, however, not political, but academic and financial. The fall in student numbers was slight, and in no way comparable to that in 1914–18, but the fact that a fair number of students interrupted their courses to join the forces or take up some other war-work in Britain, and doubtless some potential students went straight from school to the war, suggests that had there been no war the student numbers would have moved upwards. Even in Britain, of course, the disruption of university life was far less than it had been in 1914–18, and this was so *a fortiori* in neutral Dublin. The fairly large scale on which deferment of call-up was agreed in Britain meant that Irish students could grant themselves deferment without feeling that they were shirking the issue. But the general atmosphere was unsettling; considerations of public duty or of private interest did not provide clear answers as to whether to go or stay, and although the insouciance of youth shielded many against these worries, the more intelligent and sensitive did not find the peace of mind necessary for academic work at its best.

The effect on the staff was more immediate and more conspicuous. Four Fellows (all born in Britain or Northern Ireland) received leave of absence to take up civil service posts in Britain; Bigger, the Professor of Bacteriology, went to serve with the Royal Army Medical Corps in England, and Walter Starkie took charge of the British Council office in Madrid, where he made such a success of the post, building it up into virtually a rival embassy to the official one under Sir Samuel Hoare, that he never returned to his chair in Dublin. Some six or eight lecturers also departed, either to join the armed forces or to other forms of government service in Britain. Substitutes were found – not always very satisfactory – and no courses were cancelled, but the effects of undermanning soon became apparent, all the more so as death struck heavily during the war years; Provost Thrift, four Fellows (Goligher, Bell, Fry and Rowe) and one Professor (Rudmose-Brown) died during the years 1940–3. Replacements were not easy to obtain, and in any case it was held, at least as far as Fellowships were concerned, that it would be unfair to those away on some form of war service to fill the posts before the war ended. In consequence the surviving staff became overstrained, and it was very difficult to find from the depleted ranks of the Fellows suitable men for the various administrative posts. When Bailey was promoted from Junior Dean to Registrar in 1942 it was only after considerable pressure from the Provost that Charles Rowe agreed to take over the former post. He was a sensitive, introverted mathematician, held in great esteem by a small circle of intimate friends, but although he did his best he was not suited to his new duties, and a realization of this was one of several factors that led to his tragic suicide eighteen months later.

By the end of 1943 the shortage of staff had become so obvious that earlier attitudes had to be modified. The number of Fellows had sunk to twenty-two and of these only seventeen were at work in the College. The tutors were overworked and some departments were seriously understaffed. It had already been agreed a few months earlier that, war or no war, a Fellowship in Law should be offered in 1944, and in due course J.A. Coutts, who had been lecturing in the school since 1937, was elected. But this in itself did not solve the general problem. An Ordinance was prepared, therefore, providing for the election in 1944 of two further Fellows from among the existing lecturers; selection was to be primarily on the basis of published or unpublished work, but general usefulness to the College was also to be taken into account, and those elected were bound to accept a tutorship if offered one. Some twelve lecturers appeared as candidates, and on a table outside the Board Room was laid out for each his curriculum vitae and his reprints or typescripts. One elderly Senior Fellow, to whom a reprint from a learned journal was an unfamiliar object, was heard to refer to the candidates as 'those bloody pamphleteers'. The Board soon decided on G.F. Mitchell as a suitable man; he had already laid a solid foundation for his life-work in quaternary studies, and he had shown his public spirit by his efficient organization of the College fire-fighting service. Agreement on a second name was more difficult to obtain, and it was not until the autumn that the Board decided that E.G. Quin, an Irish scholar and philologist, was an acceptable and uncontroversial candidate. By this time the prospects of a fairly early conclusion to the war were becoming brighter, and in response to some feelers sent out by the College two or three of the Fellows were released from their war jobs before hostilities ceased.

By the summer of 1945 it was quite possible, without doing an injustice to absentees, to make plans to fill the vacant posts. Three Fellowships were agreed for 1947, and three Fellows were elected, all from among the existing lecturers. But when it came to recruiting Professors in a subject in which there was no suitable internal candidate a new difficulty arose. The income of the College had not kept pace with wartime inflation; the English universities, with increased grants, were recruiting in large numbers; it was, in fact, a seller's market for university posts, with Trinity in a very weak position. It was unfortunate that the chair which most urgently needed filling was French, for the salaries for chairs in modern languages had always been near the lower end of the professorial scale, and the Board could not, without risking discontent among the other Professors, advertise the post at a higher salary than £700, rising to £900. Only one well-qualified candidate applied, E.J. Arnould, reader in French at the University of Exeter, and he was offered the post.[31] He was immediately offered a chair by Exeter. The Board had, therefore to raise its offer to a starting salary of £900. The College was lucky to acquire such a good scholar at the price, but it was in no position to stand firm over details, and it is remarkable that Arnould ended up as the only Professor without a retiring age, and the only Professor with two sets of rooms.

(xiii)

It is convenient to consider here three incidents which, although not connected with the war, took place between 1939 and 1945 and were of some consequence to the College. These were the death of Provost Thrift in 1942, the appointment of John Charles McQuaid as Catholic Archbishop of Dublin in 1940, and the campaign against the College Library initiated in 1941 by Stanley Unwin on behalf of the Publishers' Association.

On the death of Thrift the example set at the previous vacancy of convening a meeting of Fellows and Professors was followed. Only two

28   Ernest Henry Alton. Provost, 1942–52. (Leo Whelan, Trinity College.)

candidates emerged: Alton, Professor of Latin and Vice-Provost, and K.C. Bailey, Professor of Physical Chemistry and Junior Dean. Alton had in his favour the fact that he was the only Senior Fellow who could seriously be considered; he was in good standing with the Government, thanks to his long service in Dail and Senate, and to the candid but very moderate manner in which he had supported the cause of the Protestant and Anglo-Irish minority. He was generally popular in College, was a good host and a good talker, and a man devoted to scholarship. Against this he was sixty-eight – not impossibly old but above the optimum age – and he was in many respects a muddler, who gave the impression (partly, though not entirely true) that he was incapable of orderly administration. Bailey, on the other hand, was in the eyes of many rather too young (only forty-five), and would have been, if appointed in 1942, the youngest Provost since Andrews. To some of the younger nominators, however, this was a point in his favour. His energy and loyalty were beyond question; if his conversation was less cultured than Alton's his publications were much more substantial, and several of his scientific colleagues thought that the time for a scientist as Provost was overdue. Alton, however, secured a substantial majority. Despite some hysterical rumours current among the more extreme ex-Unionists that De Valera intended to install as Provost a virtually monoglot Gaelic enthusiast, the College's nomination was accepted immediately without demur.

On the whole Alton made a good Provost. He was wise in appointing Bailey as Registrar, and they worked well in harmony. His choices for the other major offices were not so happy, but he was severely handicapped by the depleted state of the College staff brought about by the war, and the ties of friendship and the pressure of tradition combined to force him into making and continuing appointments with which he was not at all satisfied. For the rest, he showed himself a humane man, who could rebuke without humiliating, and who was genial and hospitable to junior members of the staff even if he forgot their names the next day. In general his heart ruled his head, but it was a generous heart; he had many prejudices in favour of people and only a few against them. His speeches at dinners and meetings were spiced with some splendid phrases, but you had to be sitting almost next to him to hear them; similarly, his reputation as a lecturer had been that some of his best remarks were made from the next room, where he had gone to verify a reference. On paper, however, he was able to discipline his mind, and could write good letters and memoranda. If sometimes laughed at, he was generally loved, and when he died the College felt, as it had not felt since the death of Salmon, that it had lost a father.

(xiv)

By 1939 the relationship between Trinity College and the Catholic Church appeared to have reached equilibrium. There was disapproval and there were warnings, but there was no openly-expressed hostility except in the cheaper Catholic press and from a few eccentrics like Alfred O'Rahilly, ostensibly Professor of Mathematical Physics at University College, Cork, but in fact a self-appointed oracle on every aspect of politics, sociology, economics and religion. To parents who presented a well-prepared case permission to send their children to Trinity was seldom refused. The proportion of Catholics in the annual intake had fluctuated during the inter-war years in a manner that is difficult to account for, reaching a peak of 24 per cent in 1926, and then declining to 8 per cent in 1937.

The Archbishop of Dublin in these years had been Edward Byrne, a somewhat inconspicuous figure who had been completely eclipsed as a public spokesman by the redoubtable figure of Cardinal Macrory of Armagh. In 1940, however, Archbishop Byrne died and was replaced by John Charles McQuaid, a man of great energy, ability and (as far as personal contact was concerned) suavity and charm. The force of his personality was enough to transfer the primacy, if not *de jure* then *de facto*, from Armagh to Dublin. He had been headmaster of Blackrock College, and preserved as Archbishop a headmaster's interest in detail and a determination that his wishes should be carried out without question and without compromise. And the most prominent of his aims was to make the Catholic Church the unchallenged arbiter of all questions in which it could reasonably claim to have an interest. Protestants and infidels were entitled to their civil rights and to the direction of their private institutions, but they need not expect any share in the direction of public education, welfare, medicine or even famine relief. Ireland was to be in as full a sense as possible a Catholic country. This attitude was not enunciated with any arrogance, or even very explicitly, but it was implemented by continuous hints, directives and pressures, and more than one mixed committee for charitable work had to be dissolved and reconstituted on sectarian lines. McQuaid was able to carry out his policy all the more effectively because he was obviously a devout, and indeed a holy man, and was not primarily in pursuit of personal power.

Trinity College could not hope to escape his attentions, and sure enough within two years of his appointment the terms in which the faithful were annually warned of the dangers of sending their children to Trinity were altered. For a warning was substituted a positive veto, from which the Archbishop alone could give a dispensation. Immediately McQuaid became a sort of bogy-man, not only to Protestants, but to an at first cautious, but later more outspoken, minority of liberal Catholics, and his motives, activities, prejudices, shortcomings and virtues were endlessly discussed in Trinity. The reaction was natural enough, but it was to some extent needless, for McQuaid's inflexibility on paper contrasted strangely with his accommodating attitude in personal interview; and neither from the diocese of Dublin nor from Ireland as a whole did the number of Catholics admitted to the College show a significant decline in the years that followed his appointment (see appendix 2). It is possible that his attitude prevented a more rapid rise, but at least from 1945 onwards the spirit of the times was working against him, and although he loyally carried out its decrees, much of the proceedings of the second Vatican Council must have darkened his last years.

(xv)

Even though the University as a whole was to experience little expansion between 1921 and 1945, there was one department which could not help but expand, and that was the Library. By 1919 it contained about 365,000 volumes, and was receiving some 4,000 a year under the terms of the Copyright Act. The expedient of enclosing the colonnade in 1891 had provided some further shelf-space, but already by 1919 the books were too numerous to be housed in the main building, and they overflowed into the Provost's stables and disused O.T.C. huts. In the early thirties the Provost with some difficulty persuaded the Board to put away some money for expansion, and a new octagonal reading-room, with an underground connexion to the main building and entered through the hall of honour which had already been erected as a war memorial by public subscription, was opened in 1937. It is not a very satisfactory building, but it served its essential purpose, and the second half of the colonnade was made available for book storage.

Meanwhile, however, the position of the Library under the Copyright Act was under attack. In 1922 two publishers maintained that as it was no longer in the United Kingdom its privileges should lapse, and they refused to send it their books. They had no legal case, and after a solicitor's letter from the College they complied 'under protest'. There was to be no further trouble for twenty years, but in 1941 the attack was renewed by Stanley Unwin, whose firm had been one of the recusants in 1922. Unwin, deploring the rights of all the copyright libraries, but striking at what he saw to be the weakest spot, declared that it was preposterous that British publishers had to subsidize a neutral country; but the Copyright Act made no mention of belligerence, and it was rather naive to expect Parliament in the middle of a war to pass a bill to exclude Trinity College from its provisions. A year later, however, he renewed the attack with the more damaging assertion that the Library was not well administered, that it was very difficult for a stranger to obtain admission, that many of the books claimed from the publishers were not easily available, and that some of them did not seem to be available at all, presumably because they had been sold.

Some of these charges were, unfortunately, true, but luckily for the

College Unwin spoilt what could have been a good case by mixing in with them others which were inaccurate. Spokesmen for the College replied that any genuine scholar was always admitted to the Library, and that it was completely untrue to say that any books received free were ever sold. Since Unwin accepted this denial only half-heartedly they declined to pursue the controversy any further.[32] What was, however, unfortunately true was an assertion of Unwin's, buried among exaggerations and irrelevancies, that many of the books received under copyright were difficult of access. A copyright library with limited resources is in the embarrassing position of a charitable trust presented with a large mansion with no endowment for its upkeep. Ideally such a library should consider not only the needs of contemporary scholars, but also the unpredictable whims of posterity. But when storage space and cataloguers are both in short supply it is obvious and right that *Tractatus logico-philosophicus* should be given a higher priority than *Tiger Tim's annual*. What had for many years been happening in Dublin was that books which could reasonably be regarded as of contemporary scholarly interest, and a few others, were catalogued and shelved fairly promptly; the remainder, including most novels, children's books, maps, music and much else, were 'postponed', which was a euphemism for 'neglected'. Some were card-indexed and shelved, others merely shelved, while all too many lay around in piles.

For this state of affairs the Librarian must take the blame. J.G. Smyly, who had been appointed to the post in 1914 was from the start a *fainéant* Librarian; he sat in the Librarian's room and edited Greek or Latin texts or medieval deeds, but unlike his great predecessors Todd, Ingram, and Abbott, he did nothing towards improving or extending the catalogues of manuscripts or other specialized material; he left virtually all the administration to his staff. Up to 1929 the Assistant Librarian had been a graduate and a man of general culture, even if untrained in librarianship. But in that year De Burgh retired, and was succeeded by Joseph Hanna, who had worked his way up from the position of junior clerk. Hanna was a hard-working, loyal, conscientious and obliging man, but he was unfitted to be the virtual head of a great Library. Since 1927 Smyly had sat on the Board, and with a little enthusiasm, pertinacity and diplomacy he would certainly have been able to persuade his colleagues to increase the Library grant by £1,000 a year (from 1922 to 1942 it had varied only from £3,300 to £4,100, except in 1937, when the move to the new reading-room had incurred some extra expense), and this would have sufficed to pay for a trained assistant and leave a balance to increase the pitiably small sum spent on foreign books. But he did nothing beyond presenting annually a report written by Hanna and, in his later years, greeting with scepticism and sometimes with open opposition any proposals for change.

Unwin's campaign, however, gave the Board a fright, and efforts were made to improve the position. Somewhat belatedly, in 1946, the College publicly committed itself to a policy of returning to the publishers any books which were not to be catalogued (though it was found, when Smyly died two and a half years later, that this promise had been very imperfectly kept). A Library committee was appointed, which managed to bring about some useful minor reforms, although its proposals for rationalizing the public exhibits in the Long Room were vetoed by the Librarian. The Friends of the Library, founded in 1945 at Provost Alton's suggestion, organized exhibitions, bought a few desiderata and stimulated interest in the Library among bibliophiles. At last it was seen that some life was stirring in the place.

Smyly died in December 1948, and six months later, Parke, Professor of Ancient History, was appointed in his place. With energy, determination and knowledge from his Oxford days of what a great library should be like, he set about clearing the Augean stables, and a report which he made to the Board after five years in office showed that, although much remained to be done, he had made notable progress. When the Librarian (Parke) and Luce gave evidence before a committee of the Board of Trade appointed in 1961 to take evidence germane to a new copyright act, they were able to convince the committee of the merits of the Library's case, and in 1966 its privileges were confirmed in the new Act. Since then the Library, though it still has its problems, has gone from strength to strength, but one is forced to admit that, dubious though his motives and methods may have been, most of the credit for initiating its reform must be given to Stanley Unwin.

(xvi)

In January 1946, the salaries committee of the Board reviewed the problem which had been revealed by the difficulties in filling the chair of French. The financial outlook was bleak. The Fellows and lecturers released for war service were mostly back and were drawing their full salaries. Posts left vacant for the duration of war had now to be filled. Arrears of maintenance work had been piling up. Interest rates were tending to fall. And, worst of all, academic salaries in Britain had risen considerably, and very soon Trinity would be unable to compete. Loyalty or inertia might retain much of the existing staff at low salaries, but the more able men would tend to drift away, and the College would be unable to fill vacancies at an acceptable level of competence. The committee, in a lucid report, filled in this sombre picture in some detail, and then went on to consider what seemed to be the only three possible sources of increased revenue: higher fees, private benefactions and a government grant. Although an increase in student numbers might bring in an extra £10,000 or so in fees it would also stimulate demands for more staff, and it was not yet by any means clear that the increase would be anything more than a short-lived post-war boom, similar to that of 1919. The scale of fees had been raised only two years earlier, and an immediate further increase would drive away students. There was, therefore, little to be looked for under this head. A public appeal for subscriptions had been tried once before. In 1927 a devoted and optimistic group of graduates, headed by Sir Robert Woods, set out to raise a fund of £250,000 to re-endow the University and replace the grant which had been recommended by the Geikie Commission. But after twenty years' effort the Educational Endowment Fund which they established amounted only to £20,000, and there was no reason to think that a similar appeal in 1946 would be more successful, especially in view of the fact that the sum needed now was a full million, rather than a quarter.[33] The third possibility, assistance from the Government, appeared to be the only hope, but by many members of the Board (and by several outside it) this solution was viewed with pessimism, alarm and distaste. The history of the College's appeal in 1923 had not been encouraging, and many felt that the College would only receive a humiliating rebuff. Others were more afraid of the conditions which the Government might impose as the price of a grant; of these, compulsory Irish at matriculation (which the National University had imposed from its foundation) was the most probable and almost the most distasteful. But as there seemed to be no alternative the Board, after some months' hesitation and some prodding by the Junior Fellows, prepared under Bailey's guidance a persuasive booklet setting out its case, and asked that the Provost and Registrar should be received by Mr De Valera to expound it verbally. De Valera, who had been given private intimation that the request was imminent, received them on 20 February 1947, accompanied by his Minister of Finance, and immediately made it clear that the Government conceded in principle that the College had a sound case, though it admitted that the sum asked for – £35,000 a year – was rather larger than had been expected. But the following day the representatives of the College were told that the Government had decided that the case presented by the College was 'simple and straightforward', and that a grant of £35,000 would be included in the estimates to be published in March. The grant was to be 'for the general purposes' of the College, and no explicit conditions were made, but there were some personal requests, and some hints were dropped. De Valera requested that the money should not be used to increase the larger salaries, nor to raise any above those of comparable posts at University College, and, somewhat tentatively, he expressed a hope that the College might now find it possible to experiment with some teaching through the medium of Irish. The College representatives confined themselves to pointing out that it might not be easy to find lecturers of the necessary competence nor pupils willing to attend their courses, but raised no difficulties in principle.[34] It was decided later that a conciliatory gesture should be made, and for a few years there were lectures in Irish on mathematics and on Irish archaeology. Their quiet disappearance seems to have caused no adverse comment, and the College could congratulate itself that it had secured its survival without any serious sacrifice of principle.

(xvii)

This first and important step towards integration with the new Ireland and official recognition by the State as an institution of national importance was accompanied, paradoxically enough, by a change in the composition of the student body which pointed in the opposite direction, and which some years later was to raise embarrassing queries as to the assumptions on which a government grant was given. For in the fifteen years which succeeded the war the student body, which had hitherto been almost entirely Irish, became strikingly cosmopolitan, with students of British birth becoming more and more numerous. In 1938–9 the number of students of Irish birth matriculating annually stood fairly steady at around 310, which represented slightly over 80 per cent of the total intake; 10–12 per cent had been born in Britain and 8 per cent abroad, but of this last category at least half were of Irish-born parents. Of the Irish students, between a quarter and a third came from the six counties of Northern Ireland. The figures for 1945 showed little change, but by 1946, while the absolute figure for admissions had risen by nearly 50 per cent, well over half of this increase was attributable to students born in Britain, and a significant fraction to those born overseas. Although the absolute figure for admissions fell off in 1950–1 the changes in proportions continued, so that by 1952 only 34 per cent of the admissions were from the Republic of Ireland, 30 per cent were from Great Britain, and 18 per cent each from Northern Ireland and overseas.

Although this change was destined eventually to lead to political criticism and the imposition of quotas, in its first few years it attracted no unfavourable comment, and it produced a welcome diversification of the student body, which hastened on the recovery from the atmosphere of isolation which had been generated by war and neutrality. Moreover, since in 1946–7 a large proportion of the students from Britain had seen service in the war, and for some years after that a significant number had done their military service before matriculating, they were more mature, and, with a few exceptions, more rewarding to teach and more enterprising in the range of extra-curricular activities which they initiated. The students from overseas still included, of course, some of British or Irish stock, but there were sizeable contingents from Nigeria, Malaya and Hong Kong, a sprinkling of Cypriots, Greeks and displaced Poles, and occasional representatives of other nations. The diversity was sufficient to enable a 'Carnival of Nations', consisting mainly of national songs and dances in national costume, to form a popular event for several years.

In absolute numbers the expected post-war boom was followed by a slight drop, so that in 1951, although the student population was higher than it had been for over a hundred years, it was not obvious that these numbers would be maintained. Expansion was, in fact, resumed soon after 1952, but there were not many in the College at that time who imagined that the student population was likely to stabilize at a figure above 2,500. The opportunities and the strains provided by an expansion to almost 6,000 over the next twenty-five years lie outside the scope of our narrative.

14

Epilogue

1947–1952

(i)

The reader will probably have noticed a difference between the last chapter and its predecessors; it is more diffuse and detailed, dealing with numerous persons and processes rather than with a limited number of broad issues. This change of style, artistically regrettable but historically necessary, we attribute to a change which began in all universities in the second quarter of the twentieth century, and has continued with constant acceleration ever since – an increase in the diversity of their activities (and consequently in the size of their staffs) and a weakening of central control. Up to around 1925 the head of a university was in the position of a managing director. Nowadays he is comparable to the chairman of a holding company, receiving reports from his subsidiaries and trying in some measure to co-ordinate their activities. The collegiate traditions and the compact, unitary campus of Dublin did something to delay this change, but they did not stave it off completely.

In this epilogue, however, we shall eschew the lesser developments of 1947–52 (some of them have been anticipated in chapter thirteen, and the remainder are of small importance) and concentrate on three major topics: the continuing financial crisis, the mounting discontent over the administration and government of the College, and the appointment of A.J. McConnell as Provost, together with the consequential changes.[1]

(ii)

Soon after the receipt of the government grant in 1947 a new salary-scale was approved,[2] which, although it lagged slightly behind the British scale, was effectively competitive, for at that time taxation was lower in Ireland, and rationing, apart from a serious shortage of fuel, was less severe and life in general less austere. But this happy state of affairs did not last for long. 'Inflation' was not yet a word on every-

477

body's lips, but one noticed that prices often went up and seldom came down, and soon people began to talk of 'the diminishing purchasing power of the pound'. This in itself might not have produced more than a little mild grumbling, as the war had accustomed people to doing without many of the things they wanted, had it not been for the fact that in the United Kingdom academic salaries had responded rapidly to the rise in the cost of living, and it was clear by the end of 1948 that the Dublin salaries were no longer competitive. There were several years in which the headline that a member of the College dreaded above all others to see on opening his paper was 'Further rise in university salaries in the U.K.', and when he saw it he was subjected to a feeling of impotent gloom.

The only remedy seemed to be a request for an increase in the government grant, and such requests were made in November 1948, and again in 1949 and 1950. Each year, naturally enough, the sum requested was larger, and by 1949 it amounted to an annual grant of £88,000 and a capital grant of £250,000. But De Valera had fallen from power in 1948 and a coalition (or, as it preferred to call itself, 'inter-party') government was now in power. Its two dominant elements were Fine Gael, with a tradition of economy and pre-Keynesian finance, and Labour, with insistent demands for greatly increased spending on social welfare. This did not leave much for the universities, and for three successive years the grants for the general purposes of Trinity and of University College, Dublin both remained unchanged.[3] But in the spring of 1951 University College was given an increase of over £100,000 in its annual grant, while Trinity at the same time was given what may be fairly described as a derisory increase of £10,000. The total grant to University College was now to be £233,000 per annum and that to Trinity was £50,000. As the income of the latter from its original endowment amounted to at most £60,000, it was clear that there was a discrepancy too large to be justified by the difference in student numbers.

The explanation was, for a Trinity man, not hard to find. Ever since 1922 University College had been a stronghold of the party which now called itself Fine Gael, and Patrick McGilligan, the Minister of Finance, still retained the part-time post of Professor of Law in University College. This remarkable combination of offices would have made it difficult for the most unprejudiced man to hold the scales even, and whatever virtues might be ascribed to McGilligan, freedom from party spirit was not among them. A very able lawyer and a successful politician, he was also a man of the most passionate party loyalties, and he was famous, both at the Bar and on political platforms, for the verbal duels in which his polished but lethal rapier-thrusts were made all the more effective by his rasping Derry accent and the soft, apparently consumptive cough with which they were punctuated.

Suspicions of McGilligan's hostility were changed to certainties when Provost Alton and the Registrar (who was now, following Bailey's resignation on account of illness, A.J. McConnell) were given an interview on 19 March 1951, with John Costello (head of the coalition) and McGilligan. A memorandum had been sent to the Government earlier; it concentrated on the disparity of treatment between the two colleges, and the representatives of Trinity College asked for an explanation. They were soon answered. McGilligan said that he had ceased reading the memorandum when he discovered what was its basis, as in his view no comparison between the colleges was valid. University College was part of what was justly called the National University; Trinity College was a private institution catering for a small minority. Its teaching was in many of its courses offensive to Catholics, and such Catholics as attended it did so only because they did not want to learn Irish or because they were put off by the higher intellectual standards of University College. There could be no question of parity of treatment. Costello when asked whether he agreed with the views of his Minister of Finance, shifted uneasily in his chair and made a non-committal reply. In a letter, which he wrote immediately after the interview, Alton lamented that he could not have talked to Costello alone, as whenever he spoke he was interrupted by McGilligan. But some interruptions seem to have come from his Registrar as well. The interview, in fact, soon developed into an argument before two impotent spectators between a Ballymena Presbyterian and a Derry Catholic – a confrontation that was unlikely to end in *détente*.

The Provost lost no time in circulating a memorandum of the interview to the University's representatives in the Senate and in consulting Senator Douglas and one or two other government supporters friendly to the College. From Douglas he received a guarded hint which we interpret as indicating that the unsympathetic attitude of the Government arose in part from a desire to appease Archbishop McQuaid at all costs, and this in its turn was due to a serious dispute among the ministers, which was soon to become public knowledge and to bring the Government down. Noel Browne, Minister for Health, had proposed a far-reaching scheme for ante- and post-natal care (known as the Mother and Child scheme), but only ten days before the interview with Alton and McConnell the Archbishop had informed the Government that many clauses in the proposed bill, by their transference to the State of functions which properly belonged to the family, made it unacceptable to the Catholic Church. Browne refused to give way, and the Government was faced with the prospect of either a head-on collision with the Hierarchy or the jettisoning of a minister who had justly made himself popular by his successful anti-tubercular campaign. On 19 March the nerves of all the ministers must have been on edge; an argument about university finance must have seemed merely an irritating side-issue to be disposed of as quickly as possible; and the fact that Browne was a Trinity graduate cannot have helped to make them sympathetic to his *alma mater*.

Before an effective post-mortem on the interview could be held, the Mother and Child scheme was abandoned, Browne resigned, the Government was defeated in the Dail, and at the ensuing general election De Valera was returned to power. By the middle of June the Provost was able to write to Costello to say that he need no longer trouble him for his version of the interview and to thank him 'for the sympathy which he had shown', and on the same day, with less caution and more gusto to De Valera. 'I cannot forget', he wrote, 'your kindness and understanding; no one has understood better what the idea of a university is.' The understanding continued, and early in 1952 Alton's last days were gladdened by the news that a substantial increase in the annual grant was to be expected. There was, in fact, an increase of £40,000, and also a special grant of £10,000 for the repair of the College's historic buildings. This was *ad hoc* and non-recurrent, but it was repeated for many years and enabled the College to overtake slowly the results of many years of neglect by eliminating dry-rot and repairing defective stonework. The financial problems of the College were not solved, but they were greatly reduced, and it was given hope of fair treatment in the future – a hope which has not proved illusory.

(iii)

The constitutional reforms of 1911, which added four elected members to the Board and gave the possibility of a further counterbalance to the Senior Fellows in throwing open to all Fellows the major administrative offices, were generally accepted at the time as a reasonable compromise. Although the Geikie commission of 1920 recommended a more representative governing body the political tensions of the next few years were not conducive to internal disputes, and up to about 1937 most of the Junior Fellows, though perhaps deploring the constitution in theory, admitted that it gave reasonably satisfactory government and administration. But by 1937 the Bursar (Russell) was clearly failing, and his replacement next year by Harry Thrift was not a great success; Fry was still efficient as Senior Lecturer, but becoming more rigid and more irascible; Goligher died in 1940, and there was nobody as effective as he had been in pushing the Board to a decision. Among the remaining Senior Fellows, Smyly, Tate and Fraser were passengers as far as administration and policy-making were concerned, except in so far as they could be counted on to oppose almost any change. And the war was bringing new problems, especially in the sphere of supply, for it needed initiative and outside contacts to obtain scarce materials, and sympathy and imagination to allocate them fairly. None of these qualities was shown in large measure. The war brought other difficulties, which we have already described, for which the Board cannot be blamed, but it was only because the Senior Fellows were becoming unpopular for other, more rational, reasons that there was a subconscious tendency to hold them accountable for a bad winter or a shortage of petrol. At all events the Junior Fellows converted themselves in 1940 into a vocal and coherent body which decided to meet at least once a term. In the following year they debated the need for extra representation on the Board, and in May 1941, it was decided by thirteen votes to three (with one abstention) that the number of Junior Fellow representatives should be raised from two to four, and that the Board be asked to receive a deputation to hear their case. Six months later, however, it was decided that the matter should be postponed for a year. The reasons for this postponement are not entirely clear, but one may guess that some, at least, of the Junior Fellows believed that constitutional reform was impossible within the next few years (for the absence of several Fellows on war-work could always be pleaded as an excuse for postponement), or at best could be achieved only by a prolonged and bitter battle in which they did not wish to become involved.

Another factor which discouraged activity on the constitutional front during the years 1942–50 was the lack of co-operation from the non-Fellow Professors. In 1905–10 they had been in the van, with the more conservative Junior Fellows trying to restrain their ardour. Things were very different now, and on more than one occasion the Professors declined to associate themselves with the Junior Fellows' proposals for reform, declaring themselves perfectly satisfied with the existing constitution. Why they should have trusted the Senior Fellows any more than the Junior is not immediately obvious – their attitude in 1908 had been very different, and it changed again in 1951 – but it can in part be explained by the composition of the Professorial body during the war years. Several of them (Werner, H.H. Dixon, Jamieson, Hewson, Sir Arthur Ball) were elderly men, contemporaries of the Senior Fellows or older. Others, such as Liddell, Miss Maxwell and Miss Moran, were of strongly conservative instincts and disliked upsetting the existing order; they could escape the difficult task of defending it by criticizing the tactics, the manners, or even the accents of the reformers. Others again, like John Purser, Moorhead, Pearson and to some extent Bigger, were of authoritarian temperament and disliked outspoken criticism of those in authority. There were several Professors of at least mildly liberal disposition, but they were mostly timid men, unwilling to take the lead, or else too busily engaged in their departments to spare time for academic politics. From 1935 to 1945 Moorhead, and from 1943 to 1950 Purser sat as one of the Professors' representatives on the Board, so that if it came to a vote the Senior Fellows could count on at least some support from the Professors. One of the first signs which the Senior Fellows received of the imminent cracking of the ice was when in June 1950 Purser was voted off the Board and replaced by L.B. Smyth. Thrift was furious and declared it to be the work of a caucus. But a Junior Fellow, when the news reached him just before Commons, stood wine for the entire High Table.

The non-cooperation of the Professors was embarrassing to the Junior Fellows for two reasons. In the first place it enabled the conservatives to represent the reform movement as the work of a clique of a dozen Junior Fellows, without the support of the academic body as a whole. Secondly it increased the gravity of the problem, already inherent in the constitution, that whereas the number of Junior Fellows on the Board could be increased to any number by an Ordinance (requiring only the consent of the Board, the Visitors and a majority of the Fellows),[4] the number of representatives of the non-Fellow Professors was frozen at two by the terms of the Letters Patent of 1911, and could not be altered except by parliamentary legislation. And obviously equity demanded that if the Junior Fellows were to receive extra representation the non-Fellow Professors should also be given it. Rather naively, perhaps, the Junior Fellows suggested that the Professors might elect a Fellow to represent them, but this revived among the Professors the ancient distrust: a Fellow could never represent them, as he would always, in the last analysis, work for the interests of the Fellows and against those of the Professors.

The Junior Fellows turned, therefore, in 1942 to the problems of the pass course and the grievances of the tutors. On the first topic they made little progress. They agreed that there should be fewer examinations, but the Board was not convinced; and on the structure and content of a revised course, although there was some agreement it was not sufficient to enable a coherent proposal to be made to the Board. In the matter of tutorship the Junior Fellows backed the tutors in their requests for more tutors, more money and more secretarial assistance. On the first point the Board was accommodating, and by the end of 1944 the shortage of tutors was no longer acute. In the matter of emoluments the Board not unreasonably deferred the matter until all salary-scales came up for consideration. But on the relatively trivial third point a battle royal was joined, and the obduracy on this issue of the Senior Fellows and their allies on the Board served as the spark to set off an explosion which robbed them of their power for ever.

A little caution on financial grounds in meeting all the tutors' requests could probably be justified, but this was not the basis on which most of them were refused (the refusal being sometimes followed later by grudging and partial concessions). It was rather a determination that nineteenth-century methods of doing business should be continued into the middle of the twentieth century. There was an old-established convention whereby all transactions between a student and the Senior Lecturer or Bursar were carried out, not directly, but through his tutor. As a means of protecting administrators from too many trivial interruptions it was sensible enough, but it was quite needlessly extended to postal transactions. As late as 1942, therefore, a tutor would receive from the Bursar a pile of 'incidentals' accounts (covering electricity, milk, Commons, etc.) for his pupils in residence, and the tutor had to send them out and see that they were paid. Even more astonishingly he received once a quarter a cheque for all the prizes and scholarship payments due to his pupils; he had to lodge this to his private account and himself write out and sent out cheques to the individual pupils, and pay for the stamps. And for the typing of letters he had to scrounge around to find a secretary who wasn't occupied by business given her by one of the senior officers.

Slowly, though at the cost of much time and temper, some progress was made, and in February 1950, it was agreed that the long-since obsolete office of Senior Tutor should be revived to handle all pre-matriculation correspondence, which, soon after the war, had increased suddenly to an alarming extent. But instead of transferring one of the more experienced tutors to the office it was given to R.M. Gwynn, by now seventy-two years old. He struggled manfully with his new duties, but he had no administrative talent, and it is doubtful whether his office really saved the tutors much work.

The tutors continued to draw the Board's attention to the handicaps under which they had to work, and in November 1950 a committee was appointed to deal with their complaints, with Luce as chairman. It was an unfortunate choice, partly because Luce, like many of his generation, was unaccustomed to secretaries and preferred to write or type his own letters, and did not see why everybody else should not do the same, and partly because he was at this time in his most authoritarian mood. The Board, in his eyes, did not administer or even govern the College; it 'ruled' it. He exasperated the tutors continually by his attitude of *de haut en bas*; refusals were accompanied by lectures (such as an assurance that parents preferred handwritten to typed letters from the tutor), and concessions were doled out according to the formula followed with fatal effect by so many colonial powers: too little, too late.

The final explosion came early in 1951. The tutors had asked for an extra typist, and also for a senior secretary who would decide priorities, look after the filing, and generally superintend the work of the tutorial office. The extra typist was conceded, the senior secretary refused. The tutors wrote back to thank the Board for the first, but added that they 'must insist' on the urgent need for the senior secretary. Luce interpreted the word 'insist' as insubordination; the request was refused again with some asperity, and as a punishment the appointment of the typist was to be deferred for three months. The tutors brought the matter to the Junior Fellows, and they decided that this was the end of the road. A meeting of the whole academic staff must be summoned to demand constitutional reform.

Tiresome as Luce's handling of this matter had been, and feeble as the Board had been in giving him his head, it would not have forced the Junior Fellows to seek a final solution if it had not taken place against a background of discontent over many other issues. Of these the most important were the secrecy in which the Board conducted all its business and the administrative incompetence of certain academic officers. The fact that some of the discussions and decisions of the Board were rightly regarded as confidential served as an excuse for regarding all its proceedings as confidential. Important discussions were often omitted from the minutes, and documents presented to the Board which its majority found distasteful or embarrassing were not preserved in the College records. But even with these precautions the Registers, containing the minutes of the Board meetings, were regarded as 'classified' material. Fellows, by an old-established privilege, were entitled to consult them, but non-Fellow Professors and lecturers were not. When the two authors of this book (at that time lecturers, but not Fellows) began to interest themselves in the history of the College they were denied access even to the Registers of the early nineteenth century. The annual accounts were shrouded in even deeper secrecy. An abstract was submitted to the Board, and presumably if a member of the Board had pressed for further details he would have been given them privately. But the Junior Fellows were not allowed to see even the abstract until 1951.[5] Under these conditions it was naturally impossible to make really constructive criticisms, and, arising as they did from a background of ignorance, some of the suggestions of the Junior Fellows for increased expenditure on particular projects could be rejected as irresponsible.

Cognate to this secrecy, and a source of recurrent discontent, was the failure of the Board (not on every occasion, but on far too many) to consult the Junior Fellows before taking a decision about the timing, conditions and subject when a new Fellow was to be elected. Sometimes the Board went ahead and presented the Junior Fellows with a *fait accompli*; at other times it received representations from the Junior Fellows in advance and rejected them. There are at least half a dozen entries in the Junior Fellows' minute book relating to such controversies.

In the matter of administrative inefficiency, criticism was focused on Smyly, Thrift and R.M. Gwynn. Smyly's shortcomings have already been dealt with; it remains only to add that if, in his case, the discontent bore some small fruit in the creation of the Library committee and its few modest reforms, this was largely because Provost Alton loved the Library and was prepared to exercise on its behalf more pressure on a Senior Fellow than he would for other causes. Criticism of the gross defects of Gwynn's administration was inhibited by the affection in which he was generally held as a man; nevertheless it was sufficient to induce the Junior Fellows to send a delegation to the Provost in June 1951, to request that neither Gwynn nor Thrift should be renominated to their offices. The Provost received the delegation sympathetically but non-committally, promised to have a talk with Gwynn, and a fortnight later renominated both of them.

It was chiefly the tutors who suffered from Gwynn's lack of business method; Thrift as Bursar presented a target to almost everyone, and above all to the resident staff. On the purely financial side his faults were mainly negative ones – intense conservatism and lack of foresight – but occasionally these had serious immediate consequences. It was only with the greatest of difficulty that he was persuaded in the post-war years to accept from local authorities in Great Britain fee-payments at a time of year and in a manner which conflicted with the age-old College regulations. Moreover, he must take much of the blame for the fact that the College lagged at least five years behind the Church of Ireland (whose legal position was very similar) in taking steps to emancipate itself from the strait-jacket of fixed-interest trustee stock and to make up part of its portfolio from equities, which, for at least fifteen years or so after the end of the war, were far more attractive financially.

But the Bursar was at that time not only the treasurer and paymaster of the College; he was also in charge of all its domestic arrangements, and it was here that he gave the greatest dissatisfaction from a combination of negligence and obstinacy. He rarely spent more than three or four hours a day in his office; he pushed all difficult decisions on

Bailey; and he left matters such as redecoration, repair and maintenance entirely in the hands of unskilled subordinates. That most of the lecture rooms had broken chairs, that the student lavatories were a disgrace and those for the staff inadequate, that nearly all doors were repainted with artificial graining, no matter where they were situated, that the greenhouses in the Botanic Gardens were falling to pieces from lack of paint – none of these things worried him, because he rarely saw them; his orbit was confined to his office, the Board Room and the Common Room. The one thing to which he devoted some pains was the organization and financing of College sport, and for that a few were prepared to forgive him everything else. But only a few, for by this time organized sport had become a minority interest among the academic staff. Moreover, he had a peppery and somewhat bullying manner and took as a personal insult any criticism of the activities for which he was nominally responsible. In an attempt to circumvent this, the Junior Fellows requested the Board in June 1948 to set up a 'House committee' by which suggestions and criticisms relating to domestic arrangements could be brought to the Bursar's notice in a constitutional and impersonal manner, and by which he could make his point of view known to the academic staff. It was turned down, mainly on the initiative of Thrift and Luce; the latter thought he had disposed of the matter when he said that it would be a 'grouse committee' (which, of course was true).

Each one of these grievances was in itself a fairly small matter, but they added up to produce a dangerous atmosphere of frustration and, here and there, of personal hostility such as College had not known for the past forty years. The proposal to summon a general meeting of the academic staff to discuss constitutional reform had been agreed in principle on 1 March 1951. But it took some time to agree on the wording of the resolution to be proposed, especially in view of the declaration of the non-Fellow Professors that they would not support any change which merely increased the representation of the Junior Fellows on the Board. They made no allowance for the fact that there were legal difficulties in the way of any other scheme, and made no suggestions as to how the legal difficulties might be circumvented. The Junior Fellows, therefore, consulted counsel at their own expense on the question whether additional Professors, not members of the corporation, could sit on the Board. The reply was inconclusive but on the whole negative. And while these discussions were going on the Senior Fellows added substantial fuel to an already healthy fire by proposing that they (and the Provost) should receive a 10 per cent increase in their salaries, and carrying the proposal on the Board by their own seven votes against three from the Registrar and the two representatives of the Junior Fellows (the Provost and the Professors' representatives not voting). When the Junior Fellows heard of this they protested that it was a clear breach of the undertaking given to De Valera in 1947 that the highest salaries should not be increased. On 18 June the Board, by the same majority, rejected the protest, and refused to enter it or the voting in the minutes. Once more the Junior Fellows protested, and asked their representatives to insist that the matter should be properly minuted. The Board refused.

Whether the fall in the value of money between March 1947 and June 1951 meant that even the pre-1920 Fellows should in equity receive an increase was perhaps a question on which there was something to be said on both sides. But that the Senior Fellows should be prepared to act with such assurance as judges in their own cause, when it was quite clear that a large number of their colleagues condemned their action, and should then refuse to leave a record whereby posterity could judge the case – this lost them much of their residual support, and there was scarcely anybody now outside their own ranks who would defend without some reservation their predominance in the government of the College. It did not escape notice that not one of the men (nor indeed any of those who were Senior Fellows between 1943 and 1949) who thus elected to defy the opinion of their colleagues had ever received the vote of confidence implicit in being elected as a representative of the Junior Fellows on the Board. The Junior Fellows elected men as diverse in opinions, temperament and seniority as Alton, Bailey, Duncan, Goligher, McConnell, Moody, O'Meara, W.E. Thrift and G.R. Webb, but they had never felt inclined to trust the representation of their interests to Smyly, Fraser, R.M. Gwynn, Tate, Harry Thrift, Luce, Johnston or Godfrey.

The Senior Fellows at this stage began to realize their isolation and responded in the manner of musk-oxen: they formed themselves into a circle with their horns directed outwards. In retrospect one can see an element of pathos in their position. Each had his faults and virtues, and, as we have suggested earlier, two or three of them should never have been in academic life. But they were victims of the system, of which they had the misfortune to be the last, anachronistic survivors. For years they had looked forward to a day when they would be wafted up into Olympus and find themselves, enriched by years of experience and for this reason regarded with deferential respect by their juniors, spending their latter years, not so much in *otium* as in *negotium cum dignitate*. Instead of this they found themselves perpetually in the centre of violent controversies, faced with novel problems and rapid change, and subject alike to personal and to collective criticism. Their total failure to understand the attitude of their juniors was due in part to an unusually wide age-gap. In June 1951, the average age of the Senior Fellows was seventy-three and the youngest was sixty-seven; only one of the Junior Fellows was over fifty.

The meeting of the academic staff (Junior Fellows, non-Fellow Professors, and lecturers of at least three years' standing) took place on 28 June. It was well attended, went off quietly, and was, indeed, something of an anticlimax in the opinion of some of the more militant radicals. But the reform party realized that there was a considerable body of opinion only slightly left of centre whose support was essential at this stage; while the conservatives realized that some change was inevitable and that they would be well advised to join in the discussions to see that it was gradual and limited in scope. The motion put to the meeting, therefore, proposed by Parke as the most senior of the Junior Fellows, and seconded rather surprisingly by John Purser, merely asserted that the present constitution was unsatisfactory, that there should be 'a more representative Board, consisting mainly of elected members', and that a draft scheme had been prepared as a basis for discussion, providing for a smooth transition from the present Board to a mainly elected one, without depriving any of the present Senior Fellows of their membership. The resolution was signed by nineteen Junior Fellows out of twenty-one, twenty-four non-Fellow Professors out of twenty-eight, and nineteen lecturers. No record of the attendance at the meeting has survived, so it is not known how many attended but refused to sign; it is certain, however, that they were very few. Poole was inclined to refuse up to the last minute, but when Purser came up to him and whispered earnestly in his ear he was heard to say, 'All right, hang it all, I'll sign.'

Although the resolution concluded with a request that the Board should give the matter its immediate attention, nothing was done until Michaelmas Term. On 6 October it was briefly and inconclusively discussed and postponed. Shortly afterwards two of the Senior Fellows demanded more detailed criticisms; what, they asked, was exactly the basis of the discontent? The elected representatives (Wormell and D.A. Webb for the Junior Fellows; Torrens and L.B. Smyth for the Professors) agreed to draw up a document to answer this question. J.D. Smyth, one of the more radical of the Junior Fellows, who had been largely responsible for inciting the tutors to revolt, had already drawn up a list of grievances; this was edited and added to by Webb and passed on to Wormell for drafting in appropriate language. The document, dated 24 October, covers over seven pages of foolscap, and expresses in some detail the discontents which have been summarized in the last few pages. As a judicial summary it is obviously open to criticism, but as a case for the prosecution it reads well enough; only a few sentences are inaccurate or exaggerated. A week later a reply to this indictment was circulated to members of the Board by Luce. It is a remarkable and entirely characteristic document, consisting in part of shrewd rebuttals of the weak points in the indictment, and in part of statements which can only be described as fantasy. Two examples of the latter will suffice. He maintained that the system of government by Senior Fellows recruited by co-option was a 'representative, democratic system', on the grounds that the statutes enjoined the Senior Fellows to co-opt the most senior of the Junior Fellows to fill a vacancy in their ranks only if they considered him 'worthy'. The fact that in 171 out of 173 of the co-options which had taken place since the Restoration the most senior of the Junior Fellows *was* considered worthy was passed over as a coincidence. Secondly he dealt with the statement that the Royal Commissions of 1906 and 1920 had both recommended a more representative constitution for the Board by the assertion that 'The Royal Commissions are dead and buried. Their recommendations hinged on a grant of some £45,000 a year – which never materialized.'[6]

The representatives considered whether a reply to Luce's reply should be made, and a draft was prepared; whether it was circulated or not we cannot tell, on account of the lack of documentation on this controversy in the muniments. It pointed out that Luce had lectured the authors of the indictment because their statement was ill-documented, unbalanced, one-sided, devoid of sustained argument and unity of aim, untrue, inaccurate, unverifiable, misleading and marred by emotive statements. It suggested that all these adjectives could be applied to Luce's reply. But its most significant passage was this:

Dr Luce's reply reveals an attitude of mind so profoundly different from ours that we see no point in discussing individual points with him. We believe in government by consent; he plainly does not. Between his concepts and ours of what a Governing Body ought to do, and what are the natural rights and proper functions of elderly Fellows there yawns an abyss which no words can bridge.

Whatever the rights or wrongs of the arguments, this was plainly true.

On the same day as Luce's document was circulated the Junior Fellows, without, of course, committing themselves to every sentence of their representatives' indictment, reaffirmed their lack of confidence in the existing constitution and expressed their full support for their representatives' efforts for its reform. But a new excuse for postponement arose immediately: the Board decided on 3 November that a truce should be called in the constitutional dispute while the statement to the Government of the College's financial needs was drawn up in the now auspicious circumstances of De Valera's return to power. Meanwhile the Junior Fellows had come to the conclusion that it was probable that when the resolution of the academic staff did eventually come up for decision it would be rejected. It was agreed, therefore, that the Board should be asked to receive a deputation containing Junior Fellows, Professors and Lecturers to expound the resolution to them, and that the Junior Fellows' representatives on the Board should draw up more specific resolutions to indicate just where the irreconcilable differences lay. The Board agreed to receive the deputation, and did so on 9 January 1952. A full-dress discussion and vote was again postponed for one reason or another, and on 22 January there was a significant shift in the balance of power: Sir Robert Tate died, and a few days later Parke, a committed reformer, was co-opted in his place. It was agreed that a special meeting of the Board should be held on 16 February to debate the resolution, but once more it had to be postponed, for on 14 February the Provost had a stroke and four days later he died. It was generally agreed that a topic of this importance should not be decided *sede vacante*.

(iv)

In April 1947 Provost Alton had fallen ill; the illness proved serious, and he was not able to return to work until October. As he was by then seventy-four years old, men's minds naturally turned to the question of his successor – a problem never far below the surface in an academic society. During his absence, Luce, who had been appointed Vice-Provost six months earlier, took charge, and for a few weeks he dazzled the College by the crisp and energetic decisiveness with which he settled questions over which Alton had been dawdling for months. There is little doubt that if Alton had died in June Luce would have been a strong candidate for the succession. He had a character which is impossible to portray in anything less than a long essay, or to sum up in words that will seem adequate to those who knew him; but it must be made clear that the rather hostile portrait of him given in the last few pages, though true enough, does justice to only one side of his complex character. He had passed through two major crises in his life: in the First World War he suffered severely from the psychological disturbance then known as shell-shock, and this probably inclined him towards extreme views and controversial attitudes; and in 1940 on a family fishing outing his wife and daughter were drowned almost before his eyes – a blow which he overcame by an impressive exercise of will-power, and which helped to mellow him. Most men contain some qualities which seem inconsistent with each other, but in Luce the opposites were to be seen in conflict almost every day. The courteous host and the frosty disciplinarian; the conscientious and devoted servant of the College and the tenacious fighter for his rights and emoluments; the single-minded seeker after truth and the master of a repartee based on unfair pseudo-logic; the stern moralist and the very unorthodox churchman; the man of the world and the ill-informed provincial; the stylist in words and the ignoramus in the sphere of the fine arts – what was one to make of such a mixture? At his best there were few men in College who commanded such respect and admiration; at his worst he drove his colleagues mad. And during the latter months of his deputizing for the absent Provost some of his less popular characteristics began to get the upper hand: energy began to be seen as meddling, firmness as dictatorship, and decisiveness as disastrously bad judgment. By the time the Provost returned to work Luce's stock had fallen badly.

Men's minds reverted, therefore, to one who had for long been regarded as the favourite, and who had had some success against Alton in 1942 – K.C. Bailey. By 1948 most of the College saw his succession to the provostship as inevitable. He had many undeniable qualifications. He was extremely hard-working and rarely took a holiday; his loyalty to the College knew no limits, and he was prepared to serve it by taking on any chore when he was asked to do so; he had a good reputation in scholarship, first in classics and later in chemistry, where he did some useful work on negative catalysis, as well as combining his two fields of learning in a commentary on the elder Pliny's chemistry and an etymological dictionary of chemistry and mineralogy. He was even-tempered and seldom ruffled, and was good at soothing down angry or over-excited colleagues. He had sat continuously on the Board from 1931, first as representative of the Junior Fellows and then as Registrar, and had been a generally successful, if at times somewhat schoolmasterly, Junior Dean for over ten years. As Registrar he was Provost Alton's indispensable right-hand man, and he also did much of the Bursar's work for him. He saw his role as a mediator between the Seniors and the Juniors, and was often successful; and he was trusted by all the Seniors and many of the Juniors. What more could one ask for?

And yet, and yet... There were many who did not feel entirely happy at the prospect. Bailey had few faults, but he had some undoubted limitations. He was not an active philistine, but the arts meant little to him, and what praise he bestowed in this sphere was usually on the second-rate. His Panglossian optimism in everything concerning the reputation of the College, though founded on good nature, could be irritating; it was well displayed in his history of its fifty years since the Tercentenary,[7] where there is scarcely a note of criticism of anybody except Oscar Wilde. He had a rather prudish morality and took a needlessly severe view of an occasional daring *double entendre* in undergraduate publications. He rarely travelled, and although he knew the Protestant world of Dublin inside out, he knew little of the wider world. Under his rule, it was thought, the College would be efficient but very provincial and rather self-satisfied.

But was there an alternative? One other name began to be mentioned, that of Joseph Bigger, Professor of Bacteriology and Dean of the Medical School. A vigorous, plain-spoken Ulsterman, he had Bailey's capacity for hard work, but his temperament was very different. He was undisguisedly ambitious, with plenty of push, and he knew how to delegate, which Bailey did not. He was a vigorous and go-ahead director of his department and the author of a deservedly popular textbook, and he was alive to the problems facing the medical school. But he had none of Bailey's suavity or capacity for compromise; when he saw what he wanted or what he thought should be done he went for it bald-headed, and instead of healing quarrels he tended to promote them, being perpetually at odds with the two successive Professors of Pathology with whom he had to share a building. Nevertheless, despite the roughness of texture in his manner and speech, he commanded respect as a man of drive and vision, and he was that rarity among academics, an excellent chairman. He added a handsome feather to his cap when in October 1947 it was announced that Miss Grania Guinness (later Lady Normanby) had offered to provide for the College at a cost of £50,000 (subsequently raised to £85,000, which was quite big money in those days) a building to house the departments of Bacteriology and Social Medicine – the latter to be a new development – in memory of her father, the first Lord Moyne, who had been assassinated in Cairo during the war. The building was to be planned in consultation with Bigger, who was to be its first director.[8]

It would seem, therefore, that if there was to be a vacancy in the Provostship in 1948 or 1949 Bailey would be the favourite, with Bigger quite a strong runner-up. But Alton, having made a good recovery from his illness, was at work until a few days before his death in February 1952. Meanwhile there had been an extraordinary *coup de théâtre*. In June 1950 Bigger learnt that he was suffering from leukaemia and resigned from all his appointments. Two months later Bailey, who had been ailing for some time from stomach trouble, learnt that it was cancer; an operation gave some hope for a short time, but not for long, and both men died within a month of each other in 1951. The College had lost two of its most dynamic members, and the question of the succession, with Alton nearing his seventy-eighth birthday, was wide open again.

Nobody immediately took the field as favourite, or anything like one, for a few months. The name of T.C. Kingsmill Moore, one of the Visitors and a very loyal graduate who kept in close touch with the College, was occasionally mentioned, but there was a general feeling against going outside the ranks of the Fellows unless these showed a disastrous lack of talent. Gradually, however, A.J. McConnell began to emerge as at least a possible Provost. He had been appointed Registrar when Bailey had been given sick leave in 1950, partly, no doubt, on grounds of seniority, for he was by then the most senior of the Junior Fellows except for Parke, who was busy with his new post as Librarian, but also because he was obviously alert and businesslike. He was making a good job of the Registrarship; he was an open advocate of constitutional reform; and he had wider contacts outside the College than had many of his contemporaries, both in the other Irish universities and in government circles. Parke, his immediate senior, and Duncan, his immediate junior, were also mentioned; both had the same general outlook as McConnell on university administration, and both, like him, were Ulstermen. Each had his supporters, but a larger number tended to favour McConnell, partly because, as Registrar, he was more in the public eye, partly because he gave the impression of being the superior of Duncan in *suaviter in modo* and of Parke in *fortiter in re*, and partly because, being a better talker than either of the others, he had impressed men by the breadth of his interests and his capacity to make worthwhile comments on a wide variety of topics.

When Alton died, therefore, there was a fairly open field, with McConnell the probable, but not the incontestable favourite. This situation was, of course, viewed with alarm by the pre-1920 Fellows and some of the non-Fellow Professors. There was no solid conservative candidate to be found outside their own ranks, and from within them only Luce and Godfrey appeared to be 'possibles'. Godfrey declined nomination; he was not an ambitious man, and was perfectly happy with his small empire as Senior Lecturer. They had, therefore, to pin their hopes on Luce. Stanford and Moody were nominated as the two most likely men of the younger generation, and as representing the relatively conservative element among the Junior Fellows; and belatedly there came in, from the side as it were, an unusual candidate in the shape of Fearon. He was, in a sense, a protest candidate, the nominee of the romantically minded who did not care what happened at the Board so long as there was a man of distinction and style in the Provost's House, and who were repelled equally by the old-fashioned starchiness of Luce and the impersonal efficiency and Ballymena accents of McConnell and Duncan. Fearon was ambitious, despite his diffident manner, but he lacked the push which ambition requires to be effective, and he had the reputation of dodging controversial issues rather than facing them.

When the Fellows and Professors assembled on 11 March in the Common Room for the nomination, they had, then, seven names before them: Duncan, Fearon, Luce, McConnell, Moody, Parke and Stanford. The Government, while anxious to consult the wishes of the College, had asked that three names should be submitted to it (in order of preference if desired), so that it might have at least some opportunity for independent judgment. Voting took place by elimination, one candidate being eliminated at each vote. The atmosphere was tense and the room overheated; half-way through the voting the cellarer was sent down to bring up some hock, and the voters could be seen sipping it judiciously while the candidates gulped it nervously. Moody and Stanford were eliminated first, as too junior and untried; Luce was the next to go, showing that true-blue conservatives constituted only a small minority; he was followed by Duncan, so that the three names to be sent to the Government were McConnell, Parke and Fearon, and the concluding votes determined that that was the order in which they were to be placed. De Valera, who knew McConnell well and liked him, was happy to confirm the College's choice, and he was admitted Provost on 18 March, at the age of forty-eight. Duncan was appointed Registrar in his place.

As the nominators dispersed after the meeting Johnston was heard to murmur to Godfrey, 'Now we're for it', and he was not far wrong. The new Provost soon made it clear that he was determined on far-reaching administrative reform, and that, although he was not going to pick unnecessary quarrels, personal considerations were not going to deflect him from his course. His first few weeks were spent in settling in and clearing off arrears of routine business, but the oft-postponed constitutional issue was scheduled to come up for discussion and, it was hoped, decision on 24 May. Wormell and Webb had, with the consent of the Junior Fellows, drafted three resolutions for decision. The first was to the effect that nobody should remain a member of the Board after he had reached the age of seventy-two; the second, that the number of representatives of the Junior Fellows should be increased from two to four; the third, that the rule would be abolished whereby a Senior Fellow absent from a Board meeting was fined two guineas, which was paid to the most senior Junior Fellow, who was called up to replace him. This last was a very trivial affair and represented a perhaps somewhat unworthy attempt by the reformers to diminish the regularity of attendance of the more elderly or apathetic Senior Fellows.

At first sight it seemed as though the prospects for the passing of the resolutions was good. There were five certain votes against them, from the pre-1920 Fellows; Fearon's attitude was unpredictable, but it was hoped that he might abstain.[9] The Provost, Parke, Duncan, Wormell and Webb would certainly vote in favour, and so, it was hoped, would the Professors' representatives. L.B. Smyth's support was regarded as fairly certain; about Torrens there was some doubt, as he was a man of strange moods and obscure grievances, but in fact these suspicions were groundless. Only, therefore, if Fearon were to vote with the Seniors and Torrens to defect could the motions fail. But once more illness intervened in a dramatic manner. Five days before the meeting at which the motions were to be proposed L.B. Smyth went to his doctor for a diagnosis of some internal trouble from which he had been suffering. He was told that he had advanced cancer of the liver and had not long to live. He went home to die with quiet dignity, and attended no more meetings of the Board. When the votes came, therefore, his seat was vacant, and on the first two motions Fearon voted with the pre-1920 Fellows. They were therefore lost on an equality of votes. On the third and least important motion Fearon changed sides, and it was carried, but this was of little consequence.

It seemed, therefore, that the deadlock could not be broken until one of the Senior Fellows were to die. But a little reflection showed that this was not so. The annual elections for the principal offices were due in June. The Letters Patent of 1911 had provided that the offices of Bursar, Senior Lecturer and Registrar should be open to Junior as well as to Senior Fellows; but never had more than one of them (usually that of Registrar) been held by a Junior Fellow, and there had been a period of seven years as recently as 1935–42 when they had all been held by Senior Fellows. What if they were all given to Junior Fellows? Their voting power on the Board would be increased by two without any constitutional change. It was the custom for the Provost to nominate to the Board all the annual statutory officers a week or a fortnight before the day of election; in the interval any member of the Board could make an alternative nomination, and the matter would then be put to the vote, but it was almost unheard of for the Provost's nominations to be challenged. McConnell in nominating his officers was primarily concerned to secure good administrators, but this second aspect can hardly have escaped his notice. On 14 June he made his nominations; Parke as Vice-Provost in place of Luce, Duncan as Bursar in place of Thrift, Wormell as Senior Lecturer in place of Godfrey, Mitchell as Registrar in place of Duncan, Moody as Senior Tutor in place of Gwynn, Thrift as Auditor in place of Johnston, and Godfrey as Senior Dean in place of Gwynn.

Everybody had expected changes, but not on this scale. The Seniors threatened with displacement were, of course, indignant, and even among the Junior Fellows there were a few who thought that things were going too fast. The new appointments to the Bursarship and Senior Tutorship were welcomed; most people thought that Luce had had a long enough run for his money as Vice-Provost; and Mitchell seemed a good choice for Registrar. But about the displacement of Godfrey some grave doubts were expressed. Within the traditional limits of the post he was doing his duties well; nobody could accuse him of inefficiency. But he was very inflexible, and McConnell knew well that any proposed changes in his sphere of influence would be fought with tenacity and skill, and, even if carried at the Board, might not be implemented. A meeting of the Junior Fellows was summoned in response to this disquiet, and Moody and Stanford attacked the proposed displacement of Godfrey with some vigour; there was much talk of humanity and *pietas*. Wormell and Webb said that they felt committed to support the Provost's nominations and, although they saw that there was something to be said on both sides, they could not now in conscience change their policy. It eventually became clear that a few were clearly opposed to the change, a slightly larger number favoured it, and the majority, though a bit doubtful, did not feel inclined to make a major issue of it. No resolution on the subject was moved.

When the day for the elections arrived on 28 June the old guard decided to make a last stand. It was no use fighting the issue of the Vice-Provostship, for in this case the Provost had a statutory veto on anybody whom the Board might try to elect against his wish. But Thrift was proposed for re-election as Bursar and Godfrey as Senior Lecturer, while Luce, to console himself for the loss of the Vice-Provostship proposed himself as Registrar. The voting strength of each side was of course exactly the same as it had been on 24 May, so it seemed fairly certain that once again there would be an equality of votes, and so it turned out. But there was this vital difference. The statutes provided that the Provost should have a casting vote in elections, though not on other issues. All his contested nominations were therefore carried by his casting vote. It was an embarrassing way in which to win, but there was no alternative.

With this vote our story ends, for 28 June 1952 represents the end of one epoch and the beginning of another. Although, on account of various legal and political complications, Senior Fellows still sit on the Board as of right, they no longer form an identifiable group, their presence is not resented by the Junior Fellows and few, if any of them would refuse to relinquish their seats, if called upon to do so. A convention has been established, which would be very difficult to break, that all the major offices should be held by Junior Fellows, selected for their (at least alleged) competence and not on grounds of seniority. It is no longer possible for the Board to ignore a resolution sent to it by any substantial part of the academic staff. And if at times a small group among the officers has pushed through a measure which has turned out to be unpopular it was only because the opposition was irresolute, divided or inert.

What is remarkable is that all these changes were brought about by what has been fairly nicknamed a 'palace revolution'; no constitutional changes were needed. It demonstrated the fact that the dissatisfaction with the archaic constitution of the Board was fuelled purely by its inefficiency or insensitivity; theoretical democracy had its vigorous advocates, but primarily as a means to an end – to get X and Y out of power. The increase in the number of Junior Fellow representatives on the Board – that oft-repeated request as the *sine qua non* of reform – did not take place until 1958. The changes in administration and policy which followed the 'palace revolution' were numerous and rapid, and most of them were generally welcomed. Naturally, after a honeymoon period, the new administration found itself involved in controversies, but they had nothing of the bitterness that characterized the battles of 1942–52. The majority of the Fellows, though they would not have admitted it openly, found themselves in agreement with Pope:

> For forms of government let fools contest;
> Whate'er is best administered is best.

497

Appendix 1

Provosts of Trinity College
since the foundation

1592–4	Adam Loftus	1758–74	Francis Andrews
1594–8	Walter Travers	1774–94	John Hely-Hutchinson
(*vacant* 1598–1601)		1795–9	Richard Murray
1601–9	Henry Alvey	1799–1806	John Kearney
1609–27	William Temple	1806–11	George Hall
1627–9	William Bedell	1811–20	Thomas Elrington
1629–34	Robert Ussher	1820–31	Samuel Kyle
1634–40	William Chappell	1831–7	Bartholomew Lloyd
1640–1	Richard Washington	1837–51	Franc Sadleir
(*vacant* 1641–5)		1852–67	Richard MacDonnell
1645–50	Anthony Martin	1867–81	Humphrey Lloyd
(*vacant* 1650–1)		1881–8	John Hewitt Jellett
1651–60	Samuel Winter	1888–1904	George Salmon
1660–75	Thomas Seele	1904–14	Anthony Traill
1675–8	Michael Ward	1914–19	John Pentland Mahaffy
1679–83	Narcissus Marsh	1919–27	John Henry Bernard
1683–92	Robert Huntington	1927–37	Edward John Gwynn
1692–5	St George Ashe	1937–42	William Edward Thrift
1695–9	George Browne	1942–52	Ernest Henry Alton
1699–1710	Peter Browne	1952–74	Albert Joseph McConnell
1710–17	Benjamin Pratt	1974–81	Francis Stewart Leland Lyons
1717–58	Richard Baldwin	1981–	William Arthur Watts

Of the fourteen Provosts who held office during the first hundred years, eight were educated at Cambridge, three at Oxford and three at Dublin. Since 1692 all have received their education at Trinity College, Dublin.

Appendix 2

Statistics relating to students

(i) Fluctuations in student numbers

As we explain on p. 524 (n. 28) the annual matriculations form a better guide to fluctuations in student numbers than do figures for the students on the books. Fig. 1 shows the variation in the number of annual matriculations from 1668 (the earliest date from which reliable figures are continuously available) to 1945. The figures plotted are, however, not the actual matriculations for each year, but a five-year running average centred on that year. This smooths out short-term changes of no real significance and enables the more lasting trends to be seen much more easily. The smoothing of the curves is, however, achieved at the cost of slightly reducing the peaks and troughs; in 1798, for example, only 102 students matriculated, although the minimum shown on the curve is 115. Similarly the peak at 1824 shows a maximum of 436, although the actual number of matriculations in that year was 466. Since, however, the student population in any year is a function of the number of matriculations over the past five years, our curves represent the fluctuations in this population better than would absolute figures.

The first fact to note is that the numbers, which had shown relatively little variation in the late seventeenth and early eighteenth centuries, doubled in the short space of eleven years between 1763 and 1774, and maintained this level, apart from the decade 1795–1805. Moreover, recovery in 1805 to the 1774 figure was followed not by a stabilization, but by an even more dramatic rise, for in the following nineteen years (1805–24) the numbers were more than trebled, and never thereafter sank to a lower level than that of 1812. The scale of the College, therefore, underwent two rather sudden transformations. The first expansion may be held to reflect the flowering of Georgian Ireland, and the second the rise of the middle class. Neither is surprising in its incidence, but both are surprising in their suddenness.

Of the other fluctuations, a few of the minima can be easily explained: those of 1691, 1800 and 1923 are due mainly to the practical difficulties and general uncertainty produced by the political disturbances of 1688–91, 1798–1800 and 1920–3 respectively; the minimum of 1916 is due entirely to the First World War; and that of 1853–7 was intensified, if not entirely caused, by the economic distress which followed the famine of 1846–8. The pronounced minimum at 1902 remains, however, largely mysterious. The Protestant population of Ireland was falling in 1880–1900, but no more rapidly than it had fallen between 1860 and 1880, a period which had seen a rise in student numbers.

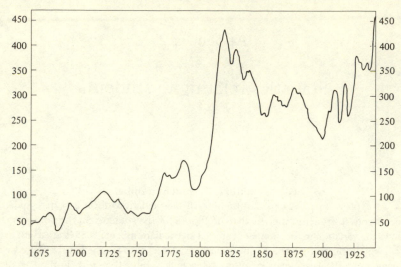

Fig. 1   Annual matriculations, 1668–1950, plotted as five-year running averages.

The maxima are even harder to explain. For those of 1699 and 1724–7 we can offer no suggestion; nor do we know why the numbers should have started to decline in 1790, when the political horizon was still clear. The great increase in numbers in the early nineteenth century becomes slightly less mysterious when we realize that it is closely paralleled at Cambridge (Table 1) – so closely, indeed that we present the figures in a table rather than as a graph, for in a graph the curves would be for much of their course so close as to be almost indistinguishable.

But we are still left with a query: why did the rise stop at 1824 in Dublin, to be followed by a small but distinct decline, while at Cambridge the rise continued for another five years, and was followed not by a decline, but by a plateau? We can point to no economic or demographic factor which came into operation around 1825 and which would be likely to encourage university recruitment in England and discourage it in Ireland.

A consideration of these figures leads to two conclusions, both rather negative. The first is that rises and falls in student numbers admit of no simplistic explanation; they are the resultant of the action of a large number of different forces. In saying this we speak, of course, of the world before 1945; after that date a radical change in the attitude of society and the state to university education has meant that student numbers are mainly determined by government budgeting. But it is only in the very last years of our history that this change affects our figures. We have not plotted the figures later than 1945, partly because they would break through what is otherwise a convenient ceiling for the graph, but also because, in a period of rapid change, five-year running averages can be misleading. In 1945 there were 378 matriculations; by 1948 the figure had risen to 617, but this represented a post-war 'bulge' rather than a long-term social trend, for by 1951 the figure had fallen to 462. Thereafter it oscillated rather irregularly for the next four years, until in 1951 a new and permanent increase began.

Statistics relating for students

Table 1. *Average over five-year periods of annual matriculations at Cambridge and Dublin*

	Cambridge	Dublin
1751–5	121	61
1756–60	122	72
1761–5	111	68
1766–70	118	91
1771–5	130	133
1776–80	143	144
1781–5	162	138
1786–90	179	178
1791–5	160	175
1796–1800	146	119
1801–5	176	128
1806–10	226	162
1811–15	288	240
1816–20	354	352
1821–5	423	427
1826–30	445	370

Our second conclusion is that, in Dublin at any rate, there was up to 1952 little or no correlation between student numbers and the reputation of the University or its achievements in scholarship. The idea that a large department is necessary to produce first-rate scholarship is a very modern one; Trinity College was more productive and more highly regarded, both in Ireland and abroad, in 1900 than it had been in 1825. Up to 1952 the principal effect of a rise or fall in student numbers was financial.

(ii) Women students

From soon after their admission in 1904 the number of women students, whether expressed in absolute numbers or as a percentage of the total, rose fairly steadily up to 1920–3, when they constituted 26 per cent of the total. The next twenty years showed a slight decline, but the rise was resumed about 1940, and in 1947–52 the percentage was fairly constant at 29–30. Although later developments lie outside our scope, it is worth recording that the period 1954–63 showed an unexpected decline, the proportion of women entrants falling as low as 23 per cent in 1959, but thereafter the rise has been uninterrupted – by 1966 41 per cent of the entrants, and by 1978 something like 47 per cent were women. They have not yet, however, as we write, attained to full equality with men.

(iii) Relation between matriculation and graduation

In every university some of the students who matriculate leave without a degree. Failure in examinations is the commonest cause, but there are others: ill health or death, financial disaster, dislike of the pattern of collegiate life, change of mind as to intended career. There were also until recently a sprinkling of wealthier students who never intended to graduate; they came to College to play games or to make congenial friends.

The number of such 'drop-outs' is higher in Trinity College than most people would expect, but over long periods it is only slightly higher than the corresponding figure for Cambridge.

If we arrange the figures by decades we find that in twelve of the twenty-five decades from 1700 to 1949 the ratio of B.A. degrees awarded to the number of matriculations five years earlier varies only between 67 per cent and 72 per cent. Here and there, in other decades, the ratio is as high as 76–77 per cent, while in the middle of the eighteenth and nineteenth centuries it sank as low as 60–61 per cent. The explanation of these variations eludes us, but the very low ratios for 1790–9 and 1910–19 were clearly brought about by rebellion or war, and the very high ratio for 1920–9 is caused by the considerable number of graduates whose academic career had been interrupted by the war.

(iv) Numbers in the professional schools

Fig. 2 shows the fluctuations in numbers of those who graduated with professional qualifications in divinity, medicine or engineering – that is to say a divinity testimonium, a degree or licence in medicine, or a diploma, licence or degree in

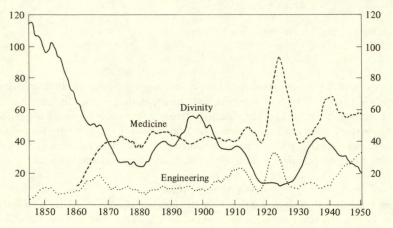

Fig. 2   Number of qualifications awarded annually in Divinity, Medicine and Engineering, plotted as five-year running averages.

engineering. Accurate figures for divinity testimonia are available from 1840 onwards, but we start our curves in 1845, when the new engineering school had found its feet. For medical qualifications, however, we thought it best to start our curve at 1860; records of medical degrees and licences go back far beyond that date, but they are misleading in that up to the middle of the century there were many students in the school who received their final qualification at Edinburgh or elsewhere, not least because of the punitive stamp duty which had to be paid on a Dublin M.B. It was only after the establishment of an effective school of surgery in Trinity and the passing of the Medical Registration Act in 1858 that the figures for qualifications bear a realistic and fairly constant relation to the number of students in the school.

If we may continue the boating metaphor used by Dr Lyons in his foreword, we can see that Divinity, which started as head of the river, was twice bumped by Medicine, and twice by Engineering. In each case it managed to avenge the first of these bumps, but not the second, so that it ended in the lowest place. In view of the general secularizing tendency of the century covered by the curves this causes no surprise, but the steepness of the descent from 1845 to 1873 is unexpected, as are also the two recoveries which led to temporary maxima in 1899 and 1936–8. The initial fall, however, must be viewed against the fact that it started from a very high figure which was probably unprecedented. In 1846 as many as 135 divinity testimonia were issued, although in 1840 the number had been only 64. It is this dramatic peak in the mid-forties (when slightly over half the students in the College must have been reading for orders) that demands an explanation as much as the decline over the next thirty years.

The curve for Medicine rises very rapidly from 1860 to 1870, as a result of the factors already mentioned and of the vigorous direction of the school by Haughton, who was appointed Registrar in 1863. By 1872 the annual qualifications were averaging forty, and they remained remarkably close to that figure for the next forty years. A brief rise starting in 1911 was checked by the outbreak of war, but the small decline produced by the war was followed by an astonishing post-war boom which reached its climax in 1924 (the year in which most of those who matriculated in 1919 would have qualified). A further increase, starting in 1932 (*i.e.* with students who would have entered in 1927), was again checked by war, though not very severely, and the figure soon stabilized around fifty-five. Since then it has been governed less by demand than by the accommodation and facilities available to meet the requirements of the General Medical Council.

The story of Engineering follows that of Medicine fairly closely. Apart from a short-lived boom in 1862–70 it shows the same constancy in its output from 1853 to 1901. The curve then begins to rise, perhaps because of the diversification of the course initiated soon after 1900, but as with Medicine there is a war-time trough, followed by a post-war peak. From 1930, however, the fortunes of the two schools begin to diverge, for Engineering remains steady up to 1940, but then, despite the war, begins on a steady rise to 1950, heralding the advent of the new world of technology.

As there is no qualification awarded by the University which is recognized as a sufficient qualification for admission to the ranks of either barristers or solicitors, we are unable to present any figures for the School of Law.

(v) Religious affiliations

Fig. 3 presents the figures for the matriculation of Roman Catholics and Presbyterians from 1845 to 1950. To have included a curve for Anglicans would have meant reducing the vertical scale to an inconvenient extent; we therefore present instead a curve for the total of non-Anglicans – that is to say, Catholics, Presbyterians and 'others', who include not only members of the smaller Protestant churches (Methodists, Quakers, Congregationalists, Baptists, Unitarians, Plymouth Brethren and Christian Scientists are those which recur most regularly), but also Jews, who average 2–3 per cent over most of the period, and a sprinkling, very small before 1920, but increasing thereafter, of Orthodox Christians, Moslems, Hindus and sceptics. These 'others' made up less than 5 per cent of the total up to 1855; by 1910 they had risen to 10 per cent and by 1950 to 16 per cent. Their curve follows rather closely that of the Presbyterians, so that it may be said that of the students who did not belong to one of the episcopalian Churches usually about half were Presbyterians.

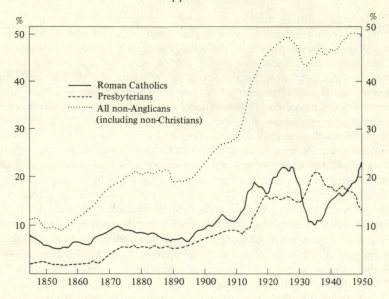

Fig. 3   Annual matriculations of Roman Catholics and Presbyterians, and of all non-Anglicans (including non-Christians), plotted as five-year running averages.

Turning now to the major denominations, we can see, by subtracting the values of the dotted curve from 100, that Anglicans were completely predominant up to the beginning of this century, 1902 being the first year in which they made up less than 75 per cent of the total. Over the succeeding quarter-century they declined fairly rapidly to just over 50 per cent, but the decline was then arrested, and it is only as our history ends that they lost their absolute majority.

Up to 1900 the proportion of Catholic entrants varied only between 5 per cent and 10 per cent but a rise then began, which carried the number up to well over 20 per cent in the years from 1923 to 1930. The thirties, however, showed a sudden and most mysterious decline, the entry in two years in the middle of the decade falling as low as 8 per cent. Recovery began in 1938 and continued without interruption, until by 1950 the figure once more stood at 23 per cent. Ecclesiastical discouragement was certainly no heavier during the mid-thirties than before or after, and the advent of Archbishop McQuaid is reflected by no more than a slight tremor in the rising curve.

Curiously enough, the drop in Catholic numbers in the nineteen-thirties coincides exactly with an equally mysterious rise in the number of Presbyterians, whose curve shows otherwise no very remarkable features.

One interesting feature of the curves in Fig. 3 deserves mention. In 1873 Fawcett's Act opened to men of any religion or none various posts in Trinity, and especially Fellowship, which had hitherto been reserved to Anglicans. Yet it was immediately after 1873 that the number of Roman Catholics admitted started on a twenty-year decline, while the curve for Presbyterians, which had been steadily rising, levels off at 1876 and continues unchanged for twenty years. Correspondingly the brisk decline in the proportion of Anglicans which had been going on since about 1855 was halted, and their figures remained steady till the end of the century. These facts suggest that the grievances which Fawcett's Act set out to remove were symbolic and theoretical rather than substantial and practical.

(vi) Place of birth

The entrance books record the place of birth of most students, but not their place of domicile at matriculation. In earlier times these were usually identical, or at any rate not far apart, but as long-distance travel gradually became more frequent, so also did the divergences. Migration could, of course, proceed in either direction, and to some extent the opposing streams cancelled each other out. But as proximity to domicile is always one factor in determining the choice of a university, we must assume that the figures, at any rate after about 1860, for students born in Ireland are slightly lower than for those domiciled in Ireland during their student days.

With this caution we may consider the figures presented in Table 2. They have been pooled over fairly long periods of time when no great changes were taking place, but when the pace of change was rapid they are presented for shorter periods or for a single year.

Table 2. *Birthplaces of students, expressed as percentages of the total*

Years of matriculation	Twenty-six counties (see text)	Six counties (see text)	Total for Ireland	Britain	Overseas
1800−5	86	12	98	2	0
1825−33	80	11	91	8	1
1851−64	68	12	80	16	4
1881−5	63	16	79	16	5
1911−13	68	16	84	10	6
1922−8	69	17	86	8	6
1938−9	56	25	81	11	8
1945	53	30	83	11	6
1946	46	22	68	18	14
1947−51	33	21	54	29	17

We have divided the Irish birthplaces into those falling within the present territory of the Republic of Ireland and of Northern Ireland respectively, but as these terms are anachronistic before 1921 we head the columns 'Twenty-six counties' and 'Six counties' respectively.

It will be seen that the number of students born overseas increases slowly but steadily from 1800 to 1939, and then, after a brief decline in the wartime years, rises sharply between 1945 and 1951. There was, however, a change in the ethnic composition of these foreign-born students along with their rise in number. Up to 1939 at least half, and perhaps nearly two-thirds were born abroad of Irish parents. After 1945 the majority were genuine 'foreigners', some from America, some from Asia or Africa, and some refugees or displaced persons from Europe.

The figures for students born in Britain show a less regular pattern. Their high value between 1850 and 1900 represents perhaps the overspill of those who desired a university education but were unable or unwilling to take it in Oxford, Cambridge or London; by the end of the century the provincial universities in England were providing a cheaper and more convenient alternative to Dublin. We have commented elsewhere (p. 475) on the dramatic rise in British-born students after 1945.

Within Ireland it can be seen that the proportion of students from the Ulster 'heartland' has risen fairly steadily from 1800 to 1945. Even after 1945 it should be noted that although the figures show a drop when expressed as a percentage of the total intake, if recalculated as a percentage of those of Irish birth they continue their rise.

(vii) Age at entrance

The available data on this subject do not admit of precise statistical analysis or of presentation in tabular form. For an age given as '17' may mean anything from 17 to 17.9 years old, and there is some evidence to suggest that in earlier years it often meant 'rising 17', *i.e.* 16.8 or thereabouts. Moreover the period between the entrance examination (when the student gave his age) and the date on which he actually took up his studies varies a lot. Finally, the spread of ages at entrance has always been large: the two most popular years never account for more than 60 per cent of the total, and usually only about 50 per cent. Our remarks on this subject must, therefore, be of a very general nature.

In the first few decades of the College's existence boys seem to have entered in their early teens, but already by 1640 the average age was rising rapidly, for in 1638–44 we find that although 30 per cent were admitted before they were sixteen, 60 per cent were between sixteen and nineteen. As always in the aftermath of war or political disturbance, the proportion of mature students rose during the Civil Wars, so that in 1656–65 those who were at least twenty at matriculation amounted to 17 per cent. The number of these mature students soon sank again, and between 1666 and the early years of the nineteenth century it varied only between 2 per cent and 7 per cent. Meanwhile the normal age of admission was creeping up, from fifteen or sixteen in 1665–9 to seventeen or eighteen in 1684–9. There was a short-lived reaction between 1695 and 1714, when fourteen-year-olds became frequent again and half the intake was aged under seventeen, but from 1725 to 1800 there was a fairly steady rise in the average age, so that in the first third of the nineteenth century only about 15 per cent entered before they were sixteen. The next two decades saw a further rise, so that by mid-century the pattern was very like what we regard as normal today – that is to say 10 per cent below seventeen, 50–55 per cent aged seventeen or eighteen, 15 per cent aged nineteen and 20–25 per cent aged upwards of twenty.

(viii) Social background

We had hoped to present tables showing changes from time to time in the social class from which the students came, but although every entrant was asked his father's occupation the data are almost impossible to classify. In the first place the answer 'dead' was deemed sufficient; there was seldom any information as to what the father did before he died. Secondly, the aspiring student was often vague or misleading; one boy might describe his father as a cattle-dealer while two years later his younger brother would say that he was the son of a landowner. Both statements might be literally true,

Table 3. *Occupations of students' fathers, expressed as percentages of the total*

	1800–5	1851–5	1891–5	1922–8	1950–1
Gentlemen	36	21	9	3	2
Professional class					
Clergymen	20	21	21	10	4
Lawyers	8	13	9	8	4
Doctors	4	6	8	8	10
Others	7	13	16	18	22
Total, professional class	39	53	54	44	40
Manufacturers and traders	13	18	16	23	27
Administrators and clerks	1	4	11	17	20
Farmers	11	2	8	10	8
Others	—	2	2	3	3

Note: 'Gentlemen' implies people of independent means who do not adopt a profession or trade. The professional class is here understood to include teachers, army officers, and followers of literary or artistic occupations. 'Administrators' are largely civil servants of various grades.

but there is a world of social difference between them. Furthermore, in the realm of trade, although the description might be precise, we found it impossible to draw a line anywhere in the smooth gradation between a small shopkeeper in Co. Kerry and a Dublin maltster or a midland miller who might dine with baronets and Q.C.s.

If we accept these limitations, however, and make it clear that we do not attempt to divide students' fathers into the classes beloved by sociologists, the data presented in Table 3 are not without interest.

The steady decline in the proportion of 'gentlemen' will surprise nobody, but it is interesting to see how much their numbers had been reduced even before land purchase took its toll. The 2 per cent survivors in 1950–1 consisted largely of African chiefs and exiled Polish counts.

What emerges clearly is that the professional class, although it was only in the second half of the nineteenth century that it constituted an actual majority, has always been the backbone of those who sent their children to Trinity. Within this class we can follow the rather sudden decline of the clergy early in the present century, the gradual rise of the doctors, and the great increase in recent years of 'others', who are largely engineers, surveyors, accountants and the like. Businessmen steadily increase, as might have been expected, but even more striking is the rise from almost nothing in the administrators and clerks – an indication of the coming of a bureaucratic age.

While we are on the subject of social class, a word might be said about fellow-commoners and noblemen. The former, who in the early part of the nineteenth century had made up anything from 13 per cent to 20 per cent of the total, started on their final decline in 1831, the last year in which they exceeded 15 per cent. By 1841 they were down to 10 per cent and by 1857 to 5 per cent. The last man to matriculate as a fellow-commoner entered in 1902.

The number of 'noblemen' in the technical sense – that is, students who matriculated as *filius nobilis* or *nobilis ipse* and were prepared to pay four times the normal fee in return for an abbreviated course and a gown with gold tassels – was always minute,

Table 4. *Absolute numbers of students of noble birth who matriculated in each quarter-century, 1700–1850*

1700–25	16
1726–50	19
1751–75	22
1776–1800	40
1801–25	23
1826–50	18

for several peers preferred to enter their sons as fellow-commoners. But even these peers were never really numerous. There is a persistent legend that in the closing decades of the eighteenth century most of the Irish peers sent their sons to Trinity, and that this came to a sudden end with the Act of Union. There is a grain of truth in this legend, but only a grain, for the fact is that many peers did not send their sons to a university at all, and even before 1800 some went to Oxford or Cambridge.

We may define a 'student of noble birth' as one who is either a peer, the son of a peer, or one who succeeds later to a title which was in existence when he entered College. The last category consists for the most part of nephews or grandsons of peers without living sons, and therefore heirs-presumptive. The numbers of students of noble birth on this definition who entered in each quarter-century from 1700 to 1850 are shown in Table 4.

There was, admittedly a maximum in the days of Hely-Hutchinson, but an entry of less than two noble students a year can hardly have transformed the College, especially if we remember that most of them read an abbreviated course, and many of them lived at home with a tutor and came up to College only for the quarterly examinations. In the years 1788–90 the entry averaged five a year, so that the early nineties may have given the tuft-hunter some encouragement, but his golden age was of short duration. It should also be realized that Table 4 gives absolute numbers; if they were expressed as a proportion of the total entry we should find that the years 1745–7 make as good a showing as do 1788–90. In no year, however, did the intake of noble students exceed 1.4 per cent of the total, and their influence on the general lifestyle must have been small. Trinity College has always been a fundamentally middle-class institution.

Appendix 3

College finance and academic salaries

(i) College finance

A full analysis and discussion of the College finances lies altogether outside the scope of this work, but as scholarship and teaching are at least in part dependent on a satisfactory financial background, we present some data to give a general idea of the College finances from 1850 to 1950. Before 1850 the Bursarship rotated rapidly, and the methods of accountancy – at best rather cursory and uninformative – changed every few years, so that it is very difficult to find strictly comparable figures before that date. We can say, however, that the total revenue was nearly doubled (from about £32,000 to over £60,000) between 1800 and 1850, about 30 per cent of the increase coming from higher yield from the estates, and the remainder from the extra fees paid by the greatly increased number of students. The fee itself remained nearly constant throughout the nineteenth century, the total in fees required over four years for a B.A. degree being £70 in 1820 and £83 in 1900. After the First World War it was raised to £101, in 1944 to £126 and in 1947 to £168.

Fig. 4 shows curves for the period 1850–1950 for the total income, the endowment income (rents plus dividends) and the annual surplus or deficit, all being plotted as 5-year running averages. The vertical distance between the two upper curves provides a measure of the other sources of income, of which fees and government grants alone are of any importance, though the latter were non-existent before 1906 and were (except for the period of *ad hoc* – one might almost say *ad misericordiam* – grants in 1919–25) negligible before 1947. The surplus or deficit is reckoned in strictly cash terms and ignores internal accountancy devices such as the building fund. A year showing a deficit may, therefore, have realized a surplus of 'ordinary income' over 'ordinary expenditure', but expenditure on a new building (for which earlier surpluses had been earmarked) has converted this into a deficit.

Our figures differ substantially from those in many published sources, as we have included *all* sources of income, including tutorial fees (which did not pass through the Bursar's accounts before 1919), income from benefactions (earmarked endowments) and the Provost's private estate. On the other hand we have excluded from both income and expenditure such 'in-and-out' items as payments for Commons, and we have set off chamber rents against maintenance of buildings.

Our curves start in the economic doldrums which followed the famine, though the College, thanks to its policy of letting largely to middlemen, suffered much less than did most landlords. Nevertheless, arrears of rent and fall in student numbers combined to drag the total income down from about £73,000 in 1830 to £55,000 in the middle

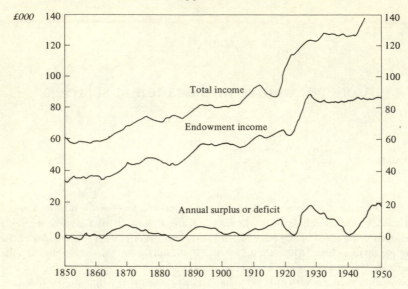

Fig. 4   Five-year averages for total income of the College, income from endowments, and annual surplus or deficit.

fifties. Soon after 1860, however, recovery began, and the curve for income rises slowly but steadily, with only small and short-lived setbacks, until the departure of students to war in 1914 caused a sudden and fairly serious fall. As may be seen from the lower curve this steady rise was due mainly to a rise in endowment income; it was only after 1900 that increases in income from fees made a significant contribution.

After 1918 two conflicting tendencies were at work. The great post-war boom in fee-paying students coincides with a sudden check to the rising endowment curve, caused by the difficulty of collecting rents during the political troubles of 1919–23. The latter was followed, however, by a remarkably brisk recovery, to which a number of different factors contributed: investment of considerable wartime surpluses; a reinvestment programme which, even within the narrow limits of trustee securities, gave a higher yield; a few substantial benefactions; recovery of the arrears of rent; and the temporary gain (to be paid for later, in 1927–32, by land purchase on unfavourable terms) brought about by the settlement made with the Government in 1923 (p. 428). Thereafter both total and endowment income remain fairly constant until the increase in fee income, starting in 1944, sends the former up rather sharply. The advent of government grants in 1947 would send it up through the ceiling, so we terminate it in 1945.

The lowest curve shows that for all but brief periods in the eighteen-fifties, the early sixties, and again in the middle eighties, the College enjoyed a net surplus on its cash account. There were deficits in 1906–7, 1922–3 and 1941, but surpluses in the neighbouring years saw to it that the curve here touches the zero line but does not fall below it. Although the five-year average surplus never rose above £7,000 in the nineteenth century, this figure must be viewed against the extensive expenditure incurred on new buildings. Only in the sixties was this on a small scale; the fifties (Museum Building), the eighties and nineties (medical and scientific buildings), and the first decade of the new century (Graduates' Memorial Building) each showed an average annual expenditure of £3,000–£4,000, and the total expenditure on buildings between 1854 and 1905 amounted to £168,000. But even after these bills had been paid the total net surplus for the same period amounted to £106,000, and the investment of this made a contribution to the steady rise in the endowment curve, although the rise in the value of land and the accession of benefactions were both of more importance.

After 1914 the story is a different one. From 1914 to 1950 the surpluses totalled over £375,000 (over £10,000 a year), while new buildings cost only £21,000. But the investing of these large surpluses brought about, at any rate after 1927, not an increase in the endowment income but merely its maintenance. This was because interest rates were falling over most of the period; expenditure, therefore, had to be kept well below income if the latter was not to fall. Even in 1947 the problem was not a cash crisis, for the College adhered to its policy of avoiding a deficit at all costs; it was the fact that within this constraint it could not offer adequate salaries.

If we examine the different heads under which income and expenditure can be classified we find that the pattern remained remarkably constant over a long period. There is one exception, of course: within the endowment income the proportion arising from rents has steadily declined while that from dividends (with which we include bank interest and fixed rent-charges) has steadily increased. In 1856–7 96 per cent came from rents, but their contribution declined to 80 per cent in 1886, 62 per cent in 1911, 50 per cent in 1921, 25 per cent in 1931 and 10 per cent in 1936. By this time the rents were confined to the City estate, and they maintained a value of about 10 per cent up to 1952. Table 5 shows the figures for the main items of income and expenditure, and we can see that up to 1943 the proportion of the total income derived from endowments varied only between 66 per cent and 72 per cent while fees contributed 26–33 per cent. 1951 shows a radically different pattern, with fees exceeding endowments, and government grants amounting to nearly a quarter of the total. The pattern of expenditure shows an even more remarkable constancy, extending in most items even to 1951: salaries vary only between 57 per cent and 61 per cent of the total and general upkeep and maintenance only between 10 per cent and 15 per cent. The expenditure on the scientific and medical departments alone shows a constant increase.

(ii) Academic salaries

Any attempt to present a clear picture of the size and range of academic salaries throughout the period of our history is hampered by four serious difficulties. Firstly, before about 1800 the relevant muniments are scrappy and incomplete, so that it is now very difficult to ascertain the basic facts. Secondly, the income of most members of the academic staff was until quite recently an aggregate of an astonishingly large number of different types of payment, some of which passed through the Bursar's books while some did not. We have, therefore, to add to the basic salary of a Fellow, Professor or lecturer (sometimes on an incremental scale) such items as salaries of administrative offices, tutorial fees, capitation fees, dissecting-room fees, lecture fees, examination fees, fees for preaching or reading the service in chapel, poundages on fees or rents handled by certain officers, decrements (a fraction of student fees), renewal fines on leases, achates (fees on sealings) and the Provost's private estate. Some of the more old-

Table 5. *Analysis of average annual income and expenditure for selected periods*

(Figures are in thousands of pounds)

	1868–72	1899–1905	1926–30	1934–43	1951
Income					
Rents	42.2	44.9	27.4	8.5	7.2
Dividends	2.5	13.6	59.2	74.2	78.9
Total endowment	44.7	58.5	86.6	82.7	86.1
Fees	22.4	22.1	31.5	37.6	90.6
Government grants	—	—	4.6	5.3	52.8
Miscellaneous	0.9	0.3	0.4	0.6	0.5
Total income	68.0	80.9	123.1	126.2	230.0
Expenditure					
Salaries	37.0	45.6	63.4	72.4	122.1
Student prizes, scholarships and grants	6.6	9.6	12.1	13.5	16.1
Library	1.3	3.0	3.6	4.2	8.9
Scientific and medical departments	2.3	4.7	8.4	11.0	23.2
General maintenance	7.5	8.1	12.4	14.6	32.5
Miscellaneous	5.1	3.9	4.6	4.8	11.4
New buildings	1.5	4.4	—	1.1	—
Total expenditure	61.3	79.3	104.5	121.6	214.2

fashioned of these items were abolished in the latter part of the nineteenth century, but the concept of a consolidated salary dates only from 1947. The importance of these supplementary payments may be demonstrated by the fact that as late as 1919 the salary of a Junior Fellow *qua* Fellow was only £36 18s. 8d. and that in 1905 the Professor of Chemistry, with a basic salary of £275 actually enjoyed an academic income of £939. Thirdly, there was always great variation in income between different members of what one might hope to regard as a homogenous class. In 1905, for example, the total emoluments of the Professor of Romance Languages was £652, while that of the Professor of German was only £402. Finally, there is the difficulty of knowing how much allowance should be made for payments in kind. The Provost and Fellows have always been entitled to free lodging and free Commons (as have also, at times, some of the lowest-paid Professors), and the Professors of Astronomy had a free house. But the value of chambers and commons was as a rule greater to a bachelor than to a married man, and cannot, therefore, be easily expressed in cash terms.

If we consider first the Junior Fellows, the earliest period at which we can make a reliable assessment of their economic position is in the late eighteenth century. During Hely-Hutchinson's provostship it would seem probable that the average income of a Junior Fellow was around £320 a year, though variation in the size of the tutorial chamber meant that some were getting much more and others much less. In the last decade of the century the serious decline in student numbers reduced this average to about £260, which prompted a protest in 1800 (T.C.D. MSS Mun P/1/1140). A modern touch is given to this protest by the stress which it lays on 'comparability' – the relation of a Fellow's income to that of other professional men – though here, perhaps, the Fellows' position was not as strong as they might have wished, as a major in an infantry regiment received only £270 in 1799. They were, however, successful; the Crown, at the request of the Board, raised the annual tutorial fee from £6 to £9 2s. 0d. This soon brought the Fellows' income back to the level at which it had stood ten or twelve years earlier, and as at the same time the student numbers started on their enormous rise, culminating in the peak of 1826, the tutors soon became relatively wealthy (though harder worked) and the poor infantry major was left far behind. By 1830 the average income of the Junior Fellows was about £800. The new tutorial system of 1834 meant that variation in income now depended on seniority rather than popularity, and except in his first two years a Fellow could count on an income of £400, rising over the next fifteen years or so to £850–£900. And about half way through his term as Junior Fellow he received a bonanza of some £900 in the year in which he was Junior Proctor.

From 1846 onwards there was at the bottom of this scale a poverty-stricken class of non-tutor Fellows, but they were no worse off (and had no heavier duties) than the worse-paid Professors, and their numbers, and consequently the length of time they had to wait before getting a tutorship, was progressively reduced over the next half-century.

Through the latter part of the nineteenth century the income of the Junior Fellows rose slowly but steadily, not from an increase in tutorial fees, but from an increase in the number of 'pickings' such as examination fees, salaries of newly founded chairs, fees for extra honor lectures, and so on – indications of the increasing diversity of academic teaching. By 1905 the average emoluments of a Junior Fellow had risen to £750, and several were earning more than £1,000. The reorganization of tutorial finance in 1919 removed some anomalies but scarcely altered the average emolument, and even in 1947 and 1951 the adjustments to the salary scales only gave on each occasion an increase of about £100 a year.

All this, however, was for the greater part of the period covered by our history only a foretaste (for those who survived and were not lured away to a College living) of the richer pastures of Senior Fellowship. From a modest £400 or so in the late eighteenth century the emoluments of a Senior Fellow rose very rapidly, and throughout the period 1840–1950 they averaged something close to £1,500 a year.

If we turn now to the non-Fellow Professors we find once more an enormous contrast between the best- and the worst-paid. Some, such as the Regius Professor of Divinity or of Feudal and English Law, had to be paid enough to induce them (as the statutes required) to resign their Fellowships. At the other end of the scale there were many who were paid only £100, but their duties were light, and they were expected to use their College position as a base from which to look for other earnings. For some, indeed, such as the Professor of Surgery, the title meant much more than the salary. The emoluments of many of the Professors depended largely on capitation fees, whose magnitude varied both with the total number of students and with fluctuations in the popularity of the subject. As we have already noticed, the Professor of Chemistry in 1905 derived less than 30 per cent of his academic income from his basic salary; the remainder was from capitation and examination fees. In 1850 only four non-Fellow Professors (Astronomy, two in Divinity and one in Law) were receiving more than £500 a year, and most of the remaining eighteen fell very far short of this figure. By 1905 the pattern, though not without its anomalies, was more reasonable, for twelve Professors were now receiving over £500, and these included, with two exceptions, all the chairs which could reasonably be called 'central' or of primary importance. The two exceptions were the Professor of German who received only £402, and the Professor of Modern History, who received £242. For the latter there was, if not a justification, at least a historical explanation, for the chair up to 1902 had always been held by a Fellow, for whom £200 was a quite adequate salary. Why the chair of German should have lagged so far behind is not so clear, but the consequence became clear when Williams resigned it in 1912 for a chair at Belfast, with a gain of about £100 a year.

For it was during the first decade of the twentieth century that competition from redbrick universities made itself felt. Trinity did not lose its Professors to them, except in the one case of German, but although it had been able to attract Young from his chair in Bristol in 1903, thereafter it was only readers or lecturers from the new universities who applied for chairs in Dublin. For although there were in 1905 twelve non-Fellow Professors who received more than £500 only four of these earned more than £700, and Redbrick was fast rising to their level. Here also there were large discrepancies: in 1899 A.E. Housman was getting £445 as Professor of Latin in London while the Professor of Chemistry at Manchester was earning over £1,300. But from about 1905 onwards a man hesitating between the attractions of a chair in Dublin and one in Cardiff or Leeds would be swayed more by the imponderables than by the small difference in salary.

As the twentieth century proceeded the Professors gradually edged their salaries upwards, but this was done piecemeal. Occasionally the Board decided that increases were needed for several chairs, but more often an individual Professor struck a private bargain with the Board by reciting a hard-luck story or by threatening to go elsewhere. It was obviously undesirable that the other Professors should know of this, and it was partly for this reason that the Board minutes and the College accounts were guarded with such jealous secrecy.

Any attempt to compare Dublin salaries with those at Oxford and Cambridge comes up against the difficulty that the latter varied in an equally complex manner, and in accordance with variables with which we are not familiar. Our general impression, however, is that from 1830 to 1914 the great majority of the dons at Dublin did rather better than their opposite numbers at Oxford or Cambridge. Against this one must set the fact that their perquisites were less attractive: they had plainer living, less spacious rooms, and probably less services such as heat and light provided free. (Even Provost MacDonnell was beaten in a strenuous battle he waged with the Board to make the College provide free coals for the Provost's House.) Of course these things varied greatly from college to college, but the aspirations of the average Fellow of Trinity (who had few contacts with the aristocracy or the really wealthy) would have been satisfied with the standards of Balliol, and did not hanker for those of Christ Church or of Trinity College, Cambridge. He preferred to bank an extra £100 each year.

Comparison with the other professions is even more difficult, not least for the reason that the don usually sees his alternative life not as that of the average, but of the leading surgeon or barrister. When G.F. Shaw complained (p. 261) that he had sacrificed his professional prospects to run for Fellowship, it was true that some barristers were earning more than he was, but many were earning less.

To sum up, we give as our impression (and it can be little more) that although there were always a few hard cases, judged even by the standards of the age, most of the academic staff were adequately paid between 1780 and 1914, and in the central part of that period were perhaps rather over-generously rewarded. After 1914 there were a few lean periods, but for most of the succeeding thirty years the emoluments were reasonable in relation to those of comparable posts elsewhere. Only in the last seven or eight years of our history did they fall clearly below this level.

Notes

1. EARLY DAYS: 1592–1640

1. For the foundation and early history of the College see J.P. Mahaffy, *An epoch in Irish history* (1903); W. Urwick, *The early history of Trinity College, Dublin* (1892); J.W. Stubbs, *The history of the University of Dublin* (1889), 1–84, 348–409; H.L. Murphy *A history of Trinity College, Dublin* (1951).
2. [J.H. Todd], *Dublin University Calendar for 1833*, 13–17; W. Monck Mason, *The history of the cathedral church of St Patrick*, 100–2.
3. 1591 Old Style. This has led to constant confusion as to the date of the foundation, which has been added to by the fact that in December 1591 (Old and New Style alike) the Queen wrote a letter to the Lord Deputy signifying her approval of the proposed foundation. This letter is referred to by Stubbs, *History*, who dates it correctly to 1591 on p. 7, but on pp. 354–6, where he prints the text of the letter from a copy in the Bodleian, the date of 1592 is given both at the beginning and the end. This is certainly an error.

    It should be explained that in this book we express the year in New Style, but the date of the month, up to 1752, in Old Style. Thus 3/13 March 1591/2 is here expressed as 3 March 1592.
4. 'Collegium Sanctae et Individuae Trinitatis juxta Dublin ... mater universitatis ... pro educatione, institutione, et instructione juvenum et studentium in artibus et facultatibus ... ut eo melius ad bonas artes percipiendas colendamque virtutem et religionem adjuventur.' The Elizabethan charter is printed in the *Statutes*, vol. 1, pp. 1–9, and *The consolidated statutes* (1926), 128–32. (For details of the official publications of the College see bibliography, pp. 560–1.)
5. This is the earliest of the muniments to survive which deals with the internal affairs of the College. It was published in facsimile by Mahaffy in 1904.
6. The Senate of the University was made a corporate body by Letters Patent of 1857, with the usual rights of corporate bodies to own property, to sue and be sued, etc. But the Senate is not the same as the University, and in fact it has never owned any property, never sued, and has only once been sued (in a technical suit, with Trinity College as the plaintiff), when it lost its case.
7. *The College and the University* (1871).
8. *Statutes*, vol. 2, pp. 507–32.
9. 'Cumque dictum Collegium sit et habeatur universitas ...'
10. Mahaffy, *Epoch*, 167.
11. The earliest complete code of College statutes is dated 1629, and was drawn up by William Bedell during his brief tenure of the provostship. They are, however, largely based on the statutes then in force, and most of them probably date from as early as 1610. Bedell's code is printed by Mahaffy, *Epoch*, 327–75. But there

exists also an incomplete version of University statutes drawn up by Provost Temple in 1615 or 1616, in which the qualifications for the different degrees are prescribed. These statutes have never been printed; some of their provisions have been summarized by Stubbs, *History*, 44–6.

12. The most serious of these was in 1659; see Urwick, *Early history*, 62.
13. As the result of pressure from some of the bishops Hebrew was made a compulsory part of the Divinity course in 1856, but the protests against this regulation soon mounted up, and it was repealed in 1859.
14. J.B. Mullinger, *The University of Cambridge from 1535 to the accession of Charles the First* (1884), 387–8, 414.
15. Printed respectively in J. Lamb, *A collection of letters* (1838), 315–54, and Mullinger, *The University of Cambridge*, 579–627.
16. Mullinger, *The University of Cambridge*, 402–3.
17. *Ibid.*, 409–13.
18. *Dublin, 1660–1860* (1952), 3.
19. Published in Dublin in 1602 and 1608 respectively.
20. It may be noted that all these activities are extra-curricular. Even as dedicated an enthusiast as Bedell did not venture to introduce such a utilitarian subject into the course to be read for a degree. This was true also of the revivals of Irish under Narcissus Marsh and in the nineteenth century; it was not until 1908 that the study of Irish helped towards the obtaining of a degree.
21. See M.H. Risk, *Hermathena*, 102 (1966), 16–25. Lynegar's name does not appear in the Register, and he was probably paid no salary, but given a room and allowed to charge fees. He died in poverty, and it seems probable that he received no active encouragement from the College after Hall resigned the vice-provostship in 1713.
22. The average age at entrance rose rapidly, however, during the period of the Civil War and Commonwealth, and, by 1670, was almost seventeen (see p. 506).
23. No formal, permanent Professorships existed before 1668, but the title was given now and then to somebody charged with the principal duties of instruction in the subject.
24. Dublin, 1641.
25. Quoted by Stubbs, *History*, 73.
26. This is the word normally used, but in fact the College still holds the Elizabethan charter. A large part of it was explicitly confirmed by the new one, and from the legal point of view neither charter can be properly interpreted without reference to the other.
27. The phrase used by Laud to justify the increase in the Provost's powers falls strangely on modern ears: 'Quia in omni societate bene constituenda paritas membrorum maxime caveri debet . . .' (*Statutes*, 1 (1844), 35). The other important changes were the transfer from the Fellows to the Crown of the right to appoint the Provost, the giving of a life tenure to Fellows, and the imposition on them (with two exceptions, the *Medicus* and the *Jurista*) of a requirement to take holy orders.
28. The identification is not certain, but for confirmatory evidence see W.F. Pyle, *Hermathena*, 71 (1948), 83–92.

2. SEDITION, PRIVY CONSPIRACY AND REBELLION: 1640 – 1717

1. He was appointed Bishop of Cork in 1638, but was ordered by Strafford to retain the provostship, although this contravened a statute enacted only a year earlier.
2. Only three Provosts of Trinity College have been educated at Oxford. Two fled

under the stress of rebellion or civil war; the third complained of having to live 'in this lewd and debauched town' (Diary of Narcissus Marsh, quoted by Stubbs, *History*, 114).

3. It has been stated that he was also Professor of Laws, but there is no evidence for this in the College records. It may be that the statement was based on a misinterpretation of his degree of Doctor of Laws. In the eighteenth century Doctors of Divinity were often given the title of S.T.P. (Sanctae Theologiae Professor), and it may be that in the seventeenth century a similar title was used for Doctors of Laws.

4. See T.P.C. Kirkpatrick, *History of the medical school* (1912), 49—71.

5. Mahaffy, *Epoch*, 313.

6. *Ormonde MSS* (Hist. MSS Comm.), new series, vol. 6, p. 421.

7. Nathaniel Hoyle made a sixth, and it would appear that Caesar Williamson was accepted as a seventh, although his title was no better than that of any of the other Commonwealth Fellows. Perhaps he was included on the strength of his service in the King's army; but it may have been the result of an administrative muddle, for as early as 1661 a *mandamus* arrived to elect Edward Veale to a Senior Fellowship. This can only have been drafted on the assumption that Williamson's place was vacant. The Board replied that it could not admit him as all seven places were filled; he was elected a Junior Fellow but ejected a few months later for refusing to conform. Another possibility is suggested by the fact that Joseph Travers, elected Fellow in 1634, was in the College in June 1660, and signed the congratulatory address to Ormonde on his return from England (T.C. Barnard, *Hermathena*, 109 (1969), 44). But there is no evidence of his having acted as a Fellow later than 1655, and it seems unlikely that Williamson (who had facilitated the Convention in its first move, in March 1660, to eject Winter) should not have been appointed to a Fellowship at all.

8. Hely-Hutchinson (*experto crede*) declares that this appointment was made so that he could hold the provostship 'with proper dignity' (MS History, book 4, 182—3).

9. Henry Jones, recently dispossessed of the vice-chancellorship in favour of Jeremy Taylor, Bishop of Down, was given, as Bishop of Clogher, a place in the procession, but it was held to be unsuitable for such an active collaborationist under Cromwell to participate in the laying on of hands.

10. These figures make it rather difficult to accept the estimate of '340 young men and boys' of whom Provost Marsh complained he was quickly wearied (Stubbs, *History*, 114). Allowing for 5 per cent wastage per year in each class, the number of undergraduates can hardly have exceeded 210, and to make up Marsh's total every student would have had to stay on until of M.A. status, which was certainly not the case. About 290 seems a more probable figure.

11. Stubbs, *ibid*.

12. *Ormonde MSS*, new series, vol. 6, pp. 515—36.

13. *Elegies on the much lamented death of the right honourable the Earl of Mountrath* (Dublin, 1661); *Threnodia in obitu honoratissimi Wentworthi, Kildariae comitis* (Dublin, 1664).

14. For an account of this society see K.T. Hoppen, *The common scientist in the seventeenth century* (1970).

15. 'I was the first', wrote William Molyneux, 'that recommended to the revd. provost of our university, Dr. Ashe, a most learned and ingenious man, your Essay, with which he was so wonderfully pleased and satisfied, that he has ordered it to be read by the bachelors of the College, and strictly examines them in their progress therein' (John Locke, *Correspondence*, ed. E.S. de Beer, vol. 4 (1979), 601—2).

We find ourselves unable to agree with H.F. Kearney in his *Scholars and gentlemen* (1970), 153, when he says that 'far too much has been read into this by historians anxious to demonstrate the modernity of the general intellectual atmosphere of the college'. He bases this assertion on the flimsy evidence of a few borrowings, spread over many years, by Fellows from the Library of somewhat old-fashioned scholastic treatises. But the period of these borrowings was 1685–97, *before* Locke's *Essay* arrived on the scene. Kearney also gives an extraordinary description of the College as 'Oxford's Irish offshoot'. For only nine years (1679–88) was it ruled by Provosts from Oxford, and although Marsh's *Institutiones logicae* (1681) may have marked a slight change in the orientation of philosophical teaching, the fact that it does not seem to have been reprinted suggests that his influence was not long lived, and Marsh's successor, Robert Huntington, had little interest in philosophy. There is no evidence whatsoever for any Oxford influence in T.C.D. after 1688.

16. Of the twenty men appointed to Irish sees from 1691 to 1699 nine had been Fellows of Trinity College, and in 1699 there were eight ex-Fellows on the Bench.
17. MS History, book 6, 241–2.
18. John Shadwell to the Revd Laurence Howell, 26 September 1703 (Rawlinson MSS, C 842); summarized in *Analecta Hibernica* 2 (1931), 74–5.
19. A biography of Peter Browne has recently been published by A.R. Winnett (1974).
20. This incident has been misinterpreted by past historians; see E.H. Alton, *Hermathena*, 58 (1941), 148–65. Although some difficulties remain, it seems certain that Alton's interpretation is substantially correct.
21. *Commons Journal, Ireland*, 1 June 1709.
22. Hely-Hutchinson, MS History, book 6, 257–8.

3. GEORGIAN STASIS AND GEORGIAN SPLENDOUR: 1717–1794

1. George Berkeley discharged the duties of a Fellow for only two years during Baldwin's provostship.
2. A satirical pamphlet of about 1726 (*The conclave dissected*) deals out even-handed justice by censuring the Provost and nine Fellows for arrogance, self-indulgence or frivolity, while it praises ten for learning, humility or integrity. Gilbert, Helsham and Delany are numbered among the sheep, as also is Lambert Hughes, who was expelled by the Provost in 1739 (Stubbs, *History*, 167–8).
3. The silence of the University as a whole, however, lasted for only twenty-two years, as Thomas Molyneux published his *Discourse on Danish forts* while Regius Professor of Physic in 1725, and Bryan Robinson, a later occupant of the same chair, published a book on nutrition in 1747. Helsham's *Lectures on Natural Philosophy* were not published until after his death.
4. *The book of Trinity College*, 84.
5. Walter Bagehot, *Collected works*, vol. 1, ed. N. St John Stevas, (London, 1965), 219.
6. Craig, *Dublin 1660–1860*, 96.
7. For further details see Kirkpatrick, *History of the medical school*, *passim*.
8. C.E. Mallet, *A history of the University of Oxford*, vol. 3 (1927), 126; D.A. Winstanley, *Unreformed Cambridge* (1935), 164–5.
9. The phrase was intended, it seems, to cover pathology and physiology, but in fact such teaching in physiology as was given up to 1874 was given by the Professor of Anatomy.
10. *Correspondence*, ed. H. Williams, vol. 3 (1963), 312.

11. Winstanley, *Unreformed Cambridge*, 154—62.
12. The course is written on the blank page of one of the Senior Lecturer's ledgers (T.C.D. MSS: Mun V/27(1), 6). It is printed in Stubbs, *History*, 200, but in a very garbled and scarcely comprehensible form, with many errors in transcription.
13. The list actually reads 'Clerk's Logic; Art of Thinking' suggesting two separate works. But no author is given for the latter, and it seems safe to assume that the subtitle of Le Clerc's work became detached from the title by mistake.
14. 'The sad story of Dr Colbatch', *Portraits in miniature* (London, 1931).
15. *Life of Thomas Parnell* (London, 1773), p. ii.
16. *Correspondence*, vol. 1, ed. T.W. Copeland (1958), 28.
17. J.E.B. Mayor, *Cambridge under Queen Anne*, 252. Abbreviated English translations had appeared in Cambridge from 1701 onwards — an early indication of the impending disappearance of Latin as the universal language of scholarship.
18. Mallet, *History of University of Oxford*, vol. 3, p. 127.
19. Mention should be made here of Provost Marsh's *Institutiones logicae* (see chapter 2, note 15), which was presumably used as a textbook in the last years of the seventeenth century.
20. We have searched many library catalogues without finding any mention of a book which might correspond to this. One must presume that the author was Jacques-Nicolas Colbert (1655—1707), who became Archbishop of Rouen in 1691. In 1678, a year before his ordination, he published in Paris his *Philosophia vetus et nova, ad usum scholae accommodata*, and extracts from this may have been republished later as textbooks.
21. A circular for schoolmasters drawn up by the Board in 1759 is printed by Stubbs, *History*, 206. It advised that 'every young gentleman be completely instructed in the Common Rules of Arithmetic before he shall think of entering the College', and recommended them 'to exercise your scholars in these Rules by examples taken from the coins, weights and measures of the Ancients'. Even simple arithmetic had to be taught through the medium of the classics.
22. Mayor, *Cambridge under Queen Anne*, 53.
23. Translated from *De officio hominis et civis*, first published in 1675. It is a condensation of Pufendorf's earlier and more celebrated work, *De iure gentium et naturae*.
24. Cited by Stubbs, *History*, 204.
25. There is some uncertainty as to the date of his birth.
26. E.g. by Mahaffy in *The book of Trinity College*, 56—7.
27. In 1731 Boulter rather half-heartedly recommended Baldwin for appointment to Ossory, but expressed his relief when he heard that an Englishman had been preferred to him. See his *Letters* (1770), vol. 2, p. 73.
28. Pelissier had been elected to Fellowship by the arbitrary *fiat* of Baldwin, despite the opposition and protest of most of the Senior Fellows.
29. F. Hardy, *Memoirs of the life of James Caulfield, Earl of Charlemont* (1810), 75—7.
30. G. Montagu to Horace Walpole, 27 November 1761 (*Correspondence of Horace Walpole*, ed. W.S. Lewis, vol. 9 (London and New Haven, 1941), 404).
31. The semi-clandestine marriages among the Fellows, described on pp. 106—7, had by this time become fairly common, and certainly Clement and Leland were married.
32. *Lachrymae academicae* (1777), *passim*.
33. Craig (*Dublin 1660—1860*, 206) praises him as 'at least as good a Provost as Andrews', and dismisses Duigenan as 'an Orange boor'.
34. A parliamentary committee found that he had used improper influence in

securing the election of his son in 1776, and visitations in 1776 and 1791 found against him on a disciplinary dispute and on the Provost's power of veto in elections. In view of the usual reluctance of the Visitors to find against the Provost or the Board, and of the fact that the two Vice-Chancellors concerned – Primate Robinson and Lord Chancellor Fitzgibbon – could scarcely be described as radicals or indifferent to the rights of properly constituted authority, it is clear that in both hearings the case against the Provost was strong.

35. See pamphlets in T.C.D. Library, Press E 4 7a (27, 28).
36. Dublin, 1775.
37. *An account of some regulations made in Trinity College, Dublin, since the appointment of the present Provost* (1775), 5. The pamphlet is anonymous, but is generally ascribed to Hely-Hutchinson himself.
38. A grinder is the equivalent of an Oxford or Cambridge coach.
39. *Dictionary of National Biography.*
40. *Complete Peerage, sub tit.* Mornington.
41. For a fuller assessment of Lawson's work see Stanford, *Ireland and the classical tradition* (1976), 52–4.
42. Not the Provost, Francis Andrews, as is erroneously stated in many lists.
43. He is best known as having been Bishop of Killala in 1798 when the town was captured by the French, who held him prisoner for a month. He wrote a vivid narrative of the episode, in which the tributes he paid to the generally courteous and civilized behaviour of the French officers made him unpopular in conservative circles.
44. Stanford (*Ireland and the classical tradition*, 211) suggests that the strongly pro-Athenian and democratic enthusiasm of Lawson and Leland in their published works may, as it came through in their lectures, have inspired the Whiggish policies of such men as Flood, Grattan and Curran, who could have heard them as students. This may be so, but it is worth noting that Leland (whose allegiance had been secured by a dispensation for his unstatutory marriage) was an unwavering supporter of Hely-Hutchinson in his somewhat Macedonian methods of ruling the College.
45. It appears in a pamphlet of 1783, often attributed to Arthur Browne, but more probably by John Forsayeth, entitled *Thoughts on the present state of the College of Dublin.*
46. The first Professor of Astronomy, Henry Ussher, was a Fellow, as was C.J. Joly, who held the chair from 1897 to 1906, but the remaining seven Professors were not. The Professor of Feudal and English Law was bound by statute to resign his Fellowship on appointment.
47. The College seems to have possessed a telescope about 1685, but it did not survive the Jacobite occupation.
48. No attempt was made to set up a similar chair at Cambridge, which had to wait till 1800 for the Downing Professorship. There were, however, some lectures in English law from about 1785.
49. Hely-Hutchinson, MS History, book 7, 32.
50. There was a technical hitch over his appointment, as it was found at the last minute that he did not fulfil the condition required by the statute that he should have practised for two years at the Bar. A man of straw, John Armstrong, was elected to fill the chair for two months until Palmer received a dispensation from the requirement.
51. Printed in Stubbs, *History*, 257–8.
52. *Observations on the course of science* (1792).

53. Hely-Hutchinson, MS History, book 7, 37, gives Andrews the credit for this, and declares that as a result 'the modes of argument' used in the learned professions have shown 'great advances in clear reasoning'.

54. See E.J. Furlong, *Hermathena*, 60 (1942), 38. The edition usually cited is Dublin, 1782, but an edition of 1759 is to be found in the Haliday collection of the Royal Irish Academy.

55. This applies only to the pass course; Locke continued, of course, to be studied by honor students.

56. Dublin, 1787. The only copy of the first edition which we have been able to trace is in private hands.

57. Newton survived until 1727, but all the work on which his fame rests was done before 1700.

58. It is easy to forget that Locke was a graduate of Oxford.

59. Mallet, *History of University of Oxford*, vol. 3, p. 128.

60. *Thoughts on the present state*, 11 (see note 45 in this chapter).

61. Oxford, 1762; Dublin, 1763.

62. Kenyon *MSS* (Hist. MSS Comm.), 540.

63. T.C.D. MSS 2244–5.

4. LIMBO: 1794 – 1830

1. College opinion, which had unanimously condemned the rebellion, was largely opposed to the Union. Only five Fellows (Fitzgerald, Elrington, Browne, Graves and Prior) were known to favour it. A few were indifferent; the majority, including Stokes, Magee, Miller and Davenport, was hostile, as was also Provost Kearney (Matthew Young to Castlereagh in Castlereagh, *Memoirs and correspondence*, ed. C. Vane, vol. 3 (1849), 229–30). It is interesting to note that those favouring the Union included liberals (Fitzgerald and Browne) as well as staunch conservatives (Elrington and Prior).

2. See pp. 507–8.

3. Vice-Chancellor of the University and Lord Chancellor of Ireland, later Earl of Clare. Fitzgibbon was an imperious and hot-tempered man, and would have given short shrift to anyone who, no matter how pure his intentions, wished to oppose a nominee of the Crown.

4. See further, on these manoeuvres, T.C.D. MSS Mun P 1/1062–1130; also Stubbs, *History*, 271–7; J.C. Martin and M. O'Sullivan, *Remains of Rev. S. O'Sullivan*, vol. 2 (Dublin, 1853), 271–5; Edmund Burke, *Correspondence*, vol. 8, ed. R.B. McDowell (1969), pp. 6, 11 and 28.

5. This provoked the first of very numerous edicts of the Board, reiterated at intervals throughout the first half of the nineteenth century, and sometimes raised to the dignity of decrees by the concurrence of the Visitors, forbidding students to attend political meetings or to become members of debating societies.

6. 'The wild opinions of Paine were at this time widely and zealously disseminated, and had been eagerly embraced . . . even by some among the fellows.' From a note written by William Magee on the flyleaf of a sermon preached in the College in May 1791; it is printed on p. xxxii of the *Memoir* by A.H. Kenney prefixed to Magee's *Works* (2 vols., 1842).

7. Wolfe Tone, who declared that Stokes was 'the very best man I have ever known', also said of him, 'I very much fear that his very metaphysical unbending purity, which can accommodate itself neither to man, time nor circumstance, will always prevent him being of any service to his country . . . what he would highly,

that he would holily, and I am afraid that in the present state of affairs that is a thing impossible' (*Life of Theobald Wolfe Tone*, ed. W.T.W. Tone, vol. 2 (1826), p. 489). This generous judgment was sound enough as far as political action was concerned, but one regrets that Tone was unable at this time to view service to Ireland in any terms other than violent political action.

8. He was forbidden for three years to hold a tutorship or to sit on the Board.
9. *Dublin University Magazine*, 26 (1845), 484.
10. A copy of the second edition (Dublin, 1798) in the National Library of Ireland is the only one we have seen; the book is not in the Library of Trinity College nor of the British Museum.
11. Kearney and Kyle were promoted direct from the boardroom; Hall and Elrington spent five or six years in a College living before returning as Provost.
12. Hall never took up his duties as Bishop, as he died five days after his consecration.
13. W.B.S. Taylor, *History of the University of Dublin* (1845), 256.
14. T. Moore, *Memoirs*, ed. Lord John Russell, vol. 1 (1853), 50, 69–70, 104–5.
15. *Personal recollections* (1849), 9.
16. Prior's diary (T.C.D. MSS 3367–9), 1 January and 13 February 1817.
17. *Ibid.*, 15 July 1835.
18. Evidence of the Government's motives may be found in letters from Talbot (Lord-Lieutenant) to Gregory (Under-Secretary), 4 February 1820 (*Mr Gregory's letter-box, 1813–30*, ed. Lady Gregory (London, 1898), 139–40), and from Talbot to Sidmouth (Home Secretary), 22 July 1820 (Home Office 100/199).
19. *The book of Trinity College* (1892), 82–9.
20. This passage was written during the preparations for the Tercentenary, when Mahaffy's tremendous appetite for magnificence and display found itself severely curbed by the financial caution of the Bursar and by Provost Salmon's strong distaste for anything savouring of ostentation. In consequence Hely-Hutchinson, whose manner of living was extravagant and grandiose, is defended on nearly all counts – even for melting down College silver to make a dinner-service for use in his wife's house at Palmerstown – while his more parsimonious successors are mercilessly derided.
21. *Cambridge University Calendar* for 1802.
22. It was a short-lived generation. Of the nine men elected to Fellowship in the decade 1770–9 six died before they were fifty and the oldest at sixty-seven.
23. Many of the most popular stories appeared in Lever's *Charles O'Malley*, but they deserve no more credence than other anecdotes in that entertaining but scarcely realistic tale. Lever, however, wrote an article on Barrett in the *Dublin University Magazine* for May 1841, and the stories recounted here, though mostly at second-hand, are probably based at least in part on fact. A few stories derive from other sources.
24. An American, after dining with Elrington in 1817, remarks: 'The Provost's table presented a luxurious display of viands, and the glasses as they briskly circulated sparkled with wines of ruby brightness and rarest excellence' (A. Bigelow, *Leaves from a journal* (Edinburgh, 1824), 126). One feels that this naive provincial was easily impressed. The oft-repeated description of the reception given to George IV in 1821 had an unmistakable note of vulgarity in its splendour. Admittedly the King was greatly pleased, but his taste was easily swayed by his vanity.
25. An increase in the number of students between 1770 and 1790 led to a demand for more accommodation, and work on this square was begun about 1794. But it had not gone far before the sharp decline in student numbers led to the suspension of building, and the greater part of the square dates from about 1812.

26. The effects of this change could be traced up to about thirty years ago in the library of many of the country houses of Ireland, where there was inevitably a sound, if unadventurous selection of standard eighteenth-century writers, followed by a miscellaneous jumble of nineteenth-century works in which studbooks, military memoirs and volumes of the Badminton Library tended to predominate. Most of these libraries are now, however, broken up.

27. The generation of Burke, Goldsmith, Sheridan, Grattan and Flood was followed by that of Tone, Castlereagh, Wellington, O'Connell and Moore (all born between 1763 and 1779). The next twenty years, the generation of Byron, Shelley and Keats, seems to present in Ireland an absolute blank; and even of the men born between 1800 and 1820 the most distinguished are Cullen, Lever, Rowan Hamilton, Davis, Butt and Salmon, who can scarcely be said to hold their own with their English contemporaries, Newman, Macaulay, Gladstone, Disraeli, Darwin and Tennyson. Later on the supply is resumed: Lecky, Mahaffy, Parnell, Wilde, Shaw, Carson and Yeats were all born between 1838 and 1865.

28. This is much the most satisfactory index of size. The total number of students given in Calendars or government returns is subject to arbitrary variation following changes in administrative practice or in the academic timetable. The total number of students, at any rate for the period 1750–1914, is seldom far removed from the total intake of the past five years. For a further discussion of this topic see appendix 2.

29. The Cambridge figures are derived from J.A. Venn, *A statistical chart to illustrate the entries at the various colleges in the University of Cambridge, 1544–1907* (1908). We have summed the figures shown in his chart for the various colleges.

30. Curiously enough Venn, in the booklet accompanying his *Statistical chart*, refers to a 'slow increase' at Cambridge between 1807 and 1826, and suggests that its slowness was due to 'troubles on the Continent'. But the increase over this period of nineteen years amounted in fact to more than 120 per cent.

31. An average of 40 students were admitted to the medical school annually between 1810 and 1813; over the period 1824–30 the average was 96. In addition to these, external students attended on a fee-paying basis, and the numbers attending Macartney's classes rose from 53 in 1814 to 188 in 1831.

32. Of the 111 students admitted to the school in 1828, 12 had been born in England and 3 in Scotland.

33. *Address delivered before the King and Queen's College of Physicians in Ireland* (Westminster, 1851), 4.

34. James Drought, the retiring Professor, was succeeded by his son-in-law, Richard Graves, but the appointment was a sound one, and indicates not nepotism but the small world of intellectual Protestant Dublin.

35. That is to say *valde bene* in all subjects but one, in which *bene* was allowed.

5. THE COLLEGE IN 1830

1. This arrangement was made partly because the medical school was frequented by extern students over whom the Board had no adequate disciplinary control, but also because of the low moral reputation of Park Street.

2. *Charlemont MSS* (Hist. MSS Comm.), vol. 2, p. 32.

3. Hardwicke to Hawkesbury, 31 August, 9 September and 23 October 1805; Hawkesbury to Hardwicke, 6 and 14 September, 6 October 1805. Hardwicke papers (Brit. Lib. Add. MSS 35710).

4. In 1805 the Duke of Cumberland, on assuming the chancellorship, appointed as Vice-Chancellor the Lord Chief Justice of Ireland, instead of the previous Vice-Chancellor, Lord Redesdale, who was at that time Lord Chancellor of Ireland. Redesdale was an extremely able lawyer, but his vigorously expressed anti-Catholic views were embarrassing to the Government (though not, one would have thought, to Cumberland). A few weeks later, when the 'ministry of all the talents' was formed, Redesdale was dismissed from the office of Lord Chancellor, but not before the Board had sent him a message of confidence and sympathy which came near to a vote of censure on their new Chancellor.

5. Strictly speaking the Chancellor, or in his absence the Vice-Chancellor. But the Chancellor, though occasionally consulted by letter, never seems to have visited.

6. Varied, however, in 1829 by an unexpected diversion. Boyton, the Junior Dean, had appealed to the Visitors against the Board for their failure to punish a radical undergraduate as severely as Boyton (an extreme Tory) thought appropriate. The Visitors (the Archbishops of Armagh and Dublin) disagreed publicly, and had to retire to patch up in private a face-saving compromise (*Dublin Evening Post*, 3 and 5 November 1829).

7. The duties of this office, which dates back to the seventeenth century, consisted in the general superintendence of examinations and to some extent of lectures, and the keeping of the academic records of students.

8. Leveson-Gower, the Chief Secretary, wrote of him: 'the Provost is a man of weak character, more obsequious than sincere, and undoubtedly unfitted for his situation in these difficult times, though he might make a quiet and respectable head of a house on our side.' He maintained that Kyle's opinions, though not openly expressed, were 'of a very deep Orange; he is entirely guided by the Bishop of Ferns [ex-Provost Elrington], a very violent and eccentric, though conscientious man. They now carry on a correspondence in cipher.' (Leveson-Gower to Singleton, 23 March and 26 May, 1829 from his letter books in the Public Record Office of Ireland.)

9. Croker to Peel, 25 May 1818 (Brit. Lib. Add. MSS 40330).

10. All these offices were confined by statute to the Senior Fellows, except the Senior Proctorship (about which the statutes were curiously silent) and the Librarianship. But it was not until 1914 that a Junior Fellow was appointed Librarian, and that was mainly because in that year all the Senior Fellows were over seventy.

11. This is perhaps not quite fair to Sadleir, who probably saw at least that the books were well looked after. In 1831 we find him, as Bursar, reporting to the Board that the manuscripts were 'in a state of decay by worms', and that he had shown them to the bookbinder, who had said that they must be unbound and washed. The task of College historians would be easier if all Bursars had been as vigilant.

12. The statutes were not quite as explicit as the Junior Fellows might have wished, but at least for the Bursarship and the Professorships qualifications were required which were inconsistent with automatic rotation, and for the other offices the Visitors declared the system to be, even if not postively illegal, at least inexpedient.

13. These estates amounted to some 170,000 acres, scattered through twelve counties, and provided throughout the nineteenth century the major part of the college's income.

14. These estimates, which are likely, if anything, to be too low, are based mainly on the information supplied to the Royal Commission of 1851, taking into account changes in student numbers and agricultural conditions between 1830 and 1850.

15. 'The Board', wrote Barlow (then Vice-Provost) in his statement to the Royal

Commission of 1906, 'enjoys the perhaps undesirable privilege of being the most heartily and universally abused body in Ireland. This is no peculiarity of the present Board; unpopularity seems to be an essential attribute of a Senior Fellow; my own personal knowledge of this sad fact goes back as far as 1843, in which year I was a Junior Freshman, and I have rarely heard the Board spoken of without the prefix of some uncomplimentary adjective.' As will be seen later, there was a short period around 1852 when this was not true, but Barlow at that time belonged to the most under-privileged and discontented body in College (the non-tutor Fellows), and doubtless one of the uncomplimentary adjectives was often on his lips.

16. Of the eight men who composed the Board in December 1824, seven were still sitting on it in November 1836.

17. Eighteen of these advowsons were presented to the College very early in its history by James I. Three were purchased later. All the livings were in Ulster.

18. These estimates are derived from figures published by the *Dublin University Commission: Evidence* (1853), 252–3, supplemented by some figures from Prior's diary for 1831.

19. Undeterred, apparently, by the fact that William Davenport, his colleague till recently on the Board, had blown out his brains after a year's experience of the same living (Prior's diary, 26 July 1823).

20. S.C. Sandes and Charles Graves resigned their Senior Fellowships for bishoprics in 1836 and 1866 respectively, and Singer, to become Regius Professor of Divinity, in 1850.

21. This trend, as will be seen, was temporarily reversed around 1850.

22. Phipps, in some mysterious manner, managed to retain the office of Registrar from 1840 to 1843 though he attended only a single Board meeting throughout this period.

23. He had, however, been given permanent leave of absence in 1874.

24. Meetings were held at this time not infrequently in the middle of the long vacation, and on more than one occasion on Christmas Eve, not for any sudden emergency, but because it was regarded as a working day.

25. D.A. Winstanley, *Early Victorian Cambridge* (1940), 432–3.

26. *Statutes*, vol. 1, p. 52.

27. A.H. Kenney, *Memoir*, prefixed to W. Magee, *Works* (1842), p. xxviii.

28. W.G. Carroll, *A memoir of the Rt. Rev. James Thomas O'Brien* (1875), 8. This curious work is outstanding among episcopal biographies for its remarkable frankness.

29. R.H. Graves, *Memoir*, prefixed to the collected works of Richard Graves, Dean of Ardagh, *Whole works* (1840), p. xxix.

30. *Dublin University Magazine*, 26 (1845), 484.

31. R.P. Graves, *Life of Sir William Rowan Hamilton*, vol. 1 (1882), 241.

32. T.R. Robinson, *A system of mechanics* (Dublin, 1820), pp. vi–vii.

33. The average age at election between 1810 and 1830 was twenty-six.

34. A.H. Kenney, *Memoir*, p. xxii.

35. W. Phelan, *Remains* (1832), 16.

36. Matthew Young was ready to present himself as a candidate in 1771, but, by what his biographer calls 'an unprecedented fatality' ('lack of fatality' might have been the more accurate phrase) he had to wait until 1774 for a vacancy (T. Elrington, memoir appended to *A sermon preached . . . on the death of the Right Reverend Matthew, Lord Bishop of Clonfert* (Dublin, 1800)).

37. A.H. Kenney, *Memoir*, p. xxiv.

38. A second Jurist's place had been established in 1761. Most of the Fellows took

orders willingly enough, as may be seen from the fact that the post of *Medicus* lay vacant sometimes for several years. The requirement that orders should be taken within three years of the M.A. degree, instead of (as might have been expected) within three years of election, offered, however, a means of postponement. In 1839 Provost Sadleir, noting that four of the Junior Fellows had failed to take their M.A. when qualified to do so, ordered them all to take the degree at the next Commencements. They obeyed, and all subsequently took orders except A.S. Hart; he was saved by the death of Hodgkinson in 1840, which left vacant one of the lay Fellowships.

39. 'Si quem etiam Sociorum ... uxorem duxisse ... compertum sit, eum societatis omni jure privari volumus' (*Statutes*, vol. 1, p. 42). It was maintained that 'compertum sit' implied the formal notification of the marriage to the Board and Visitors.

40. E.g. Hodgkinson, in 1808. As a layman his position was especially precarious, as he could not fall back on a living if things went wrong.

41. *Dublin University Magazine*, 26 (1845), 489—90.

42. Plunket and Croker, the rival candidates, both emphasized the influence they could exert upon the Government to grant dispensations in individual cases, and the latter was pressed by one of his supporters (Bartholomew Lloyd) to investigate the possibilities of repeal of the statute (*Crokeriana* (1818), iv).

43. Liverpool to Wellesley, 7 June 1822, Wellesley papers (Brit. Lib. Add. MSS 37299).

44. *Gentleman's Magazine*, 4 (1835), 457.

45. Griffin had been a friend of Robert Emmet in their undergraduate days, and when Emmet was sentenced to death he rushed to the dock and gave him a parting embrace (J.R. O'Flanagan, *The Irish Bar* (London, 1879), 308).

46. Kenny to Sidmouth, 6 and 14 August, 18 September 1820 (Home Office, 100/199).

47. *Gentleman's Magazine*, 44 (1855), 544.

48. James Kennedy in classics, H.H. Harte in mathematics, J.T. O'Brien in theology, Humphrey Lloyd in physics and Mountiford Longfield in economics.

49. Three of these died relatively young, and cannot, therefore, be fairly assessed.

50. Fifty-three future Fellows took their degree between 1816 (when the new medal course first took effect) and 1853 (when the better representation of classics in the Fellowship examination began to be seriously discussed). Of these, twenty-five won a medal in mathematics alone at the degree examination, eleven in both mathematics and philosophy (or, in the years before 1833, in the two combined), two in philosophy alone, one in classics and philosophy, and one in classics alone. Thirteen (including, rather surprisingly, McCullagh and Todd) did not win high enough marks for the nature of their specialization to be apparent.

51. He offered to resign, but for reasons which are now obscure, the Provost, albeit with tears in his eyes, expelled him.

52. R.P. Graves (*Life of Hamilton*, vol. 1, p. 179) says of him that 'his judgment was not always equal to his erudition, and his language, not only in his writings but in his conversation, was famed for polysyllabic pedantry'.

53. Even as late as 1880 membership of the Common Room was confined to the Fellows.

54. A remark is attributed to Einstein that the best post for a pure mathematician is that of lighthouse keeper; the next best that of Astronomer Royal of Ireland in the early nineteenth century.

55. This figure must be assessed in the light of what is said below about non-resident students.

56. The annual fee for a pensioner was at this time £15.

57. *Minutes of evidence taken before a Select Committee of the House of Lords appointed to inquire into the state of Ireland*, H.C. (181) 1825, IX, 158.

58. D. McSweeney, *The case of Daniel McSweeney* (1819). Since 1843 the sizars have dined with the other students.

59. The number of Corkmen among the Fellows of the early nineteenth century is also very striking. Of the forty Fellows elected between 1832 and 1858 no fewer than fifteen were born in the city or county of Cork.

60. [Hely-Hutchinson], *An account of some regulations* (1775), 8.

61. The earliest publications to deal in any detail with the non-resident students are T. Andrews, *Studium generale* (1867) and H.Y. Thompson, *The system of non-residence at Trinity College, Dublin* (1872).

62. Thompson, *System of non-residence*, 3.

63. *Dublin University Commission: Evidence* (1853), 212.

64. Thompson, *System of non-residence*, 4–5.

65. G.A. Studdert Kennedy, who took his degree in 1904, 'worked at home with occasional fleeting migrations to Dublin' (*G.A. Studdert Kennedy, by his friends* (London, 1929), 29). A.A. Luce, though later a Moderator and Fellow, started his academic career with a steamboat degree in 1905.

66. Samuel Butler, *Life and letters of Dr Samuel Butler*, vol. 2 (London, 1896), 206–7.

67. John Jebb, who initiated this controversy towards the end of the eighteenth century, had spent a year at Trinity College, Dublin before migrating to Cambridge.

68. Even as late as 1844. See Lombe Atthill, *Recollections of an Irish Doctor* (1911), 80.

69. *Discipline of Dublin University* (2nd edn, 1828), 6.

70. The course for 1828 is given in the *Discipline*, 17–24. This book was an unofficial and anonymous student's guide to courses and regulations. Its publication seems to have supplied the stimulus for the College to bring out an annual Calendar, in which the same information (and a good deal more) was provided with an official *imprimatur*. The first Calendar appeared in 1833; it was produced on the initiative of J.H. Todd, and much of it (including the elaborate historical introduction) was written by him. The College took it over a few years later, and it has been published annually since then (though only in skeleton form during the war years 1942–5).

71. Dublin, 1826. This book, which has been described as 'beautifully written, with very elegant notation', was produced specifically for the undergraduate course. T.R. Robinson's *System of Mechanics* (Dublin, 1820) had also been designed for the same end, but had proved unsuitable. As Lloyd politely remarks in the preface to his own work, 'the information it conveys is dealt with according to the riches of the store from which it proceeded, rather than to the wants of those to whom it is offered'.

72. At King's College, Aberdeen, the Moral Philosophy class in their last year studied natural theology, jurisprudence, political economy, rhetoric and *belles-lettres*. At Marischal College the course in Natural and Civil History included galvanism, zoology, metrology, ancient history and chronology. At Edinburgh the chair of Rhetoric was founded to teach scientific criticism by 'referring the productions of genius in all departments of elegant design to those operations and laws of our sensitive nature, to which everything that designs to please must be accommodated'. But circumstances limited this ambitious plan; 'from the low state of grammatical instruction in this part of the island, and the local and provincial idioms prevalent even in the works of the learned' the Professor had to spend most of his time in giving elementary lessons in English. *Report by a Royal*

Commission of inquiry into the state of the Universities of Scotland (1831), 129.

73. Entrance scholarships, which had been introduced on an open basis at Cambridge not many years earlier, were condemned in 1879 by an influential body of university opinion, and survived only because of the support they received from headmasters (D.A. Winstanley, *Later Victorian Cambridge* (1947), 349).

74. *Discipline*, 25.

75. There were at this time, as at Oxford, four terms in the year.

76. There is a cryptic reference to an 'ordeal' known as the *Consuetum Examen* in the *Oxford University Commission: Report* (1852), 58.

77. *Statutes*, vol. 1, 73.

78. There were virtually no public examinations in the Scottish universities at the time of the Royal Commission of 1831.

79. *Report by a Royal Commission into the universities of Scotland* (1831), 10.

80. The fact that until about 1955 this bell tolled to summon a rather dingy handful of undergraduates to a pass examination, while the élite of the College proceeded to its honor and moderatorship examinations without any accompanying solemnity, is a reminder of the absolute precedence in earlier days of the pass course, to which honor courses were but slowly and grudgingly admitted as alternatives.

81. These had been started at St John's about 1767, adopted by Trinity in 1790, and were gradually taken up by the smaller colleges during the early nineteenth century. By 1830 they were held in all but three or four. Nothing of the kind seems to have existed at Oxford.

82. B.D. Walsh, *A historical account of the University of Cambridge* (1837), 80.

83. See especially J.R. Seeley in F.W. Farrar, *Essays on a liberal education* (London, 1867), 161.

84. R. MacDonnell, *A letter concerning the undergraduate examinations* (1828).

85. We are indebted for the first of these stories to the late J.G. Smyly (Fellow, 1897–1948), and for the second to the late Dr Eva Jellett, daughter of Provost Jellett.

86. *A history of Greece* (London, 1862 edn), vol. 5, p. 77.

87. Ezra, i, 9.

88. The book prizes awarded today for first-class honors at the annual examinations are the lineal descendants of the premium system, which was initiated in 1731 at the suggestion of Samuel Madden. Their real value, however, has shown a sad decline.

89. An enthusiastic commentator on the scheme when it was first instituted justly observed that it was founded 'on the strongest and noblest principle of education, a love of merited applause, by which young and ingenious minds are more powerfully activated than by any other passion' (*An essay ocassioned by the Rev. Mr Madden's Scheme* (Dublin, 1731)).

90. *Memoir*, prefixed to Richard Graves, *Whole works*, p. xii.

91. R. Henderson, *A memoir of the late Rev. George Armstrong* (1859), 3.

92. In many cases preparation for the Fellowship examination began a year before graduation.

93. E. Jane Whately, *Life and correspondence of Richard Whately, D.D.* (1866), vol. 1, p. 166.

94. Oriel and Corpus Christi had reformed their methods of election at the beginning of the century; they were soon followed by Balliol, and more slowly by some of the other colleges. But even in 1852 it appeared that 'at Queen's . . . the Scholars . . . till lately succeeded to Fellowships without any examination. At Christ

Church the Students are nominated by the Dean and Canons in turn ... it is notorious that Studentships are often given as a matter of favour, and that relatives or friends of Canons are likely to be preferred. At Merton and All Souls Colleges ... it would be useless for candidates, however qualified, to present themselves if their claims were not supported by personal interest or high connections' (*Oxford University Commission: Report* (1852), 168). In many cases too the Scholarships, which were the passports to Fellowships, were mainly rewards for having been born in the same county as a benefactor of two or three centuries earlier.

95. *In linguarum peritia, in historiis, et poetis, et in toto genere humanioris literaturae* are the words of the statute. The examination in fact covered classical literature, ancient history, chronology and Hebrew.

96. According to Prior (Diary, 30 May 1836), under the 'old system' Mooney would have been elected to the third Fellowship in 1836 instead of Charles Graves, as Graves was superior to Mooney in mathematics alone, but in all other subjects inferior, and did not offer Hebrew at all.

97. A substantial minority of the Fellows of the early nineteenth century turned back to the classics or related subjects after they had won their Fellowship mainly in mathematics. But the traces of the mathematical training can be seen in the fact that most of them favoured a linguistic, rather than a literary or historical approach. Of the twelve Fellows elected between 1800 and 1860 who made a worthwhile contribution in the field of *litterae humaniores* eight concerned themselves with grammar or philology. Of these five (George Longfield, Ingram, John Gwynn, Abbott and Ferrar) had taken Moderatorship in Mathematics; Hincks and Wall graduated before the institution of the medal system, and Byrne took a pass degree. One can appreciate that for Hincks's almost cryptographic work on cuneiform inscriptions higher algebra might well prove a better training then the study of Thucydides or Horace. The remaining four Fellows (Kennedy, Todd, Barlow and McIvor) were historians, philosophers or literary critics. Of these Barlow alone was a Moderator in Mathematics; McIvor took his degree in Classics and Philosophy; Kennedy took a pass degree, as did Todd, who, although he competed for a medal, failed to win one.

98. Henderson, *Memoir of George Armstrong*, 3.

99. Lever entered College in 1822.

100. *Dublin University Magazine*, 5 (1835), 353–5.

101. Hamilton was a friend of Wordsworth, and visited him several times at Grasmere; he was also a prolific but mediocre poet. He sent his poems for criticism to Wordsworth, who answered with a judicious mixture of candour and tact.

102. R.P. Graves, *Life of Hamilton*, vol. 1, 497–8.

103. The last of these survived until about 1935. By that time, however, the number of honors-men who took grinds was very small indeed.

104. Winstanley, *Early Victorian Cambridge*, 410–13.

105. We have traced eighty-five works published between 1800 and 1850 which seem to be directly inspired by the requirements of the entrance examination or the undergraduate course in arts.

106. D. Lardner, *A series of lectures on Locke's Essay* (Dublin, 1824).

107. A.M., *A contraction of Locke's Essay* (Dublin, 1829).

108. J. Walker, *The first, second and sixth books of Euclid ... for the use of younger students* (Dublin, 1808).

109. According to the *D.N.B.* he earned five times this sum in the course of a single lecture-tour in the United States and Cuba.

110. He had, however, acted since 1827 as deputy for Graves, who was incapacitated by illness.

111. He resigned his position as chaplain to the Lord-Lieutenant in 1837 because, having been invited to preach at the Chapel Royal on Sunday, 5 November, he discovered that the Dean intended to treat it as an ordinary Sunday, instead of reading the special service for deliverance from the Gunpowder Plot, which was still ordained by the rubrics.

112. C.S. Parker, *Sir Robert Peel*, vol. 3 (1899), 38.

113. *University of Dublin: Returns*, H.C. (264), 1831–2, XLV, 3.

114. The graduates who were ordained within a few years of 1830 include Bishops Brown and Russell, of Sierra Leone and North China respectively; W.C. Magee, Archbishop of York; Archibald Boyd, Dean of Exeter; R.C. Singleton, first Warden of Radley; and such well-known writers and preachers as John Jebb, Moses Margoliouth, J.S.B. Monsell and William Pennefather.

115. *Dublin University Commission: Evidence* (1853), 25.

116. C.A. Cameron, *History of the Royal College of Surgeons in Ireland* (2nd edn, 1916), 656.

117. See Alexander Macalister, *James Macartney, a memoir* (1900). It must be borne in mind that the author, who held for some years the same chair as Macartney, had felt dissatisfied with his own treatment by the Board. Parts of the book, therefore, are to be read rather as a manifesto than as a dispassionate biography.

118. Macartney had suggested that before the formal examination in Latin there should be a preliminary 'screening' examination in English. The Board asked the other Professors for their opinion, and Hill replied, 'Examinations in English as introductory to a learned Profession are so absolutely contrary to the conceptions which I entertain of a literary education, as to render it impossible that I would tolerate them in any case in which I possessed any influence ... How could I possibly be satisfied through such examination of the candidates being *doctrina idoneum*?' (Kirkpatrick, *History of the medical school*, 237.)

119. His uncle had been a Fellow, and his father a Fellow and Professor of Mathematics; his son was to succeed him as Regius Professor of Physic; his great-grandson became Professor of Pathology. Two of his grandchildren were scholars of distinction, though not connected with the College, and Sir George Gabriel Stokes, the physicist, was his cousin.

120. The *London Medical Gazette*, 1 (1828), 533, said of Crampton's lectures that 'his mode of delivery, which is generally cold and spiritless, is occasionally varied by being dry and sour'.

121. T.C.D. MSS P/1/1643,1648.

122. In 1828 111 students entered the medical school. Of these only eleven matriculated as full members of Trinity College, of whom six proceeded to their B.A. degree and three to the degree of M.B.

123. Complaints were made from Edinburgh that Trinity College had disingenuously styled this diploma a doctorate *of* medicine, and a full degree a doctorate *in* medicine. We can find no corroboration for this assertion, and such a deception would have run entirely contrary to University policy, which was to prevent medical men of insufficient general education from passing as graduates.

124. Of the 677 persons who graduated in medicine at Edinburgh in the six years ending in 1826, eighteen had received all and 150 had received part of their medical education in Dublin. (*Commission for visiting the universities of Scotland: Evidence, Vol. 1* (1837), Appendix, 150.)

125. *Ibid.*, 300.

126. It is only fair to record that his biographer (Kenney, *Memoir*, p. xxii) attributes the characteristic backward tilt of his head to frequent nose-bleeding in early youth.

127. Richard Graves, later Regius Professor, was the author of *An essay on the character of the Apostles and Evangelists, designed to prove that they were not Enthusiasts* (Dublin, 1798).

128. This spirit expressed itself most happily in hymnody. Apart from 'While shepherds watched their flocks' and 'Rock of ages', which belong to an earlier epoch, 'Abide with me', 'Praise, my soul, the King of Heaven', 'Fight the good fight', and 'Hark, ten thousand voices sounding' were all written by T.C.D. men.

6. REFORM UNDER BARTHOLOMEW LLOYD: 1831–1837

1. *Westminster Review*, 4 (1825), 152, 166. It could be fairly replied that Canning, who had been educated at Christ Church in an atmosphere of Catullus and curricles, though perhaps weak on cotton-spinning, did as much as anyone at this time to restrain the Holy Alliance.

2. Wall to Beresford, 3 May 1832. Beresford papers, 66.

3. By a curious irony the effect of the Reform Bill was to convert the representation of Dublin University from one doubtful seat to two safe Tory ones. In 1831, with the restricted franchise of Provost, Fellows and Scholars, Lefroy beat Crampton only by 44 votes to 36 (30 of Crampton's votes coming from the Scholars). In 1832, with two seats, and an electorate consisting mainly of Masters of Arts, the two Tories polled 2,594 votes; Crampton and his fellow Liberal only 813.

4. *Nation*, 27 April 1844.

5. W.B. Yeats, 'Seven Sages' in *The Winding Stair* (1933).

6. If Prior (Diary, 10 May 1833) is to be believed, the transaction was reminiscent of a cattle fair. Sadleir, who had left the room while the Board debated their terms, came in and asked for £1,400, then came down to £1,300 and later £1,200; he was with difficulty eventually persuaded to settle for £1,000.

7. *Dublin University Magazine*, 7 (1835), 347; 11 (1837), 140. Mulgrave to Morpeth, 27 April 1836 (Castle Howard MSS).

8. Prior's diary, 1 July 1835 and 13 April 1833.

9. *Ibid.*, 18 February 1832.

10. *Ibid.*, 4 and 5 July 1835.

11. Register, 23 December 1833.

12. See A.J. McConnell, 'The Dublin mathematical school in the first half of the nineteenth century', *Proceedings of the Royal Irish Academy*, 50A(1945), 75.

13. We have already (p. 528) referred to the excellence of his textbook.

14. The corresponding reform at Cambridge had been initiated by Woodhouse ten years earlier than in Dublin, but had been blocked for some time by opposition from Newtonian fundamentalists. For a few years around 1815, therefore, Dublin was ahead of Cambridge in practice, though not in aspirations. See Winstanley, *Early Victorian Cambridge*, 157–8.

15. *Système du monde* (Dublin, 1830); *Mécanique céleste* (Books I and II) (Dublin, 1822–7); *Traité de mécanique* (London, 1842). It has been claimed that Harte's are the first translations of Laplace into English. This is not quite true, as John Pond, the Astronomer Royal of England, published a translation of the *Système du monde* in 1809, and a translation by J. Toplis of one of the books of the *Mécanique céleste* appeared in Nottingham in 1814. Harte's editions were, however, of value

for their explanatory matter rather than as mere translations, and they were of great service, in England as well as in Ireland, in popularizing the new French methods among the general run of mathematicians.

16. It was alleged by Wall in a letter to the Vice-Chancellor (Beresford papers, 66) that Harte, who might also have been a strong candidate, was tricked into resigning his Fellowship for a living by assurances that he would still be eligible for the chair, but that the regulations were then changed, making the new Professor one of the examiners for Fellowship, a duty which could hardly be carried out by a non-Fellow. Harte, however, although he had accepted the living, was still a Fellow when the examination for the Professorship was held, and if he had been really anxious for the post he could have competed and, if successful, abandoned his claim to the living.

17. In 1833 he made the rather spectacular experimental verification of the phenomenon of conical refraction, which had been predicted on theoretical grounds by Rowan Hamilton.

18. This prohibition took the form of a proviso that the lecturer should *ipso facto* vacate his office on ceasing to be a Junior Fellow, which he would, of course, have to do if he accepted a living.

19. *Memoir*, by Samuel Butcher, prefixed to Thomas McNeece, *Sermons* (1863).

20. London, 1713.

21. Richard Mant, Bishop of Down, declared that 'an approval of the Irish National Education System is incompatible with our stipulated obedience to God in his Holy Church (cited by C.R. Elrington, *A few suggestions . . . upon . . . the question respecting National Education in Ireland* (Dublin, 1847)). On the other side Provost Sadleir refused to allow the Church Education Society to hold its annual meeting in Trinity College in 1840.

22. We have referred elsewhere (p. 104) to his eccentricities of manner.

23. Chichester (1839) and Wells (1840) were the earliest of these colleges which catered primarily for university graduates. There were already in existence three or four others which prepared for ordination men who had not been to a university; these included St Bees and St David's, Lampeter.

24. He was a bishop from 1805 until his death in 1862. Although twenty-six years senior to Whately on the Bench, he died only a year before him.

25. Of the twenty-five Fellows, Sadleir, Wray, Sandes, Hare and O'Brien alone failed to sign. Sadleir and Sandes were staunch Whigs, and Wray an intermittent one. O'Brien had perhaps some sympathy with the Archbishop's theological views. Hare was probably absent from College.

26. Our information about this episode is derived largely from the Wellesley papers (Brit. Lib. Add. MSS 37306–7), the Register for April and May 1834, and June 1839, and E. Jane Whately, *Life of Richard Whately* vol. 1 (1866), pp. 200–4, 215–8, 434–5. A good summary is given by E.J. Young, *Church of Ireland Gazette*, 14 August 1932.

27. R. Whately, *Report on the address on the conclusion of the first session of the Dublin Statistical Society* (Dublin, 1848). (Reprinted in the first volume of *Transactions Dublin Statistical Society*, 1849.)

28. For further information on Longfield see L.S. Moss, *Mountifort Longfield* (1976).

29. R.D.C. Black, *Hermathena*, 70 (1947), 69–73.

30. This regulation was relaxed two years later, students who had won an honor at any term examination being allowed to present themselves for Moderatorship without taking the pass degree examination first.

31. *Dublin University Commission: Suggestions* (1853), 290.
32. It was only at the beginning and end of a Fellow's career as tutor that the size of his chamber had some effect on his income.
33. E. McParland, *The Buildings of Trinity College, Dublin* (1977); reprinted from *Country Life*, nos. 4114–16 and 4137–8 (1976). This handsomely illustrated booklet gives a critical and scholarly account of all the College buildings up to 1855.

7. DEVELOPMENT IN EARLY VICTORIAN TIMES: 1837–1851

1. Even with the statute in force there were in 1815–16 two successive years without an election, and this was repeated in 1826–7.
2. *Dublin University Commission: Report* (1853), 22 and 25. Clogherny was a singularly unsuccessful investment. The incumbent at the time of purchase lived on for a further twenty-five years so that the College had only one chance to present to the living before its rights were abolished at Disestablishment.
3. This Act, which united some bishoprics and regularized the more anomalous ecclesiastical incomes (using the money thereby liberated to build new churches), was the rather improbable starting-point of the Oxford Movement, as it was denounced by Keble in his assize sermon under the title of National Apostasy.
4. Of the nineteen Fellows elected during the period 1812–30 no fewer than thirteen resigned as Junior Fellows after an average tenure of eleven years; four died young; and only two (Humphrey Lloyd and J.L. Moore) had the patience to restrain their matrimonial impulses until after 1840, and ended up as married Senior Fellows. For Fellows elected after 1830 the chances of their release from compulsory celibacy had become fairly bright by the time they were old enough to chafe against it.
5. Beresford maintained that the Chancellor (the King of Hanover) was against the repeal, and that it was contrary to the statutes to take a step of such importance against the wishes of the Chancellor. But the concept of celibacy entertained by one of Queen Victoria's uncles was probably different from that which the Primate was trying to maintain.
6. Excluding two exceptional cases: the most junior, who had only recently become a tutor, and the Junior Proctor, who received in the single year in which he held the office an additional £900 or so from fees.
7. *Dublin University Commission: Suggestions* (1853), 290.
8. *Dublin University Commission: Report* (1853), 25.
9. *Personal recollections of English engineers, by a Civil Engineer* (London, 1868), 46.
10. After a long period of disuse this building, which, in the form of a small Greek temple, was one of Frederick Darley's happier efforts, served for some years as a manuscript room for the Library, but in 1971 had to be taken down to make room for the new Arts Building. It was given to University College, and re-erected in their grounds at Belfield.
11. This is the title in the original Board minute, and the one used today. In the early years of the School the Professor was often called the Professor of Practical Engineering, and some issues of the College Calendar used the two titles on different pages, and at times even a third (Professor of the Practice of Engineering). It seems probable that the Board preferred the first title, the Professor the second.
12. All·salaries in the field of the natural sciences were at this time held down by the

fact that Whitley Stokes was still receiving £800 a year as lecturer in Natural History, although he was by now virtually retired. Many of the appointments include a clause promising an increase in salary on Stokes's death.

13. As Professor of Geology alone. Mineralogy was handed back to Apjohn, who thus enjoyed from 1845 to 1875 the rare distinction of holding three Professorships at once.

14. There had been various efforts before this to organize a Common Room for the Fellows and other senior members of the College, but its existence seems to have been very spasmodic, and there are no records of its location. Two documents (T.C.D. MSS Mun P/1/148, 170) suggest that a coffee-room with newspapers existed in Provost Andrews's day, for the use of Fellows, Masters of Arts and Fellow-Commoners. Thackeray, in his *Irish Sketch-book* (chapter 32) gives a somewhat fanciful account of his entertainment in the College in October 1842, which implies the existence of some sort of Common Room. After assuring his readers that he really did dine on commons (for it was less than ten years since guests had been admitted for the first time) he continues: 'If the fellows of Colleges in Oxford or Cambridge were told that the fellows of Trinity College, Dublin only drink beer at dinner they would not believe *that*. Such, however, was the fact; or maybe it was a dream, which was followed by another dream of about four-and-twenty gentlemen seated round a common-room table after dinner, and by a subsequent vision of oysters in the apartments of a tutor.'

15. He failed to see how quickly trade unions would tread on the heels of applied science.

16. Leaving aside degrees in Surgery, which were made almost obligatory by the legislation of 1858, these degrees of B.A.I and M.A.I. seem to have been the first given by any university in the British Isles outside the traditional faculties of arts, divinity, law, medicine and music.

17. Rowan Hamilton offered himself as a candidate for this post, in exchange for that of Astronomer Royal. But the Professor of Mathematics had to be a Fellow, and no way could be found to elect Hamilton to a Fellowship except by allowing him to compete at the examination in the ordinary way against men twelve years his junior. Not unnaturally he refused this condition.

18. So styled in the Register for 1847 (and also in the Act of 1723 by which it was established). In the intervening period, and after 1847, it was usually, though not invariably, called a Professorship. The fact is that before about 1850 few people drew a clear distinction between the two words.

19. It was given the title of Regius Professor by Letters Patent in 1868. It may be noted here that although six Professorships in Dublin have been given the title of Regius by Letters Patent, in no case has the Crown claimed a right in the appointment, as is the normal practice in England and Scotland.

20. Martin Tuomy, who held the King's Professorship of the Practice of Medicine from 1812 to 1828, was a Catholic, although in his student days he had been prepared to conform sufficiently to be elected a Foundation Scholar.

21. The principal documents relating to this controversy are printed in *Dublin University Commission: Evidence* (1853), 238—52.

22. *Diseases of the lungs and windpipe* (Dublin, 1837); *Diseases of the heart and aorta* (Dublin, 1854).

23. E. Hayes, *Report of cases argued and determined in the Court of Exchequer* (1837), 611—41. See also T.C.D. MSS Mun P/1/1383. W.B.S. Taylor, *History of the University of Dublin*, 191—2, states that a Professor of Irish was appointed, and continued

despite the adverse legal decision, but that his successor was dismissed in 1814 for 'having expressed himself too freely at a public meeting, on a political question'. We can find in the College records no confirmation for these statements.

24. Beresford gave a further £1,000 towards the endowment in 1861.

25. Some passages translated by him appeared in *Blackwood's Magazine* in 1820, and appear to be the first published translations into English of any part of the work. Anster's complete translations of parts 1 and 2 appeared in 1835 and 1864 respectively.

26. H.B. Leech, a later Regius Professor of Laws, writing in some irritation because Longfield had not supported his scheme for registration of land titles, said of him that he 'had succeeded in impressing his contemporaries with the idea that, as regards questions concerning land, he made as near an approach to infallibility as is permitted to a finite intelligence'. (*Registration of title v. registration of assurances* (London and Dublin, 1891), 58.)

27. *A treatise on the theory and practice of music* (Dublin, 1853).

28. This change of function only twenty years after the room had been built and named suggests that it was during the latter half of Andrews's provostship that the disputations finally became reduced to unimportant formalities.

29. Among other species named after him are the big-cone pine (*Pinus coulteri*) and the large, white Californian poppy (*Romneya coulteri*). The generic name of the latter is based on that of Thomas Romney Robinson, former Fellow of the College and a friend of Coulter's, whose obituary notice, in *Proceedings of the Royal Irish Academy*, 2 (1844), 553–7, provides the main source of our knowledge of his life.

30. These include the oldest dated specimen in the herbarium, a plant of *Thesium divaricatum*, collected in 1753. It is still in good condition.

31. His work on the Bryozoa has only recently been superseded, and his monograph on hydroids can still be consulted with profit.

32. For a fuller assessment of Harvey see D.A. Webb, *Hermathena*, 103 (1966), 32–45.

33. The Museum attracted more than 14,000 visitors in 1852. There was at that time no counter-attraction, as the National Museum had not yet been founded.

34. *Evidence*, 153–69.

8. THE ROYAL COMMISSION AND ITS AFTERMATH: 1851–1860

1. The Scottish universities had been the subject of a Royal Commission in 1837.

2. Register for October 1850, and April 1851.

3. Brady was out of office for a year during the sittings of the Commission, for the period of Lord Derby's short-lived administration of 1852.

4. E.J. Young, *Church of Ireland Gazette*, 14 August 1931.

5. Curiously enough the Cambridge Commissioners also included two astronomers.

6. T.C.D. MSS 387, no. 73.

7. Clarendon papers, Box 10.

8. The Provost and Senior Fellows were fortunate in that one point on which they had been open to serious criticism had been resolved only two years previously. The renewal fines on estates, which had formerly been paid to them personally (p. 101), were in future to be paid direct to the Cista Communis. The compensation which they received for this change (£800 a year each) was generous, but it did not provide such an easy target for criticism as the previous arrangement.

9. *Dublin University Commission: Suggestions* (1853), 332.

10. *Ibid.*, 333–42.

11. *Ibid.*, 333–4, 343, 346, 332.

12. Omitting Hare, who was at this time a more or less permanent invalid, with a dispensation which allowed him to be absent from College. He was, in fact retired in all but name, and Hart, the most senior of the Junior Fellows, who sat regularly on the Board in his place, has here been reckoned a member of the *de facto* Board.

13. Williamson had his revenge on the succeeding generation, for after attaining to a Senior Fellowship in 1897 he held it for eighteen years before retiring. More pathetic are cases such as that of Townsend (Fellow, 1845–84), who, after serving in bondage for thirty-eight years, survived for only nine months in the promised land.

14. *Dublin University Commission: Suggestions* (1853), 290.

15. *Ibid.*, 314. The evidence given by Graves strikes the reader of today as more modern in its tone and presuppositions than that of any other member of the College. He combined foresight with common sense, and although not an active campaigner for reform, he was remarkably untrammelled by the prejudices of his age. His removal to a bishopric in 1866 represented a serious loss to the College.

16. E.g. Martin Tuomy (Scholar, 1788).

17. A petition was presented to the House of Commons on 25 June 1832, by the National Political Union, who asked that 'the sacramental test so unjustly enforced by the Board of Trinity College without the authority of any statute as a qualification for scholarship' should be abolished by Act of Parliament.

18. *Dublin University Commission: Report* (1853), 93.

19. Non-foundation Scholarships were reinstituted in 1906 to meet the demands of a new class of 'unenfranchised helots' in the form of the women students.

20. The difficulties of interpretation were further increased by the fact that as the original statutes were in Latin specific amendments to them by Letters Patent had to be in the same language. Entirely new provisions with statutory force were, however, enacted in English.

21. Apart from the Register, our information about the negotiations which followed on the Commission's report is derived mainly from the Beresford papers, 564–737.

22. The issue of such dispensations and the election to the lay places are sometimes, but not always, recorded in the Register, so that the succession of those occupying the Jurists' places cannot be drawn up with certainty. But from 1720 onwards the number of lay Fellows (excluding those recently elected, who would probably take orders later) always exceeded by one, and sometimes by two or three, the number permitted by the statutes.

23. In the twenty years from 1839 to 1858 there had been an average of just over one double Moderatorship a year. In the next twenty years, from 1859 to 1878, the average was about three, and in 1879–98 exactly four.

24. *Dublin University Commission: Report* (1853), 88.

25. Beresford papers, 550.

26. Beresford papers, 678, 683.

27. W.R. Furlong, *Report of the case of Angeli v. Galbraith* (1857).

28. In February, on the occasion of the state entry into Dublin of the new Lord-Lieutenant, the crowd in College Green, which included many students, bored with waiting, began to tease and taunt the police, who reacted with unnecessary violence and injured several innocent spectators, including some students, in a baton-charge. The riot had no political significance, and has been somewhat over-emphasized by College historians, chiefly because it is the subject of a well-known print.

29. On at least four occasions in the late fifties and early sixties the customary

Commencements dinner was cancelled in the interests of economy. In 1855 the Board had appointed a committee to consider means of retrenchment, and in 1856 there were several sales of stock, and finally a request to the Government for a loan of £20,000.

30. *Dublin Evening Mail*, 9 July 1874.

31. The incident is described by Todd in a letter to the Chancellor (Beresford papers, 697).

32. J.F. Waller, *Report of a visitation holden in Trinity College Dublin, May 24 and 25, and June 1 and 3, 1858* (1858).

33. The Board had second thoughts, and a few weeks later proposed that one of the new offices should be a chair of Latin, with a salary of £700 a year, and the other a Senior Tutorship with £900. But the Junior Fellows with selfish and pedantic obstinacy held the Board to its earlier promise of two posts at £800 (Salmon, to his credit, dissenting). The Professor of Latin could not be paid more than £700 without raising jealousy among other comparable Professors, and the establishment of the chair was thus set back for twelve years.

34. In a letter to Lord Naas, dated 4 June 1858, printed and inserted in the Register. It is not clear from the context what is meant by 'the tribunal'.

35. Under the Caroline statutes an auditor was to be appointed only if the Provost and Senior Fellows thought it desirable. The Queen's Letter of 1855 made it mandatory, and the auditor's report had to be forwarded to the Visitors. This 'internal' auditor was always, up to the abolition of the office in 1957, a Senior Fellow.

36. One exception must be noted: James McIvor performed the remarkable feat of graduating with a double Moderatorship in Classics and Philosophy in 1841 and winning a Fellowship in 1844. He must have taught himself mathematics to a high standard in the intervening period.

37. Professors of this type were paid only a very small salary, and had to supplement it by taking in private pupils, as well as by the fees they received from students.

38. From 1855 to 1871 an average of seven were chosen each year. After 1871 a change in the age-limit led to a falling off, but the figures picked up again after 1900, and by 1912 a total of 180 had passed into the service.

39. Cited by J.M. Compton, *English Historical Review*, 83 (1968), 271.

40. This has usually been its official title; popularly it has usually been called the Engineering School. Only the geological and mineralogical parts of the Museum were housed in it. Today it is occupied mainly by the departments of geology and geography.

41. The same team was employed, far less successfully, on the New Museums at Oxford; an entertaining account of their difficulties is given in Kenneth Clark, *The Gothic revival* (2nd edn, London, 1950), 282–6. Unfortunately the author twice confuses the Museum Building of Trinity College with its Library.

42. For these buildings see also McParland, *Buildings of Trinity College*, and R.B. McDowell, *Trinity*, 4 (1952), 21–3.

9. SHIFTING LANDMARKS: 1861 – 1880

1. Published as *The Inspiration of Holy Scripture* (London and Dublin, 1854).

2. He had also quarrelled with the Provost as the result of a rebuke administered to him for an unsuitable (though quite orthodox) sermon delivered at an ordination service. See N.J.D. White, *Some recollections of Trinity College, Dublin* (1935), 30.

3. In a review of Darwin's *Descent of Man*, in *Dublin Quarterly Journal of Medical Science*, August 1871.

4. *Manual of geology* (Dublin, 1865), chapter 4.
5. *Annual address delivered to the Geological Society of Dublin, February 8, 1859* (Dublin, 1859), 16–18.
6. In 1873, however, the Protestant Defence Association wrote to the Board protesting that such a man, who had referred to the acts of the General Synod as 'schismatical', was unfit to teach Divinity students. Gibbings, the Professor of Ecclesiastical History, also came under their ban for referring to the majority of synodsmen as 'misinformed enthusiasts and sectaries' (T.C.D. MSS Mun P/1/2180). One guesses that Salmon may have asked them to moderate their language, but otherwise no action was taken.
7. The College Calendar for 1871 gives lists of all incumbents of the various College livings, and concludes with the remark: 'All these rights of patronage were summarily swept away by the Irish Church Act'.
8. There were some dissentients. Provost Lloyd in the early stages of the controversy, and Haughton throughout its course, preferred to leave Trinity unchanged but were willing to see a parallel college for Catholics set up and endowed. Lloyd would have joined this with Trinity in a single university; Haughton would not.
9. Critics were quick to point out that by the same criterion (number of students in relation to annual budget) there was an even stronger case for extinguishing Magdalen College, Oxford.
10. This choice of 'sensitive' subjects shows that Gladstone's intellectual interests, though much wider than those of most politicians, were limited. The bishops declared that geology, biology and English literature were equally sensitive and must remain under their control, while Fawcett ridiculed the idea of trying to discuss the economics of the Poor Law without referring to the dissolution of the monasteries.
11. This refers to the college in St Stephen's Green, which concerned itself with arts and theology. The medical school in Cecilia Street showed much more vitality and more hope for the future.
12. Gladstone's arithmetic, by which he demonstrated that the College would not really be worse off at the end of the day, was more ingenious than convincing.
13. Thirty-five Irish Liberals, of whom nine were Protestant, and eight English Liberals, including Fawcett, voted against the Government. For information on Fawcett's campaign, Gladstone's bill and the reaction of the College see Humphrey Lloyd's letter-book (T.C.D. MSS 3487); Gladstone papers (Brit. Lib. Add. MSS 4437–8); *The Times*, 7 and 30 April 1870, and January to March 1873; *Trinity College (Dublin) . . . copy of the memorial*, etc., H.C. 1870 (110), LIV.
14. Russell, Mooney, Kennedy, Goligher, Henry and Johnston.
15. Frederick Purser. His election in 1872 was the subject of an appeal to the Visitors, which became something of a *cause célèbre*. The Board elected him, knowing that he was a Moravian, but hoping that the differences between this church and the Church of Ireland were not enough to prevent him from making the Fellow's declaration. On the following day, however, he declined to make the declaration required by the statutes, asking (in the belief that Fawcett's bill would shortly become law) that this formality be deferred. G.A. Minchin, the *proxime accessit* in the examination, asked that Purser's election be declared invalid. The Visitors found that the election was valid, but that Purser had vacated his Fellowship by declining to make the declaration; the Fellowship was therefore vacant, but could not be filled until the following year. By 1873 Fawcett's Act was passed; Purser competed again, but was unsuccessful (as also was Minchin), but was finally elected in 1878.

16. Maguire and W.B. Kelleher died nine and thirteen years respectively after election; W.J.M. Starkie resigned after eight years.
17. R.A.Q. O'Meara had, however, been elected to the Board in 1945 as a representative of the Junior Fellows.
18. *University Education in Ireland* (1868), 7.
19. Well exhibited in W.M. Dixon's *Trinity College, Dublin* (1902), a scholarly and well-written book, but strongly influenced by Mahaffy, who believed, broadly speaking, that if a student led a respectable life and learnt some classics and enough social graces to mix with the gentry, his religious affiliation was not of great importance.
20. The atmosphere was not improved by pinpricks such as that given by the Vicar-General of the diocese of Dublin in 1873, who, in support of a request from a Catholic Scholar to be excused from the duty of reciting the statutory graces before and after Commons, declared that 'no Catholic could with safe conscience take any part active or passive in such a prayer' (T.C.D. MSS Mun P/1/2159). The only conceivable objection to the grace from a Catholic standpoint is that in it the College gives thanks to God for its foundress, who was, of course, the Heretic Usurper deposed by the bull *Regnans in Excelsis*. It was only when the Church was riding high on the ultramontane tide that such a judgment could be given, and during the present century dozens of Catholic Scholars have said grace without the propriety of their action ever being questioned.
21. From the death of Todd in 1869 to the co-option of Haughton nearly twelve years later no member of the Board was familiar with any branch of scholarship other than mathematics, physics, philosophy, theology, and to some small extent classics. By 1895, with Haughton, Ingram, Shaw and Barlow on the Board, the spread of interests was far wider. But the youngest of this quartet was by then sixty-nine years old.
22. The Council did not nominate to Professorships in the Divinity School, nor to those for which the mode of election was specified by Act of Parliament or deed of trust.
23. A refusal on these grounds was made in 1877. It turned on a procedural question, whether it was the members of Council, who nominated, but with a virtually mandatory nomination, or the members of the Board, who actually elected, who should take the statutory declaration to elect the most suitable candidate without fear or favour. The majority of the Council declined to take the declaration, and the Board refused to elect. The Visitors, on appeal, upheld the Board's point of view, so the members of Council had to swallow their pride and take the declaration before re-nominating. It was a silly dispute; no great harm would have been done if both Board and Council had regarded themselves bound by the statute until the matter was clarified.
24. A clause in the original constitution of the Council made its members ineligible for Professorships.
25. T.C.D. MSS Mun P/1/2261. In the same document (a printed flysheet for circulation among his colleagues) he declares that 'having burnt the whole of my candle in T.C.D it is now in my interest to burn the remaining inch there. The expiring wick may, of course, for a long time continue giving but a murky light, and signalizing its existence chiefly by sputter and odour of tallow; but for this eventuality I am not responsible.' He continued to 'sputter' for a further twenty-three years (for he was only in his middle fifties when this affecting passage was written), and for nine of them he enjoyed the emoluments of a Senior Fellow.
26. For further information on this quarrel see Stanford and McDowell, *Mahaffy* (1971), 174—5.

27. *Brief suggestions in reference to the undergraduate curriculum in Trinity College, Dublin* (1869).
28. This was rather an exaggeration.
29. Of the ten men who won top place in classical Moderatorship from 1851 to 1860, four were called to the Bar and two entered the Indian Civil Service.
30. At the same time an attempt was made to find a place in the mathematical school for John Casey, another Catholic graduate who had won a considerable reputation for himself as a mathematician, and was at that time a schoolmaster in Kingstown. Unfortunately the offer from the College came too late, for Casey had accepted nomination to a Professorship in the Catholic University, and had to decline with regret (T.C.D MSS Mun P/1/2202–4).

    Casey behaved as an honourable man in not throwing over for a better-paid offer a post which he had accepted. It is stated, however, in *A page of Irish history* (*Compiled by fathers of the Society of Jesus*, Dublin, 1930), 88, that he was persuaded by Cardinal Cullen *after* he had been offered a post in Trinity College to reject it in favour of a lower-paid chair at the struggling Catholic University. The letters cited above make it quite clear that Casey had accepted the latter post and agreed on its terms before any offer came from Trinity.
31. Doubtless some others answered in philosophy at the Fellowship examination, but only, one must suppose, as the result of cramming, and with little real love for the subject.
32. He had competed in 1860 and won the Madden prize, being defeated only by Ferrar. Two Fellowships had become vacant in the previous year, but in January 1859, the Board and Visitors issued a decree suppressing one of the non-tutor Fellowships. Webb disputed the validity of this decree and appealed to the Visitors. He presented a very plausible case, but as the Visitors could not find in his favour without admitting the invalidity of the decree which they had signed, they surprised nobody by dismissing Webb's appeal without giving their reasons.
33. To the modern reader Anster's version is preferable, partly, perhaps, because Anster was himself a minor poet. Webb's may here and there be closer to the original, but his attempt to follow its sound and rhythm by the free use of feminine rhymes (which come naturally in German, but awkwardly in English) give to many of his pages a stilted tone which proclaims them obviously a translation.
34. The appointment was for five years, with the possibility of renewal for subsequent terms, but at each vacancy the post was advertised, and sometimes as many as thirteen applications were received. Butler, Webb, Maguire and Beare were nominated to second terms without serious opposition, but in 1852 Moeran, and in 1872 McIvor were quite rightly displaced by better qualified candidates.
35. 'My plan ... has been to act independently of the College terms ... the time of students is so occupied during term-time with many branches of learning which our authorities render *necessary* that frequently little is left for those which, like modern languages, are *voluntary* so far as the College is concerned.' I.G. Abeltshauser, *The study of modern languages: an introductory lecture* (1857), 5.
36. From 1873 to 1876 Italian and Spanish were also available as options for the second language, but as nobody chose them they were dropped.
37. For a sympathetic sketch of Abeltshauser see M.M. Raraty, *Hermathena*, 102 (1966), 53–72.
38. The Board sought advice from Lord Rosse, tentatively suggesting one of the Fellows (Galbraith). But Rosse firmly recommended Brünnow, and his advice was taken.

39. We should, perhaps, point out that trouble of this kind is not an invariable concomitant of the name.

40. J.H. Todd to the Bishop of Cork (Kyle), 1 March and 8 June 1838 (T.C.D. MSS 2214).

41. The Library contained 88,000 printed books in 1840. By 1846 it had reached the 100,000 mark.

42. In 1856 Sophister students were granted reader's tickets. Only fourteen years earlier a request from the Scholars for the same privilege had been refused with some asperity. The Board disapproved the encouragement of 'those desultory habits which admission to so extensive a library at an early period of their studies would tend to produce. There is a lending library from which the undergraduate is permitted to take to his own apartments any books which it would be in the least degree useful for him to study . . . The junior Scholars are not the best judges of their real interests, as there are few young men who would not wish to have access to more extensive collections of books than it would be expedient to place within their reach' (Register, 17 December 1842). The uncompromising tone of the reply may in part, perhaps, be attributed to the fact that the Scholars had been unwise enough to couple with their request another which asked for an increase in their salary. But Carson was of the same opinion even in 1852; in his evidence given to the Royal Commission he regretted the time which he had spent 'reading the magazines' when he obtained access to the shelves on election to Fellowship.

43. For an appreciation of Todd, see G.O. Simms, *Hermathena*, 109 (1969), 5–23.

10. THE END OF THE VICTORIAN AGE: 1881–1900

1. Address of welcome from the Senate to Lord Londonderry on his arrival as Lord-Lieutenant, October 1886 (printed and inserted in the Register).

2. Cf. Yeats's epigram in *Last poems and plays* (London, 1940), 35:

> Parnell came down the road, he said to a cheering man:
> 'Ireland shall get her freedom, and you still break stone.'

3. T.H. Huxley, a man of generally radical cast of mind, was a strong Unionist and Imperialist, and in his letters there are many contemptuous references to Gladstone and the Home Rule movement.

4. *Fragments from old letters, E.D. to E.D.W., 1859–82*, ed. E.D. Dowden, second series (1914), 170 and 181.

5. The only disputes were about different shades of Unionism. In 1892, when Edward Carson was nominated for the University seat in Parliament, there were growls from some Conservatives, including his namesake, Joseph Carson, and T.T. Gray. The University had always been represented by a Conservative; why should a Liberal Unionist, who had seen the light only six years ago and jumped on the Conservative band-wagon, be foisted on us now?

6. This claim is made for Salmon, Haughton, Ingram, John Gwynn, Mahaffy, Palmer, Tyrrell, Fitzgerald, L.C. Purser, Bernard, Bury, Sir Robert Ball, Sollas, Atkinson, Dowden, Cunningham and Bastable. To adopt crude but objective criteria of a more than local reputation, all but one are noticed in the *D.N.B.*; all but four received honorary degrees from universities outside Ireland; six were Fellows of the Royal Society and five of the British Academy; two were knighted. All except Sollas and Cunningham were originally Dublin graduates.

7. Traill to Chaine, 8 April 1880; Traill to Gibson, 9, 14, and 18 April 1880 (Ashbourne papers, House of Lords Record Office).
8. Cowper to Gladstone, 29 January and 6 February 1881 (Brit. Lib. Add. MSS 44468).
9. R. Ffolliott, *The Pooles of Mayfield* (Dublin, 1958), 113.
10. Stanford and McDowell, *Mahaffy*, 199.
11. N.J.D. White, *Some recollections*, 29.
12. *Ibid.*, 16–17.
13. Conner, Abbott, Gray and Macran. The first three were all conservative, and in any case they rightly guessed that they would be co-opted to the Board within the next three years. Macran's abstention probably indicated merely his lack of interest in College politics.
14. Had this proposal been adopted the existing Senior Fellows would all have been removed by 1897, and the average length of tenure of Junior Fellowship before co-option reduced by over ten years. But it would have advanced the advent of a reliably liberal Board by only three years at most.
15. Barlow was, in fact, only sixty-eight.
16. Barlow also proposed a characteristically ingenious and perverse scheme for increasing the income of the Junior Fellows in a year in which no place on the Board fell vacant, thus 'no doubt greatly damping the zeal of the Junior Fellows for our removal'.
17. The history of this controversy can be traced in a series of documents (many of them printed) in T.C.D. MSS Mun P/1/2490–2506.
18. Mahaffy and E.P. Wright had protested against the decision to hand over on long loan to the National Museum some Polynesian weapons, hitherto in the College Museum. The Registrar replied that 'it would be impossible for the Board to get through their business if, after they had come to a decision with due deliberation, it was necessary for them to spend further time in discussing with irresponsible persons whether or not their decision had been the best and wisest'. Cited by K.C. Bailey, *A History of Trinity College, Dublin, 1892–1945* (1947), 75.
19. Erasmus Smith's Professorship of Mathematics fell vacant in 1862. Salmon, for reasons which we have been unable to discover, did not offer himself as a candidate, although he was senior to the two Fellows who did compete (Michael Roberts and Townsend) and better qualified than either. He can scarcely have been reserving himself for the Regius Professorship of Divinity, as the occupant (Butcher) was only eight years older than Salmon, and his resignation at the age of fifty-seven to become Bishop of Meath could not have been predicted.
20. Compare his reply to a Catholic who asked him, 'After all, Dr Salmon, where was your Church before the Reformation?' 'Where was your face before you washed it?' Very neat, but not exactly what we would say today.
21. His gifts to the College which are set out in official records amount to more than £6,000, and there must have been many others which remain unchronicled. His largest gift was to endow a fund for giving financial help to needy students.
22. One example may be cited. In a discussion on corporal punishment Mahaffy declared rather ponderously, 'I was only once caned, and that was for telling the truth,' but before he could launch into his reminiscence Salmon cut in with, 'Well, it certainly cured you, Mahaffy.' (Stanford and McDowell, *Mahaffy*, 85.)
23. The other was a sermon consisting of a detailed anatomical and physiological analysis of the causes and nature of death by crucifixion.
24. See also W.J.M. Jessop, *Hermathena*, 116 (1973), 5–26.
25. Mahaffy, *Epoch*, xii–xiii, published six years after Stubbs's death, excuses the

defects of *The book of Trinity College*, a large, elaborate and on the whole very satisfactory souvenir volume presented to guests at the Tercentenary, by 'the jealousies and oppositions then brought to bear upon it. It therefore does not represent a tithe of what could have been done with a little more generosity and sympathy on the part of the Bursar.'

26. He was, rightly or wrongly, attacked in an anonymous lampoon of 1869 for his unfairness as an examiner in Scholarship, and in the same year the tutors complained that he was neglecting his duties as Junior Bursar by insufficient attendance at his office.

27. T.C.D. MSS 2386.

28. His methods of securing pupils were at times unusual. R.M. Gwynn in *Of one company*, ed. D.A. Webb (1951), 83, relates how on entrance as a freshman he had been assigned to Beare as a tutor, but how Traill, recognizing him when the youths were lined up behind their tutors for the Entrance Breakfast, said that no cousin of his should go to another tutor, and carried him off *vi et armis* to join his own band. Gwynn was Traill's second cousin once removed.

29. Mahaffy is said to have asked a dull student in a classical *viva voce* examination, after he had missed two questions, 'Why was Dr Barlow made a Fellow?' Again the student did not know. 'Quite right. You get a mark for that. Nobody does' (Stanford and McDowell, *Mahaffy*, 72). On the Council there was hardly a year in which Traill did not either oppose Barlow's re-election as secretary, or move that he should be given extra duties or that his salary should be decreased.

30. *The immortals' great quest* (London, 1909).

31. Volumes 3–7 were produced under the joint names of Tyrrell and Purser, but in the preface to Volume 2 Tyrrell acknowledges the 'invaluable assistance' he has received from Purser, and it is generally agreed that most of the work for the later volumes was done by Purser.

32. R.M. Gwynn, *Some tributes to the departed* (1932), 6.

33. *Royal Irish Academy, Abstract of minutes*, session 1921–2, 6.

34. He is best remembered as the author, with A.W. Panton, of *The theory of equations* (Dublin, 1881; 7th edn, 1928).

35. *Nature*, 25 February 1892.

36. From a letter to his uncle, Dr Johnstone Stoney, cited in the preface to his *Collected works* (1902), p. xxxvii.

37. He resigned on Raymochy, one of the poorer livings, but with the option of transferring to a better one at the next vacancy, and a few months later he succeeded to Cappagh. Later on he held the sinecure office of Dean of Clonfert.

38. *Classical Review*, 2 (1888), 220–1.

39. The modern reader may need some reminders of the value of money in 1892. Within the social world to which most of the Fellows belonged, a young bachelor could live easily enough for a few years on £200 a year. Perhaps on £350, and certainly on £400, he would be prepared to marry. By early middle age he might be making about £750, and he would be satisfied if he reached £1,000 some years later. With anything over £1,000 a year he was 'comfortable'; with over £1,500 'well-off'. A Georgian house of five storeys might cost him between £2,000 and £2,500; a satisfying meal for two in a comfortable restaurant with a bottle of sound wine would cost about seven and sixpence. A trip to London with his wife, with a theatre and two nights in a hotel, would probably leave some change out of £20.

40. He read divinity as a student, intending to proceed to orders, and changed his mind only at the last moment.

41. *New studies in literature* (London, 1895), 19.

42. This was not, however, the only or even the dominant note in Irish Unionism; it was largely confined to urban intellectuals. The landed gentry tended to look down on the English almost as much as on the mere Irish; they were intensely loyal to the Queen and the flag, but they did not whole-heartedly concede to England the place of 'predominant partner' in the Union, and they believed, not entirely without justification, that the efficient maintenance and defence of the Empire depended to a large extent on the Anglo-Irish. Mahaffy was forever trumpeting the superiority of the Anglo-Irish over both of their parent stocks, and T.T. Gray, who came of a family of midland landowners, let out a characteristic growl when he told the Royal Commission of 1906 that 'a great many people have begun to think that everything in England is much superior to everything in Ireland'.
43. H.O. White, *Edward Dowden, 1843–1913* (1943), 19.
44. Distinguished for his work on Indian law, as well as on Celtic philology. He was the son of William Stokes, Regius Professor of Physic.
45. Bachelors or Doctors of Music *nondum graduati in Artibus* were, however, ranked in the official order of precedence below the humblest B.A.
46. N.J.D. White, *Some recollections*, 43.
47. The title dates only from 1922, when the College, in order to free itself from the obsolete provisions of the School of Physic Acts, set up four new chairs (Physiology; Plant Biology; General Chemistry; Human Anatomy and Embryology) parallel to the old-established King's Professorship of the Institutes of Medicine and the University Professorships of Botany, Chemistry and Anatomy. The salaries were attached to the new chairs, which were under the control of the Board and Council of Trinity College; the College of Physicians was then, after a shorter or longer interval, invited to elect these Professors to the historic chairs for the sake of continuity. Legislation in 1961, which abolished many of the provisions of the School of Physic Acts, allowed Trinity College to abolish these 'parallel' chairs, since the historic chairs were now completely under its control.
48. For an interesting discussion of this question in relation to fluctuations in numbers at Oxford, see *The university in society*, ed. L. Stone, vol. 1 (1975), pp. 3–110, and especially pp. 5–6.
49. It may be noted, however, that in the late seventeenth and early eighteenth centuries several families in West Wales sent their sons to Dublin rather than to Oxford, because the journey was not only cheaper, but also safer.
50. The fees at this time amounted to about £85 for a four-year arts course (they were more for professional students). £80 was regarded as a minimum annual allowance, £120–£150 as a generous one, *Dublin University Commission: Evidence* (1906), 173–4.
51. T.C.D. MSS Mun P/1/2591.
52. *Nature*, 1 December 1892.
53. It was possible up to 1918 to keep all terms as of right by examination only; after this it was possible only after permission had been granted by the Lecture Committee or the Senior Lecturer. The practice died out gradually and inconspicuously during the thirties and forties.
54. Except at the very end. An aspiring moderator was not compelled to sit the ordinary degree examination.
55. The engineering students of this period constituted a remarkably homogeneous group. Out of the forty-three who graduated between 1891 and 1895 only one was a Catholic and only three were born outside Ireland. All but six were the sons of gentry, army officers or professional men.

56. A magazine written by and for undergraduates and young graduates. It started publication in 1895 and flourished until about 1960, when it began to suffer from the competition of other and more militant periodicals. It eventually petered out in 1976.

57. In 1892 these comprised only rackets and lawn tennis. Hurling, which had enjoyed a brief period of popularity, had died out, and had not yet been replaced by hockey; golf was played only by a few; association football was temporarily in eclipse; and squash had not yet been invented. For further details of sports clubs see Bailey, *History*, chapter 7.

58. *Daily Express*, 21 June 1892.

59. Except to Barlow, the most senior of the Junior Fellows, who boycotted the proceedings in protest against his exclusion from office and power, despite forty-two years' service as a Fellow. This did not, however, prevent him from making a vigorous defence to the Royal Commission of 1906 of the same system of elderly oligarchy against which he had protested, but of which he was by that time enjoying the fruits.

60. The final cost of the celebrations was just over £4,000.

61. The celebration in 1764 of the bicentenary of Shakespeare's birth seems to stand alone in earlier centuries.

62. This date was chosen apparently because it was in 1594 that the first students were admitted, but in any case the College was still suffering too severely in 1692 from the scars of the Jacobite occupation to stage any kind of celebration. The year 1894 was for this reason suggested for the Tercentenary celebrations, but was overruled in favour of 1892.

63. *The book of Trinity College*, 82–3.

64. The degrees of Litt.D. and Sc.D. had been instituted in 1891, though there was substantial opposition in the Senate from those who considered such new-fangled millinery unnecessary. At the Tercentenary Commencements the honorary degrees comprised five Doctorates of Laws, six of Medicine, twenty-four of Science, thirty-three of Literature and one of Music, as well as two degrees of Master of Engineering.

65. The proceedings are fully described in *Records of the Tercentenary festival of Dublin University* (1894), which is known to have been edited by Arthur Palmer, though his name does not appear on the title-page. There are also in the College Library two volumes of press-cuttings and other souvenirs.

66. *Irish Builder*, 5 June 1902.

67. For a detailed account of this struggle see T.S.C. Dagg, *College Historical Society* (1969), 281–331.

11. THE ADMISSION OF WOMEN

1. The three men who occupied the Provost's House from 1904 to 1927 (Traill, Mahaffy and Bernard), though divided on many issues and differing widely in temperament, were all vigorous campaigners for the higher education of women.

2. The endowment in 1895 of the Hermione lectures on art history and appreciation, and later of the Ardilaun lectures on history, has continued up to our own day the tradition of lectures by visitors of distinction, whom Dubliners would otherwise have little chance of hearing.

3. Counsel supported their opinion by stating that the admission of women was bound to disturb the discipline of the College and the maintenance among the men of that decorum and propriety towards women which are essential features

of a liberal education. Any clubman could have said the same from the depths of his armchair, and one gets the impression that neither for the first nor for the last time counsel, when consulted on the charters and statutes of the College, disguised with a rather thin legal top-dressing a prejudice in favour of keeping the College as it was in their youth. In 1955, when counsel were asked whether women could be admitted to Foundation Scholarship they returned a confident negative, on the grounds that the relevant Latin words in the charter were masculine in form. It was only when, some years later, a Fellow of the College pointed out that either they had read the wrong section, or else that their Latin grammar was rusty (the only relevant word, by a curious irony, being a feminine one, *persona*), and also that they had overlooked the Sex Disqualification (Removal) Act of 1919, that behind a learned smokescreen they ate their words.

The law officers of the Crown took a very different view in 1903 from that of Jellett and White, for the King's Letter when it eventually appeared took the form of a declaration resolving doubts as to whether the admission of women *might* be inconsistent with the charter.

4. The women had a reply to this: why not, instead of B.A. and M.A., confer degrees of G.A. (Graduate in Arts) and P.A. (Proficient in Arts)?
5. Our account of this campaign is based to a large extent on documents preserved in T.C.D. MSS Mun P/1/2526, 2598–9, 2607–9.
6. Salmon to Dudley, 4 July 1903 (State Paper Office, CSORP/1911/17982).
7. The corresponding success in Mathematics had to wait till 1970, and gold medals in Classics, Economics and Legal Science have yet to be won by women.
8. Cambridge compromised in 1919 by giving women the 'title' to a degree; that is, the right to put letters after their name, but not to vote.
9. For some reason not now apparent the numbers from Cambridge greatly exceeded those from Oxford.
10. Frances Moran held the Professorship of Laws (1934–44) and later the Regius Professorship (1944–63), but not as full-time posts.
11. For further details on the early years of women in Trinity College see Olive C. Purser, *Women in Dublin University, 1904–1954* (1954).

12. THE LAST DAYS OF THE ASCENDANCY: 1901–1919

1. Madden to Balfour, 26 January and 18 February 1904 (Brit. Lib. Add. MSS 49815). See also two letters from Balfour to Wyndham printed by R.B. McDowell in *Hermathena*, 96 (1962), 31–7.
2. For several public appointments at this time (not least the Lord-Lieutenancy of Ireland) a substantial private income was an almost essential qualification. Balfour, misled perhaps by the fact that almost half the Provost's income came from the 'private estate' and was not shown in the Bursar's accounts, may have assumed that this was true also of the provostship. In fact Traill, who was of Scottish stock, attempted no great splendour in his entertainment in the Provost's House.
3. A good example is given by Stanford and McDowell, *Mahaffy*, 200. At the unveiling of the statue to Lecky in 1906 the Provost remarked that four men who had subsequently distinguished themselves had presented themselves for the entrance examination on the same day: Lecky, himself, Chief Justice Fitzgibbon and Mahaffy. As *T.C.D.* remarked ironically, 'With becoming modesty he placed himself second.'

4. Even a friendly critic complained that a speech delivered to the Cecilia Street medical school on the University Question on 7 November 1889, filled ten columns of small print in the *Freeman's Journal*.

5. Mgr Persico, the Papal legate sent to Ireland in 1887 to report to Rome on the degree of involvement of the Irish clergy in extremist politics, wrote of him that 'the public meets the Archbishop daily – not in person, but in the newspapers, either in the form of letters to the editor or in articles. The latter deal mostly with political and literary matters, rarely with religion.' (A. Rhodes, *Encounter* (February 1980), 12.)

6. A generous selection of the Archbishop's speeches and writings from 1885 to 1895 was published under the title of *The Irish University Question* (1897).

7. *Ibid.*, 373.

8. These various statements are reprinted in the *Royal Commission on university education in Ireland* (1902), appendix to first report, 383–8.

9. Archbishop Walsh devoted an enormous amount of space to trying to prove that this was the case, despite the adverse judgment of the Master of the Rolls in the Reid case (p. 4; see also *Statutes*, vol. 2 (1898), 507–32). But the question was entirely irrelevant; if the Government had wished to create a second college in the University of Dublin it could legislate to that effect, no matter what Queen Elizabeth or King James I may have said or thought. What was overlooked, however, by all supporters of such a scheme was the very great difficulty of making an equitable separation between university and college property, and of including other colleges in the University of Dublin without rewriting the constitution of Trinity College *de novo*. Archbishop Walsh was not alone in trying to prove historical sanction for his policy; Chief Baron Palles also appended a personal statement to the report of the Royal Commission of 1906, which amounted to a long-delayed and unofficial reversal, given in chambers as it were, of the judgment of the Master of the Rolls. We hesitate to criticize the views of such an eminent lawyer as the Chief Baron, but it appears to us that the corporation whose existence he was trying to prove (the University of Dublin) must have been a very odd one, for it had no formal charter; an unsuccessful attempt had been made to procure a charter for it; its supposed existence was repeatedly ignored in Letters Patent and Acts of Parliament; and the wording of the Letters Patent of 1857 deliberately avoided a formal incorporation of the University.

10. It was generally assumed that this would hold good for the College Library, and in so far as it applied to books received under the Copyright Act this was morally justifiable. But nearly all the older books and a fair number of modern ones had been received by gift or bequest to the College (not the University). Similarly there was ample scope for argument on the question of how much of the capital owned by Trinity College could fairly be regarded as state endowment. Much of it certainly could, but it comprised also gifts and bequests, as well as savings derived from economy and prudent management.

11. T.C.D. MSS Mun P/1/2461.

12. *The Irish University Question*, 87. The Archbishop later devoted much space to explaining away these remarks and declaring how misleading they were when quoted out of context. He may have expressed himself with unusual freedom on this occasion without realizing that reporters were present.

13. *Intermediate Education (Ireland) Commission* (1899), appendix to first report, 159; appendix to final report, 33, 637–45.

14. *Royal Commission on university education in Ireland* (1902), appendix to third report, 371–2.

15. John Lane edn (1937), 153.
16. Chapter 5.
17. The reader unversed in Irish academic history might welcome here a summary of the changes in the places of higher education other than Trinity College subsequent to the foundation of the Queen's University in 1850 (p. 202). In 1854 there was founded at 86 St Stephen's Green the 'Catholic University', of which Newman was the first Rector. Newman, however, resigned in 1858, his idea of a university and of his duties as Rector differing from those of Cardinal Cullen, and although the foundation-stone of a grandiose building at Drumcondra was laid in 1862, the building never materialized, and the university (which had received a charter from Rome, but none from the Crown) gradually went downhill until 1883. Meanwhile, however, its medical school, founded in 1856 and located in Cecilia Street, had proved much more successful. It was unable to confer degrees recognized by the General Medical Council, but its students obtained a registrable qualification from the conjoint board of the Royal Colleges of Surgeons and Physicians.

In 1879 it was enacted that the Queen's University should be dissolved and that the Royal University should be established in its place. The Queen's Colleges were left unaltered, and the new university was designed primarily as an examining university on the model of London, to which any college with adequate academic standards could become affiliated. It had a majority of Catholics on its Senate, and it provided for the first time a channel by which Catholics could take degrees without attending instruction in a college condemned by the bishops. In 1883 the premises of the Catholic University in St Stephen's Green, which were by now almost destitute of students, were made over by the bishops to the Jesuits. They re-named the place University College, prepared students for degrees at the Royal University, and, although the numbers remained small, built the college up, under the direction of Father Delany, to form a lively centre of Catholic academic life, with Gerard Manley Hopkins the best-known (though also probably the most discontented) of its professors. There was close co-operation between University College and the Cecilia Street medical school, although there was no formal constitutional link, the latter being still part of the Catholic University, under the control of the bishops.

Apart from conducting examinations and conferring degrees, the Royal University provided, by means of Fellowships which it had at its disposal, an indirect state endowment on a small scale for University College. The Royal University was, however, a cumbrous and unloved body, and the Royal Commissions of 1901 and 1906 alike started from the premise that it must be either remodelled or replaced.
18. Balfour to Cadogan, 23 February 1901; Cadogan to Balfour, 23 April 1901 (Brit. Lib. Add. MSS 49802).
19. *Royal Commission on university education in Ireland* (1902), appendix to the first report, 37.
20. *Ibid.*, 85 and 92.
21. Although Bishop O'Dwyer (*ibid.*, 17) had stated that the Queen's Colleges had been condemned as dangerous, but that individual Catholic students had never been formally and expressly forbidden to attend them, and implied that the same was true of Trinity College, Bishop Clancy of Elphin (*ibid.*, 129) regarded the Church's attitude as a definite prohibition (to which occasional exceptions might be allowed), rather than a mere discouragement. When pressed on this point he was quite categorical. Of course what sounded like a friendly warning if de-

livered over a cup of tea at Clongowes College might well sound like a prohibition when delivered from the altar steps at Ballaghaderreen.

22. Stanford and McDowell, *Mahaffy*, 212.

23. 'A University Scandal', *New Ireland Review*, 12 (1899), 169. Although it was not directly mentioned, the knowledge, both among the College officers and their critics, that Hyde had been rejected for the chair of Irish in 1896 in favour of Murphy, a Church of Ireland clergyman, a fluent Irish speaker and a well-educated man, but with no claim to scholarly distinction, heightened feelings in the controversy. It is clear from a letter written by Provost Salmon to Lecky (who as M.P. for the University was one of the trustees with whom the appointment lay) that it was the Board's suspicion of Hyde's nationalist politics, supported by the supposedly impartial, but in fact malicious, judgment by Atkinson on his linguistic competence, that ruled him out, despite the fact that Salmon realized his abilities, at least in part. Atkinson had told Salmon that Hyde's fairy-tales were written 'in Baboo Irish . . . a queer mixture of modern colloquialisms with the old literary Irish, of which Hyde . . . has a very imperfect knowledge' (T.C.D. MSS, Lecky papers, 1233a, 1254). It does not seem to have occurred to Atkinson that this 'queer mixture' might have been just the language used by elderly story-tellers of the day.

24. The report is very fully indexed; we have not, therefore, thought it necessary to give page references for such quotations from it as can readily be traced through the index.

25. Archbishop King's Lecturership in Divinity is here reckoned as a chair, which it was to become a few months later. The chair of Biblical Greek was vacant.

26. Men as diverse in outlook as E.J. Gwynn and John Joly were agreed on this limitation. It did not arise from simple social snobbery, as they would have welcomed the son of a Protestant shopkeeper or small farmer if he was diligent and reasonably intelligent. But for a Catholic to 'fit in' it was held (with some justice) that he must come from a background in which he was used to meeting Protestants on terms of equality, and would therefore be free from the aggressiveness that arises from insecurity.

27. But not, of course, in practice. Except for the few occasions on which episcopal denunciation of the extremer manifestations of nationalism was ignored and even publicly controverted, the average Irish Catholic was prepared, at least up to about 1945, to receive with respect a bishop's views on almost any subject.

28. In a letter to the *Irish Independent* written shortly before his death, which is reprinted in the *Royal Commission on Trinity College and the University of Dublin* (1906), appendix to final report, 479.

29. The new University College, Dublin was formally distinct from the body of the same name which had been governed by the Jesuits since 1883. But it took over the 'good-will' of the former college, most of its students, many of its professors, and, indeed, much of its atmosphere.

30. This was, however, made over to University College, Dublin, by the Free State Government in 1926.

31. It is of interest to note that the first Professors of Old Irish (Bergin), Modern Irish (Hyde), Welsh (Lloyd-Jones) and Irish Archaeology (Macalister) were all Protestants.

32. The average number of entrants rose from 7 per cent around 1895 to 12 per cent around 1911, and in absolute terms from seventeen to thirty-six over the same period.

33. Thompson resigned the chair of Physiology in Belfast in 1902 to come to Dublin.

34. The principal documents relating to this controversy up to July 1906 are printed in the *Royal Commission on Trinity College and the University of Dublin* (1906), appendix to First Report, 82–106.

35. In a letter to the Board (Companion to the Register, vol. 1, p. 55) he wrote: 'No outside body shall have any voice in the control of our Divinity School until they bring in their hands an ample sum of money (say £50,000) as an endowment for additional chairs in that School. When they do this they will be in a position to negotiate with us, but not till then.'

36. Bernard papers, 89.

37. As there was no provision for a retirement pension, a statute made provision for the appointment of a permanent deputy for an elderly Regius Professor.

38. The College received from Miss Anne Donnellan in 1794 a bequest 'for the encouragement of religion, sound learning and good manners'. It was applied to found an annual series of lectures, but up to 1914 these took the form of six sermons delivered in the College Chapel, always on a religious topic. From 1914 onwards the lectures were to be given in a College hall, and the lecturer might be a layman. Up to 1919, however, the topic remained a religious one, and the lecturer a clergyman. The first lectures on a secular subject were given in 1920 by A.A. Luce; the first lay lecturer was Lord Haldane in 1921. Thus by a curious irony it was under Provost Bernard that their exclusively religious nature was abolished.

39. Mahaffy, as Vice-Provost, was deputizing for Traill, who was by now in poor health.

40. Bernard papers, 89.

41. The 'ban' on the entry of Catholics to Trinity College was finally removed in 1970. Its removal was, no doubt, due in part to the change of spirit that followed the second Vatican Congress, but it was hastened by proposals of the Government for a 'merger' of Trinity with University College, Dublin, which implied a concentration of certain faculties in one college or the other.

42. *The impending fate of Trinity College*, by 'a Heretick' (1871).

43. Hereinafter referred to simply as 'the Professors' when mentioned in a constitutional rather than a scholarly context. The constitutional position of a Fellow was the same whether he held a chair or not.

44. The minutes of this committee are preserved in the College muniments (Mun V/8b).

45. These were defined as the Professors of Astronomy, Chemistry, Applied Chemistry, Botany, Zoology, Geology, Romance Languages, German, English Literature, Political Economy, Anatomy, Institutes of Medicine (= Physiology) and Engineering.

46. It is remarkable that this final compromise was exactly that which had been recommended by Lecky in a letter to Bernard written in June 1899 (Bernard papers, 5e).

47. Companion to the Register, vol. 5, p. 46.

48. The appointment of Leslie in 1870 and of W.E. Thrift in 1901 to Erasmus Smith's Professorship of Natural and Experimental Philosophy (*i.e.* Physics) might be cited as exceptions. But the tradition of appointing a Fellow to this chair had been unbroken, and the terms of the endowment allowed, in practice, no alternative. The Council, however, seems to have felt uneasy about the position, for in 1910, when the chair of Natural Philosophy (*i.e.* Applied Mathematics) fell vacant they asked the Board to seek advice from the Visitors as to the legal restrictions (if any) on the field from which candidates could be considered. The Board agreed, but then temporized, and finally the Council was persuaded to nominate M.W.J. Fry, a Junior Fellow aged forty-six; he had published a few papers on his subject,

but was scarcely of professorial calibre. It seems probable that the dissatisfied members of Council had their eye on Edward Whittaker, Professor of Astronomy since 1906, who was admirably qualified for a chair of Applied Mathematics.

49. The Board always allowed itself to be guided by the examiners, who sent in precise marks, which were subsequently published. Only once, to our knowledge, was this tradition broken, when in 1905 the Board elected Alton, although R.M. Gwynn had gained a slightly higher mark. They justified this on the grounds that Alton was an older man, and would not compete again; Gwynn did, and was successful in 1906. The Board made a less easily defended decision in 1908 when it awarded the Madden prize (a valuable prize earmarked for the *proxime accessit*) to Harry Thrift, although Canning had a substantially higher mark. The decision caused much indignation (see *T.C.D.*, 20 June 1908) and has never been satisfactorily explained.

50. *The Red Hand of Ulster* (1912), 13.

51. T.C. Kingsmill Moore in *Of one company*, ed. D.A.Webb (1951), p. iv.

52. 'To dissipate one's energies by working at too many subjects does not lead to academic success nowadays, though it was our tradition half a century ago.' Bernard to Henry, 6 November 1922 (Bernard papers, 375).

53. His obituary by Alton in *T.C.D.* (30 November 1933) is memorable for its exquisitely ambiguous phrase, 'How much his translation of the *Alexander* of Lycophron has been appreciated by scholars is shown by the fact that this book has been out of print for many years past.'

54. *Irish Times*, 20 August 1917.

55. See his revealing entry in *Who was Who* (1941–50).

56. This idea did not command universal assent. Barlow wrote to the Registrar on 9 May 1907, denouncing the idea of introducing 'a gang of frog Fellows into this unfortunate College' (Companion to the Register, vol. 4, p. 35). He was probably afraid of Gerothwohl's election.

57. T.C.D. MSS Mun P/1/2637.

58. Although most of the discussion centred on modern languages, there was also some disquiet about the fact that the very theoretical nature of the examination in physics could not be relied on to produce men capable of carrying on Fitzgerald's tradition of experimental laboratory work.

59. For a full (if slightly hagiographical) account of Joly's life and work see H.H. Dixon, *John Joly: presidential address to the Dublin Experimental Science Association, 1940* (privately printed, 1941).

60. Rosse to Mahaffy, 6 June 1899 (Joly papers, T.C.D. MSS 4007, no. 1).

61. There were only 237 subscribers, but 47 of these gave sums of £100 or more.

62. For details of the campaign for financing the development of science at this time, see T.C.D. MSS 2325 and 4006–7.

63. The jurisprudence element in this mixed course had been dropped in 1903.

64. 'In Ireland a lecture on Modern History must be regarded as an incitement to a breach of the peace ... we must view as something absolutely portentous the courage of a lecturer who, unbacked by the police, takes as his subject a period of Modern Irish History.' J.W. Barlow, *A History of Ireland during the period of parliamentary independence: a lecture* (Dublin, 1873).

65. In 1898 R.H. Charles, whose knowledge of apocalyptic literature is described in the *D.N.B.* as 'vast and accurate' was appointed to the chair of Biblical Greek, and in the same year H.J. Lawlor, a man of great erudition both in patristics and in the history of the Irish Church became Professor of Ecclesiastical History.

66. *Committee on military education: minutes of evidence*, H.C. (Cd. 982) 1902 x, 203–6.

67. T.C.D. MSS Mun P/1/2846.

68. We use this word as the most neutral; for some curious reason 'rebellion' is interpreted as hostile, 'rising' as sympathetic.

69. T.C.D. MSS 3332(15); *Irish Times*, 20 November 1913; J.R. White, *Misfit* (1930), 243–4, 253.

70. Strictly speaking the Board appoints the Vice-Provost, but as the Provost has a veto the appointment lies in practice in his hands.

71. *Reminiscences and anticipations* (1920), 218–64.

72. 19 June 1916.

73. Archbishop Bernard, in a letter to *The Times*, published on 5 May 1916, deplored the prevalent rumour that martial law was to be suspended. 'This is not the time', he declared, 'for amnesties and pardons; it is the time for punishment swift and stern.' Many Unionists and some Nationalists were of the same opinion, but it seemed rather strange that an Archbishop should be the man to express it so forcibly.

74. In a straitened age he stood out as a generous patron, and in a world of falling standards disdained to lower his own.

13. LOW PROFILE: 1919–1947

1. R.M. Gwynn, *Tributes*, 12–13.

2. MacNeill had been sentenced by court martial to life imprisonment for treason. His position was rather ambiguous, for although he was an extreme nationalist his only role in the insurrection had been a partly successful attempt to call it off.

3. Campbell to Law, 12 May 1919; Iveagh to Samuels, 17 May 1919; Bernard to Law, 2 June 1919 (Bonar Law correspondence, 97/3/14).

4. See especially N.J.D. White, *Some Recollections*, 23–4.

5. Professor W. McC. Stewart, a Scholar of 1919, who kindly gave us his memories of the incident.

6. In the case of Trinity College, Dublin one must add 'from a parliament of the United Kingdom'. The Irish parliament had been, as we have seen, lavish with capital grants for building from 1698 to 1787. But the question of an annual subsidy had never been raised.

7. Geikie to Bernard, 5 December 1919 (T.C.D. MSS Mun P/1/2904 (10)).

8. This bill, which was enacted in December 1920, provided for Home Rule independently for Northern and Southern Ireland. Its provisions were the basis of the Belfast parliament from 1921 to 1972; in the south the parliament was boycotted by Sinn Fein and was entirely abortive.

9. Bernard to Midleton, 7 November 1921 (T.C.D. MSS Mun P/1/2922 (20)).

10. T.C.D. MSS Mun P/1/2949. See also, for these negotiations, Mun P/1/2956, 2961, and Bernard papers, 380, 462.

11. See Companion to the Register, vol. 6, pp. 17 and 23.

12. Bernard papers, 2922.

13. Had he perhaps read *The Red Hand of Ulster*, from which we have quoted earlier? The narrator (a moderate Unionist) declares with some justice that' in Ireland we only hoist flags with a view to irritating our enemies, and ... the Union Jack is of all flags the most provocative. Any other flag under the sun, even the Royal Standard, might be hoisted without giving any very great offence to anyone. But the Union Jack arouses the worst feelings in everybody' (G.A. Birmingham, *Red Hand*, 176–7).

14. Sadleir to Tate, 11 February 1936 (Alton papers).

15. This meant in practice graduates of Dublin, Oxford or Cambridge, since an Oxford or Cambridge graduate could take a Dublin degree under the formula of *ad eundem gradum*.

16. Starkie, Synge, McConnell, Duncan and Bell respectively. The election of Broderick in 1930 was the result of Synge's resignation shortly before the election date, for the Board decided hastily that a second Fellow in Mathematics was needed.

17. These were Fearon and Poole in 1921; Bailey and Bell in 1926; Stanford and Graham in 1934. In each pair the name of the successful candidate is given first.

18. These resulted in the election of Rowe, Ditchburn, Parke, Wormell and Moody. Rowe was a Dublin graduate, but he had first graduated at University College, Cork; Ditchburn and Wormell were from Cambridge, Parke from Oxford and Moody from London. Moody was the first Fellow in the history of the College to have been a graduate neither of Oxford, Cambridge nor Dublin.

19. Companion to the Register, vol. 5, 160.

20. 'Post-1919' would be more accurate, but 'post-1920' was the phrase always used.

21. In the early thirties, Luce, a Fellow and tutor of some standing, and R.B.D. French, a junior lecturer, were keeping hall together. Luce took advantage of the opportunity to attack French vigorously, and indeed somewhat imperiously, for having failed one of his pupils in an English essay. French replied nervously that his academic conscience would permit no higher mark. Luce said, 'Well, I'll see the Senior Lecturer about it' and swept out. Five minutes later he returned, silent and thoughtful. Eventually French ventured a query, 'Well, Sir, what did the Senior Lecturer say?' Luce, to his credit, replied candidly, 'I'm sorry to say, French, that he threw me out.'

22. The Yquem cost five and nine pence a bottle; the Haut Brion was rather cheaper.

23. *T.C.D.*, 16 May, 1940.

24. Asof and Apnu were not, as might be thought from the context, local deities, but were mnemonics for certain rules in logic.

25. This was the dingiest of all College examinations, at which pass-men who had failed in June, and again in October, but only in a single subject, were allowed, if their performance in other subjects had been reasonably good, a last chance to save their year by sitting a special examination in this one subject.

26. He invented a variant of chess with four players, and dukes and emperors as additional pieces, and trained three of his colleagues to play it with him. He is said to have sent the rules to Capablanca for comment; Capablanca (then world champion) replied that he found ordinary chess difficult enough.

27. Expenditure under this head rose from £55,300 in 1919–20 to £69,400 in 1939–40.

28. Bailey was, of course, also making a substantial contribution in Physical Chemistry.

29. Of the ninety-eight Moderators in Modern Languages in the years 1935–9 all but nine chose French as one of their languages. Twenty-seven were men, sixty-two women.

30. This account is based on a file in the Alton papers, aided by the recollections of one of the authors, who was an eyewitness of much of the proceedings. The accounts in the contemporary newspapers are misleading on several points.

31. The only other candidate was Dr Owen Sheehy Skeffington, who had been lecturing in French for over ten years. He was, at least in his early years, a popular and effective interpreter of Gide and other near-contemporary authors to his classes, but he put none of this down on paper, for he sacrificed (one must

presume deliberately) his scholarly to his political interests, and for many years played effectively the part of a left-wing gadfly, too independent for any party to harbour him. For some years, however, he represented the University in the Senate.

32. For this controversy see *The Times* for 6, 10, 11 and 14 February 1941; 26 and 29 January and 3, 6 and 10 February 1942.

33. Not long after 1947 the Educational Endowment Fund (soon to be reconstituted for technical reasons as the Trinity Trusts) began to show more signs of life, and over the course of the next thirty years brought in enough money to enable it to give substantial grants to various aspects of College life, which the Board might not have been able to do without creating awkward precedents. By 1979 it had an income from subscriptions and investments of nearly £24,000 a year, but it never reached a scale sufficient to make a significant contribution to the salaries problem.

34. A report of this interview is to be found in the Companion to the Register, vol. 6, p. 181.

14. EPILOGUE: 1947–1952

1. The information in this chapter is derived primarily from the College muniments (Registrar, Companion and Minutes of the Junior Fellows' Meetings) and also from the Alton papers; but this has had to be supplemented largely from the memory of the authors and documents in their possession, for there is a surprising number of important matters on which the official records have no documentation. These include the 'remonstrance' of 24 October 1951, and Luce's reply, the protest from the Junior Fellows about the increase in Senior Fellows' salaries, and, most surprisingly of all, the nominations to the annual offices made on 28 June 1952 in opposition to those made by the Provost, and the record of the voting on this issue. The record of the resolutions of the tutors and their exchanges with the Board is also defective.

   Such documents as relate to these issues and are in the possession of the authors are to be lodged in the College muniments as soon as this book has gone to press.

2. This scale was anticipated by a rather daring move in 1946, when the Professorship of Chemistry was advertised at a salary of £1,150, a figure considerably above the current scale. It was a gamble, probably made at Bailey's suggestion, on the likelihood of a grant being made by the Government; but at the time nothing can have been known except possibly a hint through indirect personal channels that the Government was prepared to examine an application. The gamble paid off well, as Wesley Cocker was secured for the post; within a very short time he had initiated some long overdue modernization and had set up an active school of research into the organic chemistry of natural products.

3. University College was also given during this period some non-recurrent grants, amounting to £42,000 in all, for equipment and adaptation of premises. These were certainly badly needed, but Trinity had some of the same problems, albeit on a smaller scale, arising from the rise in student numbers, and a corresponding grant to Trinity of, say, £15,000 would not have been unreasonable.

4. The Board had done its best to conceal this fact in the *Consolidated statutes* of 1926. The Letters Patent of 1911, while reserving to the Crown the power to alter certain 'entrenched' clauses in the statutes, had given to the Board, Visitors and majority of the Fellows power to alter all other clauses 'including Ordinances varying from time to time the constitution of the Board'. In the statute of 1926

which recited a large part of the 1911 Letters relating to the machinery of statutory change by Ordinance, the phrase relating to the composition of the governing body was omitted. Its omission had, of course, no legal effect in the absence of any entrenched clause *forbidding* an Ordinance altering the composition of the Board, but it represented a deliberate decision of the Board (Register, 28 February 1925) to avoid putting ideas into the heads of Junior Fellows.

5. This arose from a decision made about 1925, similar to that mentioned in the preceding note. It will be recalled that the Royal Commission of 1851 recommended that the accounts of the College should be published. This was too much for the Board, but as a compromise they inserted in the decree of 1858, which specified that an external auditor should be appointed and defined his duties, a clause saying that the balance sheet so audited 'shall be open at stated times to be fixed by the Provost, for the inspection of all Fellows who may desire to examine the same'. Whether any Fellows took advantage of this we do not know, but in the *Consolidated statutes* of 1926 the decree about the external auditor, his duties and salary are repeated, but the clause about the accessibility of the accounts is omitted, and by this omission was repealed.

6. The Commission of 1906 made no recommendation for a grant; that of 1920 established no logical connexion between the recommendation of a grant and the recommendation for constitutional reform. Luce's sentence can only mean, 'Since we never got the money we can ignore the Commissions' recommendations.'

7. *A history of Trinity College, Dublin, 1892–1945.*

8. Although Bigger was extremely energetic and effective in expediting the building, much of the credit for directing Miss Guinness's generosity in the direction of Trinity College must be given to Martin Fallon, formerly University Anatomist.

9. He had a great dislike of controversy on committees, and an even greater reluctance to take sides. His usual technique was first to propose that the matter be postponed for a year; if that failed he would suggest a novel proposal of his own, which would be in no sense a compromise between the two contending parties, but rather the third corner of an equilateral triangle of which they formed the base. It seldom won support, and at the final vote he would often be absent on the plea of a doubtless genuine but equally doubtless psychosomatic cold. His steady support of the pre-1920 Fellows in 1951–2 is not easy to explain, as in private conversation he could be extremely critical of them. When taxed by one of the reform party with his votes he would explain that he was a liberal and in favour of reform, but that the reformers were 'going about it the wrong way'. What the right way was never became very clear.

Bibliography

I. MANUSCRIPT SOURCES

(i) Library of Trinity College, Dublin

(a) *College muniments*

The College muniments were arranged and catalogued by Miss Margaret Griffith between 1971 and 1976, and we are fortunate in being the first historians of the College to benefit from her excellent organization of its records. Our only problem has been an *embarras de richesse*, and if we can claim in some areas to be pioneers, favoured by fortune, we have to admit that there are many seams which we have not had time to exploit.

We have made especial use of the following:

The Particular book (Mun V/1 (i)). This is the oldest muniment to survive which deals with the internal affairs of the College; it consists of a very miscellaneous collection of documents dating from the period 1595–1641. It was published in facsimile, with an introduction and appendices, by J.P. Mahaffy (London, 1904).

The Registers (minute books) of the Board, 1627–1928 (Mun V/5).

The Companions to the Registers, 1887–1922 (Mun V/6).

The University Council minute books, 1875–1949 (Mun V/3).

Minute book of meetings of the Junior Fellows, 1902–64 (Mun V/8a).

Minute book of meetings of the joint committee of representatives of the Junior Fellows and of the Professors, appointed in accordance with a resolution passed in December, 1907 (Mun V/8b).

Entrance books, 1637–1961 (Mun V/23–5).

List of candidates for Fellowship, 1821–58 and 1891–1962 (Mun V/37–8).

Bursar's yearly accounts, 1800–1956 (Mun V/58).

Junior Bursar's books, 1830–1936 (Mun V/53).

Bursar's salary books and schedules, 1836–1945 (Mun V/63–4).

Loose papers from the muniment room, 1592–1911 (Mun P/1).

Files transferred from the Provost's House in 1980 (uncatalogued).

(b) *Other manuscripts*

E.H. Alton papers (P 46)

C.F. Bastable, correspondence (5879)

Lord John George Beresford, correspondence (2770–4)

J.H. Bernard, correspondence (2388–93)

J.H. Bernard, scrapbooks (2386–7)

J. Carson, notebook (3494)
A.F.Dixon papers (3332)
J. Hely-Hutchinson, History of Trinity College (1770–4b)
J. Joly papers (2304–9a, 2312, 2324–5, 4006–7)
W.H. Lecky, correspondence (1827–36)
H. Lloyd, letter-book (3487)
T. Prior, account of 1798 visitation (3373)
T. Prior, diaries (3363–9)
J.H. Todd, correspondence (2214)
M. Wycherley, notebooks (2244–5).

(ii) Other Dublin collections
(a) *Public Record Office*
Leveson-Gower letter-books (M 736)

(b) *State Paper Office*
File relating to Trinity College (CSORP/1911/17982).

(iii) London
(a) *The British Library*
Balfour papers (Add. MSS 49802–3, 49815)
Campbell-Bannerman papers (Add. MSS 41211, 41240)
Gladstone papers (Add. MSS 44437–8, 44468)
Hardwicke papers (Add. MSS 35710)
Peel papers (Add. MSS 40330)
Wellesley papers (Add. MSS 37299, 37306–7)

(b) *House of Lords Record Office*
Ashbourne papers
Bonar Law correspondence

(c) *Public Record Office*
Home Office papers (H.O. 100/199)

(iv) Oxford: the Bodleian Library
Clarendon papers
Rawlinson MSS

II. PRINTED SOURCES
(i) Printed collections of documentary material
Burke, Edmund. *Correspondence*, ed. T.W. Copeland, 9 vols. Cambridge and Chicago, 1958–78.
Castlereagh, Viscount. *Memoirs and correspondence*, ed. C. Vane, 12 vols. London, 1848–53.
Locke, John. *Correspondence*, ed. E.S. de Beer, 8 vols. Oxford, 1976–
Swift, Jonathan. *Correspondence*, ed. H. Williams, 5 vols. Oxford, 1963–5.
Historical Manuscripts Commission:
    Charlemont MSS (vol. 2)
    Kenyon MSS (14th Report, appendix, part 4)
    Ormonde MSS (new series, vol. 6)
'Report on Rawlinson MSS (Class D)', *Analecta Hibernica*, 2 (1931), 44–92.

Bibliography

(ii) Parliamentary proceedings and papers

Hansard's Parliamentary debates, third and fourth series.

House of Commons Journals (Ireland).

Report ... by a Royal commission of inquiry into the state of the universities of Scotland. H.C. 1831 (310) XII.

University of Dublin (Trinity College) returns ... H.C. 1831–2 (264) XIV.

Evidence ... taken and received by the commissioners for visiting the universities of Scotland: Vol. 1, University of Edinburgh. [92] H.C. 1837 XXXV.

Oxford University Commission. Report ... together with the evidence and an appendix. [1482] H.C. 1852 XXII.

Cambridge University Commission. Report ... together with the evidence and an appendix. [1559] H.C. 1852–3 XLIV.

Dublin University Commission. Report of Her Majesty's Commissioners appointed to inquire into the state, discipline, studies and revenues of the University of Dublin and Trinity College ... [1637] H.C. 1852–3 XLV.

Report of the commissioners appointed to consider the best mode of reorganizing the system for training officers for the scientific corps ... [0.52] H.C. 1857 VI.

Roman Catholic University (Ireland): copy of correspondence relative to the proposed charter to a Roman Catholic university in Ireland. H.C. 1867–8 (288) LIII.

Roman Catholic University (Ireland): copy of further correspondence ... H.C. 1867–8 (380) LIII.

Trinity College (Dublin) ... copy of the memorial from the Provost and Fellows ...; copy of the petitions of the Provost, Fellows and Scholars ... dated the 12th day of June, 1868 ... and of the petition of certain graduates ... presented on the 6th day of March, 1868. H.C. 1870 (110) LIV.

Trinity College (Dublin). Returns of the number of Fellows in Trinity College, Dublin, and their average incomes ... H.C. 1870 (295) LIV.

Dublin University and Trinity College: returns of the total revenue from all sources ... of the expenditure of the sum paid ... by the Irish Church temporalities commissioners to Trinity College, and allocation of such sums. H.C. 1874 (344) LI.

Dublin University Commission. Report of Her Majesty's commissioners appointed to inquire into certain matters relating to the College of the Holy and Undivided Trinity of Queen Elizabeth, near Dublin, with minutes of evidence and appendix. [C. 2045] H.C. 1878 XXIX.

Intermediate Education (Ireland) Commission:
  First report, with appendix [C – 9116–7]; *Final report* [C – 9511] H.C. 1899 XXII.
  Appendix to final report, part I [C – 9512] H.C. 1899 XIII; *part II* [C – 9513] H.C. 1899 XXIV.

Royal Commission on university education in Ireland (the Robertson commission):
  First report, with appendix [Cd. 825–6]; *Second report, with appendix* [Cd. 899–900] H.C. 1902 XXXI.
  Third report, with appendix [Cd. 1228–9] H.C. 1902 XXXII.
  Final report, with appendix [Cd. 1483–4] H.C. 1903 XXXII.

Royal Commission on Trinity College and the University of Dublin (the Fry commission):
  First report [Cd. 3174]; *Appendix to first report: statements and returns* [Cd. 3176] H.C. 1906 LVI.
  Final report, with appendix (minutes of evidence and documents) [Cd. 3111–2] H.C. 1907 XLI.

Royal Commission on the University of Dublin (Trinity College) (the Geikie commission):
  Report [Cmd. 1078] H.C. 1920 XIII.
  Appendix [Cmd. 1167] H.C. 1921 XI.

Bibliography

(iii) Official publications of the College, and reports of visitations and meetings of the University Senate

Numerous editions of the College statutes were printed from time to time during the eighteenth and nineteenth centuries, both in Latin and English, but since 1844 only those listed below were generally regarded as authoritative. The volumes of 1844, 1898 and 1917 contain, in addition to the charters and what may properly be called statutes, numerous other documents relevant to the interpretation of the statutes. These include decisions of the Visitors, Acts of Parliament and judicial decisions which relate to the internal affairs of the College, decrees of the Board and Visitors, etc.

Chartae et Statuta Collegii Sacrosanctae et Individuae Trinitatis Reginae Elizabethae juxta Dublin. Dublin, 1844. Reprinted in 1898 as a companion volume to the following, and then numbered as vol. 1.

Chartae et Statuta Collegii Sacrosanctae et Individuae Trinitatis Reginae Elizabethae juxta Dublin, vol. 2. Dublin, 1898.

Chartae et Statuta Collegii Sacrosanctae et Individuae Trinitatis Reginae Elizabethae, juxta Dublin, usque ad initium termini S. Michaelis, MCMXVII, vol. 3. Dublin, 1917.

The consolidated statutes of Trinity College, Dublin, and of the University of Dublin. Dublin, 1926. A self-contained code, which repealed all earlier statutes. The volume contains also the charters and some other material.

The 1966 consolidated statutes of Trinity College, Dublin, and of the University of Dublin. Dublin, 1966.

Dublin University Calendar. Issued annually since 1833. Up to 1900 volumes are dated by the calendar year; from 1901 onwards by the academic year. In 1876 and 1877, and again from 1901 to 1919 it was published in two volumes; in some years examination papers were issued as a supplementary volume, and from 1952 to 1957 lists of examination results, prizes and degrees were issued as separate supplements.

Dublin University Calendar, vol. III, being a special supplemental volume for the year 1912–1913. Dublin, 1913. A historical record. Similar, but less complete supplemental volumes had been issued in 1901 and 1906; all their material is incorporated in the above.

Trinity College record volume. Dublin, 1951. An updating of the preceding entry, including some of its material reprinted, with corrections.

A catalogue of graduates who have proceeded to degrees in the University of Dublin . . . to December 16th, 1868. Dublin and London, 1869. Supplements have been issued from time to time, numbered as later volumes:

Vol. 2 (1868–95, with corrigenda to vol. 1). Dublin, 1896.
Vol. 3 (1895–1905). Dublin, 1906.
Vol. 4 (1906–17). Dublin, 1917.
Vol. 5 (1917–31). Dublin, 1931.
Vol. 6 (1931–52). Dublin, 1952.
Vol. 7 (1953–69). Dublin, 1970.

Alumni Dublinenses: a register of the students, graduates, professors and provosts of Trinity College in the University of Dublin (1593–1846), edited by G.D. Burtchaell and T.U. Sadleir. London, 1924. New edition, with supplement, Dublin, 1935. The supplement covers matriculations from 1846 to 1860, with some corrigenda to the first edition.

Register of the alumni of the Trinity College, Dublin. A list of the living alumni, with addresses, reissued from time to time. The first edition appeared in 1928, the ninth in 1970.

Bibliography

School of Engineering, Trinity College, Dublin. A record of past and present students. Dublin, 1909. Second edition, Dublin, 1921. Third edition, Dublin, 1960. Fourth edition, Dublin, 1966. Fifth edition, Dublin, 1981.

The book of Trinity College, Dublin, 1591–1891. Belfast and Dublin, 1892. Presented to guests at the Tercentenary celebrations.

Records of the Tercentenary festival of the University of Dublin held 5–8 July, 1892 [ed. by A. Palmer]. Dublin and London, 1894.

University of Dublin: Trinity College. War list, February 1922. Dublin [1922].

MacDonnell, H.H.G., and Hancock, W.N. A report of the case of Denis Caulfield Heron against the Provost and Senior Fellows in the visitational court of Trinity College, Dublin. Dublin, 1846.

Waller, J.F. Report of the proceedings at a visitation holden in Trinity College, Dublin, on May 24th and 25th and June 1st and 3rd, 1858 ... Dublin and London, 1858. The appeal of Shaw and Carmichael against their censure by the Board.

Report of the arguments of counsel, and decision of the court of Visitors, as to the mode of election of the principal officers of Trinity College, Dublin. Dublin, 1871.

Elrington, S.N. Election of Fellows of Trinity College, Dublin: report of the proceedings at a visitation holden in Trinity College, Dublin ... on Tuesday, 11th, Saturday, 15th, Tuesday, 18th June and Saturday, the 6th of July, 1872. Dublin, 1872. The disputed election of Frederick Purser to Fellowship.

The School of Physic – rights of the Professor of Anatomy: visitation holden on Monday, the 3rd, Tuesday, the 4th and Wednesday, the 12th February, 1873 ... Dublin, 1873.

Report of the proceedings at a special meeting of the Senate of the University of Dublin ... to consider Mr. Gladstone's University Education Bill (Ireland). Dublin, 1873.

Report of the proceedings at a special meeting of the Senate of the University of Dublin, on Saturday, April 18th, 1874, and continued by adjournment for six following meetings to consider a draft Queen's Letter for revising the statutes of Trinity College and establishing a Council. Dublin, 1874.

(iv) Histories of the College

Bailey, K.C. A history of Trinity College, Dublin, 1892–1945, Dublin, 1947. A companion volume to Maxwell's history (infra).

Dixon, W. Macneile. Trinity College, Dublin. London, 1902.

Heron, D.C. The constitutional history of the University of Dublin. Dublin, 1847.

Kirkpatrick, T.P.C. History of the medical teaching in Trinity College, Dublin, and of the School of Physic in Ireland. Dublin, 1912.

Mahaffy, J.P. An epoch in Irish history: Trinity College, Dublin, its foundation and early fortunes, 1591–1660. London, 1903. Reprinted, Port Washington and London, 1970.

Maxwell, C. A history of Trinity College, Dublin, 1591–1892. Dublin, 1946.

Murphy, H.L. A history of Trinity College Dublin from its foundation to 1702. Dublin, 1951.

Stubbs, J.W. The history of the University of Dublin from its foundation to the end of the eighteenth century. Dublin, 1889.

Taylor, W.B.S. History of the University of Dublin ... London, 1845.

Urwick, W. The early history of Trinity College, Dublin, 1591–1660. London and Dublin, 1892.

(v) Newspapers, periodicals and proceedings of learned societies

British Academy, Proceedings

Church of Ireland Gazette

The College Pen (1929–30)
Dublin Evening Mail
Dublin Evening Post
Dublin Statistical Society, *Transactions*
Dublin University Magazine
Edinburgh Review
Gentleman's Magazine
Hermathena (1874–   ) Articles dealing with the history of the College are to be found
    in nos. 28, 41, 57, 58, and frequently from no. 69 onwards.
Irish Times
Kottabos (1869–91)
The Nation
Royal Irish Academy, *Proceedings* (1836–1902); *abstract of minutes* (1902–   )
Royal Society of London, *Proceedings*
T.C.D. (1895–1976)
Trinity: an annual record published by Trinity College, Dublin (1952–72)
Westminster Review

(vi) Other printed works

Abeltshauser, I.G. *The study of modern languages: an introductory lecture*. Dublin, 1857.

Andrews T. *Studium generale: a chapter of contemporary history*. London, 1867.

Armstrong, G.F. *Life and letters of Edmund J. Armstrong*. London, 1877.

Atthill, L. *Recollections of an Irish doctor*. London, 1911.

Ball, W.V. (ed.). *Reminiscences and letters of Sir Robert Ball*. London, 1915.

Barnes, W.A. *Inaugural address delivered . . . at the opening of the session 1910–11* [of the
    School of Agriculture]. Dublin [1911].

Bellot, H.H.L. *University College, London, 1826–1926*. London, 1929.

Birrell, A. *Things past redress*. London, 1937.

Boulter, H. (Archbishop of Armagh). *Letters . . . containing an account of the most
    interesting transactions which passed in Ireland from 1724 to 1738*. 2 vols. Dublin,
    1770.

Brooke, W.G. (ed.). *Statement of the proceedings from 1892 to 1895 in connection with the
    movement for the admission of women to Trinity College, Dublin*. Dublin, 1895.

Burrowes, R. *Observations on the course of science taught at present in Trinity College,
    Dublin, with some improvements suggested therein*. Dublin, 1792.

Cameron, C.A. *History of the Royal College of Surgeons in Ireland*. 2nd edn, Dublin, 1916.

Carroll, W.G. *A memoir of the Rt. Rev. James Thomas O'Brien, with a summary of his
    writings . . . Dublin, 1875.

Cloncurry, Lord. *Personal recollections . . . Dublin, 1849.

Compton, J.M. 'Open competition and the Indian civil service', *English Historical
    Review*, 83 (1968) 265–84.

Craig, M. *Dublin, 1660–1860*. Dublin and London, 1952.

Dagg, T.S.C. *College Historical Society*. Privately printed, 1969.

Davidson, E.F. *Edward Hincks: a selection from his correspondence, with a memoir*.
    Oxford, 1933.

Dixon, H.H. *John Joly; presidential address to the Dublin University Experimental Science
    Association, 1940*. Privately printed, 1941.

Dowden, E.D. and Dowden, H.M. (ed.). *Letters of Edward Dowden and his corres-
    pondents*. London and New York, 1914.

Duigenan, P. *Lachrymae academicae: or the present deplorable state of the College of the
    holy and undivided Trinity . . . Dublin, 1777.

Elrington, T. *A sermon preached ... on the death of Matthew [Young], Lord Bishop of Clonfert*, 3rd edn, Dublin, 1800.

Fisher, H.A.L. *James Bryce*, 2 vols. London, 1927.

Fitzgerald, G.F. *Scientific writings ... collected and edited with a historical introduction by J. Larmor*. Dublin, 1902.

Furlong, W.R. *Report of the case of Angeli v. Galbraith*. Dublin, 1857.

Gibson, S. 'The University of Oxford', *The Victoria history of the county of Oxford*, vol. 3, pp. 1–39. London, 1954.

Graves, Richard (Dean of Ardagh). *The whole works of Richard Graves ... with a memoir of his life and writings by R.H. Graves*, 4 vols. Dublin, 1840.

Graves, R.H. *see* Graves, Richard.

Graves, R.P. *Life of Sir William Rowan Hamilton*, 3 vols. Dublin, 1882–9.

Gregory, Lady (ed.). *Mr Gregory's letter-box, 1813–30*. London, 1898.

Gwynn, R.M. *Some tributes to the departed*. Privately printed, 1932.

Hardy, F. *Memoirs of the political and private life of James Caulfeild, Earl of Charlemont*. London, 1810.

Haughton, S. *University education in Ireland*. London and Dublin, 1868.

Hayes, E. *Reports of cases argued and determined in the Court of Exchequer in Ireland from Hilary term 10 and 11 Geo. IV to Easter term 2 William IV*. Dublin, 1837. Includes the judgment disallowing the College's claim to the Flood bequest.

Henderson, R. *A memoir of the late Rev. George Armstrong*. London, 1859.

Hoppen, K.T. *The common scientist in the seventeenth century: a study of the Dublin Philosophical Society, 1683–1708*. London, 1970.

Joly, John. *Reminiscences and anticipations*. Dublin, 1920.

Kearney, H.F. *Scholars and gentlemen: universities and society in pre-industrial Britain, 1500–1700*. London, 1970.

Kenney, A.H. *see* Magee, W.

Lamb, J. *A collection of letters and other documents ... illustrative of the history of the University of Cambridge*. London, 1838.

Lee, W. *Suggestions for reform in the University of Dublin ...* Dublin, 1854.

Lloyd, H. *Praelection on the studies connected with the School of Engineering ...* Dublin, 1841.

Macalister, Alexander. *James Macartney, a memoir*. London, 1900.

McConnell, A.J. 'The Dublin mathematical school in the first half of the nineteenth century', *Proceedings of the Royal Irish Academy*, vol. 50A, pp. 75–8.

MacDonnell, R. *A letter to Dr Phipps, Registrar of Trinity College, concerning the undergraduate examinations in the University of Dublin*. Dublin, 1828.

McGrath, F. *Newman's university: idea and reality*. London, New York and Toronto, 1951.

McNeece, T. *Sermons preached in the chapel of Trinity College, Dublin*. Ed. Samuel Butcher. Dublin, 1863.

MacNeill, Eoin. *Irish in the National University of Ireland: a plea for Irish education*. Dublin, 1909.

McParland, E. *The buildings of Trinity College, Dublin*. [Dublin], 1977. Reprinted from *Country Life*, nos. 4114–16 and 4137–8 (1976).

McSweeney, D. *The case of Daniel McSweeney (late of Trinity College) and the rights of the independent members of the University vindicated ...* Dublin, 1819.

Magee, W. *Works ... with a memoir of his life by A.H. Kenney*, 2 vols. London, 1842.

Mallet, C.E. *A history of the University of Oxford*, 3 vols. London, 1924–7.

Mason, W. Monck. *The history and antiquities of the collegiate and cathedral church of St Patrick, near Dublin ...* Dublin, 1820.

Mayor, J.E.B. *Cambridge under Queen Anne* . . . Cambridge, 1911.

Miller, D.W. *Church, state and nation in Ireland, 1898–1921*. Dublin, 1973.

Miller, G. *An examination of the charters and statutes of Trinity College, Dublin, in regard to the supposed distinction between the College and the University.* Dublin, 1804.

Moody, T.W., and Beckett, J.C. *Queen's, Belfast: the history of a university*, 2 vols. Belfast, 1959.

Moore, T. *Memoirs, journal and correspondence*, ed. Lord John Russell, 8 vols. London, 1853–6.

Moss, L.S. *Mountiford Longfield, Ireland's first Professor of Political Economy.* Ottawa (Illinois), 1976.

Mullinger, J.B. *The University of Cambridge from the Royal injunctions of 1535 to the accession of Charles the First.* Cambridge, 1884.

Murray, R.B. *Archbishop Bernard: professor, prelate and provost.* London, 1931.

Napier, Sir Joseph. *The College and the University. Communicated to the governing body of the College, and to the Senate of the University.* Dublin, 1871.

O'Flanagan, J.R. *The lives of the Lord Chancellors and keepers of the great seal of Ireland* . . . 2 vols. London, 1870.

Oldham, C.H. *Trinity College pictorial . . . illustrated from photographs by L.R.F. Strangways and E.M. Cosgrave. A tercentenary souvenir.* Dublin, 1892.

Parker, C.S. *Sir Robert Peel*, 3 vols. London, 1891–9.

Phelan, W. *Remains . . . with a biographical memoir by John* [Jebb], *Bishop of Limerick. Ed.* Margeret Phelan, 2 vols. 2nd edn, London, 1832.

Purser, Olive C. *Women in Dublin University, 1904–1954.* Dublin, 1954.

Reichel, C.P., and Anderson, W. *Trinity College, Dublin, and university reform.* Dublin and Belfast, 1858.

Roach, J.P.C. 'The University of Cambridge', *A history of the county of Cambridge and the Isle of Ely*, vol. 3, pp. 150–312 (Victoria history of the counties of England; London, 1959).

Robinson, R. *A refutation of the charge of perjury, alleged by Theophilus Swift, Esq., against the married Fellows of Trinity College, Dublin.* Dublin, 1796.

Rowan, A.B. *Brief memorials of the case and conduct of Trinity College, Dublin, 1686–1690.* Dublin, 1858.

Stanford, W.B. *Ireland and the classical tradition.* Dublin and Totowa (New Jersey), 1976.

Stanford, W.B., and McDowell, R.B. *Mahaffy: a biography of an Anglo-Irishman.* London, 1971.

Starkie, W.F. *Scholars and gypsies, an autobiography.* London, 1963.

Stephen, L. *Life of Henry Fawcett.* London, 1885.

Stokes, W. *Address delivered before the King and Queen's College of Physicians in Ireland on . . . May 10th, 1851.* Westminister, 1851.

   Medical education in the University of Dublin . . . Dublin, 1864.

Stokes, Sir William. *William Stokes, his life and work (1804–78).* London, 1898.

Stone, L. (ed.). *The university in society*, 2 vols. Princeton and Oxford, 1975.

Stoney, G.J. *University reform in 1874.* Dublin, 1874.

Swift, T. *Animadversions on the Fellows of Trinity College.* Dublin, 1794.

Thompson, H.Y. *Higher education in Ireland.* Privately printed, 1872.

   The system of non-residence at Trinity College, Dublin. Privately printed, 1872.

Tierney, M. (ed.). *Struggle with fortune. A miscellany for the centenary of the Catholic University of Ireland, 1854–1954.* Dublin, [1954].

Tone, W.T.W. (ed.). *Life of Theobald Wolfe Tone* . . . 2 vols. Washington, 1826.

Venn, J.A. *A statistical chart to illustrate the entries at the various colleges in the*

University of Cambridge, 1544–1907. [Accompanied by a descriptive text.] Cambridge, 1908.

Walsh, B.D. *A historical account of the University of Cambridge and its colleges* . . . 2nd edn, London, 1837.

Walsh, W. (Archbishop of Dublin). *The Irish University Question: the Catholic case. Selections from the speeches and writings of the Archbishop of Dublin* . . . Dublin, 1897.

   The Irish University Question, with special reference to Trinity College, Dublin and its medical school. . . . Dublin, 1906.

Webb, D.A. (ed.). *T.C.D.: an anthology, 1895–1945.* Tralee [1947].

   Of one company: biographical studies of famous Trinity men. Dublin, 1951.

Whately, E. Jane. *Life and correspondence of Richard Whately, D.D., late Archbishop of Dublin,* 2 vols. London, 1866.

White, H.O. *Edward Dowden, 1843–1913.* Dublin, 1943.

White, J.R. *Misfit.* London and Toronto, 1930.

White, N.J.D. *Four good men.* Dublin, 1927. Includes biographical sketches of Luke Challoner and Narcissus Marsh.

   Some recollections of Trinity College, Dublin. Dublin, 1935.

Whyte, J.H. *Church and state in modern Ireland, 1923–1970.* Dublin and London, 1971.

Winnett, A.R. *Peter Browne, provost, bishop and metaphysician.* London, 1974.

Winstanley, D.A. *Unreformed Cambridge. A study of certain aspects of the University of Cambridge in the eighteenth century.* Cambridge, 1935.

   Early Victorian Cambridge. Cambridge, 1940.

   Later Victorian Cambridge. Cambridge, 1947.

Woodlock, B. *Catholic university education in Ireland; a letter to the Rt. Hon. W.H.F. Cogan, M.P.* Dublin, 1868.

The following are anonymous or pseudonymous works (in chronological order):

The sad estate and condition of Ireland as represented in a letter from a worthy person, who was in Dublin on Friday last . . . London, 1689. Dated Chester, 4 March 1689, and signed A.A. Evidently written by one of the Fellows of the College who had fled to England as a result of the harassment by the government of James II.

The state of the protestants of Ireland under the late King James's government . . . [By W. King, later Archbishop of Dublin.] London, 1691.

Heads of a scheme for applying part of the increase-rents of Erasmus Smith lands to the use of the college or university of Dublin, drawn up by order of the Governors. [Dublin, c. 1724.]

A proposal for the general encouragement of learning in Dublin College. [By S. Madden.] Dublin, 1731.

A letter to G — W —, Esq., concerning the present condition of the college of Dublin, and the late disturbances that have been therein. [Dublin], 1734.

A second letter to G — W —, Esq., concerning the present condition of the college of Dublin and the late disturbances that have been therein. [Dublin], 1734.

A general account of the regulations, course of study, and expenses . . . *in the seminary to be opened on Monday the 8th day of January, 1759, by the noblemen and gentlemen associated for the improvement of education in Ireland* . . . Dublin, 1758.

Pranceriana: a select collection of fugitive pieces. Dublin, 1775. Lampoons on Provost Hely-Hutchinson, by several authors.

An account of some regulations made in Trinity College, Dublin, since the appointment of the present Provost. [By J. Hely-Hutchinson.] Dublin, 1775.

Minutes of evidence taken before the select committee on Trinity College election. [Dublin, 1778.]

Thoughts on the present state of the College of Dublin, addressed to the gentlemen of the University. [Probably by J. Forsayeth.] Cork [1782].

An enquiry how far the Provost of Trinity College, Dublin, is invested with a negative on the proceedings of the senior fellows by the charter & statutes. [By M. Young.] Dublin, 1790.

A full and accurate report of the proceedings in the case of the borough of Trinity College, Dublin. Dublin, 1791.

Statement of the case respecting the right of the Provost of Trinity College, Dublin, to exercise a controlling negative at the college board ... [By M. Young.] Dublin, 1792.

A brief statement of the causes which led to the dissolution of the Historical Society of Trinity College, Dublin. By a member of the late Society. Dublin, 1815.

Crokeriana: or 'familiar epistles' published and dedicated to Trinity College, Dublin. Dublin, 1818.

Discipline of Dublin University; being a concise account of all duties of students in Trinity College .... Dublin, 1823: 2nd edn, 1828; 4th edn, 1830.

The Dublin academic calendar, containing university intelligence for the preceding half year ... *to which is prefixed an article on premature entrance into College and a syllabus of the courses required for the different examinations* ... Dublin, 1830.

The idler in college, or the student's guide. Dublin, 1850.

Personal recollections of English engineers and of the introduction of the railway system into the United Kingdom. By a civil engineer. London, 1868.

Brief suggestions in reference to the undergraduate curriculum in Trinity College, Dublin. [By H. Lloyd, Provost.] Privately printed, 1869.

The impending fate of Trinity College considered. By 'a Heretick'. [J. Barlow.] Dublin, 1871.

Remarks on the Vice-Chancellor's judgment and the late college visitation. By an ex-Fellowship candidate. Dublin, 1872.

The Trinity College Divinity School: correspondence between the committee of the Church of Ireland Protestant Defence Association and the Board of Trinity College, Dublin ... [Dublin, 1873.]

Dublin University defence: pamphlets bearing on Mr Bryce's proposed university legislation for Ireland. Dublin, 1909.

Fragments from old letters, E.D. to E.D.W., 1869–1892. [By E. Dowden.] 2 vols. London and New York, 1914.

Alexandra College, Dublin: its history and its work ... *Jubilee, 1866–1916.* Privately printed, 1916.

A page of Irish history: the story of University College, Dublin, 1883–1909. Compiled by fathers of the Society of Jesus. Dublin, 1930.

Index

Fellows of the College are distinguished thus: *; non-Fellow Professors thus †.

Peers are indexed under their title, unless they are referred to in the text by their surname; in this case a cross-reference is given under the title.

*Abbott, Thomas Kingsmill: as scholar, 171, 269, 283, 304–5, 530; as Librarian, 99, 305; other references, 298, 348, 381, 419, 543
†Abeltshauser, Ignatius George, 225, 271
†Adams, Robert, 276
administrators, non-academic, 443–4
Agriculture, School of, 415–16
Airy, Sir George Biddell, 113
Alcock, Sir John William, 425
†Alexander, Thomas, 321, 393, 406
Alexandra College, Dublin, 344, 346, 351
algebra, 48, 90
†Ali, Mir Alaud, 234, 272
All Hallows, monastery of, 2
†Allman, George Johnston, 196, 209
†Allman, William, 143
*Alton, Ernest Henry: as classical scholar, 400, 459; in politics and public life, 401, 429; as Junior Fellow, 487, 552; as Provost, 443, 468–9, 479–80, 485; illness and death, 490, 493; other references, 398, 403, 491, 492, 552
Alvey, Henry (Provost), 7
Anatomy, Professors of, 42–3, 59, 141–2, 186, 274–5, 320, 454
*Andrews, Francis: appointed Provost, 50; his provostship, 37, 52–3, 56, 58, 385; confused with William Andrews, 521; his death and legacy, 53, 58, 64
*Andrews, William, 60
†Angeli, Basilio, 199, 224–5
Anne, Queen, politics in the reign of, 33–6
†Anster, John, 193, 230, 268, 541
†Apjohn, James, 182–3, 196, 197, 317, 535
Apothecaries' Hall, 140

Arabic (and later Persian and Hindustani), Professors of, 234, 449
Aristotle, 15, 31, 32, 46
†Armstrong, John, 521
Army School, 415
Arnold, Thomas, 148
Arnould, Émile Jules François, 467
Arran, Richard Butler, Earl of, 25–6
Ashbourne, Lord, see Gibson, Edward
*Ashe, St George (Provost), 29–31
Astronomy: Professors of, 64–5, 111–13, 207, 273, 315, 432; courses in, 47, 70
†Atkinson, Robert: as philologist and linguist, 272, 283, 311, 313–14, 542; his opposition to the Gaelic revival, 363, 550; other references, 263–4, 375, 403

Bacon, Francis, 7, 32
Bacteriology, Professors of, 455, 492
*Bailey, Kenneth Claude: as Junior Fellow, 445, 487, 554; candidate for Provostship in 1942, 468; as Registrar, 466, 474–5; qualities and limitations as possible future Provost, 491–2; premature death, 492
*Baldwin, Richard (Provost), 34, 36, 37–41, 45, 49, 50, 56, 97, 284
Balfour, Arthur James, 358, 360–1, 368, 377
†Ball, Sir (Charles) Arthur Kinahan, 481
†Ball, Sir Charles Bent, 393
Ball, John Thomas (Vice-Chancellor), 250, 290
Ball, Robert (Director of the Museum), 197, 230, 317
†Ball, Sir Robert Stawell (Professor of Astronomy), 263, 273, 315
†Banks, Sir John Thomas, 276

†Barker, Francis, 143, 183
*Barlow, James William: his religious heterodoxy, 241, 385; character and achievement, 300–1; as Senior Fellow, 358, 388, 390, 543; as Professor of History, 412, 530; boycotts Tercentenary celebrations, 546; opposition to constitutional reform, 525; other references, 272, 381, 552
†Barnes, William Arthur, 416
*Barrett, John, 81–2, 99
Barrington, Jonah, 85
†Bastable, Charles Francis, 314, 392, 405, 414, 453, 460, 542
Bath, sixth Earl of, see Bourchier, Henry
†Baxter, James Sinclair, 414, 453
*Beare, John Isaac, 298, 302–3, 372, 390–1, 392, 404, 541
Bedell, William (Provost), 9, 11
Bedford, John Russell, fourth Duke of (Chancellor), 52
*Bell, James, 466, 554
Belmore, Somerset Richard Lowry-Corry, fourth Earl of, 381
†Bennett, Edward Hallaran, 318
Bennett, William (Bishop of Cloyne), 76, 106
Beresford, Lord John George de la Poer (Vice-Chancellor, and later Chancellor; Archbishop of Armagh): as Vice-Chancellor, 96; opposes Archbishop Whately's proposed divinity college, 166–8; favours maintenance of celibacy rule, 179; endows chair of Ecclesiastical History, 191; proposes retirement pensions for Fellows, 191, 201; succeeds to Chancellorship, 206; his views on recommendations of the Royal Commission, 214, 220, 223; presents the Campanile, 237; other references, 166, 216, 228
Beresford, Marcus Gervais (Archbishop of Armagh), 245
*Berkeley, George, 30, 32, 170
Bernal Osborne, Ralph, 204
*Bernard, John Henry: as scholar and lecturer, 268–9, 283, 318, 398, 542; supports constitutional reform, 287, 388; considered for Provostship in 1904, 356–8; on the Irish University Question, 372–3; appointed Provost, 423–4; fights for a government grant, 425–9, 551; death, 439; other references, 162, 299, 304, 383–4, 399
Biblical Greek, Professors of, 164, 171, 552
†Bigger, Joseph Warwick, 455, 465–6, 482, 492
Biochemistry, chair of, 454

Birkenhead, first Earl of, see Smith, Frederick Edwin
'Birmingham, George A.' (J.O. Hannay), 397, 553
Birrell, Augustine, 377–8
bishoprics, promotion of Provosts and Fellows to, 23, 34, 50, 64, 78, 83, 107–8, 155, 526
Blackburne, Francis (Vice-Chancellor), 206, 214, 223
Blackstone, Sir William, 65
Blythe, Ernest, 445
Board of the College, 55, 80, 97–103, 208–11, 290–1, 346–8, 394–5, 444, 484–5, 496–7
Botany, Professors of, 42–3, 59, 142–3, 196–7, 274, 317, 410, 456. See also herbarium
Boulter, Hugh (Archbishop of Armagh), 50
*Bourchier, Henry, sixth Earl of Bath, 13
Boyle, Michael (Archbishop of Dublin, and later of Armagh), 25
Boyne, battle of the, 24, 29
*Boyton, Charles, 155, 525
Brady, Maziere (Lord Chancellor of Ireland), 205, 207, 216, 222
†Brady, Thomas John Bellingham, 267–8
†Brinkley, John, 65, 71, 80, 108, 112, 131, 160
*Broderick, Timothy Stanislaus, 432, 554
Brown, Sir Arthur Whitton, 425
†Brown, Samuel Lombard, 453
*Browne, Arthur, 61, 67, 77, 80, 81, 82, 193, 522
*Browne, George (Provost), 24, 31
Browne, Noel Christopher, 479–80
†Browne, O'Donel Thornley Dodwell, 455
*Browne, Peter (Provost), 32–4
†Brünnow, Franz, 273
Bryce, James, later Viscount Bryce, 368, 376–8
buildings of Trinity College, 23, 41, 50, 53, 55, 83–4, 89, 93–5, 115, 176, 236–7, 289, 339–40, 407, 411, 471
Burdon-Saunderson, Sir John Scott, 337
Burke, Edmund, 49, 75, 78
*Burnside, William Snow, 304, 395
*Burrowes, Robert, 66–8, 69, 71
Bursars, 99, 208, 296, 442, 485–6
Burton, Decimus, 236–7
*Bury, John Bagnell, 264, 283, 298, 302–3, 356–7, 398, 412, 542
*Butcher, Samuel, 191–2, 543
Butcher, Samuel Henry, 368, 375
Butler, Samuel (Bishop of Lichfield), 117

†Butler, William Archer, 170, 270, 541
†Butt, Isaac, 134, 169, 245
Byrne, Edward (Archbishop of Dublin), 470
*Byrne, James, 308–9, 530

Cadogan, George Henry Cadogan, fifth Earl, 549
†Cairnes, John Elliott, 169, 218, 230
Cairns, Hugh McCalmont, Earl Cairns (Chancellor), 290, 381
Calendar, College, 277, 528
Cambridge, University of, 4, 6, 7, 16, 47, 86, 97, 124, 351–2. *See also* Oxford and Cambridge compared with Dublin
Campbell, James Henry Mussen, later first Baron Glenavy (Vice-Chancellor), 424
Canning, George, 532
*Canning, Hugh, 400–1, 552
*Carmichael, Robert Bell Booth, 227–8
Carson, Sir Edward Henry, 424, 542
*Carson, Joseph: as examiner, 126, 296; on ecclesiastical issues, 245, 381; as Senior Fellow, 251, 264, 290–1, 296; helps to oppose Gladstone's Irish Universities bill, 254; opposes admission of women to the College, 345, 347; death, 348; other references, 197, 337, 542
Casey, John, 541
catechetical course, 129, 331, 387
*Cathcart, George Lambert, 272, 304, 374, 395, 423, 430
Catholic Bulletin, 431–2
Catholic emancipation, 76–7, 79, 154, 238
Catholic University of Ireland, 253–4, 541, 549. *See also next entry.*
Cecilia Street Medical School, 378, 539, 549
celibacy statute, 102, 106–7, 177–9, 204, 260
Challoner, Luke (Vice-Chancellor), 2, 83
Chamberlain, Joseph, 354
Chamberlain (Joseph) Austen, 430
Chancellors of the University, 13–15, 17, 36, 52, 95–6, 99, 206, 223, 525, 534
Chapel services, 129, 383–4, 385–7
*Chappell, William (Provost), 3, 9, 11, 16, 17, 22
Charlemont, James Caulfeild, first Earl of, 66, 95
†Charles, Robert Henry, 552
charters, 2, 3, 14
Chemistry, Professors of, 42–3, 59, 131, 182–3, 315, 317, 456, 555
Choral Society, 194
Church of Ireland, 138, 149–51, 308, 379–82
Church of Ireland Training College, 450

†Churchill, Fleetwood, 276
civil wars and Commonwealth, 17–21
Clancy, John (Bishop of Elphin), 549
Clare, Earl of, *see* Fitzgibbon, John
Clarendon, George William Villiers, fourth Earl of, 207
†Clark, David, 455
classics, 61, 69, 118, 121, 265–8, 301–3, 459. *See also* Greek *and* Latin
*Clayton, Robert, 40
†Cleghorn, George, 42–3, 59
*Clement, William, 42–3, 50, 53
*Cocker, Wesley, 555
Coffey, Denis Joseph, 368–9, 376, 379
College of Science, 371, 377, 378, 416
Commerce, diplomas and degrees in, 416, 449, 462
Common Room, 184, 527
Commonwealth, *see* civil wars.
Comparative Anatomy, chair of, 274–5
†Coneys, Thomas De Vere, 191
*Conner, Richard Mountiford, 299, 348, 543
constitutional reform, 287–9, 387–96, 480–2, 486, 488–90, 494–5, 497
Cooper, Edward, 205–6
Corporation (body corporate) of the College, 392–5
Costello, John Aloysius, 479–80
Coulter, Thomas, 196
Council, University, 258–9
*Coutts, John Archibald, 453, 466
†Crampton, John, 143
*Crampton, Philip Cecil, 107, 110, 139, 155
Croker, John Wilson, 98, 527
Cromwell, Henry, 18
Cromwell, Oliver, 11
Cullen, Paul (Cardinal-Archbishop of Dublin), 255, 361, 385, 541, 549
*Culverwell, Edward Parnell, 298, 307, 372, 377, 389, 417, 423
Cumberland, Duke of, *see* Ernest Augustus
†Cunningham, Daniel John, 320, 337, 413, 542
Cunningham, Margery, 351
†Curtis, Edmund, 412, 458
†Cusack, James William, 188

Daly, Robert (Bishop of Cashel), 226
*Daniel, William, 9
Darley, Frederick (architect), 176, 534
*Darley, John, 128
*Davenport, William, 522, 526
Davis, Thomas, 155, 185, 200
degrees, proliferation of, 460–3

*Delany, Patrick, 40, 45

Delany, William (President of University College), 375, 379, 549

dentistry, 461

Derby, Edward George Geoffrey Smith Stanley, fourteenth Earl of, 206

Descartes, René, 31–2

De Valera, Eamonn, 433, 444, 463, 469, 474–5, 480, 489, 494

†Dickson, Alexander (Professor of Botany), 274

*Dickson, Benjamin, 262, 286

discipline, 20–1, 34–6, 38, 77

Disestablishment of the Irish Church, 244–6, 250–1

*Disney, Brabazon, 50

Disraeli, Benjamin, 250

*Ditchburn, Robert William, 456–7, 554

Divinity: early Professors of, 11–13; Regius Professors of 41, 90, 136–7, 192, 318–19, 452; Archbishop King's Lecturers and Professors, 44, 100, 161–2, 164, 318, 452; School of 136–8, 161–4, 189–93, 379–84, 451–3, 502–3; School Council, 382

†Dixon, Andrew Francis (Professor of Anatomy), 392, 437, 454

†Dixon, Henry Horatio (Professor of Botany), 410, 423, 430, 437, 456, 481

*Dixon, Robert Vickers, 186, 245

*Dodwell, Henry, 25

Donegall, Arthur Chichester, first Earl of, 30

Donnellan lectures, 241, 384

*Dopping, Anthony, 24

Douglas, James Green, 479

†Dowden, Edward: as critic, 263, 311–12, 542; as Professor of English Literature, 230, 271, 284, 312–13, 457; as positivist, 293; as politician, 282, 312; attitude to Irish literary revival, 312; in constitutional negotiations, 392

†Downing, Samuel, 184

Doyle, Bernard, 28

Drew, Sir Thomas, 339

*Drought, James, 524

Dublin Philosophical Society, 30

Dublin Statistical and Social Enquiry Society, 169

Dudley, William Humble Ward, second Earl of, 358

*Duigenan, Patrick, 55, 66

Dun, Sir Patrick, 43, 87

*Duncan, George Alexander, 449, 460, 487, 493–5, 554

Durham, University of, 165, 180, 347

Ecclesiastical History, chair of, 164, 191–2, 318, 352–3, 552

economics, *see* Political Economy

Edinburgh, University of, 88, 89, 145, 531

Education, School of, 307, 417, 450

Educational Endowment Fund, 474

Edward VIII, 434

Einstein, Albert, 527

Elizabeth I, 2–3

*Elrington, Charles Richard (Regius Professor of Divinity), 80, 110, 136–7, 163–4, 192, 231, 276

*Elrington, Thomas (Provost), 78–9, 80, 120, 136, 522, 523, 525

Emmet, Robert, 527

Engineering: Professors of, 182, 183–4, 321, 455–6; School of, 180–5, 331, 406, 410–11, 503

English literature, Professors of and courses in, 230–1, 271, 311–13, 457–8

entrance examination, 49, 118, 229, 520

Ernest Augustus, Duke of Cumberland and King of Hanover (Chancellor), 96, 206, 525, 534

ethics, 5, 46, 48–9, 71–2. *See also* Philosophy

estates of the College, 3, 15, 17, 23, 100–1

*Eustace, Maurice, 13

examinations, undergraduate, 90, 121–7, 173–4, 296, 327–9

Fallon, Martin, 556

Fawcett, Henry, 250–2, 255, 258

Fawcett's Act, 256–7, 268, 380, 384–6

*Fearon, William Robert, 397, 437, 454, 493–4, 554

fellow-commoners, 3, 114, 127

Fellows: nominated in the charter, 3; tenure in the early seventeenth century, 10; changes in their number, 3, 59, 90, 179, 262, 438, 466–7; tenure during the civil wars and at the Restoration, 18–19, 21–2; appointment by *mandamus* or King's Letter, 19, 22–3, 29; examination for the election of, 61, 105–6, 127–9, 231–2, 396–7, 402–5, 435–6; election without examination, 405, 436, 466–7; remuneration, 438–9, 512–13; women Fellows, 353; lay Fellows, 14, 25–7, 42–3, 50, 106, 107, 217–19; non-tutor Fellows, 179–80, 221–2. *See also* Senior Fellows *and* Junior Fellows

*Ferrar, William Hugh, 110, 232, 263, 530, 541

Fisher, Herbert Albert Laurens, 425

*Fitzgerald, George Francis: his character and achievement, 305–7; as physicist, 273, 283, 542, 552; as constitutional and educational reformer, 284, 326, 390, 417; campaigns for scientific expansion, 406–8; death and memorial scholarship, 408

*Fitzgerald, Gerald, 59, 66–7, 522

†Fitzgerald, William (professor of Moral Philosophy), 206–7

Fitzgibbon, John, first Baron Fitzgibbon, and later first Earl of Clare (Vice-Chancellor), 75, 77, 78, 521

flags, 433–4, 464–5

Flood, Henry, 189

†Foley, Daniel (Professor of Irish), 191, 226–7

*Foley, Samuel, 24

Forbes, Edward, 33–4

foundation of the College, 1–3

*Foy, Nathaniel, 24

*Fraser, John, 398–400, 447, 481, 487

Freeman, Thomas Walter, 450

French, Professors of, and teaching of, 57, 225, 271–2, 403, 458, 467. *See also* Modern languages.

French, Robert Butler Digby, 447, 554

Fry, Sir Edward, 368, 375, 392

*Fry, Matthew Wyatt Joseph, 304, 392, 441–2, 448, 466, 480, 551–2

*Fullerton, James, 13

†Fynne, Robert John, 417, 450

Gaelic revival, 363–4, 370, 490

*Galbraith, Joseph Allen, 224–5, 234–6, 245, 254, 281, 295, 541

games and sports, 148–9, 333–4, 401–2

†Gatenby, James Brontë, 456

Geikie, Sir Archibald, 426

Geography, 450

Geology, 182–3, 229, 273, 315, 411, 456. *See also* Haughton, Samuel, *and* Joly, John.

geometry, 47, 70

George V, 434

George Augustus, Prince of Wales, later George II (Chancellor), 36, 95

George Augustus Frederick, Prince of Wales, later George IV, 82, 95, 108, 523

German, Professors of, and teaching in, 57, 225, 271–2, 403. *See also* Modern languages

†Gerothwohl, Maurice Arthur, 403, 552

†Gibbings, Richard, 192, 539

Gibson, Edward, first Baron Ashbourne, 231

*Gilbert, Claudius, 38, 519

Glasgow, University of, 180

Glenavy, Lord, *see* Campbell, James Henry Mussen

Gloucester, Duke of, *see* William Henry

Gladstone, William Ewart: as Chancellor of the Exchequer, 213; as Liberal leader, 243, 285; proposes Disestablishment of the Irish Church, 244–5; attempts to solve Irish University Question; 248–9, 252–5, 359, 362, 377; advocates Home Rule, 282, 362; declines invitation to Tercentenary celebrations, 337

*Godfrey, Francis La Touche, 401, 420, 432, 439, 487, 493, 495–6

Gogarty, Olive St John, 454, 459

*Goligher, William Alexander, 398, 401, 442, 459, 466, 480, 487

Good, John, 449

†Goodman, James, 191, 314

*Gougleman, Lambert, 22

Government, financial assistance from, 34, 50, 425–8, 474–5, 477–80

Graham, Douglas Leslie, 554

Grattan, Henry, 76, 78

*Graves, Charles, 185, 211, 241, 348, 526, 530

*Graves, Richard, 80–1, 104, 127, 136–7, 522, 524, 532

†Graves, Robert James, 143–4, 188–9

*Gray, Thomas Thompson: as Junior Dean, 299; his political conservatism, 378, 430, 542; as unyielding opponent of constitutional reform, 299, 348, 390, 395, 419, 543; as Senior Fellow, 348; other references, 381, 415, 423, 545

Greek, 5–6, 8, 15, 19, 46, 59, 100, 327. *See also* classics

Greene, Arthur, 28–9

†Gregg, John Allen Fitzgerald (Archbishop of Dublin, and later of Armagh), 424, 452

*Griffin, Henry, 108, 527

Griffith, Arthur, 527

grinders, *see* private tuition

Guinness, Hon. Grania, later Marchioness of Normanby, 492

*Gwynn, Edward John: as supporter of constitutional reform, 287, 373, 389, 395; as scholar, 320, 398, 414–15; his attitude to the Irish University Question, 373–5, 377; appointed Provost, 439–41; illness and retirement, 441; other references, 363–4, 403

*Gwynn, John, 162, 218, 245, 283–4, 318–20, 542

*Gwynn, Lucius Henry, 334, 400

*Gwynn, Robert Malcolm, 398–400, 418, 483, 485, 487, 495, 544, 552

†Haig, Sir Thomas Wolseley, 449
Haldane, Richard Burdon, 377–8, 551
*Hales, William, 59, 62–3, 309
*Hall, George (Provost), 78–80
*Hall, John, 10, 34
*Hamilton, Hugh, 53, 63, 71, 108
*Hamilton, James, 13
*Hamilton, William, 67
†Hamilton, Sir William Rowan: intellectual
   brilliance and precocity, 111–12; election
   to Professorship while an undergraduate,
   104, 112–13; as Professor of Astronomy,
   111, 199, 207; as mathematician, 113, 160,
   199; unable to transfer to chair of
   Mathematics, 535
†Hancock, William Neilson, 169, 206
Hanna, Joseph, 472
Hanover, King of, *see* Ernest Augustus
Harcourt, Vernon, 255
*Hare, Charles, 533, 537
†Harrison, Robert, 186, 188
*Hart, Sir Andrew Searle: as lay Fellow, 217,
   527; as member of the Board and Vice-
   Provost, 210, 241, 251, 264, 285; other
   references, 245, 254
†Hart, Eric George (Professor of Arabic, etc.),
   449
†Hart, George Vaughan (Professor of Feudal
   and English Law), 413–14
*Harte, Henry Hickman, 80, 160
†Hartford, Richard Randall, 452
†Hartigan, William, 89
Harvard, University of, 5, 19
†Harvey, William Henry, 196–7, 199, 242,
   274, 317
*Haughton, Samuel: his evidence to Royal
   Commission of 1851, 209; starts Indian
   Civil Service School, 234–6; Registrar of
   Medical School, 275; possible Provost in
   1881, 286; as member of the Board, 290,
   348; opposes theory of evolution, 242–3;
   his work on animal musculature, 263, 274;
   his views on the Irish University Question,
   254, 257; character and achievements,
   294–6, 542; other references, 231, 381
Hebrew, 5–6, 19, 44, 59, 98, 100, 277
*Helsham, Richard, 38, 43, 45, 71, 519
Hely-Hutchinson, John: appointment as
   Provost, 53; his rule and character, 54–6,
   175; his innovations in the curriculum and
   leisure activities, 56–8; insists on appointment of Brinkley as Professor of Astronomy, 64–5; his death, 75; his treatment by

historians, 56, 523; other references, 31, 66
*Henry, James Maxwell, 399, 400, 417, 465
herbarium, 196–7, 317
Hermathena, 263–4
Heron, Denis Caulfield, 213–14
†Hewson, George Henry Phillips, 481
Higgins, Paul, 9–10
higher degrees, 460–3, 546
†Hill, Edward, 142–3, 531
*Hincks, Edward, 109, 231, 309, 530
Historical Society, 79, 184
history: ancient, 267, 459; economic, 458;
   modern (incl. medieval), 44–5, 59–61, 100,
   230, 300–1, 302–3, 411–3, 458
*Hodgkinson, Francis, 97, 99, 100, 131,
   157–8, 527
Home Rule, 245, 279–83, 418
honors courses, 172–4
honors degrees, *see* Moderatorships
Hopkins, Gerard Manley, 549
Houghton, Robert Offley, second Baron, later
   first Marquess of Crewe, 281
*Hoyle, Joshua, 12–13
*Hoyle, Nathaniel, 18, 21–2, 518
*Hughes, Lambert, 519
Huntington, Richard (Provost), 24, 519
Huxley, Thomas Henry, 240, 542
Hyde, Douglas, 283, 363, 368–9, 376

Indian Civil Service, 229–30, 232, 234–6
*Ingram, John Kells: as scholar, 264, 283,
   292–3, 530, 542; founder of the School of
   English Literature, 230, 271; as Librarian,
   99, 267; as Senior Fellow, 290, 337, 540; as
   positivist, 241–2, 293; on the admission of
   women, 346, 348; retirement, 348; other
   references, 209, 218, 219, 285–6, 294, 337
Institutes of Medicine, *see* Physiology
insurrection of 1916, 421
Irish: early teaching of, 9–10, 189; Professors
   of, 164, 190–1, 226–7, 314; added to
   School of Modern Languages, 448; lectures
   through the medium of, 475; scholarly
   work in Old Irish, 277, 313, 320, 441
Irish Free State, relations with its government, 427–9
Irish University Question, 246–55, 359–62,
   365–79
Irving, Henry, 338
Italian, 57–8, 224–5, 272, 448. *See also*
   Modern languages
Iveagh, Edward Cecil Guinness, first Earl of,
   411, 424

Jackson, Henry, 368, 376
James VI of Scotland and I of England, 13, 526
James II, 27–9
†Jamieson, John Kay, 454, 481
Jebb, John (Cambridge reformer), 528
Jebb, John (Bishop of Limerick), 105
Jebb, Richard Claverhouse, 264, 368
Jellett, Eva, 349, 529
*Jellett, John Hewitt (Provost), 186, 223, 245, 263, 273, 284, 285–6, 293, 345
John III, Pope, 422
*Johnston, Joseph, 400, 460, 487, 494, 495
*Joly, Charles Jasper, 398
*Joly, John: as scientist, 315, 322, 408–10; as representative of non-Fellow Professors in constitutional negotiations, 392–3; elected Fellow, 405; proposed for Provostship; 423; other references, 420–1, 426, 456, 550
*Jones, Henry (Vice-Chancellor), 17–18, 518
*Jones, John, 27
Jones, William, of Nayland, 72
†Jourdan, George Viviliers, 452–3
Joyce, James, 365, 401
Junior Dean, 104, 299, 303, 465, 491
Junior Fellows, 3, 103–5, 298–308, 481–4, 496–7

Kane, Sir Robert, 224, 259
*Kearney, John (Provost), 78–9, 80, 95, 522
*Kelleher, Stephen Barnabas, 368–9, 375, 391, 400–1
*Kennedy (later Kennedy-Baillie), James, 61, 80, 110, 231, 527, 530
*Kennedy, William, 398, 400–1, 539
*Kenney, Arthur Hugh, 109
Kettle, Thomas, 370
†King, Sir Lucas White, 432, 449
King, William (Archbishop of Dublin), 34, 44
King's College, London, 165, 180
King's Inns, 193, 331
King's Professors in the School of Physic, 43–4, 87–8, 183–4, 212
*Kyle, Samuel (Provost), 78–9, 97, 130, 152

†Lane-Poole, Stanley, 449
Lanyon, Sir Charles, 237
Lardner, Dionysus, 134
Latin, 45–6, 265–7, 538. *See also* classics
Laud, William (Archbishop of Canterbury; Chancellor), 11, 13–16, 17, 31
Law, Andrew Bonar, 423–4
Law: Professors of, 19, 41, 65–6, 81, 97, 100, 107, 193–4, 321, 413–14, 453–4, 518; School of, 138–9, 193–4, 330–1, 413–14, 453–4
†Lawlor, Hugh Jackson, 192, 552
†Lawson, James Anthony, 169
*Lawson, John, 50, 60–1
†Leahy, John James, 143
Lecky, William Edgar Hartpole, 241, 294, 378–9, 550, 551
lecturers, 321–2, 451
*Lee, William, 162, 231, 246
†Leech, Henry Brougham, 321, 413–14, 536
Lefroy, Thomas Langlois, 105, 155, 279
*Leland, Thomas, 53, 56, 60–1, 520, 521
*Leslie, John Robert, 273, 551
Lever, Charles, 85
Library, 29, 36, 41, 82, 99, 145–7, 225–6, 277–8, 305, 471–3, 485
†Liddell, Maximilian Friedrich, 481
Little-go, 328, 447–8
livings in the gift of the College, 62, 102, 178, 246, 261–2, 308–9, 318
*Lloyd, Bartholomew: as Senior Fellow, 98; passed over for Provostship in 1820, 79; appointed Provost in 1831, 152; as academic reformer, 152–3, 157; his influence on mathematical teaching and scholarship, 159–61; reorganizes the Divinity School, 161–4; institutes the chair of Moral Philosophy, 169; reorganizes the academic year, 171–2; institutes Moderatorships, 172; helps to reorganize the tutorial system, 174–5; starts the building of the New Square, 176; criticized by Todd, 276; his death, 177; other references, 75, 93, 100, 165, 166, 168
*Lloyd, Humphrey: as scholar, 191, 264, 273, 527; appointed Professor of Natural and Experimental Philosophy, 161; helps to found the Engineering School, 181, 184; his marriage delayed by the celibacy statute, 534; considered as possible Provost in 1851, 206; appointed Provost in 1867, 264; his attitude to Fawcett's Act, 250–1, 539; old age and death, 284–5; other references, 185, 218, 245, 264–5, 380
Lloyd George, David, 281, 423, 427
Locke, John, 30, 47, 70, 72–3, 78–9
Loftus, Adam (Provost), 2, 7, 53
logic, 5, 7, 15, 46–7, 305
Logue, Michael (Cardinal-Archbishop of Armagh), 367, 371
London, University of, 117, 203, 344

Londonderry, Charles Stewart Vane-Tempest-Stewart, sixth Marquess of, 542
*Longfield, George, 530
*Longfield, Mountiford: as lawyer and judge, 107, 193, 263; as Professor of Political Economy, 169, 527; considered for the Provostship in 1851, 207; member of the Royal Commission of 1851, 205–7; advises the College on legal and parliamentary matters, 254
†Lottner, Carl Friedrich, 278
low profile, policy of, 429–30
*Luby, Thomas, 181, 197, 210, 251
*Luce, Arthur Aston: serves in 1914–18 war, 420; as philosopher, 400, 458–9; as Vice-Provost, 483–4, 490; activities during the constitutional disputes of 1947–52, 486, 489, 495–6; personality of, 490–1; candidate for Provostship in 1952, 494; other references, 353, 383, 430, 439, 487, 551, 554
*Lyngard, Richard, 27

M.A. degree, 6, 10, 99, 136, 527
†Macalister, Alexander, 242, 263, 274, 531
†Macan, Arthur Vernon, 318
†Macartney, James, 80, 89, 141–2, 186, 275
Macaulay, Thomas Babington, 93, 222, 232
MacCarthy, Teigue, 29
*McConnell, Albert Joseph, 436, 460, 477, 479, 487, 493–6, 554
*McCullagh, James, 147, 160, 161, 181, 185–6, 197, 273
*MacDonnell, Richard: as academic reformer in his youth, 125, 157, 173, 175; as Bursar, 99, 207; appointed Provost in 1851, 206–7; his evidence to the Royal Commission, 179, 211, 214, 220; his attitude to implementation of the Commission's recommendations, 216; other references, 201, 224, 230, 241
†McDowel, Benjamin George (Professor of Anatomy), 274–5
*McDowell, George, 218–19
McGilligan, Patrick, 478–9
*McIvor, James, 241, 530, 538, 541
Mackay, James Townsend, 144
†Mackintosh, Henry William, 317
*McNeece, Thomas, 162, 164
†McNeile, Alan Hugh, 452
MacNeill, Eoin, 370, 424
MacNeill, James (Governor-General of the Irish Free State), 434
†McNeill, John Benjamin, 182–3

McQuaid, John Charles (Archbishop of Dublin), 467, 470–1, 479
*Macran, Henry Stewart, 397, 403, 458–9, 543
Macrory, Joseph (Cardinal-Archbishop of Armagh), 470
Madden, Dodgson Hamilton (Vice-Chancellor), 358, 404
Madden, Samuel, 529
Madden prize, 456, 552
*Magee, William, 78, 80, 82–3, 102, 104–8, 150, 522
Magee College, Londonderry, 417
Magennis, William, 370
*Maguire, Thomas, 171, 214, 263, 268, 270, 282, 302, 540, 541
*Mahaffy, John Pentland: elected Fellow, 265; as classical scholar, 61, 263–5, 283, 292, 301, 542; as historian of the College, 40, 80; his work on Kant, 263, 268–9; as a 'character' and subject of anecdotes, 82; his views on his colleagues, 286, 297, 369, 544; on the Irish University Question, 254, 362, 375; co-opted to the Board, 348; favours the admission of women, 348, 546; fails to win the Provostship in 1904, 355–9; his attitude to constitutional reform, 390; opposes the revival of Irish, 363, 415; his brush with the Gaelic Society over Pearse, 419; his exuberant proposals for an Army School, 415; elected Provost, 419; his provostship, 419–22; other references, 293, 336, 384, 406, 423, 435, 461, 543, 545
Manners, Lord John, 255
Manning, Henry (Cardinal-Archbishop of Westminster), 255
Mant, Richard, 533
†Marani, A.C., 224–5, 272
Marsh, Narcissus (Provost), 9–10, 24, 519–20
*Martin, Anthony (Provost), 17
Martyn, John, 43
Mathematics: absence from the curriculum in early years, 7, 47–8; introduced to undergraduate course, 69–70; lecturerships and chairs in, 19, 30, 41, 59, 100; Professors of, 19–20, 59, 63, 100, 185, 303–4, 459–60, 551–2; encouraged and developed by Murray, 63; continental methods introduced by Bartholomew Lloyd, 159–60; medal course, 121–2; Moderatorship in, 174; predominant position in Fellowship examination, 128–9; Salmon's achievements in, 291

*Mather, Samuel, 19
†Maturin, Charles, 414
†Maxwell, Constantia, 352, 412, 432, 458, 481
Meath Hospital, 89, 144
Mechanics, 70, 447
Medical School, 41–4, 55, 87–9, 139–45, 186–9, 275–6, 295, 330, 454–5, 502–3
Medicine (Physic), Regius Professors of, 19, 42, 142–3, 186, 188–9
†Micks, Robert Henry, 455
*Miller, George, 60–1, 67, 131, 522
Minchin, George Minchin, 539
Mitchel, John, 200
*Mitchell, George Francis, 466–7, 495–6
Moderatorships, 173–4, 198, 229–31, 329–30, 414, 448–9
Modern East Indian Languages, Professor of, 449
Modern languages, 57–8, 270–2. *See also under the individual languages.*
†Moeran, Edward Busteed, 231, 541
Molloy, Monsignor Gerald, 375
Molony, Sir Thomas (Vice-Chancellor), 432
†Molyneux, Thomas, 30, 519
Molyneux, William, 518
†Monck, William Henry Stanley, 259
†Montgomery, William Fetherstonhaugh, 143
*Moody, Theodore William, 458, 487, 494–5, 554
*Mooney, George William, 374, 395, 400, 459, 539
Mooney, Robert Gerald, 530
*Moore, John Lewis, 210, 231, 260, 534
Moore, Michael ('Head of the College', 1689), 29
Moore, Theodore Conyngham Kingsmill, 421, 493, 552
Moore, Thomas, 78, 85
†Moorhead, Thomas Gillman, 455, 482
†Moran, Frances Elizabeth, 453, 481, 547
†Mornington, Garrett Wesley, first Earl of, 52, 58, 194
Moyne, Walter Edward Guinness, first Baron, 492
Murphy, Harold Lawson, 412
†Murphy, James Edward Harnett, 191, 550
*Murray, Richard (Provost), 63, 75–6, 78
Museum, 194–8, 543
Music, Professors of, 52, 58, 194, 314–15

Naas, Lord (Richard Southall Bourke, later sixth Earl of Mayo), 228
Napier, Sir Joseph (Vice-Chancellor), 4, 254

national anthems, 434
National University of Ireland, 378–9
Natural and Experimental Philosophy, *see* Physics
Natural Philosophy, *see* Mathematics
natural sciences, 30, 47, 70–1, 273–4
Newman, Henry (Cardinal), 254, 549
Newton, Sir Isaac, 30, 72–3

*O'Brien, James Thomas, 104, 108, 162, 164, 527, 533
O'Connell, Daniel, 114
O'Conor, Charles, the O'Conor Don, 249
O'Dwyer, Edward Thomas (Bishop of Limerick), 365–6, 549
†Oldham, Thomas, 183, 197
O'Mahony, Eoin, 434
†O'Mahony, Thaddeus, 191
*O'Meara, Robert Allen Quain, 436, 487, 540
O'Rahilly, Alfred, 469–70
Oratory, 19, 44–5, 59–61, 230
ordinary course in arts, *see* undergraduate course
Oriental languages, Moderatorship in, 448–9
Ormonde, James Butler, twelfth Earl and first Duke of (Chancellor), 8, 17, 24, 25
Ormonde, James Butler, second Duke of (Chancellor), 34, 36, 95
*O'Sullivan, Alexander Charles, 299, 300, 303, 389, 420, 423
†Oulton, John Ernest Leonard, 452
Oxford, University of, 12–13, 18, 24, 25, 27, 47, 128, 168, 351–2, 519, 538. *See also succeeding entry*
Oxford and Cambridge compared with Dublin; 14, 41, 43, 45, 64, 69, 72, 74, 80, 91–2, 101, 109–10, 117, 118, 120, 122–4, 154, 165, 202–4, 246–7, 347, 401, 405–6, 425–6, 514

Paine, Thomas, 78
Palles, Christopher (Chief Baron of the Exchequer), 368, 375–6, 548
*Palliser, William, 24
*Palmer, Arthur, 263–5, 267, 283, 301–2, 542, 546
†Palmer, Patrick, 66
Palmerston, Henry George Temple, third Viscount, 216
*Panton, A.W., 544
*Parke, Herbert William, 459, 473, 490, 493–5, 554
parliamentary representation of the University, 55–6, 81, 98, 155, 432–3, 542

pass course, *see* undergraduate course
Pastoral Theology, chair of, 164
Pathology, Professors of, 300, 454
Patten, James, 195
Pattison, Mark, 265
Peacocke, Joseph Ferguson (Archbishop of Dublin), 231, 383
†Pearson, William, 455, 482
Peel, Sir Robert, 202–3, 248
*Pelissier, John, 50
†Perceval, Robert, 88, 89
Persico, Monsignor Ignatius (later Cardinal), 548
*Phelan, William, 105
†Phillips, John (Professor of Geology), 183
Phillips, Owen Hood (Lecturer in Law), 453
†Phillips, Walter Alison (Professor of Modern History), 413, 458
Philosophy, 19, 32, 169–71, 268–70, 458–9
*Phipps, Robert, 97–8, 157–9, 172, 526
Physic, *see* Medicine
Physicians, Royal College of, 19, 30, 43–4, 87–8, 140, 144, 186, 545
Physics: foundation of a chair of, 44; modification of its terms of tenure, 160–1; Professors of, 45, 100, 161, 185–6, 305–7, 456–7, 551; courses in, 70–1, 198; laboratory provided for, 411
Physiology, 320, 454, 519
Pigot, David Richard, 259
Pius IX, Pope, 201, 243, 257
†Plummer, Henry Crozier, 432
Plunket, David Robert, Baron Rathmore, 250, 255, 411
Plunket, William Conyngham, later first Baron Plunket, 527
Political Economy, 168–9, 293–4, 314, 449, 460
*Poole, Hewitt Robert, 218, 290, 298, 348
*Poole, John Hewitt Jellett, 437, 456–7, 488, 554
†Pope, John van Someren, 449
Porter, Andrew Marshall (Master of the Rolls), 4, 548
Porter, Andrew Marshall (undergraduate), 334
positivism, 241–2, 293
*Pratt, Benjamin (Provost), 34–6
Presbyterian church, 383–4
Preston, John, 12
†Pringle, Harold, 454
*Prior, Thomas, 79, 98, 157–9, 172, 184–5, 522, 530
private tuition, 132–3

Professors, non-Fellow, 110–11, 160, 258–9, 261–2, 309–21, 388–9, 391–5, 481–2, 513–14
†Prout, Ebenezer, 375
Provost, powers of, 37, 56, 97, 495–6, 517, 520
Public administration, diploma in, 450
*Pullen, Tobias, 24
Puritanism, 8–9, 18–21, 23, 24
*Purser, Frederick, 273, 298, 304, 539
†Purser, John (Professor of Engineering), 455–6, 482, 488
†Purser, John Malet (King's Professor of the Institutes of Medicine), 276, 320, 337, 413, 420
*Purser, Louis Claude, 267, 283, 302, 389, 398, 423, 441, 542

Queen's Colleges, and Queen's University of Ireland, 202–3, 218, 248, 253, 365, 367, 377, 549
Queen's University, Belfast, 378–9
*Quin, Ernest Gordon, 467

†Radice, Evasio, 111, 224
Raleigh, Sir Thomas, 368, 376
†Rambaut, Arthur Alcock, 322
Ramus, Petrus, 7, 15
Rathmore, Lord, *see* Plunket, David Robert
rebellion of 1798, 76–7, 78, 91
Redesdale, John Freeman-Mitford, first Baron (Vice-Chancellor), 525
reform, parliamentary, 99, 154, 176, 238
Registrars, 442, 469, 495–6, 526
Regius Professors, significance of the title, 535
religion in College, 149–51, 239–44, 333, 386–7. *See also* catechetical course, Chapel services, Divinity School *and* Theological Society
religious tests, 88, 212–14, 246–8, 249–50, 255–6, 361, 379
Restoration, 21–2
revolutions of 1848, 200–1
†Reynolds, James Emerson, 276, 315–17
rhetoric, 5, 7
*Richardson, William, 62
Ridgeway, William, 267
Roberts, Frederick Sleigh, first Earl Roberts, 354
*Roberts, Michael, 218, 273, 303, 543
*Roberts, William, 260
*Roberts, William Ralph Westropp, 298, 304, 390, 392, 423, 441

Robertson, James Patrick Bannerman, first
  Baron Robertson, 365
†Robinson, Bryan (Regius Professor of
  Physic), 43, 519
Robinson, Richard (Archbishop of Armagh,
  later first Baron Rokeby), 521
*Robinson, Thomas Romney, 104–5, 109, 536
*Rogers, Reginald Arthur Percy, 389, 400
Roman Catholic church, its spirit in 1860–90,
  243–4; its attitude to the Queen's Colleges,
  203; its attitude to Trinity College, 257–8,
  358, 362, 365, 367, 370–2, 374, 469–71
Romance languages, Professors of, *see* French
Rosenhead, Louis, 436
Ross, Sir John, 426
Ross, Laurence Parsons, fourth Earl of
  (Chancellor), 290, 410, 411
Rosse, William Parsons, third Earl of
  (Chancellor), 205–7, 541
*Rowe, Charles Henry, 460, 466, 554
Royal Commission of 1851, 202–25
Royal Commission of 1877 (Belmore
  Commission), 262, 380–1
Royal Commission of 1901 (Robertson
  Commission), 357, 365–7
Royal Commission of 1906 (Fry Commission),
  357, 368–76, 382, 383, 389–91
Royal Commission of 1920 (Geikie
  Commission), 426
Royal Irish Academy, 61, 66–8, 424
Royal Society of London, 30, 377
Royal University of Ireland, 344, 349, 378,
  549
Rücker, Sir Arthur, 368, 375
†Rudmose-Brown, Thomas Brown, 430, 458,
  466
Ruskin, John, 237
Russell, Lord John, 154, 204
*Russell, Robert, 298, 304, 369, 372, 389, 439,
  442, 480, 539

*Sadleir, Franc: as Senior Fellow, 98–100,
  103; as Professor of Mathematics, 156, 161;
  as Bursar, 525; as staunch Whig, 155–6; as
  Provost, 167, 177, 194; death, 206
*Sadleir, William Digby, 210
St Columba's College, 218, 277, 318
St Patrick's Cathedral, 1, 22, 339
salaries, academic, 450–1, 477–8, 511–15
*Salmon, George: general assessment, 291–2;
  his evidence to the Royal Commission of
  1851, 208–9; as mathematician, 273, 303;
  as Regius Professor of Divinity, 254, 273,
  318, 358, 539; as Provost, 286, 290, 469,

523, 550; opposes the admission of women,
  345, 347–9; his lack of enthusiasm for
  scientific research, 407; his role in the
  General Synod after Disesablishment,
  245–6; suggests constitution for the
  Divinity School, 382; old age and death,
  354–5, 357; other references, 240–1, 296,
  538, 542
*Sandes, Stephen Creagh, 108, 155, 167, 526,
  533
Sanskrit and comparative philology, 232–4,
  272
Sayce, Archibald Henry, 264
Scholars of the House, 3, 23, 120–1, 178,
  213–14, 229, 256, 353, 542
scholars, non-Foundation, 214–15, 353, 537
science, campaign for the expansion of,
  406–11
†Scott, Robert, 89
Scottish universities, 120, 123. *See also*
  Edinburgh
*Seele, Thomas (Provost), 22–3
Seely, Sir John Robert, 265
†Selss, Albert Maximilian, 271, 311, 403
Senate of the University, 33, 97, 223–4, 226,
  254, 381, 396, 516
Senior Fellows, 3, 97–103, 260, 292–8,
  480–1, 486–8, 536. *See also* Board
Senior Lecturers, 98–100, 441–2, 493, 495–6
*Shaw, George Ferdinand, 218, 227–8, 261,
  290, 298, 337, 540
*Sheridan, Thomas (Jacobite), 27
Sheridan, Thomas (schoolmaster), 56
Shipley, Sir Arthur, 426
Sibthorpe, Humphrey, 43
†Siegfried, Rudolph Thomas, 232–4, 278
*Singer, Joseph Henderson, 108, 192, 526
sizars, 3, 114–15
Skeffington, Owen Sheehy, 554
†Smith, Aquilla (King's Professor of Materia
  Medica), 276
Smith, Erasmus, 44
Smith, Frederick Edwin, later first Earl of
  Birkenhead, xviii, 430
*Smith, George Sidney, 208
†Smith, John (Professor of Music), 194
†Smith, Robert William (Professor of
  Surgery), 187–8
*Smyly, Josiah Gilbart, 398, 400, 432, 459,
  472–3, 481, 485, 487
*Smyth, James Desmond, 488
†Smyth, Louis Bouvier (Professor of Geology),
  456, 482, 488, 495
social medicine, 492

†Sollas, William Johnson, 315, 542
South African war, 354
Spanish, 57–8, 224–5, 272, 448, 458. *See also* Modern languages
Spillan, Daniel, 133–4
*Stack, John, 64, 71
*Stack, Richard, 67
*Stack, Thomas, 231, 290, 298
'stagnation', problem of, 211, 259–62, 287–9, 388
*Stanford, William Bedell, 459, 493–4, 496
*Starkie, Walter Fitzwilliam, 432, 436, 458, 466, 554
*Starkie, William Joseph Myles, 302, 303, 366, 372, 389
statutes of the College, 5, 14–15, 215–17, 516, 555, 556
*Stearne, John, 19, 25, 42
Steevens's Hospital, 89
†Stewart, Sir Robert Prescott, 194, 314–15
*Stewart, Samuel George, 400, 420
*Stock, Joseph, 61–2, 108, 110, 200
†Stokes, Adrian (Professor of Bacteriology), 455
*Stokes, Gabriel, 56
†Stokes, George Thomas (Professor of Ecclesiastical History), 318
*Stokes, John, 60–1, 455
*Stokes, Whitley: censured at the visitation of 1798, 77; opposed to the Union, 522; as physician and medical professor, 80, 143; resigns his Fellowship from religious scruples, 111, 143; lecturer in Natural History, 131, 143, 195, 534–5; death, 186
Stokes, Whitley (Celtic scholar and jurist), 313
†Stokes, William (Regius Professor of Physic), 89, 143, 186, 188–9, 199, 276, 545
Strafford, Earl of, *see* Wentworth, Thomas
*Stubbs, John William, 197, 290, 296–8, 348, 381
Studdert Kennedy, Geoffrey Anketell, 528
students: variation in their numbers, 23, 28, 85–7, 113, 199, 322–3, 475, 499–501, 518, 523; awards to 90, 120–2, 126–7, 174; non-resident, 115–17, 199, 326; social background, 114–15, 324–6, 506–8; birthplace, 115, 323–4, 475–6, 505–6; religious affiliations, 323, 470, 503–5; recreations, life-style and general outlook, 148–9, 331–5, 344–5
Studentships, 221
*Styles, Henry, 25–7
*Sullivan, Francis Stoughton, 50, 65–6

†Sumner, Miles, 19–20, 30
Surgeons, Royal College of, 140, 187–8
Surgery, Professors of, 187–8
Swift, Jonathan, 38, 45
Swift, Theophilus, 68
*Synge, John Lighton, 436, 445, 460, 554
Synge, John Millington (playwright), 283
†Synge, Victor Millington (King's Professor of the Practice of Medicine), 455

*Tarleton, Francis Alexander, 273, 303–4, 345, 348, 390, 394, 423
*Tate, Sir Robert William, 399, 400, 439, 481, 487, 490
Taylor, Jeremy (Vice-Chancellor), 518
teaching methods, 5, 7, 129–32
Temple, William (Provost), 7, 23, 31, 49
Tercentenary celebrations, 335–9, 523
terms and vacations, 171–2
textbooks, 49, 133–4, 291
Thackeray, William Makepeace, 535
Theological Society, 192–3
theology and biblical studies, 10–13, 25, 291–2, 318–20, 425
†Thompson, Sir William Henry, 420, 550
*Thrift, Harry: as Fellowship candidate, 552; as Junior Fellow, 439, 456, 487; as Senior Fellow, 482; as Bursar, 442, 480, 485–6, 495–6; unsuited to academic life, 398–400
*Thrift, William Edward: as supporter of constitutional reform, 389, 392; as Junior Fellow, 400; as representative of Junior Fellows on the Board, 487; as Professor of Physics, 456–7, 551; as parliamentary representative, 432–3; possible Provost in 1927, 439; as Vice-Provost, 434, 441; as Provost, 1937–42, 443; death, 466, 467
toasts, 434
*Todd, James Henthorn: as Librarian, 99, 234, 277–8; as staunch Anglican and high-churchman, 192, 207, 241, 251, 276–7; considered unsuitable as Provost, 207, 264, 278; as scholar, 231, 277; as College historian, 277, 528; other references, 197, 210, 222, 527, 530, 540
*Toleken, John, 102, 217, 262
Tone, Theobald Wolfe, 522–3
†Torrens, David Smyth, 454, 488, 495
Townsend, John Sealy Edward, 426
*Townsend, Richard, 209, 273, 303, 543
*Traill, Anthony: as Junior Fellow, 245, 254, 260; as tutor, 298–300; attempts to buy the Provostship, 285; supports the admission

Index

of women, 345, 348; his successful struggle
for the Provostship, 355–7, 358–9; as
Provost, 369, 377–8, 383–4, 387, 390, 394,
395, 406, 419; other references, 292,
299–300, 336, 352, 382
*Travers, Joseph, 518
Travers, Walter (Provost), 7, 9
Trench, Richard Chenevix (Archbishop of
Dublin), 246
†Trench, Wilbraham Fitzjohn, 457
Trinity College, Cambridge, 6, 56, 80, 103
Trinity College Defence Committee, 377
Trinity Hall (seventeenth century), 19, 42
Trinity Hall (twentieth century), 351–2
Trouton, Frederick, 322
†Tuomy, Martin, 535, 537
tutors, 103–4, 160, 174–5, 220, 298, 482–4
*Tyrrell, Robert Yelverton, 263, 265–6,
283–4, 292, 301–3, 542

undergraduate course (leading to pass B.A.):
in the seventeenth century, 5–8, 15; in the
eighteenth century, 31–2, 45–9, 69–73; in
the nineteenth century, 118–20, 172–3,
198, 229, 326–9; in the twentieth century,
445–8, 482
Union, Act of, 74, 78, 81, 84–5
Unionism, 280–4, 312, 321, 426–7, 430–3
University College, Dublin, 378–9, 478–9,
549, 555
University College, London, 180
University of Dublin, 4–5, 95–7, 548
Unwin, Sir Stanley, 467, 471–3
*Ussher, Ambrose, 12
*Ussher, Henry (Archdeacon of Dublin), 2
*Ussher, Henry (Professor of Astronomy), 64,
67
*Ussher, James (Archbishop of Armagh),
10–13, 17, 137

*Veale, Edward, 518
veterinary science, 450
Vice-Chancellor, office of, 11, 17, 18, 96
Vice-Provost, office of, 99, 419, 441
Victoria, Queen, 354
Victoria University, 367
†Vieyra, Antonio, 58
Visitors and visitations, 23, 34, 77, 96–7, 99,
213–14, 227–8, 275, 386, 404, 521, 539,
540, 541

*Walker, John, 61, 80, 110, 133–4, 143
*Wall, Charles William: as Hebrew scholar,
98, 100, 231; as conservative, and op-
ponent of Lloyd's reforms, 154–5, 158,
161; other references, 99, 200, 210
†Walsh, Richard Hussey, 169
Walsh, William (Archbishop of Dublin), 335,
360–1, 362, 364, 365–6, 375, 383
*Walton, Ernest Thomas Sinton, 436, 457
war of 1914–18, 405, 418, 420–1
war of 1939–45, 463–4, 465–7
*Ward, Michael (Provost, and later Vice-
Chancellor), 23–4
Ward, Samuel (of Ipswich), 12
†Wardell, John Henry, 393, 412
Washington, Richard (Provost), 17
†Weaver, John Reginald Homer, 412
*Webb, David Allardice, 488, 494–6
*Webb, George Randolph, 400–1, 487
*Webb, Thomas Ebenezer, 171, 218, 232,
268–9, 413, 541
Wentworth, Thomas Wentworth, first
Viscount, later Earl of Strafford, 13, 16, 17,
517
†Werner, Emil Alphonse, 317, 322, 393, 456,
481
Wharton, Thomas Wharton, first Marquess
of, 34
Whately, Richard (Archbishop of Dublin),
127–8, 165–9, 205, 207
Whigs, ascendancy of, 36–8, 72
†White, Herbert Martyn Oliver, 313, 457–8
White, Captain James Robert, 418
†White, Newport John Davis, 384, 452
†Whittaker, Edmund Taylor, 375, 552
†Wigham, Joseph Theodore, 454
Wilde, Oscar Fingall O'Flahertie Wills, 267,
492
*Wilder, Theaker, 50, 59
*Wilkins, George, 302–3, 374, 395, 416, 462
Wilkins, William, 221
William Henry, Duke of Gloucester
(Chancellor), 75, 95
†Williams, Robert Allan, 379, 403
*Williamson, Benjamin, 211, 218, 303–4,
341, 348, 394, 411, 419
*Williamson, Caesar, 18
†Williomier, Charles, 111
*Wilson, James, 102
Wilson, James (Bishop of Cork), 205
Windle, Sir Bertram, 375
Winter, Samuel (Provost), 13, 17–22, 31
Wolfe, Arthur, later Lord Kilwarden, 75
women: admission of, 341–9; their sub-
sequent role in the College, 349–53; num-
bers, 501
Woodhouse, Robert, 532

Index

Woods, Sir Robert Henry, 474
Woodward, Benjamin, 225, 237
*Wormell, Donald Ernest Wilson, 459, 488, 494–6, 554
*Wray, Henry, 98, 157, 533
†Wright, Edward Perceval, 230, 242, 263, 311, 317, 543
†Wright, William, 234

Wycherley, Michael, 73
Wyndham, George, 357–8, 368

Yeats, William Butler, 155, 239, 431, 542
*Young, Matthew, 63–4, 67, 80–1, 108, 522, 526

Zoology, 229–30, 273–4, 456

580